Praise for *The Pushcart Prize, XVII:*

"Once again, this perennial favorite collects short stories, essays, and poems from small magazines and book publishers across the country. Some of the more familiar names among the 60 writers are William Gass, Gary Soto, Sharon Olds, Francine Prose, and William Matthews, but the real excitement of these anthologies is the discovery of new names, new points of view, new voices. So don't stop now; add this to the *Pushcart* lineup."

—*Booklist*

"A solid addition to literary collections."

—*Library Journal*

Praise for Previous *Pushcart Prize* Editions:

"A fascinating peek at the vast and largely hidden world of noncommercial publishing."

—*Time*

"Solid accomplishments from writers to watch.

—*Publishers Weekly*

"A showcase that displays some of the year's best writing."

—*Philadelphia Inquirer*

"An anthology of literature to nourish the human spirit."

—*Milwaukee Journal*

THE
PUSHCART PRIZE, XVII:
BEST OF THE
SMALL PRESSES

THE PUSHCART PRIZE XVII

BEST OF THE SMALL PRESSES

Edited by
Bill Henderson
with the
Pushcart Prize
editors.
Poetry Editors:
Christopher Buckley,
Chase Twichell
Essays Editor:
Anthony Brandt

A Touchstone Book
Published by Simon & Schuster
New York   London
Toronto   Sydney
Tokyo   Singapore

TOUCHSTONE
Simon & Schuster Building
Rockefeller Center
1230 Avenue of the Americas
New York, New York 10020

10 9 8 7 6 5 4 3 2 1

Library of Congress Cataloging-in-Publication Data is
available

ISBN: 0-671-73436-9

*Note: Nominations for this series are invited from any
small, independent, literary book press or magazine in
the world. Up to six nominations—tear sheets or copies
selected from work published, or about to be published,
in the calendar year—are accepted by our December 1
deadline each year. Write to Pushcart Press, P.O. Box
380, Wainscott, NY 11975 for more information.*

Acknowledgements

Introduction ©1992 Bill Henderson
From the Meadow © 1991 Aralia Press
Vespers: Parousia © 1991 Tikkun
I Would Call It Derangement © 1991 South Florida Poetry Review
Grid © 1991 Poetry Northwest
Helen © 1991 Orchises Press
The Wrestler's Heart © 1991 Colorado Review
To The Muse © 1991 American Poetry Review
To A Wren on Calvary © 1991 Missouri Review
Lost Fugue for Chet © 1991 Kenyon Review
Four Days: Earthquake © 1991 Kenyon Review
Oh, By The Way © 1991 Ploughshares
Quick Eats © 1991 Boulevard
Wheatfield Under Clouded Sky © 1991 Paris Review
Parents © 1991 Gettysburg Review
Insomnia © 1991 Painted Hills Review
My Father's Body © 1991 Gettysburg Review
Worldly Beauty © 1991 Ploughshares
Snow Figures © 1991 Ohio Review
Apple Rind © 1991 American Poetry Review
When I Was Saved © 1991 Shenandoah
But Bird © 1991 Georgia Review
Ray © 1991 American Poetry Review
Inscriptions © 1991 Paris Review
Reading With the Poets © 1991 Antaeus
Good Heavens © 1991 Gettysburg Review
Circumstance © 1991 Ploughshares
Mannequins © 1991 Michigan Quarterly Review
Twelve O'Clock © 1991 Paris Review
Train Whistles In the Wind and Rain © 1991 Shenandoah
The Columbus School for Girls © 1991 Georgia Review
Mine Own John Berryman © 1991 Gettysburg Review
Red Lipstick © 1991 TriQuarterly
Blood Brother © 1991 Ontario Review
On Dumpster Diving © 1991 Threepenny Review
Whitewing © 1991 Shenandoah
My Best Soldier © 1991 Agni
A Note on the Type © 1991 Review of Contemporary Fiction
Simplicities © 1991 Review of Contemporary Fiction
Prolegomena © 1991 Fiction International
Rubber Life © 1991 North American Review
The Telegraph Relay Station © 1991 Missouri Review
A Day At The St. Regis With Dame Edith © 1991 American Scholar
Freeway Bypass © 1991 Witness
Hush Hush © 1991 Boulevard

This book is for Barbara Lish

INTRODUCTION

by Bill Henderson

Ten years ago I stopped writing the introductions to these annual celebrations. After seven introductions I decided I had said my all about the obvious importance of small presses.

I asked Gail Godwin, Jayne Anne Phillips, George Plimpton, Cynthia Ozick, Frank Conroy, Richard Ford, Tess Gallagher, Russell Banks and Edward Hoagland to take over this spot, in that order. I thank them for helping to keep our common vision bright.

After a year of extraordinary national arts alarms, I resurface here briefly to repeat the original assertion of this series, first stated in 1976. That assertion is simply that words are too important to be left to the corporate and political moneymongers. Writers who create for the small presses—a term that includes both book publishers and little magazines—do not do so for money. They may have other vices, but money-lust is not one of them. For those who write for and work in the commercial publishing establishment money is always a factor. For those who bankroll the commercial establishment, words *are* money.

Steven J. Ross earned compensation of $78 million in 1990 for running Time Warner, where words were spun into magazines, books, movies, videos and television. Time Warner bestrides world media and Steve Ross bestrides Time Warner. Soon after he collected his 78, Ross fired 605 staffers in Time Warner's publishing division. His compensation was over two times what they earned collectively.

In the political news—by now ancient but classically important history—we were astonished by a tragic-farce for four actors:

Senator Jesse Helms (R. N.C.), a heavy in matters sexual and excretory; Patrick J. Buchanan, lightweight phrase slinger; John E. Frohnmayer, fired chairman of the National Endowment for the Arts; George Bush, President of the world's remaining super power.

At stake: $175 million in NEA funds and the very survival of that endowment.

Jesse Helms stirred up the religious right—The American Family Association of Tupelo, Mississippi in particular—when he chanced on two publications of the NEA funded Portable Lower East Side press: *Queer City* and *Live Sex Acts*. Helms and the people from Tupelo lifted these minor efforts out of context from the thousands of grants awarded to literature, the visual and performing arts and others by the NEA, grants that have brought about a cultural renaissance in this country for over two decades. Helms and the Tupelo people, champions of our moral heritage, shaded the truth a bit (they lied) to convince a portion of the electorate that the NEA was a prime source of evil and should be abolished.

Meanwhile Buchanan challenged Bush in the New Hampshire Republican primary and parroted Helms and the Christian (sic) right: "The NEA is the upholstered playpen of the arts-and-crafts auxiliary of the Eastern liberal establishment," squawked Buchanan.

On the eve of the New Hampshire primary I was visiting with Joe David Bellamy, director of the NEA Literature Program and a Pushcart author. I hadn't seen Joe in several years and I wanted to hear his take on politics and the fortunes of small presses after two years at his post in Washington. "Small presses are in a very fragile financial state. Many of them could blow away in a slight breeze," Joe reported. He added: "I think Bush will fire Frohnmayer if Buchanan does well in New Hampshire tomorrow."

I thought this was an unlikely script. Why would the President of the United States seek a scapegoat in the NEA?

The next day Buchanan did well. Bush fired Frohnmayer.

Political terrorists had exploded their bomb in the art's foundation.

Seventeen years ago, I worried in the first *Pushcart Prize* introduction about the power of "big bucks conglomerates."

11

That concern remains, whether the conglomerates are political or commercial. Behemoths will crush writers and editors if it is expedient.

Steven Ross will fire 605 publishing staffers and pocket over double their salaries himself to improve Time Warner's bottomline.

Helms and Buchanan, would-be assassins of the NEA, will conspire to create a monster out of straw for political expediency. After his firing, John Frohnmayer was reminded of a Nazi stunt titled "Degenerate Art," a collection of modern paintings paraded by the Nazis to condemn German artists of the 1930s. The headline then: "Your tax money goes to support this filth." Helms-Buchanan tagged the NEA with the same smear.

But we are not without heroes.

Vaclav Havel, Salman Rushdie and David Hamilton are a few of mine.

Vaclav Havel, President of Czechoslovakia, warned in New York Times Op Ed piece of the principal threats in the world today: AIDS, ozone depletion, and world domination by commercial media, like Time Warner.

Salman Rushdie, under Iranian death sentence for his *Satanic Verses*, and the ultimate symbol of what horror political expediency can inflict on an individual writer, dared to appear in the United States for a speech this spring. Flanked by bodyguards he said "I have tried repeatedly to remind people that what we are witnessing is a war against independence of mind, a war for power . . . it is a battle that can only be won because the consequences of losing it are horrendous."

David Hamilton is editor of *The Iowa Review,* circulation 1,200; three issues a year; poetry, essays, fiction; to my mind one of the best little mags in the country. He is among those in charge of our fragile small press culture.

Last year, Hamilton was instructed by central administration at the University of Iowa that the construction of a laser center and a new building for the business school were more important than *The Iowa Review.* He was on his own for funding.

Hamilton reports his reaction: "We scrambled as best we could . . . by writing to a group of alumni subscribers, then to all the writers whom we had published in the last ten years, and for whom we had addresses, then to all the faculty of the

12

University of Iowa, and finally to some business leaders, principally in Iowa. We raised over $19,500 in gifts, new subscriptions, and pledges . . . over 230 people responded."

Thanks to Hamilton and friends—and a belated matching grant from the University—*The Iowa Review* will survive for another two years.

David Hamilton is typical of the editors and writers that the *Pushcart Prize* has attempted to honor in the past seventeen years. We have been helped in our honoring by over 150 Contributing Editors and hundreds of individual publishers who suggest thousands of poems, essays and fictions for each edition. These nominations are read by dedicated people like Christopher Buckley and Chase Twichell (poetry editors of PPXVII), Tony Brandt (essays editor) and a staff of fiction readers including myself. All of us labor for nothing, or for a pittance that is far below minimum wage (fed inspectors please note).

We ask for and receive no grants—federal, state, or corporate.

And thus the *Pushcart Prize* series has thrived for seventeen years, not however without criticism—we couldn't possibly please all readers—and not without flaws. One developing flaw is the lack of space for the plethora of extraordinary work. We can't reprint all that we admire. So we are reduced to a Special Mention section, a situation that satisfies nobody.

Why this abundance of literary talent in an age that is fixated on videos, movies and television? Why do our poets, essayists and fictioneers bother to revere honest words?

Perhaps because they still care about finding the truths in our funny, sad, lonely, brave lives on this blue globe lost in space. They sense that something important may be going on here, perhaps sacred, and attention must be paid.

Those interested in financial and political power just don't get it. They think small presses are the tryout farm teams. Not so. Today, small presses are the majors. For what is truly minor, look to the mass media moguls.

In the Pushcart Press office, a garage in the woods at the eastern end of Long Island, New York, I have scribbled a reminder and tacked it to the wall: "One perfect sentence, read and remembered by one reader, is worth all the throw-away sentences read by millions of readers and forgotten the next minute."

The Iowa Review may circulate only 1,200 copies each issue. But years from now issues of *The Iowa Review* and other small press books and journals will be cherished while the current sloppy bestsellers and perfumed glossies sink deeper into the landfills.

On the following pages you will discover our 17th annual collection of evidence for that assertion.

THE PEOPLE
WHO HELPED

FOUNDING EDITORS—*Anaïs Nin (1903–1977), Buckminster Fuller (1895–1983), Charles Newman, Daniel Halpern, Gordon Lish, Harry Smith, Hugh Fox, Ishmael Reed, Joyce Carol Oates, Len Fulton, Leonard Randolph, Leslie Fiedler, Nona Balakian (1918–1991), Paul Bowles, Paul Engle (1908–1991), Ralph Ellison, Reynolds Price, Rhoda Schwartz, Richard Morris, Ted Wilentz, Tom Montag, William Phillips, Poetry editor: H. L. Van Brunt.*

EDITORS—*Walter Abish, Ai, Elliott Anderson, John Ashbery, Ed Sanders, Teo Savory, Grace Schulman, Harvey Shapiro, Leslie Silko, Charles Simic, Dave Smith, Elizabeth Spencer, William Stafford, Gerald Stern, David St. John, Bill and Pat Strachan, Ron Sukenick, Anne Tyler, John Updike, Sam Vaughan, David Wagoner, Derek Walcott, Ellen Wilbur, David Wilk, David Wojahn, Jack Gilbert, Louise Glück, David Godine, Jorie Graham, Linda Gregg, Barbara Grossman, Donald Hall, Helen Handley, Michael Harper, Robert Hass, DeWitt Henry, J. R. Humphreys, David Ignatow, John Irving, June Jordan, Edmund Keeley, Karen Kennerly, Galway Kinnell, Carolyn Kizer, Jerzy Kosinski, Richard Kostelanetz, Seymour Krim, Maxine Kumin, James Laughlin, Seymour Lawrence, Naomi Lazard, Herb Leibowitz, Denise Levertov, Philip Levine, Stanley Lindberg, Thomas Lux, Mary MacArthur, Jay Meek, Daniel Menaker, Frederick Morgan, Cynthia Ozick, Jayne Anne Phillips, Robert Phillips, George Plimpton, Stanley Plumly, Eugene Redmond, Russell Banks, Joe David Bellamy, Robert Bly, Philip Booth, Robert Boyers, Harold*

Brodkey, Joseph Brodsky, Wesley Brown, Hayden Carruth, Frank Conroy, Paula Deitz, Steve Dixon, Rita Dove, Andre Dubus, M. D. Elevitch, Louise Erdrich, Loris Essary, Ellen Ferber, Carolyn Forché, Stuart Freibert, Jon Galassi, Tess Gallagher, Louis Gallo, George Garrett, Reginald Gibbons, Bill Zavatsky.

CONTRIBUTING EDITORS FOR THIS EDITION—*Jane Hirshfield, André Bernard, DeWitt Henry, J. R. Humphreys, Lloyd Schwartz, William Kennedy, George Plimpton, Gordon Lish, Cynthia Ozick, Michael Waters, Richard Kostelanetz, Barbara Thompson, Ted Wilentz, Rick Bass, Mark Doty, Alberto Alvaro Rios, Josip Novakovich, Barbara Einzig, Carolyn Kizer, Christina Zawadiwsky, Herb Leibowitz, Hugh Fox, Sam Vaughan, Gary Gildner, Maxine Kumin, David Jauss, Jim Moore, Robert Phillips, Robert Pinsky, Arthur Smith, Kristina McGrath, David Romtvedt, Susan Mitchell, Bin Ramke, M. D. Elevitch, Frankie Paino, Josephine Jacobsen, Stephen Dunn, Robert Wrigley, Jim Simmerman, Rosellen Brown, Philip Dacey, Helen Norris, Gerry Locklin, Ben Groff, David Lehman, Michael Bowden, Richard Currey, Carl Dennis, Wally Lamb, Kim Herzinger, Lisel Mueller, Sharman Russell, Ron Tanner, Kenneth Gangemi, Diane Williams, H. E. Francis, Edward Hirsch, George Keithley, Donald Revell, Sandra McPherson, Pamela Stewart, Lynne McFall, John Allman, Joan Murray, Tony Quagliano, Kent Nelson, Toi Derricotte, Rita Dove, Kathy Mangan, Daniel Hayes, Jeanne Dixon, James Solheim, Wesley McNair, Jane Flanders, Susan Straight, Dan Masterson, Sigrid Nunez, Harold Witt, Melissa Lentricchia, Patrick Worth Gray, Stuart Dybek, Maura Stanton, Joyce Carol Oates, Laura Jensen, Ellen Wilbur, Kenneth Rosen, Judith Ortiz Cofer, Sherod Santos, Jennifer Atkinson, Shay Youngblood, Sandy Huss, Greg Pape, Will Baker, Naomi Clark, Mary Peterson, Lynda Hull, T. R. Hummer, Stephen Corey, Lou Mathews, David Wojahn, Robert McBrearty, Thomas Kennedy, Kelly Cherry, William Stafford, Laurie Sheck, Mark Jarman, Brenda Hillman, Marilyn Hacker, Eileen Pollack, Tony Hoagland, Gibbons Ruark, Henri Cole, Lee Upton, Colette Inez, Gary Soto, Len Roberts, Clarence Major, Philip Appleman, Ursula Le Guin, Mary Karr, Michael Collier, Walter Pavlich, Robin Hemley, Naomi Shihab Nye, Reginald Gibbons, John Drury, Christopher*

17

CONTENTS

INTRODUCTION
    Bill Henderson   10
THE COLUMBUS SCHOOL FOR GIRLS
    Liza Wieland   23
MINE OWN JOHN BERRYMAN
    Philip Levine   37
FROM THE MEADOW
    Peter Everwine   62
RED LIPSTICK
    Yolanda Barnes   63
BLOOD BROTHER
    Ayla Nutku Bachman   74
ON DUMPSTER DIVING
    Lars Eighner   88
APPLE RIND
    Carol Frost   101
READING WITH THE POETS
    Stanley Plumly   102
WHITEWING
    Janet Peery   104
MY BEST SOLDIER
    Ha Jin   125
PROLEGOMENA
    Ken Bernard   136
PARENTS
    Robert Wrigley   137
INSCRIPTIONS
    Eavan Boland   138
RAY
    Hayden Carruth   140

SIMPLICITIES
    William H. Gass   142
RUBBER LIFE
    Francine Prose   162
INSOMNIA
    Timothy Geiger   173
WHEATFIELD UNDER CLOUDED SKY
    Campbell McGrath   177
THE TELEGRAPH RELAY STATION
    Norman Lavers   179
A DAY AT THE ST. REGIS WITH DAME EDITH
    Perdita Schaffner   194
CIRCUMSTANCES
    Richard Jackson   203
FOUR DAYS: EARTHQUAKE
    Gary Young   205
FREEWAY BYPASS (Detail From Map)
    Fred Pfeil   207
HUSH HUSH
    Steven Barthelme   223
MANNEQUINS
    Laurie Sheck   239
TO A WREN ON CALVARY
    Larry Levis   241
AGAINST DECORATION
    Mary Karr   244
A NOTE ON THE TYPE
    Alexander Theroux   268
VESPERS: PAROUSIA
    Louise Glück   271
GRID
    Mark Jarman   273
BORDER WATER
    Gretchen Legler   274
FOUR STORIES
    Lydia Davis   286
OH, BY THE WAY
    Ed Ochester   290
MY FATHER'S BODY
    William Matthews   292
ACTS OF KINDNESS
    Mary Michael Wagner   294

CHRISTA
　　Sigrid Nunez   305
BUT BIRD
　　Paul Zimmer   333
TO THE MUSE
　　Carol Muske   335
WAR
　　Molly Giles   338
CRITTERWORLD
　　Steve Watkins   348
QUICK EATS
　　Charles Simic   361
WORLDLY BEAUTY
　　T. R. Hummer   363
BODIES
　　Susan Moon   366
A CLARION FOR THE QUINCENTENARY
　　Eliot Weinberger   373
WHEN I WAS SAVED
　　Andrew Hudgins   377
GOOD HEAVENS
　　Pattiann Rogers   379
LIKE HANDS ON A CAVE WALL
　　Karen Minton   382
LOOK ON THE BRIGHT SIDE
　　Dagoberto Gilb   399
SNOW FIGURE
　　David Baker   411
LOST FUGUE FOR CHET
　　Lynda Hull   413
I WOULD CALL IT DERANGEMENT
　　Gerald Stern   416
THE WRESTLER'S HEART
　　Gary Soto   419
THE OTHER LEAGUE OF NATIONS
　　Alberto Alvaro Rios   422
TWELVE O'CLOCK
　　Carolyn Kizer   434
TRAIN WHISTLES IN THE WIND AND RAIN
　　Henry Carlile   439
KERFLOOEY
　　Sharon Sheehe Stark   442

20

THE LOOM
    R. A. Sasaki   460
THE PULL
    Sharon Olds   476
BLACK AND BLUE
    Charles Wright   478
HELEN
    C. K. Williams   480
GLIMPSES: RAYMOND CARVER
    Sam Halpert, James Linville   488
SPECIAL MENTION   525
PRESSES FEATURED IN THE PUSHCART PRIZE
    EDITIONS (1976–1992)   530
CONTRIBUTORS' NOTES   535
CONTRIBUTING SMALL PRESSES   541
INDEX   550

THE COLUMBUS SCHOOL FOR GIRLS

fiction by LIZA WIELAND

from THE GEORGIA REVIEW

"IT'S THE OLDEST story in America," Mr. Jerman says, "only no one seems to know it. When Christopher Columbus went to ask Queen Isabella to bankroll his voyage to the east, she just laughed at him, and she told him it was about as likely he could make that trip as it was that he could make an egg stand on its end. But that Columbus, he said, okay Isabella, watch closely. And he took out an egg—the one he always carried for state occasions just like this—and tapped it ever so gently on one end, not enough to shatter it, but enough to flatten that end just slightly, and there the egg stood, and Isabella gave Columbus the dough, and the rest is history."

We love this story, and we love the teacher who tells it to us and girls like us, year after year at The Columbus School for Girls. We love the way he stands over the lectern at Chapel, right in front of the red-and-white banner that says *Explore thyself!* below the headmaster's favorite words of wisdom, copied from money, IN GOD WE TRUST. We like to sit left of center and close one eye. Half-blind we see Mr. Jerman's face like a hieroglyph in the midst of wisdom, a blessed interruption, and the words say IN GOD WE RUST.

We don't care much for the other teachers, the ones who tell us to spit out our chewing gum, pull up our knee socks, and button our blouses all the way up, the ones who warn us we'll never amount to anything. We know how they fear us—we're walking danger to them, the way we whoop in the halls, the way we dance in slow circles to no music—but still they dream of having us for their daughters, of taking us home and seeing what, given the proper tools and rules, we might become. We smoke cigarettes in the bathroom. We've been known to carry gin in vanilla bottles and have a swig or two after lunch.

Mr. Jerman, though, we would be his daughters in a heartbeat. We would change our names, we would all become Jermans. We would let his wife, Emily Jerman, be the mother of us all. We see her rarely, at wind-ensemble concerts, at dances, and at field-hockey games, standing on the sidelines behind the opposing team. Tiny thin Emily Jerman, always so cold that we'd like to build a fire right at her feet. Emily Jerman, always wearing one of her husband's sweaters, smiling at us, leaning her thin bones against her husband's arm and talking into his ear in a voice we've never heard but guess must sound like baby birds. We want to be like her, so we steal our fathers' sweaters, our brothers' sweaters, our boyfriends'. We let ourselves grow thin. Emily Jerman and Bryan Jerman—we say their names over and over at night into the darkness of the Upper Five Dormitory where the air is already hazy with girls' breath. We pass his name between the beds—*have you had Bryan Jerman yet?*—like he's something you could catch.

In the morning when we wake up, their names are still hanging over us, and it's still November, always November. November is by far the cruelest month at The Columbus School for Girls. By then nothing is new anymore, not the teachers, not the books, not the rules and the bravest ways to break them. November is Indian summer, and then it's rain. November, Mr. Jerman says, is longing, and we agree. We long for Thanksgiving, but we don't know why, because it will only lead to real winter, killer winter when nothing moves. All month, we long to go back to the days when our school uniforms were new and tight across our hips, when our notebooks were empty, when no one had discovered us yet.

"Girls," Mr. Jerman says in the middle of this cruel November, "I have been thinking about you."

We could say the same thing, especially since he has been reading us Emily Dickinson these past weeks. We have come to

24

think of Emily Dickinson as Emily Jerman and vice versa. We whisper about Emily Jerman's closet full of white dresses and her strange ideas about certain birds and flowers and angleworms. We think this must be what Emily Jerman does all day in the bungalow behind Lower Four Dormitory: she writes hundreds of poems on the backs of school memoranda that Mr. Jerman has folded and torn in quarters, just the right size for one of her poems about yellow daisies beheaded by winter, that white assassin.

"I have been thinking," Mr. Jerman says again, "that we need to do a little more exploring. We have been sitting like bumps on logs reading these poems when we could do so much more."

We look at him, making our smiles bright and trusting the way we think he must like them, letting him lead us on.

"I could take you to Emily Dickinson's house," Mr. Jerman says, and we lean forward over our desks. It feels like he's invited us into his own home. "If you're interested, I can call up there this afternoon. We can take one of the school vans. I'm sure my wife would love to come along too. She's always wanted to go there."

We can imagine. We can imagine Emily Jerman going to the home of her namesake, her other, her true self. We can imagine our own selves being the Jermans' daughters for a whole weekend, far away from The Columbus School for Girls, deep in what we think must be the savage jungle of western Massachusetts.

*

Mr. Jerman has a hard time convincing the headmaster to let us go. We listen to them discuss it late the next afternoon while we're waiting for tardy slips.

"Bryan," the headmaster is saying, "think about it. All of *them*. And just you and Emily. What if something happens? What if one of them goes berserk? Or gets arrested? Or smuggles along contraband?"

"Leo," Mr. Jerman says, "nonsense. The girls will be perfect ladies. It will be good for them to get out, see some more of the world. And Emily will be along to take care of any, you know, girl problems."

"I just don't think so," the headmaster says. "I'm not sure these are girls you can trust."

"Rust," we say.

"Of course I can trust them," Mr. Jerman says. "That gin at lunchtime business is all a made-up story. They're chafing at the bit a little, that's all. This trip will be just the thing. I've told their parents to call you about it."

"Oh God, Bryan," the headmaster says.

"Oh God," we say.

"Girls," the headmaster's secretary says, "you know there's none of that on school grounds."

The telephone on the secretary's desk rings in a stifled *brrrr*. We're sure it's our parents—all of them making one huge impossible conference call to tell the headmaster to keep us at this school forever, until we grow old and die. We can't stand it anymore. We forge the signatures on our tardy slips and beat it to smoke cigarettes behind Lower Four. From there we can see the Jermans' bungalow, and we keep smoking until Mr. Jerman comes home. We think his shoulders look awfully slumped, and we notice, too, the way the fiery late-afternoon light seems to have taken all the color out of his face. The front door opens, and Emily Jerman is standing there, a yellow halo surrounding her whole tiny body from head to toe. When she reaches up to touch Mr. Jerman's face, we try to look away but we can't. Our eyes have become hard cold points of darkness fixed on them, on their tenderness, and learning it. Emily and Bryan Jerman go inside their bungalow and the door closes. We watch them move from room to room past the windows until it's so dark we have to feel our way back to Upper Five, crawling on our hands and knees, lighting matches to see what little of the way we know.

At night we dream Emily Jerman has come to stand at our bedside. She is putting small pieces of paper under our pillow— Columbus School for Girls memoranda, torn in quarters. *Lie still,* she commands. *If you move, they will explode.*

The next day is Saturday, when we always have detention, and then Sunday, when we have Chapel. The opening hymn is "A Mighty Fortress Is Our God." Mr. Jerman has told us you can sing most of Emily Dickinson's poems to the tune of "A Mighty Fortress Is Our God," so we try it. The headmaster glares at us, but we stare at the word RUST beside his head, rising like the balloon of talk in a comic strip. We sing to him, enunciating like there's no tomorrow, and he watches our mouths move, trying to

26

discover our blasphemies, the mystery of us. Was there ever one of us he understood, he must be asking himself; was there ever one of us who did not have a black heart and carry a knife in her teeth?

*

"Girls," Mr. Jerman says on Monday morning, "grab your coats and hats, pack your bags. It's all set. We leave Friday afternoon. Friday night in Pennsylvania. Saturday at the Emily Dickinson Homestead."

We're stunned, and then we cheer until Mr. Jerman's eyes move from our faces and out to the middle distance. We turn in our desks to see Emily Jerman standing at the window. She waves to us and moves off across the garden.

"She wanted to get a look at you," Mr. Jerman says, his voice strangling in his throat.

We watch her as she gathers wood for kindling: birch, alder, even green pine. Her arms are full of wood and purple thistles, her red hair falling forward to cover her face and throat.

Oh Emily Jerman! Her name rises, almost to our lips. We burn for her, all day long, wherever she goes—our long hair fallen like hers, in flames.

*

By the time we're ready to leave Friday afternoon, it's getting dark. The Jermans are going to drive three hours apiece to get us as far as Harrisburg, Pennsylvania, where we've got rooms in a motel. We look out the windows and watch the back of Emily Jerman's head. She has said hello to us, but nothing after that. She rides up in front next to her husband, and sometimes their arms touch, his right and her left across the space between the seats. We stare at them when this happens, our eyes glittering and hungry, and we play charades. By the time we get an hour out of town, all we can see is night rising on the soft shoulders of the road and our own faces reflected in the windows. The highway is our own hair streaming behind us, and the moon is our eye. For miles and miles, there haven't been any lights. We're all there is in this world, just us and the Jermans.

27

In Zanesville, we stop for supper. Mr. Jerman drives off the highway and through a web of back streets to a Chinese restaurant—the "Imperious Wok," he calls it, glancing over at his wife, who turns to him and smiles. When we get to the parking lot, the marquee says, "The Imperial Wok," and we laugh, even though we don't get the joke and we don't like them having secrets between themselves, a whole history we can never know. Inside, Mr. Jerman explains the menu and shows us how to use chopsticks. He is amazed that we've never had Chinese food before. He toasts us with his tiny bowl of tea.

When the waiter comes, Emily Jerman orders a cocktail. Mr. Jerman looks at her and raises his blonde eyebrows, but doesn't say anything. We realize this is the first whole sentence we have ever heard Emily Jerman say: *I would like a double vodka on the rocks.* Her voice is surprisingly low and sweet. We have always thought she should have a high voice to go with her tiny frail body, but instead it's a voice like being wrapped in a smoky blanket. We hope she'll keep on talking. Right now we want to be Emily Jerman's daughters more than anything else in the world.

The waiter brings our food, announcing each dish quietly, with a question, like he's trying to remind himself what it is. After each name, Mr. Jerman says "ah" and his wife laughs, a low, thrilling laugh, and we know we're going to have to spend all night in our motel room trying to imitate it exactly. She orders another double vodka.

"Dear," Mr. Jerman says, "who's going to help me drive for the next four hours?"

"We will," we say, reaching into our coat pockets for our driver's licenses. We hand them over to Emily Jerman, who looks at the pictures and then up at us, squinting her eyes to get the true likeness.

"Seventeen," she says, "Damn. I remember that." Then she laughs her low laugh—like a car's engine, we think, finely tuned.

Mr. Jerman hands around the dishes of steaming food. We still don't know what any of it is, but the strange new smells are making us not care. We feel a little drunk now, chasing gobbets of meat and snaking onion around on our plates with these wooden knitting needles. A triangle of something bright red flies from someone's plate and lands in Mr. Jerman's tea bowl, and grains of rice ring our placemats where we've let them fall. We lean our heads back and drip noodles into our mouths, noodles that taste like peanut butter. We lick the plum sauce spoon. We take tiny little sips of tea. We watch Emily Jerman get looped.

"Seventeen. Oh God, do I remember seventeen. It was before you," she says to her husband, leaning against him in that way that makes us stare at them with hard bright eyes. "I was at The Columbus School for Girls, can you imagine? Things were by the book then, no drinking gin at lunch, no blouses open down to here, no overnight trips. The goddamn earth was flat then. That's why it's called The Columbus School for Girls, to show how far you could go in the wrong direction."

"Emily," Mr. Jerman says, exactly the way he says the name in class, like he's a little afraid of it.

"Oh don't Emily me, sweetheart," she says thrillingly, her low laugh like a runaway vehicle. "I'm just giving your girls some true history, that's all."

"What was it like?" we ask.

"The same, really. We read Emily Dickinson, too. Or some of us did, 'A narrow fellow in the grass,' " she says, to prove it.

"What house did you live in?" we want to know.

"Cobalt," she says, naming a dormitory we've never heard of. "But the boiler exploded and it burnt to the ground ten years ago. Nobody likes to talk about it."

We glance over at Mr. Jerman, who seems lost to us, shaking his head.

"A girl nearly died," Emily Jerman says, looking us straight in the eye. "And the gardener did die. They were, you know, in her room. It was a big scandal. Hoo boy."

"Emily," Mr. Jerman says in a way that lets us know everything his wife is saying is true.

"He loved Emily Dickinson," Emily Jerman tells us.

"Who did?" her husband says. But we already know who she means.

"The gardener. He'd been to see her house. He had postcards. He gave me one."

"You never told me that." Bryan Jerman stares at his wife. Already we're miles ahead of him, and we can see it all: the girl who is Emily Jerman grown young, and the gardener there beside us, then the two bodies tangled together, singed, blackened by smoke.

"Fortune cookies!" Emily Jerman cries, clapping her hands. "We'll play fortune-cookie charades. It's just like regular charades, only when you get to the part about movie, book, or play, you do this."

She brings the palms of her hands together, pulls them in close to her chest, and bows from the waist. Mr. Jerman is smiling again, looking at his wife like he can't believe how clever she is. The fire, the girl, and the gardener drift from the table, guests taking their leave.

"A bit of mysterious East for you," the waiter says. "Many happy fortunes."

Look below the surface, truth lies within. Unusual experience will enrich your life. Positive attitude will bring desired result. Time is in your favor, be patient. The rare privilege of being pampered will delight you. The fun is just beginning, take it as it comes. Beware of those who stir the waters to suggest they are deep.

Our charades make Emily Jerman laugh until tears come to her eyes and run down her cheeks into her mouth. We watch her taste them and she watches us back, holding our eyes just as long as we hold hers. Then Mr. Jerman tells us it's time to get *on the road again,* singing it like Willie Nelson. Out in the parking lot, he takes his wife's hand and presses it to his heart. Light from the Imperial Wok falls on their coats, turning black to tender purple.

"See?" he says, and together they look east to where the lights of Zanesville die away and there's only stars and West Virginia and Pennsylvania and finally the great darkness of western Massachusetts. We stare at them, our eyes going clean through their bodies. Then we look east too, but we can't for the life of us tell what they're seeing.

Hours later, we wake to hear Emily Jerman singing along with the radio. "And when the birds fly south for a while," she sings, "oh I wish that I could go. Someone there might warm this cold heart, oh someone there might know." Her voice breaks on the last line, and we close our eyes again.

At the Holiday Inn in Harrisburg, the Jermans unload us one by one, right into our rooms, right into bed. We stay awake as long as we can listening to Emily and Bryan Jerman in the next

30

room, imagining we can hear the words and other sounds that pass between them when they're all alone.

In the morning, it's Scranton, New York City, Hartford, and on into Amherst. Emily Jerman looks terrible, her hair hanging loose, her skin the color of old snow, but she drives first and Mr. Jerman takes over after lunch. Then she stares out the window. We think something has happened to her during the night. At first we believe it has to do with love, but soon we see how wrong we are, how lost, and for a split second we wish we'd never left The Columbus School for Girls. We've been moving east with Emily Jerman, weightless, like swimmers, but now she's holding on to our uniform skirts, and she's dragging us under. When we get to the Dickinson Homestead in the middle of the afternoon, the air is so wet with snow that we're having to breathe water, like the nearly drowned.

Emily Jerman hasn't said a word all day, but when we're all out of the van, she tells us she's going to stay put. She's been moving too fast, she says, and now she needs to sit for a while. Mr. Jerman hands her the keys, squeezes her knee, and leads us inside the house. We try to catch a glimpse of her out the window as we're standing beside Emily Dickinson's piano, listening to Mr. Jerman make introductions.

The tour guide tell us she is the wife of an English professor who studies Emily Dickinson, and for a whole year when they were first married, he would talk about her in his sleep. That, she explains, is how she learned most of what she knows about the poet, by listening in on her husband's dreams. She looks straight at Mr. Jerman.

"It's how most husbands and wives come to know anything at all," she says.

He stares back at her out of his great blue unblinking eyes, and for the first time ever, we think he looks bullish and stupid. It unhinges us, and we have to sit down on Emily Dickinson's chintz sofa.

The professor's wife keeps talking. She tells us what belongs to Emily Dickinson and what doesn't. She lets us touch a teacup and hold a pair of wine glasses the color of fresh blood. We feel as though they want to leap out of our hands and smash on the floor. We almost want to throw them down to get it over with— the same way we think about standing up in Chapel and shouting

31

out something terrible. Then we wonder if we haven't already done it. At that moment, the back door opens and Emily Jerman walks into the hall. The professor's wife drops the guest book and its spine breaks. Pages and pages of visitors wash over the floor.

"See Bryan," Emily Jerman says to her husband, "I told you I shouldn't have come." As we pick up the pages of the guest book, she walks over to the piano. She stays there with her back to us for a long time, and we can tell that she is crying. We want Mr. Jerman to do something, but he stays with us, listening to the tour guide wander through all her dreamed facts, and we hate him for that.

Upstairs we see the dress and the bed, the writing table, the window that looks out over Main Street, the basket used to lower gingerbread down to children in the garden. We stick our noses inside like dogs and sniff to see if the smell of gingerbread is still there, and we tell each other that it is. When the guide's back is turned, we touch everything: the bed, the shawl, the hatbox, the dress, even the glass over the poet's soft silhouette.

We watch Emily Jerman move down the hall and into this room like she's walking in a trance. We see her eyes are red and her face is swollen. The professor's wife is talking about incontinence, and then about the Civil War, but we don't know how she got there. We watch Emily Jerman, more whisper than woman's body, a sensation in this house, a hot spirit distant from her husband and from us. We stare at the two of them, and all at once we know we will never remember anything Mr. Jerman has taught us, except this: that the world is a blind knot of electric and unspeakable desires, burning itself to nothing.

*

As we're leaving, the professor's wife makes us promise not to miss the graveyard, and we assure her that we won't. We tell her that we have already dreamed of it, just like her husband, and she tells us to button up our blouses. It's cold out, she says.

"We'll save that for tomorrow," Mr. Jerman says. "It's too dark now."

"Oh no," Emily Jerman tells him, the light beginning to come back into her voice, "it's perfect now, perfect for a graveyard."

32

She takes the keys out of her coat pocket, unlocks the van for the rest of us, and gets in behind the wheel.

"I know the way," she says. "I already looked on the map."

Emily Jerman makes three left turns and we're in West Cemetery where it's pitch dark. Mr. Jerman asks if she knows where the grave is and she nods, but then she drives us once around all the graves anyway. When we come back to the entrance road, she pulls a hard left and drives up on the grass. There in front of the van's lights are three headstones behind a black wrought-iron fence.

Emily Jerman climbs down quickly and opens the van doors from the outside. We're surprised at how strong she is, how determined she is for us to be here. She leads us to the graves, pushing us a little from behind, pointing to the marker in the middle. "Called Back," it says. She shows us all the offerings there—dried flowers, coins, somebody's ballpoint pen with its red barrel looking like a swipe of blood.

" 'Just lost when I was found,' " Emily Jerman says behind us, " 'just felt the world go by, just girt me for the onset with eternity when breath blew black and on the other side I heard recede the disappointed tide.' "

"Saved," Mr. Jerman says. "It's *saved*."

"Just lost when I was fucking *saved* then," his wife calls back. " 'Therefore as one returned I feel odd secrets of the line to tell. Some sailor skirting foreign shores.' "

We've turned around to look for her, for Emily Jerman, but she's standing in between the van's headlights, leaning back and against the grille, so we can't see her, only the smoky mist her breath makes in the cold as she speaks.

"Do another one," we say, but she won't.

"That's my favorite," she says. "It's the only one." She tells us to leave something at the grave. She says it doesn't matter what.

There's nothing in our coat pockets but spare change, wrappers from starlight mints, and our driver's licenses. We don't know what to do. We can feel panic beginning to take fire under our ribs, and we look up first at the evening sky, clear and blue-black, then across the street to the 7-Eleven, where the smell of chili dogs is billowing out the doors. We lean over and take hold of the hems of our Columbus School for Girls skirts. We find the

33

seam and pull sharply upward, and then down, tearing a rough triangle out of the bottom of the cloth. Cold air rushes in at our thighs and between our legs.

"Girls!" Mr. Jerman says, but his voice gets lost in the sound of his wife's laughter.

"What a waste," he says, but we tell him it isn't. At school, sewing is compulsory, and we know that with an extra tuck and the letting out of one pleat at the other seam, our skirts will look exactly the same again.

*

At dinner, Mr. Jerman hardly says a word while his wife orders double vodkas and tells us more about her days at The Columbus School for Girls.

"Those graduation dresses you have now," she says, "they were my idea."

We look at Mr. Jerman, who nods his head.

"I just couldn't stand the thought of black robes, and so I drew up a pattern and took it into the headmaster—who's dead now, by the way, and what a blessing *that* is."

"What did he say?" we ask.

"He said absolutely no, he wasn't going to have a bunch of girls traipsing around in their nighties. He wanted us fully covered. But I went ahead and made one dress and wore it every day. Every day for all of March and most of April. I got detention every day, too, and served them all, and finally he gave in."

We wonder why Emily Jerman would now be passing the rest of her life at a place that had treated her so badly. We think she must love Bryan Jerman beyond reason. We can't imagine that she wants to go back tomorrow, not any more than we do.

"It was a beautiful place then," she says. "The gardens were kept up. Outside was like Eden. The gardener could do anything, bring anything back to life. He was a genius."

"Emily," Mr. Jerman says, "I believe you had a crush on that gardener."

"Darling," she says, "we thought you'd never guess—didn't we, girls?"

His laugh dies to a choking sound as his wife stares at him, breathing hard and smiling like she's just won a race. The silence

34

is terrible, beating between them, but we won't break it. We want to watch and see how it will break itself.

"To the new girls," Emily Jerman says finally, toasting us with her third vodka. We can see how, inside the glass, our own faces look back at us for a split second before they shatter into light and fire and gluey vodka running into Emily Jerman's mouth.

*

We don't know how long we've been asleep when Mr. Jerman comes in to wake us up. It's still dark outside. We have been dreaming but we couldn't say about what. Mr. Jerman stands beside our beds and reaches out to turn on the lamp. When he can't find the switch, he takes a book of matches from his pocket, lights one, and holds it over our heads. We think maybe we have been dreaming about that, a tongue of flame hissing above us, or about everything that is going to happen now.

Mr. Jerman tells us to put on our shoes and socks, our coats over our nightgowns, and then he leads us outside, down to the parking lot where the motel's airport van is waiting. The heat inside is on high, so we can barely hear what passes between Mr. Jerman and the driver, except when he says he couldn't very well leave young girls alone in a motel, now could he?

We know they're taking us back to Amherst, and when we pull into West Cemetery, we know why. There, exactly where Emily Jerman had parked it in the early evening, is our school van, the lights on, shining on the wrought-iron fence and the three headstones behind it. Emily Jerman is standing behind the fence, her right hand curled around one of the thin black posts rising up to shoulder height.

Two West Cemetery guards stand off to her left, motionless, watching, their bodies balanced slightly ahead of their feet and their heads hung down as if they had been running and then had to stop suddenly to keep from going over the edge of the world.

"Girls," Emily Jerman says when she sees us standing with her husband. "Look at you, traipsing around in your nighties. How far do you think you're going to get in this world dressed like that? You have to learn how to keep warm. When I was your age, I learned how. When I was your age, I was on fire. On *fire*, do you understand?"

35

We do. We see the two bodies pressed close, Emily Jerman and the gardener who could bring almost anything back to life. We hear his whispering and smell her hair in flames.

Mist rises in front of the van's headlights. The cemetery ground between us and Mr. Jerman looks like it's burning, but this does not surprise us. It only makes us curious, like the night birds that rise now from the leaves to ask *whose fire? whose fire?* and then drop back to sleep.

We know what will happen next. Mr. Jerman will walk through this fire and it won't consume him. He will move past us toward his wife, and we'll feel his breath as he passes, sweet and danger-ously cold. This time, we'll look away when they touch. We won't have to see how they do it, or hear what words they use. We know what we need to know. This is the new world.

Nominated by Sandy Huss and The Georgia Review

MINE OWN JOHN BERRYMAN

by PHILIP LEVINE

from THE GETTYSBURG REVIEW

I CAN'T SAY IF all poets have had mentors, actual living, breathing masters who stood or sat before them making the demands that true mentors must make if the fledgling is ever to fly. Some poets seem to have been totally self-starting, like the cars they used to build in Detroit; I'm thinking of such extraordinary examples as Emily Dickinson and Walt Whitman, who over a hundred years ago created not only their own gigantic works but the beginnings of something worthy enough to be American poetry, and they did it out of their imaginations and their private studies and nothing more. But then they had the advantage of being geniuses. And neither was from Detroit. I think also of those poets who *had* to be poets, whom no one or nothing short of death could have derailed from their courses—John Keats, Dylan Thomas, Arthur Rimbaud—and who outstripped their mentors before they even got into second gear. There are those who were lucky enough to find among their peers people of equal talent and insight to help them on their way—poets like Williams and Pound, who for the crucial early years of their writing careers ignited each other. Though, of course, Williams tells us in the "Prologue" to *Kora in Hell* that Ezra benefited also from the scathing criticism of Williams's father William George. Williams tells us that his father "had been holding forth in downright sentences upon my own 'idle nonsense' when he turned and became

37

equally vehement concerning something Ezra had written: what in heaven's name Ezra meant by 'jewels' in a verse that had come between them. These jewels,—rubies, sapphires, amethysts and whatnot, Pound went on to explain with great determination and care, were the backs of books as they stood on a man's shelf. 'But why in heaven's name don't you say so then?' was my father's triumphant and crushing rejoinder." Pound himself showed Ford Madox Ford some early verse, serious stuff, and Fordie laughed so hard upon reading the work he actually fell on the floor and "rolled around on it squealing with hilarity at the poems." Pound said that Ford's laughter saved him two years of work in the wrong direction. Terrible conditions have driven others to take up the pen in an effort to write their way out of the deepest nightmares imaginable—Wilfred Owen in the trenches, Edward Thomas in his melancholia, Hart Crane in the slough of Cleveland. In some cases it worked.

As for those of us here in the United States of America in the second half of the twentieth century, we have developed something called Creative Writing, a discipline that not only flourishes on hundreds of campuses but has even begun to invade the public schools. It has produced most of the poets—for better or worse—now writing in the country. One can only regard it as one of the most amazing growth industries we have. Thus, at the same time as we've made our society more racist, more scornful of the rights of the poor, more imperialist, more elitist, more tawdry, money-driven, selfish, and less accepting of minority opinions, we have democratized poetry. Today anyone can become a poet: all he or she need do is travel to the nearest college and enroll in Beginning Poetry Writing and then journey through the dozen stages of purgatory properly titled Intermediate Poetry Writing and Semi-Advanced Poetry Writing, all the way to Masterwork Poetry Writing, in which course one completes her epic on the sacking of Yale or his sonnet cycle on the paintings of Edward Hopper, or their elegies in a city dumpster, and thus earns not only an MFA but a crown of plastic laurel leaves. Do I sound skeptical? Let me sound skeptical.

But I also must in fairness add that it is impossible for me to imagine myself as the particular poet I have become—again for better or for worse—without the influence of a single teacher, my one great personal mentor, and amazingly enough I found him at the head of a graduate class at that most unfashionable of writing industries, the much-maligned Iowa Writers' Workshop. He was, of course, John Berryman, not yet forty years old but soon to be so, with one book of poems to his credit and stuck with the job of teaching poetry writing—for the first time in his life and for the last.

I did not go to the University of Iowa to study with John Berryman; in 1953 his reputation was based on *The Dispossessed*, that first book, and it was no larger than it should have been. The poem "Homage to Mistress Bradstreet" had not yet appeared in *The Partisan Review*, though it soon would and would create shock waves through the then-tiny world of American poetry. The attraction at Iowa was Robert Lowell, whose second book, *Lord Weary's Castle*, had received the Pulitzer Prize, and whose singular voice had excited young poets as far away as Michigan. I among them journeyed to Iowa and enrolled in Lowell's writing workshop and audited his seminar in modern poetry; this was the fall of '53, America under Eisenhower ("Wide empty grin that never lost a vote," Berryman would later write) transforming itself into America under Joe McCarthy.

To say I was disappointed in Lowell as a teacher is an understatement, although never having taken a poetry workshop I had no idea what to expect. But a teacher who is visibly bored by his students and their poems is hard to admire. The students were a marvel: we were two future Pulitzer Prize winners, one Yale winner, one National Book Critics Circle Award winner, three Lamont Prize winners, one American Book Award winner. Some names: Donald Justice, W. D. Snodgrass, Jane Cooper, William Dickey, Robert Dana, Paul Petrie, Melvin Walker LaFollette, Henri Coulette, Donald Petersen, and an extraordinarily gifted woman named Shirley Eliason, who soon turned to the visual arts and became a master. And your present speaker. I am sure there were others among the thirteen who were excited by Lowell as teacher, for Lowell was one to play favorites. No matter how much they wrote like Lowell, some of the poets could do no wrong; in all fairness to Lowell, he praised them even when they wrote like Jarrell. Needless to say, I could write nothing that pleased Lowell, and when at the end of the semester he awarded me a B, I was not surprised. Along with the B he handed me a little card with scribbled notes regarding my poems and then told me I had made more progress than anyone else in the class. "You have come the farthest," he drawled, which no doubt meant I had started from nowhere. "Then why the B?" I asked. "I've already given the A's out," he said. This was at our second and last fifteen-minute conference—which did not irritate me nearly as much as our first, when he accused me of stealing my Freudian insights and vocabulary from Auden. "Mr. Lowell," I had responded (I never got more intimate than Mister and he never encouraged me to do so), "I'm Jewish. I steal Freud directly from Freud; he was one of ours." Mr. Lowell merely sighed.

Lowell was, if anything, considerably worse in the seminar; we expected him to misread our poems—after all, most of them were confused and, with very few exceptions, only partly realized, but to see him bumbling in the face of "real poetry" was discouraging. The day he assured the class that Housman's "Lovliest of Trees, the Cherry Now" was about suicide, Melvin LaFollette leaned over and whispered in my ear, "We know what he's thinking about." His fierce competitiveness was also not pleasant to behold: with the exceptions of Bishop and Jarrell he seemed to have little use for any practicing American poet, and he once labelled Roethke "more of an old woman than Marianne Moore." He was eager to ridicule many of our recent heroes, poets I for one would have thought him enamored of: Hart Crane and Dylan Thomas. Still, he was Robert Lowell, master of a powerful and fierce voice that all of us respected, and though many of us were disappointed, none of us turned against the man or his poetry. As Don Petersen once put it, "Can you imagine how hard it is to live as Robert Lowell, with that inner life?"

During the final workshop meeting he came very close to doing the unforgivable: he tried to overwhelm us with one of his own poems, an early draft of "The Banker's Daughter," which appeared in a much shorter though still hideous version six years later in *Life Studies*. Someone, certainly not Lowell, had typed up three-and-a-half single-spaced pages of heroic couplets on ditto masters so that each of us could hold his or her own smeared purple copy of his masterpiece. He intoned the poem in that enervated voice we'd all become used to, a genteel Southern accent that suggested the least display of emotion was déclassé. I sat stunned by the performance, but my horror swelled when several of my classmates leaped to praise every forced rhyme and

40

obscure reference. (The subject was Marie de Medici, about whom I knew nothing and could care less.) No one suggested a single cut, not even when Lowell asked if the piece might be a trifle too extended, a bit soft in places. Perish the thought; it was a masterpiece! And thus the final class meeting passed with accolades for the one person present who scarcely needed praise and who certainly had the intelligence and insight to know it for what it was: bootlicking.

His parting words were unqualified praise of his successor, John Berryman, not as poet but as one of the great Shakespearean scholars of the age. And then he added that if we perused the latest issue of the *Partisan* we would discover the Mistress Bradstreet poem, clear evidence that Berryman was coming "into the height of his powers," a favorite phrase of Lowell's and one he rarely employed when speaking of the living. In fairness to Lowell, he was teetering on the brink of the massive nervous breakdown that occurred soon after he left for Cincinnati to occupy the Elliston Chair of Poetry. Rumors of his hospitalization drifted back to Iowa City, and many of us felt guilty for damning him as a total loss.

How long Berryman was in town before he broke his wrist I no longer recall, but I do remember that the first time I saw him he was dressed in his customary blue blazer, the arm encased in a black sling, the effect quite dramatic. As person and teacher, John was an extraordinary contrast to Lowell. To begin with, he did not play favorites: everyone who dared hand him a poem burdened with second-rate writing tasted his wrath, and that meant all of us. He never appeared bored in the writing class; to the contrary, he seemed more nervous in our presence than we in his. Whereas Lowell always sprawled in a chair as though visibly troubled by his height, John almost always stood and often paced as he delivered what sounded like memorized encomiums on the nature of poetry and life. Lowell's voice was never more than faintly audible and always encased in his curiously slothful accent, while Berryman articulated very precisely, in what appeared to be an actor's notion of Hotspur's accent. His voice would rise in pitch with his growing excitement until it seemed that soon only dogs would be able to hear him. He tipped slightly forward as though about to lose his balance, and conducted his performance

41

with the forefinger of his right hand. The key word here is performance, for these were memorable meetings in which the class soon caught his excitement. All of us sensed that something significant was taking place.

Beyond the difference of personal preferences and presentation was a more significant one. Lowell had pushed us toward a poetry written in formal meters, rhymed, and hopefully involved with the griefs of great families, either current suburban ones or those out of the great storehouse of America's or Europe's past. We got thundering dramatic monologues from Savanarola and John Brown that semester. For Berryman it was open house. He found exciting a poem about a particular drinking fountain in a bus station in Toledo, Ohio. Lowell certainly would have preferred a miraculous spring in that other Toledo—though now that he was no longer a practicing Catholic, sainthood seemed also to bore him. Berryman was delighted with our curious efforts in the direction of free verse, on which he had some complex notions concerning structure and prosody. He even had the boldness to suggest that contemporary voices could achieve themselves in so unfashionable and dated a form as the Petrarchan sonnet. To put it simply, he was all over the place and seemed delighted with the variety we represented.

Their contrasting styles became more evident during the second meeting of the class. Lowell had welcomed a contingent of hangers-on, several of whom were wealthy townspeople dressed to the nines and hugging their copies of *Lord Weary's Castle*. Now and then one would submit a poem; Lowell would say something innocuous about it, let the discussion hang in mid-air for a moment, then move on to something else. Berryman immediately demanded a poem from one of this tribe. The poem expressed conventional distaste for the medical profession by dealing with the clichés of greed and indifference to suffering. (We later learned it was written by a doctor's wife.) John shook his head violently. "No, no," he said, "it's not that it's not poetry. I wasn't expecting poetry. It's that it's not true, absolutely untrue, unobserved, the cheapest twaddle." Then he began a long monologue in which he described the efforts of a team of doctors to save the life of a friend of his, how they had struggled through a long night, working feverishly. "They did not work for money. There was no money in it. They worked to save a human life because it was a human life and thus precious. They did not know who the man was, that he was a remarkable spirit. They knew only that he was too young to die, and so they worked to save him, and failing, wept." (It turned out the man was Dylan Thomas, but Berryman did not mention this at the time.) A decent poet did not play fast and loose with the facts of this world, he or she did not accept television's notion of reality. I had never before observed such enormous cannons fired upon such a tiny target. The writer left the room in shock, and those of us who had doubts about our work—I would guess all of us—left the room shaken.

We returned the next Monday to discover that Berryman had moved the class to a smaller and more intimate room containing one large seminar table around which we all sat. He was in an antic mood, bubbling with enthusiasm and delighted with our presence. He knew something we did not know: all but the hard-core masochists had dropped, leaving him with only the lucky thirteen. "We are down to the serious ones," he announced, and seemed pleased with the situation; he never again turned his powerful weapons on such tiny life rafts. In truth, once we'd discovered what he'd accomplished, we too were pleased not to have to share his attention with writers we knew were only horsing around.

Now came the hard task for him of determining what we knew and what we didn't know. At least half of us were trying to write in rhyme and meter, and a few of us were doing it with remarkable skill. It was at this meeting that he asked each of us to turn in a Petrarchan sonnet so that he might have some idea how far we'd come on the road to grace and mastery in the old forms. (The logistics were simple: we turned in our work on the Friday before our Monday meeting, and John selected the work to be dittoed and discussed in class.) He presented us with two models, both recited from memory.

THE SIRENS *by John Manifold*

Odysseus heard the sirens; they were singing
Music by Wolf and Weinberger and Morley

43

About a region where the swans go winging,
Vines are in color, girls are growing surely

Into nubility, and pylons bringing
Leisure and power to farms that live securely
Without the landlord. Still, his eyes were stinging
With salt and seablink, and the ropes hurt sorely.

Odysseus saw the sirens; they were charming,
Blonde, with snub breasts and little neat posteriors,
But could not take his mind off the alarming
Weather report, his mutineers in irons,
The radio failing; it was bloody serious.
In twenty minutes he forgot the sirens.

Recited in Berryman's breathless style, it sounded like something he might have written; he had an uncanny knack of making a great deal of poetry sound like something he might have written. And who was John Manifold? An obscure Australian poet who fought in ww II, someone we should discover if we were serious, as he was, about poetry. The second sonnet was Robinson's "Many Are Called?" which begins "The Lord Apollo, who has never died. . . ." After reciting it John went back to a passage in the octave:

And though melodious multitudes have tried,
In ecstasy, in anguish, and in vain,
With invocation sacred and profane
To lure him, even the loudest are outside.

"Who are those multitudes?" he almost shouted. Petrie, a great lover of Robinson, answered, "The poets." "Exactly, Mr. Petrie, the poets. Certainly the poets in this room." It was perfectly clear he did not exclude himself.

Much to my horror my Petrarchan sonnet was selected for discussion on that third meeting. (I believe the poem no longer exists; I had the good luck never to have had it accepted for publication.) Actually, it was not that bad: it was about food, which had been an obsession of mine for several months; I was running out of money and so ate very little and very badly. To be more precise, the poem was about my mother's last Thanksgiving

44

feast, which I had returned home to participate in; since my mother was a first-rate office manager and a tenth-rate cook, the event had been a disaster. John discussed four poems that day. The first was not a Petrarchan sonnet, and as far as he could determine had no subject nor any phrasing worth remembering. The second did have a subject, but John went to the board to scan its meter. "This is NOT iambic," he said. After getting through four lines, he turned and headed directly toward the cowering poet, suspended the page over his head, and finally let it fall. "This is metrical chaos. Pray you avoid it, sir." I was next. Much to my relief, John affirmed that, yes, this was a Petrarchan sonnet; it was iambic and it did possess a fine subject—the hideous nature of the American ritual meal become a farce. He paused. "But, Levine, it is not up to its most inspired moments—it has accepted three mediocre rhymes, it is padded where the imagination fails. If it is to become a poem, the author must attack again and bring the entirety up to the level of its few fine moments." In effect John was giving us a lesson in how poems are revised: one listened to one's own voice when it was "hot" (a word he liked) and let that "hot" writing redirect one toward a radical revision. "No hanging back," he once said. "One must be ruthless with one's own writing or someone else will be." (I tried but failed to improve the poem. Even at twenty-six, I had not learned to trust the imagination.)

It was clear that among those poems considered, mine had finished second best, and for this I was enormously relieved. What follows is the best, exactly in the form we saw it on that late February Monday in 1953:

SONNET *by Donald Justice*

The wall surrounding them they never saw;
The angels, often. Angels were as common
As birds or butterflies, but looked more human.
As long as the wings were furled, they felt no awe.
Beasts, too, were friendly. They could find no flaw
In all of Eden: this was the first omen.
The second was the dream which woke the woman:
She dreamed she saw the lion sharpen his claw.

As for the fruit, it had no taste at all.
They had been warned of what was bound to happen;
They had been told of something called the world;
They had been told and told about the wall.
They saw it now; the gate was standing open.
As they advanced, the giant wings unfurled.

After reading the poem aloud, John returned to one line: "As for the fruit, it had no taste at all." "Say that better in a thousand words," he said, "and you're a genius." He went on: "One makes an assignment like this partly in jest, partly in utter seriousness, to bring out the metal in some of you and to demonstrate to others how much you still need to learn. No matter what one's motives are, no teacher has the right to expect to receive something like this: a true poem." Class dismissed.

A week later a telling incident occurred. The class considered a sonnet by one of its more gifted members, a rather confused and confusing poem which Berryman thrashed even though one member of the class found it the equal of the Justice poem from the previous week. The tortured syntax suggested Berryman's own "Nervous Songs," but he saw little virtue in the poem and felt it was more in the tradition of Swinburne than any contemporary poem should be, writing that tried to bully its readers with rhetoric rather than move them with the living language of the imagination. "Write good prose diction in a usual prose order," he said, "unless you've got a damn good reason for doing otherwise." (It was clear he must have felt he had a damn good reason for doing otherwise when he wrote "Bradstreet.") After class, as we ambled back to the student union for coffee and more poetry talk, the same student who had defended the poem informed Berryman that the author had recently had a sheaf of poems accepted by *Bottege Oscura*, then the best-paying and most prestigious literary magazine in the world. Berryman froze on the sidewalk and then turned angrily on the student and shouted, "Utterly irrelevant, old sport, utterly irrelevant!" He assured the man that absolute "shit" appeared in the so-called "best" publications, while much of the finest poetry being written went begging. (No doubt his own difficult early career had taught him that.) "You're stupid to have raised the subject, stupid or jejune." He paused a moment. "I'll give you the benefit of the doubt: jejune." John smiled, and the incident passed. He was incredibly serious about poetry, and one of us had learned that the hard way. In her gossipy *Poets in Their Youth,* Eileen Simpson would have us believe that all the poets in "the Berryman circle" ached to be the elected legislators of the world and suffered deeply because they were not among the famous and powerful. Everything I saw during the semester contradicted that view: the reward for writing a true poem was the reward of writing a true poem, and there was none higher.

In spite of his extraordinary sense of humor, the key to Berryman's success as a teacher was his seriousness. This was the spring of the Army-McCarthy hearings, the greatest television soap-opera before the discovery of Watergate. John, as an addicted reader of *The New York Times,* once began a class by holding up the front page so the class might see the latest revelation in the ongoing drama. "These fools will rule for a while and be replaced by other fools and crooks. This," and he opened a volume of Keats to the "Ode to a Nightingale," "will be with us for as long as our language endures." These were among the darkest days of the Cold War, and yet John was able to convince us— merely because he believed it so deeply—that nothing could be more important for us, for the nation, for humankind, than our becoming the finest poets we could become. And there was no doubt as to how we must begin to accomplish the task; we must become familiar with the best that had been written, we must feel it in our pulse.

"Levine, you're a scholar," he once roared out at me in class. "Tell us how you would go about assembling a bibliography on the poetry of Charles Churchill." A scholar I was not, and John knew it, but he had a point: that poets had to know these things. The ignorant but inspired poet was a total fiction, a cousin to Hollywood's notion of the genius painter who boozes, chases girls, and eventually kills himself by falling off a scaffold in the Sistine Chapel. "Friends," John was saying, "it's hard work, and the hard work will test the sincerity of your desire to be poets." He rarely mentioned inspiration, perhaps because he assumed that most of us had been writing long enough to have learned that it came to those who worked as best they could through the barren periods, and this was—he once told me—a barren period

47

for him. So we knew how to begin the task of becoming a poet: study and work. And how did it end? Here John was just as clear: it never ended. Speaking of the final poems of Dylan Thomas, he made it clear they were merely imitations of the great work of his early and middle period. "You should always be trying to write a poem you are unable to write, a poem you lack the technique, the language, the courage to achieve. Otherwise you're merely imitating yourself, going nowhere because that's always easiest." And suddenly he burst into a recitation of "The Refusal to Mourn the Death by Fire of a Child in London," ending:

> Deep with the first dead lies London's daughter,
> Robed in the long friends,
> The grains beyond age, the dark veins of her mother,
> Secret by the unmourning water
> Of the riding Thames.
> After the first death, there is no other.

"Can you imagine possessing that power and then squandering it?" he asked. "During our lifetime that man wrote a poem that will never be bettered."

No doubt his amazing gift for ribaldry allowed him to devastate our poems without crushing our spirits, that and the recognition on his part that he too could write very badly at times. He made it clear to us from the outset that he had often failed as a poet and for a variety of reasons: lack of talent, pure laziness ("Let's face it," he once said to me, "life is mainly wasted time"), and stupid choices. "There are so many ways to ruin a poem," he said, "it's quite amazing good ones ever get written." On certain days he loved playing the clown. One Monday he looked up from the class list sent to him by the registrar and asked Paul Petrie why he was getting twice as much credit for the course as anyone else. Paul said he wasn't sure. "Perhaps," said John, "you're getting the extra units in Physical Education and Home Economics. I'd like you to arrive twenty minutes early and do fifty laps around the room and then erase the blackboard. You might also do a few push-ups or work on your technique of mixing drinks." He then discovered my name was not on the roll. (The truth was, lacking sufficient funds, I had not registered.) He asked me if I thought the registrar was anti-Semitic. No, I said, just sloppy.

"You realize," he said, "that until your name appears on this list you do not exist. Tell me," he added, "does anyone else see this Levine fellow? Sometimes I have delusions." As the weeks passed my name continued not to appear on the roster, and John continued to make a joke out of it. "Levine, should I go see the registrar and remedy this hideous state of affairs?" I assured him it was unnecessary, that it was just a meaningless slip-up, and I wasn't taking it personally. "You're quite sure it's not anti-Semitism, Levine? These are dark times." Indeed they were for many Americans, but for the young poets in this workshop they were nothing if not glory days.

"Levine," he said on another day, "when was the last time you read your Shakespeare?" "Last week," I said. "And what?" "*Measure for Measure*." "Fine. I've noticed you consistently complain about the quantity of adjectives in the poems of your classmates." This was true. "Is it the number that matters or the quality?" I failed to answer. "Remember your Blake: 'Bring out number, weight, & measure in a year of dearth.'" I nodded. " 'Thy turfy mountains where live nibbling sheep.' Two nouns, two adjectives. Any complaints, Levine?" I had none. "Who wrote the line?" "Shakespeare," I said, "What play?" Again I was silent. His long face darkened with sadness. LaFollette answered, "*The Tempest*." "Levine, do not return to this class until you have reread *The Tempest*. I assume you've read it at least once." I had. " 'Fresher than May, sweeter / Than her gold buttons on the boughs . . . ' Recognize it?" I did not. "There is great poetry hiding where you least suspect it, there for example, buried in that hideous speech from *The Two Noble Kinsmen*, Act III, Scene I." Much scratching of pens as the class bowed to their notebooks. "We must find our touchstones where we can."

Knowing I had gone to Wayne University in Detroit where John had once taught, he asked me if I'd studied with the resident Shakespeare scholar, Leo Kirschbaum, whom I had found a brilliant teacher. "Amazing fellow, Dr. Kirschbaum; singlehandedly he set back Lear scholarship two decades." Little wonder I'd failed to recognize the line from *The Tempest*. While he was on the subject of Shakespeare, he required the entire class to reread *Macbeth* by the next meeting. " 'And yet dark night strangles the travelling lamp.' Hear how the line first strangles and then releases itself. Read the play carefully, every line, let it heighten

49

your awareness of the extraordinary possibilities for dense imagery. You should know that Shakespeare had less than two weeks to complete the play. Why was that, Mr. Justice?" Don, well on his way to his doctorate, explained that the ascendancy to the English throne of James VI of Scotland called for a play in praise of James's Scotch ancestry. Berryman nodded. "Took him no time at all to write it, and yet it would take half the computers in the world a year to trace the development of the imagery that a single human imagination created and displayed in a play of unrivalled power." So much for the school of Engineering. We were never to forget that men and women of the greatest intellect and imagination had for centuries turned toward poetry to fulfill their private and civic needs.

Certain classes were devoted to special subjects relating to poetic practices, prosody for example. For two hours John lectured on the development of this study and how amazingly fragmented and useless the literature was. People of great learning and sensitivity had come to preposterous conclusions, and nothing in print was reliable. It was our duty to master this literature and discover what was useful and what was nonsense. "A man as learned as George Saintsbury, a man who had read and absorbed so much that in old age he took to studying doctoral dissertations from American universities just to keep busy, a man of that breadth of knowledge, gave us a three-volume study of prosodic practices in British and American poetry, and on almost every significant point he is wrong." Still, he urged us to read the work, for if nothing else it was a brilliant anthology of the diversity and richness of poetry in English. We, the hungry students, demanded to know to whom he went for "the scoop," another of his expressions. He laughed and pointed to his ear. There was no such book, and as in everything else we were thrown on our own. We would develop a prosody that would allow us to write the poetry we needed to write, or we wouldn't, in which case that poetry would never be written. And in order to do it right, we had to learn from those poets who had already done it—for as John made clear, those who best understood prosody—Shakespeare, Milton, Keats, Blake, Hopkins, Frost, Roethke—had better things to do than write handbooks for our guidance.

"Let us say you are appalled by the society in which you live—God knows it is appalling—and you want to create a poetry that speaks to the disgusting human conditions around you. You want to mount a powerful assault, you want to be the prophet Amos of the present age. To which poet would you turn for aid?" Silence from the class. "You want to evoke your rage, your righteous indignation, in numbers that will express the depthless power of your convictions. To whom do you turn?" A voice from the class: "Robert Lowell." "Good choice, but there is a danger here, correct?" The voice: "Yes, I already sound too much like Lowell. I'm doing my best to avoid him." Berryman: "Indeed you are. When I first saw your poems I thought you'd borrowed Cal's old portable Smith-Corona. Why not go to Cal's source, the poet upon whom he based the movement and the syntax of his own work? And who would that be?" Another voice from the class: "Pope." "No, no, you're blinded by his use of the couplet. Milton, our great Milton." Affirmative nods from the class; how could we not know something so obvious. John quoted "On the Late Massacre in Piedmont," using his forefinger to mark the ends of the lines so we heard how powerful the enjambment was. "Bring the diction three hundred years toward this moment and you have one of Cal's early sonnets." More nodding of heads. "And the key to such rhythmic power is . . . ?" Silence. "Speed, achieved by means of a complex syntax and radical enjambment. Speed translates always into rhythmic power, and speed is unobtainable in a heavily end-stopped line."

Then he turned to me. "For the power you so dearly aspire to, Levine, you must turn to the master, Milton, the most powerful poet in the language, though you might do well to avoid the Latinate vocabulary. Have you studied Latin?" Levine: "No." "You might consider doing so; that way you'll know what to avoid when you're stealing from Milton. Do you have another favorite among your contemporaries?" Levine: "Dylan Thomas." Berryman: "It doesn't show, Levine, it doesn't show; you've done a superb job of masking that particular debt. How have you managed that?" Levine: "I didn't. I wrote through my Dylan Thomas phase and quit. It was impossible for me to write under his influence and not sound exactly like him except terrible." Berryman: "Levine, you've hit upon a truth. Certain poets are so much themselves they should not be imitated; they leave you no room to be yourself, and Thomas was surely one of them, as was Hart Crane, who probably ruined the careers of more young poets than

51

anything except booze. Levine, you might go to the source of Dylan's own lyrical mysticism, and who would that be?" Silence. "Mr. Justice?" Justice: "Blake." "Exactly, you might go to Blake, who is so impossibly lyrical and inventive no one in the world has the talent to sound like him." In an unusually hushed voice he recited all of Blake's early "Mad Song," ending:

> I turn my back to the east,
> From whence comforts have increased;
> For light doth seize my brain
> With frantic pain.

"Better to learn from a poet who does not intoxicate you," said Berryman, "better to immerse yourself in Hardy, whom no American wants now to sound like. A great poet seldom read." After class Henri Coulette said to me that he'd passed over Blake's "Mad Song" a dozen times and never heard it until John incanted it.

No one escaped unscathed. John advised Petrie to set aside his Shelley and Elinor Wylie and leap into modernism. Coulette was told to loosen up his strict iambics, to try to capture the quality of living speech. Strangely, he under-appreciated the formal elegance of William Dickey's work. Neither Petersen nor Jane Cooper was productive that semester; Jane later said she was put off by John's sarcasm. Shirley Eliason's work he found wonderfully dense and mysterious; he wanted more. "Write everything that occurs to you," he told us all; "you're young enough to still be searching for your voice. You certainly don't want to find it before you find your subject, and you're still young enough to accept failure." LaFollette seemed the greatest enigma to him. "Yes, yes, you have a genuine lyrical gift," he said one day in class, "but who encouraged you never to make sense, always to be opaque?" LaFollette eagerly revealed that he'd just finished a year's work with Roethke. "Yes," said John, "I can see the influence of Roethke, but Ted's best early work is remarkably straightforward on one level. Of course there is always the shadow of something more formidable, darker. Did Cal encourage this sort of obscurity?" LaFollette revealed he had also studied with Richard Eberhardt. John's mouth fell open as he stood speechless for several seconds. "You let Dick Eberhardt read your poems, and you are here to tell the tale. Amazing!"

He always wanted more work from Robert Dana, though when Dana finally gave him a poem of ninety-eight lines, he mused over it for a time and finally noted two good images. His parting words were, "If you're going to write something this long why don't you try making it poetry?" Meeting after meeting produced the same advice: "Write everything that occurs to you; it's the only way to discover where your voice will come from. And never be in a hurry. Writing poetry is not like running the four hundred meters. Coulette, do you remember what Archie Williams said his strategy was for running the four hundred meters?" (Coulette, the resident sports maven, did not know. Williams had won the gold at the '36 Berlin Olympics.) John went on: "Archie said, 'My strategy is simple; I run the first two hundred meters as fast as I can to get ahead of everyone, and I run the second two hundred meters as fast as I can to stay there.' Now that is NOT the way we write poetry, we are not in a race with anyone, but all of us are getting on in years and we'd better get moving." In other words, go as fast as you can but don't be in a hurry; we had a lifetime to master this thing, and with our gifts it would take a lifetime.

Even Justice got mauled. John found his "Beyond the Hunting Woods" a bit too refined, a bit too professionally Southern. Those dogs at the end of the poem, Belle and Ginger, all they needed were a few mint juleps. And Levine? Levine got his. According to John, Levine's best poem that semester was "Friday Night in the Delicatessen," in which a Jewish mother laments the fact that her sons are growing away from her, becoming Americans, becoming—you should forgive the expression—*goyim*. At one point she describes them with "hands for fights and alcohol." "Hands for fights, yes," said John, "but hands for alcohol? No. We drink alcohol, Levine, as I know you've learned—we absorb it through the digestive system. The fact we hold a glass of whiskey in our hands is not enough. The parallel structure is false, but this is an amazingly ambitious poem." (I lived on that word, "ambitious," for weeks, even after a friend said, "He forgot to add, 'Ambition should be made of sterner stuff.' ") Again I had finished second best. This poem was written to fulfill John's

53

assignment for an ode, the clear winner was "A Flat One," by De Snodgrass, a poem of enormous power that depicted the slow and agonizing death of a ww I veteran, and the vet's relationship with a hospital orderly who must kill to keep him alive. Even in this earlier "static semi-Symboliste version" (Snodgrass's description), it was a startling poem. (Although Lowell is generally credited for being the mentor behind the poems of *Heart's Needle* ["A Flat One" actually appears in De's second book, *After Experience*], De now claims that Lowell discouraged the writing of those poems, and quite forcefully. "Snodgrass, you have a mind," he'd said to him. "You mustn't write this kind of tear-jerking stuff." Berryman never found the poems sentimental; he tried to move De's writing further from traditional metrics toward something— as De put it—"more like his own experiments at the time . . . more like regular speech . . . less like the poetry being written at the time.")

A later class also began with a demonstration from the front page of *The New York Times*. "Allow me to demonstrate a fundamental principle of the use of language, which is simply this: if you do not master it, it will master you. Allow me to quote Senator McCarthy speaking of his two cronies, Cohen and Shine." Roy Cohen and David Shine were two assistants—investigators, he called them—of the Senator for whom he had gained extraordinary privileges which allowed Shine, for example, an ordinary enlisted man in the army, to avoid any of the more onerous or dangerous work of a soldier. "The Senator said the following: 'I stand behind them to the hilt.' We now know what Mr. McCarthy thinks we do not know, that he is about to stab them in the back, abandon them both as political liabilities." John was of course correct; within a few days the deed was done. "Because he is an habitual liar, Mr. McCarthy has blinded himself to the ability of language to reveal us even when we're taking pains not to be revealed. Exactly the same thing holds true with poetic form; if we do not control it, it will control us." He went on: "I do not mean to suggest that each time we enter the arena of the poem we must know exactly where we're headed. We have all learned that that is preposterous, for the imagination leads us where it will, and we must be prepared to follow, but—and this is the crucial point—should we lack the ability to command the poetic form, even if that form is formlessness, toward which our writing travels, we shall be mastered by that form and what we shall reveal is our ineptitude." He then turned to a student poem in formal meters and rhymed couplets and painstakingly analyzed it from the point of view of how the need to rhyme and to keep the meter had produced odd and unconvincing movements in the poem's narrative, as well as needless prepositional phrases and awkward enjambments. "A poem of real fiber, a rhymed poem, will find its rhymes on subjects, objects, and especially verbs, the key words of its content." He then quoted a poem of Hardy's which ended:

> So, they are not underground,
> But as nerves and veins abound
> In the growth of upper air,
> And they feel the sun and rain,
> And the energy again
> That made them what they were!

Again with his forefinger he scored the key words, and finally repeated that final line, " 'That made them what they were!'—my friends, what they were! That is the artist in command, that is triumph!"

Once again he seemed a walking anthology of poetic jewels, and once again we learned how exacting this thing with the poetry was. Later in Kenny's tavern, where many of us assembled after class, one poet recalled that Ignacio Sanchez Mejias, the matador elegized in Garcia Lorca's great poem, had once remarked, "This thing with the bulls is serious," and thus we produced a catch phrase for John's class: "This thing with the poems is serious."

What became increasingly clear as the weeks passed was that while John was willing on occasion to socialize with us, he was not one of us; he was the teacher, and we were the students. He had not the least doubt about his identity, and he was always willing to take the heat, to be disliked if need be. In private he once remarked to me that teaching something as difficult as poetry writing was not a popularity contest. "Even a class as remarkable as this one," he said, "will produce terrible poems, and I am the one who is obliged to say so." He sensed that the students had themselves developed a wonderful fellowship and took joy when

55

any one of them produced something fine. Whether or not he took credit for any of this I do not know. To this day I can recall Bill Dickey studying a Justice poem almost with awe. "Do you see those rhymes?" he said to me. "I'll bet this is the first time they've been used in all our poetry!" I shall never forget Don Petersen's welcoming me up the mountain of poetry—at that time Don seemed to believe he was the guardian of the mountain. He told me in his curiously gruff and tender voice that a particular poem of mine was in fact a poem, and though the class—including John—had not taken to it, it was evidence that I had become a poet. His words were welcomed and genuine. I can recall my own thrill on seeing a particular poem by Jane Cooper in which her portrayal of a nocturnal hedgehog came so vividly to life I shuddered. I expressed my wonder openly and knew she heard it. One day both Henri Coulette and Robert Dana took me aside to tell me they could scarcely believe how far I'd come in a single year. We were all taking pride and joy in each other's accomplishments.

This fellowship was a delicate and lovely thing, a quality that always distinguishes the best creative writing classes. We were learning how much farther we could go together than we could singly, alone, unknown, unread in an America that never much cared for poetry. I don't honestly know how large a role John played in the creation of this atmosphere, but I do know it had not existed during Lowell's tenure; his favoritism, his intimacy with some students and visible boredom with others, tended to divide us into two hostile factions, the ins and the outs. In John's class we were all in and we were all out, we were equals, and instead of sinking we swam together. In spite of John's willingness to be disliked, he clearly was not disliked. Of course he was a marvelous companion, and on those evenings he sought company we were all eager to supply it, but we never forgot that come Monday afternoon the camaraderie would be forgotten and he would get to the serious business of evaluating and if need be decimating poems.

Sometimes his seriousness could be more than a little intimidating. On one occasion over drinks, before going to dinner with a group of student writers and faculty, John began to muse over a remarkable poem by the Welshman Alun Lewis, "Song: On seeing dead bodies floating off the Cape." Berryman believed that

Lewis was one of the great undiscovered talents of the era. He quoted a portion of the poem, an interior monologue by a woman who has had a vision of her lover's death at sea; then his memory failed him, and he apologized to the group. It so happened one of the poets present knew the poem and took up the recitation:

> The flying fish like kingfishers
> Skim the sea's bewildered crests,
> The whales blow steaming fountains,
> The seagulls have no nests
> Where my lover sways and rests.

His memory primed, John completed the poem, which ends with the woman lamenting the "nearness that is waiting in" her bed, "the gradual self-effacement of the dead." After a moment's silence John remarked, "The dead do not efface themselves; we, the living, betray their memories." John seemed lost in his reverie on the life and early death in war of the poet when another poet present, an enormous man who worked in town as a bartender and bouncer, began to praise one of John's own war poems which had appeared in *The Dispossessed*. Suddenly awakened, John shouted in the man's face, "We are talking about great poetry, do you get it, old sport, great poetry, and not the twaddle you have in mind. I do not appreciate bootlicking." A silence followed, and the moment passed. This thing with the poetry was indeed serious.

That semester Berryman conducted the most extraordinary seminar on other writers I've ever been a part of; again, for lack of funds, I was not registered, but I missed only a single class and that when the obligation to make some money took me elsewhere. The students were assigned a single long paper of considerable scope, the subject agreed upon by teacher and poet—for all the registered students were from the workshop. The papers themselves were never presented in class, but not because Berryman found them inadequate. Indeed he raved about their quality. The reason was simply that John felt he had news to bring us on the subject of poetry in English from Whitman to the present. The highlight of the semester was his presentation of the whole of "Song of Myself," which included the most memorable and impassioned reading of a poem I have ever in my life heard, along with the most complex and rewarding analysis of Whitman's design, prosody, and imagery ever presented. When he'd finished the reading, he stood in silence a moment and then from memory presented the final section again, concluding:

I bequeath myself to the dirt to grow from the grass I love,
If you want me again look for me under your boot-soles.

You will hardly know who I am or what I mean,
But I shall be good health to you nevertheless,
And filter and fibre your blood.

Failing to fetch me at first keep encouraged,
Missing me one place search another,
I stop somewhere waiting for you.

He stood for a moment in silence, the book trembling in his hand, and then in a quiet voice said, "Do you know what that proves? That proves that most people can't write poetry!"

When the semester began I was the only non-enrolled student attending, but so extraordinary were his performances that the news spread, and by the time he gave his final Whitman lecture the room was jammed to the bursting point. Crane, Stevens, Bishop, Roethke, Eliot, Auden, Dylan Thomas, and Hardy were also subjects of his lectures. These were not talks he gave off the top of his head. Far from it. He entered the room each night shaking with anticipation and armed with a pack of note cards, which he rarely consulted. In private he confessed to me that he prepared for days for these sessions. He went away from them in a state bordering on total collapse. It would be impossible to overestimate the effect on us of these lectures, for this was an era during which Whitman was out, removed adroitly by Eliot and Pound, and kept there by the Ironists and the New Critics who were then the makers of poetic taste. In 1954 in Iowa no one dreamed that within a few years Williams would be rescued from hell, the Beats would surface, and Whitman would become the good gray father of us all. (John himself later claimed the Beats didn't know how to read Whitman and mistook his brilliant rhythmic effects for prose. "They don't write poems," is the way he put it.) I cannot speak for the entire class, but I know that Petrie, Jane Cooper, Dana, Coulette, Justice, Snodgrass, and I were convinced that "Song of Myself" was the most powerful and visionary poetic statement ever made in this country. Those lectures not only changed our poetry, they changed our entire vision of what it meant to write poetry in America, what it meant to be American, to be human. "There is that lot of me and all so luscious," I suddenly sang to myself, and believed it, and thanks to John and father Walt I still believe it. Whitman had laid out the plan for what our poetry would do, and so large was the plan there was room for all of us to take our part, as for example, Roethke was doing, that poet who according to John "thought like a flower."

Unlikely it seems now that Berryman should have performed that task, for was he not an Eastern intellectual poet and part-time New Critic himself, a protégé of Mark Van Doren and R. P. Blackmur? Like so much that concerns Berryman, the answer is ambiguous. His reviews often sounded very much like what the New Critics were turning out, except they were far wittier and often more savage; in savagery only Yvor Winters could measure up to him. Who else would be bold enough to invent a poem that a poet might have written, nay should have written, as John did in a review of Patchen, and then define Patchen's weaknesses on the basis of the poem Berryman and not Patchen had written? But unlike Winters and the rest of the New Critics, he was unashamedly Romantic at the same time as he was distrustful of the "cult of sincerity." He was, as in so many things, his own man and in a very real sense a loner.

Before we parted that semester he performed two more services for me. The day before he left for New York City—he was going East to teach at Harvard that summer—we had a long conversation on what a poet should look like. The Oscar Williams anthology, one of the most popular of that day, included photographs of most of the poets at the back of the book; John and A. E. Housman were the only exceptions—they were represented by drawings. John's was very amateurish and looked nothing like him. I asked him why he'd used it instead of a photograph. He claimed he wanted neither but Oscar had insisted, and he'd taken the lesser of the two evils. He thought either was a distraction, though the drawing did make it clear he was ugly enough to be a poet. I didn't catch his meaning and asked him to explain. "No poet worth his salt is going to be handsome; if he or she is beautiful there's no need to create the beautiful. Beautiful people are special; they don't experience life like the rest of us." He was obviously dead serious, and then he added, "Don't worry about it, Levine, you're ugly enough to be a great poet."

The next day at the airport he was in an unusually manic mood. "Think of it, Levine, in a few hours I shall be mine own John Poins." Not knowing Wyatt's poem written from exile in rural England to Poins in London, I asked him what he meant.

> I am not he, such eloquence to boast
> To make the crow in singing as the swan,
> Nor call the lion of coward beasts the most,
> That cannot take a mouse as the cat can . . .

He quoted from memory. "Wyatt, Levine, Wyatt, his rough numbers would be perfect for your verse, you crude bastard." ("Crude bastard" was his highest form of compliment.) Before boarding he invited me to send him four or five poems in a year or so, and he'd be sure to get back to me to tell me how I was doing. Having seen an enormous carton of unopened mail in his apartment, I doubted he'd ever answer, but nonetheless a year-and-a-half later I sent him four poems. His response was prompt and to the point; with xs to mark the lines and passages he thought a disaster and checks where he found me "hot," along with specific suggestions for revision; there was not a single line unremarked upon. There was also a brief letter telling me things were going well in Minneapolis and that he was delighted to know I was fooling editors with my "lousy poems." He looked forward to seeing me one day. There was not the least doubt about what he was in fact saying: our days as student and teacher had come to an end. We could not exchange poems as equals in poetry because we were not equals and might never be, and yet I had come too far to require a teacher. I felt the same way. I'd had one great poetry writing teacher, I had studied with him diligently for fifteen weeks. From now on I had to travel the road to poetry alone or with my peers. This was his final lesson, and it may have been the most important in my development.

As the years pass his voice remains with me, its haunting and unique cadences sounding in my ear, most often when I reread my own work. I can still hear him saying, "Levine, this will never do," as he rouses me again and again from my self-satisfaction and lethargy to attack a poem and attack again until I make it the best poem I am capable of. His voice is there too when I teach, urging me to say the truth no matter how painful a situation I may create, to say it with precision and in good spirits, never in rancor, and always to remember Blake's words (a couplet John loved to quote): "A truth that's told with bad intent / Beats all the Lies you can invent." For all my teaching years, now over thirty, he has been a model for me. No matter what you hear or read about his drinking, his madness, his unreliability as a person, I am here to tell you that in the winter and spring of 1954, living in isolation and loneliness in one of the bleakest towns of our difficult Midwest, John Berryman never failed his obligations as a teacher. I don't mean merely that he met every class and stayed awake, I mean that he brought to our writing and the writing of the past such a sense of dedication and wonder that he wakened a dozen rising poets from their winter slumbers so that they might themselves dedicate their lives to poetry. He was the most brilliant, intense, articulate man I've ever met, at times even the kindest and most gentle, and for some reason he brought to our writing a depth of insight and care we did not know existed. At a time when he was struggling with his own self-doubts and failings, he awakened us to our singular gifts as people and writers. He gave all he had to us and asked no special thanks. He did it for the love of poetry.

Nominated by Joyce Carol Oates, Edward Hirsch, Robert Phillips, Wesley McNair, Len Roberts, The Gettysburg Review

FROM THE MEADOW

by PETER EVERWINE

broadside from ARALIA PRESS

It isn't that you were ignorant:
star thistle, bloodroot, cruciform . . .
beautiful words, then as now,
unlike pain with its wooden alphabet,
its many illustrations, which are redundant.

You had imagined vistas, an open meadow:
on the far side, water trembles its lights;
cattle come down to their shadow lives
beneath the trees;
the language of childhood is invented anew.

But now you know, right? what lies ahead
is nothing to the view behind?
How breathtaking these nostalgias rising
like hazy constellations overhead!—

little to go by, surely,
though from the meadow where you stand looking
over your shoulder, that tiny figure you see
seems to be calling someone,
you perhaps.

Nominated by Aralia Press

RED LIPSTICK

fiction by YOLANDA BARNES

from TRIQUARTERLY

Lettie's coming.

She's coming. On her way.

That was her calling on the telephone. Telling me she'll be here soon.

Lettie.

Jesus Lord. So much to do.

"Who is this?" I said. "Who?" My voice harsh, not like me at all. That ringing phone had pulled me from my bed, that's how early it was, and I'm up by seven every morning. It's been that way for years. "Who?"

"Albee?" she said. I didn't know her voice. Imagine that. She spoke again, this time adding a weight to her words, leveling her tone with authority, calm. "Albertine."

"Lettie."

Lettie Lettie Lettie. Her name rolls along in my mind like a prayer, a curse. Like the singsong of a children's nursery rhyme, a chant to jump rope by: Here comes Lettie. Here she comes. Lettie. Lettie. My best-best friend. Lettie Lettie. The one I loved. *Oh, but that was a long time ago.*

On her way back to me at last. I stood in the hallway after we hung up, wearing just a nightgown, my feet bare against the hallway floor, bumps on my arms and the back of my neck, a chill I was feeling and at the same time not feeling. I was bound to get sick, I was thinking, in spite of the flu shots. Nothing would save me. Such strange thoughts. About my heart, leaping so against my chest. It would jump out, I was certain, and I crossed my arms, trying to hold it back. All these bits jumbled inside me. Until I couldn't think at all, like the times now I am driving and suddenly people honk their horns at me, an ugly, rude chorus, when I have no idea what wrong I have done, making me stop in my tracks, same as the little brown rabbit startled in the woods, black eyes bright and body stiff, stopped in the middle of the intersection and so nobody can go until I'm able to breathe again.

I have to reach for breath after Lettie calls. The weight of my crossed arms squeezed against my breasts. What a sight I would make for the woman doctor who worries about my blood pressure. Until I begin to rub my arms, my cheeks, the still rabbit coming back to life. Lettie's on her way and I have to prepare.

First move I make is to pull on my old housedress with the green and brown and yellow checkered squares, torn and stitched with safety pins beneath the right arm. Tie a kerchief around my head on the way to the front yard, the first sight that will greet Lettie. I carry the broom for sweeping the curb where dirt and slips of paper and soda cans have collected. But first the lawn. Down on hands and knees, my eyes narrowed and searching the grass for weeds, I crawl about, snatching at dandelions and crabgrass until green streaks stain my palms. When the walk catches my sight. My new walk that Mr. James in the green house on the corner just finished building without taking a penny. Mr. James with his pretty wife who nudges him to help the old widow down the street. He laid the walk just the way I asked, with bricks of different colors—pink, of course, but also coral and burgundy, yellow and green and gray. Like a crazy quilt, that's what I told him. Like Joseph's coat.

I squeeze my eyes tight and see Lettie strolling along that new walk. The way she was years ago, wearing one of her dresses, bright-colored and the skirt swinging, brushing the back of her knees. Her plump cheeks and skin the shade of black plums. Her hats—the straw one with the scarves tied around the brim, the tails drifting down her back and that man's hat tilted on her head, shadowing one eye. I see her hair dyed yellow. (How my Harald talked her down for that! "A woman with skin that black," he said, like it was some crime. "She's got no *business*.") I see tripled strands of fake pearls slapping against her breasts as she stepped, and her lips, slick and shiny red, open and stretched across laughing teeth.

"Miz Clark?" I hear, and open my eyes. Sonya from across the street stands on my lawn. "Miz Clark?" she says. They all call me that. "How you doing today, Miz Clark?" they say; "You getting along all right, Miz Clark?" No longer Albertine. Nobody remembers Albertine but me. "Miz Clark?" Sonya is saying. "You doing O.K., Miz Clark?" Her little boy and girl dressed in blue uniforms, on their way to the Christian school. They hold Sonya's hands and stare at me with dark brown eyes, the girl's hair all in braids and fastened with blue-and-white barrettes.

"You've been working hard," Sonya says. "I saw you." Her voice is weak, surprising because Sonya's a big woman. A big yellow woman. The way she fusses at me is how I imagine a daughter would. I know I should be thankful for neighbors like her. "Maybe you should rest," she says, but I just grin and pat her fleshy arm. Tell her to stop worrying. That's all I say. She wouldn't understand the rest, that I haven't felt so good in a long, long time.

Lettie never said what she wanted when she called. But I know. The same as how I know almost everything about Lettie. More, probably, than in those days we talked all the time. I know about that new house of hers and how each of her daughters turned out, about each wedding, each birth of a grandchild, each baptism, communion, graduation. I know about her boy, her baby. How his motorbike skidded on an oil-slicked road. He was nearly killed and I know that nearly killed her. There are people who tell me these things, Essie in particular, but sometimes I wonder if I need them. I feel I would know no matter what. I would just know.

"Can I come over today, Albee?" she said. "I've got something to ask you." What answer possible, except "Of course, Lettie." All this time her words swirling in my mind until, finally, while working in the yard their meaning comes to me, makes me sit back on my heels although this causes great pain in my legs. Already my palms sting, my back hurts from all the pulling and stooping but I have taken certain pleasure in all these aches, accepted any sufferings stemming from Lettie's visit as natural and expected. Now, at this moment, I don't feel a thing. "So that's

65

what she wants," I say, then snap my mouth shut, in case Sonya's back across the street, watching.

There's a sickness eating through Lettie, Essie told me. She says it can't be fought. "They put her in the hospital time after time," Essie said. "But she always comes out." I could picture Essie on the other end of the telephone, shaking her head, black curls trembling. But I know better. Lettie is a cat. What else Essie tells me, that Lettie's alone. "Alonso's left her," she lowered her voice when she told me this, and on my end of the phone I nodded my head. My whole body nodding, my shoulders rocking back and forth, my toes in it too, tapping the floor. Ah, Alonso. Couldn't take any more. Lettie's carryings-on and her lies. Her arrogance. See there. I'm not the only one. "And the children," Essie said. "All gone too." That boy turned out no better than her. Traipsing around the country. Living with one woman after another. The twins, Claire and Carla. "They won't have nothing to do with her." Essie's tone hushed. Gleeful. "Won't even let her in their homes."

"It's payment due," I said. "Fortune's wheel turning round. All Lettie's deeds coming back to her. All the evil, all the lies, all that boozing, all her selfishness. All the suffering she's caused." I had to catch myself, listen to Essie's silence. It made me press my lips tight. Nobody wants to hear me talk that way.

Alone. That's why Lettie's coming back. She needs my help.

She'll be here soon, and so I move inside to the living room. She'll only pass through here, Lettie and I were never living-room friends. Still I take my old dust rags and wipe the Beethoven bust on the piano. I grip the bench and lower myself one knee at a time to clean the instrument's feet, pushing my fingernail through the cloth to get at the dust in the carved ridges. I pour lemon oil on the coffee table and knead it into the wood. The centerpiece is an arrangement of silk-screen flowers. It would be nice to replace it with a token from Lettie, but there is nothing. A punch bowl that Harald dropped years ago. When we were children I'd give Lettie presents. Little bracelets with dangling charms and necklaces with mustard seeds captured in glass balls. I stole from my mother's jewelry box a pin shaped like a bird with rhinestones in its breast. Lettie and I believed they were diamonds. How Mama whipped me when she found out. I gave Lettie the toy circus animals my daddy bought me when I was sick with chicken pox. Tiny, tiny things. When I shut my eyes now I can see them still: a lion, a monkey, a capped bear holding a little red ball. Lettie won't remember.

In the kitchen I fill a bucket with ammonia and hot water, sink my bare hands in and swirl the rag about. My fingers look strange, puffy, bloated, plain except for the wedding band I still wear though Harald's been gone, what?, almost ten years. In the moment it takes to squeeze the rag my hands have turned a raw red. I was the fair-skinned one with the pretty hair. Lettie standing in the schoolyard behind me, playing with my ponytail, saying "this is good stuff." Combing it with her fingers, plaiting it, dressing it with ribbons. She chose me, I remind myself as I clean. "Me." Wiping down the windowsill above the sink where I keep my pot of violets, the ceramic swan with the white, curved neck, the goldfish bowl. Harald's glasses. The last pair he owned, cracked in the brown frame. Oh, Harald never liked Lettie. He saw before I did. The way his face turned mean at the sight of her children here. But I didn't mind taking care of them, I tried to tell him, since we couldn't have any of our own. "Fool," he said. He knew what Lettie was doing, how she got those fancy hats and bottles of perfume cluttering her glass-topped vanity. "Fool," he said, and I thought he meant Alonso.

I want Lettie to see those glasses. And the drawings held by magnets to the refrigerator. Sonya's children colored those and signed them with love and kisses. I want Lettie to take note of the cabinets beneath the sink; Mr. James built those, yes, the same one who did the walk. And the large bowl on the table, let her see that, too, filled with figs and oranges and lemons and tomatoes and yellow squash. My neighbors pick these from their trees and gardens and carry them over in grease-stained paper bags. All this will show Lettie. "See, I have friends. See what my friends do for me, Lettie? Do you hear? I have a good life. I keep busy. I substitute-teach and lunch twice a month with Essie. I attend all the meetings of the neighborhood block club, elected secretary two years in a row."

I shake my head. Standing in the middle of my kitchen, hands on hips, the rag dripping ammonia-water on the floor, I have no time for this, there is much more to do. A new, fresh tablecloth and the good curtains, yellow ones that match my kitchen, I need to get them down from the hall cabinet. I will fix tuna sandwiches, cut in triangles and trimmed of crusts, just how she likes, and put the rest of the coconut cake on the party platter with the red and yellow tulips decorating the border. When Lettie comes I will put on a pot of coffee. We used to sit at this very table and drink cup after cup. Lettie making me laugh. If I had more time I would get on hands and knees and scrub the floor. I would wipe down the cabinet doors, the woodwork, the walls till free of fingerprints and grime and grease. Sort through the cupboards, throw out the clutter, the excesses, and reline the shelves with fresh, new paper. I would clean this house to its bones, its soul. I would cook Lettie her favorite meal, gumbo with sausage and crab and shrimp. All that and more if I had the time. But a million years would not be enough to prepare for Lettie.

It's remarkable to me that I didn't know her voice. Of course it's been several years since we spoke on the telephone or anywhere else. But that doesn't mean I had stopped hearing Lettie. No. I've heard her voice often. Still it follows me around, sits on my shoulder and whispers in my ear, pops up at the strangest times. Once when I was slicing eggplant and something about it, its deep black purpleness, I think, like Lettie's color, made me think of her and I swear I heard her laughing. Another time I was humming some nonsense tune I made up as I leaned over the backporch sink washing my clothes and her voice rose up over mine, singing one of those common, nasty songs she used to know. I must hear her in my sleep too, because sometimes I wake in the night answering her.

Something to ask me, that's what she said, and that is just like Lettie. Seems like she was always wanting something from me. Never the other way around. Didn't Harald say that? And Essie? Oh, I was a good friend to her, everybody knows that. But I've learned my lesson now. I'm stronger than before. "Where are my little toy animals now?" My voice bounces against the tile walls of the bathroom. I hear in it the frantic pain of the old crazy woman filthily dressed who stands at the bus stop and shouts all her business. With trembling fingers I unbutton my old plaid dress and soap a washcloth to rub against the back of my neck, my ears, beneath my arms. Fill the basin with water and bring my face down.

People wondered after I let Lettie go. Prying, nudging questions. Essie tried to find out, oh, how she tried. She was so certain it was some one, huge thing. She questioned me about Lettie and my Harald; she knew how Lettie was. But I never answered. Let Essie think whatever she wants, tell her tales. But this is how Lettie and I came to end.

The Christmas party at Essie's house and me still in my widow's black although Harald had been gone more than two years. At this party I was sitting on Essie's flowered couch, a paper plate on my lap, listening to Chloe. I was eating one of those big black olives, nodding my head to whatever talk she was talking when I heard Lettie's voice coming from the kitchen (who did not hear?) saying, "No, I don't think it's time Albertine stopped wearing black. Black suits Albertine." And then she laughed. I heard her laugh.

I went home after that and took off that black dress. I sat on my bed dressed only in my slip, my arms folded against the chilled night air, and began to think about Lettie and me. I combed through our history together.

Pulling memories like loose threads. One for the time after my third miscarriage when Lettie said to me, "Obviously the Lord doesn't intend for you to have babies, Albertine. Not every woman is meant to be a mother." A thread for the time creditors were after me, when I could have lost this home Harald and I worked so hard for (and I'll let you all know I never asked for a dime) and Lettie's answer: "Every tub must stand on its own bottom." Another for those two days Harald stayed in the hospital, those terrible last days, and she never came. Every insult, every hurt, every slight since childhood. All thought forgotten or excused or forgiven. All that I had chosen not to see. I sat there in the dark with goosebumps on my bare arms, pulling them from a place deep within me, weaving these threads together. Lettie had never been my friend. She had never loved me as I loved her.

The face I wash is old and full, skin loose and drooping beneath the chin, at the neck. Never have I been one of those women to worry about vanity and I do not try to hide my age now, I pat on a little bit of powder and line my mouth with lipstick, pale pink, not red like Lettie. Once, foolishly, I asked Essie, "Does she ever mention me?" Anything would have pleased me, even spiteful words. "Does she?" And Essie waited, I could hear her thoughts weighing whether to spare me, before answering what I knew to be true. "No," she said. "Not once." I hold my brush with tight, curled fingers. My knuckles hurt. Twist my hair and pin it in two tightly wound coils.

At the closet I fumble through my hanging dresses. Which one? The black dress with the white polka dots. No. Eh heh. Nothing black today. The green one? The striped one? None of them seems right. Lettie will show up here in something red, hem swinging, slapping. She'll wear a hat with a feather sprouting out, or the brim trimmed with fur. Strutting up my walk without shame.

I could say no. That would serve her right. Laugh at Lettie when she asks for my help. Like she would do me. Leave her deserted. Yes. Exactly what I should do.

Such unChristian thoughts ruling my mind as I stand before the closet. Finally, I shake my head and get back to business. It's the striped dress I finally choose.

Getting time now. She'll be here. Here. I rush over to press my dress, scorching my arm below the wrist. A bad burn, but the hurt will come later. For now I am free. Standing next to the ironing board, it takes long minutes to button up that dress. Lettie.

Sometime past two o'clock I wrap the sandwiches in wax paper and push the plate far back in the refrigerator. Cover the cake and set it back on the counter. She should have been here two hours ago. Just like Lettie. To keep me waiting. And then I realize, such a horrible thought it makes me sink into one of the kitchen chairs. I brace my elbows against the table. She's not coming.

Has nothing changed?

I hear her first. Jump up and run to the window with loud thudding steps that shake the floor, stand behind the sheer yellow curtains. Lettie's here. That's her car. The gold Cadillac. I

70

remember how she fussed and nagged until Alonso bought it though they barely had money enough for a house to live in. I step back from the window, clap my hands, lift my feet and turn in a circle. I have to do something with all this feeling bouncing inside me. "Lettie," I sing.

Does she ever think of the time she took me to the beach? I watched through the window that day too when she drove up in the Cadillac, new and gleaming then. "Let's go somewhere," she said, and I tugged the kerchief from my head. We drove, little Alonso not even born yet and the twins mere toddlers, fussing in the back seat, nearly two hours along the coast to a mission town. Lettie wearing her straw hat that time with a yellow scarf tied around the brim, the tail fluttering out the window. We came to a beach with the prettiest, clearest water I've ever seen, white pebbles that hurt my stockinged feet.

Lettie left us behind, her two babies and me, to climb the rocks. She found herself a place to settle, her straight black skirt pulled up, showing her thighs, and a bottle of orange pop in one hand. Her hair still colored yellow then, Harald was right: a common-looking false blond. I remember the babies crawling over my stomach, their reaching, slapping hands in my face struggling for attention, when all I wanted was to stare at Lettie sitting so bold on her rock. Not seeing us at all. And I was thinking, "We ought to take these babies. Harald and me. Away from her. Raise them right." Treacherous thoughts, not like me at all, and I tried to shrug them off, a burdensome cloak around my shoulders, heavy, anchoring me. "We could run into the ocean," I whispered to those babies, gathered in my arms. "Disappear. Drown. She'd never know." And though it was hard I waited and waited until it seemed enough time had passed so I could stand and call to her, wave her back to us, shouting, "Lettie. Lettie. Let's go home."

All the times I have remembered that day and what warning I should have taken. But I've learned. I won't be a fool again.

I hurry back to the window. "It's her. Lettie." Starting up my new walk. "What will she say about that?" I whisper. "My walk of different colors? About my dress? What cruel things?"

And then I see her. I see Lettie.

She's got skinny. Too skinny. Oh, that's a bad skinny.

71

A step closer to the window, my face pressed into the curtains. Where is her hat? She wears a wig, a cheap one, too obvious; it is brown with strands thick and straight as a horse's mane. She wears a black dress.

Black!

Lettie is dying.

Essie was right, I can see that now. This sickness has defeated her and now me too. Robbed me of my Lettie. Left me empty-handed. What business have I got against this woman here? I leave the window, don't want to see anymore. Betrayed again.

Racing all around my kitchen, the nervous little brown rabbit. All the things that should give me comfort. I reach up and take Harald's glasses from the windowsill, hold them to my lips. But from them get nothing. No power. Compared to Lettie it's worthless. Everything in my pretty yellow kitchen, worthless.

So I walk back to the window and push the curtains aside. A ghost stands on my front porch, and inside myself I feel something falling. Falling.

"Lettie." Her name leaves my mouth in a wail. It carries through the glass pane and causes her to look my way. Through the window our eyes meet. Startled eyes, wondering, watchful. And then I see, what I have been searching for all along. Her red lips. Red. Red. Nothing but red. Oh, Lettie's always worn the brightest red lipstick, ever since she was a girl and her mother couldn't slap her into stopping. *See there.*

At once I am laughing. *Lettie's here. Still. She hasn't left me. Not yet. Why, I'd bet anything, beneath that wig, she still dyes her hair blond. Scarce, nappy, yellow hairs. I'd bet my life.*

She stares at me. And then, slowly, smiles.

I let go the curtain, fall back and lean myself against the wall. Breathless.

She will ask me for this favor, I know it, and without hesitation I will answer. Yes. Always yes. Anything to keep Lettie near.

And I begin to imagine the caring of Lettie. Shopping in the market, picking out the finest okra, the best green beans. For her. Plaiting Lettie's hair, pinning it up at night so she can sleep in comfort. Peeling potatoes to simmer in a stew to feed her. Washing her soiled underclothes. Bathing her, soaping and scrubbing her pathetic, racked limbs. Sitting by her bedside, squeezing her hand when she cries out in pain.

72

All these visions bring me joy. My victory.

Now I stand in the middle of my kitchen, alone on the checkered tile floor, and listen to the doorbell ring. Twice more I hear it, dainty and distant, but still I have trouble moving. Finally, after what seems an instant, what feels my lifetime, I take my first step. On my way toward greeting Lettie.

Nominated by TriQuarterly

BLOOD BROTHER

fiction by AYLA NUTKU BACHMAN

from ONTARIO REVIEW

MY BROTHER IS a boy. Mother says so. "You know your brother is a boy," she says when she really wants to say, he doesn't have to, you can't make him, I won't allow it. I know what she means, but I play the fool.

"And I am not?"

"No, you are not. I mean, yes, you are not."

"How do you know?"

"Don't you?"

This is what boys are: careless, violent, ungrateful; they forget what they eat, where they sleep; they don't have what you and I call memory. But it's only fair. They concentrate on more important things.

"Like?"

Like the questions your brother asks, haven't you heard? "How far are the stars?" "How deep are the oceans?" Questions Mother collects as trophies to present to my father when he comes home. She rolls my brother's socks, ties his shoelaces and buckles his belt.

I have to be closely watched. Once, I plugged in the iron and tried to press the dress on my back. Once, I tied a helium balloon on my finger and pretended to rise with it, stepping over the furniture in my shoes. Mother wouldn't buy me a watch, so I bit my wrist, hoping to read the hour and minutes inside my teeth marks.

"You and I," Mother says. "We understand each other."

"Don't you understand Omar?"

"I didn't say that."

I am beginning to see: what one does not understand, one loves.

Omar is two years older than me, but we look like twins. Everyone says so, even Mother. We have our father's doe eyes, her colt legs and a mule's intransigence. She doesn't know where we acquired that. She looks at me when she says the word mule.

Omar is small, but strong.

I am built like a frame and filling out, the way girls are supposed to do.

His thin arms grow into thick rose bushes, scratching at my face. His small feet are tucked inside velvet slippers; but, at a moment's notice, he turns them into mallets, pounding tiny kicks into my shins.

We wrestle on the living-room rug. He grabs and throws me to the floor, pinning down my shoulders. When I am up, he chases me down the corridor and before I know we are in a race, he wins. If I am ahead, I slow down, turning my hare's hops into a turtle's crawl. Nobody tells me to. I am willing to carry him on my back as if he were my shell.

I am going to get the answer very soon; I know the question; but I don't know how to ask. I think "why" is only a sound, the sound babies make, wailing in the dark when they cry.

*   *   *

Hatije is calling us, "Omar, Aisha."

I am ready.

Her forehead is pressed against the glass of the door to the balcony; her cheeks are flushed with excitement. She grips our hands; her hands are moist; she flips us over. An upside down moment: Omar and I become one whole person. We toss her to the floor, and she lets us ride her like a donkey. Her scarf is loose; tiny wooden combs fall out of her black hair. Omar and I tug at the thick braid down her back to lead her wherever we wish to go, but she pushes us away and gets up.

"Look at the boys," she says, lifting me in her arms. My feet touch the top of the cold radiator. I try to reach the brass handles that unlock the iron bars on the windows. I see the terracotta roofs of the apartment buildings across the street; the galvanized exhaust pipes of the coal furnaces stick out their tongues, spitting soot over the balconies. The sky like olive oil, faithfully, rises above the streets and the people—don't step outside, it's the vinegar of life, Mother says.

Hatije kicks the door open and the three of us step out on the tiny balcony, overhanging the cobblestoned street. Our knees touching, we crouch over the mosaic tiles smeared with pigeon droppings and peer out of the arabesque black iron rails.

I love the humid air caressing my arms, the scent in Hatije's hair, a brew of sandalwood, fried oil and soap, the street vendors' cries; the horse-drawn carts bump their wooden wheels over the uneven cobbles and the tram tracks.

The man with the handlebar moustache is pushing a handcart; he is singing, "Tomatoes, cucumbers, ripe, ripe."

"Old suits, dresses, I take old t-h-i-n-g-s." A hunchback has thrown a burlap sack over his shoulder.

The knife sharpener's wooden wheel is in the middle of the street. He is pumping the lever with one foot and rocking over the scissors he pries open. The flintstone kicks blue shavings of light up to his face. He spits, wipes the blade on his trousers.

I hold on to Hatije's knee. I don't want to fall through the rails. The woman on the next balcony is beating her prayer rug with her cane.

Hatije points at the four brothers, walking hand in hand on the street; the oldest is thirteen, the youngest six. "*Masallah, masallah,* they've gone and become Allah's children." She sighs like an old woman.

The white satin pajamas on the boys gleam like fresh yogurt poured on a platter. The red sequins stitched in spiraling crescents and stars on the back of their red capes look like Omar's cheeks when he had scarlet fever. The hats slip over the boys' brows like fezzes, studded with rhinestones in Arabic. Silk banners cross their hearts.

"They are men now." Hatije cups her mouth and giggles. "Like Omar will be tomorrow."

I turn around to see tomorrow and meet her eyes. Their caramel hue is as sweet as my favorite candy.

"I want one of those." My brother points at the pinwheel the youngest boy is holding. The breeze is pedaling the wheel; the silver and vermillion foil sparkles.

"Just wait," Hatije says.

Omar spits through the rails. The youngest looks up.

"I got him," Omar shouts as we duck down.

"What does it say on the ribbon?" I can't read Arabic.

"Allah's name." Hatije whispers back. She's learned about prayers and God in her mountain village. "The boys lie in a bed of down, white as snow . . . the girls sing and dance." She is snapping her henna-stained fingers over her head. "The barber cuts right here," she touches between her legs, "the blood runs with God speed, spills into a thimble and out, the man seals the skin. They say, it is easy; blood-letting, that's what they call it."

"Who says?"

"Folk, who else?"

The father of the boys, the doorkeeper of the building across the street dressed in his worn brown-tweed cap and rumpled suit, is looking up at us. His wife's head is covered with a black scarf. She walks obediently behind her sons.

"Now you've done it. You've gone and got us into mighty big trouble with your mother."

A door slams in the cool distance of the cavernous apartment. "Bring them inside." Mother is standing over us in her sling--back white heels with the tiny silver buckles. "I told you not to let them out on that balcony. Go and wash your hands, all of you, go."

Hatije locks the window and the world with people, sunshine and voices, suddenly, turns into a mute picture behind the glass.

"Only peasants go around parading like that," Mother says. She is wearing her navy dress with the pinhead white polka dots and piqué collar.

"I want to . . . I want to be a peasant." I cling to her skirt.

She pulls my hands free. Gazing into Omar's eyes, "we'll see," she says, combing through his hair with her polished red fingernails.

* * *

Tomorrow is not like today. The curtains in the living room are down, the dust covers of the furniture are stripped, the forbidden sienna brocade upholstery is showing. Hatije is on top of the ladder under the chandelier with a bowl of alcohol in which she is soaking the tear-shaped crystal pieces and drying them with strips of cotton.

In the living room, the chairs and tables are pushed aside; a man is building a platform, covering the plywood floor with a roll of red felt cloth. He's got a hammer and a box of thumbtacks.

I wonder if Omar and I tore the house apart while we were dreaming the night away.

Our aunt, Ahmet's mother, and his father's relatives, who have journeyed overnight in a bus from their village in Anatolia, have moved into the guest room. I hear the women's voices raised in giggles or prayers, but when they come out of the room, their eyes are downcast, mouths swaddled inside headscarves. In the morning, as I pass by their open door, I see the women rolling up the thin cotton mattresses off the floor or unrolling the prayer rugs they keep in scrolls behind the door. They stand at prayer five times a day, their gold bangles rattle as much when they bow toward Mecca as when they shake their bedsheets and pat their cotton-batted pillows.

Our cousin Ahmet crows like a rooster, He can do a dog and a horse, too. I hate Ahmet's wisdom. He says girls should play with dolls, but mostly, girls should play with girls; he knows what to put on cuts—wet bread and onion—why not to look directly at the sun, the mirror inside the eye would crack, and how tightly to tie the scarf in blindman's buff.

He is short and stocky; his head grows out of his shoulders. His thick black eyebrows meet over the bridge of his nose. I can outrun him. He wobbles. He has to wear heavy rubber shoes with metal inserts in them.

Mother leads me with her cotton-gloved hand out to the vestibule. "We'll be back," she calls to whoever is listening. We go down the dark stairwell slowly; my heart beats to the tap of her high heels.

Our flat is in a five-story stone building. The marble steps are speckled with veins, the color of egg yolk; the moldings are chiseled with gilt. The walnut banister curving around the stairs is a snake nestled around a tree and whenever Omar and I are alone, we ride the back of the animal all the way down, but not now.

Now with Mother, I am a girl going shopping with her mother.

We close the heavy iron and etched glass door behind us and step out into the sunshine.

* * *

The shop in the bazaar smells of dust, sweat and pine-resin glue. From floor to ceiling, the walls are fitted with cubbyholes; bolts of fabric, silk, satin, brocade, velvet, are arrayed in a rainbow of colors. On top of the counter, a gossamer piece of chiffon, the color of pistachios, takes my breath away. I want it. It is fluttering in the wake of a desk fan. There are spools of thread, sequins, rhinestones, chiffon, dyed cock feathers. The brass blade on the ceiling is whirring, rustling the white packaging paper folded over a piece of wire.

"Madam, I'll be with you," the owner is holding a tape measure around the waist of a little boy who is standing on top of a shaky stool. His mother, dressed in a black chador, is holding the boy's hand as the bald man hobbles around the boy, licks the tip of his colorfast purple pencil and makes some notes on the back of a cigarette box. Mother and I stand in the doorway, watching him take down a bolt of red satin and whip it open.

Without taking the scissors off the gold chain around his neck, he slashes the fabric in one stroke. The threads give, like blood out of a fresh cut, filaments spring at the seam. He rolls the fabric and wraps it in paper, pulling twine from a spool, knotting it, then rolling the package over, knotting it again, before handing it to the woman.

The man heaves a sigh as they leave. He turns to me. His eyes are as oily as his bald pate. "That one is going to look like a young sultan in his bed," he laughs.

"We want the cape in your window." Mother speaks.

I see it. It is what the boys on the street were wearing. I jump with excitement. Mother is going to buy it for me.

The man's eyes flicker over my white organza apron with the daisies embroidered on the pockets. He is staring at my bobbed hair.

"The cape, pretty hah, but this one is much better for her." He ambles over to the wall and pulls down a bridal veil from the ceiling. He is grinning as he puts the fabric into my hands.

79

My fingers slip through the holes of the white lace. It is like an expensive handkerchief, pretty, but too rough to dry one's tears on.

"Girls don't have to get circumcised to have such pretty things," he says in consolation.

I drop the fabric and step back, my shoe catches on a nail in the floorboards. The man catches my elbows in the cup of his palms. They are soft, padded like a cat's paw. I run and hide behind Mother whose alligator clutch bag is hanging open. She takes out a roll of bills; without taking off her white cotton gloves, she counts the bills into the man's hand. In silence, we wait for him to wrap the cape.

The brass clip on Mother's purse shuts with the spring of a brand-new mousetrap and we step out. She doesn't speak.

I don't ask.

* * *

Across from our apartment building, Mother releases my hand. "Go and play. There is Omar and Ahmet." The photographer is camped in front of the iron gates of the municipal park across from the two bronze lion statues. His camera is set on a tripod, ready to snap the photos of children who clamber over the animals. I have a photo of myself taken there. My hair is in a topknot; I am looking torn between the two lions, riding neither, refusing to favor one over the other.

Mother waves the man away, she lets me run past the gates into the narrow paths of the garden, bordered with clipped hedges and honeysuckle vines. The ground is covered with the pebbles the city dredges from the Black Sea every spring. I kick the stones on my way to Omar and Ahmet who are playing in the sand. I pick a stone and lift it up to the sun; it turns into a fiery opal. I find another one and another one. This one is for Omar; it is milky white, streaked with black lines. It is hard to tell which color is in the foreground; my eye gets caught between the black and white and flickers. I drop the stone in his lap and catch him glance at it before he slips it inside his shirt pocket.

Ahmet glowers. He didn't expect to see me. I don't care. He is showing Omar a thick branch he pulled down from the ash; he wants the two of them to turn it into a sling. He's already got the

80

rubber band. The crows will make the perfect prey. All we have to do is aim, he tells my brother.

I watch Ahmet take out a pocket knife and start whittling. The branch is getting shaved, the wood turning naked like butter. The rubber band is red, thick and juicy. I start collecting all the stones I can get my hands on. All that Ahmet will want as his bullets; I am racing against the clock. Omar looks over at what I am doing; he winks, saying, I would rather play with you, but I can't.

I hear the snap of the rubber and the thud of the stones on the bark of the ash. They have won; I see the tree shudder and shed leaves. A nurse is sitting on the bench under the tree, rocking a baby pram with her feet.

Ahmet aims at me, draws the rubber taut then releases it. The pebble hits my foot. I cry; the pain pierces my toe and travels to my heart. I try to get up, but I can't. I pull a fistful of pebbles together and shower Ahmet with them.

Omar has tackled Ahmet to the ground. The sling is in his possession, but he's cut his finger. "Wait," I say. "Let me." I wipe the blood with a leaf, then put my lips to the wound. I am astonished to discover that blood is warmer than skin, as salty as the sea and as sweet as cotton candy, which sticks and spreads over my palate at once.

Ahmet chases me all the way to the lions. I jump on the back of the beast. His mane is warm. Omar beats Ahmet; he gets up on the mate of my animal. The two of us are riding together when Ahmet catches up with us. He sticks his hand into the mouth of Omar's animal, daring him to bite it off. The photographer catches us; he claps his hands to scare us off. A couple with their newborn infant in their arms are waiting to have their picture taken.

I run inside the hedge behind the animals and wait there for a minute. The man passes. I stumble to get free of the barbed twigs. I twist and turn; I see Ahmet. He's undone the buttons on the front of his short trousers. I hear the sound of his water hitting the ground.

I want to close my eyes, but I can't. I am looking. I am so close, I can touch him if I wish, but I don't. His is like the furry tail of a new-born puppy. It wags. When he sees me seeing, he cups himself with his hands.

Omar is standing behind us. His cheeks are red. We step out of the bushes together. When Ahmet pulls up his trousers, my eyes brush over the mound between his legs. I won't turn my eyes away again.

He is rolling up his shirt sleeves to show me his biceps.

"Here, I have two good arms, too," I say and push up my short melon sleeves. The tight elastic has left its mark on my skin.

"Girls don't play this game." He leans over, ready to pull my sleeves down.

I push him away. I call Ahmet muscle head. I have heard Father use that word. Brains will outdo muscles anyday, I tell him.

"I will show you," he shakes his fist in my face.

I laugh. I have already seen what he can show me.

* * *

We hold hands and together cross the street to reach our apartment. After the August afternoon sun, the damp rooms of the house are like cool compresses placed on our foreheads.

I hear voices when I pass by my parents' door. My father is home. Shadows are moving in and out of the keyhole. I see the pink quilt on my parents' bed, the cover embroidered by my grandmother, which my mother says will become mine someday.

"He should have a new blood count."

"He's good and ready."

"The iron shots helped him, but he's so thin." I hear her brush strokes. I can see her sitting in front of her vanity, tugging at her auburn hair with her ivory and silver brush.

"Omar will always be thin, like you . . . Do you want to wait another year?"

I cannot hear her. A tram is passing in front of the building, the iron wheels screech and the ground under the house shakes.

"He's getting too old."

"If only you would listen to me." His voice is raised, "We don't have to do it."

"Everyone would know," she whispers.

"Let's not shackle our children with old religious rituals."

"He is not going to be different from any other Moslem boy." She snaps. There is silence, then I hear her tearful voice. "I

82

won't let him wear the satin and parade in the streets. I am not going to turn him into a peasant."

My father blocks the keyhole. He is wearing an undershirt. His hands are down at his sides. "Needless public show."

"Your sister can dress Ahmet as she sees fit."

"Such a contrast. That boy is an ox." Father walks away from the door and pulls out a drawer.

I run away and hide in Hatije's room next to the kitchen. It has clean whitewashed walls and a window which looks out on the alley. The trunk in which she's brought all her belongings from her village is pushed against one wall. When she is not using her prayer rug, she drapes it over her trunk.

I marvel at the simplicity in her life; that all her belongings should fit inside this square box about the size of my toy chest. Her bed is covered with a sheepskin. It has long white hair like the flowing white beard of an old man. Over her bed, there is a pillowcase she has been embroidering. It has Omar's initials in red thread and the crescent moon in green—the color of Islam. I see Omar's red cape and white satin pajamas on the ironing board. I touch the satin; in the dim light, the rhinestones shine like cat's eyes. I place the cape over my shoulders, and slowly turn toward the window to catch a glimpse of my face on the glass. I am beautiful.

I hear footsteps, throw the clothes on the bed and hide behind the door. Omar is in the room; he turns on the single light bulb hanging over Hatije's bed. "Come now, before Mother starts looking for you."

His brown hair is wet, parted on the side. He has on his short leather pants held up with straps. Something is going to happen to him. He will start wearing long trousers tomorrow. Father is trapped. Mother is scared and sad but doesn't want us to be different.

"Did you hear . . ."

"No, what?" He turns off the light and ushers me out of Hatije's room.

"I will dance tomorrow." I snap my hands over my head, the way I have seen Hatije do.

"No, I didn't know." He chases me down the corridor into the living room.

83

"There you both are." My parents are dressed, having tea in the sitting room. Ahmet is buried in an armchair, his mouth full of almond cookies.

"What kind of a day did you three have?" Father asks.

* * *

The next morning, the shutters of the large living room are open. Sunshine is pouring over the oil-painted yellow walls, the sienna couch, the newly polished golden parquet floors. The chandelier is sparkling; miniature rainbows bounce off the walls.

The platform is complete, red felt floors, red velvet curtains hang from the ceiling in front of it, creating a small stage. My parents' bed is on top of the platform; it looks like a throne for two. The brass gleams. Helium balloons, red and white carnations are tied to the four posts. Streamers hang from the ceiling over the bed, secretly kissing the creamy sheets and pillowcases here and there.

The flowers the guests send are delivered in white wicker baskets with gladiolas, roses and carnations inside. Mother has Hatije place the baskets at the head and foot of the bed.

The curtains are inscribed with prayers. Arabic reminds me of chipped beads recklessly strung together. If moved, the words threaten to fly off into the corners of the room, collecting dust under the furniture.

"Today, you have to do everything Hatije tells you," Mother says.

Hand in hand, she and I walk down the hall. As we stop at her door, we see the practitioner coming towards us. My father is carrying the man's black leather medicine bag in one hand, offering him support with his other hand. The man is tall with puffy eyelids and pouches under his eyes. He gasps for air. Passing by me, "Aha," he wheezes in my father's ear, "you have only one boy!"

Hatije gives me a bath and helps me put on my mother-of-pearl blue taffeta dress. She wraps the starchy wide ribbon around my waist, tying it in a large bow as crisp as a freshly cut rose. Her dress is new, too, made out of soft brushed flannel printed with brooding pansies.

84

The cook chases Hatije out of the kitchen, but she comes away with a prize. The honey-filled baklava she's brought melts in my mouth. She laughs. "Girl," she says, "eat it, eat it, you'll grow into a flower, I know it."

She leads me out of the apartment. Mother wants us to go to the lobby to greet guests who are arriving late. Gently, she shuts the lacquered wooden door behind me.

In the pitch-black stairwell, I shiver. The doorkeeper's cat slithers, rubbing my ankle with his tail. I jump. "Where is Omar? I want Omar."

Hatije blocks the door with her body; her hand is on the brass doorknob. I push and pull at her; she lets her arm go limp like a rag doll's. I punch her stomach. I want her to get out of my way and let me back into my house. She takes me in her arms.

"Soon enough, he's done and gone nowhere," she murmurs as she seizes my wrist.

I escape and mount the banister.

As the snake takes me away, I hear Omar's scream tear down the hallways, stairways, all the way down to the lobby. Hatije runs after me, trying to grab the ruffles on my sleeve. Someone upstairs has turned on the record player. An African drum song, Omar's favorite, blares down the five floors. The door of our apartment flies open,

"Hatije, hurry, hurry, bring the ammonia." My father is leaning over the banister.

Hatije runs back. I reach the lobby. I sit on the marble steps, my thighs chilled with fear.

"Your mother was on the floor. She fell." Hatije tells me later, when she finds me on the stairs.

The ammonia was for my mother who fainted. I am glad it wasn't for Omar; I know that ammonia hurts when it is put on cuts.

*   *   *

In the evening, the curtains on the stage are parted and the boys are lying in my parents' double bed. The guests are gathered in groups. Patiently, they wait for their turn to mount the platform, to present their gifts to the boys. From time to time, one of them looks up to see if the boys are ready to receive their blessings.

85

Music blares from the phonograph. Tangos and sambas are playing, some songs are in Turkish, some in French.

Hatije is keeping a strong grip on my arm as we enter the living room. I look up at the bed. The lights are dim. The guests are standing under the chandelier, talking in a close whisper.

In the dining room, I hear applause, young couples stand against the wall, clapping to the music.

Ahmet's relatives have spread a quilt on the floor. They sit with their legs folded under them. One woman is knitting a sock, another eating Turkish delight out of a kerchief between her legs. Ahmet's mother is talking; she stops to dab at her eyes with the hem of her long skirt. I cannot hear what she is saying. She must be talking about Ahmet: how brave he was, not a sound escaped his lips; he's kept his promise to his mother: I'll make you proud, *ana*. The woman eating the candy wipes her fingers on her trousers, then rubs her eyes. She, too, is crying.

Hatije and I tiptoe up the steps to the platform and hide inside the red curtains. Omar is lying on his stomach with his head buried under the ivory satin quilt. Next to him, Ahmet is propped up on the pillows. He is wearing his hat, cape, playing the host, receiving the gifts for both of them.

"Is he all right?"

"Didn't your Hatije tell you!"

One of Father's friends and his wife stand by as Ahmet opens their gift, a box of watercolors; he is taking out the sable brushes one by one and testing them on the palm of his hand. As he tickles himself, he titters. The couple is smiling. Omar's box is at the foot of the bed, untouched, inside its original wrap.

Mother's lips are drawn in a smile, but the furrow between her eyebrows dimples like a scar. She and my father are shaking hands and offering their cheeks to the guests who greet them. Mother looks over Father's shoulder, to see if Omar is awake, but she doesn't leave the arms of her husband.

Ahmet waves. I hide inside the curtains. I don't want to hear him boast about the watches, fountain pens, globes and slide rules the two of them have acquired in one day. I am sure he is going to tell me that the scream I heard did not come from him.

Hatije pushes me forward. "Go, give him a kiss, go on," she says.

Quickly, I run to Omar's side and kneel at the head of the bed. He has turned on his back, his eyes are open, fixed on the ceiling. Pointing to the cracks in the plaster, I smile, "How many faces did you find?"

He looks at me. His face is pale. His eyes, full of tears, glisten like black grapes. I swallow.

"Don't let . . . them . . . " he says, "Don't let them do it to you."

I rest my face against his. "I won't," I promise, but my voice is a stranger, elbowing us apart.

My parents are dancing. His arm is around her waist; hers nestles into his neck. I stare at the red stone on her bracelet which burns like charcoal.

I want to tell Omar, Can't you see? They won't do it to me, I am here and they are there.

I turn and peck his cheek, then run to safety inside the folds of the velvet. Hatije lifts me up in her arms. She is a sprig of lavender in the dark. I will be her girl.

I stick out my tongue and lick my tears. They are sharp and sweet, like memory—like blood.

Nominated by Ontario Review

ON DUMPSTER DIVING

by LARS EIGHNER

from THE THREEPENNY REVIEW

LONG BEFORE I began Dumpster diving I was impressed with Dumpsters, enough so that I wrote the Merriam-Webster research service to discover what I could about the word "Dumpster." I learned from them that "Dumpster" is a proprietary word belonging to the Dempsey Dumpster company.

Since then I have dutifully capitalized the word although it was lowercased in almost all of the citations Merriam-Webster photocopied for me. Dempsey's word is too apt. I have never heard these things called anything but Dumpsters. I do not know anyone who knows the generic name for these objects. From time to time, however, I hear a wino or hobo give some corrupted credit to the original and call them Dipsy Dumpsters.

I began Dumpster diving about a year before I became homeless.

I prefer the term "scavenging" and use the word "scrounging" when I mean to be obscure. I have heard people, evidently meaning to be polite, use the word "foraging," but I prefer to reserve that word for gathering nuts and berries and such which I do also according to the season and the opportunity. "Dumpster diving" seems to me to be a little too cute and, in my case, inaccurate because I lack the athletic ability to lower myself into the Dumpsters as true divers do, much to their increased profit.

I like the frankness of the word "scavenging," which I can hardly think of without picturing a big black snail on an aquarium wall. I live from the refuse of others. I am a scavenger. I think it a sound and honorable niche, although if I could I would naturally prefer to live the comfortable consumer life, perhaps—and only perhaps— as a slightly less wasteful consumer owing to what I have learned as a scavenger.

While my dog Lizbeth and I were still living in the house on Avenue B in Austin, as my savings ran out, I put almost all my sporadic income into rent. The necessities of daily life I began to extract from Dumpsters. Yes, we ate from Dumpsters. Except for jeans, all my clothes came from Dumpsters. Boom boxes, candles, bedding, toilet paper, medicine, books, a typewriter, a virgin male love doll, change sometimes amounting to many dollars: I acquired many things from Dumpsters.

I have learned much as a scavenger. I mean to put some of what I have learned down here, beginning with the practical art of Dumpster diving and proceeding to the abstract.

What is safe to eat?

After all, the finding of objects is becoming something of an urban art. Even respectable employed people will sometimes find something tempting sticking out of a Dumpster or standing beside one. Quite a number of people, not all of them of the bohemian type, are willing to brag that they found this or that piece in the trash. But eating from Dumpsters is the thing that separates the dilettanti from the professionals.

Eating safely from the Dumpsters involves three principles: using the senses and common sense to evaluate the condition of the found materials, knowing the Dumpsters of a given area and checking them regularly, and seeking always to answer the question "Why was this discarded?"

Perhaps everyone who has a kitchen and a regular supply of groceries has, at one time or another, made a sandwich and eaten half of it before discovering mold on the bread or got a mouthful of milk before realizing the milk had turned. Nothing of the sort is likely to happen to a Dumpster diver because he is constantly reminded that most food is discarded for a reason. Yet a lot of perfectly good food can be found in Dumpsters.

Canned goods, for example, turn up fairly often in the Dumpsters I frequent. All except the most phobic people would be willing to eat from a can even if it came from a Dumpster.

Canned goods are among the safest of foods to be found in Dumpsters, but are not utterly foolproof.

Although very rare with modern canning methods, botulism is a possibility. Most other forms of food poisoning seldom do lasting harm to a healthy person. But botulism is almost certainly fatal and often the first symptom is death. Except for carbonated beverages, all canned goods should contain a slight vacuum and suck air when first punctured. Bulging, rusty, dented cans and cans that spew when punctured should be avoided, especially when the contents are not very acidic or syrupy.

Heat can break down the botulin, but this requires much more cooking than most people do to canned goods. To the extent that botulism occurs at all, of course, it can occur in cans on pantry shelves as well as in cans from Dumpsters. Need I say that home-canned goods found in Dumpsters are simply too risky to be recommended.

From time to time one of my companions, aware of the source of my provisions, will ask, "Do you think these crackers are really safe to eat?" For some reason it is most often the crackers they ask about.

This question always makes me angry. Of course I would not offer my companion anything I had doubts about. But more than that I wonder why he cannot evaluate the condition of the crackers for himself. I have no special knowledge and I have been wrong before. Since he knows where the food comes from, it seems to me he ought to assume some of the responsibility for deciding what he will put in his mouth.

For myself I have few qualms about dry foods such as crackers, cookies, cereal, chips, and pasta if they are free of visible contaminates and still dry and crisp. Most often such things are found in the original packaging, which is not so much a positive sign as it is the absence of a negative one.

Raw fruits and vegetables with intact skins seem perfectly safe to me, excluding of course the obviously rotten. Many are discarded for minor imperfections which can be pared away. Leafy vegetables, grapes, cauliflower, broccoli, and similar things may be contaminated by liquids and may be impractical to wash.

Candy, especially hard candy, is usually safe if it has not drawn ants. Chocolate is often discarded only because it has become discolored as the cocoa butter de-emulsified. Candying after all is one method of food preservation because pathogens do not like very sugary substances.

All of these foods might be found in any Dumpster and can be evaluated with some confidence largely on the basis of appearance. Beyond these are foods which cannot be correctly evaluated without additional information.

I began scavenging by pulling pizzas out of the Dumpster behind a pizza delivery shop. In general prepared food requires caution, but in this case I knew when the shop closed and went to the Dumpster as soon as the last of the help left.

Such shops often get prank orders, called "bogus." Because help seldom stays long at these places pizzas are often made with the wrong topping, refused on delivery for being cold, or baked incorrectly. The products to be discarded are boxed up because inventory is kept by counting boxes: a boxed pizza can be written off; an unboxed pizza does not exist.

I never placed a bogus order to increase the supply of pizzas and I believe no one else was scavenging in this Dumpster. But the people in the shop became suspicious and began to retain their garbage in the shop overnight.

While it lasted I had a steady supply of fresh, sometimes warm pizza. Because I knew the Dumpster I knew the source of the pizza, and because I visited the Dumpster regularly I knew what was fresh and what was yesterday's.

The area I frequent is inhabited by many affluent college students. I am not here by chance; the Dumpsters in this area are very rich. Students throw out many good things, including food. In particular they tend to throw everything out when they move at the end of a semester, before and after breaks, and around midterm when many of them despair of college. So I find it advantageous to keep an eye on the academic calendar.

The students throw food away around the breaks because they do not know whether it has spoiled or will spoil before they return. A typical discard is a half jar of peanut butter. In fact nonorganic peanut butter does not require refrigeration and is unlikely to spoil in any reasonable time. The student does not know that, and since it is Daddy's money, the student decides not to take a chance.

Opened containers require caution and some attention to the question "Why was this discarded?" But in the case of discards from student apartments, the answer may be that the item was discarded through carelessness, ignorance, or wastefulness. This can sometimes be deduced when the item is found with many others, including some that are obviously perfectly good.

Some students, and others, approach defrosting a freezer by chucking out the whole lot. Not only do the circumstances of such a find tell the story, but also the mass of frozen goods stays cold for a long time and items may be found still frozen or freshly thawed.

Yogurt, cheese, and sour cream are items that are often thrown out while they are still good. Occasionally I find a cheese with a spot of mold, which of course I just pare off, and because it is obvious why such a cheese was discarded, I treat it with less suspicion than an apparently perfect cheese found in similar circumstances. Yogurt is often discarded, still sealed, only because the expiration date on the carton had passed. This is one of my favorite finds because yogurt will keep for several days, even in warm weather.

Students throw out canned goods and staples at the end of semesters and when they give up college at midterm. Drugs, pornography, spirits, and the like are often discarded when parents are expected—Dad's day, for example. And spirits also turn up after big party weekends, presumably discarded by the newly reformed. Wine and spirits, of course, keep perfectly well even once opened.

My test for carbonated soft drinks is whether they still fizz vigorously. Many juices or other beverages are too acid or too syrupy to cause much concern provided they are not visibly contaminated. Liquids, however, require some care.

One hot day I found a large jug of Pat O'Brien's Hurricane mix. The jug had been opened, but it was still ice cold. I drank three large glasses before it became apparent to me that someone had added the rum to the mix, and not a little rum. I never tasted the rum and by the time I began to feel the effects I had already ingested a very large quantity of the beverage. Some divers would have considered this is a boon, but being suddenly and thoroughly intoxicated in a public place in the early afternoon is not my idea of a good time.

I have heard of people maliciously contaminating discarded food and even handouts, but mostly I have heard of this from people with vivid imaginations who have had no experience with the Dumpsters themselves. Just before the pizza shop stopped discarding its garbage at night, jalapeños began showing up on most of the discarded pizzas. If indeed this was meant to discourage me it was a wasted effort because I am a native Texan.

For myself, I avoid game, poultry, pork, and egg-based foods whether I find them raw or cooked. I seldom have the means to cook what I find, but when I do I avail myself of plentiful supplies of beef which is often in very good condition. I suppose fish becomes disagreeable before it becomes dangerous. The dog is happy to have any such thing that is past its prime and, in fact, does not recognize fish as food until it is quite strong.

Home leftovers, as opposed to surpluses from restaurants, are very often bad. Evidently, especially among students, there is a common type of personality that carefully wraps up even the smallest leftover and shoves it into the back of the refrigerator for six months or so before discarding it. Characteristic of this type are the reused jars and margarine tubs which house the remains.

I avoid ethnic foods I am unfamiliar with. If I do not know what it is supposed to look like when it is good, I cannot be certain I will be able to tell if it is bad.

No matter how careful I am I still get dysentery at least once a month, oftener in warm weather. I do not want to paint too romantic a picture. Dumpster diving has serious drawbacks as a way of life.

I learned to scavenge gradually, on my own. Since then I have initiated several companions into the trade. I have learned that there is a predictable series of stages a person goes through in learning to scavenge.

At first the new scavenger is filled with disgust and self-loathing. He is ashamed of being seen and may lurk around, trying to duck behind things, or he may try to dive at night.

(In fact, most people instinctively look away from a scavenger. By skulking around, the novice calls attention to himself and arouses suspicion. Diving at night is ineffective and needlessly messy.)

Every grain of rice seems to be a maggot. Everything seems to stink. He can wipe the egg yolk off the found can, but he cannot erase the stigma of eating garbage out of his mind.

That stage passes with experience. The scavenger finds a pair of running shoes that fit and look and smell brand new. He finds a pocket calculator in perfect working order. He finds pristine ice cream, still frozen, more than he can eat or keep. He begins to understand: people do throw away perfectly good stuff, a lot of perfectly good stuff.

At this stage, Dumpster shyness begins to dissipate. The diver, after all, has the last laugh. He is finding all manner of good things which are his for the taking. Those who disparage his profession are the fools, not he.

He may begin to hang onto some perfectly good things for which he has neither a use nor a market. Then he begins to take note of the things which are not perfectly good but are nearly so. He mates a Walkman with broken earphones and one that is missing a battery cover. He picks up things which he can repair.

At this stage he may become lost and never recover. Dumpsters are full of things of some potential value to someone and also of things which never have much intrinsic value but are interesting. All the Dumpster divers I have known come to the point of trying to acquire everything they touch. Why not take it, they reason, since it is all free.

This is, of course, hopeless. Most divers comes to realize that they must restrict themselves to items of relatively immediate utility. But in some cases the diver simply cannot control himself. I have met several of these pack-rat types. Their ideas of the values of various pieces of junk verge on the psychotic. Every bit of glass may be a diamond, they think, and all that glistens, gold.

I tend to gain weight when I am scavenging. Partly this is because I always find far more pizza and doughnuts than water-packed tuna, nonfat yogurt, and fresh vegetables. Also I have not developed much faith in the reliability of Dumpsters as a food source, although it has been proven to me many times. I tend to eat as if I have no idea where my next meal is coming from. But mostly I just hate to see food go to waste and so I eat much more than I should. Something like this drives the obsession to collect junk.

As for collecting objects, I usually restrict myself to collecting one kind of small object at a time, such as pocket calculators, sunglasses, or campaign buttons. To live on the street I must anticipate my needs to a certain extent: I must pick up and save warm bedding I find in August because it will not be found in Dumpsters in November. But even if I had a home with extensive storage space I could not save everything that might be valuable in some contingency.

I have proprietary feelings about my Dumpsters. As I have suggested, it is no accident that I scavenge from Dumpsters where good finds are common. But my limited experience with Dumpsters in other areas suggests to me that it is the population of competitors rather than the affluence of the dumpers that most affects the feasibility of survival by scavenging. The large number of competitors is what puts me off the idea of trying to scavenge in places like Los Angeles.

Curiously, I do not mind my direct competition, other scavengers, so much as I hate the can scroungers.

People scrounge cans because they have to have a little cash. I have tried scrounging cans with an able-bodied companion. Afoot a can scrounger simply cannot make more than a few dollars a day. One can extract the necessities of life from the Dumpsters directly with far less effort than would be required to accumulate the equivalent value in cans.

Can scroungers, then, are people who *must* have small amounts of cash. These are drug addicts and winos, mostly the latter because the amounts of cash are so small.

Spirits and drugs do, like all other commodities, turn up in Dumpsters and the scavenger will from time to time have a half bottle of a rather good wine with his dinner. But the wino cannot survive on these occasional finds; he must have his daily dose to stave off the DTs. All the cans he can carry will buy about three bottles of Wild Irish Rose.

I do not begrudge them the cans, but can scroungers tend to tear up the Dumpsters, mixing the contents and littering the area. They become so specialized that they can see only cans. They earn my contempt by passing up change, canned goods, and readily hockable items.

There are precious few courtesies among scavengers. But it is a common practice to set aside surplus items; pairs of shoes, clothing, canned goods, and such. A true scavenger hates to see good stuff go to waste and what he cannot use he leaves in good condition in plain sight.

95

Can scroungers lay waste to everything in their path and will stir one of a pair of good shoes to the bottom of a Dumpster, to be lost or ruined in the muck. Can scroungers will even go through individual garbage cans, something I have never seen a scavenger do.

Individual garbage cans are set out on the public easement only on garbage days. On other days going through them requires trespassing close to a dwelling. Going through individual garbage cans without scattering litter is almost impossible. Litter is likely to reduce the public's tolerance of scavenging. Individual garbage cans are simply not as productive as Dumpsters; people in houses and duplexes do not move as often and for some reason do not tend to discard as much useful material. Moreover, the time required to go through one garbage can that serves one household is not much less than the time required to go through a Dumpster that contains the refuse of twenty apartments.

But my strongest reservation about going through individual garbage cans is that this seems to me a very personal kind of invasion to which I would object if I were a householder. Although many things in Dumpsters are obviously meant never to come to light, a Dumpster is somehow less personal.

I avoid trying to draw conclusions about the people who dump in the Dumpsters I frequent. I think it would be unethical to do so, although I know many people will find the idea of scavenger ethics too funny for words.

Dumpsters contain bank statements, bills, correspondence, and other documents, just as anyone might expect. But there are also less obvious sources of information. Pill bottles, for example. The labels on pill bottles contain the name of the patient, the name of the doctor, and the name of the drug. AIDS drugs and anti-psychotic medicines, to name but two groups, are specific and are seldom prescribed for any other disorders. The plastic compacts for birth control pills usually have complete label information.

Despite all of this sensitive information, I have had only one apartment resident object to my going through the Dumpster. In that case it turned out the resident was a University athlete who was taking bets and who was afraid I would turn up his wager slips.

Occasionally a find tells a story. I once found a small paper bag containing some unused condoms, several partial tubes of flavored sexual lubricant, a partially used compact of birth control pills, and the torn pieces of a picture of a young man. Clearly she was through with him and planning to give up sex altogether.

Dumpster things are often sad—abandoned teddy bears, shredded wedding books, despaired-of sales kits. I find many pets lying in state in Dumpsters. Although I hope to get off the streets so that Lizbeth can have a long and comfortable old age, I know this hope is not very realistic. So I suppose when her time comes she too will go into a Dumpster. I will have no better place for her. And after all, for most of her life her livelihood has come from the Dumpster. When she finds something I think is safe that has been spilled from the Dumpster I let her have it. She already knows the route around the best Dumpsters. I like to think that if she survives me she will have a chance of evading the dog catcher and of finding her sustenance on the route.

Silly vanities also come to rest in the Dumpsters. I am a rather accomplished needleworker. I get a lot of materials from the Dumpsters. Evidently sorority girls, hoping to impress someone, perhaps themselves, with their mastery of a womanly art, buy a lot of embroider-by-number kits, work a few stitches horribly, and eventually discard the whole mess. I pull out their stitches, turn the canvas over, and work an original design. Do not think I refrain from chuckling as I make original gifts from these kits.

I find diaries and journals. I have often thought of compiling a book of literary found objects. And perhaps I will one day. But what I find is hopelessly commonplace and bad without being, even unconsciously, camp. College students also discard their papers. I am horrified to discover the kind of paper which now merits an A in an undergraduate course. I am grateful, however, for the number of good books and magazines the students throw out.

In the area I know best I have never discovered vermin in the Dumpsters, but there are two kinds of kitty surprise. One is alley cats which I meet as they leap, claws first, out of Dumpsters. This is especially thrilling when I have Lizbeth in tow. The other kind of kitty surprise is a plastic garbage bag filled with some ponderous, amorphous mass. This always proves to be used cat litter.

City bees harvest doughnut glaze and this makes the Dumpster at the doughnut shop more interesting. My faith in the instinctive wisdom of animals is always shaken whenever I see Lizbeth attempt to catch a bee in her mouth, which she does whenever bees are present. Evidently some birds find Dumpsters profitable, for birdie surprise is almost as common as kitty surprise of the first kind. In hunting season all kinds of small game turn up in Dumpsters, some of it, sadly, not entirely dead. Curiously, summer and winter, maggots are uncommon.

The worst of the living and near-living hazards of the Dumpsters are the fire ants. The food that they claim is not much of a loss, but they are vicious and aggressive. It is very easy to brush against some surface of the Dumpster and pick up half a dozen or more fire ants, usually in some sensitive area such as the underarm. One advantage of bringing Lizbeth along as I make Dumpster rounds is that, for obvious reasons, she is very alert to ground-based fire ants. When Lizbeth recognizes the signs of fire ant infestation around our feet she does the Dance of the Zillion Fire Ants. I have learned not to ignore this warning from Lizbeth, whether I perceive the tiny ants or not, but to remove ourselves at Lizbeth's first pas de bourrée. All the more so because the ants are the worst in the months I wear flip-flops, if I have them.

(Perhaps someone will misunderstand the above. Lizbeth does the Dance of the Zillion Fire Ants when she recognizes more fire ants than she cares to eat, not when she is being bitten. Since I have learned to react promptly, she does not get bitten at all. It is the isolated patrol of fire ants that falls in Lizbeth's range that deserves pity. Lizbeth finds them quite tasty.)

By far the best way to go through a Dumpster is to lower yourself into it. Most of the good stuff tends to settle at the bottom because it is usually weightier than the rubbish. My more athletic companions have often demonstrated to me that they can extract much good material from a Dumpster I have already been over.

To those psychologically or physically unprepared to enter a Dumpster, I recommend a stout stick, preferably with some barb or hook at one end. The hook can be used to grab plastic garbage bags. When I find canned goods or other objects loose at the bottom of a Dumpster I usually can roll them into a small bag that I can then hoist up. Much Dumpster diving is a matter of experience for which nothing will do except practice.

Dumpster diving is outdoor work, often surprisingly pleasant. It is not entirely predictable; things of interest turn up every day and some days there are finds of great value. I am always very pleased when I can turn up exactly the thing I most wanted to find. Yet in spite of the element of chance, scavenging more than most other pursuits tends to yield returns in some proportion to the effort and intelligence brought to bear. It is very sweet to turn up a few dollars in change from a Dumpster that has just been gone over by a wino.

The land is now covered with cities. The cities are full of Dumpsters. I think of scavenging as a modern form of self-reliance. In any event, after ten years of government service, where everything is geared to the lowest common denominator, I find work that rewards initiative and effort refreshing. Certainly I would be happy to have a sinecure again, but I am not heartbroken not to have one anymore.

I find from the experience of scavenging two rather deep lessons. The first is to take what I can use and let the rest go by. I have come to think that there is no value in the abstract. A thing I cannot use or make useful, perhaps by trading, has no value however fine or rare it may be. I mean useful in a broad sense— so, for example, some art I would think useful and valuable, but other art might be otherwise for me.

I was shocked to realize that some things are not worth acquiring, but now I think it is so. Some material things are white elephants that eat up the possessor's substance.

The second lesson is of the transience of material being. This has not quite converted me to a dualist, but it has made some headway in that direction. I do not suppose that ideas are immortal, but certainly mental things are longer-lived than other material things.

Once I was the sort of person who invests material objects with sentimental value. Now I no longer have those things, but I have the sentiments yet.

Many times in my travels I have lost everything but the clothes I was wearing and Lizbeth. The things I find in Dumpsters, the love letters and ragdolls of so many lives, remind me of this lesson. Now I hardly pick up a thing without envisioning a time I will cast it away. This I think is a healthy state of mind. Almost everything I have now has already been cast out at least once, proving that what I own is valueless to someone.

Anyway, I find my desire to grab for the gaudy bauble has been largely sated. I think this is an attitude I share with the very wealthy—we both know there is plenty more where what we have came from. Between us are the rat-race millions who have confounded their selves with the objects they grasp and who nightly scavenge the cable channels looking for they know not what.

I am sorry for them.

Nominated by Threepenny Review

APPLE RIND

by CAROL FROST

from AMERICAN POETRY REVIEW

Someone else was afraid and spoke to me
and I couldn't answer . . . swallowing oxygen
from a tube. And then? The cool blade
freeing rind from an apple,
like the first touch of day. How long
I'd been in someone's still life—the blade
hidden, dividing—and was helpless.

Perfectly drugged, I lay just shy of winter
in my own mind. My cut chest felt nothing,
no terror, no pain. And there were morphine's sweet-
and-fruit boxes piled on the white terrain
like reasons for lives and death.
The orchard was weathered to admonitory bareness
except for a few frozen apples
above a disturbance of snow—the hoof prints
of deer coming by several routes to this late harvest,
the dim haunches and various limbs
afloat on movement that can break
or double back into the gray calm of woods.

How to explain directions a mind takes
or why I told no one how much I wanted
to come back to this beautiful, stupid world?

Nominated by Michael Waters, Mark Jarman, Arthur Smith

READING WITH THE POETS

by STANLEY PLUMLY

from ANTAEUS

FOR STANLEY KUNITZ

Whitman among the wounded, at the bedside,
kissing the blood off boys' faces, sometimes stilled
faces, writing their letters, writing the letters
home, saying, sometimes, the white prayers, helping,
sometimes, with the bodies or holding the bodies
down. The boy with the scar that cuts through his speech,
who's followed us here to the Elizabeth
Zane Memorial and Cemetery, wants
to speak nevertheless on the Civil War's
stone-scarred rows of dead and the battle here
just outside of Wheeling equal in death to
Gettysburg because no doctor between the war
and Pittsburgh was possible. Boys dressed like men

and men would gangrene first before the shock of
the saw and scalpel. Three days between this part
of the Ohio River and Pittsburgh. He
knows, he is here since then a child of history
and knows Elizabeth Zane saved all she could.
Keats all his wounded life wanted to be a healer,
which he was, once at his mother's bedside, failed,

102

once at his brother's, failed. Whitman in Washington
failed: how many nights on the watch and it broke
him, all those broken boys, all those bodies blessed
into the abyss. Now the poem for Lincoln,
now the boy with the scar almost singing, now

the oldest surviving poet of the war
reading one good line, then another, then
the song of the hermit thrush from the ground cover.
Lincoln's long black brooding body sailed in a train,
a train at the speed of the wind blossoming,
filling and unfilling the trees, a man's slow
running. Whitman had nowhere to go, so I
leave thee lilac with heart-shaped leaves, he says at
last, and went to the other side with the corpses,
myriads of them, soldiers' white skeletons,
far enough into the heart of the flower
that none of them suffered, none of them grieved, though
the living had built whole cities around them.

Keats at his medical lectures drew flowers.
Not from indifference, not from his elegance:
his interest couldn't bear the remarkable
screams of the demonstrations. He sat there, still
a boy, already broken, looking into the living
body, listening to the arias of the spirit
climbing. So the boy at the graves of the Union
singing, saying his vision, seeing the bodies
broken into the ground. Now the poem for Lincoln.
Now the oldest surviving poet still alive
weaving with the audience that gossamer,
that thread of the thing we find in the voice again.
Now in the night our faces kissed by the healer.

Nominated by Linda Bierds, Henry Carlile

WHITEWING

fiction by JANET PEERY

from SHENANDOAH

ALTHOUGH SHE WAS a law unto herself in our small south Texas town, my mother listened every morning to Waldron Ming's phone calls reporting the fires and prowlers, deaths and mischiefs within the city limits of Martha. He called each weekday at exactly seven-thirty, just as my sister and I were getting ready to go to school, Evelyn Patsy to her sheltered elementary outside McAllen, me to Harlan Bloch High, where I served a lackluster term as vice president of the sophomore boys Swim Club and slogged through every course but English, which I liked. When we heard our mother say, "Yes, Waldron, and you have a fine day, too," we went in to breakfast.

My mother cracked an egg against the side of the griddle. "Mr. Ming tells me the plate glass at the Luz Palmetto looks like a bloodbath. They think it's V-8 juice." She slid the insides of the egg into melted bacon fat, then turned to me. "You wouldn't know anything about it, would you, Will?"

"No, ma'am," I said. When she turned back to the stove, I looked across the table at Evelyn Patsy to see if she would give me away, but she was staring out the window at a hummingbird in a firecracker bush. My mother said she was a "simple spirit," but my sister seemed often preternaturally wise, and knew the very things I wished she didn't.

"I didn't think so," my mother said. "I told him you wouldn't." She cracked another egg onto the griddle, sprinkled water on the hot fat, then clamped a pan lid over the eggs. "I hope," she said, turning toward me, "I'm not defending you injudiciously."

104

I flicked my knee so my napkin would fall and I could duck to retrieve it. "No, ma'am." My voice was thick with the rush of blood to my head.

"That man," she said, warming to her subject, "is really something."

"He sure is," I said. I hoped she would go on a while about him, so I shook my head and said, "Boy, howdy, he sure is, Mama." I drank some orange juice, waiting, half-listening.

Waldron Ming was a turkey-necked cotton grower who wrote a weekly column for the *Valley Evening Sun*. Years before, when he was young and the Rio Grande Valley was at the height of citrus-planting fever, he had written the words to "The Magic Valley," a booster-anthem that had since been bastardized by several generations of wit. Most of the versions supplanted the word "citrus," used in the song as profusely as the orange groves that lined our roads, with the word "Meskins," who were also profuse, but a good deal more indigenous. By the time my contemporaries got around to their own version, which was in the early sixties, no one except perhaps Waldron Ming remembered the original lyrics, and by now they are probably as lost as the way of life in the Valley when I best knew it, when Mingo, as we called him, made his daily round of calls to express outrage he divided between the Anglo teenagers who raced between the palms along the flat caliche roads, and the people who lived in the dusted-over tangle of *tacquerías*, domino parlors, and wooden shacks set among bright rows of cannas on the northern edge of town.

My mother tolerated him, and in those days it seemed to me she suffered fools too gladly. Widow of Martha's once and only lawyer, my father, she was a lightning rod for the culturally deprived of Hidalgo County. She numbered among her friends several devotional poetesses, a mad-eyed sculptor of custom coats-of-arms, half a string quartet which scoured the Valley for a bassist (my mother was their cellist), and the unforgettable Mr. Boelker, a tortured wraith whose hand-written manuscript *My War with Mammon* spilled from three bushel baskets he carried on the back seat of his oyster-colored '49 Chevrolet, occasional sheets of foolscap flapping out the windows like yellow birds set free, Mr. Boelker after them in hot pursuit.

My mother was from an odd, artistic Louisiana family, and used to eccentricity. Born Evangeline Garb, she had been, as my

105

father loved to tell our guests and always in her hearing, the only Cajun Jewish cello-player at Sophie Newcomb, and he had married her—here he paused, straightfaced, stage-reflecting, and that pause held her smile, his laugh, their love, and us, as surely as his broad hand held his glass of Beam—because by-God-somebody-had-to. It had been their plan, my mother once told me, to rear their children with progressive artistic, spiritual and social attitudes, even in a place like Martha. Especially in a place like Martha.

Much of this was lost on me. I preferred the company of Brush Dudley and Snakey Hurdman, white-socked, wheat-jeaned Texas boys who knew beans about art and music, who, if asked, might have said that Mahler's First was one god-awful round of tag-team wrestling, rooting for the Mauler. Our taste ran to the gunfighter ballads of Marty Robbins, "El Paso" at the top, though the steel guitar of Santo and Johnny's "Sleepwalk" could twang in us a rapturous chord as we drove around the Valley in Brush's rusted Dodge, the Green Latrine, so called for both its odor and condition. How could I tell my mother, when she wondered aloud what I saw in my friends, that it was for these inexpressible reasons I loved and defended them? She was a dark-eyed pretty woman, with the gentle affect of her Southern upbringing, but with opinions about honor and conduct set as hard as I liked the yolks of my eggs.

She brought our plates to the table and set them in front of us. "Don't stare so, Pats," she said. She tucked a strand of hair behind my sister's ear, then followed her gaze toward the hummingbird. "Such a pretty thing," she said. "Just think how fast its heart must beat." She sat down, poured cream into her coffee, then turned to me.

"I wish you didn't see so much of that Dudley boy."

I picked up my knife and fork, planning to chop my eggs and bacon into a red-and-yellow, pepper-flecked mash I would then fork onto a piece of toast. "Brush?"

At the sound of my friend's name, Evelyn Patsy turned her attention to the table. Brush Dudley said sweet teasing things to my sister, flustering her into prettiness.

"Where do you suppose he picked up that awful sobriquet?"

I jammed a mash-spread toast corner into my mouth. Brush was Brush because he was the first among us to sport a full and wiry pubic escutcheon, which he liked to show off in gym class. His real name was Harold. No one remembered the origin of Snakey's nickname. "Mmnnh," I said, my mouth full, "good chow."

My mother fixed me with a look of disgust, then turned to talk to Evelyn Patsy about school, allowing me to finish my egg project and to go over our steps of the night before. I was trying to decide if we'd left anything that would tie us to the juice-smeared window of the Luz Palmetto, a *tacquería* on East Seventh.

It was Brush who led us on our raids. Vigilantes, we thought ourselves, and we had a name, the Valley Lords, and a special handshake which featured a lot of brace and shove. The Luz Palmetto had been our target because little Lupe Palacio had called Snakey a *maricón* when we went in to try to buy some beer. Brush decided things were getting out of hand if a seventh-grader could call one of the Valley Lords a faggot. Juicing was the perfect retaliation, as just that day Snakey's father, manager of the canning plant, had caught two wetback workers pissing into a vat of tomato juice. It had to be thrown away, so we had all the material. We'd been sure to park the Green Latrine a block away, and we threw the five-gallon cans in the arroyo. I didn't think we'd left any traces. I got up from the table, picked up my books, kissed my mother and sister and went outside to wait for Brush.

From our front porch I could see the stretch of Mile Six Road down which the Green Latrine would come before it turned into our long, flat drive. Just as I saw the flash of chrome in the distance, a movement near the mesquite thicket at the edge of our property caught my eye, and a dark-skinned stranger—the man who would become my mother's husband—came out from behind the trees and walked across the yard toward our tool house. His walk was quiet, but determined, a guarded walk, but not particularly sneaky. I wondered what he was trying to do, walking toward the shed in full daylight, Brush's car approaching, its radio blaring. I watched until he popped the complicated door latch, so easily I thought he must have done it before. When Brush pulled the car up beside me, I set my books on the hood and stuck my head in the passenger window. "Some guy's in the toolhouse."

"A wet?"

"I think so."

"Don't just stand there, man. Run him off." He reached under the seat for his Indian club. "You want the masher?"

"Nah," I said. "Guy's a runt." I gave the roof of the car a smart pat and started across the yard.

The door stood open and I could see him by the workbench, rummaging in a bin. When I was close enough, I called out, "Hey, buddy."

He looked up, then grinned. In his right hand he held tools, a wrench and an auger. He extended them and grinned again. "*Si*," he said. "Okay."

"Put 'em down," I said.

He continued to hold the tools, nodding.

"Com-prend-ay," I said. "Down." I didn't speak Spanish, just what was necessary to get along with our maid Remedios and what I picked up in the halls at school. I pointed to the tools, then to the workbench. "Put the damn things down."

"Okay," he said, still clutching the tools, still nodding.

I took a step toward him, blocking his exit. He wasn't acting like the thieving wets Brush talked about running off. I didn't know what to do, wondered what Brush would do. I stepped inside and grabbed the tools. "Get out," I said.

He stopped smiling and dropped his hands to his sides. I stood there breathing hard: who did he think he was? I decided to hold my ground, make him walk around me. "Move," I said. I clenched my jaw. I felt mean and stupid and ugly. "Move!"

Something about it—the close, hot smell of him; the way his shoulders set, somewhere between challenge and surrender; maybe just because it came to me that I could—made me wheel as he passed me, slam the heel of my hand into the flat place between his shoulder blades. The sound he made was thick and dull, hollow as the breath heaved from him. He kept walking, not looking back, not acknowledging the blow, across the yard toward the mesquite. I shook my arm. My hand felt heavy, swollen, the way it felt if I slept with it hanging over the edge of the bed.

"You get him?" Brush asked when I got into the car.

"He's gone."

Brush shifted into first, narrowed his eyes at me. "You chickened out, man. Didn't you? Level with ol' Daddy Brush."

"I got him."

"Whoo-boy!" Brush beamed. "You're gettin' there." He popped the clutch and we lurched onto the drive. "Damn wets," he said. "Kill you as look at you." He went on about a grower in Mission who'd had his shotguns stolen. I listened, rubbing the heel of my hand along my jeans leg. "The Valley's getting worse," he said. "Tell your mama to lock up better."

"Mingo's wise," I said, remembering the Luz Palmetto.

"Mingo doesn't know anything. They got that crazy Otón on it. The Palacios fired him for being drunk again and they figure he did it to get even. He already confessed, I heard. Cried like a baby."

We pulled into the Hurdman's driveway where Snakey waited, black-hornrimmed, skinny. He got into the back seat. "Men," he greeted us. "A perfect day for tomatofish."

Snakey was a reader. His hero that year, and several before it, was J. D. Salinger, for the chapel-fart scene, which Snakey could recite. If Brush was the muscle for our excursions, Snakey was the brains.

"Snake the Great," Brush said. "We pulled it off."

"Vengeance is mine." Snakey leaned forward, resting his arms on the seatback as we drove along Mile Six toward school.

Brush looked in the rearview. "What's that gunkus all over your face?"

I turned to look. Snakey's forehead, cheeks and chin were covered with puckered spots, like dried egg white. Flecks sprinkled his shirt like chips of mica.

"My secret formula." He flicked a speck from his glasses. "Equal parts alum and Elmer's Glue. Cheaper than Clearasil."

"Man," Brush said, shaking his head, and we all hooted, just to hoot. Brush turned up the radio while Richie Valens sang "Donna," and we pulled into the Harlan Bloch parking lot, howling and moaning with the song. In the swell of students entering the school, I forgot about the intruder for a while, and if I thought of him, or of the way I'd treated him in the tool house, in the days that passed before I saw him again—this time in our living room—it was with the uneasy notion that I had somehow wronged him, and that the wrong would come home to sit on my shoulder when my mother found out about it. When I told her I had seen someone in the tool house, she looked up from sewing a

109

hem into Evelyn Patsy's skirt, snipped off a bit of thread, and said, "That's nice."

Friday night Brush and Snakey and I went to McAllen to cruise the main street. Radio at full volume, we drove around, arms resting on the rolled-down windows, trying to look uninterested. All the songs seemed to be about girls—Donna, Carole, Peggy Sue. The Valley Lords had none, unless we counted Brush's bouts with Paula Rainwater. Cruising along on warm Valley nights, though, singing the girl-songs, we felt the promise of them, that we were getting closer to some great something that was just around the corner, and I imagine each of us thought he was alone in pretending it meant nothing. The pretense was easy during the tough, macho songs, the driving songs, but when a tender lyric came along, I turned into wistful, hopeful, moon-struck mush, mush I would have hooted at if Brush or Snakey had confessed to it, mush so fraught with yearning it was almost holy.

"I bet old Phoebe Caulfield turned into the greatest girl," Snakey said, his sneakered feet resting on the seatback.

Brush slowed the car beside a group of Mexican girls on the sidewalk outside the Orpheum theater. "Look at that."

"Cowabunga," Snakey said.

I slid down in the seat a ways, holding the girls in the corner of my vision until we passed. I didn't dare look at them full on. White, black, brown: if they'd been green they couldn't have looked more beautiful to me, innocent, mysterious, all of them, all of girlkind, all of womankind, and none of them, except the knowing ones you didn't want, could know how much you wanted them.

Something about the night laid us low. Maybe it was the lack of women, or rather girls; it could have been the changes brought about by September and the start of school or even the weather, which had a lonely touch of coolness in it. Whatever it was, it seemed to swirl through the open windows of the Green Latrine as we drove back to Martha, subdued and disheartened, and when I walked onto our porch to let myself in, I felt for the first time empty, wanting, that even home was not enough.

Music came from the living room, from the old Deutsche Grammophon recording of the Ninth Symphony, the final movement with Schiller's *Alle Menschen werden Brüder* refrain, my father's favorite. I opened the front door and walked down the hall toward the sound.

A single lamp was on behind my mother's chair, its yellow light gathering all the sadness of that manlorn house the daylight made me forget. When I saw her reach out to touch my father's chair, and I saw the jut of a knee, I realized she wasn't alone. I moved sideways into the room to stand inside the doorway so I could see.

I didn't try to make sense of it. My mother's guest was the man from the tool house. He had cleaned up. He wore black trousers and a short-sleeve white dress shirt. Even in the dim light I could see the comb tracks in his hair. He was crying. Flat-handed, he wiped tears from his face. My mother touched his arm. I remembered how my hand felt on his back, and it came to me that I wanted to shove him again.

When the music ended my mother rose to lift the needle arm. Seeing me, she said, "Come in, Will."

He stood, wiping his palms on his pants.

"This is my friend Andrés." She took my arm and pulled me closer. "Will," she said to him, "my son." He extended his hand.

Jackass, I called myself as I took it. My mother talked, but I didn't hear what she was saying, and when I took my hand from his it was moist.

She went on talking, out of breath, overbright. Finally, she said, "He plays the violin," and sank into her chair.

He said something in Spanish, and she looked at the two of us and said, "Yes, that's probably best." She rose and they walked toward the front hall. I followed them. She turned on the porch light and opened the door for him. Moths began to flutter around her and she made girlish shooing motions.

He caught one of her hands, then kissed it. "Evangelina," he said. Something in Spanish. Then, "Thank you." He looked at me, and for an instant I wondered if he even remembered the tool house. "Bye-bye, Will," he said. My mother closed the door.

I followed her down the hall to the kitchen. "Bye-bye?"

She wouldn't look at me. "He was a guest in our house." She ran water into two wineglasses that sat on the drainboard.

"That's the guy I saw in the tool house."

"I told him he could." She dabbed at a lipstick smudge on the rim of the crystal. "Borrow things. I thought I told you." She

111

lifted the drainboard, then picked up a sponge and began wiping the counter. She wrung out the sponge, then stopped to look at me. "I forget how big you are."

"He's a wetback, Mama. What do you think you're doing?"

"Keep your voice down, you'll wake your sister." Her eyes seemed tired, and her face had the bruised look that made me feel responsible for it, for my father's worn-out heart. "I just wanted him to have a nice evening. He's a nice man. And he isn't Mexican, if that's what's bothering you. And you must stop using that ugly phrase." She opened the cabinet and began straightening glasses. "And I'll entertain Eskimos and Hottentots in this house if it pleases me."

A glass tipped over, rolling along the shelf in a bottom-heavy arc. She righted it, then giggled, oddly.

"What's the matter with him?"

"Nothing's the matter with him. He was an engineer. Is. He played with the symphony in San Salvador."

"Looks like he slept in a cave."

She brightened. "He's living out at the Seabury place, in the fruit shed. Miz Seabury told me about him and I went to visit." She shook her head. "No running water, no electricity. He sleeps on an old *lona*, Will. He's helping her with some . . ."

"What the hell's he used to, the Taj Mahal?"

"Keep your swearing outside. I won't have it in this house."

I got a glass, ran water into it and started to drink, but the warm mineral-salty Valley liquid reminded me suddenly of the way he had smelled in the tool house. I swallowed. "You'll have everything else in here."

She closed the cabinet door. "You are treading on thin ice, Mister."

"If he's so great, what's he doing up here? He kill somebody?"

"It was political. He supported the wrong man. Or wrong for him."

"That's stupid."

"It's not for us to say."

"How do you think this makes me look? Don't you think people are going to talk?"

She laughed. "This place," she said, "this *place*. And what do you suppose they'll say that they haven't said a thousand times?"

I set my glass down. "That you're breaking the law."

112

She was silent, considering, and for one moment I imagined that this would be the end of it. I decided to press my advantage. "He show you his papers?"

She laughed. "Oh, Will, I don't need papers. And you needn't stand there glowering at me like a county judge." She pulled out a chair and sat at the table. "I suppose this has to do with your friends."

"They don't know about it."

"I mean your attitude." She sighed. "I can't imagine what your father would think of this."

Her words struck me like a punch, and I felt sick. "Daddy wouldn't have let any wetback kiss his hand."

Before she could say anything, I left the kitchen.

The next day I avoided my mother, spending the afternoon with Brush and Snakey. We cleaned our guns for opening day of whitewing season, which would be the following Saturday. I had a Remington .20 gauge, Brush a Winchester, and Snakey used an old .410 which we hooted at routinely, but Snakey maintained the gun had mystical, lucky properties. My father had a beautiful Parker Brothers, double-barrel .16 I could have used, but I was happy just to know I had it if I wanted it. Brush and Snakey and I had gone on opening day since we were eleven, and we waited for it all summer, resisting the urge to bag a few before time. None of us saw the irony in our strict observance of the hunting rules while at the same time using the same shotguns to turn road signs into sieves.

That night my mother seemed careful with the things she said to me. She talked mostly with my sister, and I took a measure of mean satisfaction, beyond any power I imagined I had, in my silence, in picturing the state of things if I were gone. Later, as I lay on my bed listening to KRGV, she came to stand in the doorway. The Coasters were singing "Poison Ivy."

"Try to understand, Will."

"What's to understand?"

She looked at me for what seemed a long time. "I'm helping him with his English."

"Right."

"Was that smart-lip, young man?"

113

"No, ma'am." I rolled over and turned up the radio, then closed my eyes and felt a wave of longing for my former self, for the times I'd lain in bed content to *think* about being a man— bigger shoulders, deeper laugh, a hat maybe, a pipe, wide hands that unscrewed jar lids—before this mystic urge to *be* one. I don't know how long she stood in the doorway, but when I turned over she was gone.

My mother set a table as hybrid as her pedigree: Coca-Cola-baked ham, boiled greens and butter beans, gumbo, dirty rice, borscht, latkes. She left the Mexican cooking to Remedios, who made tortillas, cornshuck-wrapped tamales, pots of *olla podrida* with chorizo and garbanzos. My mother said she couldn't get the hang of it. When I came home from school the next Friday and found her in the kitchen chopping onions, Evelyn Patsy beside her, the counters and table strewn with peppers and corn meal, an oddly spiced meat mixture simmering on the stove, I knew something was up. I set my books on the table. "What's that smell?"

My mother looked up. "Finer, Pats," she said to my sister, "they need to be the size of little grains of rice." To me, she said, "We're making papusas. They're Salvadoran."

"For him?"

"If you mean Andrés, yes."

"He can't find his own food?"

She banged her knife on the cutting board. "I won't have this attitude." She hacked at the onion. "He is an educated man."

"If he's so educated, why's he living in a fruit shed?"

She shook her head. "Someday," she said, "someday perhaps you will learn compassion."

I would like to say that her remark stung me, made me see how stupidly I was behaving. But I was fifteen, and I have since discovered that any lesson learned by me is of the head-bang, hard-knock, bashed-forward-from-bullhead stripe, and only I can do the bashing. Her remark stung, of course, but it served only to give me a tighter grip as I clung to my Valley logic, to make me dig my thick-wit ditch a little deeper, so that when I peered out of it I saw what I wanted to see, what everyone else in the Valley (except my mother) knew: that Mexico was a hopeless, dried-up dirtball of a country and that El Salvador, at the bottom

114

of it, could only be worse. There was no beauty there. They all wanted to leave, cross the border any way they could. What they touched turned lurid and pathetic as their painted saints, their bright red lilies that concealed tumbledown shacks, turned into the trashy leavings of a carnival. No music but the yipping see-saw of mariachi bands. No honor; they stole everything you didn't nail down. They wanted what we had. I yanked open the refrigerator and took a bottle of Coca-Cola. "I won't be home for supper."

"He's going to play for us," Evelyn Patsy said. Her vague gaze seemed to go beyond our kitchen walls.

"Great," I said. "Just great."

I found Brush and Snakey on Hurdman's screened porch, playing with Snakey's parakeets, Holden and Phoebe. Snakey let them fly around the porch. "Don't let them out," he warned.

I closed the screen door and sat in a seat-sprung lawn chair. Blue Phoebe flew to perch on my shoulder, pecking at my collar, "Tell her not to crap on me."

"She has her pride," Snakey said.

Holden, a small green missile, buzzed my ear as he flew to the screen behind me. I heard his claws picking their way along the mesh. "You know that wet?" I told them what was going on at my house.

Brush took out his pocket knife and began to clean his nails. "It's no secret, man. I heard the guy's just about camped out on you all's doorstep."

"Mingo," Snakey said. "The Voice of the Valley." He made a clicking noise to call the birds. "There's a lot of that on TV. Look at Louis Prima and Keely Smith. Xavier Cugat and Abbe Lane. Lucy and Ricky. Shoot. Maybe it's not so bad." He shrugged.

"It's not like that," I told them. "She feels sorry for him."

Brush slouched in his chair, giving me a heavy-lidded look. "What you going to do about it?"

That night the Valley Lords went riding. We drove out toward the Seabury place, swinging by Paula Rainwater's so Brush could see if Mason Vestring's car—a blue Ford sedan we called the Dipmobile—was there. It was. We drank from bottles of home brew Snakey filched from his father. The more we drove around, the clearer it became that we should teach Andrés a lesson of place.

115

"Tomatoes?" Brush suggested.

"Too close to Operation Luz Palmetto."

"Eggs are good."

I suggested an anonymous letter.

"You know Spanish?" Snakey asked.

"Just food and the dirty stuff."

"Great," Snakey said. " 'Dear Cabron: Chinga yourself and get out of town before sundown or we'll bash you with our big tamales.' Great, Will."

We hooted. I was starting to feel better, knowing we would do something.

"I have it!" Snakey said. He cupped his hand around his mouth, making it a tube he spoke through. "Modess," he said, " . . . because." He waggled his eyebrows.

"What?"

"A product I have tested in my labs. Absorbency. Adhesion. Turn the car around. To Rexall, men."

"It's closed."

"The grocery, then."

We sped back to Martha. Snakey refused to give us any clues. "Keep it running," he said as he jumped out the back door. He disappeared into the grocery store, then came back out with a blue box wrapped in cellophane.

"Tampax?" Brush read. "They let you just go in and buy those things?"

Snakey pointed toward Acacia Street. "The Dairy Maid."

At the drive-in he ordered a cup of warm water, tipping the car hop a penny. "Keep-o el change-o," he said. She sneered at him and we drove back to the country.

The Seabury place had been a family citrus operation before most of the land was sold to big growers. Miz Seabury still lived there, alone unless a migrant helper stayed in the fruit shed. She kept a small business in cabbage and tomatoes and hand-picked cotton. We walked across a cabbage field to get to the shed, a cinder-block and corrugated-tin structure that rose ramshackle in the moonlight.

Snakey unwrapped the box, slid a tampon from the cardboard tube and held it by the string. Brush and I watched. I had never seen one; my mother was discreet, and I had seen only a large blue box beneath the bathroom sink, in loopy script above a pic-

116

ture of a carnation the words "Modess . . . because." The single flower looked wilted and sad, and I suppose because my discovery of them coincided with my father's death and my curiosity about what my mother did for so long behind the closed bathroom door, I decided the thick white pads were something ladies used when they cried, put them over their eyes, maybe, "because" the word that had to do with unspeakable grief.

Snakey dipped the tampon into the water, then swung it by the string, spattering us with the drops. He aimed at the shed and let fly, flung it hard against the wall where it stuck with a wet, gorged, satisfying splat.

"Whoo-boy," Brush said. "Let me."

"Brilliant," I said. Against the gray block wall the tampon looked like a fat, white rat, obscene tail dangling. We took turns flinging them until Snakey said, "Wait. Cut your finger." He held out his pocketknife.

"What do you want to cut mine for?" Brush said. "Cut your own damn finger."

"I'll do it." I took the knife and drew blood from my middle finger, then dabbed it on the wet white cotton. I threw it against the wall.

"Ooo-eee!" Brush yelled.

When all the tampons were gone we stood back to look at our work. The side of the shed looked profane, infested, and I felt that the perfect message of gore, of shame, of violence and blemished purity had been sent. As we walked back to the car, I could hardly stop turning around to get a new look at it, to see it fresh, to see what it meant, to be glad and horrified; the fruit shed looked the way he made me feel.

He was still at our house when Brush dropped me off. I heard music, and I went to stand by the front window to look in. Evelyn Patsy sat at his feet, my mother behind her chair, leaning on folded arms, watching him play. I waited outside until the music ended.

The house still smelled of their odd dinner. My mother smiled at me. "You missed a lovely time, Will."

"I cried," Evelyn Patsy said, pleased.

"Yeah, well," I said. I looked at him, gave a wave that was half-salute, half-dismissal.

"You cut yourself," my mother said.

117

I looked at my finger. "Car door."

"You'd better put something on it."

Andrés came forward to shake my hand, but I held it up to show the cut. "Sorry," I said.

My mother beamed. "I'll just show you to the door, Andrés."

She said something to him in Spanish, then turned to me, smiling. "You put something on that hand, now. Hear?"

"Yes, ma'am." I stood aside as they walked to the door, then I went to the kitchen to make a sandwich.

She came to stand in the doorway. "It's nice to see you getting along with Andrés."

I slathered mustard onto Wonder bread. "I don't guess he'll be around here much longer anyway."

"Why, of course he will. He was just telling me how much he likes it here."

I shrugged. I put a piece of ham on the bread and clapped the sides together, then I leaned back against the counter and bit into the sandwich.

"He lost his father early, too, Will. He told me he knows how you must feel about, oh, things. I was telling him about your trip tomorrow and he said he'd like to come along."

Stunned, I swallowed too soon, felt the bread lodge at the bottom of my throat.

"It would really be nice," she said. "I think he could be a friend to you."

"I've got friends already." My voice felt choked. I went to the refrigerator and took a big swallow of milk from the carton.

My mother opened the cabinet and handed me a glass. "Well, it won't hurt for him to come along. He'll be here for lunch tomorrow. I told him you all leave around one."

I smashed my fist into the sandwich. "You can't do that. You can't just goddamn invite somebody on somebody else's trip!"

"I'm afraid it's done. And mind your talk."

"This is crazy! He can't come. Brush . . . " I thought about what Brush would do, what he would want me to do. "You have to tell him he just can't come!"

"You tell him," my mother said. "You tell him when he gets here. You tell him you don't want him on your hunting trip. You tell him why!"

118

I picked up the smashed sandwich and threw it in the sink. "I bet he doesn't even have a gun."

"I told him he could borrow Daddy's."

"Not the Parker Brothers?"

She shook out a dish towel and folded it, hung it on the towel bar. "That one in the case," she said. "You never use it."

"I wanted to," I said. Until this time I had been happy just to unzip the fleece-lined case, to run my hand along the burled stock. "I clean it all the time." I wanted to run get the gun from the closet and show it to her, as an article of proof she could see, and when she saw it—polished, clean, well-oiled—realize what she was doing, stop, and things could settle back the same as before.

"Well, it's done," she said. She turned, flicked off the kitchen light.

"I'm not going," I said. "I'm flat not going."

"That's your choice." She left the kitchen.

I went to bed wishing it had been a dream. I wanted to call off the trip, but my friends would go without me. I thought of sneaking off, spending the night with Brush, and I was almost out the window when I began to picture my mother tracking me down at the milo field where we hunted. The more I thought about what she had done, the angrier I became, the further from a solution. As I drifted off to sleep, occasionally an idea brushed past me, just below the surface, like the whir of Holden's wings behind my ear, but when I opened my eyes and tried to catch it, to remember harder, it flew away.

The Valley air was hot and wet, thick as the cotton lint that flocked the power lines, when Brush and Snakey arrived at one o'clock. I came out from behind the garage where I had hidden from my mother's lunch. When the Green Latrine pulled up beside me, I said, "He's coming with us."

Brush cut the engine. "Not the guy?"

My mother and Andrés came out onto the porch and waved at us. Brush handed me the keys so I could open the trunk. Snakey smirked. "Where'd he get those pants, man?" Andrés wore black dress pants, too short, too shiny.

"Stole 'em off a dead matador," Brush whispered. "That your daddy's gun?"

119

Andrés approached the car, my mother following. He wore my father's shell vest, the clay-colored fabric jutting from the shoulders as though it remembered his shape. The vest seemed to swallow Andrés, his deltoids skinny in the ample armholes. For one stupid second I thought I might cry. I took the Parker Brothers from him and put it in the trunk next to my Remington.

We got into the back seat and my mother leaned toward the window. "You make the introductions, Will." She smiled at Brush and Snakey. "You boys have a good time. I'll fix you all a big dove supper."

"Yes, ma'am," they said. They tried to look busy in the front seat—Brush checking the gearshift position, Snakey patting his vest for shells—and I knew, because of her ability to shame me, that she had shamed them, too.

Our hunting place was a milo field owned by Brush's uncle. Bounded by mesquite, it provided the camouflage we thought we needed, though we knew the birds were trusting and would fly over anything. The canal was close by for the water they sought on their afternoon and evening flights, and the land was posted, so we weren't likely to meet other hunters. The first few miles passed in silence, with Brush saying only, "Hotter than hell in a bucket." When it hit us that Andrés couldn't understand us, we loosened up.

"A wet with a gun," Brush said. "Terrific."

"My dream come true," Snakey said.

"He's Pancho Villa," I said. "Santa-fucking-Anna."

Andrés grinned at us.

"He thinks we're cute," I said. I grinned back at him.

"Just keep your eye on him," Brush said. "He's your baby."

"It's not like it's my fault."

"Same as."

When we got to the field Brush opened the trunk. We took out our guns and shells. Snakey handed around bottles of home brew. He gave me two, so I handed the extra bottle to Andrés. "*Gracias,*" he said. "*Frio.*"

I knew he meant the bottle was cold from the cooler, but I pretended I didn't understand.

We found places near the mesquite and sat, waiting for the first flyover. Andrés raised his bottle. "*Las alas blancas.*"

We knew he meant to toast the hunt, but we didn't drink with him.

"To white rats!" Brush said, and we laughed, the three of us, and drank. We made the motions of our secret handshake.

"What a dope," I said.

We sat around in silence until a javelina shoat crashed out of the stubble at the edge of the field, surprising us.

"Oh, man," Snakey yelled. "Where's his mama?"

We jumped up, ready to shoot or run if the mother came squalling out of the thicket; javelinas just farrowed were a dangerous thing in the scrub around the valley. Andrés took aim.

"Don't!" I shouted at him, but he fired a shot that I couldn't believe was anything but lucky, and the shoat fell.

"Damn," Brush said in the silence after the Parker Brothers' report.

We looked around, expecting a full-grown javelina to charge, but the pale stubble was still as the heavy air. Andrés nodded vigorously, grinned, then went to get the shoat. He brought it back, holding it by the hind legs, and offered it to me.

"No shoot, you idiot." I made flying motions with my arms. "Shoot whitewing."

"*Sí,*" he said. "*Las alas blancas!*" He gave me an encouraging smile, as though he'd just taught me something. He extended the shoat.

I shook my head.

"Cook," he said. He rubbed his belly. "*Delicioso.*"

"Sit down," I said. "Just sit the hell down." Hot, sweating, miserable, I sat near a clump of *huisache*. My stomach gnawed at me because I'd missed lunch. Andrés sat a few yards away. Snakey passed more beer.

About three o'clock we saw the first flyover, six or seven birds, white-bellied, wing tips black as beetles against the blanched sky. "Here they come," Snakey whispered. We raised our barrels. I heard the clap from Brush's shotgun, a thinner pop from Snakey's. I squeezed the Remington's trigger, hit one.

Beside me, Andrés sat, gun across his knees. "Whitewing," he said when the birds wheeled and flew off.

"Why didn't he shoot?" Brush asked.

"Who the hell knows," I said.

Andrés smiled. "*Las alas blancas.* Whitewing."

"Right, asshole. Whitewing."

"*Pequeños.* Little."

"You bet, leetle. Next time shoot. Shoot the leetle whitewing."

We passed the afternoon drinking beer, trying to stay in the mesquite shade. I ridiculed Andrés, tricked him with words he didn't know, called him names I hadn't known I knew. Brush and Snakey moved away. From time to time they laughed at something I said, but for the most part they left us alone.

All that wickedly hot afternoon we sat, me beside him, my insults thick as the clouds of midges around us, rising with the mercury, with our blood alcohol, until his very smell ignited me, the way he grinned and shambled for approval, his clothes, my father's vest. Everything he was and everything he wasn't grew inside me until I grew strong and foul with my own sweat. I reeked with anger and I was happy in it and I knew I was going to hit him. I stood up. "Watch this," I called to Brush and Snakey. "Call him an asshole and he smiles. He likes it. Call him anything. He's a goddamn puppet."

I turned to Andrés. He stood. "Hey asshole. Whitewing."

"*Las alas blancas,*" he agreed. "Shoot whitewing, *si?*"

I took a step toward him. "Punch wetbacks. *Si.*"

He held his hand palms up, puzzled. He looked at the sky.

"Come on, Will," Snakey said. "Lay off. It's hot."

"You don't want to do this, man." Brush said.

I ignored him, moving toward Andrés, watching his eyes. "I'm doing it."

Brush yelled at me. "Cut it, Will!"

In that wild state where reason finally left me completely, I held Andrés to blame when the thing I wanted most not to happen just then happened, when a flock of doves appeared over the field, a host of black-tipped wings, white flash of underbelly, a hundred, maybe more together than I had ever seen. Snakey said, "God-damn," broke the .410's action, loaded, aimed. Brush picked up his Winchester, shouldered the butt. I went for mine. "This is it," I called to Andrés. "Now you shoot."

He didn't move, but stood watching as the birds flew in, eyes moving from the flock to me, the flock to me. I raised the barrel, aimed. "Now! Shoot whitewing."

"Shut the hell up, Will," Brush said. "It doesn't matter."

Andrés didn't move.

I yelled at him. "You stupid idiot!" I crossed the distance between us and punched him in the solar plexus. His belly was hard, but he buckled, guarding. I turned away, brought the stock to my shoulder, raised the barrel toward the sky. "Shoot!"

I didn't hear him coming—smelled him first, beer and dirt, sweat rancorous as mine. He stood at my right shoulder, breathing hard, gripped my barrel with his left hand, swung his right, slamming his fist into my jaw. I felt my neck wrench, lost balance, recovered, tasted blood. Andrés drew back, spat.

I stood stockstill, my jaw inflamed and swelling, my vision scintillating whorls of sparks and blind spots, trying to focus on the flock, hold the shotgun rigid, aiming at the center; fired, broke action, loaded, fired again, again, again, felt the power that held the barrel upward and away from him, felt it buckle, give, then hold; shot and shot and shot.

We all shot, Brush, Snakey, Andrés, me; firing and reloading as the whitewing fell or swooped or scattered, and for those moments nothing mattered but explosion and recoil, aim and trigger. The doves were gone and still we fired, wild, like boys with firecrackers, until our shells were spent and pale-red cylinders littered the dirt around us, our fingers stiff and crabbed, the nitrate smell of powder acrid clouds around our legs. The silence in the late afternoon resounded like the cessation of the chirr of locusts, the loudest silence.

We retrieved the birds. I walked upfield beside Andrés. His shoulders seemed to sag, and his face had gone blank and empty, nothing in it of what had happened. He didn't look at me, but fixed his gaze along the furrows, looking for felled birds. From across the field I heard the sound of Brush and Snakey arguing over which of them had shot a clutch of doves, an argument that I imagine has found a thousand subjects over the years they spent together in the Valley, but maintains its one unchanging form.

We sat around the cooler, opened beers. Brush raised his bottle, then, speechless, lowered it.

"The dumbest hunt we've ever gone on," Snakey said.

I nodded, tired, dumbstruck still. We drank. The sun looked huge and full, descending, slanting light across the milo stubble. Brush and Snakey began to filet the doves, removing each small, plump, grain-fed breast. Down and feathers filled the air as the pile of discarded bodies grew.

I looked again at Andrés. Moisture beaded the brown glass of his bottle, sweat runneled the dirt on his face. His head, held low, seemed to bob in an odd way, and I realized he was laughing.

He looked at us. "Ratones blancos," he said. He wagged his finger, smiling, his teeth white against the dust-filled orange light. "No, no, no. White rats." Again he smiled.

"Whoo-boy," Brush said. Snakey, shrugged, smirking.

Something about it—the way he sat, hunkered down in his bullfighter pants and borrowed vest, the pile of stiffening doves at his feet; the way he wagged his finger, chiding us the way old Mingo might, the way a father would; maybe just his dogged self—struck me funny, struck me simple, backward past myself and then beyond. It came to me then as it would come to me again years later when I would see that, like my mother and Andrés, I would leave the Valley, that certain moments are foregone, that fight them, they would come to be. This struck me as both sad and funny, and I felt my shoulders shaking in a way I couldn't stop. Even though it seared my jaw and racked my head, awooze with beer and blood and sun, and made me feel as if a box of shot had spilled, was loose and skittering behind my eyes, I couldn't stop. I wasn't laughing and I wasn't crying but I couldn't stop not doing either. I looked at Brush and Snakey to see if they'd been watching, but they were working at the doves and I could hardly see their faces through the feathers rising in the air.

Nominated by Shenandoah

MY BEST SOLDIER

fiction by HA JIN

from AGNI

I COULDN'T BELIEVE it when I saw that the photograph sent over by the Regimental Political Department was Liu Fu's. How clumsy he looked in it: a submachine gun slanted before his chest; above his army fur hat, at the right corner, stretched a line of characters—"Defend My Motherland"; his smile was still a country boy's smile lacking the sternness of a soldier's face. He had been in my platoon for only about ten months. How could he, a new soldier, have become a secret customer of Little White Fairy in Hutou Town so soon?

Our political instructor, the Party secretary of our company, interrupted my thought, "I have already talked with him, and he admitted he had gone to that woman six times this year."

"Six times?" Again I was surprised. "He is new. How could he get to know her so quickly?"

"I've asked the same question." Instructor Chang tapped his cigarette lightly over an ashtray and raised his head, looking across the small room in which we were sitting. He wanted to make sure that the orderly was not in the next room. "I think there must have been a pimp, but Liu Fu insisted he got to know the Fairy by himself when he had his hair cut in her barbershop. Obviously, he is a novice in this business. No old hand would leave his picture with that weasel."

"You're right." I remembered last year a bulletin issued by the Regimental Political Department had carried a report on this young woman. After having been caught in bed with an officer,

125

Little White Fairy was brought to the Regimental Headquarters, where she confessed that many soldiers and officers had visited her. Once she had received six army men in a single night, but she didn't know any of their names. Each man would give her a two *yuan* bill and then go to bed with her. That was all. Regimental Commissar Feng swore to have those men found out, as they must have belonged to our Fifth Regiment, the only army unit in Hutou. But those were old dogs and would never leave any traces.

"You should also talk with him." Secretary Chang exhaled a small cloud in the air and continued, "Comrade Wang Hu, your platoon has done everything well this year except this Liu Fu matter. Don't get lost in doing military exercises and in improving fighting skills. Mind modeling is more important. You see whenever we slacken a little in ideological education, serious problems emerge among our men."

"Secretary Chang, I will talk with him immediately. From now on I will pay more attention to ideological education."

"That's good."

It seemed he didn't want to continue the talk, so I left the company headquarters to rejoin my platoon.

I was somewhat upset by Liu Fu's case. What a shame! I had always considered him as a potential successor of a squad leader. His squad leader, Li Yaoping, was going to be demobilized next year, and I had planned to promote Liu Fu to take over. To be fair, Liu was in every way an excellent soldier. He surpassed all my men in hand-grenade throwing. He could throw a grenade seventy-two meters. In our last practice with live ammunition, he scored eighty-four points with nine shots, which was higher than everybody except me. I got eighty-six. If we had a contest with the other three platoons, I would certainly place him as our first man.

Needless to say, I liked him, not only for his ability and skills but also for his person. He was a big fellow, over a hundred and eighty centimeters tall and a little heavily built but very nimble. His wide eyes reminded me of a small pony in my home village. His square mouth and bushy brows resembled those of the ancient generals in Spring Festival pictures. All the other soldiers liked him a lot too, and it seemed he had quite a few friends in our Ninth Company.

I can never forget how he became a figure of poetry. That spring when we sowed soybeans, I assigned the Third Squad to pull a plough, since we didn't have enough horses and oxen. On the first day the men were soaked with sweat and complained that it was animal's work. But the next day was different. Liu Fu and two other boys in the Third Squad appeared with bald heads. They said a bald head would make the sweating more endurable and the washing easier after the work. The atmosphere in the field came alive, because the three shining round heads were wavering about like balloons in the team pulling the plough. Everyone wanted to get some fun out of it. As Liu Fu was taller and had a bigger head, he became the main butt. By and by a poem was composed in his honor, and soon the whole company chanted:

> When Big Liu takes off his hat
> The county magistrate shakes his head:
> "Such a vast piece of alkaline land,
> How can the grain yield reach the Plan!"

> When Big Liu takes off his hat,
> The hardware store is so glad:
> "With such a big shining bulb,
> How many customers can we attract!"

> When Big Liu takes off his hat,
> The saleswoman is scared out of breath:
> "Having sold condoms for so many years,
> I've never seen such a length and breadth!"

Big Liu was never offended by the doggerel. He even chanted it with others, but he would replace the name "Big Liu" with "Small Wang," "Old Meng," and so forth. As his popularity increased he was welcomed everywhere in the company. A boy like him could be a very able leader of a squad or a platoon. This was why I had planned to promote him to be a squad leader the next year. But who knew he was a "Flowery Fox"!

Our Party Secretary was right: there must have been somebody who introduced him to Little White Fairy. Hutou was over fifty *li* away from Mati Mountain where we garrisoned; at most

Liu Fu had gone to the county town seven or eight times on Sundays. He had seen the White Fairy six times? Almost every time he went there? It was impossible, unless at the very beginning somebody took him directly to the woman. I remembered Li Dong had gone with him for his first visit to the town, and the second time Zhao Yiming had accompanied him. Both of the older soldiers were pretty reliable; it was unlikely that either of them could be a pimp. But to know a man's face is not to know his heart. I must question Liu Fu about this.

Our talk did not take long. He looked crestfallen and deeply ashamed, but he denied there had been somebody else involved and insisted, "A good man must shoulder the outcome of his own action."

In a way, I appreciated his only blaming himself for the whoring, because if another whoremonger was found in my platoon, I would have trouble clearing our name. People would chuckle and say: the First Platoon has a whoring gang. Besides, that would give Liu Fu himself a hard time too, as he would surely be treated by the other men as a sort of traitor.

But I took this case seriously, for I had to stop it. We garrisoned the border line to defend our country, and we must not lose our fighting spirit by chasing women. Unlike the Russians on the other side, we Chinese were revolutionary soldiers, and we must not rely upon women to keep up our morale. Every Saturday night we saw from our lookout tower the Russians having many college girls over in their barracks. They would sing and dance around bonfires, kiss and embrace each other in the open air, roll and fuck in the woods. They were barbarians and Revisionists, whereas we were Chinese and true Revolutionaries.

So I ordered Liu Fu to write out his self-criticism, examining the elements of bourgeois ideology in his brain and getting a clear understanding of the nature of his offense. He wept and begged me not to take disciplinary action against him, for his family would know it and he would carry the stain all his life. I told him a disciplinary action would have to be taken, and I was unable to help him with that. It was better to tell him the truth.

"So I am done for?" His dimmed horsy eyes watched my mouth expectantly.

"Your case was sent down by the Regimental Political Department, and you know our company cannot interfere with a decision from above. Usually, an offender like you *is* punished with a disciplinary action. But this doesn't mean you will have to carry it for the rest of your life. It depends on your own behavior. Say from now on if you behave well in every way, you may have it taken out of your file when you are demobilized."

He opened his big square mouth, but he didn't say anything, as if he swallowed down some words that had been stuck in his throat. The word "demobilized" must have struck him hard, since a soldier like him from the countryside would work diligently in order to be promoted to be an officer. It would be a misfortune for him to return to his poor home village, where no job waited for him, and without a job no girl would marry him. But with such a stigma in his record, Liu Fu's future in the army had been fixed: he would never be an officer.

Two days later he turned in his self-criticism. On eight white sheets were lines of big, heavily scrawled words and a few ink stains. A country boy certainly couldn't say extraordinary things. His language was plain, and many sentences were broken. The gist of his self-criticism was that he had not worked hard enough to purge the bourgeois ideology from his head and he had contracted the disease of bourgeois liberalism. The Seventh Rule for the Army stated clearly: "Nobody is allowed to take liberties with women," but he had forgotten Chairman Mao's instruction and violated the rule. He also had forgotten his duty as a soldier staying on the Northern Frontier: when the enemies were sharpening their teeth and grinding their sabers at the other side, he was indulging himself in sexual pleasure. He was unworthy of the nurture of the Party, unworthy of the Motherland's expectation, unworthy of his parents' efforts to raise him, unworthy of the gun that the people had entrusted to his hands, unworthy of the new green uniform . . .

I knew he was not a verbal person, so I spared him the trouble of putting more self-scathing and remorseful words in the writing. His attitude was sincere; this alone counted.

He looked a little comforted when I told him that I would try to persuade Secretary Chang to ask the Regimental Political Department to administer less severe punishment to him. "This is not over yet," I warned him. "But you must not take it as a heavy burden. Try to turn over a new leaf and work hard to make up for it."

He said he was grateful and would never forget my help.

Two weeks passed. We had not heard anything from the Political Department about the decision on Liu Fu's case. Neither our Party secretary nor our company commander ever requested an action. It would be unwise to do that, for the longer we waited the more lenient the punishment would be. Time would take away the interest and the urgency of the case. In fact, none of our company leaders would welcome a severe action against Liu Fu. Liu was their man, and no good leader would like to see his own man being punished.

A month passed. Still nothing happened. Liu Fu seemed very patient and was quieter than before. In order to prevent him from being involved with Little White Fairy again, we kept him at Mati Mountain on weekends. We also became very strict about permitting other men, especially new soldiers, to visit Hutou Town.

One night it was my turn to make the round through all our sentry posts, checking the men on duty and making sure they did not doze off. We had five posts, including the new one at the storehouse where we kept our food and a portion of our ammunition. I hated to do it at midnight when you had to jump out of your bed and pretend to be as awake as a cat. If you didn't look spirited in front of them, the men on duty would feel doubly sleepy.

I went to the parking yard first, where our trucks and mortars stood, and caught the sentry smoking in the dark. I ordered him to put out his cigarette. The boy complained it was too cold and he couldn't keep his eyelids apart if he had nothing to to. I told him everybody had to stand his hours on cold nights. Nobody but the Lord of Heaven was to blame for the cold. As for his sleepiness, he'd better bear in mind that we were merely four *li* away from the Russians. If he didn't stay alert, he put his own neck at risk. The Russians often sent over their agents to find out our sentry positions and our deployment. They would get rid of a sentry if they found it necessary and convenient. So for his own safety, he'd better keep his eyes open and not show them where he was.

Then I went to the gate post and our headquarters. Everything was fine at those two places. I chatted with each of the men for a few minutes and gave them some roasted sunflower seeds. Then I left for the storehouse.

The post was empty there, so I waited inside the house, believing the sentry must have been urinating or emptying his bowels somewhere outside.

After ten minutes nobody showed up. I began to worry and was afraid that something unusual might have happened. I couldn't shout to summon the sentry over. This was the last thing you would do at night, for it would wake up the whole company, and the Russians might hear it as well. But I had to find out where the sentry had hidden himself. He must have been dozing away somewhere. There were no disordered footprints in the snow; it was unlikely that the sentry had been kidnapped or murdered. I picked up a line of footprints that looked new and followed it for a little distance. They were heading towards our stable. I raised my eyes and saw a dim light at the skylight on the stable's roof. Somebody has to be there. What's he up to in the stable? Who is on duty now? I looked at my luminous watch—1:30—and couldn't recall who was the sentry.

Getting close to the door I heard some noise inside, so I hastened my steps. With my rifle I raised a little the cotton door-curtain to have a view inside and to make sure that nobody was hiding behind the door waiting to knock me down.

It was Liu Fu! He was standing beside our gray mule, buckling the belt around his pants. His gun leaned against the long manger, and his fur hat hung on its muzzle. Beyond the mule stood a dozen horses asleep with downcast heads. So he is the sentry. The rascal, he's using the stable as a latrine. How luxurious, keeping his butt warm here!

No, I noticed something unusual, for behind the gray mule's hindquarters was a bench. On the bench there were some particles of snow and some wet smudges. The beast! He has been screwing the mule! Looking at him, I found his sweating blood-stained face distorted with an awkward but clear expression, as if saying to me: *I can't help it, please I can't help it!*

131

I sprang at him and grabbed him by the front of his jacket. Though he was much bigger and stronger than I was, I felt he went limp in my hand. Of course, a spent beast! I started slapping him on the face and cursing, "You—mule-fucker! You never give your cock a break! I will geld you today and throw your itchy balls to the dogs!"

He didn't resist at all and merely moaned, as if my cursing and slapping made him feel better. He looked so ashamed. Not encountering any resistance, I soon cooled down. You couldn't go on for long beating a man who didn't even raise his hands to defend himself. I let him go and ordered, "Back to the storehouse. We'll settle it tomorrow."

He picked up his gun, wiped away the tears on his cheeks with his hat, and went out quietly. In the stable all the animals were out of sleep now, their eyes open and their ears cocked up. One horse snorted.

I couldn't wait for tomorrow, so I had Li Yaoping, his squad leader, awakened. We had to talk before I reported it to our Party secretary. I must know more about Liu Fu. It was understandable if a long-deprived monk screwed a girl in the town, since there was no woman on the mountain. But to screw a dumb animal like that, who could imagine it! It nauseated me.

Li was not completely awake when he came into my room. I gave him a cigarette and struck a match for him. "Sit down. I want to talk with you."

He sat on a stool and began smoking. "What do you want to talk about on a dark—" He looked at his watch. "It's already half past two in the morning."

"I want to talk about Liu Fu. Just now I found him in the stable fooling around with the gray mule." I wouldn't say: "He screwed the mule," since I didn't see him do it. But I was sure of it, as Liu Fu himself did not deny it when I cursed him, so I was ready to explain further to Li what I meant.

"Oh no, you mean he did it again?" Li shook his freckled face.

"Yes. So you knew everything already?" I was surprised.

"Ye—yes." He nodded

"Why didn't you inform me of that before? Who gave you the right to hide it from me?" I was angry and would have yelled at

132

him if some of my men were not sleeping in the adjacent room.

"He promised me he would never do it again." Li looked worried. "I thought I should give him a chance."

"A chance? Didn't we give him one already when he was caught with Little White Fairy?" I felt outraged. Apparently this thing had been going on in my platoon for quite a while, but I had never got a whiff of it. "Tell me when did you see him do it and how many times."

"I saw him with the mule just once. It was last Saturday night. I saw him standing on a bench and hanging on to the mule's hindquarters. I watched for a while through the back window of the stable, then I coughed. He was scared and immediately fell off. When he saw me come in, he knelt down begging me to forgive him and not to tell on him. He looked so piteous, a big fellow like that, so I told him I wouldn't tell. But I did criticize him."

"What did you say? How did you conduct your ideological instruction, Comrade Squad Leader?" I felt it strange—he sounded as if he might have sold his sister if he took pity on a man.

"I asked him why he had to screw the mule." Li looked rather cheerful.

"What a stupid question. How did he answer it?"

"He said, 'You know, Squad Leader, only—only mules don't foal. I promise, I'll never touch any—any of these mares.'" Li started tittering.

"What? It's absurd. You mean he thought he could have got those mares with babies? What a silly fellow! So moral, he's afraid of being a father of horsy bastards!" I couldn't help laughing, and Li's tittering turned into loud laughter too.

"Sh—," I reminded him of the sleepers.

"I told him even the mule must not be 'touched,' and he promised not to do it again." Li winked at me.

"Old Li, you're an old fox."

"Don't be so hard on me, my platoon leader. To be fair, he is a good boy in every way except that he can't control his lust. I don't know why. If you say he has too much bourgeois stuff in his head, that won't fit. He is from a pure poor peasant family, a healthy seedling upon a red root—"

133

"I don't want you to work out a theory, Old Li," I interrupted him. "I want to know how we should handle him now. This morning, in a few hours, I will report it to our Company Headquarters. What should we say and how should we say it?"

"Well, do you want to get rid of him or keep him?"

This was indeed the crucial question, but I didn't know the answer. Liu Fu was my best man and would need him in the future. "What's your opinion then? At least, we must not cover it up this time." I had realized that Old Li didn't tell on Liu Fu because he wanted to keep him in his squad.

"Certainly, he had his chance already, How about—"

The door burst open and somebody rushed in. It was Ma Pingli, our youngest boy, who was to stand the three o'clock shift at the storehouse. "Platoon Leader," he took the fur mask off his nose, panting hard, "Liu Fu is not—not at the post, and all the telephone wires are cut. We can't call anywhere."

"Did you go around and look for him?"

"Yes, everywhere."

"Where's his gun?"

"The gun is still there, in the post, but his person's gone."

Hurry up! Bring over the horses!" I ordered. "We'll go and get him." Ma started running to the stable.

I glanced at Old Li. His looks showed he understood what was happening. "Take this with you." I handed him a semi-automatic rifle, which he accepted mechanically, and I picked up another one for myself. In an uneasy silence, we went out waiting for Ma.

The horses sweated all over, climbing towards the border line. I calculated that we would have enough time to stop him before he could get across. He had a climb a long way from the southern side of the mountain in order to avoid being spotted by our lookout tower. But when we three reached the Wusuli, a line of fresh footprints stretched in front of us, winding across the snow-covered surface of the river, extending itself into the other side, and gradually losing its trail in the bluish whiteness of the vast Russian territory.

"The beast, stronger than a horse and faster than a hound," I cursed. It was unimaginable that he could run so fast in the deep snow.

"He's there!" Ma Pingli pointed to a small slope partly covered by gray bushes.

Indeed, I saw a dark dot moving towards the edge of the thicket, which was about five hundred meters away from us. Impossible. Surely he was too smart not to put on his white comouflage cape. I raised my binoculars, and saw him carrying a big stuffed gunnysack on his right shoulder and running desperately for the shelter of the bushes, a camouflage cape secured around his neck flapping behind him like a huge butterfly. I gave the binoculars to Old Li.

Li watched. "He's taking a sack of *Forwards* with him!" he said with amazement.

"He stole it from the kitchen. I saw the kitchen door broken," Ma reported. We all knew our cooks stored *Forwards*, the newspaper of Shenyang Military Region, in sunny sacks as kindling. We had been told not to toss around the paper, because the Russians tried to get every issue of it in Hong Kong and would pay more than ten dollars for it.

"The Russians may not need those back issues at all," I explained. "They've already got them. They only want recent ones. He's dumb."

Suddenly a yellow light pierced the sky over the slope. The Russians' lookout tower must have spotted him; their Jeep was coming to pick him up.

Old Li and I looked at each other. We knew what we had to do. No time to waste. "We have no choice," I muttered, putting a sighting glass onto my rifle. "He has betrayed our country, and he is our enemy now."

I raised the rifle and aimed at him steadily. A burst of fire fixed him there. He collapsed in the distant snow, and the big sack fell off his shoulder and rolled down the slope.

"You got him!" Ma shouted.

"Yes, I got him," I replied. "Let's go back."

We mounted on the saddles; the horses immediately galloped down the mountain. They were eager to get out of the cold wind and return to their stable.

All the way back, none of us said another word.

Nominated by Lloyd Schwartz, Agni

PROLEGOMENA

fiction by KEN BERNARD

from FICTION INTERNATIONAL

LET US GRANT that anything I say may be used against me.

Let us grant that whatever I say it is all untrue but may for various expediencies be accepted as true, that we are entered here, as in an unholy matrimony, into an agreement to play the game, abiding by its rules, and pretending to enjoy its satisfactions, breath by dying breath.

Let us grant that this pretense is no different from any other pretense, except that it is understood that some games are considered better than others but opinions vary as to which.

Let us grant that although I claim to be the author of these words and am reading them, I do not exist.

Let us grant that although I do not exist, neither do I wish to be harmed. Even so, if I bleed, I will continue to deny that I exist, even as I continue to admit that I wrote these words and seek medical care for myself.

Let us grant, however, that I do not claim to write (or speak) these words in blood.

Let us grant that you do not exist either. Although you are listening and responding to what I read, you have no understanding of it because you do not know what it is. Further, you are each responding differently to what you don't understand, but because of the seating arrangements, the ticket price, the program, and other such formalities it might seem that you share something or that we share something or that there is something to share.

Nominated by Richard Kostelanetz

PARENTS

by ROBERT WRIGLEY

from THE GETTYSBURG REVIEW

Old two-hearted sadness, old blight
in the bones, the history of sugar
and the daily syringe, show tunes,
Shalimar, car after car after car.

Here are my names, all three
trochees ratcheted out like comeuppance,
here my oldest living forebear,
the Depression, my big nose, my love for jazz.

Let us locate our first marriages
festering in the cedar closet.
You show me proximity, I'll show you
the blank expansiveness of the west.

O roads, varicose and meandering,
bloody Kansas after Kansas between us—
there are days I'd kneel to kiss
the knuckles most like my own, other days

when a blue Pacific sky shows me all
that's possible, whole oceans of air
I can dream myself a kind of prince in,
a kind of bird, who believes he reigns there.

Nominated by Robert Phillips, Henry Carlile

INSCRIPTIONS

by EAVAN BOLAND

from The PARIS REVIEW

About holiday rooms there can be
a solid feel at first. Then, as you go upstairs,
the air gets
a dry rustle of excitement

the way a new dress comes out of tissue paper,
up and out of it, and
the girl watching this thinks:
Where will I wear it? Who will kiss me in it?

Peter
was the name on the cot.
The cot was made of the carefully-bought
scarcities of the nineteen-forties:
oak, tersely planed and varnished.
Cast-steel hinges.

I stood where the roof sloped into
paper roses—
half a world away from where I lived—
in a room where a child once went to sleep;
looking at blue, painted lettering:

As he slept,
someone had found for him
five pieces of the alphabet which said

the mauve petals of his eyelids as they closed out
the scalded hallway moonlight made of the ocean at
the end of his road.

Someone knew
the importance of giving him a name.

For years I have known
how important it is
not to name
the coffins, the murdered in them,
the deaths in alleys and on doorsteps,
happening ninety miles away from my home;

in case they rise out of their names
and I recognize

the child who slept peacefully,
and the girl
who guessed at her future in
the dress as it came out of its box, falling free in
kick pleats of silk.

And what comfort can there be
in knowing that

in a distant room
his sign is safe tonight,
and reposes its modest blues in darkness?

Or that outside his window
the name-eating elements—the salt wind, the rain—
must find
headstones to feed their hunger?

Nominated by Laurie Sheck, Marilyn Hacker, The Paris Review

RAY

by HAYDEN CARRUTH

from AMERICAN POETRY REVIEW

How many guys are sitting at their kitchen tables
   right now, one-thirty in the morning, this same
time, eating a piece of pie?—that's what I
   wondered. A big piece of pie, because I'd just
finished reading Ray's last book. Not good pie,
   not like my mother or one of my wives
could've made, an ordinary pie I'd bought at the
   Tops Market in Oneida two hours ago. And how
many had water in their eyes? Because of Ray's
   book, and especially those last poems written
after he knew: the one about the doctor telling
   him, the one where he and Tess go down to
Reno to get married before it happens and shoot
   some craps on the dark baize tables, the one
called "After-Glow" about the little light in the
   sky after the sun sets. I can just hear Ray,
if he were still here and this were somebody
   else's book, saying, "Jesus," saying, "This
is the saddest son of a bitch of a book I've
   read in a long time," saying, "A real long time."
And the thing is, he *knew* we'd be saying this
   about his book, he could just hear us saying it,
and in some part of him he was *glad!* He
   really was. What crazies we writers are,
our heads full of language like buckets of minnows
   standing in the moonlight on a dock. Ray

140

was a good writer, a wonderful writer, and his
    poems are good, most of them, and they made me
cry, there at my kitchen table with my head down,
    me, a sixty-seven-year-old galoot, an old fool
because all old men are fools, they have to be,
    shoveling big jagged chunks of that ordinary pie
into my mouth, and the water falling from my eyes
    onto the pie, the plate, my hand, little speckles
shining in the light, brightening the colors, and I
    ate that goddamn pie, and it tasted good to me.

Nominated by Maura Stanton, Laura Jensen, Len Roberts

SIMPLICITIES

by WILLIAM H. GASS

from THE REVIEW OF CONTEMPORARY FICTION

1

JUN'ICHIRO TANIZAKI WRITES that we "Westerners are amazed at the simplicity of Japanese rooms, perceiving in them no more than ashen walls bereft of ornament." What he writes is true. We are amazed. Often, furthermore, we deeply approve; for simplicity—severity even—plainness—are pioneer virtues still held in high esteem by us, if rarely practiced now. Indeed, the simple, in our covered-wagon days, was directly connected, as a tool might be, to the hand and what the hand made. This simplicity implied less skill than it demanded determination, and it emerged from coarse necessity the way the vegetables we grew in the dirt near our farmhouse kitchen did: products equally of effort and rough chance, crude as our first fence, and cultivated no farther than you would dig a well—not an inch beyond the reach of water.

The shelters we built were like the ground we broke and the implements we made—plain as their names: house, field, food, cloth, plough—simple as the simple liberties we enjoyed, though these were not freedoms from Nature, certainly, since Nature hemmed us in and made life hard, or from thieves or Indians or illness, dangers common and recurrent as nighttime; but from society, from other people's profiteering regulations, from laws we didn't like, servitude and our own past failures, from the exasperating complications of a civilization caught in the toils of Time, tied down by custom and privilege.

In a land whose very features were unfamiliar, where even the rules of life were strangers, where the past had been abolished so that everyone could feel they were starting life as equals from a line of opportunity which was also the same for all; in such a land, with such a task, you had to learn to depend on yourself, to make a religion, as Emerson did, out of "self-reliance," and become a handyman, a "jack-of-all-trades," as it was put; but it was also true that when you did need others, you desperately needed them—to form a posse, raise a roof, to bridge a stream—nor did you have the time or training to divine obscure intentions, or engage in elaborate ritual games, in order to discover whether another person was a friend or an enemy, a worker or a wastrel, dependable or weak, an honest man or a rustler; so you wanted to know immediately "how the land lay," and the frank and open countenance was consequently prized, as were the looks of a man who had worked long and hard in the wind and sun, who appeared to fear God (for you were often beyond the reach of any other law), who had the confidence that came from overcoming many obstacles, who "put on no airs," "wore his heart on his sleeve," was entirely "up front," and, as the salacious saying is now, "let it all hang out"—presumably his wash. Nowadays, even a candid, blunt, abrasive boss can be admired because he has been "straight" with you, letting you know "where you stood."

The simple, like the straight and the plain, is relatively featureless. It reduces the number of things with which you have to cope. After all, when crossing the country by covered wagon, you took winding trails only when rivers and mountains made the circuitous the shortest way. And in the Bible, didn't God promise to make the crooked straight and the rough places plain? We liked the land we settled to be level, well-drained, free of rock. We often preferred the companionship of animals because they couldn't talk at all, and could be expected to act within their species as if in a cage. It was the body which dealt with the day's difficulties. It was the body which built, which plowed, which planted, and which, on occasion, danced and sang and played. The body baked. The body begot. It was not the brain.

So our breath was supposed to be too short for long sentences. Democracy didn't encourage subordination, not in people, or for any part of their speech, whether it was to fancy words, or flattering phrases, or complicated clauses. Honesty was suspicious of

143

endless ramifications. Adverbs which didn't contribute to their action were needless frills. If it didn't matter to the bite of the blade what the color of the ax's handle was, you didn't write it down or say its name. Events were the chief ingredient in stories, and the main thing was not to dawdle, but to offer up the verb, and then get on with it. Ideas fuddled you far worse than alcohol. Theories couldn't thread a needle. You read a bit from the Good Book of an evening because, otherwise, God might blight your wheat. And you went to the Sunday Meeting for the society of it, and for the same wary reason you read. What's more, there was always another row to hoe.

How different this simplicity was from the sort praised by the subtle Tanizaki, and how misled we Westerners were when we admired an innocence we thought was our own. Those ashen walls, with their unadorned surfaces, the candles which lit them, the unpretentious wood which framed the windows, the plain mats which softened and warmed the floor, were there to receive the indefinite wavers of the flame, to grow uneven with revelation and concealment, to move, as if alive, inside their planes, and provoke the profoundest contemplation.

While the walls of the American settlers existed to keep out the cold and be forgotten . . . existed to keep out the vast space of the prairie which lay around every cabin like an endless sea . . . existed to keep out the high sky you could fall into like a pit.

The traditional Japanese room might give out onto a garden of gravel, a small raked space with one or two stones which stood for a world or any mountain, each tame as a household bird. What of the planks whose grain will emerge only after years of timidity and suspicion, the mats that greet each footstep with a whisper which they pass among their fibers? and what of the corners in such a room, carved from darkness, where perhaps a thread of gold gleams from the flank of an otherwise invisible lacquer chest, where the dimmest hint of an ardent desire may lie wrapped in alternating layers of shadow and silk so that an additional breath bends the candle flame? These conditions, these qualities, speak to us not of simplicity, not in our sense, but of the indirect and devious, and suggest—there is the word!— they suggest that these plain surfaces and impassive features are

144

screens on which one reality plays while another lurks behind them, and may move, when it moves, in metaphysical earnest.

One simplicity is reached, then (we cannot say "achieved"), when skills and means and time and energy are minimal. It is the sort of simplicity which looks not at the causes of things, but only at their effects. Who cares, it says . . . who cares what drove the nail, if now its head rests in the right place? When the larder holds only a bit of ground corn, a corn cake is what we shall have. Two "I do"s shall marry a couple as well as any cathedral ceremony.

Another simplicity is reached by removal and erasure, by denial and refusal. It begins with features already played upon by the artist, with surfaces into which the candle's flicker has been cut, and dark corners created with charcoal, so there need never be an actual niche or a real lantern, but only a steady indifferent glare of light; for absences will have to be understood to be as solidly in place as any wooden headrest, waiting the head that will sleep. It begins by looking at decoration as if it were a disease, as a form of social mold, a sign of spiritual decay, another case of the showy bad taste of some nouveau riche, or the loud cosmetics of a whore. Beneath these excrescences, these layers of gilt, these scabs of fashion, is an honest beam, more richly grained and more interesting than all these distracting carvings; beneath this powder and this creme is a natural beauty who might again send the Achaeans against Troy; behind these nervous variations is a mighty theme; let us hear it. Just one time. So cleanly, so clearly, we cannot be confused, nor any flaw disguised. We want to grasp the lines, follow the form, find the true source of our sensation. Then, when real simplicity has returned, when the essential has been restored to its few rightful properties, we may let fall upon it the pale light of our mind; we may shadow it with the darkness that lives in a few of our own thoughts; we may allow to cross it the slow movements of our meditations.

Let us reconsider, for a moment, the simple objects which our ancestors made: a plain wooden bowl, for example, hollowed from a sawed round of tree trunk. A chisel bites into the heart of that wood, eats into the center of its rings of yearly growth, so that shortly a spoonful of milk could be placed in it, and then a cup's worth, although there will be bark remaining around the rim.

145

The rind is peeled off, needless bulk is cut away, and by continued gnawing at the core, the tools of the carpenter create a basin we can begin to recognize as a bowl. Or perhaps hot coals burn the hollow in it. Its interior should be smooth enough to let liquids slosh, a spoon to scoop, a larger one to ladle, and it should rinse out easily. The wood must be hard and dense so that warm soup won't penetrate its fibers. Beyond this, little needs to be done. For the utilitarian, the means cease the moment the end is reached. A little sand will scour the bowl; a little seasoning will secure the grain. If it were a size to conveniently stack—that would be a plus. Our sentences should similarly fly to the mark, deposit their message and disappear, as if a pigeon were to become its poop, so when any one of us looked up to complain because our shoulder had been stained, there'd be no bird there.

Then why did we ever worry about the exact slopes of the hollow our tools had chipped, the precise sheen of the wood, the slim line and smooth run of the rim? We certainly should have cared about how sturdily the dish sat, and how its sides widened so the soup could cool; but why were we concerned about the match of its rings, the quality of the grain in the base and bowl, the shape of the shadows which crept from beneath its sides?

This bowl is ceasing to be simple. Hardship forces the makeshift upon us; primitive conditions produce primitive results; urgent needs aren't choosy; indeed, the sharp teeth of need close like a trap on any victim; but when circumstances are no longer as straitened as they once were, and a bit of leisure, some small level of satisfaction, has been reached, the mind can let go of the plough's handle, can turn aside from its single thought, and transform its lust into a little love.

The bowl has ceased to be simple. A word like *perfection* has us by the ear. Now we are seeking a smoothness, an evenness, an achievement in its completion which will take us days— months—beyond an efficient use of our time. We become obsessed (is it suddenly or slowly?) by geometry, by geometry's deceptive simplicities, its lucent beauty, and we see how the bowl is but a nest of circles whose circumferences are steadily shrinking and whose diameters retract.

The bowl is a celebration of complexity. We've had to set several versions aside in order to start over, trying to improve its proportions, passing before our mind's demanding eye, as though they were bathing beauties, images of other utensils whose alluring features may help us with the one we're composing. What is this resulting bowl, then, whose shaping requires the failure of so many others, who devours this base and that rim, accepts a surface, adapts a form, distorts a tendency—acquiring qualities the way an actor takes on personalities in order to realize a role; what is this object whose making is directed by memory as much as by the pots which are broken when they fail to satisfy, or the bowls which are burned as kindling when the wind turns cold, or the words which are sent away from the sentence they were to serve in, and linger near it like disconsolate shades? what is this thing built so solidly of ghosts?

This simplicity I seek is not the product of a simple mind; it is the consequence of complex steps and subtle choices; it is the consequence of long study and patient learning: I must house a whole history within myself; I am what I have preferred; I am what I have abhorred. For when I create any kind of container now, do I not consider the character of its likely companions? how long and often it will rest unseen in a cupboard, the special occasions in which it will be summoned forth, and borne to the stove to be filled, and borne to the table to be emptied? and whether the teeth marks of greedy men will mar it, knives and spoons scratch it, falls abrade or dent? and how it will feel to hold, and to look down upon when steaming with cooling stew? and whether it shall contain its own memories, too, of cereal and milk and mornings, or pudding and custard, illness and sadness, and what it will be like when the stained old bowl is packed to be moved, packed to be given away or sold, as part of the normal sweepings of spring cleaning, the settlement of a bankruptcy, or the offer of it by a legacy, when death has claimed its most companionable plate?

How reluctantly, in the United States, have we come to recognize that civilization is refinement; that it requires leisure, judgment, taste, skill, and the patient work of a solitary mind passing itself, as though it were both a cleaner and a cleansing cloth, back and forth across an idea, back and forth until the substance of it—in wood or marble or music, in syllables seeking their place in some song—back and forth until the matter of it begins to gleam deeply, from its buried center, deeply where thought and thing are one, and therefore not solely from its surface where a

147

glitter may sometimes be glibly emitted, a glitter which comes just after a bit of light has struck, a glitter, a glit before the beam has bounded off—a glitter, a glit—a spark, after which there will be only the light which has gone.

Apart from the simplicity associated with the pioneer spirit of America, we developed, also very early, a simplicity of a second sort, though certainly in some sympathy with the first; this was exemplified by the distilled designs, the purified life, and even purer dreams, of a sect called Shakers (so named because of their custom of dancing during their religious services, and of being frequently and literally moved by their love of God). They were separatists, forming withdrawn and self-sustaining communities. They were pacifists like the Quakers (another name signifying uncontrolled movement), and believed in equality, and in the actual, rather than the rhetorical, Brotherhood of Man. They were celibate, and endeavored to live a life free of sexual tension and gender competition. They were undogmatic, preferring to follow their faith rather than preach it, drawing communicants not by argument and propaganda, but by shining example. Since Shakers did not breed, they were never guilty of corrupting their children with their principles, and converts came to them entirely out of free choice and when in possession of a presumably mature mind.

"When a World's Fair was held several years ago in Japan" (June Sprigg, a student of the Shakers, writes), "one of the most popular features was an exhibit of Shaker furniture. Chairs without carving, tables without knickknacks, the simplicity of Shaker stoves and baskets, even the white walls and bare wood floors—all these made sense to the Japanese, who recognized and appreciated the same simplicity based on spiritual principle that characterizes traditional Japanese culture."

I wonder if the visitors to the Fair saw how directly the Shakers translated moral qualities into principles of craftsmanship: spare, straight, upright, plain, simple, direct, pure, square, tight, useful, orderly, unaffected, neat, clean, careful, correct. For every chair there was a peg on the wall from which it would hang while the floor was thereby more swiftly swept, and every peg was perfect. Since the chair was hung by its heels, as it were, what dust there was would settle on the bottom of the seat and not on the side where one sat. Beds also folded up into the wall, and drawers drew out of anywhere. A sewing box might be fitted in a rocker, for example, shutters slid up and down instead of swinging out into the room, and boxes were invariably nested. Every space was made of appointed places, and the tools that cleaned those hard-to-reach corners were hooked alongside a horsehair sieve sometimes, or a fluted tin mold for maple sugar.

Yet the Shakers used only the finest maple, the truest oak, and clearest pine, the best slate. Grooves and pegs which were internal to a piece, and therefore never seen were finished as finely as if they would live their whole life out-of-doors. Drawers not only slid out smoothly, they said they slid, in the look of them, in the shush of their sliding; and the ingenious nestling of things, the creation of objects which did double duty, the ubiquitous ledges and holders and racks and pegs, spoke of order, and neatness, and fit—the Godliness of Utility; for though their chairs were stiff and forthright, their tables, wide and unencumbered, and their solutions to problems quite evidently inspired by necessity, there was nothing humble about their materials, pure and as prized as silver and gold. There was nothing humble about the days of careful labor that obviously went into them. There was nothing humble and spare about houses with double doors and double stairs—one for each sex. Nor is there anything humble about a building built to stand a thousand years, or in some handmade things so supremely finished they provoke us to exclaim: "handmade, maybe, but what careful fingers, what holy hands!" There is nothing humble about perfection.

And the hidden joints, the concealed beds, the matched grains, the boxes which live their carefully concealed lives in other boxes: these are tricks of the High Baroque.

Unlike pioneer simplicity, which was perforce crude and incomplete, Shaker simplicity spoke eloquently about its moral ideals. Every room was as much God's place as a church. Every object was, in its expense of spirit, in its richness of refinement, in its strenuous demands on occupants and employers, a symbol of Divinity and Divine Law.

Sometimes, when we look at a Shaker surface, or when we take into account the requirements of Tanizaki's ideal toilet, we believe we see things so simple that there is really nothing there; but the decoration of a Shaker surface is completed by the Shaker craftsman's care; it colors the wood as no paint could; it

149

composes—wooden wall and window, wooden beam—as no carver or designer could contrive. The eye is full to overflowing. And if we recall how Tanizaki wrote about his toilet; how it would be built in a grove fragrant with leaves and moss, apart from the house, yet at the end of a passage; how high slim windows would let in a dim soft light; how it would be, this plain chamber of relief, so cut off from the other concerns of ordinary life that you could say it was made of quiet; and how in that quiet you could hear the hum of the mosquito, the scrape of the cricket, each gentle drop of rain tippling along from leaf to leaf and falling from an eave; then we have to realize, once again, that the simplicity he desired was one which would allow natural complexities their full reach, and that this simple place of his was decorated by no less than the moon, for instance, which would hang its half-light there to be enjoyed, or by the sky which would offer a streak of blue like a sash, and by the sound of insects in the deep grass.

2

Simplicities, in short, are not all the same. When, in her master-piece, a story of black people and the problems of love called "Melanctha," Gertrude Stein resorts to the plainness of the pioneer style, she does so to render the rhythms of black Baltimore speech, and to convey the handmade quality of such talk, as it struggles to express powerful and complex feelings through the most ordinary of words, and by their rhythms, rhymes, and repetitions.

Melanctha told Rose one day how a woman whom she knew had killed herself because she was so blue. Melanctha said, sometimes, she thought this was the best thing for her herself to do.

Rose Johnson did not see it the least bit that way.

"I don't see Melanctha why you should talk like you would kill yourself just because you're blue. I'd never kill myself Melanctha just 'cause I was blue. I'd maybe kill somebody else Melanctha 'cause I was blue, but I'd never kill myself. If I ever killed myself Melanctha it'd be by accident, and if I ever killed myself by accident Melanctha, I'd be awful sorry."

Although Ernest Hemingway's style gets some of its substance from Gertrude Stein (it is even more deeply indebted to Sherwood Anderson), its aim is less complex than hers. He borrows a bit of machismo from the Pioneer, some of his ostentatious simplicity from the Shaker, and sharpens this by means of a selectivity which is severe and narrow. If Adolph Loos, architecture's enemy of ornament, felt we should sweep walls free, and wipe planes clean, Hemingway's purpose was to seize upon the basics right from the beginning, and therefore be in a position to give an exact description of "the way it was." He would remove bias and cliché, our conception of how things had always been, our belief in how things ought to be, and replace them with the square-shouldered resoluteness of reality.

> Out through the front of the tent he watched the glow of the fire, when the night wind blew it. It was a quiet night. The swamp was perfectly quiet. Nick stretched under the blanket comfortably. A mosquito hummed close to his ear. Nick sat up and lit a match. The mosquito was on the canvas, over his head. Nick moved the match quickly up to it. The mosquito made a satisfactory hiss in the flame. The match went out. Nick lay down again under the blanket. He turned on his side and shut his eyes. He was sleepy. He felt sleep coming. He curled up under the blanket and went to sleep.

Brevity may serve as the soul for wit, but it is far from performing such a service for simplicity. The economy of most of Hemingway's writing is only an appearance. To shorten this passage we could have encouraged the reader to infer more, and said: "The fire brightened when the night wind breathed upon it. The swamp was as quiet as the night." If images, implications, and connectives are allowed, a condensation can be sought which is far from simple. "A mosquito sang in his ear so he sat and lit a match." Matches do go quickly out. No need to mention that. Moreover, Nick could be put to sleep far less redundantly. But

Hemingway needs to state the obvious and avoid suggestion, to appear to be proceeding step by step. He needs the clumsy reiteration. It makes everything seem so slow and simple, plain, even artless, male.

Hemingway's search for the essential was characteristically American; that is, it was personal; he sought a correct account of his own experience, because anything less would be fraudulent and insincere. The simplifying came prior to the writing; it was to be built into the heart and the eye, into the man—hunting or fishing, running with the bulls, going to war, mastering his woman. On the whole, Hemingway's work has not held up very well, and that is perhaps because he didn't see or feel any more than he reports he felt or saw, because the way it was was really only Heming's way.

According to Democritus, the atom was so simple it could not be divided, and that simplicity, Plato thought, was the source of the soul's immortality. Only if you had parts could you come apart, and only if you came apart could you decay and die and disappear. Change itself, Parmenides argued, depended upon such minuscule divisions, but it required, in addition, the space to come apart in, for when separation occurred, something (which was a swatch of Nothing, in most cases) had to fill the breach in order to ensure the cut would continue and not heal around the knife. So the atom remained an atom because it was a plenum and contained not even a trace of the real agent of decay, empty space.

Behind the search for the simple is a longing for the indivisible, the indestructible, the enduring. When a noun is reified, its elements fuse. It obtains an Essence. It becomes One, Primitive, Indefinable. God is God. A rose is a rose. And that is that.

These ultimate simples were invisible, not only because they were very very small, but because they were pure. Purity is a property of simplicity. It is often what is sought in seeking the simple. Atoms had no qualities. Atoms had nothing to say to the senses. Atoms were geometries. They had shapes; you could count them; they weighed; they fell through the Void like drops of rain; they rebounded; they combined; and when these combinations came undone, they remained as unaffected by their previous unions as any professional Don Juan.

Visibility is impurity. Invisibility belongs to the Gods, to the immaculate Forms, to the primeval seeds. It is not morally pure, ethereal spirits, but those ghosts clotted with crime, who hang about like frozen smoke in the still air. The soul, as a penance, is encumbered with flesh. Thought is brought to us in terms which can't help but demean it, as if our sincerities were written in neon. Sin and sensation together veil the truth. Simplicity serves the essential, so the simple style will stick to the plainest, most unaffected, most ordinary words; its sentences will be direct and declarative, following the basic grammatical forms; and to the understanding, it will seem to disappear into its world of reference, more modest than most ministers' wives, and invisible as a perfect servant.

These ultimate simples were near enough to numbers as to make the move from Materialism to Idealism a small step. The logician, in an exactly similar fashion, seeks the supreme, unfactorable unit to begin with, and to that unit he then applies his intuition of the first fundamental logical operation, namely addition. One, and then: one more. One. And one. And one. Like Roman numerals or a prisoner's days. Bars, mars, nicks, accumulating in the direction of a unapproachable infinity. Others argue that anything either Is (like a light switch, On), or it Isn't (and like a light switch, Off); that a "yes," or a "no," suffices. To build a machinelike mind. Plato's Demiurge lets the right triangle flop about like a stranded fish, and in that way it forms squares, cubes, and other polyhedrons, or it spins itself into a cone (for a cone is a triangle revolving like a door), while this shape, pivoting on its peak, will turn itself, in turn, into a sphere. With every essential figure drawn and every atom formed, the remainder of the universe is easy.

At one extreme, then, we find mathematicians, logicians, and those quantitative scientists who shave with Occam's razor; whose concepts have one (and only one) clear meaning; whose rules are unambiguous and conclusions rigorously drawn; while, on the other hand, there are the pious craftsmen who think with their hands, reverence their materials, and build their own beds.

As simple as the simple is, and as basic as butter to French cuisine, it never seems to be nearby or abundant, but has to be panned, like silver or gold, from a muddy stream. Surfaces have to be scrubbed, disguises divested, impurities refined away,

153

truths extracted, luxuries rejected, seductions scorned, diversions refused. Because, if some things in life are simple, quite a lot is not; quite a bit is "buzzing, blooming confusion." There is, of course, deception's tangled web. There are the many mysteries of bureaucracy, the flight path of bees, the concept of the Trinity; there are the vagaries of the weather, the ins and outs of diplomacy, business, politics, adultery; there is poetry's indirection, the opacity of German metaphysics, the ornamentation of Baroque churches, and the cast of the Oriental mind.

Simplicity is not a given. It is an achievement, a human invention, a discovery, a beloved belief.

In contrast to the bubbling stew we call our consciousness (and to reprise), there are the purities of reason which require clear rules of inference and transparent premises; there are the invisible particles of matter, those underlying elements out of which the All is made Universal by the Few; there are nascent conditions of existence, unsullied by use or age or other kinds of decay; there are definitions brief and direct as gunshots; there are modes of being which streamline the soul for its afterlife flights. Consequently, beneath simplicity itself, whenever it serves as an ideal, lie moral and metaphysical commitments of considerable density. If the foundations of Reality are simple, the grounds of Simplicity are complex.

Those who champion simplicity as a way of life are aware of the political and moral statement they are making. Gustav Stickley, who contributed so substantially to the Arts and Crafts Movement in America around the turn of the century, certainly was. For him, simplicity was not a Spartan lunch of caviar and champagne, or a lazy day sunning on the deck of the yacht. In his first collection of *Craftsman Homes*, Stickley writes:

> By simplicity here is not meant any foolish whimsical eccentricity of dress or manner or architecture, colonized and made conspicuous by useless wealth, for eccentricity is but an expression of individual egotism and as such must inevitably be short-lived. And what our formal, artificial world of today needs is not more of this sort of eccentricity and egotism, but less; not more

conscious posing for picturesque reform, but greater and quieter achievement along lines of fearless honesty; not less beauty, but infinitely more of a beauty that is real and lasting because it is born out of use and taste.

For Stickley, his movement's heroic figure was an Englishman, Edward Carpenter, whose writings he much admired and frequently quotes. *England's Ideal* (which is the title of one of Carpenter's books) appears to be agrarian, anticolonial, puritan, roundhead, and reformist. Our labor should not be a stranger to all that sustains us; our culture should be of our own contriving, and not something we have purchased in a shop; the true character of life ought not to be shamefully concealed; the head must have a hand, both to help it and hold it in check. Possessions, in particular, are like unwanted immigrants—the first family to arrive is soon followed by boatloads of their relatives. Carpenter is vivid:

> It cannot be too often remembered that every additional object in a house requires additional dusting, cleaning, repairing; and lucky you are if its requirements stop there. When you abandon a wholesome tile or stone floor for a Turkey carpet, you are setting out on a voyage of which you cannot see the end. The Turkey carpet makes the old furniture look uncomfortable, and calls for stuffed couches and armchairs; the couches and armchairs demand a walnut-wood table; the walnut-wood table requires polishing, and the polish bottles require shelves; the couches and armchairs have casters and springs, which give way and want mending; they have damask seats, which fade and must be covered; the chintz covers require washing, and when washed they call for antimacassars to keep them clean. The antimacassars require wool, and the wool requires knitting-needles, and the knitting-needles require a box, the box demands a side table to stand on and the carpet wears out and has to be supplemented

155

by bits of drugget, or eked out with oilcloth, and beside the daily toil required to keep this mass of rubbish in order, we have every week or month, instead of the pleasant cleaning-day of old times, a terrible domestic convulsion and bouleversement of the household.

Of course, for the person who does not hear the Turkey carpet call for a stuffed couch, or accede to its demands for a walnut-wood table, or fill the table's polishing requirements, or the bottle's for a shelf, as if they were medical prescriptions; for such a person the growing snowball of belongings will never overtake and amalgamate the sagging seat or soiled cover, because the simplest thing to do with dust is never to disturb it, while wear can be watched with the same interest one watches a sunset, and juxtapositions of hilarious quaintness or stylistic jar can often be appreciated as accurate images of the condition of life. Simplicity carries at its core a defensive neatness which despairs of bringing the wild world to heel, and settles instead on taming a few things by placing them in an elemental system where the rules say they shall stay. Corners full of cupboards, nooks full of crannies, built-in shelves, seats, and drawers, deny each corresponding desire for change, for adjustment. They may begin as conveniences, but they end as impositions. It is their insistence that every function has its implement, every implement its place, every place is a station, and every station has its duties, as they wish the world does, and had, and did.

Labor-saving devices like the sewing machine, Carpenter argues, only provide more time for fashioning frills and flounces. Economy, like purity, like neatness, is one of simplicity's principal ingredients. We must be frugal with what we have when what we have (of premises or provisions) is so limited; but we need to be frugal whether our possessions are many or few, because frugality is inherently virtuous. In describing economy's consequences, Carpenter does not conceal the religious implications, but records them, albeit with a saving smile.

For myself I confess to a great pleasure in witnessing the Economics of Life—and how seemingly nothing need be wasted; how the very stones that offend the spade in the garden become invaluable when footpaths

156

have to be laid out or drains to be made. Hats that are past wear get cut up into strips for nailing creepers on the wall; the upper leathers of old shoes are useful for the same purpose. The under garment that is too far gone for mending is used for patching another less decrepit of its kind, then it is torn up into strips for bandages or what not; and when it has served its time thus it descends to floor washing, and is scrubbed out of life—useful to the end. When my coat has worn itself into an affectionate intimacy with my body, when it has served for Sunday best, and for week days, and got weather-stained out in the fields in the sun and rain—then faithful, it does not part from me, but getting itself cut up into shreds and patches descends to form a hearthrug for my feet. After that, when worn through, it goes into the kennel and keeps my dog warm, and so after lapse of years, retiring to the manure-heaps and passing out on to the land, returns to me in the form of potatoes for my dinner; or being pastured by my sheep, reappears upon their backs as the material of new clothing. Thus it remains a friend to all time, grateful to me for not having despised and thrown it away when it first got behind the fashions. And seeing we have been faithful to each other, my coat and I, for one round or life-period, I do not see why we should not renew our intimacy—in other metamorphoses—or why we should ever quite lose touch of each other through the aeons.

Just suppose, though, that carelessness is the way of the world; that natural selection proceeds by means of an immense waste; that survival is hit or miss and fitness is genetic. Suppose that the deepest of energy's rhythms are random, and that nature may conserve matter but callously use up each of its particular forms. Suppose that order is only a security blanket; that there are no essences; that substance is another philosphical invention like soul and spirit and ego and the gods, like mind and will and cause and natural law. Suppose that life will run every whichaway like a dispersed mob; that the words for life are *proliferation* and

157

opportunism, and that ends are absent and meaning too, purposes pointless and pointlessness the rule: what will simplicity explain in such a case? what will it justify? how will its economies console? its purities protect? its neatnesses regulate?

So many simplicities! How is one to know where one is? what one has? We sometimes admire the naive directness of the primitive painter, failing to notice that what is attractive is often what is not there, rather than what is; and the simplicity we associate in the United States with the Shakers can be found in the mystically inspired Piet Mondrian, as well as in other artists for whom purity of color, line, and shape represents a holiness otherwise out of reach, although what each reaches is obscured behind a different mist; then there is the meditative simplicity of someone like Tanizaki, which seems to require only a cleared space, a bare screen, a benevolent silence, into which he can cast shadows like so many heavy sacks, or project a dance of light and mind, or provoke the mosquito into speaking, or the moon; perhaps nearby we can place the duplicitous simplicity of the drape or curtain behind which plots may be planned, or bring out the bland expression which lids a kettle of seething rage, or maybe we can unfold a calm screen, like a newspaper held in front of our breakfast face, behind which caresses unscheduled by any passion can continue themselves to their self-canceling conclusion; while finally we must find a spot beside the psychological essentialism of a writer like Hemingway, or alongside the ontological researches of a painter like Basho, where we can put the expressive simplicity of minimalists such as Samuel Beckett and Mark Rothko, who brood upon their motifs like Cézanne his mountain, or Flaubert his Bovary, until any silly little thing, so intensely attended to—as words often are, as symbols are, as bodies, as beliefs—until any ugly old tatter, attended to, touched by concern, becomes as full of the possible as an egg, an embryo, a soft explosion of sperm; and we stare at the striations of a stone, for instance, as at a star, as if time itself wore every scar the stone does, as if the rock were that world of which the poet so often speaks—that world made cunningly; that world held in the palm of the hand; that flower, wooden bowl, or grain of sand, of which the poet so often speaks—speaks to another world's inattentive ear.

"Limitation of means determines style." That is the pat answer to many a mikelike question. "With one hand tied behind my back . . . "is the common boast. The simple can be a show of strength; it can place a method or a bit of material under significant stress so as to see what it is capable of, what its qualities can achieve. In the small and simple atom is a frightful force, a heat equivalent to a nation's hate, if it is unanimously released, as meaning in a lengthy sentence sometimes waits to the last syllable to explain itself, or a life of persistent disappointment bursts suddenly down the barrel of a gun, years of pent-up letdowns set loose.

Simplicity can be a boast—"see how I deprive myself"; it can be an emblem of holiness, a claim to virtues which might otherwise never be in evidence; the peasant-loving prince, the modest monarch, unspoiled star, humble savior, rich man's downcast door. But most of all it is a longing; for less beset days, for clarity of contrast and against grays, for certainty and security, and the deeper appreciation of things made possible by the absence of distraction, confusion, anxiety, delay. Simplicity understands completeness and closure, the full circle, something we can swing a compass round, or—to hammer out the line—get really straight.

What it does not understand so well is exuberance, abundance, excess, gusto, joy, absence of constraint, boundless aspiration, mania, indulgence, sensuality, risk, the full of the full circle, variation, elaboration, difference, lists like this, deviousness, concealment, the pleasures of decline, laughter, polyphony, digression, prolixity, pluralism, or that the devil is the hero in the schemeless scheme of things. If our North Pole is Samuel Beckett and our South Pole is Anton Webern, our equator is made by François Rabelais with Falstaff's belt.

Thinking now of how complex simplicity is, perhaps we have an answer (though I do not remember previously posing any question). Before the buzzing, blooming abundance of everyday, facing the vast regions of ocean and the seemingly limitless stretches of empty space; or—instead—wincing at the news in the daily papers (you had not thought the world—as wide as earth, water, and air are—could contain so much crime, such immense confusion, this daunting amount of pain); or—instead—reading the novels of Henry James and James Joyce and Melville and Mann, or living in Proust or traveling in Tolstoy, you are again impressed by immensity, by the plethora of fact, by the static of statistics and the sheer din of data, by the interrelation of everything, by twists and turns and accumulations, as in this sentence going its endless way; yet as one proceeds in science, as one proceeds through any complex aesthetic surface, as one proceeds, the numerous subside in the direction of the few (the Gordian Knot is made, it turns out, of a single string), the power of number grasps vastness as though each Milky Way were the sneeze of a cicada; so that slowly perhaps, steadily certainly, simplicity reasserts itself. The simple sentence is achieved.

Thinking then of how simple complexity turns out to be, I can understand, when we began with a bowl chipped from a bit of wood, how its innocence drew suitors. Soon considerations had multiplied as though put in a computer. Simplicity disappeared the way a placid pool is broken when a bit of bread brings a throng of greedy carp to boil, or when the mind turns plain mud or simple wood into moving molecules, those into atoms, orbiting alarmingly, these into trings, trons, and quarks, until the very mind which made them gives up trying to calculate their behavior. At such times, and in such times as these, don't we desire the small garden into which we can carry our battered spirit, or perhaps a small room at the top of some tower, a hut in a forest, a minibike instead of a Toyota, a bit of smoked salmon on an impeccable leaf of lettuce, a small legacy from a relative long forgotten whose history is no burden and no embarrassment?

Tanizaki explains to us how the high shine of lacquerware (whose surface under electric light is so harsh and vulgar) becomes softly luminous in the candlelight it was meant for; how the voluminous folds of a lady's garment may hide her body from us only to seduce us with her wit. He allows us to see that the simplest step is nevertheless a step in a complex series, a series whose sum is simple. Cultures are both complex and simple the way the world is. Having reached that world, with the poet's help, from a grain of sand, and found that stretch of sand peopled with every sort of sunbather, we must remember to disembody bather and sand again, to simplify the beach and its sighing surf, so that now we watch the water run up that sand, as full of foam as ale is, only to slow and subside and slip back into the sea

again, leaving a line at each wave lap—a line as pure as a line by
Matisse, a line as purely sensuous as the outline of some of those
bathers, lying on a beach one grain of which we'd begun with,
when we said we could see the world in a bit of grit.

Nominated by The Review of Contemporary Fiction (Dalkey Archive Press)

RUBBER LIFE

fiction by FRANCINE PROSE

from NORTH AMERICAN REVIEW

That winter I read a lot and worked in the public library. A fog settled in on my heart like the mists that hung in the cranberry bogs and hid the ocean so totally that the sound of the waves could have been one of those records to help insomniacs fall asleep. Always I'd been happy when the summer people left, but that fall I couldn't look up when the geese flew overhead and I avoided the streets on which people were packing their cars. Always I'd felt that the summer people were missing something, missing the best part of something, but now it seemed that I was the one being left as they went off, not to their winter office life, but to a party to which I had not been asked, and I felt like you do when the phone doesn't ring and no mail comes and it's obvious no one wants you. Of course I had reason to feel that way. But oddly, I hadn't noticed. How strange that you can be satisfied with your life till the slamming of some stranger's car trunk suddenly wakes you up.

I was trying to be civilized, cooking fresh produce till the market ran out, although it was only for me. The house I was caretaking had a microwave oven that seemed important to resist. The microwave surprised me. It was a colonial whaler's house, white clapboard with a widow's walk, so perfectly restored and furnished so obsessively with period pieces that all the comforts of modern life were tucked away grudgingly in some hard-to-find wing or upstairs. There was a cherrywood table on which I read while I ate. I had promised myself: no television till 10:30, when

Love Connection came on. I loved that show with its rituals of video dating, its singles who rarely loved each other as much as they'd loved each others' images on TV.

The house was supposed to be haunted—but so was every house in our town; a resident ghost could double what you could ask for summer rent. The Carsons' who were returning from Italy in the spring, told me their house had a ghost they'd never seen or heard; they could have been referring to some projected termite problem that never materialized. I didn't listen too hard. I'd heard similar stories in several previous houses, and such was my mood that fall that it depressed me to admit that ghosts were yet another thing that I no longer believed in.

I read through the evenings and weekends. I found out how not to O.D. When I got tired there were books I could read for refreshment, fat nonfiction bestsellers detailing how rich people contract-murdered close relatives. I skimmed these books as fast as I could and let their simple sentences wash through my brain like shampoo. I couldn't read at work, except on quiet mornings. We were surprisingly busy. Our town had a faithful daytime library crowd—young mothers, crazies, artists, retirees, the whole range of the unemployed and unattached. The best part of my job was seeing them come in from the briny winter cold, into the shockingly warm, bright library where the very air seemed golden with the fellowship and grateful presence of other people.

At first I read mostly new books, picked indiscriminately from the cartons that came in. Most of them were boring, but I liked knowing how to live with tennis injuries and diseases I hoped never to live with. I preferred these to the exposés of environmental poisoning and books about why women lose men, books that made me so anxious I'd fall asleep reading and wake up long before dawn. It was a winter of lengthy biographies: lives that seemed longer than lives lived in actual time. I read a book about Edith Wharton and Henry James, and then I read Edith Wharton. I felt so close to Lily in *The House of Mirth* that when she took opium and died, an odd electric shiver shot across my scalp. We had six Edith Wharton books. When I finished them nothing else seemed appealing and for awhile I felt lost.

Then I became interested in a man named Lewis and the problem of what to read was solved because now I could read what he read. I put the books he returned aside and later took them

163

home. To start, these were mainly cookbooks with photos in which dusty bits of Mexico or Tuscany peeked disconsolately at you from behind shiny platters of food. The first time I noticed Lewis—one of the summer helpers must have issued his card— he was returning a book he opened to show me a huge plate of black pasta on which some mussels had been fetchingly strewn.

"Isn't it wild?" Lewis said. "Isn't it pornographic?"

"How do they make it black?" I said.

"Squid ink, I think," Lewis said. He looked at me almost challengingly, perhaps because our town was very health conscious, on strict natural and macrobiotic diets that would probably not include squid ink—though you might ask why not. The previous week, at a potluck Sunday brunch, I got up to help clear the dishes and was scraping grapefruit shells into the compost when my hostess said, Stop! it wasn't compost, it was the tofu main course. After that, the black pasta looked as magnificent as the walled Tuscan city behind it, and when I said, "Have you ever made this?" there was a catch in my voice, as if we were gazing not at pasta but at a Fra Angelico fresco.

Lewis said, "No, I use the pictures for attitude. Then I make up the recipes myself."

I wondered whom he cooked for, but didn't feel I could ask. It crossed my mind he might be gay—but somehow I thought not. After that I paid attention: Lewis came in about twice a week, often on Mondays and Thursdays; I always wore jeans and sweaters, but on those days I tried to look nice. One day a Moroccan cookbook seguéd into a stack of books about Morocco which I checked out for him, longing to say something that wasn't obvious ("Interested in Morocco?") or librarian-like ("Oh, are you planning a trip?"). If he was en route to Marrakech, I didn't want to know. When he returned the Morocco books I guiltily sneaked them home. That night I sat at my table and read what he'd read, turned the pages he'd turned, till a hot desert wind seemed to draft through the house, and I felt safe and dozed off.

He chose topics apparently at random, then read systematically; theater memoirs, histories of the Manhattan Project, Victorian social mores, the Dada avant garde, Conrad, Appolinaire, Colette, Stephen Jay Gould. I read right behind him, with a sense of deep, almost physical connection, doomed and perverse, perverse because to read the same words he'd read felt like sneaking into his room while he slept, doomed because it was secret. How could I tell him that, with so many books in the library, I too just happened to pick up *The Panda's Thumb?*

No matter what else Lewis borrowed, there were always a couple of art books. He renewed a huge book on the Sistine Chapel three times and, when I finally got it home I touched the angels' faces and ran one finger down the curve of the prophet's defeated shoulders. He often had paint on his clothes, and when I'd convinced myself that it wasn't too obvious or librarian-like, I asked if he was an artist. He hesitated, then went to the magazine shelf and opened a three-month old *Art News* to a review of his New York show. There was a photo of a room decorated like a shrine with tinfoil and bric-a-brac and portraits of the dead in pillowy plastic frames. He let me hold it a minute, then took it and put it back on the shelf. I was charmed that he'd given me it and then gotten shy; other guys would have gone on to their entire resumés. I wanted to say that I understood now how his work was like his reading, but I was ashamed to have been paying attention to what he read. After he left I got the *Art News* and reread it again and again.

Then two weeks passed and Lewis didn't appear. One afternoon a woman brought back Lewis's books. I noticed the proprietary intimacy with which she handled them; they might have been dishes, or his laundry, unquestionably her domain. She had red hair and a pretty, Irish face, endearingly like mine. She looked around, intimidated. Were it anyone else, I would have asked if she needed help, but I have to confess that I liked it when she left without any books.

The next time Lewis came in, he stood several feet from my desk. "Stand back" he said, "I've still got the flu."

I said, "Look, look at this," babbling mostly to cover the fact that my face had lit up when I saw him. As it happened we'd just received a new book—a history of the 1918 influenza epidemic. He took it and returned from the shelves with an armload of medical history. In one volume of sepia photos, hollow-eyed Civil War soldiers stared into the camera; for all their bandages and obvious wounds, they perched on the edge of their cots, as if, the instant the shutter snapped, they might jump up and go somewhere else. Lewis said, "I think I'll go home and get over this flu and meditate on a new piece."

Nothing is so seductive as thinking you're someone's muse—even when you aren't—and in that instant the library became for me a treasure trove of possibilities for conversation with Lewis. The cellophane bookcovers seemed to wink with light, and as I browsed among them, I felt like a fish in clear silver water, swimming from lure to lure. Each week I set something aside and rehearsed what I wanted to show him, but always I was defeated by an adrenaline rush. One day he was practically out the door when I called him back and flung open a coffee table book. I turned to a photo of an altar from a West African tribe that boasted an elaborate dream culture in which you constructed little personal shrines with doll figures representing everyone you had ever slept with in a dream.

Lewis studied it a while. Then he said, "My gallery isn't big enough." I laughed but it hurt me a little. I thought, Well, it serves me right. Honestly, I couldn't believe what I'd picked out to finally show him. Lewis said, "And who do *you* dream about?" It was a smarmy, lounge-lizard kind of question he seemed shocked to hear himself ask. Then he got embarrassed and I got embarrassed and I said, "Last night I dreamed I was trapped in Iran with terrorists looking for me and—"

"Oh," said Lewis, semi-glazed over. "The evening news dream. Do you get cable? The worst dreams I ever have are from falling asleep watching C-Span government hearings from D.C."

A week or so later I ran into Lewis on Front Street. I had never seen him out in the world. It took me a second to recognize him; then my heart started slamming around. I walked toward him, thinking I would soon get calm but when I reached him I was quite breathless and could barely speak. He walked me to the library. I noticed that we moved slower and slower the closer and closer we got; it made me feel I should be looking around for the woman Lewis lived with. He said he was driving to Rockport next week and did I want to go? He left me at the library without coming in, even though it was Thursday, one of his regular days.

On the way to Rockport Lewis told me his idea. He was planning to make a kind of wax-museum diorama, all manner of Civil War wounded and maimed behind a plexiglass panel that tinted everything sepia except in large gaps through which you could see the scene in all its full gory color. When I asked what he needed in Rockport he said, "I don't know. Store mannequins. Ace bandages. Ketchup. Half my art is shopping."

I tried to imagine the piece, but kept being distracted by how many layers of meaning everything seemed to have. For example: the ashtray in his car was full and smelled awful. Normally, I'd have shut it, but he wasn't smoking, so it must be the woman he lived with who smoked, and I feared my shutting the ash tray might be construed and even intended as a movement towards him, against her. I felt she was there with us in the car; in fact it was her car. I can't remember quite what I said but I know that it wasn't entirely connected to Lewis saying, "It's Joanne's car. Joanne, the woman I live with."

"How long have you lived together?" I asked; my voice sounded painfully chirpy.

"Forever," said Lewis, staring off into space. "Forever and ever and ever."

By then we were walking through Rockport at our usual hypnotized crawl; really, it was so cold, you'd think we might have hurried. Lewis bought a wall clock, the plain black-and-white schoolroom kind. In a drygoods shop, he asked to see the cheapest white bedsheets they had and the salesman looked at me strangely. We walked in and out of antique stores; several times Lewis made notes. More often, we just window-shopped. In front of one crowded window, Lewis pointed to a large porcelain doll in a rocking chair. He said, "People always say 'lifelike' when they just mean nicely painted. But that one really looks like an actual dead child."

"Or a *live* one," I said, over-brightly. Though the doll was fairly extreme, I probably wouldn't have noticed. Whatever I was drawn to in antique shop windows, it wasn't, hadn't been for years, the Victorian doll in the rocker with the corkscrew curls and christening dress. But when Lewis said look, I looked.

It would have seemed impolite not to ask him in for a drink when he drove me home, and when it got late and I said, "Won't Joanne be expecting you?" and he said, "She's in Boston," it would have seemed silly not to invite him to dinner. Hadn't my asking after Joanne made my good intentions clear? If you believe *that*, you'd believe that my showing him the African dream-lover altar was meant to convey not the fact that I'd dreamed of sleeping with him (which, actually, I hadn't) or that I wanted to sleep with him, but rather that I would be satisfied if it only happened in dreams.

There was never any telling when he would show up. Sometimes at night he would rap on the window, very *Wuthering Heights*, and my heart would jump. I'd think first of psycho killers and then of the house's ghost; then I'd realize it was Lewis and get scared in a different way. We were very discreet because of the woman he lived with. He clearly felt torn for deceiving her and would never come, or say he would come, unless she was gone or too busy to ever suspect or find out. In the library we were distant, no different from before. It was remarkably erotic. Once more I brought home the books he returned, read what he had read, though now these were sometimes on woodworking and the chemistry of glue. Strangely, I never mentioned this. I think I was superstitious that his knowing might spoil my pleasure, pleasure I badly needed to fill the time between his visits. I was disturbed that time had become something to fill, and sometimes I couldn't help wondering if I hadn't been happier before.

But of course I never wondered that when Lewis was around. I made him watch *Love Connection* with me, and for the first time, my feelings for the video-date couples were unmixed with personal fear. He seemed so happy to see me that I thought, without daring to think it in words, that what he felt was love. Perhaps I was underestimating myself to think that Lewis's interest in me had to have been deep. But how could I know the truth about this when I never knew him well enough to confess we read the same books? There were some things I knew. He used to bring me presents: sewing baskets, beaded purses, bits of antique fluffery that somehow I knew he'd tried out unsuccessfully in his work. Lewis often talked of his work in the most astonishing ways. Once he told me about making a figure for his new piece, a Confederate dummy. Just as he finished painting the face, he was for an instant positive he'd seen it blink, and he felt that if he sat down beside it on its cot he might stay there and never get up.

One night he gave me a cardboard box long enough for the dozen roses I hoped were not inside, but reassuringly wider. In it was the Victorian doll we'd seen in the Rockport window. Though it wasn't something I wanted, I nonetheless burst into tears and, like an idiot, I hugged it. I stood there lamely, cradling the doll, wondering where to put it. I thought of pet shop goldfish and of how one was cautioned to find them a water temperature just like the one they had left, and I remembered the antique mini-rocking chair in the Carsons' living room, with the tiny woven counterpane tossed artfully across it, always at the ready to keep the colonial baby warm. The doll was larger than it appeared, and it was a bit of a squeeze. For awhile we remained looking down at it until it had stopped rocking.

That night when we were in bed we heard footsteps from downstairs. "Did you hear that?" I said, though I could tell Lewis had. It had stopped us cold. Lewis put on his pants and picked up a poker from the fireplace in my bedroom, a hearth I suddenly wondered why I had never used. "Wait here," he said, but I put on my nightgown and followed him.

We skulked through the house, flinging doors open, like in the movies. But there was no one there. The door was locked, the windows shut. Nothing had been disturbed. "Mice," Lewis said.

"Mice in tap shoes," I said.

Then Lewis said, "Look at that." The doll we'd left in the rocker was sitting in one corner of the living room couch. He said, "How did you do *that*?"

"I didn't!" I said shrilly. "I was upstairs with you." I felt too defensive to be frightened or even amazed. Did he think I'd staged this for his benefit? I'd read all those books for his benefit, and I couldn't even admit that. "Well, the house is supposed to be haunted," I said, and then got terribly sad. It struck me that finding yourself in a haunted house with someone should unite you in a kind of fellowship, the camaraderie of the beseiged, of spookiness and fear. But I didn't sense any of that. What I did feel was that Lewis had moved several steps away. "Put it back in the rocker," he said.

"I don't think it liked it there," I said.

"Put the doll back in the rocker," he said. I did, and we went upstairs. We got into bed and curled back to back, staring at opposite walls. Finally he said, "I'm sorry. I take these things too seriously. I guess it was being raised Catholic. I can't help thinking it has something to do with Joanne."

I couldn't see what a walking doll could have to do with Joanne. I hadn't known he was Catholic—why had that never come up? I didn't know why this was stranger than thinking a Confederate dummy had blinked at him. Though maybe, it occurred to me, that had never happened; it had just been a figure of speech. "I'm Catholic, too," I said. "But the ghost is a Protestant ghost."

Just then the footsteps resumed. We rolled over and looked at each other. It was exactly like those awful moments when you wake up in the morning and the pain you've been worried about is still there. Downstairs, we found the doll on the couch. This time I got frightened. Lewis's face looked totally different than I'd ever seen it look.

"You know what, Bridget?" he said to me. "You are one crazy chick."

After that everything changed and ground to a gradual halt. After that the doll stayed put and we never discussed that night. To mention it would have risked letting him know how wronged I felt, not just over his coolness, his punishing me for what obviously wasn't my fault, but because he'd left me so alone, alone with my own astonishment. I'd been mystified, too, confused, even a little irritated to find myself so chilled by something I couldn't explain and didn't believe in. I kept thinking that meeting a ghost with someone who actually loved you might actually have been fun. Anyway what was happening with us seemed beyond discussion. In the library, we acted the same as before, but it was no longer exciting. It left me nervous and sad. I stopped reading the books he brought back. All I had to do was look at them and a heaviness overcame me, that same pressure in the chest that on certain days warns you it's not the right time to start leafing through family albums of the family dead.

In any case I stopped reading. Without that awareness of what Lewis might choose, I'd lost my whole principle of selection. Out of habit, I browsed the shelves; nothing seemed any less boring than anything else. I gave up *Love Connection*, but often fell asleep watching TV, not for entertainment so much as for steadiness, comfort and noise. For a while I forgot the doll, then considered throwing it out. I wound up tossing the counterpane over its head and leaving it in its chair; the doll showed no reaction. I remember waves of a tingly frostbite chill, a physical burning that sent me racing to the mirror. Naturally, nothing showed. It should not have been so painful, the whole thing had been so short-lived, not nearly so bad as, say, the break-up of a long marriage, losing someone you've shared years and children with. That pain is about everything: your life, your childhood, death, your past. Mine was purely about the future.

That winter the future took a very long time to come. I felt that time had become an abyss I would never get across. And then at last it was spring. The Carsons returned from Italy. Their eyes kept flickering past me till they'd reassured themselves that the house was in perfect shape. Then they thanked me for forwarding their mail, inquired after my winter, told me that Florence had been marvelous fun, and asked if I'd seen the ghost. No, I said. I hadn't.

"No one has," said Mrs. Carson. "But once you know about it . . . Now that you're leaving I can tell you, I'm always reluctant to lease this place to couples with small children because the ghost, oh, it's horrible, the ghost is supposed to be that of a child."

For just a moment I got the chills. I refused to let this sink in. I wondered if her reluctance really had to do with the supernatural or with damage control. I said. "Well, if that's the case, I'm leaving the ghost a present." I indicated the doll. They weren't exactly thrilled. The doll, after all, was Victorian, hopelessly out-of-period. They seemed already tired of me and impatient for a reunion with their possessions.

Outside, packed, was the car I had just bought; even its monthly-payment book seemed a sign of faith in the future. I was moving to Boston to enroll in a library science program. I said goodbye to the Carsons and got in my car and drove off. On my way out of town, I drove past the golf course on which, from the corner of my eye, I spotted what looked like a sprinkling of brilliant orange poppies. It took me a while to realize that they were plastic tees.

Moments of recovery are often harder to pinpoint than moments of shock and loss, but I knew then at what precise instant I'd stopped grieving over Lewis. It had been late April, or early May, a few weeks before the Carsons came home. The tulips were in bloom. I'd been at work, shelving books, deep in the stacks. A volume on Coptic religious texts had fallen open to reveal a magazine hidden inside. It was a fetish magazine called

The Best of Rubber Life. A price tag said seven dollars. Inside were color photos of mostly plump, mostly female couples. Some of the women wore baby doll pyjamas, others were in rubber suits or in the process of putting them on. Most were in quasi-sexual poses though no one seemed to be touching or making love. Everyone gazed at the camera, full frontal stares in some hard-to-read middle between totally blank and bold.

I wondered whose it was, I considered some (mostly elderly) men who seemed like possible candidates. I thought meanly: maybe it was Lewis's. But I didn't think it was Lewis. Perhaps I should have been disgusted, it was really extremely sordid, or even frightened of being in the library with whoever had hid it there. In fact I felt nothing like that, but rather a funny giddiness, an unaccountable lightness of heart. I felt remarkably cheered up. Standing there in the stacks, turning the pages, I realized, as never before, what an isolated moment each photograph represents, one flash of light, one frozen instant stolen from time, after which time resumes. It was what I'd thought when I'd first seen those Civil War pictures but had never known how to tell Lewis. Perhaps I'd been worried that if I told him, the camera would click and he'd move.

I looked at the women in the rubber magazine, and I began to laugh, because all I could think of was how soon the strobes would stop flashing, the cameras would click one last time, how that day's session would end, and they would collect their checks and rise from their rubber sheets and fill the air with hilarious sounds as they stripped off their rubber suits. It was almost as if I could hear it, that joyous sigh and snap—the smacky kiss of flesh against flesh, of flesh, unbound, against air.

Nominated by C. E. Poverman, Richard Burgin and North American Review

INSOMNIA

by TIMOTHY GEIGER

from PAINTED HILLS REVIEW

The rain off and on
all night, the space
heater humming,
a long gray slur
between no dreams.
And this morning
a saucepan of re-heated coffee,
the burning white nail
of a Marlboro Light . . .

*

In a barn in Huntsville
a farmer's widow
is trimming fat
from the year's healthiest
slaughtered pig.
Flies stutter in orbits
around her head, around
the red stump
of the pig's discarded heart.
The blood dries
on her hands,
beneath her fingernails,
up to the knuckles,
bone-deep in the silence
of gristle.

173

*

Last week's news
had the story
of a man in Ohio
who lost his only daughter
to the slow and severe
deductions of cancer.
Told how, after
seven sleepless weeks,
the girl finally gave in
and he did not,
until later
when, heavily sedated,
he finally slept
through funeral and burial.
And how they found him
early the next morning,
digging,
with his bare hands,
to reclaim
one more thing
missing from his life.

*

Coldest night
of January, 1972.
A boy's father
lifts him to his shoulder
and whispers,
"What are you thinking?"
but the boy is either
too tired to answer,
or already asleep
among the stars.
Then, somewhere past
Orion's bow, he's dreaming
the song of new days,

174

the single white arrow
never finding its mark.

      *

Now, October again
and I find myself recalling
what small proof
the living are left with.
How our grief
adds little significance
to whatever doesn't
remain behind.
How the cold,
colorless theorems
of dust return,
how every night
conceals
more than the dark
stones of our faith
shimmering on the hill
beyond this window,
like broken teeth
in the pre-dawn glow . . .

      *

Five a.m.
and I cannot return
to that six-year-old boy,
his warm cheek
on the shoulder
of winter air.
Just as the man
on the six o'clock news
must accept his part
in the story
which he is required
to tell again at eleven,
so too,

the farmer's widow
will learn to expect
the seasonal failures
of corn and cabbage,
the hollow eggshells
which remind her of luck,
which she quietly watches
spinning away
out the window
of that blue
moment before sleep
that will not end.

Nominated by Painted Hills Review

176

WHEATFIELD UNDER CLOUDED SKY

by CAMPBELL McGRATH

from The PARIS REVIEW

Suppose Gauguin had never seen Tahiti. Suppose the
    bêche-de-mer and sandalwood trade had not materialized
and the Polynesian gods held fast in the fruit of Nuku Hiva and
    the milk-and-honey waters of Eiao.
Suppose that Europe during whichever century of its rise toward
    science had not lost faith in the soul.
Suppose the need for conquest had turned inward, as a hunger
    after clarity, a siege of the hidden fortress.
Suppose Gauguin had come instead to America. Suppose he left
    New York and traveled west by train
to the silver fields around Carson City where the water-shaped,
    salt-and heart-colored rocks
appeased the painter's sensibility and the ghost-veined filaments
    called his banker's soul to roost.
Suppose he died there, in the collapse of his hand-tunnelled
    mine shaft, buried beneath the rubble of desire.
Suppose we take Van Gogh as our model. Suppose we imagine
    him alone in the Dakotas, subsisting on bulbs and tubers,
sketching wild flowers and the sod huts of immigrants as he
    wanders,
an itinerant prairie mystic, like Johnny Appleseed. Suppose what
    consumes him is nothing so obvious
as crows or starlight, steeples, cypresses, ghettos, absinthe,
    epilepsy, reapers or sowers or gleaners,
but is, like color, as absolute and bodiless as the far horizon, the
    journey toward purity of vision.

177

Suppose the pattern of wind in the grass could signify a deeper
   restlessness or the cries of land-locked gulls bespoke the
   democratic nature of our solitude.
Suppose the troubled clouds themselves were harbingers.
   Suppose the veil could be lifted.

Nominated by Michael Collier, Reginald Gibbons

THE TELEGRAPH
RELAY STATION

fiction by NORMAN LAVERS

from THE MISSOURI REVIEW

THREE DAYS BEYOND the fort on the stage, following the line of
telegraph poles like a spider slowly clambering its web. The dry
grass prairie is sere and burned looking, like brown skin with a
worn ghost of hair on it, the buffalo far to the south at this time
of year—Thanksgiven day—but packs of white wolves standing
and looking at us curiously. What can they find to eat? All morning long we look forward to seeing the telegraph relay station,
mainly because there is utterly nothing else to see. That is the
place where I will depart from my two fellow passengers and wait
for the stage that comes through from the north, and will take me
south to my destination.

There 't is! Curly hollers back down to us, and we bump each
other to be first to crane our heads out the window, squinting our
eyes into the dust and bits of broke-off dry grass. It's a low cabin
of adobe, the same color of the bare dirt, but with a steep peaked
roof to shrug off the winter snows, no trees or bushes about it.

When we get closer, we see extra poles at the front, where the
telegraph wire we are following goes into the building, then
comes back out on the other side and rejoins the line of poles
continuing straight ahead. But it is a crossroads, and the wire
from the line of poles coming down from the north also enters
the building, then reemerges and continues south, following the
southern road.

179

Well before we reach it, a man has emerged from the front door, a fur cap with ear flaps, buttoning his coat as he runs and stumbles towards us. He reaches us, shouting happily up at Curly, then walks alongside, directly in our dust, escorting us to the station. He is looking in the window at us, face gawped in grin, waving to us repeatedly, so that we must answer his wave half a dozen times. I see that tears are streaming his joyful face.

We crawl out, patting the trip dust off our coats, out of our beards, beating our hats against our legs, unkinking our stiff backs, stamping our frozen feet on the hard ground. He ushers us in to the welcome of a hot stove, takes our coats from us, thrusts steaming tin cups of coffee at us, burning our hands and our lips on the metal, the whole room filled with the savory smell of fresh buffalo steaks cooking. Thanksgiven, he says. He sits us at the rough table, neatly set, and while we eat he stands and watches us, thrilled, like a child looking at his new Christmas presents, though the only gift we have for him is our brief human presence, before we carry on in our different directions.

I bid Curly, and my two fellow passengers—friends now, after two weeks of travel—adieu. And the coach, which seemed to roll so slowly when we were in it, is out of sight and hearing within minutes, and there is no sound but the steady wind whistling in the overhead wires. I turn to my host—I will be staying overnight, my connecting coach arriving the next day noon—and he is not looking down the now empty road. He is frankly staring at me, a smile hovering about his mouth, with something of the expectancy of a new groom regarding his fresh bride. I feel a little stirring of alarm, though I am certain the man is quite harmless.

Will you have more to eat? he asks eagerly.

I couldn't force in another bite, thank you very much.

My pleasure, my pleasure. No need to thank me. More coffee, then?

Yes, that would be lovely, I say (I am already sloshing).

We sit across from each other at the table. With his bulky cap and coat off, my host is a small slight mostly bald man. He watches me for any least chance to serve me, leaps to the stove to set a straw ablaze to light my cigar.

He cannot seem to stop talking.

O it's lonely lonely here, he says, then bursts out laughing.

I can well imagine.

You can't. No no I didn't mean that to sound so short and dismissing. I am sure you are a compassionate, deep imagining man, I can see it in the kindness of your eyes. But you simply can't. Nothing here to see, day in day out. The stages come by once or twice a week while the roads are open, but in winter—O, it's too terrible. Nothing, my friend, nothing. The howling wind. The endless blizzards. There is a strong rope that leads to the outhouse, though it is only fifty paces from here. It looks ridiculous now, but in another month, when the snows come, it will be dire necessity. You cling to it all the way out, and cling to it all the way back. Take your hand off it in a white-out blizzard and at once you lose direction. You can't see even your feet and you lose sense of up and down, so that you topple over. O it's too— ridiculous! Again he bursts out laughing.

I have my mouth open to say, How do you keep your sanity? But thinking better of it, say, Have you no partner here?

Ha, that is a story indeed. I had a partner when I first came here. In fact, he taught me everything. I could no more send or receive a wire than talk to the man in the moon, but he taught me. I came in, just like you, on the stage one day. Well, I had no job, no real prospects, so he convinced me to stay. In our very first winter together, he went out one night for a call of nature, and I never saw hide nor hair again. I suspect he wandered off on purpose, the skunk, just so's not to face it anymore. Anyway, I found out next spring he made it to an Indian village, where he spent the winter. But nothing could ever drag him back here again. Me, I went through the rest of that endless winter—I remember it as almost always nighttime—completely alone. All that kept mind together was the messages coming in for me to transmit onwards, and the answers returning. That world of ticking sounds under my finger became like my family. I became like a blind man with only my sense of touch and hearing to connect me to the outside. But a wonderful sort of blind man who could be in all places at once, hear everybody talking everywhere. The next summer I got me an Indian woman to stay here, not very bright or very good looking, but a sweet enough soul. But in the winter when I needed her most, she up and died on me, and I was alone again. The summers are not so bad, because sometimes, like now, I get a soul to talk to—And say! What a treat you are!—but the winters! O! O! O!—and here is another one spang upon us. Wait! Here's a call coming in.

I hear the loud tickety-tack. He rushes to his desk, takes the stub of pencil off his ear, and begins writing down characters on his notepad. Then he is tappity-tapping on his own big finger key. He waits, more tickety-tack, more writing, then he turns to me, a broad smile on his face.

It was for you, he says. They got a heavy snow up north—early this year—and your coach will be delayed a couple of days till they can dig out. Cross your fingers. If they get more snow and can't get through, there won't be no more runs till next spring.

The bitter smell of coffee awakes me. He is shoving the tin cup into my face. There is a candle lit on the table, and the fire is roaring, though he must have built it up quiet as a mouse to keep from disturbing me. It is still crisp in the room, and the sun is not up so it should be pitch dark out, but instead there is a sort of curious luminescence from the windows, a cold glowing. The wind has stopped and it is utterly still.

You'd better come have a look at this, my host says. He still has that smile playing about his mouth, the bride-groom eagerness. I struggle into my trousers, my bare feet on the frozen floor, and come with him to the window and look out.

Immense soft white flakes are curving down swiftly. They are already four inches deep on the railing outside. The sky is brightening, but there is absolutely nothing to see except sheet after sheet of swirling flakes until all is lost in an amorphous whiteness.

By noon it is a foot of snow with no surcease, by sunset two feet, and the flakes are falling even faster as I make another trip to the outhouse, my boots going clear to the ground through the soft wet snow at every step. I spend the day pacing the four corners of the tiny cabin, trying to stifle my panic. I have already read twenty times till I have memorized the stage schedule, which seems to be the only reading matter in the building. How could I have been so stupid, so improvident? How can I even contemplate six months in this worse-than-a-penitentiary? My host watches me eagerly, rushing to serve me any way he can.

182

That old expression, "keeping body and soul together," has suddenly a problematical cast.

I toss and turn all night thinking: This early freak of storm will melt off in a day or two and I can still escape, but each time I sneak over to the window, it is still pouring out of the heavens. By morning it is four feet deep, and though there was little to see before in the wide empty plain, now there is nothing whatever, a mere blank and formless white clear to the extent of vision. I sit by the fire in stunned despair, refusing breakfast, and then dinner, only drinking coffee, and gnawing at a piece of biskett to save gnawing at my own knuckle.

My host is busy. Calls are coming in constantly for him to relay north or south, east or west, people stranded in the sudden storm, connections missed, meetings aborted, a wedding cancelled.

I am a reading man, I say in agony. Is there nothing whatever in this cabin to read?

His eyes light up, and he goes at once to his cedar chest, rummages frantically, throwing out clothing in all directions, comes up with a large cloth package, unties the strings fastening it, reaches in and comes up with his treasure—and a true treasure it seems when I realize what it is. It is an immense family Bible. A whole great nation's compendium of wisdom and philosophy and morality which, such is the state of my spiritual nature, I had never been able to read past the begats. Here indeed is hope I could spend some of my time profitably. He pulls the table over by the fire, pulls up the most comfortable chair to it, and sets the great heavy tome flat on the table, and brings the lanthorn up by it.

I am in no hurry. I mean to savor every word, mull it over, draw from it its full substance, chew it and digest it. I open to the title page, where it is inscribed with his family name, and with the date of purchase, going back to a time before we were the United States. And there, one after the other, the names of various of his antecedents, all on the male side, and later on, to judge by the dates, brothers of his, and finally his own name some two or three times, and after each signature, the date, and a solemn pledge never again to imbibe in spiritous liquors.

I turn to page one, and read: In the beginning God created the heav'n & the earth. & the earth was without form, & voyde; &

darkness was upon the face of the deep. & the Spirit of God moved upon the face of the waters.

It stops snowing for a few days, but it does not melt. Only, the four feet settles into one foot, and develops sufficient crust that it will support our snowshoes and we can tramp about with a gun looking for game, though there is none. Then it snows more feet, then settles, and so on. Each morning one or other of us digs out the back door and the path to the outhouse. There is a covered porch that leads to the barn with our food supplies and fuel (dried buffalo chips). The front door is blocked by drifted snow which comes halfway up the windows, reducing what little light there is from outside.

I am once more bogged down in the begats. My host knows from his experience that it is best for us to pursue our separate occupations, only coming together to talk at meals, and after supper at night when we sit together about the fire. He is surprisingly busy relaying messages during the day. In quiet moments he rolls and smokes cigarettes and sits by the partially occluded window. I scribble notes in my notebooks, try to plow forward in the Bible. We make shift to pass the day, he much better at it than I. At meals now he is serene and I am the one who cannot stop talking. We have told each other every last wrinkle of our life histories. He seems tranquilly happy at the unexpected boon of my company. For my own part I feel, at moments, a scream starting from somewhere deep in my bowels. I think, if I hear one more tappity tap from his tinny machine I will launch my head through each of his window panes in turn. I envision lifting up the stove and shaking its burning faggots out on the floor. I daydream artillery barrages.

He is sensitive to my moods, watching me from the tail of his eye. I stand up with the idea of taking the shotgun outside and merely firing it off. He rises too, with a smile, and says, Come here, you might as well learn how this operates.

I am told about inventor Samuel F. B. Morse and his ingenious international code based on long and short sounds electrically transmitted down hundreds of miles of wire. At each point where resistance in the wire begins to slow and weaken the signal, there is a relay station where an operator "reads" the message, then sends it off fresh on a new wire to continue its journey. In this way virtually instantaneous communication can connect thousands of square miles of territory, in time our entire nation.

He takes a page of my notebook, and with his pencil writes down the code for me. A . _ ; B _ . . . ; C _ . _ . ; and so on. I have a quick memory and study it all day until I have it by heart. Now I listen with new interest in the tickety tack, but it is too fast, I can't catch the rhythm, I can't break in to see where it starts and stops. He laughs at my frustration—I was the same, he says. In a quiet moment he says: Get your pad and take this— and with his pencil he taps a message on the wood of the table, slowly and carefully. He has to repeat it several times before I get it all.

W-H-A-T-H-A-T-H-G-O-D-W-R-O-U-G-H-T

Then I try, and, haltingly, referring back to my notebook, I send the same message back to him, then again, doing it swifter.

The next morning there is a purpose to get up. I sit at the desk beside him, taking down the messages on my own notepad, then comparing with him. At first I only get a letter or a word here and there, but then more and more. Finally I get an entire message perfectly. He jumps to his feet, I jump to my feet, and we embrace.

You've got the calling, he says. Those with the calling catch on at once, the others never.

We send messages back and forth by pencil tapping, and finally he says I am ready to transmit a message. The first is a botch, I am so frightened and tentative on the big electric key, and he has to come in after me and re-send it. But then I get the touch— he's right, I do have a gift—and I am able to send slowly and accurately, then faster, not so fast as him by a long shot, but tolerable.

One day he says, you're my partner now. I'm not afraid to obey a call of nature, or take a snooze, or go out scouting for game, because I know you are here to back me.

To prove it he leaves me for an hour to ramble around on his snow shoes, and messages start coming in at once, and a couple of times I have to ask for repeats, and a couple of times I have to

185

apologize and make a second transmission, and at first I am sweating profusely—but by the time he gets back I feel competent and professional.

Nevertheless, it is a long time before I am relaxed enough to begin paying attention to the messages themselves. At first they are mere alphabetical counters I am receiving and relaying on, and that takes every ounce of my concentration. But little by little they begin to flesh out into words, become voices that I hear in my head almost as I hear spoken voices. The speakers begin to take on human form in my mind. And—since we have no sense of the passage of time here, and our minds seem to sleep between transmissions—even though answers come a day or several days after an original message, in our senses, suspended in our memories, the replies seem to come close after, as if we were overhearing actual conversations.

TO ED WOBURN AT FT CLAPTON HAPPY BIRTHDAY THIS DAY YOUR FOND BROS TOM MOSE JOSIAH WALTER

TO ANYONE INDIAN TERRITORY WORD OF MY HUSBAND JIM THOMPSON REWARD ELIZ THOMPSON

TO ANYONE FT CLAPTON AREA OR SOUTH WIDOW 38 HARD WORKER SAVINGS LOOK ALRIGHT PLUMP SEEK MAN W LAND PURP MATRIMONY FLO BUSKIRK

TO RICK CRUM AT PAWNY CORNERS CANT GET THRO SNOW SEE YOU NEXT YR BIG DRINKING PARTY THEN SAM

TO FLO BUSKIRK AT FT LEAVENWORTH AM 33 HAVE 138 ACR SOME CATTLE HORSES PROSPECTS GOOD SLIGHT LIMP FT CLAPTON AREA ED WOBURN

TO FLO BUSKIRK AT FT LEAVENWORTH HAVE 5000 ACR MANY CATTLE HORSES TANNERY MILL GOOD WATER FT CLAPTON AREA AM 73 CY MCCLINTOCK

186

TO FLO BUSKIRK AT FT LEAVENWORTH AM 21 GOOD
LOOKING PAWNY CORNERS AREA BUY LAND W YR SAV-
INGS RICK CRUM

Wait, my host says. Don't send those last three on.
What do you mean?
We've got to think about them first. If you sent her the one of
that probably worthless flighty pup Rick Crum, think what will
happen. She's newly widowed. I know what that's like when your
mate is suddenly gone. You're no longer getting what your body
is used to, your blood is up in you. She might make a terrible
even if fully understandable mistake.
I start laughing. So—what?—do we only send on the one from
the well-heeled Cy McClintock?
No. That's no good either. After her loss, she may be down,
she may have lost confidence in the future, she might make a
cautious choice for the old geezer, and get trapped into a marriage with no tenderness in it. She's still relatively young. It's got
to be Ed Woburn. He's a good man. See how much his brothers
like him. Just send that one on.
You can't be serious! We don't know any of this. "Slight limp"
may mean wooden leg. We can't take this kind of responsibility
for someone else's life. We just have to send the offers on and let
her make her own choice. People have to be free to make their
own mistakes. That's what life's about.
You don't know this place as well as I do. That's not how we
work things here. This is my relay station.

TO JAY CHALMERS AT COTTONWOOD GROVE DADDY
SO GLAD TO HEAR YOU ARE ALIVE AND WELL WHEN
CAN YOU RETURN ALWAYS LOVE YR DTR CLEMENTINE

Don't send that one either.
Why, for goodness' sake?
I'll answer it from here, he says. And while I watch stupefied
he taps out:

TO CLEMENTINE CHALMERS IN ST. LOUIS CANT
COME THIS YR MY DEAR CAUGHT BY EARLY SNOW
NEXT SPRING FOR SURE FONDLY DADDY.

187

He looks at me sheepishly. She's been sending inquiries for her dad for a year. He's dead out there somewhere, or abandoned her. I couldn't stand her waiting so piteously for him, so I— well I manufactured some answers from him.

What're you going to do if he really answers sometime?

That already happened on another case, a woman looking for her husband. What a nightmare.

Do you mean you do this all the time?

Do you think I've probably made a mistake? he asks.

I sure do, I say, then wish I hadn't answered so quick when I see his face wince with pain and fear, and then slowly sort of cave in.

I didn't intend it to be that way. (To my astonishment he is blubbering, in tears). I just wanted to help, to be encouraging, to do something to ward off the god-awful loneliness and isolation. Now I've got dozens of them, whole families I've invented and put into contact, marriages that are going forward or being restored when one or other probably don't exist. I'm in so deep I can't get out of it anymore, I have to keep inventing more and more people in a big web and somehow keep them all separated from each other, and separated in my own mind. Once I caught myself making up a reply to another person I had made up. O me, what have I done.

He drops his head into his hands and looks so desolated I reach around and pat his shoulder.

Then he throws his head back up.

You were absolutely right, he says, I should have left them free in the first place. What do you figure I should do now?

Well, for a start, don't do any new ones. And for the others— and the whole great complex mess of it suddenly comes present to me, and I cannot stop a groan, which my host, who has been hanging eagerly to my words, matches, and sinks his head back down on the table again—For the others, I go on, I guess you can't say anything now, but you'll just have to start disengaging 'em. Kill off this one, marry off that one.

O that's so easy to say, he moans, but how can I really do it? These are human beings I have got myself involved with, how can I let them down so brutally?

You've just got to, I say. We'll work on it together. I'll stand by you, and we'll think up something case by case.

188

I've got a call of nature, he says, and heads for the door.

Your coat and hat, I say. (The blizzard has been blowing non-stop for two days.)

O. Yes, he says, and puts them on.

He pulls the door open, snow swirling in and scattering across the floor, then closes it carefully behind him.

As soon as he is gone, calls start coming in.

TO FLO BUSKIRK AT FT LEAVENWORTH AM 41 WIDOWER HAVE LAND W WATER CATTLE SOME WHEAT AT CEDAR SPRS NR CLAPTON AREA HARD WORK BUT GOOD LIFE WE HAVE BOTH BEEN HURT BUT WE CAN START AGAIN PLEASE COME JIM THOMPSON

That one sounds so good I am sure my host would have no objections to it, so I relay it forward. I had not yet sent the other three proposals; and I catch myself thinking there will be no harm waiting a bit longer, till she has had a chance to respond to this good one. But I realize I am falling into the same trap my host fell into, and so I send those three as well, giving her all four to make up her own mind about. But I admit to myself I am pulling for Jim Thompson.

More calls come in.

TO ANYONE INDIAN TERRITORY WORD OF MY HUSBAND JIM THOMPSON REWARD ELIZ THOMPSON

I have relayed it forward before the import strikes me like a blow to the head. That son of a bitch conniving bigamist Jim Thompson! Where is my host now? We've got to discuss this one.

But he does not come in. It's been an hour.

He wouldn't! That's not funny.

I put on my coat and hood and wrap my muffler about my face, leaving only the tiniest slit for my eyes. I pull open the door. New snow has already drifted in deep. The pathway is already nearly filled in, with almost no trace of his footsteps. The wind is blowing hard pellets of snow-ice directly into me, striking me like gravel. I get the door closed and plough my way forward, clinging to the lifeline with one mitten. Close to my eyes I can see the flurrying movement of the driving pellets, but farther than a foot from my eyes I can see nothing. It is midday, but it might as well be midnight, except that instead of pitch dark it is snow white. I lose my vertical equilibrium and fall to the side, for a terrifying instant almost losing contact with the line, but my fingers get a death grip in it, and I pull myself back up, though up has little meaning for me. I flounder on. I am gasping, and every time my breath rushes out, it builds a little deeper mask of ice on the wool material of my muffler right before my nose and lips and in my rising panic, that I seek to push back down, I wonder if I am slowly walling myself into a cage of my own frozen breath. I feel I have gone a mile forward, though I know the line is scarce thirty yards. I want very much to turn back, but that will answer nothing, so I continue doggedly forward, until my head strikes with a bump against the door of the outhouse. I have to dig with my hands now to clear a little space to drag the door open. I feel about inside even putting my hand the length of my arm down the hole itself. Empty. Empty. The scream is inside me like a bubble moving about in my body for an opening out of which to discharge itself.

My own path has already filled in, but it is easier returning to the cabin with the wind behind me. I have to brush away the snow that has blown inside the door before I have room to shut it fast. I hear the tickety tacking as I pull off my stiff coat and throw it to the floor. I am already taking it down in my head before I get to my pad of paper and begin writing it.

TO JIM THOMPSON AT CEDAR SPRS HAVE 1000 FROM LIFE INS YES I HAVE BEEN HURT BUT I HEAR KINDNESS IN YR VOICE HOPING FLO BUSKIRK

Grimly, I relay the message on, but every instinct tells me I should not have.

The answer when it comes is so cynical I cannot force my fingers onto the key, cannot enter into complicity with him in that way, so at least for the time being I set the message aside:

TO FLO BUSKIRK AT FT LEAVENWORTH 1ST BREAK IN SNOW I COME TO FT LEAVENWORTH IF I SUIT WE CAN MARRY TRANSFER FUNDS ETC I HEAR YR BEAUTIFUL SOUL YR JIM

190

I hear a scratching at the wall, my heart leaps and I race to the door, but it is not my host returned, it is a rat trying to scratch his way in. The walls and ceiling are filled with them. We hear them all night trying to get in when we are trying to sleep. And when the wind stops for a moment, the wolves commence howling in the most hideous manner. We see nothing outside anymore, the snow drifted above the tops of the windows. I come back and look at Jim Thompson's diabolically clever hypocritical messages to that trusting woman, I brood over his treatment of both those trusting women, his deserted wife still seeking him, fearing he is in trouble. Anger flares up in me, and I take action.

TO ELIZ THOMPSON IN ST LOUIS REGRET INFORM HUSBAND JIM THOMPSON DIED HERO SAVING CHILDREN FROM INDIANS LAST WORDS I LOVE YOU ELIZ PLEASE START NEW LIFE A FRIEND JOHN RINDO

TO FLO BUSKIRK AT FT LEAVENWORTH YOU FAT COW 1000 NOT ENOUGH WIRE WHEN YOU HAVE 10000 JIM THOMPSON

I am thinking, How could my host be so selfish? I need him here. I need to talk to him.

TO JOHN RINDO AT PLAINS CROSSING YOU SOUND NICE CAN I COME TO YOU IN SPRING FOR ADVICE RE STARTING NEW LIFE YR NEW FRIEND ELIZ THOMPSON

Hm, that was a short period of mourning. Perhaps there was more equality in that marriage than I suspected. Then a message comes down from the far north, with a notation that it has already been forwarded down from farther north from the Athabasca

TO ELIZ THOMPSON DEAREST AM ALIVE AND WELL CDNT WRITE WHILE A FAILURE BUT NOW IVE HIT IT LEAD AND SILVER WE ARE ON EASY STREET DID IT ALL FOR YOU COMING BACK TO MY DARLING IN THE SPRING ALWAYS FAITHFUL LOVE JIM

I pace round and round the four corners of the single room. It is abundantly clear that Jim Thompson cannot send messages to widow Buskirk from nearby Cedar Springs, and at the same time send messages to his wife Elizabeth from up in the high Athabasca, and be one and the same person. He could, however, send both these messages if he was in fact two unrelated, and perhaps quite decent and honorable people who happen to share, by coincidence, the same name. This comes next:

TO FLO BUSKIRK AT FT LEAVENWORTH WHY HAVENT YOU REPLIED ALL I HAVE I WANT TO SHARE W YOU EAGERLY JIM

Now how do I send that one on? Especially when this comes:

TO CY MCCLINTOCK AT FT CLAPTON AM SERIOUSLY CONSIDERING YR PROPOSAL PLEASE SEND MORE DETAILS LAND AND HOLDINGS RESPECTFULLY FLO BUSKIRK

I try this:

TO ELIZ THOMPSON REGRET TERRIBLE MISTAKE BUT HAPPY OUTCOME YR HUSBAND ALIVE AND WELL DIFFERENT JIM THOMPSON KILLED YOU WILL HEAR FROM TRUE HUSBAND SHORTLY WITH GOOD NEWS SINCERELY JOHN RINDO

The rats scratch at the walls, the ceiling, under the floor, trying to get in. The tickety tacking starts up again.

TO JOHN RINDO AT PLAINS CROSSING YOU STILL SOUND NICE HUSBAND ALWAYS A FAILURE CRAMPS MY STYLE MUST SEE YOU SOONEST DEAR BOY THINKING OF MY NEW LIFE FONDLY ELIZ THOMPSON

I do not feel very happy about it, but it is time to send forward his news of lead and silver and easy street. I do so. The next message is not long in coming, and not unexpected.

192

TO JOHN RINDO AT PLAINS CROSSING FORGET ALL FORMER CORRESPONDENCE MY WONDERFUL HUSBAND RETURNING I AM SO HAPPY RESPECTFULLY ELIZ THOMPSON

Is what I create worse than what I leave alone? Should I never have started? Should I refuse to go on? Around about is the white whirling chaos of the void, the bitter cold of non-being. Is that better, as my host evidently came to believe? My host frozen into whiteness himself, unless he made it to the Indians. The small gnawing animals scurry in the walls and chew chew chew to breach the thin envelope into my warm room. The tickety tack is going again.

TO JAY CHALMERS AT COTTONWOOD GROVE DADDY LIFE IS SO HARD PLEASE MY FATHER SPEAK TO ME ELSE HOW CAN I KNOW YOU EXIST ALWAYS LOVE YR DTR CLEMENTINE

Nominated by The Missouri Review

A DAY AT THE ST. REGIS
WITH DAME EDITH

by PERDITA SCHAFFNER

from AMERICAN SCHOLAR

A FAMILY FRIEND, a personage, visits your city for the first time. You send flowers and enclose a note. "Do let me know if there is anything I can do." You may get taken up on the offer.

My telephone rang very early one Monday morning.

"This is Edith. Osbert has been convocated. We are alone, we are desperate."

The royal We, voice in anguish.

Edith and Osbert, the Sitwells, had been lionized from the moment they stepped down the gangplank, were installed in a luxury suite at the St. Regis, and booked for lectures and readings across the United States.

Osbert had gone away for the weekend and hadn't returned, leaving not a penny in his sister's purse. There was a bank account, but she had to go in person and sign things. Where was Wall Street, she wanted to know. And shoes, she needed shoes, her favorite pair had got mislaid. Left on the ship? Or not even packed? Unclear. Her lecture shoes—she didn't know what to do. Then we would have lunch. Afterwards we would go to the Museum of Modern Art to see Tchelitchew's *Hide and Seek*, a painting she adored.

"Oh, my dear, I realize I'm battening on you, but if you could and would come to the rescue. . . ."

Of course I could and would, without delay.

It was mid-October, a steamy Indian summer day. Edith was already in the lobby, wearing voluminous robes, a scarlet turban, a heavy fur cape—her usual array of outsize sparkling jewelry.

"So good of you, dear. Now how do we get to Wall Street—the very fastest way?"

I didn't quite see Edith on the subway. The doorman hailed a cab and helped her in, an unwieldy production in itself. The traffic was fierce, the heat unbearable. Tight squeeze in back. She sat ramrod straight, obviously ill at ease, and pulled the fur cape tighter around her.

"Driver, please, I feel a terrible draught, would you be so good as to close your window."

Nonplussed, he complied.

We picked up speed on the East River Drive.

"New York—Osbert's been here before and loves it. I'm absolutely terrified, yet it's so beautiful. Oh my passport, they said I had to bring it for official identity or something absurd—don't say I forgot."

She delved into a large drab satchel—the kind old ladies used to call "my knitting bag"—extricating cosmetics, notebooks, scrib- bled poems, and jewels. At the very bottom she found the comforting navy blue square British passport.

The window jolted open a mere crack, bringing a blessed waft of fresh air.

"Oh driver, Sir, I know I'm a frightful nuisance, but . . . "

"Very happy to meet you, Miss Sitwell," said the bank manager.

The Plantagenet Queen drew herself to full height, towering over him.

"*Doctor* Sitwell."

The poor man was crushed. Edith was funny that way, obsessed with titles and rank, ever desperate for recognition. She had, some years ago, received two honorary doctorates, one from the University of Leeds and one from the University of Sheffield. She clung to them. D.Litt., D.Litt. after her name, on all her correspondence, let no one forget.

The manager was subsequently forgiven for his faux pas. She thanked him quite obsequiously, stuffed the new checkbook and a thick wad of cash into the "knitting bag."

We found a bigger cab this time. Another terrible draught assailed us through one of the back windows—jammed an inch open; nothing to be done about it.

Next on the agenda, shoes. The bane of her existence, Edith could never find any to fit. Suitable shoes were not comfortable, comfortable shoes were not suitable. These, she pointed to the clodhoppers on her feet, were the only ones she could bear, other than the mislaid pair handmade by a little man in Rome. I directed the cab to I. Miller.

Difficult feet: narrow, long, and very bony in odd places. Boxes came out by the dozen and piled up all around. This one twisted her arches, that one pinched her big toe most excruciatingly. Another was too wide at the heel, would slip and send her pitching head-first into the audience. Edith was extravagantly gracious and apologetic as she dispatched the salesman off on yet another foray. He tried so hard, to no avail.

Defeated, we walked a few blocks and came to a store with a glitzy window display where everything was on sale.

"Let's try here," she said.

Edith immediately spied a bin full of fake brocade bedroom slippers marked down to $3.99. Perfect fit on the first try.

"Do you think I can possibly get away with it?"

The robes would conceal them, I assured her. Anyway, with the spotlight on her face and her voice enthralling the audience, nobody would even notice her feet. She bought them.

Room service back at the St. Regis: a double martini for Edith, the size of a birdbath, she specified. She was quiet during lunch, withdrawn. Our expedition had taken a lot out of her. She was uneasy over Osbert's absence, and apprehensive about the weeks ahead. The Grand Tour: the Middle West, back through Boston, then Yale University, ending up with two major appearances in New York. Scary unknown territories, new audiences. How would they react, she wondered, would anyone even bother to come? I realized how intensely vulnerable she was, underneath the flamboyance, beyond her spectacular façade.

"We will now have a rest," she announced as the dishes were cleared away. "Make yourself comfortable."

She retired to her bedroom.

The Sitwells, the three of them—Edith, Osbert, and Sacheverell, known as Sashie—and my mother, the poet H. D., and her life-long companion Bryher had all known each other over the years, as cordial acquaintances. The war brought about the true meeting of minds. Restless travelers grounded on our small beleaguered island. Ardent creative spirits determined to rise above the dreariness and weariness and intermittent terrors of those times. Sashie was no longer an immediate member of the triumverate. He had a life of his own, as country squire with his beautiful wife Georgia and their two sons.

"Like the uncle of a king," is how Gertrude Stein described Osbert. Patrician, infinitely kind, courteous, elegantly understated. "Very tiresome" was his only comment on a night of bombing that had nearly blown him from his home. He and Bryher became the very closest of friends. They met every morning for a walk in Hyde Park. They exchanged long letters when separated, even wrote to each other when both were in town—afterthoughts on their earlier conversation.

Edith was anything but understated. She never faced the world until late afternoon, yet she seemed ever present through telephone calls and letters. She'd finished a poem or couldn't finish it. Her throat had flared up again, her lumbago was killing her, insomnia was driving her to the brink of madness. My mother retreated from these little dramas. Bryher loved them and would go rushing off bearing cough syrup, liniment, reference books from the London Library.

If she felt up to it, Edith would come to tea—"as strong as lye," her standard order. She always descended in full regalia, turning the most informal visit into a pageant.

She thrived on vendettas. Enemies were everywhere: stupid critics, obtuse editors, importunate neophytes who thrust manuscripts at her for a first reading, coughers and sneezers who sprayed her with deadly infections. The lunatics, she called them, one and all; she lived perpetually on their fringe. Inanimate objects joined the conspiracy: a loose carpet whipping round her ankle like a dragon's tail, collapsing beds, crashing cupboards. Her imagery was vivid, highly diverting, even if one never quite knew what to believe. Some of her complaints were mostly for show, an everlasting reaction from early life. Some scars would not heal. She was an unwanted girl, followed by two desired brothers; a strange gawky child sequestered in that somber pile, Renishaw Hall. "I have a feeling we forgot something," said her father, Sir George, as they set out on a journey. "Yes, Sir," the butler replied. "We forgot Miss Edith."

Edith was always nice to me. In turn, I was careful not to sneeze. Or to submit manuscripts—heaven forfend. She could be extraordinarily kind. She genuinely cared about people, especially about young people whose work she respected. She also burdened herself with an endless gaggle of lame ducks, most of whom sounded indistinguishable from the lunatics.

She resided at the Sesame Pioneer and Imperial Club, a Victorian enclave typical of its kind: genteel, short on capital, badly in need of repair. It offered no private bathrooms—join the queue down the hall. Frayed wicker chairs lined the lobby. The furniture in the lounge was oversized and upholstered in dark brown velvet. An unlikely venue, Edith had chosen it because she wished to be anonymous. To a degree she was. Heads turned as she passed, then the well-bred conversations continued. She took no notice of her fellow members, nor of the shabby furniture and peeling paint. The Sesame—for short—solved the housekeeping problem and lent itself to her routine. She took early morning tea at bedside, and there she remained for most of the day, surrounded by books, notebooks, pens, and pencils. A sacroiliac condition made it painful for her to sit up at a desk; bed was always her working area. She also suffered from chronic insomnia and often woke long before the tea tray arrived, working compulsively for hours.

Sometimes she dressed and emerged for lunch, depending on her mood and the day's schedule. When work was done she liked to entertain. A very clever chef performed wonders on the dull wartime fare, the staff was amiable and willing. Edith could lay things on; she arranged lunch and dinner parties for such guests as Evelyn Waugh, T. S. Eliot, E. M. Forster, and the Nicolsons, Harold and Vita.

And she did teas—little teas, big teas. I was on the tea list. The little teas were a fearful strain. Disparate groups with nothing in common, tongue-tied; each guest was expected to take the floor and shine solo.

The big teas were great fun. Edith commandeered the brown velvet lounge. Room enough to accommodate groups and subgroups, space to move around and move on. There would be a cross section of the famous, the near famous, and those who could have been either—if only we could figure out who they were. Stephen Spender showed up in a fire fighter's uniform. Lieutenant Alec Guinness, an actor beyond spear-carrying parts, was not yet *the* actor he would become, his career postponed for a while. Edith claimed him and his wife Merula as cousins, dating her lineage from Hereward and the Wake. Osbert was invariably the co-host; sometimes Sashie, too, who was similar in appearance and manner; and occasionally Georgia, of whom it was rumored she never read a book, but was so refreshing in that galère, so beautiful, that who cared. Along with other minor acolytes, I passed plates of yellow cake and played guessing games. That peppery lady over there in animated discourse with a couple of GI's. She looked like Ivy Compton-Burnett, was she, wasn't she . . . ? Circle closer, one's instincts instructed, eavesdrop.

On one of the morning walks, Osbert told Bryher of his plan, a poetry reading to benefit the Free French in England. The Queen had agreed to be a patroness, and to attend with her then young daughters, Elizabeth and Margaret. He hoped my mother, H. D., would participate. Bryher rallied his poets. For the next few weeks no one talked of anything else. Rehearsals, tea parties, endless telephone calls. The ladies practiced their curtsies and discussed what to wear. Clothes were rationed, a new dress would use up a whole year's coupons. No problem for Edith, who would wear what she always wore. The others hunted through cupboards, mended, and made do.

Beatrice Lillie was the program seller. "When is she going to sing?" Princess Margaret piped up. The poets read in alphabetical order, H. D. followed by T. S. Eliot—she tremulous, he composed but dry. The first part of the program ended with John Masefield, poet laureate. Then they filed off to an anteroom to be presented to the royal party.

So far everything was very decorous, according to plan. The unforeseen would occur, however. Lady Dorothy Wellesley—former protégée of W. B. Yeats—had fortified herself with a couple of drams. She mistook Harold Nicolson for Osbert, and attacked him with an umbrella. Beatrice Lillie broke up the fight.

Vita Sackville-West, Sitwell and Sitwell, Stephen Spender, professionals all, delivered with panache. Further down the alphabet the elderly poet W. J. Turner mumbled and bumbled inaudibly,

199

interminably, crowding scholarly Arthur Waley's slot. He had to be stopped. Lady Dorothy Wellesley had a hard time getting started. All in all a most memorable event, a lovely splash in the dark bog of 1943, when it seemed the war would go on forever.

June 6, 1944, D day at last, still a hellish long way to go. In London the worst of times since the blitz, with its abominable robots, V's 1 and 2, flying bombs and rockets, falling indiscriminately where they would, twenty-four hours a day. The V 1's sounded variously like helicopters, lawn mowers, revved-up motorboats. The V 2's were far more destructive, but descended without warning; at least we didn't have to monitor their progress across the sky. A disrupted city, inhabitants burrowing in like hysterical rabbits—just what Hitler had in mind. We went about our business as usual.

They were assembled all three, Edith, Osbert, and Sashie, at the Churchill Club, a social and cultural center for Allied officers. Osbert had read and talked of a work in progress. Edith was on stage, reading a poem inspired by the 1940 bombings, "Still Falls the Rain." We heard *it* coming, the lawn mower variety, lower and lower and louder and louder, about to tear off the roof and chop down the staircase. Nobody flinched. Edith read on, raising her voice over the racket, modulating it as the thing continued on its way. That moment, and the applause that followed, has remained one of my personal highlights of the war.

From shoes on Fifth Avenue to the firing line—quite a stretch.

Edith emerged from her room at three o'clock on the dot, rested, purposeful. We set off for the Museum of Modern Art.

We contemplated *Hide and Seek* close up, stepped back a way, and sat down, all in total silence. A disturbing picture, I thought, but I was not the one to say so. A little girl chasing a butterfly through a thicket, strange surrealist vegetation, disembodied heads.

Pavel Tchelitchew, Pavlik, was the love of Edith's life. He reciprocated, called her his muse, his sibyl, his inspiration, glass flower under glass. Separated by the war, he in America, she in England, they wrote to each other constantly. The greatest love letters of all time, it has been said, they recently have been assembled and immured in a vault at Yale University, sealed until the year 2000. He was a homosexual, however. "That of which they speak," she would lament—meaning physical passion—"I was made for it, I have never known it, I never will."

We sat for another half hour, Edith lost and gone, looking desolate.

"Nobody paints dandelion fluff like Pavlik," she finally remarked.

I didn't know the whole story. I heard it later from other sources. Their momentous reunion had taken place at dockside. Pavlik gave a big party that night. He invited her to a private viewing early the next morning before the museum opened to the public. She was shaky from a stormy passage, disoriented; longed to see his picture, but please could she wait a day or two.

Tchelitchew was offended, grudgingly agreed to a later date. Confronted by the masterpiece, volatile master at her side, she couldn't think of anything to say. He waited for her ecstatic reaction. She remained silent. He sulked and smoldered. They parted company on the sidewalk.

Edith wrote him a long letter, no doubt the most eloquent of the lot. She pleaded humility. She had been overwhelmed by an experience too great for mere words, she could never do it justice. He never forgave her, a major rift set in.

So she returned with an unbiased and uninformed companion, me. Maybe she swept in there daily. Anyway, whether on the sixth or the second viewing, her only comment was on the dandelion fluff. We walked back to the hotel.

"Dr. Sitwell," the receptionist was well trained. "Sir Osbert has just returned."

I was graciously dismissed.

"Oh, my dear, I've battened on you, taken up your whole day, but really, I don't what I would have done."

A pleasure, I assured her, an *honor*.

Dame Edith, Dame of the British Empire—with that ultimate accolade, the Doctor business went right out the window. It's now twenty-five years since her death, twenty since Osbert's. And quite recently, Sashie died at the age of ninety.

The year 2000 is no longer an abstraction out of science fiction. I hope I live to see it. Not for the date, per se, nor the new century, which will be as awful and marvellous as all the others, but I do want to read those love letters. Will they be the sensation of that new year, or will they be published quietly by some university press and soon forgotten? I ponder literary immortality. Many people have never even heard of the Sitwells. I remember their unremitting dedication, their high standards. I look at the long row of books on my shelf. Surely it must all count for something.

Nominated by Ted Wilentz

CIRCUMSTANCES

by RICHARD JACKSON

from PLOUGHSHARES

This happened just once.
Desire had stopped at some remote crossroads.
I don't know whose heart just stood there without an owner.
It was one of those little folds in time
when the absurd moon could rise without a purpose.
We all knew where melancholy could lurk
in ravines, or even lie sprawled out by the side of the road.
We all knew we could have wilted with the day lilies.
And those nail heads of stars—who would be left
to hang their sorrows on them?
That's why Boris was back in our kitchen practicing ecstasy.
It was a long way from the riots in his own Ljubljana.
It seemed the last few days were grazing
in fields south of us, swatting flies with their tails.
We were all filled with that elegiac swagger.
Somewhere a star collapsed whose cloudy image wouldn't
reach us for thousands of light years.
That's why Boris was sprinkling sugar on flowers
and eating them, inventing a story we'd remember
when times got tough. That's what made the night
scatter back into its burrows. Next morning it was
dry cat food he thought looked like Goldfish Crackers.
We were trading stories like baseball cards.
Here was laughter casting dice for a pure moment of joy.
Boris himself invented us from the smell of abandoned fruit
    stands.

I remembered lying quietly inside you while our old selves
slipped in and out of the back rooms of the soul.
We spent the rest of the day eating avocados,
and inventing a kind of love that no longer exists in the world,
a kind of love that no hordes could pillage at the outposts.
Nothing else happened. It was totally insignificant.
That night we went to the river and skipped rocks.
But I should add that it all occurred
when you could still eavesdrop on the forest,
before another remote war started out
on the road again with its beggar's cup and cane,
before the children followed like empty grain sacks,
before love had been brought to its knees like a traitor,
when we were still in the grips of the early cicadas
loitering in the trees, filling the kitchen with trellises of song,
hope still testing its toes at the water's edge
while the whole earth performed for us,
the flowers of words, the balcony of stars, the violins of light.

Nominated by Arthur Smith

FOUR DAYS:
EARTHQUAKE

by GARY YOUNG

from THE KENYON REVIEW

A<small>N</small> <small>EARTHQUAKE</small> <small>TERRIFIED</small> us all. The house trembled, the walls moved. Now the boy spins, throws himself to the ground, and laughs at this. When his eyes are closed and the world is dizzy, all fall down.

*

Those clouds didn't gather over the mountains, or drift in from the sea; they were born suddenly out of the air. If they could look down from that distance, the city, now in ruins, would be invisible.

*

I wanted a house that could float in silence over the mountains. Then a great quake tore away the earth beneath our home. A man downstream was buried alive; we can't know what he wanted. And what was he looking for at the mouth of that cave?

*

I discovered a stream that disappears underground. I found mounds of spoiled grass, a skull, and teeth standing out against the matted rot. I found mushrooms, and took them home, and washed them, and set them in a bowl to dry. It was a comfort to see the orange flesh quiver to the touch like it always had.

Nominated by Gary Soto

FREEWAY BYPASS
(detail from map)

fiction by FRED PFEIL

from WITNESS

CIRCULATION IS THE movement in which general alienation appears as general appropriation and general appropriation as general alienation.

Same billboard's still there acourse, right off the crossway from I-94. That beltway over to 78, you know. Maybe three miles in on the east side. Tween Exit 3 and 4, Black Creek Boulevard and Ardmore Ave. I donno what else to tell you. Though that one ad, the one you're talking about, they took that down a while ago. Got another one up now, couldn't tell you what.

What we know we know from newspaper and police reports, TV coverage having been both spotty and brief given the scant amount of newstime, need for brighter fillings for pre-sports and weather newsholes to maintain or increase income from ad-slots. Nobody likes it but that's the way it is, what are you gonna do? Anyway, what we know is, the guy was hit coming home from work on a Saturday night, late, Sunday morning technically, and managed to get himself over the highway to the divider there, and managed somehow, incredibly, to hold on there for three days and four nights before somebody noticed him and stopped to call 911.

Owner and leasing agent for the property, the Patrick Media Group Inc., a privately held national firm specializing in outdoor advertising. Net profits, 1990, including all divisions, $250 million.

Though the whole of this movement may well appear as a social process, and though the individual elements of this movement originate from the conscious will and particular purposes of individuals, nevertheless the totality of the process appears as an objective relationship arising spontaneously; a relationship which results from the interaction of conscious individuals, but which is neither part of their consciousness nor as a whole subsumed under them.

The image a familiar, practically generic one, and so hardly struck any startled response from Bill. A giant translucent blonde stretched across a black background raising a glass or holding a cigarette or stroking a cylindrically-shaped hair care product with one hand, the sort of thing you see every day. Only difference was, when the ad appeared out of the corner of his eye, as it did, as they do to us all, made itself slightly known to Bill's mind then disappeared, it registered as something off, something to be fixed. Though if you asked them, any of the four of them what it was like, they would have spoken awkwardly of polluted consciousness, mind control, stilted phrases like that. But between such language and the real rage, the sickness and hope at the base of it all, there was mainly this sense: the ad went by off to his right, at the edge of his vision, like a smokepuff from a small inaudible explosion, as he was coming home from work in the truck; and Bill thought, with an inward sigh of weariness plus something else, Oh yeah, okay, got to take care of that too.

This would be what he remembered later as the last moment when things were right; here atop the embankment, beside the highway, when it was still possible to see the halfmoon white as goat's milk behind the screen of clouds, beyond the throbbing dark orange of the city, its reflected warmth against the night. This serrated bone-joint of moon in its gauze of ice, this sight like a thought. It was late at night, it was after work, he was on his way back from the restaurant where he washed dishes to the room where he slept. The only sound that distant susurrus of traffic on all the roads and streets of all the city stretched around him, an omnipresence he now understood to be, in effect, this country's wind, through which, on each side of the highway in front of his eyes, these two thick smooth streams of asphalt soiled by the yellow streetlight falling down on them, he saw and heard the heightened rush of this or that stray late-night early-morning car in its occasional flight. The vehicle that struck him when he stepped out into the road might have had its headlights off, might well have been driving too fast; however it was, when he first stepped out it was invisible in this tapestry in which he too had seemed, for all the exile of his long trip to this astonishing moment, to fit. He stepped off the gravel, over the curb, onto the rolled macadam of the northbound lanes, bisected by its perforation lines of gold. Another step, another, and three more, each as simple and accentless as ordinary breath. He turned hearing the sound like the roar of a hand slicing through space held stiff for a slapping just in time to see the car's complex of dull and gleaming, sharp and curved surfaces, a single frame from a film even now still rushing past. Sick needles prickling his hands and legs, a taste or smell of must and hot engine oils flooding his head just before or just as the front fender on the right or passenger side struck his hip and upper leg on the left side flipping his body up in air.

You are familiar with our terms; for a single site with a high daily flow-rate of traffic we would be asking $4000 for a four-week rental, or somewhere thereabouts. But I would assume you would be coming to us with more than one site in mind, in which case we would want to be talking together about site patterns and price packages. And of course all the more insofar as you come to us carrying a number of clients and/or campaigns. There I think you'd find we could put together a most attractive and effective package, at a surprising—and I do mean surprisingly attractive—rate per board, depending on how many sites and/or signs you have in mind.

The structure as complementarity, set of neutralizing valences, zero-sum game. Either way you look at it, horizontally or vertically, moving across or up and down. Across, from regions with developed industrial economies and a comparatively low level of state violence, to others with a low level of industrialization, dependent on foreign investment and the export and sale of raw materials for processing in the more developed zones, and consequently with states which, given the misery of the majority of their citizenries, must employ various means of legal and extra-legal violence to maintain the status quo. From Japan or the U.S. to Guatemala and Zaire, say, with any number of slots for other nation-states along the way. And the same as we travel down within the developed "democratic" world as well, from the full world citizenship enjoyed by the wealthiest elites, individual and corporate, to the repression visited, directly or indirectly, upon those situated at or below the level of production itself. At or below: large-scale unionized manufacture, large-scale non-union, small shop, service industries, agricultural workers seasonal and year-round, under- and unemployed.

I donno what to tell you, it just makes me mad is all. Just going along back and forth to work minding your own business and then look up and see out of nowhere they've gone and ruined another of those things. I suppose you can say it's no skin off my nose and that's true as far as it goes, but somebody paid good money for that space. Course the younger ones down at the shop, they think it's pretty funny; but I'll tell you, I ever caught the ones doing it up there at it some day or night I'd write over them, I'll tell you that right now.

Their collisions give rise to an alien social power standing above them.

They were in their late 30s, early 40s, except for Steve, who worked with Bill and was 26. More or less middle-class backgrounds; various anti-war, anti-nuke, anti-intervention, anti-racist, anti-homophobic, pro-labor, pro-peace, pro-choice, pro-environment actions/groups/experiences under their belts. Jim had resisted the draft and done two years of jail time around it; Bill had been an SDS-er; Nancy, who'd also done some real time for a Trident action, had started out from the Catholic left, her favorite saint even now long since her lapsing Dorothy Day, whereas Steve simply called himself an anarchist. Nancy an RN in a poor women's health clinic about to disappear, Jim ran an off-the-books housecleaning business, Bill and Steve built cabinets and decks and did light house repair. It started out one night maybe four years ago, drunk and stoned at a party, with a couple cans of spraypaint in the back of Bill's van and a gross Be All That You Can Be army poster down the block. By now the deal was simple: whoever saw one that needed doing and was do-able went by and called the rest of them, until at least three of them had agreed on a color or colors, counterslogan, and a night.

In a striking convergence of these two axes or spectra, moreover, those at the bottom end of the vertical you'll find are often either descendants of emigrants from states at the harsh end of the horizontal, or such emigrants themselves. Put differently, we might say it is in general far easier for a given individual to move from the—impoverished, repressed, violent—losing side of the horizontal line to the downside of the vertical than for anyone to move to the up or winning side of either line. As, for example, the comparative ease with which the aforementioned victim of this story, having fled the country of his birth and reached this one, was able without papers or prior experience to find a dishwasher's job and a shared rented room in which to sleep.

Let us at least not pretend that his name is important to us: let us at least allow the man—the "poor man"?—to keep his name. He was lying on his right side, his right arm underneath, and pulled down too far towards his feet. He was lying on the road, in between the near and middle lanes, two strips of yellow paint. As soon as consciousness returned and he moved, several widespread but specific brushfires began along that side, as if a number of matches had been tossed at a given signal on the edges of baked fields called Shoulder, Shoulderblade, Hip, Thigh. In his mouth a sooty gruel of asphalt stones, dust, chips of teeth he supposed, plus an acridness he knew would signify blood. A cool breeze playing on his face bestowed upon him, absurdly, a moment of ordinary lucidity: the thought that the jacket, shirt, and pants he was wearing were all torn too badly to fix with needle and thread, and would cost money to replace. Already he knew what had happened on his left was certainly more serious than

211

the fires on his right, and that the first thing he must do now is get himself out of the road. When he rolls over onto his stomach and attempts to rise to his hands and knees his left side speaks to him at last, loudly sharply, from the regions of his ribs and pelvis, and forces an answering scream to hurl itself out of his mouth.

I

I AM

Circulation is the movement in which general alienation appears as general appropriation and general appropriation as general alienation.

AVA

AVAIL

Although the main arteries are for the most part state and federal, the city retains jurisdiction over and responsibility for rights of way, embankments, dividers and the like. So it became our problem several years back now when it was discovered that the foliage and ground cover of our most heavily utilized routes had begun to register a rather severe rate of, uh, *attrition*, in response to the concentrations of pollutants, especially those of course from auto emissions, to which such plantings were subject. Estimates were, moreover, that over the next ten years, barring the construction of additional parkways and/or superhighways, which no one expects, this problem of the dying plants and trees would only grow that much more noticeable, i.e., worse.

"She's not here," said Andrea. She shook her head, an abrupt shiver, opened the screen door, gave Bill a greeting hug out on the porch. "She had to stay after for a staff meeting. I'm sorry I'm so logey, I just woke up. I was like this all day at work today too, I don't know what it is. How are you anyway, what's up?" It was like that with Andrea: you had to wait an extra minute, but you got your chance. Bill told her about the board, asked her to ask Nancy to call. "Ask her too," he said as he finished up, "if she has any ideas for a new line or if we should just go with the usual." Andrea looked off over his shoulder, squinting at where the sun was descending, orange-swollen, over the backs of the bungalows across the street. "I wish I could help you," she said. "Not with the slogan, I mean. I mean I wish I weren't so scared of heights and chickenshit about cops." "Hey," Bill said, "don't worry about it. You do lots of stuff, you do enough." They gave each other another smile, he turned to go. "I know what she'll say about the slogan," said Andrea. "Why not stay with what works?"

The small-time boys with their two, three homebuilt boards, spiked into the sides of 8-apt. 3-flr. brick shitholes with plywood boards on their ex-windows, Hotel Junkie, the only one left up in the rubble of what once was a block. Or the ones with their paint cracked and flaking, wooden scaffoldings rotting away on some pitted two-lane off in the boonies winding from one dead small-town to the next. Carros Usados, Kobena's Hair Salon, Hidden Valley Camper Campground, pin money, chump change. Then in your larger towns and smaller cities you have your little home-grown outdoor advertising firms, typically one per such area, so even Budweiser, McDonald's, the big accounts have got to write their contracts with them. Which, of course, they'd rather do with nationals like Patrick or Gannett, themselves often as not a division or subsidiary of some yet larger transnational, Time-Warner, Phillip Morris, something like that. But just as the Patricks and Gannetts push against that next nearest surface—to supplant, to deprive of nourishment, to press to death—moving into as many mid-sized areas as is consistent with overall profit-ability, so the mid-sized locally-owned firms may also be found in every major metropolitan area, pressing back with whatever resources—pricing structure, number and placement of boards, package deals—they possess. Think of a blastular cell formation in perpetual development, always feeding on itself; think of wheels within wheels in the middle of the air.

213

It is my personal belief to this day that if the department had simply been somewhat less public about the shift in policy, few people would have noticed and fewer still cared. But just because it was a first, I suppose it was felt that the story had to be released. Then of course once it reached the papers, radio and TV that the city was taking out its real ground cover and putting in synthetics, the proverbial material hit the fan. By the end of the week the phones at the office are ringing off the hook with outraged citizens. As if they weren't the same people whose cars killed off the natural cover we put down; but that, I suppose, is another story, and in any case, you can't tell them that.

No way to write of pain without aestheticizing, speak of exploitation without abstraction: each obscenity requiring yet another merely in order to be expressed. The following morning he comes to or wakes to the sounds, smells, and breezes of a traffic registering as senseless convulsion without origin or end, a chaos of occurrences, intensities, speeds. Turning his head to one side then the other, he discerns through the bushes between which he lies one blur of wheels and colors moving up and past his head, another down and past his feet. The sun is up but has not yet been able to warm the day's air, which takes on an added chill from the contrapuntal buffetings of this traffic, these cars and vans and trucks which struck him down and now imprison him here. He knows there is something wrong with this thought but not what. The traffic is slowing, has slowed almost to a dead stop, but even now when it has become separate machines producing specific noises—brakes clamping, tires rotating, bleat of horn, blare of manic radio—the notion of calling out for help remains distant, depending as it does on the double assumption that there are people within those phantasm machines, and that there is some tie between them there and him here. So that later, even when his cries begin, it is not with any intent to communicate, really. More familiar altogether are the maroon sinews of the bushes and the green waxy leaves, edged with translucent yellow when the sun is overhead; and through those leaves, the sight he can behold with his head thrown back and turned rightward, of the smiling white woman up over road and traffic and himself, the woman lying on her side as he can almost remember from seeing her on a billboard or poster during market day back where he came from, a woman holding up her product, something he cannot see for the leaves and branches in his way, and cannot remember thanks to the pain, especially down below now, where his hip is, which was a little like a noise itself when he woke up but now is like nothing else whatsoever in the world.

AVAILA

The formative impulse behind this 'peripheral' urbanization, here and elsewhere, has been the creation of a dense nest of transactional linkages and technologically advanced production and service systems that enable increasingly vertically disintegrated industrial production processes to be flexibly and efficiently re-attached horizontally, in a burgeoning territorial industrial complex.

Far as that goes I don't see it any different than what you see anywheres nowdays. These kids want to write some filth or foolishness on a building or bus or wherever they feel like it, like so many dogs taking a piss. I don't mind telling you that's the way I see them, the way they hang out here on the streets. You can't tell me they even want to work. Just want to get messed up on drugs and beer and cheap wine and make babies and that's about it. Least the ones that get up on them billboards, they at least make something more than a doodleblotch, write *Fuck You* that some of them did across that siding I put on just two summers back. I bust their ass I catch them, same as these ones here, but at least they give you a whole sentence with some actual fuckin words.

Nevertheless the totality of the process appears as an objective relationship arising spontaneously; a relationship which results from the interaction of conscious individuals, but which is neither part of their consciousness nor as a whole subsumed under them.

Back at the house Bill told Jim about it while washing up at the kitchen sink. Jim's night to cook, and he was making a raita to go

215

with the felafel; the two of them had to move around each other somewhat delicately in the small kitchen space. Bill positioned himself in the kitchen doorway to use the phone, turning away from the sizzling and popping from the frypan on the stove. As Steve's number rang one two three four he let his mind float, looking without looking at the ensemble of Sandy, Jim's partner, folded up on the couch with her headphones on, inside one of her meditation tapes, Tonio the house mutt dozing near her on the floor, square-jawed bespectacled Emma Goldman staring down from the poster above, If I Can't Dance I Don't Want to Be Part of Your Revolution. Bill himself had been married once, too young, back straight out of school. Split up more than eight years ago, for reasons as personal as political and vice versa, a sad useless headache even to try to sort it out. Emma and Gene, 14 and 10, in Albuquerque with their mother during the school year, here with him, with the three of them in spite of the close quarters, over the summers. A certain sense, every now and then, of thinness, resonances disallowed, unacknowledged disappointments of a life correctly lived. No answer at Steve's but Jim had said Yeah sure, anytime, so if Nancy called back willing, then maybe tonight. A jolt of excitement, strictly kid's stuff but what the hell, as he hung up the phone and turned to see Jim smiling back, holding out a platter of cakes draining on a paper towel. "You want to rope Sandy back in from the cosmos, let her know it's time to eat?" "Yeah, okay. What do you want to drink?"

How many of them is it now we see every day—750? 2000? Some staggering, some inconceivable number, but who's counting anyway? What does it mean, for that matter, to "see" an ad? Isn't the degree of conscious perception involved right down there with seeing the people in the cars you drive past on your way to work, as that of hearing the traffic we hear all the time, even indoors? If so, could we say the experience of seeing an ad is roughly what it is like to run one's eyes across a stranger, a fleeting stranger on the street or in a car, as if she or he were her- or himself a commodity for sale? What it is or would be like if that oceanic sound of traffic were composed of so many cries for attention, calls for help?

Afterwards, he was interviewed only twice at the hospital where the police and ambulance finally took him. Understandable, given that his English was almost nonexistent, the reporters spoke nothing else, and it was just Human Interest anyway. Among the questions they did not ask, though, was one he asked and answered himself. The question had in fact occurred to the state trooper who responded to the billboard call and found him instead: why had the guy not only crawled over to the divider rather than the nearer curbside, but then, at the divider, dragged himself over into a thicket from which he could only be seen with difficulty even from a slow-moving or stalled car? But the cop was wrong, had picked the wrong fear. He figured the guy, given how rough the neighborhood was around here, had hid himself away so as not to get discovered, picked over, finished off by the first kid, junkie, gang to come along. But what the man himself realized was that he had without knowing it been following instructions ingrained in him from the country he was from, the people he was of, where if you are away from your village and lying hurt at the side of the road no one would dare touch or help you because the Army might be there, and if the Army is there and sees you they kill you. That was his mistake, his silly mistake, mixing up the two places; it seemed funny when he looked back on it now. So that even with the other worries on his mind, even though that mistake could have killed him, he found himself wishing someone had asked him that question in one of the interviews, either that one from the paper or the other dressed-up one from the TV, so he could have shared the joke with them.

The Burkean theory of the sublime, the apprehension through a given aesthetic object of what in its awesome magnitude shrinks, threatens, diminishes, rebukes individual human life.

So whatever your outdoor display needs, you'll find our thoroughly skilled and professional staff, from consulting agents to our display staff itself, ready to serve you and your clients here at Patrick, known coast-to-coast for quality and reliability for over 45 years.

Then on top of that you got these other ones coming in and over-running the place. See them everywhere now, all over, wanting to live here too. Just go down where I work, any direction from the shop, poke your head in first door you find open in one of them old warehouses and plants, tell me what you see. Bunch of people in there working don't even speak English. At their machines when you get there in the morning, still at it when you go back home at night. Probably sleep down there too, for all I know. Plus your people from Central America, Mexico, down there, coming over in waves and waves and waves. Like that fella they found, night I was coming home off swing shift and saw that crew up there on that billboard writing away bold as you please. One of the state boys found out there later, after I called them up and got them on it when those other jokers got away. Had it in the paper there, day or so later on. They ever find out where he was from, what the hell he was doing lying out there like that in the weeds?

A relationship which results from the interaction of conscious individuals but which is neither part of their consciousness nor as a whole subsumed by them.

AVAILABLE SP

Always a rush, the scramble from the road up through the lupine or what have you to the hollow-steel post on which the board is mounted, one carrying the ladder, the other one if only out of nervousness still jiggling the spraycan. Then with one of them holding, the other one quick up that ladder to the short set of steps on the post, swing-step around the scaffolding, go to work. Nancy stiff-arming the can before her face as though aiming from the nozzle, going over the letters a second time to make sure they stand out from the sprawled body they are written on. Not that it makes any difference to speak of, but who knows? Doing something at least means you have said to yourself that this shit does not go down. Plus to be honest, it is really a kick. And if lots more people started doing it, saying no? Jim's voice urgent from the van down below at the edge of the road. "Somebody's slowing

218

up ahead, guys—time to get down!" Bill hisses a call up to Nancy but she is already on her way. "Watch your step, watch your step," he is saying as above him she descends; muttering it to himself, adrenaline dancing through head/chest/arms/hands. Running back down the embankment, folded ladder wobbling under one arm, hearing the ragged saw of Nancy's breath behind, reviewing agreed-upon procedures for what to do, how to hang together if the bust comes down. Then, just as he throws the ladder in the side Jim has opened up and reaches out to grab Nancy in after himself, Bill looks down the road and sees this old guy walking fast down the berm from his truck, maybe a hundred yards ahead. Nancy is in, gasping, Jim pulling the van out with a yelp from the tires and the old motor whining, revving hard. "That's not a cop!" Bill says. "I never said he was!" says Jim. "Look at him, man, he's running back to his truck! He's coming after us!" The three of them look in the mirrors and out of the back window: sure enough. By now they are all laughing uncontrollably, practically laughing themselves sick. "Well," Nancy says in a rush, throwing herself back against the seat with a flourish, "we got it anyway."

People have their own lives to live, after all, for the most part, aside from the few zealous citizens we have always with us. So the following week it seemed the furor was dying down—as it generally does in such cases, truth be told. Then—I don't know, a few weeks later, sometime around the beginning of June—the first reports came in from state and local authorities to the effect that some of the synthetic coverings and plantings we had installed along and on routes with the highest utilization rates had been—well—firebombed, in effect. Specifically, it appeared that some person or persons unknown had applied something in the nature of a flamethrower to our installations in the area of, I believe it was the Crosstown, near the exit for Ardmore Ave. That first incident stayed out of the papers thanks to the cooperation of the police, our shared hope being that it would turn out to be an isolated incident. By the end of the week, though, there had been three more such occurrences, and the police felt they could no longer hold the story back. So once again, there we were in the media for replacing living foliage with so-called plastic trees on our city's most polluted highways; only now the story had guerrillas and flamethrowers as well. The following week the story was national and the copycat effect was in full swing; there were something like a dozen incidents in just three days. The City Manager had our department head in for a dressing-down; the City Council passed a special resolution requiring us to return immediately to natural cover. Which of course we have done ever since, though it represents a considerable expense to the city, since replanting and recovering needs to take place now on the average of—what's it down to?—something like every six months or less. But as we say in public service, Give the people what they want.

It remained itself but blended with other things as well. It stained the fleeting fragmentary narratives of his mother and father and sisters and brothers, his grandparents, his own wife and children, and the others in the village, and still others met on the way here, so that as they flickered and unreeled across the screen unfurled behind his eyes each became haunted by yellow hues of shame and despair. It entered his breath, shit and rust to the taste on top of the sour metal of car exhaust. Or blotted everything else out, even though when it rose and made him scream and shout he often as not still cried out words. Help me. Mother. Jesus. In his own language of course, and who knows how often or loud? The leaves over his head glowed yellow, faded black; the light on the white woman overhead came off and on. His respiration merged with the sound of the cars and when the pain woke him again when he was done screaming it would strike him that the cars were gone. But it was important not to count. Not the number of steps to the wire fence along the border then beyond it, not the number of days or weeks or months or miles away are those loved and remembered, betrayed and disappointed, in those same soiled dreams. Counting equals assessment, assessment presumes the luxury of hope. There is a thirst loose and buzzing inside him, whispering the lie that if only it were fed the pain would cease. When he shakes with laughter at smelling like a bowl of old garbage, old piss-soaked garbage version of himself in another restaurant like the one he works in used to work in here, something heavy breaks loose in his chest and belly like a new sadness, a pain like a sentence that cannot be unsaid. So he lets it be. He goes away, lets the little pieces fly off home to all who have known him, all the places where the body with his name has ever lived, even the small dirty room on the other side of this large road, the three others like himself, too tired and too frightened and too sad to talk. There is now only the body inside this body, a waiting, a dark huddled warmth. Which was where he was when he was discovered, quite by chance, by the Highway Patrol and brought via ambulance to the county hospital. To be tossed back in the stagnant water with the thrashing, gasping others of his kind, of course, upon his recovery, but minus (of course) his dishwashing job, a fact or fate which like many of these others attracted no media attention at all.

AVAILABLE SPACE

It was not enough, of course. More and better than nothing, but not nearly enough. Ideally they would have a message, a short burst of words true and witty and accessible to all, good for any billboard, not just the obviously offensive ones. Language breaking the link once and for all between pleasure, need, and desire on the one hand, things for sale on the other, exposing the link between production and purchase, who makes it and who buys it and who profits from it all. All this in a short burst of words. What would they be?

AVAILABLE SPACE
CALL 957-4653

We have offices in more than 1000 cities. We offer a full range of services. This 800 number is good anywhere, anytime, night or day. You may find us in more than 45 countries, on four continents. We would like nothing more than to welcome you into our ever-growing family of preferred clients. We look forward to hearing from you.

Their collisions give rise to an *alien* social power standing above them.

I AM NOT FOR SALE

Nominated by Witness

[Note: This story makes use of several lines quoted without attribution in the text from other writers' works: specifically, and in order of their appearance, from the *Grundrissee* of Karl Marx, *Postmodern Geographies* by Edward Soja, and "Pleasure: A Political Issue," by Fredric Jameson.]

HUSH HUSH

fiction by STEVEN BARTHELME

from BOULEVARD

WHEN PAULIE ON her way to her interview with the arts people had stopped by his office at the bank, she laughed and said, "Tilden, when're you going to move in?" He had ignored it, but now he agreed.

His office was dull, as dull as people had always said it was the first time they saw it. The first six months he had left it as he had found it, the shelves empty, the walls bare. Wooden coatrack in front of the windows. But it drew so many comments and strange looks that he had taken a weekend and moved all the furniture around; everybody else was always doing that. Then he bought Mexican rugs for the walls and, for the table, marketing and shelter magazines which, when they were superseded each month, moved to tidy stacks on the shelves. Got rid of the damn coatrack.

Still they told him it was dull, and although he thought their offices no more interesting than his—Loeffler's Pirrelli calendars and butterfly chairs—he now agreed with them about his own. Dull. Maybe a two-headed secretary out front. But where would Kelli sit? Where would she put her cat snapshots and dead seashells? Maybe some posters, for some television religion or a fifth-rate rock group, one he had never heard of, which wouldn't be hard to find, as he never listened to the radio anymore, or watched the music channels, or turned on the stereo, for that matter. Silence, Tilden thought, was sweet, as Saturday mornings had been.

The Saturday that Paulie had first arrived at his door, he had ignored her knock, sat beside the plants sipping coffee in the slanting light from the miniblinds over the windows, but she would not go away, so he finally got up and went to the door and opened it, then stood there denying he was her father, she, who should have been more embarrassed than he was, because she was outside and he was inside, just as adamantly, one foot up on a suitcase, asserting it.

He had shut the door on her, at least twice, then looked out through the blinds in the vain hope that she'd go away. She was tall, nearly six feet, muscular, dark-haired. Italian. Jeans and khaki shirt. She had settled on the top step and lit a cigarette, coughed, then, after five minutes or so, knocked again.

"Tilden," she said, through the door. "This is silly. You think you can ignore me and I'll go away? I've got no place to go." More knocking. "Nineteen sixty-six. Boston. My mother's name was Tina. You were drunk. You made a big thing about never drinking anything but vodka. Stupid, right? But what can you expect from a twenty year old? You had a show on the college radio station; you played Doors records, over and over. You have a big scar across the back of your neck. They took off a birthmark or something. Let me in."

It had ruined his morning, and all the mornings since, because now she was up before seven every day, with the blinds open and coffee brewing, like one of those women in the ads on the Weather Channel, leaping out of bed, where she had somehow mysteriously washed her face—there was never any oil on it—and her nightgown unwrinkled, so that he wondered if she had slept in it at all. He had been married twice, and women just didn't look like this in the morning, and their voices weren't light and had no lilt, and their eyes were bleary. Like his own. But Paulie came out of the back bedroom of the small apartment new-born, every morning. It was misery.

One Friday, before leaving for work, she said, "Still don't like me, do you?" and he had said, "You get in my way," and then he had thought about it all day at the office.

When he got home, she wasn't there yet, so he went to the market around the corner and bought a loaf of bread, and a jar of his brand of peanut butter, and two rib-eyes, meat, and a case of

Schaefer, which he counted on to have all the additives and un-natural junk that she claimed gave her headaches. He was arrang-ing it all on the kitchen counter when she got back.

"Where've you been?"

"What's all this stuff?" she said, throwing her hair back with her hand. "Steaks, no less. You're showing the flag, right? That's so cute!"

"Where have you been?"

"Had to work late. Some very important cultural stuff happen-ing next week, some kind of meeting. I met this very sexy British guy. His name is Ryan. Only he's short. Comes to here," she said, drawing a hand across her breasts. "If you didn't want me to work late, you shouldn't have gotten me a job."

"Does this little guy have a little apartment?"

"You mean," she said, "a little apartment I could move into? Let's not rush things. I only just met him. When do we eat?"

They ate the steaks—he cooked—and then drank the entire case of beer, save one, until to her, the headache she planned became somehow uproariously funny, and to him, she began to look more like a woman, and less like a problem, or at least like a different kind of problem, until he was shaking his head, mostly to stop looking at her, stop noticing how pretty and how perfect she was, like the pretty, perfect vegetables she brought home from the natural store, or her sweet breath, which he knew came from some kind of natural toothpaste she got at the same place.

He got up and walked from the front room into the kitchen, and opened the refrigerator. "You want this?" he said, holding the last can of Schaefer up in the triangle of light from the refrig-erator, above the door.

She shook her head. "You're jealous, aren't you?" she said. "Of Ryan? You don't want your daughter going—"

"Oh no," he said. "I've gotten rid of two wives. I'm not going to have a daughter. The price is too high." And that ended the party.

She stopped, blinked, looked at him, then started to cry, quietly.

"I'm going to sleep," he said. "I'm sorry. You forced your way in here. I got you a job. I had a nice, quiet, sensible life, before. Peaceful, goddamn it. I pay the rent. I like you, but . . . "

"But?"

225

"I'm going to sleep," he said. "There's one more can of beer. On the top shelf. And some bourbon in the cabinet. And I sleep all day Saturday, so if you get up at the crack of dawn, don't start playing the radio and singing, for God's sake." He looked at her. "Tiptoe, for God's sake. Understand?" He looked away, and walked back to his bedroom and took his clothes off and got into bed, and fell asleep before he could get angry. She was right; he was jealous, but only a little. It would pass.

The next morning, he woke up at eleven, with a headache. When he got to the front of the apartment the glare from the windows hurt. He closed the blinds, twisting one of the plastic wands until he felt it break up at the top behind the sheet metal where you couldn't see what was going on. He thought, briefly, of going to the other windows and breaking the other two, on purpose, but let it go, settled down into the couch.

"Aspirin?" she said, from the kitchen.

He nodded.

When she brought him the pills and a glass of water, she was decked out in high heels and a long rayon dress, black, all open lace over a black slip, or a bodystocking, or something. "Anything else you want?"

He squinted and blinked. "What is this?" he said, waving his hand at her clothes.

"This is the Forties' look. You like it?"

"On Saturday?" he said. "Anyway, I thought high heels were unnatural. A chauvinist conspiracy or something."

She gave him a blank look, and then said, "I need the car. Okay? I'm not walking nineteen blocks looking like this. I have to go in today. Big project." When she saw his squinting, smug expression, she said, "I'm going to work because Ryan will be there and I put on some stuff because Ryan will be there, fancy stuff, this dress, the stockings. I feel stupid enough without you staring at me." She stood looking at him. "Why're you shaking your head?"

He smiled. "I'm remembering the years I spent worrying about whether women cared about me, noticed me. The work they must have been doing that I never saw." He shut his eyes.

"If it's non-effective, I'll put my Soviet outfit back on. If it's—"

"It's effective," he said. "Maybe too effective. Just make sure old Ryan's got a nice apartment."

"I told you last night. He lives in a hotel."

He nodded. "I figure about twenty minutes for the aspirin to work. Ten more minutes."

"Tilden? Tell me something." She picked her purse out of the seat of the armchair at the end of the couch, stood pushing things around in the purse until she came up with a tiny maroon brush. She drew it slowly through her long dark hair. "Why do you live this way?"

There was a time when a woman brushing her hair was the most beautiful thing in the world to him. "This way?"

"In the dark," she said.

"I'm a mole," he said, and pointed to his eyes.

"Don't you ever want to dance? Or go to a movie or— Or a woman? People die, you know? Then it's over. I mean, you bought a brown car, for God's sake. Mamma— She told me you used to be brash. What happened?" She dropped the hairbrush back into the purse and zipped it up, put her hands on her hips. "All you do is work and eat. And sleep."

"I drink."

"Not very much," she said. "Never enough."

"If you drink too much, you have to think about it." He looked up, but the light still hurt. "The car keys are on the hook, by the door." Squinting.

"Yeah, I got them." She shook her head, opened her purse again. "I've gotta go." She leaned over and gently kissed his hair. "I could stay home. We could drink up the bourbon. Go to bed."

"Get out!"

"Just kidding, Tilden. Jesus. Calm down. You're acting like my father or something."

He lifted his feet up on the couch and turned to face the back, heard the purse zip closed again, and then her heels on the hardwood floor, finally the spring slip the bolt into the latch of the door.

Paulie was gone all day, and all day Sunday. Some time during the night she had returned the car, because when he looked out the blinds on Sunday morning, there it sat in front of the building. Brown.

He tried not to wait for her, even tried *60 Minutes* after the football games were over, but got distracted trying to tell whether the newsmen's suits were expensive, and their watches and their haircuts. He even thought of trying to call the hotel—but then remembered that he didn't know the kid's last name. He used to read, but that was no good either; he couldn't concentrate, so finally he got out the vacuum cleaner.

He straightened the rugs, pushed the chairs and the couch around, and ran the old vacuum back and forth, sweating, until the plug jerked out of the wall and he moved it to a new outlet. He left her room until last, stood before the door for a minute, and finally pushed open the door. The floor was littered with coathangers and panties, khaki shirts, sections of newspapers and crisp department store bags, leg weights, running clothes, and small balls of black hair. Tilden let the hose drop, walked over and sat on her unmade bed. He could smell Shalimar, or Emeraude, one of those.

There had been a girl, before he left school the first time, in Boston, a pretty quiet Italian so shy she could barely speak. He remembered riding her bicycle into an old church, sitting up by the altar. "I'm the bishop. You're the bishop's whore." He put his hand to the back of his neck, touched the scar. Vodka, that was right. The time he had gotten beat up on Marlborough Street, for taking somebody's liquor, she took care of him, covered his face with hot wet towels, touched his forehead, and brought him aspirin for three days. "I don't believe it," he said, out loud, and looked at the floor, settling for a moment on her discarded underwear, then quickly looking at the vacuum in the doorway.

Tilden stood up, and then sat back down, looking at a Vogue on top of a stack of magazines. He thought the telephone was ringing, in the front of the apartment, but listening harder, heard nothing. Jesus, he thought, no thank you.

The girl on the magazine cover, blond, in a three-quarter pose, her perfect face disappearing under the logo and her soft breasts nearly bare above a pale blue evening dress, holding his eyes, spaghetti straps, that's what they used to call them, ten years since he'd done this, looked at the goddamn pictures so hard it was as if you were trying to make the photograph start breathing, and he remembered knowing their names. Rene Russo, and Lois

228

what's her name, and Kim Alexis, and Lauren Hutton, of course. Verushka, way back, and Karen Graham.

"Fuck this," he said, shoving the magazines off onto the floor so that they slid over the clothes and hangers all the way to the wall. Tilden lay back on the bed, but when he felt his shoulders touch the sheet, jerked back up onto his elbows, then sat straight up and grabbed the clock from the table and threw it against the wall, and then, for good measure, finding nothing else, threw the table the clock had been on and picked up magazines from the floor and threw them too, tearing the covers, listening to the pages slap against each other until they hit the walls.

I am enjoying this, he thought, and looked at the radio, on the carpet. I am enjoying this very much. He brought his shoe down on the imitation wood grain plastic, in which there was a little too much black, and it only sort of squeaked, so he stepped back to kick it into the wall, getting a little lift so that it hit about two feet up from the floor molding, leaving a black dent in the paint and loose plastic below. "Up, and . . . good!" He was almost shouting, twisting around, turning back, looking, and he tried the bed, with both hands managing to throw the mattress against the other wall, a spinning throw which let him fall, like a dancer, on top of the box spring where he lay looking up, gasping for breath. This is it, he thought. This is the way I used to be. He laughed and looked around. Standing in the doorway, her feet in carefully chosen spots in the pretzel formed by the hose of the vacuum cleaner, Paulie was looking back at him, smiling. "You taking a break or what?" she said.

He started giggling, watching her, staring at her, the black dress, which was all holes, black faded to a sort of charcoal color, her hip cocked, her pelvis pushed front and center by the high heels like the models in the magazines, staring, and he could feel the look on his face, just past a smile, enjoying it, drunk with love, or something like love, thinking, I'm giggling, for God's sake, like everybody else.

"Tilden? Are you okay? Should I call somebody?"

He blinked. "You hurt," he said, "you know, just standing there in that goddamn dress. But . . . don't move. Are you tired?"

She stood, motionless, like a woman on display with her perfect brown eyes, perfect black hair, and glowering dark skin

229

wrapped around the muscles of her neck. "Now?" she said, reading his eyes. "Now you want to fuck?"

"No . . . " Tilden shut his eyes. "Yes. I wish you hadn't said
it that way. We could break some more stuff instead," he said.
"Let's do that." He got up, reached down for one of the pastel
blue leg weights, hesitated, and picked up the radio, the cord
wrapping itself around his leg until he kicked loose and reached
out with it, saying, "Yeah. Here. You go first. I'm buying." He
handed her the radio, which, missing only a couple of clear plastic lenses from the front, felt like a brick.

She kicked her shoes into the room and stood weighing the
radio in her hand, taking practice throws, sidearm.

"Hard," Tilden said. "Throw it hard. It's a tough little bastard."
He leaned over, kissing her neck just as she threw. The radio hit
the opposite wall and fell apart.

"Good," Tilden said. "That was good. Great. Sorry about . . . "

"It's okay," she said. "It felt . . . nice. How much shit can we
break?"

"A prudent amount."

She rolled her eyes. "You're buying?"

He nodded. "Get the bourbon," he said, and then followed her
as she walked down the hall, her long arms stretched out so that
her hands slid along the walls tearing the Jazz Festival posters in
half, leaving meandering white edges which looked like the stock
charts the newspapers published. She rose up on her toes to slap
the sickly beige cover off the smoke alarm, which immediately
began howling. In the living room she pushed over a lamp, and
Tilden stepped on the shade until the bulb shattered inside. She
cleared a bookshelf, hooked her stockinged foot under the table
in front of the couch, lifted it a quarter-inch, and yelped. Turned
around, picked up books from the carpet. "Here," she shouted,
handing him one, pointing at the three plants under the window,
and then they threw books, one by one, until the plants were
down. She turned and put her arms around his neck, sagging
against him, pulling him down. "Tilden," she said, her lips to his
ear to be heard above the screaming smoke alarm, wrapping herself around him, "let's break a rule." He reached down, put his
hands on her, feeling her through the dress, and felt as if he were
all hands.

"Tilden?" she said, in the morning, leaning over him, in the nightgown although she had slept without it, standing now with a cup of coffee in her hand, finger marks up and down her bare arms, her eyes clear, her hair shining, brushed to within an inch of its life. "You've gotta get up."

Sitting up in the bed, he set the coffee aside, and drew his fingers along her forearm. "Me?"

She nodded, sat beside him. "I bruise easily," she said, and grinned. "I was always very proud of that. If you say you're sorry, I'll break your face." She looked at her arms, and the grin turned to a broad smile. "I mean, I'd rather you didn't."

"I'm sorry."

She looked at him.

"How bad is it out there?" he said, pointing out the bedroom door. "The furniture. It's all coming back to me."

She shook her head. "Minor league," she said. "I've already put most of it back. I put that ugly plant in some water, in a mayonnaise jar. You're going to need a new lamp, though. You can probably replace that one for a buck and half."

"The lady has never bought a lamp."

"The gentleman has never been to the Salvation Army store."

"Right," he said. He put his hands on her breasts, felt her nipples through the thin nylon.

"Work," she said.

"Screw work."

"Tilden, you devil. You're going to break another rule?"

"Hey," he said. "There's only one rule. Jesus said. And then there're a lot of second-rate types making up a lot of extras. Middle management types. And Jesuits." He drew his hands away. "You in love with this Ryan person?"

"You mean, did I sleep with him?"

He laughed. "No, I meant what I said." He kissed her through the nightgown, pulled away, smiled at her. "I assumed you screwed the child's brains out. Isn't that what you young people do?"

"That's it," she said. "I mean when we aren't snorting, shooting, smoking, dropping, popping, or tearing the wings off angels. Or stealing stuff or—"

"Hush," he said. "Hush hush."

She looked at him.

231

"It's a song. Was a song. When were you born, what year?" He shook his head. "Nevermind. In olden times this blues guy, Jimmy Reed, I think he was from Dallas— He played harmonica and guitar and he had this trashy blues voice, we played him on the radio. A song called 'Hush Hush.' It was about noise. Sort of wonderful."

"I don't know whether I'm in love with him or not. Too soon to tell. He wants me to move in."

"A girl's got to find out, I guess." Tilden lay back in the bed, watching her.

"It was nice, last night, I mean throwing things and the rest of it, mostly the rest of it. I mean, I loved it. I mean, you. But look—" She was drawing circles in the sheet with her finger. "Look. When I was about six, Mamma gave me a picture, this glossy picture of you, of my father." She smiled, shook her head. "That picture was my favorite thing for about six years. You signed it. When I was about twelve, a girl told me it was Jim Morrison. The singer." She shrugged. "So I need another picture, see? Girl needs a picture."

"Let me get this straight," Tilden said. "Somehow you knew my—"

"Mamma gave it to me. Your name? I got it from Mamma."

"Okay. Anyway—"

"And Boston is right, and Baltimore, you living in Baltimore. There is a scar on the back of your neck. I've seen it. You want blood tests and shit? Paternity?"

"I want you not to be my kid. I like looking at you. Only not like you look at a daughter."

"There's lots of people to look at." She stood up, reached her hand up and split her hair between her fingers. "I've gotta go to to work. You know, Tilden, you're really fucked up," she said, and walked out of the room.

He looked toward the empty doorway. "Now!" he shouted. "I am now!"

But she didn't answer. He thought of getting up, of following her into the room and talking some sense into her, but when he imagined her shoulder in his hand, his face red and words spewing out in the southern accent that he fell into when he got angry, cared too much, the image reminded him of the bruises all over her arms, made him recall that he really didn't know what

232

to say, that two women he had married and loved and looked at ended up, after a while, looking at him, just as he ended up looking at them, sometimes fondly, each to the other a special piece of furniture. He let himself settle back into the bed, feeling comfortable and familiar, and he thought, Nestling, I'm nestling down here—just like everybody else, just before he fell asleep.

Sometime after noon, he went into work. Kelli said Loeffler had called him three times. He was supposed to be working on an incentive plan, but he spent most of the afternoon staring down out his office window at a bench and a pathetic tree set in the sidewalk, wine bottles around the tree reflecting the dirty sunlight. The bench, like all the other damn benches, had "William Donald Schaefer and the Citizens of Baltimore" painted on in script. Blue and white. He thought about calling Paulie at work but didn't, it became a test of his character, one he passed. When you make love to a woman, he thought, if you accidentally make something, you're supposed to make a son. If you accidentally make a daughter, that's all right, but you're not supposed . . . It thins out the blood or something. They make this stuff up. He put his feet on the desk and looked around. Dull, he thought, but not loud, ugly, pathetic, cruel. Decorating an office was like decorating a Buick. He closed his eyes, looking for her, and waited for five o'clock.

When he got to the apartment, she hadn't come home. Tilden fell asleep.

An hour and a half later, he woke up on the couch in the living room, in the dark, and reached up where the lamp had been, but then he remembered. So he sat in the dark. He had been having a particularly gaudy dream, he was sweating, but he couldn't remember anything except that it had something to do with work. He never remembered dreams. When he tried, all he could ever bring to mind was the dance dream, which he had had fifteen or more years earlier, a dream about his first wife. Floating around the kitchen of his parents' house in Richmond, she was dancing in the air, in a short, flimsy dress, a '60's dress from Paraphernalia, green with big yellow flowers, and he finally caught her and tied her up with white rope.

Guilt, Tilden thought. People are always talking about guilt, and this is what they mean. I'm feeling guilty, like everybody

233

else. He got up, made his way to the wall switch and stood, thinking about turning it on, decided not to.

On the steps outside the front door, he looked up and his car seemed far away, reflecting a dozen colors from the lights up and down the street. He made himself walk the fifteen feet, took a businesslike look at the traffic on the gray street, circled the brown Toyota, got in. I remember this, Tilden thought, pulling into the traffic. This is high school. He laughed.

When he got to the hotel, he left the car on the street, and was inside before he realized he still didn't know the kid's last name; Tilden stood looking. In the center of the huge, dim lobby, under a high ceiling decorated with lost chandeliers, was a flat fountain where people were pitching pennies into the water. Others sat on gray couches scattered to one side. Tourists were taking photographs of each other around the fountain, using flashes. On the far side of the fountain a recessed bar faced fat green couches set beside stingy glass tables on a gaudy carpet in a slightly darker green. The bar was railed off in brass, and packed. Another recess farther down, and corridors leading off at each corner. The elevator doors, opposite the fountain, were the same smoky marbled glass mirror as the wall. Tilden retreated to the gray couches, sat down, glanced around for short-looking men. Boys. Paulie.

Christ, he thought, it's some kind of designer whorehouse. Haven't been in a hotel for ten years. On the other couches, over-dressed women, with children standing beside them like miniatures, in crooked coats and ties. He looked around for telephones, but remembered he had no one to call. Hi, thought I'd call to say . . . well, I'm in love with my daughter . . . well, I didn't know either . . . well, she's sort of . . . tall . . . no, I'm at her boyfriend's hotel . . . well, I'm sort of spying on them . . . only I'm not spying very well . . . well . . .

He was cold, and thought of his coat, back at the apartment. He let his head sink into his hands, felt his elbows pressing into his knees, listening to high heels slap across the marble floor. His hair felt greasy. He thought of calling his wife, the second one. Beth. Her name was Beth, and she said she was going to look for somebody who'd let her have a dog. When he tried to picture her, what she looked like, he started to shake. He couldn't hear anything. Then he saw her all in white walking toward him across the lobby, from around the elevators, and, a little behind, a short guy with shaggy hair, black suit, purple shirt, cowboy boots. Paulie, he thought. Paulie, I want to talk to you.

"You don't look well, Tilden," she said, waiting for the boy to arrive beside her. "Ryan, this is my father. Tilden, Ryan."

The boy held out his hand, but then, seeing Tilden's face, withdrew it. "Hello," he said. "Paulinda has told me a great deal about you."

Tilden looked at her. She was shaking her head. This is strange, Tilden thought, he's got to think it strange. Some quaint American custom, maybe. Perhaps. They say 'perhaps.'

"I hope you're not angry," Ryan said. "I told Paulie she should call." He looked at her, for an acknowledgment, then at Tilden, and getting nothing, no smile, shook his head. "You are angry. I'm sorry. But this is a little much, you know."

Tilden nodded. "A little much," he said. "Maybe."

Paulie was smiling, carefully. She had the boy's arm, slowly pressing him backward, but he was still talking.

"I am sorry," he said. "And I am pleased to finally meet you." He turned, drew his sleeve from her. "Paulie, I'll see you up—"

Tilden grabbed Ryan's coat, pulled him up onto the balls of his feet. "Little scumbag . . . " he said. But that was all he could think of. He stared at the kid's face.

He was looking at Tilden as if the older man were a child, a particularly wearisome child, who only had to be outwaited, who couldn't win, but had nonetheless to be allowed some time before the weight of decorum hit him. Tilden let go. "Get rid of him," he said. "He says your name again, I'll kill him."

"You actually do this over here," Ryan said. He was straightening his coat. "I thought it was only in films."

Paulie had stopped smiling. "Tilden, Jesus." She and Ryan exchanged looks, she taking him by the arm and leading him the first few steps back toward the elevators.

When she walked back, she was angry. "Real shabby, daddy. What were you thinking?" She looked around, took Tilden's arm, tightly, and led him toward the marble steps down to the street door. "What the hell are you doing here, anyway? You locate some paternal instinct?" She stopped on the steps, cocked her hip, released him, and stared. "Or do you just like making scenes in hotels? You're acting like fifteen."

"I know." Tilden stood three steps down, looking back at her. "But you don't understand."

She laughed, shook her head.

She was wearing some kind of white, long, T-shirt dress, stretched over her hip in a kind of perfection that only women seemed able to achieve, and it seemed to him that because she fit so perfectly in this hotel lobby, with the Givenchy whorehouse bar, and the orgy of glass and chrome and brass, green and gray and marble and the idiot chandeliers so high no one would call them to come back, and the other people with their impossibly brisk strides and Sunday clothes—what they used to call Sunday clothes—because she fit, so did he. That's how it seemed, but he knew he didn't.

"Call me tomorrow," he said. "Tell him I haven't been well or something. Call me at work."

He smiled and turned his face away, didn't look back until he was through the glass doors and out on the sidewalk. She was posed on the broad marble steps. He stood on the sidewalk, staring back over something written in gold on the glass, her clear eyes, the black hair, soft breasts with the big nipples, her hip high, and he felt his eyes smile and felt them blink once, twice, three, four times, and he thought, You can't look at anyone this way unless you've slept with her, and she, smiling, stepped back up a step. He jerked forward, a fraction of an inch, looked down, then back up at her for another second's worth of it, then raised his hand and waved. Someone was standing behind him, a copy of the Sun under her arm, looking at him like he was some sort of space creature. Tilden smiled. He wanted to look back through the glass doors. The woman circled around him and into the hotel.

The next day, a Tuesday, she never called, but around three-thirty Tilden was looking out his window when they came up the street and stopped at the corner. A short boy and a tall girl, arguing. They worked their way toward the building and then worked their way away. She was coming; he was going. When the boy began winning the argument, they would fade toward the sad little tree and the bench for the bus. When she got the upper hand, toward the building they came. Her dress was light, nylon

236

or polyester, and swung as the boy grabbed her arm and released it, grabbed again. She threw her hands up, threw her head back, sat down on the bench. Tilden's telephone buzzed.

"Yes," he said, and then. "Okay," and then, "Oh, Kelli, when Paulie . . . If Paulie comes, just send her in," and then Tiny Loeffler came on the line.

"Let me guess," Loeffler said. "You've been busy—that teenager you had up here last month? You recall we talked about an incentive plan? We're tired of hiring new tellers every week. So think of something. You know, nifty prizes."

"We could pay them a living wage," Tilden said. He was straightening out the telephone cord. "Microwaves again?"

"That's a breakthrough," Loeffler said.

Tilden snorted. "If they aren't going to okay cash, the whole thing is a waste anyway. I can do you up a microwave plan by five this afternoon, no problem." The telephone cord was stretched out flat. They were still on the bench. Her arms were down, one hand caressing the hem of her dress, her black hair sparkling in the sunlight.

"Okay, but hurry the hell up."

His left hand, with the receiver, fell to his side; he could hear Loeffler talking distantly. "Put your arms around her," Tilden said, "you sleazy little creep." He laughed and pulled the phone back up.

"You there? Tilden? Hey, what's that little girl's name? She's in the book?"

Tilden was silent, turned away from the window. He felt blank, holding the telephone, waiting.

"Okay," Loeffler said, "but I think she needs a younger man. You're a little long in the tooth here. Aren't you? Has her daddy seen you yet? Hey?"

Tilden began to smile. "I'm her daddy," he said. "Her name is Paulinda. She's my daughter. You ought to get married, Tiny."

He heard part of a laugh, then silence, then a click, and the dial tone. Tilden, listening, stepped back to the window. She was straightening herself, patting her hair, setting seams, shifting her shoulders. Cotton. The dress was cotton. He set the telephone receiver down. I'm not a bad guy, Tilden thought, for wanting this woman to be wearing a nylon dress, for wanting to look at her, for wanting her to hush and put her hands on me, for any of

237

it. She'll be quiet now, and go away. She's already gone. Maybe sometime she'll need money and she'll call. He looked around the room. Place's okay, he thought. Peaceful. You ought to have a kid.

He stood at the tall blue windows, which stretched to the floor—it made you sick when you stood too close—and looked to his right then back to his left, but the street was empty. In his mind he saw them again, moving, talking, a mimed argument on the blue and white bench. Stand up, sit down. Stand up, sit down. I remember that, he thought. He reached out, his hand moving as if by itself, and touched the thick glass.

Nominated by Kim Herzinger, Boulevard.

MANNEQUINS

by LAURIE SHECK

from MICHIGAN QUARTERLY REVIEW

Rifle-thin, they stand in their angelic armor.
What love has brought them here, what story,
only to drop them down on this terrain of glass and chrome
smooth as an assassin's mask; cold trophies,
still aftermaths of innocence,
no longer touched by hurry or surprise?

Contagion is another world now, fear
another world. The softness that once held them has long
    vanished,
the bribes of kindness, dim corridors of night,
swift nets, swift versions, lies.
They thrive like the hard bark of leafless trees.

In their eyes all things are suspect.
The city's deformity, its standard unstoppable vanity,
spreads its glow, like ice, against them.
But they stand cloaked in a further, stranger coldness.
Fierce, telescopic, they wait, the one true dream
beneath the dream.

Out of this blank sleep, no other sleep.
Sinister hinges, the minutes tick.
Their long hair spills down like laughter
constrained behind the bright unyielding glass;
smiles flatten like closed hatches.

All day, all night, as if the future had already turned to ruin,
having brought with it the bombed deserted streets
and crumbled doorways, blasted cars,
they stand stock still, watching, and feel nothing.
This is the rubble of astonishment, it is astonishment's cold
tomb and the eyes it left there, open, as they froze.

Nominated by Edward Hirsch, Rita Dove

TO A WREN ON CALVARY

by LARRY LEVIS

from THE MISSOURI REVIEW

> *"Prince Jesus, crush those bastards . . ."*
> —François Villon, *Grand Testament*

It is the unremarkable that will last.

As in Brueghel's camouflage, where the wren's withheld,
While elsewhere on a hill, small hawks (or are they other birds?)
Are busily unraveling eyelashes & pupils
From sunburned thieves outstretched on scaffolds,
Their last vision obscured by wings, then broken, entered.
I cannot tell whether their blood spurts, or just spills,
Their faces are wings, & their bodies are uncovered.

The twittering they hear is the final trespass.

*

And all later luxuries—the half-dressed neighbor couple
Shouting insults at each other just beyond
Her bra on a cluttered windowsill, then ceasing it when
A door was slammed to emphasize, like trouble,

The quiet flowing into things then, spreading its wake
From the child's toy left out on a lawn
To the broken treatise of jet-trails drifting above—seem
Keel scrapes on the shores of some enlarging mistake,

A wrong so wide no one can speak of it now in the town
That once had seemed, like its supporting factories

241

That manufactured poems & weaponry,
Like such a good idea. And wasn't it everyone's?

Wasn't the sad pleasure of assembly lines a replica
Of the wren's perfect, camouflaged self-sufficiency,
And of its refusal even to be pretty,
Surviving in a plumage dull enough to blend in with

A hemline of smoke, sky, & serene indifference?

*

The dead wren I found on a gravel drive
One morning, all beige above and off-white
Underneath, the body lighter, no more than a vacant tent

Of oily feathers stretched, blent, & lacquered shut
Against the world—was a world I couldn't touch.
And in its skull a snow of lice had set up such
An altar, the congregation spreading from the tongue

To round, bare sills that had been its eyes, I let
It drop, my hand changed for a moment
By a thing so common it was never once distracted from
The nothing all wrens meant, the one feather on the road.

No feeding in the wake of cavalry or kings changed it.
Even in the end it swerved away, & made the abrupt
Riddle all things come to seem . . . irrelevant:
The tucked claws clutched emptiness like a stick.

And if Death whispered as always in the language of curling
Leaves, or a later one that makes us stranger,
"Don't you come *near* me motherfucker";
If the tang of metal in slang made the New World fertile,

Still . . . as they resumed their quarrel in the quiet air,
I could hear the species cheep in what they said . . .
Until their voices rose. Until the sound of a slap erased
A world, & the woman, in a music stripped of all prayer,

242

Began sobbing, & the man become bystander cried *O Jesus*.

                              *

In the sky, the first stars were already faint
And timeless, but what could they matter to that boy, blent
To no choir, who saw at last the clean wings of indifferent

Hunger, & despair? Around him the other petty thieves

With arms outstretched, & eyes pecked out by birds, reclined
Fastened forever to scaffolds which gradually would cover
An Empire's hills & line its roads as far
As anyone escaping in a cart could see, his swerving mind

On the dark brimming up in everything, the reins
Going slack in his hand as the cart slows, & stops,
And the horse sees its own breath go out
Onto the cold air, & gazes after the off-white plume,

And seems amazed by it, by its breath, by everything.
But the man slumped behind it, dangling a lost nail
Between his lips, only stares at the swishing tail,
At each white breath going out, thinning, & then vanishing.

For he has grown tired of amazing things.

Nominated by David Jauss, Jim Simmerman, Karen Fish

AGAINST DECORATION

by MARY KARR

from PARNASSUS: POETRY IN REVIEW

1

DECORATION ABOUNDS IN contemporary poetry, much of it marching beneath the banner of neo-formalism. Actually a mix of strict form and free verse, the new formalist poems juggle rhyme, meter, and various syllabic and stanzaic strategies. In the last few years, the movement has generated a rush of anthologies, such as Robert Richman's *The Direction of Poetry: Rhymed and Metered Verse Written in the English Language Since 1975.* Richman, the poetry editor of the neo-conservative *New Criterion,* selects not only distinguished writers now in their sixties such as James Merrill, John Hollander, and Anthony Hecht (all of whom, by the way, serve as chancellors for the Academy of American Poets), but also from the thirtysomething generation that includes Michael Blumenthal, Gjertrud Schnackenberg, Brad Leithauser, and Rosanna Warren. This book has already produced one outraged notice by poet-critic Ira Sadoff, who in a recent issue of *The American Poetry Review* called neo-formalism "A Dangerous Nostalgia," linking it to the political conservatism of the eighties. Once a poetry movement can boast an anthology, a starting date, and a metaphorically machine-gunning detractor, it qualifies as a movement—even if it lacks a coherent manifesto.

The fault, of course, doesn't lie with form per se. Amy Clampitt rarely employs strict forms, yet her work is almost exclusively ornamental, particularly in her overuse of historical references, which seem to increase in their obscurity over the course of her books. It's easier to know what Clampitt's read than what she's writing about (the notes for her latest, *Westward*, consume four-and-a-half pages). Critics have called her obscure, polysyllabic diction a long-awaited return to high language, likening her to Hopkins, Keats, and Milton. But Clampitt's purple vocabulary sounds to me like a parody of the Victorian silk that Pound sought to unravel. This passage could be Swinburne on acid or Tennyson gone mad with his thesaurus. In it, the sun is rising or setting:

> Seamless equipose of crossing: Nox
> primordial half-shape above the treadle,
> the loomed fabric of the sun god's ardor
> foreshortened, with a roar as if of earthly fire.

(from "Winchester: The Autumn Equinox")

Influential critics have cheered Clampitt's linguistic intricacy for its own sake. And the appreciation for ornament extends to others. In April 1990, *The New Republic* carried Helen Vendler's review of Merrill's *The Inner Room* beneath the telling headline "In Praise of Perfume." There, she aligned Merrill with writers "interested in intricacy of form, and a teasing obliqueness of content." In Merrill's "Losing the Marbles," Vendler enjoys a kind of crossword puzzle challenge:

> A poem-manuscript has been rained on, and some of
> its words obliterated. On its half unreadable "papyrus," the poem looks like one of Sappho's enigmatic
> fragments:

> body, favorite
>   gleaned, at the
>   vital
>   frenzy—

—and so on, for seven stanzas. The game is to deduce what the poem's lost cells may have been holding. . . . We become, with Merrill, scholars of the papyrus, hunters for lost words—and find ourselves (in a mockery of classical scholarly reconstructions) wholly mistaken.

There's something scary about Vendler's enthusiasm for the poem as scholastic game, particularly when her efforts leave her "wholly mistaken." I always thought that poetry's primary purpose was to stir emotion, and that one's delight in dense idiom or syntax or allusion served a secondary one. I don't mind, for instance, working hard to read *Paradise Lost,* because I return to Milton for the terror and hubris Satan embodies. If, as Vendler suggests, the sport of decoding a poem is its central pleasure, then one would no more reread such a poem than one would bother reworking an acrostic already solved. Indeed, such a poem would become disposable after one reading, the "game" played.

Yet the affection for decorative poetry extends beyond Vendler to other powerful critics, poets, and publishers: Vendler begat Clampitt and others; Harold Bloom begat John Ashbery and the poetics of coy adorableness, which in turn begat Language Poetry; Merrill begat a string of ornament-spouting progeny through his service at Yale University Press and the Academy, as well as through his general pull with New York publishers (his *blurbissimo* on book jackets is famous); Alice Quinn, poetry editor for *The New Yorker,* begat the flowery, emotionally dim poems that one reads in that magazine; *ad nauseam.*

The argument against decoration, however, runs as far back as literary criticism itself. Aristotle called metaphors of all kinds the mere "seasoning of the meat," and believed that clarity resided instead in "everyday words." Cicero and Horace basically elaborated this dichotomy between seasoning and substance. Ancient rhetoricians admonished writers to avoid—among other things— excessive use of tropes. These elaborate figures of speech could, it was argued, over-decorate a work and reduce its power to convey feeling. In fact, the *Princeton Encyclopedia of Poetry and Poetics* tells us that the poet and orator in the early Christian era had to justify the use of a limited number of tropes by demonstrating the extremity of his or her own feeling. In other words, unless the orator could convey the depth and sincerity of his or her own experience, the use of tropes fell into the realm of mere decoration. That's how I often feel about much of today's popular

246

work: The poet concentrates so fixedly on the poem's minute needlework that he or she fails to notice—like a blind man with the elephant in the old fable—that the work involves only one square inch of a tapestry draped across an enormous beast, and that the beast is moving.

I define two sins popular in much of today's poetry—particularly the neo-formalist stuff—which signify decoration and can starve a poem of value:

> 1. *Absence of emotion.* What should I as a reader feel? This grows from but is not equivalent to what the speaker/author feels. Questioning a poem's central emotion steers me beyond the poem's ostensible subject and surface lovelinesses to ultimate effect. Purely decorative poetry leaves me cold.

> 2. *Lack of clarity.* The forms of obscurity in decorative poetry are many and insidious: references that serve no clear purpose, for instance, or ornate diction that seeks to elevate a mundane experience rather than to clarify a remarkable one. Lack of clarity actually alienates a reader and prevents any emotional engagement with the poem.

Again, I do not decry decorative elements in a poem per se. One can with perfect legitimacy use a reference or create an elaborately metaphoric or linguistic surface in a poem. But when those elements become final ends, rather than acting as a conduit for a range of feelings, poetry ceases to perform its primary function: to move the reader. To pay so little attention to the essentially human elements of a poem makes a monster of poetry's primary emotional self, its very reason for being, so that the art becomes exclusively decorative and at times grotesque. Like cats in jewelry or babies in makeup, the ornaments detract from rather than illuminate their subjects.

Absence of Emotion

We can marshal evidence for the emotional vacuity of ornamental verse with the example of Merrill, who may well be the emperor of the new formalism. I contend that this emperor wears no

247

clothes—or, to use a more accurate metaphor, that the ornamental robes exist, but the emperor himself is missing—a surprising state of affairs, since Merrill is perhaps the most revered and ubiquitous poet in the country: He can boast two National Book Awards, the Bollingen, the Pulitzer, and the National Book Critics Circle Award.

Merrill's chief talent is his mastery of elegant language. And in the earlier work, the complexity of language and metaphor applies to human dramas that are grounded enough in the world to move a reader. In "Charles on Fire," for example, we hear some privileged young men at dinner discussing the difference between "uncommon physical good looks," which are believed to "launch one," and "intellectual and spiritual values," without which "you are sunk." In this poem, Merrill gives us far more narrative data than he bothers with in his more recent books. Knowing certain physical and social facts, the reader can become sufficiently engaged in the poem to marvel at Merrill's sparing use of ornament. Here is the final two-thirds of the poem:

> Long-suffering Charles, having cooked and served the meal,
> Now brought out little tumblers finely etched
> He filled with amber liquid and then passed.
> "Say," said the same young man, "in Paris, France,
> They do it this way"—bounding to his feet
> And touching a lit match to our host's full glass.
> A blue flame, gentle, beautiful, came, went
> Above the surface. In a hush that fell
> We heard the vessel crack. The contents drained
> As who should step down from a crystal coach.
> Steward of spirits, Charles's glistening hand
> All at once gloved itself in eeriness.
> The moment passed. He made two quick sweeps and
> Was flesh again. "It couldn't matter less,"
> He said, but with a shocked, unconscious glance
> Into the mirror. Finding nothing changed,
> He filled a fresh glass and sank down among us.

Charles literally *serves*, and serves to contrast with his guests, who seem more foppish than he. In fact, Charles draws the poet's pretty diction by bringing out "little tumblers finely etched," a phrase that throws in lovely sideways relief the noise of "filled with amber liquid." This diction is juxtaposed with the poem's plain speech, something which—like narrative clarity—Merrill rarely employs any more. At the instant the liquor catches fire, Merrill's staccato suspends us for an instant. Here's a wonderful example of a transforming moment that *requires* its adjectives and commas and one-syllable words to hold us at a key instant: "A blue flame, gentle, beautiful, came, went / Above the surface." And how convincing and surprising is the higher diction in the next lines when Charles, like Cinderella's footman "down from a crystal coach," briefly enters the realm of fire: "Steward of spirits, Charles's glistening hand / All at once gloved itself in eeriness." After this, the diction again irons out, becomes plain. "The moment passed. He made two quick sweeps and / Was flesh again. 'It couldn't matter less,' / He said. . . . " When Charles finds nothing changed about his outward appearance, he returns from the consuming to the mundane, from fire to flesh. In doing so, he literally sinks to the level of the others. Here the poet never embellishes a line with blowsy diction or froufrou unless it warrants such decor.

Parts of Merrill's work still show the old sparkle, but often the flourishes obscure the central subject, render it meaningless. Here, from *The Inner Room,* is "Serenade" *in toto:*

> Here's your letter the old portable
> Pecked out so passionately as to crack
> The larynx. I too dream of "times
> We'll share." Across the river: MUTUAL LIFE.
>
> Flush of a skyline. Owning up to past
> Decorum, present insatiety,
> Let corporate proceedings one by one
> Be abstracted to mauve onionskin,
>
> Lit stories rippling upside down in thought
> Be stilled alike of drift and personnel,
> Then, only then, the lyric-I-lessness
> At nightfall banked upon renew

Today's unfolder. Whose lips part. Heard now
In his original setting—voice and reeds—
As music for a god, your page
Asks to be held so that the lamp shines through

And stars appear instead of periods.

Merrill never clarifies the central characters in this memory, or
the relation between the *you* and *I*. A serenade suggests a night
song played under the balcony of the beloved. And the poem
hints at tremendous feeling—the letter so passionately typed that
the periods have pounded holes in the paper. But never does the
poet furnish the information required by the reader to understand and, thereby, feel moved. Instead, one small question after
another niggles me. I don't know who serenades whom, so I
don't know whether the letter writer's larynx cracks or the
reader-poet's larynx cracks. If the former, typing does not touch
the larynx; if the latter, there's a sick bathos to having one's voice
crack while *singing* one's own poem. I don't know what "past decorum" and "present insatiety" mean, and I very much want to,
because it sounds sexual. Unfortunately, the only excerpt from
the letter is as meaningless a line as can be found on any Hall-
mark card, "I too dream of 'times / We'll share.' " The idea and
tone suggest a foggy yearning, yet the source of that yearning
remains blurred. Merrill's peculiar diction, however, seizes our
attention: We guess at some business association with that
official-sounding language; then we slip into gushlike "lyric-
I-lessness / At nightfall." The final stanza seems to allude to the
famous musical duel between Apollo and Marsyas (the god won,
and Marsyas was flayed and nailed to a tree for his arrogance),
yet the reference seems dragged in (kicking and screaming, in my
opinion) solely to demonstrate the writer's erudition. I never understand any clear link between Apollo and Marsyas and the two
characters in the poem, or between the poet serenading and the
letter writer's star-studded letter. We guess that a parallel exists,
but how does it illuminate the poem's human situation?

I can only conclude that Merrill doesn't mind these obscurities
of character and metaphor, which leave us to gape at the poem's
gorgeous surface—the mixed diction, the clever double entendre

of "MUTUAL LIFE." Indeed, this surface seems the poet's final goal. Merrill wants to dazzle us, perhaps, with his dexterity and his ability to crank out metaphors, yet he doesn't value the ostensible subject here enough to communicate narrative data about it. The subject barely merits his attention at all, acting only as a backdrop for glittery pushpins of language and metaphor.

My test for a poem's emotional clarity is this elementary exercise: Can you fill in a blank about a poem's subject with an emotional word? *The Waste Land*, for instance, is a poem about spiritual despair. It is also about lots of ideas, not least of which is a twentieth-century decay of faith which precipitates that despair. But it strives to create that despair in the reader. That's why I return to it, not to test my knowledge of Greek myth and the Upanishads (references to which I had to look up initially anyway) but to rediscover the gravity of certain ideas with the conviction that is only born of feeling.

In my view, emotion in a reader derives from reception of a clear rendering of primal human experiences: fear of death, desire, loss of love, celebration of being. To spark emotion, a poet must strive to attain what Aristotle called simple clarity. The world that the reader apprehends through his or her senses must be clearly painted, even if that world is wholly imaginary, as, say, in much of the work of Wallace Stevens.

In Merrill's recent poems, intricate surface and form seem like mere amusements, rather than paths to or from human experience. Such decoration cuts a great gulf between form and meaning, with form favored over an attempt to communicate, word divorced from world, a kind of brittle cleverness supplanting emotion, wit elevated above clarity.

Contrast Merrill's poetry with that of Seamus Heaney, who works in form and still attends scrupulously to the human and sensory data that ultimately prompt emotion. Heaney proves, as do centuries of formal verse, that form and ornament do not in and of themselves diminish a poem's emotional possibilities. He never lets linguistic loveliness or metaphoric surface deter him from the primary task of inspiring feeling, nor does he seek to mystify facts by draping them in veil after veil of metaphor. The metaphoric and linguistic prettinesses balance somehow; they seem carefully chosen to move us. Heaney's recent sonnet sequence about his mother's death, in *The Haw Lantern*, elegantly and economically sends us all the sensory and social information we need to enter the poem's world. Here is the third sonnet from "Clearances":

> When all the others were away at Mass
> I was all hers as we peeled potatoes.
> They broke the silence, let fall one by one
> Like solder weeping off the soldering iron:
> Cold comforts set between us, things to share
> Gleaming in a bucket of clean water.
> And again let fall. Little pleasant splashes
> From each other's work would bring us to our senses.
>
> So while the parish priest at her bedside
> Went hammer and tongs at the prayers for the dying
> And some were responding and some crying
> I remembered her head bent towards my head,
> Her breath in mine, our fluent dipping knives—
> Never closer the whole rest of our lives.

Heaney begins the poem with gentle end rhymes, sometimes settling for mere consonance—*Mass* and *potatoes, one* and *iron, share* and *water, bedside* and *head*. He doesn't hit the reader on the skull with the form at first. Like Shakespeare, who endlessly varied his iambic pentameter, Heaney doesn't want the poem's noise to weigh too heavily on the ear and risk obliterating the more colloquial noises, for the poem consists of natural speech: The priest "*went* hammer and tongs at the prayers for the dying."

But after the volta—that space between the big stanza and the small one that traditionally marks a turn in the sonnet—Heaney moves to the present reality, his mother's deathbed, where he remembers their intimacy over the chore of peeling potatoes. Here the meter strengthens, becomes regular, more heavily stressed. In doing so, it gathers force. The image of the two heads bent toward each other as they peel potatoes, forever near yet forever apart, like saints in stained glass, is luminous. "Her breath in mine" is also touching: on first reading because of the physical closeness that the two almost choose to ignore by tending to their chore; on second reading because we realize that she shared her breath with him *in utero,* then lost that breath on her deathbed. Yes, the dipping knives are adjectivally "fluent," and thereby reminiscent of speech, but the resulting metaphor— fluent, expressive silence—neither distracts from nor conflicts with the human drama under study. Rather the metaphor *enhances.* The bucket of water subtly conjures both holy water and the life-giving fluid of the womb—the waters that cleanse us and slosh us forth into the world. The fluency of the knives echoes the way music—in this case potato peels weeping from a knife into water—"bring[s] us to our senses." By the remembered sound of the water, the poet re-creates in us that rare intimacy. And Heaney has no trouble making a direct statement of feeling at poem's end. Whereas Merrill would cling to emotional obliquity, Heaney earns the right to the weighty yet musical directness of his last line: "Never closer the whole rest of our lives."

Lack of Clarity

All too many contemporary poems, particularly those in the burgeoning neo-formalism canon, shy away from passion. For example, the vast majority of *New Yorker* poems favor botanical subjects, and seldom travel any farther than the poet's flowerbed. Or when poets pretend to more earnest topics, the formal elements—mere surface, the pattern in the lace, if you will— replace emotional, rhetorical, and sensory clarity. The forms of obscurity are many and insidious. I set forth the following list of those that bothered me when reading Richman's anthology:

> 1. *Obscurity of character.* Who is speaking to whom and why? What relation do the characters in the poem hold to each other? How should the reader perceive them? Even in poems that assume the intimate tone of direct speech, with the reader as eavesdropper, I seldom—in the work of Merrill or Leithauser, say— understand the relationship between the characters, or even their identities in the most prosaic sense. Are they male or female; friends, lovers, or relatives; intimates, strangers, etc.?

2. *Foggy physical world.* Where are we, and why does the poem occur here rather than elsewhere? Often physical reality remains so out of focus, with shifts in locale merely used for shifts in tone, that it's likely that the reader will be baffled. Again, I invoke Stevens's work to exemplify a wildly imagined series of overlapping places, yet each rendered precisely and appropriately.

3. *Overuse of meaningless references.* Many contemporary poets insert perplexingly obscure literary, historical, and artistic allusions, seemingly to impress us with their cleverness and sophistication.

4. *Metaphors that obscure rather than illuminate.* I. A. Richards distinguished between metaphoric tenor (the thing actually under discussion, e.g., love in "My love is a red, red rose") and the vehicle (the rose in the aforementioned metaphor.) In decorative poetry the vehicle may stand clear—the star-studded letter, for instance, in Merrill's "Serenade"—but the tenor stays out of focus, or the relation between tenor and vehicle cannot be deduced. In fact, many poets fling their metaphors (including similes, synecdoches, etc.) about like so many rhinestones, simply to change tone and, therefore, to muddle key facts.

5. *Linguistic excess for no good reason.* Polysyllables, archaic language, intricate syntax, yards of adjectives—these linguistic ornaments will slow a reader. Sometimes, this needs to happen. In "Charles on Fire," for example, the change in language used to describe a transforming moment works a kind of magic, one that *should* command our attention. Look, Merrill says, this person's world is changing. On the other hand, when Clampitt spends five lines saying that the sun rose or set while Keats took a walk, one wonders why she stopped at five. Why not six, or thirty-six?

Richman's anthology proves that a younger generation of writers has followed Merrill's lead in terms of ornament and obscurity. In

Michael Blumenthal's "Inventors," the metaphor serves to deco-
rate a startlingly banal experience:

> "Imagine being the first to say: *surveillance,*"
> the mouth taking in air like a swimmer, the tongue
> light as an astronaut, gliding across the roof
> of the mouth, the eyes burning like the eyes of Fleming
> looking at mold and thinking: *penicillin.*

Blumenthal uses metaphor the way certain bad cooks use garlic
and oregano. He mixes "swimmer" with "astronaut" with "Flem-
ing" with "mouth," all to describe something finally trivial. And
Rosanna Warren's "History as Decoration" provides an even
more meaningless text in an idiom that sounds Victorian. In a
very short space, Warren commits every decorative crime I could
imagine:

> Float over us, Florence, your banners
> of assassination, your most expensive
> reds: Brazil, Majorca, lichen, cochineal.
> Let the Neoplatonic Arno flow
> crocus yellow. Let palazzo walls
> flaunt quattrocentro dyes: "little
> monk" and "lion skin." We pay for beauty; beautiful
> are gorgeous crimes we cannot feel—
>
> they shone long ago. And those philosophies
> too pretty in spirit ever to be real.
> City of fashion, Leonardo chose
> the hanged Pazzi conspirator for a theme . . .

This sounds like an art history student, perhaps in a seminar entitled "Pigment and the Florentine Imagination," rushing to answer a very long essay question to which we as readers were not
privy. I cannot even say what this seeks to describe. Nor can I
imagine the origin of the quotes, what this has to do with Leon-
ardo, or how any river—even the Arno—can be Neoplatonic. Not
all the poems in Richman's anthology are this bad, but I reserve

the right, having plowed assiduously through fields of this kind of drivel, to choose the worst examples to make my point. If this is poetry, let us write prose.

2

Some Isms behind the Ornaments:

Some powerful "isms" lurk behind the current rage for ornamental poetry: neo-formalism I've mentioned, but I also want to consider the symbolist tolerance for obscurity, as well as the role of academic critics, who not only seem happy to take on the decorative poet's communicative burden, but whose post-structuralist theories have undermined the value of poetic clarity.

Since I've already taken a swipe at neo-formalism, I would like to start with it. I don't propose here to gauge the virtues or vices inherent in poetic forms. I agree with Coleridge when he described meter as the "yeast, worthless and disagreeable by itself . . . but giving vivacity and spirit to the liquor with which it is proportionately combined." The key word here is *proportionately*, suggesting a need to balance formal concerns with others. Good poems, in fact, always assume the precise forms required. In truth, both meaning and feeling reside in sound. As a student, I read Walter Pater's famous injunction: "All art constantly aspires toward the condition of music," which I took to mean that form in poetry should finally be indistinguishable from content in the best work. A particular musical pitch itself refers to no *thing* in the physical world, yet when we hear it in Schumann, it evokes a feeling in relation to the notes that come before and after it, so that it means something different in one concerto than in another.

So for me, sound always means something. Yeats haunts us when he writes that the heroes of the quelled Irish rebellion are not just dead but "are changed, changed utterly: / A terrible beauty is born." Here's the roll call of heroes from that famous final stanza:

> I write it out in a verse—
> MacDonagh and MacBride

256

And Connolly and Pearse
Now and in time to be,
Wherever green is worn,
Are changed, changed utterly:
A terrible beauty is born.

(from "Easter 1916")

These brief lines, like all good ones, prove the veracity of their form. Yeats plants the names in our minds with the pounding sound he's used throughout the poem. Then he challenges that expectation by varying the stanza's pattern of stresses. The caesura buried in the penultimate line lends force to the repeated word "changed": "are *changed, changed ut*terly," The form of the line climbs toward the three stresses in the middle; the peak even holds an extra instant because of the comma. The peak then slides to unstressed syllables at the line's end. The sound mirrors, in a way, the revolutionary insurgence and decline of the heroes killed in the 1916 Irish rebellion. The final three-beat iambic line, however, arrives with a different noise, in part because of what's preceded it. Whereas the penultimate line peaked and then sagged, the final line hammers home Yeats's point with a tragic-sounding, dirge-like beat; "a *terrible beauty* is *born*." The last word rings with the reverberating "n" sound like a gong being struck. The sound *is* the meaning. It's nearly impossible to imagine altering a syllable of this without ruining it.

One would think, then, that anyone who delighted in traditional formal verse (I do) would welcome the new, unless, as in Sadoff's case, you think that neo-formalism posits some offensive social agenda (I don't).

And a few of the poems in Richman's anthology—particularly the light verse pieces—work. Anthony Hecht's "The Ghost in the Martini" uses the same ironic diction I love in Larkin to render the elder poet seducing or being seduced by the twenty-year-old literary groupie. Who can fail to be amused by the first stanza:

Over the rim of the glass
Containing a good martini with a twist

257

> I eye her bosom and consider a pass,
> Certain we'd not be missed
>
> In the general hubbub. . . .

The trouble with this kind of light verse, however successful, is that like *lite* beer and *lite* salad dressing, it leaves one hungry for something more substantial. Hecht's poem may echo bouncingly through my head the next time a visiting writer swoops an attractive student away to the nearest Motel 6, but such poems do not achieve the grandeur, say, that the last section of Stevens's "Esthétique du Mal" does—a grandeur of music and meaning as well as of form.

> The greatest poverty is not to live
> In a physical world, to feel that one's desire
> Is too difficult to tell from despair. Perhaps,
> After death, the non-physical people, in paradise,
> Itself non-physical, may, by chance, observe
> The green corn gleaming and experience
> The minor of what we feel. . . .

Once I read those lines, they returned and altered my perceptions. And they returned frequently. In fact, there have been whole years of my life during which, on a daily basis, I needed to imagine that the non-physical people, these blank-faced angels— whom I think of, because of Stevens's wonderful phrasing, as a string of slightly depressed clerical workers waiting for a subway—looked down and envied in me the very passions that caused me difficulty. Hecht's poem states a social and anecdotal truth of a lower order than the great emotional or metaphysical truths that can change one's life.

In unhappy fact, most of the people who embrace neoformalism and are most closely identified with it (Merrill and Leithauser, say, rather then Kunitz) seem, unlike their putative ancestors (Keats, say), to see formal excellence as an aesthetic virtue in and of itself, betraying little emotional intention.

That said, let me iterate Richman's noble-sounding call for a revival of form. He says that neo-formalism will free us from " . . . two decades of obscure, linguistically flat poetry." In place of this grim stuff, Richman offers poems with the "sheer sensuous appeal of language." Only the most stiff-necked Anglo-Saxon farmer might shy away from the Francophile seduction of the phrase "sheer sensuous appeal"—it almost sounds like an ad for pantyhose. But behind Richman's seductive promise lurks a hoary dichotomy—linguistically flat poetry versus linguistically ornate verse. This dichotomy originates in part from a conflict in American poetry between free verse and formal.

In our memories, the free-verse advocates sought—among other things—to iron the aristocratic curlicues from poetic diction in order to make poetry sound more populist, less elitist, and, therefore, more American. Ralph Waldo Emerson first called for a purely American poet, and Whitman answered. The poets I think of as belonging to this free-verse lineage are William Carlos Williams, the Lowell of *Life Studies*, the Beats à la Allen Ginsberg with his jangling finger cymbals, the Black Mountain poets (in particular Robert Creeley), and the Naked Poets of the famous anthology (Robert Bly, James Wright, Denise Levertov, *et al.*). Common wisdom holds that the free-verse revolution in this country only follows the same path as other formal changes through history. But the revolution has not so much opposed strict form as strict form *and* a certain kind of idiom. Timothy Steele explains it best in *Modern Measures: Modern Poetry and the Revolt Against Meter,* claiming that the modern revolution

> differed from the revolution Euripides led against Aeschylean style and the revolution Horace led against the literary conservatism of the day; and it differed from—to refer to Eliot's favorite examples—the revolution which Dryden led against Cleveland and the metaphysicals and the revolution which Wordsworth led against the Augustans. . . . The Modern movement's leaders . . . identified the Victorian diction against which they were rebelling (and the subject matter associated with the diction) with metrical composition *per se*. Having made this identification, they felt that to dispose of objectionable Victorian idiom, they had to dispose of meter.

259

Shortly after the turn of the century, Steele goes on to note, T. E. Hulme equated meter with both rhetoric and stylistic excesses. And it was such meter that most annoyed Pound in the Victorians, and from which he catapulted into free verse.

It's no surprise then that by the late 1970s, when I went to school, free verse and plain diction came to predominate in the M.F.A. work-sheets. When Donald Hall claims in a recent essay that the burgeoning number of M.F.A. programs produces something called "McPoem," we who read little magazines intuitively know what he means—tone ironic, diction flat. And McPoem comes, I think, from the revolution against meter, rhetoric, and the stylistic gush that comprised the Victorian idiom. I can no more defend this line of free versers than I would seek to weigh the virtues of its form-producing siblings. I do think, however, that it's McPoem that Richman and many of the neo-formalists seek to overthrow.

And of course, there's a long and venerable tradition in America of working in meter. We think of them as sentimental and comically ornate now, but Edna St. Vincent Millay and Henry Wadsworth Longfellow used to be poetic monuments. Nor would anyone disagree that however innovative Emily Dickinson was, she drank deeply from the English wellspring. As final testimony to the powers of formal poetry, I contend that most readers can quote, if nothing else, a smidgen of Robert Frost—perhaps *the* formal poet in this century most adept at infusing measured lines and stanzas with colloquial diction, thereby satisfying both the formalists and the free versers.

Another tradition, though, that inspires much of new poetry's obliquity and lack of understandable feeling is the French symbolist tradition as it migrated here through Yeats and the High Moderns—Eliot and Stevens. Without rehashing the entire symbolist manifesto, we can say that it often suggested that poetry was, in moral and practical terms, somewhat useless. In positing this fundamental irrelevance, the symbolist idea of "art for art's sake" (Théophile Gautier's term) freed poets from many of the moral and religious imperatives that possessed, say, Milton, and haunted artists as late as the nineteenth century. It was then that John Ruskin's book *Modern Painters* held aesthetic sway. There Ruskin at one point complains that a certain painter inaccurately depicted the shape of leaves on a certain type of tree, an inaccuracy that violated painting's moral obligation to mimic the natural world. We find this notion laughable today in part because of the symbolist influence, which hinted—at times even screamed—that poetry was a purely linguistic rather than human or (to use a positivist term) synthetic experience. In fact, in this country, most formal—as opposed to moral or humanistic—criteria for judging poetry have grown directly from symbolist sources. From Rimbaud's position that poetry resulted from "a deliberate disordering of the senses," to Mallarmé's call for "pure" poetry, to Verlaine's desire to "wring the neck of rhetoric" (again, rhetoric being subtly linked in this country with Victorian excesses), the symbolists suggested that poetry needn't make much sense in terms of rational or sensory experience.

I'm saying several things with this broad characterization of recent poetic history. First, as we all know, it's not news that poets write in form. Second, neither is it news that the pendulum has swung back toward form at this particular bend in history, after several decades of increasingly plain diction. Third, while our symbolist heirs freed poetry from moral agendas, they also permitted writers not to worry much about speaking clearly (in the rhetorical and synthetic senses) to a reader.

Finally, the trend toward ornament also mirrors the end of the last century. Back then, we could also see the verse growing purpler. Like most of the pre-Raphaelites, Swinburne was a champion embellisher: Hugh Kenner slyly notes in *The Pound Era* that Swinburne once translated a single line of Sappho into eight lines of "slow-motion re-enactment." The Victorians not only embroidered language, but they managed to sentimentalize almost every subject, and to grow increasingly stern and corseted as the decade drew to a close, as if anticipating the revolution in morals (prompted by Freud's *Interpretation of Dreams*) after 1900. Poets seemed to lurch away from the new century's uncertainty by looking to the art's historical roots, honoring Greek and Latin antiquities; as a way of keeping the old cultural flame alive, lots of poets sprinkled their work with heavy references. One teacher I had in graduate school urged me to read Browning's "Sordello"—an incredibly muddled wad of nonsense about the jongleur who brought the Provençal lyric to France—in part so I might understand why Pound roared so loudly against the Victorians. Even Pound, himself anthologized as a Victorian, grumbled that you needed to learn some dozen different languages (including five dead ones) in order to read poetry. So we see at the end of the last century a reactionary lunge back toward our poetic roots, and that lunge produced some perfectly respectable results.

Sadly, the only thing that *is* news about neo-formalism is bad news. Rarely before has form been championed as a virtue in and of itself, and poems judged formally good that in fact lack any relevance to human experience. Many of the poems in Richman's anthology seem like the husks of poems, forms with the life bled out, the assumption being that impeccably rhymed and metered verse will be good regardless of poetic content, or lack thereof. This new passion for prettiness opposes, I think, the huge body of formal work that values form only as a *relative* quality. By relative, I mean that in the past the poet asked, what kind of sound will best communicate my meaning, and vice versa. So while I defend formal verse and approve neo-formalist goals—a revival of rich language and a literary history all but ignored since the free-verse revolution—I abhor its current practice as the source of perhaps the most emotionally vacant work ever written. Moreover, the acceptance of that work has given license to writers such as Clampitt who work outside strict forms, but still homestead the realm of ornament.

Despite my wince at the assembling neo-formalist canon, I believe strongly that we as readers should not scapegoat the innocent, though Sadoff's essay in *The American Poetry Review* blames political conservatism, warning readers that

> neo-formalists have a social as well as a linguistic agenda. When they link pseudo-populism ("the general reader") to regular meter, they disguise their nostalgia for moral and linguistic certainty, for a universal ("everyone agrees") and univocal way of conserving culture.

Although I suppose that, politically speaking, I stand beside Sadoff far left of center, his approach seems misconceived. His use of the word "agenda" implies a political conspiracy. And his tone almost makes me nostalgic for the political conviction (bordering on paranoia) that was the appropriate response to the evil figures of the Watergate era. While I don't doubt that Richard Nixon conspired with his pals to lower the quality of our lives, I do doubt that Merrill does, or Vendler does. When Sadoff applies this sanctimonious tone to a reading of a Merrill poem, I doubt his sociopolitical conclusions.

> One cannot read a poem like James Merrill's "Clearing the Title" . . . and admire his fluent iambic pentameter, his complicated rhyme scheme, without acknowledging that the culminating experience of this poem involves the wealthy narrator sharing a beautiful sunset with a native "black girl with a shaved skull." This "transcendent" moment allows him to make a commitment to his lover, to buy—I swear—a condo in Key West. The inherent racism of the poem . . . points out the dangers of an esthetic that ignores what is seen in favor of the pure beauty of sound.

One can discern in Sadoff's reading the same dichotomy that Richman mentioned—word versus world. Sadoff's gloss also harks back to the massive body of moral criticism after Plato. We should not, I think, look to poets or their poems for moral or political guidance, because, quite frankly, they seem to behave badly at least as often as they behave well—Larkin's misogyny and Pound's anti-Semitism pose just two examples of moral irresponsibility in our century. Nor can we as readers judge, as Sadoff tries to do, Merrill's "privileged personal stand and his obvious ambivalence toward intimacy. . . . " Who isn't ambivalent about intimacy? And how many of us writing poetry in this country aren't privileged? Moreover, the artist judged as *amoral* in his or her time—William Burroughs or Oscar Wilde, for instance—usually just proposes an unconventional moral code.

However, at a time when our national arts program must battle censors for its very life, when rap records are stripped from shelves (No, I don't like 2 Live Crew either, but I wouldn't ban them), we must take care with our moral outrage. The key argument is not, as Sadoff implies, a political one between a free-verse liberalism and a formalist conservatism. In fact, to all moral critics I suggest reading Graham Hough, who makes these distinctions between moral- and formal-based criticism:

It is quite possible to hold a formal theory and to hold also that literature should be subject to external control. . . . All that is necessary to form a formal theory is to hold that these moral controls *are* external and do not affect literary value. . . . [But] formal theories developed in isolation reduce literature to insignificance. Moral theories developed in isolation cease to be literary theories and become contributions to the social hygiene.

So if we can't blame form, or history, or a certain political or social position for decorative poetry, whom can we blame? I suggest that we blame criticism, so long as we're careful not to blame critics, for we still live, as Randall Jarrell told us back in the fifties, in the age of criticism. An inevitable consequence is that poets expect a critic to stand between the text and the reader.

Moreover, a new atmosphere of interplay between literary theory and poetic practice bears some responsibility. It's not hard to see the American rage for post-structuralist models of reading as furnishing covert manifestos for such poetries of surface as, say, Brad Leithauser's, much in the same way that the last century's social-Darwinist craze informed the naturalist movement in American fiction.

But unfortunately, poets tend to translate theoretical models into recipes for instant production. So post-structuralist theories about engagement with a text have frequently, I think, been misinterpreted by American avant-garde writers as a passport to fashionable literary chaos. Laypeople (like me) probably view a theoretician like Jacques Derrida as engaged in a creatively destructive enterprise—specifically, overturning post-Platonic separations between form and content, word and referent, in order to clear ground for new kinds of work. But in practice, working poets only receive Derrida's complex set of messages filtered obliquely through, say, articles in *The New York Review of Books*. Seldom can poets see past post-structuralism's dense surface of wordplay and a broad edict that the world itself is but text. Derrida's style, then, has probably had more effect than any of his theories, which are virtually indecipherable to most of us. In this

264

way, post-structuralism endorses an over-baroque surface that's heavily allusive and unconcerned with communication.

Furthermore, if the world itself is but text, then—or so some writers mistakenly feel—that text is doomed to be a private one, a hermetic one. Again, the liberating symbolist protest against artistic conformity to social and religious mores has perhaps transformed obscurity from something to be tolerated occasionally in a poem into something required to prove the poet's seriousness. I think of Valéry's remark that symbolist poetry after Baudelaire wanted only to "tease the bourgeois reader with difficulty." Since that injunction, the poet has learned to count on the critic to clarify any message, no matter how deeply buried. Harold Bloom stands at the ready to whisper myth and meaning into the reader's ear, and to justify said reference while scaring the hell out of the average reader with words like *historicize*. Rudolph Arnheim once warned against an art that generated chaotic forms under the guise of reflecting a chaotic world. It's that very chaos that I see in the ascendancy in much decorative poetry.

With a slight nod of culpability to Derrida and de Man, *et al.*, I do not hold deconstruction at fault in the decorative mishmash of contemporary poetry, any more than I would blame modernism for the literary confusion prompted by *The Waste Land*. But a fair measure of a theory's power is its breadth of influence, and a broad influence is doomed, in part, to be a shallow one. Deconstruction has permitted poets to be weak communicators. I'm thinking specifically of the glib meaninglessness in poets like Ashbery and his heirs, the Language Poets. It's ironic, though, that theories invented to collapse distinctions between form and content now provide writers with permission to ignore the referents of words, thereby elevating form to a communicative end in itself. As deconstructionist theories have begun blurrily appearing on our inner TV screens—part of the current *Zietgeist*— poets have begun generating a kind of literary rubble, which cannot be built upon.

I would refute ornamental poetry—represented most obviously by the neo-formalists—on aesthetic, rather than theoretical, political, or social grounds. What I posit, and indeed, what Horace posited back in the first century before Christ, is that poetry should be *dulce et util:* it should be sweet and useful, should delight and instruct; the linguistic and decorative experience of a poem should not outweigh the human or synthetic meanings.

We have collectively bemoaned how poetry's audience has dwindled to a tiny coterie, whose favor poets buy with a kind of literary jewelry. No one was wiser (or more wise-assed) about that shrinking audience than Jarrell, who wrote this forty years before poetry reached the decorative zenith it holds today:

> That the poetry of the first half of this century often *was* too difficult . . . is a truism that it would be absurd to deny. How our poetry got this way—how romanticism was purified and exaggerated and "corrected" into modernism . . . how poet and public stared at each other with righteous indignation, till the poet said, "Since you won't read me, I'll make sure you can't"—is one of the most complicated and interesting of stories.

Complicated the story still is, but I wonder if Jarrell would find the highbrow doily-making that passes for art today interesting. I scarcely do, except in the way that an exorcist might find certain demons interesting.

My opinion of ornament became cemented a few years back when I sat through a partial reading of Merrill's epic *Changing Light at Sandover*. At the crowded reception after, I stood elbow to elbow with some friends—poets and critics whose opinions I respect and who were jubilant about the performance. I asked each in turn what he or she liked in the reading, which parts were moving, because I assumed that I had *missed* something. But their faces remained empty. No one seemed to remember much. Maybe my question seemed too bone-headed to warrant an answer, but no one seized upon an instant or quoted a line to support the consensus that the reading was a smash. Yet here stood, in my opinion, a fairly elite audience. I had heard these friends in the wee hours quote Hopkins by the yard, or rehash the details of Sir Philip Sidney's *Defence of Poetry*. Yet ten minutes after an allegedly brilliant reading, the poems had merely washed past the audience, leaving no traces except for some vague murmurings.

266

I drove home feeling awful, thinking that something terrible had happened to poetry, that a trick had been played on readers, and small wonder that the number of readers continued to decline. Somehow, the poetry that made our pulses race, that could flood us with conviction and alter our lives, had been replaced by fancy decoration, which can only leave us nodding smugly to one another, as if privy to some inside joke.

Nominated by Michael Martone, Kenneth Gangemi, Parnassus: Poetry in Review.

A NOTE ON THE TYPE

fiction by ALEXANDER THEROUX

from THE REVIEW OF CONTEMPORARY FICTION

I

THE TEXT OF THIS BOOK is set in Rubberfab, a typeface designed by W(allace) A(ddison) Doody for the Menlove Linotype Company and first made available in 1949. Rubberfab cannot be classified as either "old style" or "modern." It is not based on any historical mold and hence does not echo any particular period or style of type design. It attempts nothing, in fact, and wisely avoids not only the extreme contrast between thick and thin elements which so drearily cumber the ground of most modern faces but those arresting eccentricities which catch the eye and interfere with reading. In general, Rubberfab is a simple readable typeface that gives a feeling of calm, accessibility, and submission.

W. A. Doody (1901–1953) was born in Provincetown, Massachusetts. In 1919 he moved to the island of Hydra where, forming a consortium of sorts with Paul Doberman, of horticultural fame, he built a solid reputation under the name of P. Thorne (vegetable homonyms being quite in vogue in those days) as a designer of floral handbags and of course as a calligrapher. He began an association with the Menlove Linotype Company in 1929 and over the next fourteen years, characterized as they were by both artistic and personal turmoil, nevertheless designed a number of book types of which Groines, Leatherdale, and Eggball, since widely used, name but a few. In 1944, Doody became interested in basket design, coincident with his falling out with

268

Doberman, and through the years made many important contributions to the art before being finally committed in 1948 to an institution in Coldpencil, England.

II

Hemstitched by the late Ruth Diamondstein is number 22 in the Mistermiss Series. The volume was designed and printed at the Bilitis Press in Winpisinger, N.J., in October 1963. The paper is Nutpulp "Estonian" Etching; the text is set in ten point Cloister Bold with Troy initials, both selected and arranged by Alalia Bundles which, along with her frontispiece, designed especially for the book, were printed with the kind permission of the Framingham State Prison on handmade "Milkwhistle." The binding, silk Chinese bookcloth over boards, is by Frederica Schaefer Comb who although come late to the project has since been generally recognized, along with Misses Bundles and Diamondstein, as cofounder of the Mistermiss Foundation for Creative Women in Crowborough, Vt., the abrupt dissolution of which was necessitated by a trial too celebrated to warrant review here.

This first edition is limited to 210 copies, only 91 of which, before tragedy struck, got to be signed by Ms. Diamondstein, and contains her last fatal poem, "O Radclyffe, O Hall! To F.S.C.," upon the publication of which was irretrievably lost to us an important American poet.

III

This book was set on the linotype in Shellcracker, a recutting made directly from the type cast from matrices designed by the misunderstood Czech punch-cutter, Anton Glumicich, sometime between 1660 and 1687, the year of his suicide, and first discovered in specimen sheets at Prague, then popularized by H. W. Mudgett (1839–1891) of the house of Rummery and Wegle, late of Charing Cross, by the pump, which took credit for the mold while he lived out in anonymity his last thankless years. It is an obstinate face, respelling perhaps in its too dimpled characteristics the period interest in flourish, but was nevertheless a popular one, as witness that for years it was used as the type design for the works of the twin Victorians, Lover and Lever, as well as in the logo for Pincavage Cigars.

Mudgett's was a melancholy life. He traveled, it seems, to no consequence. There were lost years. His work on Glumicich, rendering others obsolete, might have been his own biography. He visited Cincinnati, Ohio, in 1862—this we do know—and married the wealthy American widow Marion Umpelby, who with her daughter, Lalage, removed with him to the Outer Hebrides where he enjoyed that single fertile year to which can be traced several of his more successful, if controversial, typefaces, notably Forsakenness, Spoot, Deathshead, and the slightly overconsidered Roman Gondrazek which perhaps purchased more of his time than his enthusiasm, for soon after he began to suffer from Thought and taking a morbid (and decidedly unreciprocated) interest in Lalage who was by then famous at the Haymarket under the stage-name "La Sprezzatura" brained his wife the same night he took pyromaniacal revenge on his stepdaughter—ironically, with a Pincavage panatela—yelling "Theatre!" according to report, in the midst of the very fire that took their lives.

Nominated by The Review of Contemporary Fiction

VESPERS: PAROUSIA

by LOUISE GLÜCK

from TIKKUN

Love of my life, you
are lost and I am
young again.

A few years pass.
The air fills
with girlish music;
in the front yard
the apple tree is
studded with blossoms.

I try to win you back,
that is the point
of the writing.
But you are gone forever,
as in Russian novels, saying
a few words I don't remember—

How lush the world is,
how full of things that don't belong to me—

I watch the blossoms shatter,
no longer pink,
but old, old, a yellowish white—
the petals seem

to float on the bright grass,
fluttering slightly.

What a nothing you were,
to be changed so quickly
into an image, an odor—
you are everywhere, source
of wisdom and anguish.

Nominated by Henri Cole

GRID

by MARK JARMAN

from POETRY NORTHWEST

I walk those streets tonight, streets named for gems
And streets that cross them named for Spanish women.
The gem streets end at the ocean, looking out.
Each woman wears a string of them and ends
With nothing on the edge of town. They are
Juanita, Inez, Maria, Lucia, Elena.
Their jewels are Opal, Emerald, Carnelian,
Topaz, Sapphire, Pearl, Ruby, Diamond.
I'm never sure I've named them all or walked
Along them all. Some are like boulevards.
Those are the gem streets. Some little more than lanes—
Those are the women. Yet I have searched for Opal
Among dead ends and alleys and discovered it
Dangling from Maria's wrist, or Juanita's.
All the life I care about, or almost all,
Lived first along these streets. That life is gone.
And when I say, "I walk those streets tonight,"
It's only poetry. I, too, am gone.
The streets maintain their urban grid, their limits.
The gem streets end at the ocean, the blank Pacific.
And the ones that wear them, named for Spanish women,
Themselves end on the edge of town with nothing.

Nominated by David Jauss, Henry Carlile, Greg Pape, Joe Ashby Porter

BORDER WATER

by GRETCHEN LEGLER

from UNCOMMON WATERS (Seal Press)

CRAIG AND I are on our way to the Rainy River to fish for spring walleyes. The Rainy is a great, wide, slow-moving river that runs from east to west, through forests and farms, at the top of Minnesota, separating the state from Canada. Because it is a border water, you can fish the river in early April, after the ice has gone out, a full month before you can fish inland waters.

"It's hard to imagine," Craig says, as we drive along the Minnesota side of the river, looking across at the brown grass and farms on the opposite bank, "that just over there is another country." On both sides of the river there are brown grass and trees and red barns and silver silos. It looks the same. Over there, Canada, rust-colored grass and trees. Over here, Minnesota, rust-colored grass and trees. It *is* hard to imagine. But it is a different country; a place boys rowed across to in rickety boats to avoid being sent to Vietnam. It is beautiful and open and wild along the river. Behind the trees on the Canadian side there is a railroad track, and occasionally a freight train roars by with the speed trains pick up only in the country.

We have purchased Canadian fishing licenses so that we can fish both sides of the river. We have also purchased three dozen minnows and salted them down. You can use Minnesota minnows on the Canadian side as long as they are dead. If you want to use live minnows on the Canadian side, you must buy them in Canada. But you can't cross the border checkpoint at International Falls or Baudette with live minnows, so, if you want to fish

274

legally with live minnows on the Canadian side, you must launch
your boat in Canada, which means you must patronize the Canadian resorts, of which there are none on this stretch of the Rainy.

As Craig drives, I read the fishing regulations. I turn to the
fish consumption advisory. It says that on the Rainy River between International Falls and Lake of the Woods no one should
eat more than one fish meal per month of any size of any species
caught there, especially if you are pregnant or plan to be, ever,
or are nursing, or plan to ever, or if you are less than ten years
old. For years the Boise Cascade paper mill at International Falls
has dumped dioxin, mercury and other poisons into the river.
The large fish in the river taste slightly metallic. Two decades
ago, the river was a slime pit of stinking paper pulp, great pods of
which would burp open on the water and emit putrid gas. Now,
at least, old-timers say, the visible pollution is gone, the water is
clear and there are fish here again.

"Why are we coming here if all we're doing is poisoning ourselves?" I ask Craig. But, I know why, of course. We are going to
be out on the first open water of the season and to fish. That
means sitting still and thinking and maybe reading if I get bored,
talking quietly about important things, watching the sky, seeing
an eagle fly over, a few mallards whiz upriver, the brown grass on
the bank, the current bringing big sticks past.

Craig says, "Why doesn't someone sue Boise Cascade's ass? I
don't know how they can get away with polluting like that."

This is a trip Craig and I have taken for four years in a row.
"These traditional things are important," he says. "It's important
to have a history of experience together."

His eyes are on the road, and I watch his profile: a sharp
forehead and nose, cheeks, eyes and lips framed by a closely
trimmed gray-black beard, and a sloppy, sweat-stained gray Stet-
son. He looks very young to me, and slightly naive; like a Boy
Scout still. I agree with him about the importance of ritual. We
fish rainbow trout in the fall at Benjamin Lake for two weekends.
We walk the logging trails around Blackduck for grouse. Then
there is the season for ducks and geese near Thief Lake. Then we
hunt deer in the woods of northern Minnesota to fill our freezer
for the winter. When it snows we ski, and when the lakes freeze
we fish through the ice for crappies. In the spring comes the

275

Rainy River, then walking in the woods for morel mushrooms, then summer walleye fishing on big, smooth lakes. Our year together is spent in these ways. It is what we do.

But I am uneasy about the trip to the Rainy this time. For one thing, it is always difficult, physically demanding. To load and unload a boat, walk up and down the steep, slippery hill from the river to camp in heavy boots, all is wearing on my body. I get tired. I worry that I am becoming soft and weak. The weather is always unpredictable. One year as Craig and I bobbed in the current, jerking our minnow-baited jigs up and down, snow fell and ice chunks floated past us. Another year it was so warm we fished in shirtsleeves. This year the weather is in the middle. Sunny but cold. But still there is the physical work of it. Hauling. Endless hauling.

But I know my unease has less to do with this, and more to do with the first year we came here. The fishing was so good that year that the river was a solid mass of boats, gunnel to gunnel, bow touching bow, stern to bow, stern to stern. It was sunny, and everyone was having a wonderful time, lifting huge fish from the muddy water, smiling, laughing, weighing the fish, some putting the big ones back, but others keeping stringers of seven-pound fish, whole stringers of fish that would not even taste good, fish that would taste like metal.

At the boat ramp, men milled around, laughing and smoking cigarettes and drinking beer and pop. They were drunken, overloaded, dangerous. The wives and girlfriends of the fishermen stood with poodles on leashes, holding children by the hand, taking pictures of the great catches of fish. The fish-cleaning house was packed, and there was a line outside. The garbage cans in the fish house were overflowing with guts and the orange eggs of the huge spawning female walleyes. Fish heads with shining black eyes flowed out onto the ground. Flies buzzed around. It was a carnival of greed. Hundreds of people appropriating walleye flesh as if it were a right.

I was as giddy as all the rest with our success. Every cast brought in another huge green and gold fish, tugging at my line, twisting and spinning in the water, curved gracefully in the landing net, all muscle. We didn't keep them all, only the small ones. And we only kept our limit; twelve. But we were there.

We camp this year, as always, at Franz Jevne State Park on the river. It is not much of a park: a few dirt pullouts and two outhouses. The roads are winding and muddy, and the park is dark. Our small camp is in the middle of tall evergreens. I feel vaguely gloomy. Surrounded. It is dim and cool, early evening, and the men around us in other camps are lighting lanterns, starting campfires, firing up cooking stoves. I smell fish and onions and wood smoke. I see shadows moving behind the canvas walls of tents. I hear muffled, rough voices. I am the only woman here.

In the women's outhouse I sit down to pee and look at the wall in front of me. There is a crude drawing in thick black marker of a woman's vulva, a hairless mound, lips open wide, folds of flesh deep inside. The rest of the body is absent. There is no head, no face, no eyes, no mouth, no arms or legs. Just this one piece, open and dripping, as if it were cut off with a cleaver and set apart. I imagine it wrapped up in white butcher paper, the kind we'll use to wrap the walleye we catch here. "I want to fill your pussy with a lode of hot come," the writing above this picture says. Cold air is blowing up from the pit below me, hitting my warm skin. My muscles shrink. On another wall is an erect penis, huge and hairless, drawn in the same black marker. The head on the penis looks to me strangely like the head of a walleye with its gills spread wide. There is no body attached to the penis either, just a straight vertical line from which the organ springs. "I want to fuck your wet pussy. Let's meet" is scrawled next to it.

I am suddenly terrified and sickened. I hear a threat: I want to rape you; I want to dissect you. I can't pee anymore. The muscles of my stomach and thighs have pulled into themselves protectively, huddling. Between my legs now feels like a faraway cold world, not a part of me. I yank up my long underwear and wool pants, getting shirttails tucked into the wrong places, and leave with my zipper still down, happy to be outside. As I walk back to our camp I look over my shoulder and left and right into the woods. I wonder if it was that man, or that one, or that one, who wrote this violence on the wall. I am out of breath and still afraid when I tell Craig all of this. I tell him it makes me want to run and it freezes me in place. My voice is wavering. He tells me it is in the men's outhouse, too: a picture of another naked, dripping vulva and the words, "This is my girlfriend's pussy." I ask

Craig, "How would you feel if in the men's john a woman had written 'I want to cut your dick off' or 'This is my boyfriend's cock'?" I want to know if this would scare him, too. He says, "I'd watch out."

We are anchored in the current, our jigs bouncing on the bottom of the river. The river is wide and powerful and brown. It smells like cold steel. Craig wonders aloud why in all this water the poison and its smell do not dissipate. We are not catching many fish, but some. Crowded around us are men in boats. This is a good spot, on the Canadian side of the river, and the boats push together here. There are no other women on the water. Only men with other men. Some are drinking Diet Coke and munching on crackers as they wait for fish to bite. Others are swigging beer, cracking jokes, laughing. Cigar and cigarette smoke wafts up into the air. I feel as if Craig and I are being watched. A man and a woman in a boat. We watch ourselves being watched. Craig feels this, too. He says, "All these guys are out here to get away from their wives."

One of Craig's newspaper colleagues asked him once, in a voice that pleaded with Craig to come clean, to tell the truth, to join the club, "Do you really enjoy fishing with your wife?" Every time Craig remembers this he laughs. He repeats it sometimes when we are making love in the tall grass beside a trout stream, or when we are stretched out naked together under the covers in our van. He leans over now and asks, smiling, "Do you really think I can have any fun fishing with my wife?"

We are dressed in heavy wool pants and sweaters and big felt-lined boots. Craig asks me, when I am dressed up like this, if I think anyone can tell I am a woman. The sweater and down jacket hide my breasts. My long blonde hair is under a hat, my face is buried in wool, no one can see my earrings. What would be the thing that would make them know I was not a man among men? What is the line I would have to cross for them to know surely that I was different from them?

"Only when I speak," I say. "Or maybe when you lean over in the boat and kiss me. Then maybe they would think I was a woman. But I wouldn't necessarily have to be."

Until recently it never occurred to me to wonder why I was the only woman I ever knew who walked in the woods with a shotgun looking for grouse, or sat in a duck blind or a goose blind, or crouched up in a tree with a rifle waiting for deer, or went fishing on the Rainy River. It never occurred to me to wonder because I never felt alone, before now.

I used to hate being a woman. When I was very young, I believed I was a boy. I raced boxcars made from orange crates, played football with the neighbor boys and let them experiment with my body, the parts of which seemed uninteresting to me and not valuable. I was with them, watching myself in the light in their eyes, looking at me. I was flattered in high school when someone said to me, "I like you. You're just like a guy." The words I liked best to hear were: rangy, tough, smart, cynical. My father made jokes about women's libbers burning bras. I laughed, too. Throughout college I never knew what it was like to touch a woman, to kiss a woman, to have a woman as a friend. All my friends were men. I am thirty years old now, and I feel alone. I am not a man. Knowing this is like an earthquake. Just now all the lies are starting to unfold. I don't blend in as well or as easily as I used to. I refuse to stay on either side of the line.

In the boat next to ours is a quiet man with a fixed smile who has been catching all the fish. He is over a drop-off, his jig sinking exactly twenty-one feet. That is where the fish are. I ask him where he is from, my voice echoing across the water. He says he is from Warren, Minnesota. I ask him if he knows the boy I read about in the newspaper who got kicked out of West Point and was suing for his right to go back. The boy was his town's pride: a track star, a member of the choir, an honor student, handsome, full of promise. At West Point, too, he was full of promise. With his beautiful voice, he sang solo at the White House for the President. Then, on a tip from one of the boy's high school chums, the military started digging around in his past. Before they found out what he knew they would, he came forward and told them the truth. "I'm gay, sir," he told his commanding officer.

The man in the boat from Warren pushes his baseball cap back on his head and squints at the sun. He says to me, across the water, "I knew that boy really well. He was a model for the community. A model for all the younger kids." He is shaking his head. "It's hard to figure out," he says. "Just so darned hard to figure out why he'd go and do such a thing and ruin his future like that."

"I hope he wins his case against West Point," I say. There is more I ache to add. I want to yell across to him, "What's to figure out? He loves men." But, I say no more and turn away, ashamed of my silence. As I turn away, the man from Warren is still shaking his head. "It's just so hard to figure out."

Craig and I came to the Rainy partly to meet and fish with some old friends of mine, Kevin and Brad, whom I met while reporting for the *Grand Forks Herald* in North Dakota. Kevin and Brad have brought their friend John with them. John is the fishing columnist for the paper and also a professor of English. He is originally from Mississippi.

Around the campfire at night, Kevin tells us about his latest assignment. He is organizing a special section on wolves. The people of Roseau, Minnesota, believe they have a wolf problem and want the Minnesota Department of Natural Resources to get rid of some of the animals.

John is slouched by the fire with his feet straight out, taking long drinks from a bottle of root beer schnapps. Brad and Craig are standing, their hands in their pockets, looking down at the flames and coals. Kevin puts a wad of chewing tobacco behind his lower lip. I squat by the fire, hunched over a mug of tea. John passes me the bottle of schnapps, and I hesitate. For me to drink from it would be to mimic his gesture, to join in, but I am so curious to taste it. I take a small sip and make a face.

Kevin says, "Farmers think the wolf pack is purposely underestimated."

Craig asks, "You mean the government is lying about how many wolves there are so the farmers don't get upset?"

"It's more than the wolf they want to kill," I say. "It's what the wolf represents."

"What's that?" Brad says.

"Lust," I say. They laugh.

"They want control," Craig says. "They want control over nature. That's what management is all about. It's for us, not the animals. Just like with this river." Craig waves his hand toward the dark water.

"It stinks," Brad says.

"Literally," Kevin says.

"Buffalo shit," John says.

We all look at him and wait.

"Do ya'll know how much the rivers were polluted by buffalo shit? Millions of buffalo shitting in the rivers back before the white man came and after?" He's not laughing.

"Why, our screwing up the earth and killing animals, it's as natural as buffalo shit," he says. "We're part of nature, too, hell. If you fuck around with nature—try to clean up the river, protect the wolves—you'll upset the whole balance of time and evolution. Just leave things be."

There is a long, uncomfortable silence. Then Craig says, "The world has had millions of years to get used to buffalo shit. But no matter how much buffalo dung there is in a river, it still will never be as bad as dioxin."

The next day, Sunday, is the day we leave. Craig and I fish from early morning until noon. When it comes time to load the boat and return to St. Paul, one of us has to get out on shore and drive the car to the boat landing. And one of us has to take the boat by water. I want to go by water, to go fast and have the spray fly up around me and the front of the boat rise out of the river.

Craig says, "You take the boat." This is what I want to do, but I am afraid.

"Really?" I ask him. "Really, I can drive it down?" I expect not to be trusted.

"What about rocks?" I ask.

"Watch out for them," he says, very casually. He has no second thoughts. He does not understand my timidity.

Once, in the spring, a friend and I sat on the steps of Lind Hall at the University of Minnesota and watched a group of boys playing on their skateboards, jumping high in the air, knees pulled up, big, orange high-tops hovering off the ground, their skateboards flipping under them, over and over. Then the boys would land safely. Then, there they would go again, taking a running leap onto a cement bench, turning on top of it and coming off again. Graceful and noisy. My friend said, "Guys are brought up to think they can do everything."

I think of this as I pull away from the shore, waving at Craig. I think of my brothers, Austin and Edward, who climb cliffs and fly airplanes. Many women, I think, grow up believing they can't do anything. One of the tasks I believe I never will be able to do is backing the trailer into the water to load or launch the boat. I have tried and nearly every time have ruined something: cranked the trailer around to dangerous angles, smashed a tail-light, backed off the edge of the boat ramp, put the van in reverse instead of forward and driven it to the top of the wheel-wells into the water. I know that I can learn to do this physical, mechanical task. What I regret is that I do not simply *assume* I can do it. I wish I could launch into it without reserve, full of confidence, free of doubt. Like a man might.

I have learned from Craig that it is not only gender that makes for my insecurity. When we put the boat in at the Rainy River, Craig is always nervous. He believes he is being watched and judged. But, unlike me, he is protected from ridicule. When we bought the van, it came with a bumper sticker, left there by its previous owner. It says, "Vietnam Veterans of America." Craig believes this sticker gives him certain privileges and encourages respect in parking lots and at boat ramps. It prevents laughter. I often think he wishes he had earned this bumper sticker rather than bought it. He was training to be a Navy pilot when the war ended and he was sent home. Sometimes when he meets a man his age and picks up a hint or clue, he asks him, shyly, "Were you in Nam?" Sometimes they say yes and ask him if he was, and he says, almost apologetically, "No. Almost."

I drive the boat down the river, watching out for rocks. I must not hit any rocks. If I hit rocks, I will have failed. I see rocks ahead, but also a spot that looks deep. I go for what I think is the deepest water. Spray comes over the bow and sides. I am bob-bing along, zooming, my hair flying out behind me, the shore whizzing past. I am doing it all by myself. My image of my self and my self come together here. I am perfect.

Then the prop grinds against submerged rocks, the motor tilts forward and drags across them, gouging the propeller, ripping the metal as easily as cloth. I crush my teeth against one another. Again, the motor tilts forward, the engine rises in pitch and there is a grating and a crunching. Again and again this happens. I can-not see the rocks. I can't see one rock, I have no idea where they are. I feel defeated. I make it to shore, where men line the banks, and park, hitting one last rock. I pull up the motor to see the damage I have done: the prop is frayed, white paint long gone, twisted silver in its place.

I have fucked up. I never should have been trusted with this boat. I despise myself. It is not my place to drive a boat. It is too big a thing for me. Too dangerous, too demanding. Craig arrives at the boat landing. I start to cry. He says, "Don't cry. Don't cry. Don't cry. We needed a new prop anyway." I expect him to be angry. Instead Craig says, "You need to learn to do this. We should have you practice. You should always drive the boat and back up the trailer, light the stove and the lantern."

I always expect anger and sometimes feel cheated and lost when I don't get it. I expect anger now, with Craig, because that is what I learned to expect from my father. That is the way my father would have reacted if I had failed in this way in front of him.

I learned many early lessons from my father and have carried them with me into womanhood. For my father there is no middle ground between success and complete failure. I learned from him to expect and strive for perfection and to truly trust no one but myself. "If you want it done right, do it yourself," he always said. For my scientist father the world of nature, the world of personal relations and desire, the world of chance and fate, resembles a machine of sorts. Oil it, clean it, take care of it and it will run for you; you can prevent any problem from occurring. As long as you know a thing thoroughly, as long as you have control over it, as long as you command it, it can never surprise you. All of this I learned as a child, each lesson hardening into a code I would adhere to, mostly unwittingly, much of my adult life. Craig is not like my father. Instead of anger from him I get the opposite—laughter!

It has become tradition with us that while Craig puts the cover on the boat, tucks the life jackets away, winds up the stringer, I clean the fish. I take our collection of walleyes to the fish house and see that inside the screen door five men are working, slicing open the walleyes with long fillet knives, talking about their fishing day. "Is there room for another person in there?" I ask. I ask this because they are watching me stand outside the door, stringer in hand, wondering with their eyes what I am doing here. I feel unnatural and self-conscious. Perhaps they think of their own wives, or kids, at home and wonder why I am not there, too. One man, the oldest, the one with gray hair and pink

283

ears, says, "It's kind of cozy in here." I say that I will wait. I am waiting, watching them slice through the fish, peeling off an entire side of the body, then slipping the knife between the skin and the white flesh and separating the two with one or two strokes. It is remarkable to me how easy it is to slice apart a walleye—carving a breathing thing down to two essential fillets that bear no resemblance to the fish alive. The only way for me to do this is to ignore that what I've got is a fish, something that hours ago was swimming, alive. From behind me comes a man with a stringer of fish he can barely hold up. He barrels around me, steps into the fish house and throws his fish on the counter. He is in. I am still outside.

I pick up my fish and march away. Craig sees me.

"Wouldn't they let you in?"

I say, "There's no room for a goddamned girl in that fish house."

I throw down the stringer, the knife, the cutting board, the jug of water, the plastic bags and my orange cleaning tub, fall to my knees on the ground and start slashing at my fish. One, two, three. One, two, three. Three strokes and the fillet comes off clean and smooth. I am angry. I am saying to myself, "I can do this better than any of those bastards. Better than any of them." I feel defiant and confident, proud and suddenly cruel. When I do this, I realize, I am leaping across the line between the fish's life and mine, across lines that divide life into death. And I can do it as well as any. I can move as easily as anyone across this space.

Craig wants to take a new route home. I would never dare. I would simply take the freeway, the safe and easy route. He chooses a curving line that runs through the Nett Lake Indian Reservation. We wind, bump and take twice as long, but Craig likes these roads where you cannot see where you are going. There is one right angle after another.

I am exhausted and sad, but feel safe again. "I should give up and stay home," I say. "The worse it gets the more I see I don't have a place out here." I am looking out the window at the forest bumping past, thinking of the river, the outhouse, the fish house.

Around a sharp corner, a white and brown blur rises from the middle of the road. We see a hawk with a mouse in its claws, a wisp of a tail, four tiny feet hanging down, a little package being

284

carried head forward into the sky by a graceful flapping bird that goes up and up and up and over the tops of the pines. Craig slows down and we both duck our heads and peer out the windows so that we can watch the hawk until it disappears.

Craig sees that I am crying. He asks me, "What are you afraid of?"

"I am tired and afraid of being the only woman. I am so lonely," I say.

He is quiet.

"I'm afraid of the killing," I say. "I'm afraid that I wouldn't know how to live and not murder." I wipe my nose with the sleeve of my sweater. "The line is so thin," I say. "I'm afraid there is no difference between me and them."

Craig is quiet again for a long time and then says to me, "You know, if you don't take your place, then you'll lose it."

"I'm not sure I want it," I say. "Not here. Not like this. Not this place." In truth, *I am not sure.* Not sure at all. But there has to be a space for me; space for me as a woman out here. There has to be a middle ground. A space between the borderlines. A space where we can all learn to be and live and not murder.

Nominated by Seal Press

285

FOUR STORIES

fiction by LYDIA DAVIS

from CONJUNCTIONS

THE ACTORS

IN OUR TOWN there is an actor, H.—a tall, bold, feverish sort of man—who easily fills the theater when he plays Othello, and about whom the women here become very excited. He is handsome enough compared to the other men, though his nose is somewhat thick and his torso rather short for his height. His acting is stiff and inflexible, his gestures obviously memorized and mechanical, and yet his voice is strong enough to make one forget all that. On the nights when he is unable to leave his bed because of illness or intoxication—and this happens more often than one would imagine—the part is taken by J., his understudy. Now J. is pale and small, completely unsuitable for the part of the Moor; his legs tremble as he comes on stage and faces the many empty seats. His voice hardly carries beyond the first few rows, and his small hands flap uselessly in the smoky air. We feel only pity and irritation as we watch him, and yet by the end of the play we find ourselves unaccountably moved, as though he had managed to convey something timid or sad in Othello's nature. But the mannerisms and skill of H. and J.—which we analyze minutely when we visit together in the afternoons and continue to contemplate even once we are alone after dinner—seem suddenly insignificant when the great Sparr comes down from the city and gives us a real performance of Othello. Then we are so carried away, so exhausted with emotion, that it is impossible to speak of what we feel. We are almost grateful when he is gone

286

and we are left with H. and J., imperfect as they are, for they are familiar to us and comfortable, like our own people.

TRYING TO LEARN

I am trying to learn that this playful man who teases me is the same as that serious man talking money to me so seriously he does not even see me anymore and that patient man offering me advice in times of trouble and that angry man slamming the door as he leaves the house. I have often wanted the playful man to be more serious, and the serious man to be less serious, and the patient man to be more playful. As for the angry man, he is a stranger to me and I do not feel it is wrong to hate him. Now I am learning that if I say bitter words to the angry man as he leaves the house, I am at the same time wounding the others, the ones I do not want to wound, the playful man teasing, the serious man talking money, and the patient man offering advice. Yet I look at the patient man, for instance, whom I would want above all to protect from such bitter words as mine, and though I tell myself he is the same man as the others, I can only believe I said those words, not to him, but to another, my enemy, who deserved all my anger.

THERAPISTS

A friend of mine goes with her three-year-old girl to a family therapist. This therapist has guided her in her troubles with the child's bed-wetting, fear of the dark, and dependence on the bottle. One by one these problems are solved. The mother, acting on the advice of the therapist, is careful to avoid attempting to solve more than one problem at a time. The child is unhappy and nervous and holds her body in a cramped position, as though protecting herself. Her mother is also nervous, and is never still: her hands flutter and her eyebrows fly up into her forehead. There is a dark brown mole on her cheek, and this dark point is the only color in her face.

Another friend calls her husband's therapist and tells him she is going to ask her husband to move out. Naturally, the therapist

287

has to report this to his patient. The husband is hurt and indignant. My friend is adamant. Her own therapist thinks she must now be under great pressure from her husband, and this is true. Encouraged by her therapist, however, she persists in asking her husband to leave. At last he does. He now sees his children in his own apartment several times a week, including all day Sunday. Insulted by his wife's behavior, he tries to complain only to his therapist, as his therapist has advised, but he cannot help complaining to everyone—his therapist, his friends, his lawyer, his wife, and even his children. The older boy comes home angry at his mother because he does not know what is the truth anymore. He breaks two of the dining-room chairs. His mother, a frail and small woman, sits on him for several hours before he is calm enough to tell her what he is feeling.

WHAT I FEEL

These days I try to tell myself that what I feel is not very important. I've read this in several books now: that what I feel is important but not the center of everything. Maybe I do believe this, but not enough to act on it. I would like to believe it more deeply.

What a relief that would be. I wouldn't have to think about what I felt all the time, and try to control it, with all its complications and all its consequences. I wouldn't have to try to feel better all the time. In fact, if I didn't believe what I felt was so important, I probably wouldn't even feel so bad, and it wouldn't be so hard to feel better. I wouldn't have to say, Oh I feel so awful, this is like the end for me here, in this dark living-room late at night, with the dark street outside under the streetlamps, I am so very alone, everyone else in the house asleep, there is no comfort anywhere, just me alone down here, I will never calm myself enough to sleep, never sleep, never be able to go on to the next day, I can't possibly go on, I can't live, even through the next minute.

If I didn't believe what I felt was the center of everything, then it wouldn't be the center of everything, but just something off to the side, one of many things, and I would be able to see

288

and pay attention to those other things that are equally important, and in this way I would have some relief.

But it is curious how you can believe an idea is absolutely true
and correct and yet not believe it deeply enough to act on it. So
I still act as though my feelings were the center of everything,
and they still cause me to end up alone by the livingroom window
late at night. What is different now is that I have this idea: I have
the idea that soon I will no longer believe that my feelings are
the center of everything. This is a comfort to me, because if you
despair of going on, but at the same time tell yourself that what
you feel may not be very important, then either you may no
longer despair of going on, or you may still despair of going on
but not quite believe it anymore.

Nominated by Sigrid Nunez

OH, BY THE WAY

by ED OCHESTER

from PLOUGHSHARES

My friend April Fallon tells me
that blood on the exterior of the brain
is cooler than that in the interior
and that it's in the cooler blood
that dreams reside.
What do you think?
Do you love the head as much as I do?
That calcareous shell, the stoniest part
of the body. And the stone
within the skull, the maker of imperatives,
of absolutes, that directed the trains
to the death camps. The brain
has no nerves to feel pain,
that stone that gave assent
to the show trials—that Stalinist part
of the body—and the saturation bombings,
Cambodia, Dresden, you name them.
What do you think?
The overexamined life isn't worth living.
That veil of cool blood
where dreams reside: there even now
an old scholar rests his eyes
behind his hands; the farmer exerts
the requisite pressure on the cow's teats
for milk, in that pastoral memory;
the old woman wracked by pertussis

will be saved from her poverty.
Thin cool veil of blood.
What do you think?
I have to stop writing about love.
I have to stop making sense.
Cool veil of blood, old dreams:
Jeffords pushed against the bronze
school doors, red stain on white shirt,
kid with the knife:
"motherfuckin motherfucker"
(deconstruct that);
the child whispering, "Help me help me."
O thin veil of blood
where dreams reside
cool veil of blood

Nominated by Arthur Smith, Ploughshares

MY FATHER'S BODY

by WILLIAM MATTHEWS

from THE GETTYSBURG REVIEW

First they take it away,
for now it belongs to the state.
Then they open it
to see what may have killed it,
and it had arteriosclerosis
in its heart, for this was an inside job.
Now someone must identify it
so that the state may have a name
for what it will give away,
and the funeral people come in a stark car
shaped like a coffin with a hood
and take it away,
for now it belongs to the funeral people
and its family buys it back,
though it lies in a box at the crematorium
while the mourners travel and convene.
Then they bring it to the chapel, as they call it,
of the crematorium and it lies in its box
while the mourners enter and sit
and stare at the box, for the box
lies on a pedestal where the altar would be
if this were a chapel.
A rectangular frame with curtains at the sides
rises from the pedestal,
so that the box seems to fill a small stage,
and the stage gives off the familiar

illusion of being a box with one wall torn away
so that we may see into it,
but it's filled with a box we can't see into.
There's music on tape and a man in a robe
speaks for a while and I speak
for a while and then there's a prayer
and then we mourners can hear the whir
of a small motor and curtains slide
across the stage. At least for today,
I think, this is the stage that all the world is,
and another motor hums on
and we mourners realize that behind
the curtains the body is being lowered,
not like Don Giovanni to the flames
but without flourish or song
or the comforts of elaborate plot,
to the basement of the crematorium,
to the mercies of the gas jets
and the balm of the conveyor belt.
The ashes will be scattered,
says a hushed man in a mute suit,
in the Garden of Remembrance,
which is out back.
And what's left of a mild, democratic man
will sift in a heap with the residue of others,
for now they all belong to time.

Nominated by Robert Wrigley, Richard Jackson

ACTS OF KINDNESS

fiction by MARY MICHAEL WAGNER

from ZYZZYVA

Iᴛ's ᴛʜᴇ ᴅᴀʏ after payday, and all over the city people are over-dosing. Our calls have all been people celebrating. After a drop at Mount Zion, we drive up to the crest of Pacific Heights, and pull over at Vallejo and Divisadero, to look at the small patch of bay with its sailboats.

We're there five minutes, when we get a Code Three about a guy down and maybe not breathing. I'm driving, so Simon picks up the handset. As he reaches across the front seat, I notice his bare wrist, where his shirt cuff raises up. He presses his lips against the small holes of the microphone, scribbling information down on the clipboard. Another heroin overdose; we both groan. Simon drains the coffee from his Styrofoam cup, and jokes with me. The way he makes me laugh, taking the edge off things, makes me grateful. We've been on 24-hour shifts, Tuesdays and Thursdays, for six months now, and we feel like next-door neigh-bors who talk over a backyard fence and who borrow candles from each other when the electricity goes out.

I flip on the lights and siren, and we're driving, dipping low and easy through intersections. Simon's feet in dark-colored bucks are up on the dashboard. He offers me a raisin from his bran muffin, playfully wedging it between my front teeth. There is heat from his finger tips and the smell of rubbing alcohol.

When we arrive, I'm in charge of the call. Fire is already there, the lights blinking on their truck, people from the project milling around waiting to see what might be carried out. I sling

294

my bag with supplies over my shoulder, and Simon grabs the oxygen. It's a small apartment, the furniture is new-looking, grainy imitation wood. There's a nice stereo and TV and a black snake in a terrarium twined around a dry white branch. The firemen, all looking big like lumberjacks to me, are circled around the guy, who is laid out on the floor. One of them is already pumping O2 into him. I watch the guy's stomach fill with it. He's young and his shirt is pulled up. His stomach is yellowy brown and so smooth that for a second I want to touch it. The fireman with the bag-valve-mask says he was barely breathing when they got there. I feel the adrenaline in my spine and then the guy becomes a body to me, a responsibility. I kneel down and check his pulse. It is far away, reedy. His arms are clammy. Heroin is easy though, an injection of Narcan can bring practically anybody back, no matter how far away they've gone. I stab the guy twice in the upper arm with two different syringes. After a minute, he juts up, yanks off the mask, and yells, "What the fuck are you people doing in my house?"

After we drop him at General, we call back in and then drive up to Bernal Heights. Simon's laugh is machine-gunny, but soft. His Kentucky accent is all over the front of the ambulance, so that I can barely drive. The way he talks makes him seem awkward and boyish. The way his trousers, the two pockets in back, dip down low, as if his pants were too big. The way I've wanted to touch him since the first day we drove together.

Things are quiet so I park. I climb into the back and lie down on the gurney; Simon lies down on the couch that runs alongside. The aisle between us is narrow and dark. The coiled nasal canulas look eerie and reptilian above us. He tells me a ghost story he heard growing up, about the woman with the golden arm. His voice is mock-ghoulish. "Give meee back my arm. Give meee back my arm." He claws at my forearms, raising the hair there. Then he is quiet. He climbs off the couch, leans over me, picks up my arm. He feels for my radial pulse. "Bounding," he reports, "Uh oh, we've lost her pulse, cardiac arrest." He leans over to give me mouth-to-mouth. His face hovers close to mine, hesitating. His breath smells of coffee and Certs. We've played this game before, but always pulled back, so that now we both seem startled when Simon puts his mouth on mine. We both forget to breathe. I pull him down onto me. I want him to get all the way on top of me, so I can feel his whole body against mine, but he says he needs to call in and check with Central about something. The heat of his body goes away. I hear him joking with the dispatcher as I fall asleep on the gurney. Outside the tinted windows it becomes night and the electric buses make sucking sounds like the noises old men, sitting on crates, make with their teeth when I walk by in running shorts. When we have a call, he nudges me awake, his fingers shy and tentative under my shoulder.

We get off work at four in the morning. It is still dark. Simon looks haggard, driving us in his truck. We go home to my apartment. I tell him I live on a musical street. Next door is an opera singer, a couple of houses up, a trumpeter, on the other side of the street, a piano player. I tell him I go sit on the stoop of the piano player. I imagine that it is a woman and that she never stops her music, for whenever I go at night to listen, she is always playing. I sit on her cement stoop and can hear her clearly behind draped windows on the second floor.

When we get to my apartment, the opera singer is practicing. For once, I'm grateful for her rudeness, her weird hours. I open the Venetian blinds. We lie down in the small square of moon on the carpet, pulling blankets from the bed over us. The woman's voice is solemn and full. She is singing Puccini.

Simon touches my face. I think about what I've seen him do with those hands, patting arms of people who are wide-eyed afraid, maybe even dying. How those hands have brought back to life a kid who drowned in a country club pool. I feel floating and happy and want to say all the clichés I know. I want Simon to say my name over and over, as if we were in some dark place and he could only find me by calling. But as he squeezes my body, the dreaminess goes away. His tongue makes me so I can't think or protect myself. I thrash against him like a tide.

When we are finished and have kicked the blankets away, Simon whispers that he's been lonely. He whispers it like it's something to be ashamed of, like it's something he's never told anyone but me.

I wake up on the floor with Simon's legs entangled with mine. I move away and sit on my bed. I put on silk undershorts and smooth oil onto my legs, lifting my knees up to my chest. I know

296

that he is awake and watching me through the slit his arm makes over his face. I feel ashamed, so I want to overpower him in some way. Maybe I want him to fall in love with me. He pretends he's just waking up.

We have to be on shift again at four the next morning, so we spend the day together. We go see an old Fred Astaire and Ginger Rogers movie at the Castro. I don't pay attention. I think about going back to Kentucky with him. I imagine the South to be like his accent, which is lulling and outdoors-sounding. I think of us living out in the country. We'd have yellow farm equipment, yellow like my brother's Tonka trucks, machines that chew up the land. I would want a tire swing—a barn—a llama. Simon. I would want him to come to bed smelling of dogwood trees and soil and hay.

Blinking out of the movie, into the late afternoon, we laze along Castro Street. I ask him questions just to hear his accent. His voice makes me think of boys with hairless faces and paper routes, boys who play basketball in pocked driveways wearing ragged canvas hightops. I ask him to tell me about home.

He says, "You know more people die of lung cancer in Kentucky than any other state."

"Of course they do," I say, "It's all those coal mines." I think of men with their foreheads sooty like Ash Wednesday, unstrapping hats with small round lights on them.

He laughs, "No, it's the tobacco, it's the biggest crop. Everybody smokes."

I do not want to believe this. I think of Kentucky as hills and hills of impossible color, bluegrass, where people drink iced tea and sit on porch swings. I cannot see these people with cigarettes wedged between their innocent white teeth.

We make love again that night. Afterwards, before we fall asleep, Simon gets out of bed and puts on his boxer shorts and a sweatshirt. He says it's because he's cold, but under the covers it's warm. I think it is really because he feels afraid of something.

We go to work at four groggy. They tell us we won't have an ambulance until five, so I go to take a nap in the bunk beds upstairs. I can't sleep, so I put my shoes on and go back downstairs to get the book I left in the common room. The door is cracked. The light from the room is orange. I hear Simon's voice, its accent, like doorbell chimes across a yard. It makes me freeze, I don't know why. I've already walked through the slit of door-way, the conversation has already washed over me, someone else is answering him: "Jesus, in the back of the ambulance. It's probably the one I'm taking out today. You let her snail all over my gurney."

I stand there, half in the room, looking at a cigarette burning down in the ashtray. I cross my arms over my chest. I feel like these men can see inside me. I feel that Simon's the one who should feel caught. I smile, pointing at my book. "I left my book," I say.

At five we go out on our shift. I act like nothing's happened, but all morning I make mistakes. Heartbeats sound so distant I can't count them. I forget to throw away the needle from a syringe and leave it pointing dangerously on the counter. Simon picks it up and throws it away. I need to get back my rhythm of working.

We pick up someone with AIDS over on Noe. His flannel pa-jamas are big on him, like he is a child wearing his father's paja-mas as a joke. They smell of old fruit juice and urine. I can't start the IV, the man's arm seems pale and utterly veinless. Simon takes the needle from me and rubs the man's forearm, bringing a pale blue vein to the surface of his skin. He slides the needle in easily, the glass reservoir filling with blood. The man's rattling breath makes me shiver. I want to ask him how he got it. "Did somebody you love do this to you? Was it the first and only man you ever loved? Did he do something stupid and maybe even spiteful once, in a dark, curtained-off room in a grimy bar, before coming home to you?" Simon checks the vitals. I offer to drive. It begins to rain. In the mirror, I see Simon adjust the drip.

When things quiet down early in the afternoon, we stop at Denny's. I take a raincoat out of the cabinet before climbing out of the ambulance, but just carry it over my arm into the restau-rant. We both order French dips. The rain streaks the glass win-dows. It is too late in the season for rain like this. I remember when my mother made me and my brother walk to school in a storm. She opened the door, held out her hand, palm up: "See, there's not even a drop. Besides, a little rain's not going to hurt you." The sky was curdled black. But I knew about rubber, how it protected you from getting struck by lightning. I walked out in a rain coat and rubber boots, holding an old inner tube over my head. In Kansas you can see lightning for miles and miles, so you can never be sure how far away it really is. In the short gaps between houses, my brother and I seemed to be the highest things around. I crouched down as I walked—crooked spears of lightning rammed into the fields around us. My mother yelled out at us, "Just stay under the rubber hood of your slicker and keep both feet on the ground and you'll be fine."

I open my eyes. Simon is saying something to me. He's swabbing French fries through a small mound of ketchup. With the other hand, one that is also sticky with ketchup, he's playing with my fingers. He's smiling at me. He asks if I'm all right. "Fine," I say, "just cold." I pick up the slicker and ease it on over my shirt, fastening all the snaps. Then I lift my sneakered feet off his side of the booth. I press both rubbery soles firmly down onto the cold tiled floor.

We sit like that eating hot fudgecake sundaes, the vanilla ice cream making my teeth hurt, not talking or looking at each other, until we get a Code Three. Then it's not like we're on a date anymore, we don't have to be mad at each other anymore, the sound of the siren outside the closed windows is familiar and gets caught in our chests.

The rain has stopped and the clouds are thinning. The house is white, but most of the parts that haven't burned are smudged black. The fire makes the air quivery. Simon and I move inside the circle of yellow police tape, our foreheads sweaty like we've been standing too long in front of a grille in an all-night diner.

The flames have just started on the second floor. I see a face appear then disappear in the unshattered panes of glass. It is ghostly. I think I hear a voice, a child's. I yell to Fire. A few of the fireman jog up to the house carrying a ladder. In their masks and helmets, they look like insects. They lean a ladder against the sill of the window. One of them climbs up, a hose strapped under his armpit. He smashes the window with a small ax, and the people in the street sigh together like a crowd at a sporting event. For a long time he stands at the window sending water into the jagged hole in the glass. My skin is itchy and uncomfortable. I tell myself there's no way I could have heard a voice, not over the crackling of the fire and the gushing water. I ask Simon if he saw anything, and he tells me not to worry, that it was probably my imagination. He says people see things in flames that aren't there, like in clouds. I lean back against the ambulance, the scissors in the holster around my waist feeling comforting like a gun I could use if I had to.

The fireman comes out of the smoking window with a little girl held in his free arm. Simon and I run over with the gurney. The fireman sets her down. Her arms and face are blistered, but I know it's the smoke, not the burns, that might get her. The skin around her nostrils is raw and charred from inhaling the hot smoky air. Her heart's still going, but it's faint and drowned. Her throat is swollen and closed from the smoke. I hand Simon an airway, and he eases the tube down her throat. I start pumping O2 into her with the bag-valve-mask. I call for one of the firemen to drive us to the hospital, so we can both be in back in case we start to lose her. We push her through the open door to the ambulance and climb in. Someone shuts the door behind us. Simon takes the oxygen. I put a clean sheet over her gently, because this is all we can do for her burns in the field. I check her pulse and blood pressure. Her vitals are waning. Her throat is so swollen she's not getting enough oxygen. When I look at Simon, I see his jauntiness has evaporated. He seems pale and confused. His arms stick out in front of him like a sleepwalker's. The girl's burned face looks peaceful as if she weren't trying to stay alive anymore. In her ears are little gold dots. They are the kind of earrings you get when you've just had your ears pierced for the first time.

At the burn center orderlies in white are waiting for us. They whisk her away from us as soon as we have opened the ambulance door.

Even after we have filled out all the forms, Simon and I sit drinking coffee in the cafeteria, not wanting to leave. He looks so lost that I want to take him home and feed him warm, comforting things—sweet potatoes, corn pudding, turkey. I want to tell him he will never have to sleep alone again. But we have to take the fireman back, so we crumple our cups and throw them away and go back outside where he is hanging around the emergency room dock smoking a hand-rolled cigarette.

When we get back, the house is still smoking. Fire is carrying out a body, I cannot believe how brown it is, and how small. I hear people on the street say it is the little boy who lived in the

300

house. His arms are spread as if he had been running to hug someone. I can tell by the way they are carrying his burnt body that there is nothing left inside him. The medical examiner puts the child in a white bag that zips. I am told by a fireman, rolling a flat hose, that the boy had squirted barbeque-lighter fluid into the gas furnace. The girl was his babysitter.

Simon and I get another call and wave to the firemen close to us, like we've just met them for drinks or something. We climb into the front seat and I nudge the ambulance through the people still hanging around in front of the house.

I let myself fall into work as if I were falling off a very high place and all that exists are what my hands grab hold of, IV bags and wrists and blood-pressure cuffs. At four in the morning Simon drives us to my house in his truck. It is not yet light, but teenage boys ride bare-waisted down Haight Street on bikes. They don't hold onto the handlebars. I want to lean out the window and touch their long smooth backs. I have not forgotten what happened this morning. I sit far away from Simon. When we get to my house, I don't want to let him inside, but I do.

I don't want to get into my bed, I want to be asleep already. I don't take off my clothes. I lie down on the bed nudging the wall, probably getting it dirty from the grit on my uniform. I tell Simon I just want to sleep. He doesn't move to touch me. We are so light on the bed, I imagine us like the skin of onions wound around air or dry leaves.

I dream that Simon and I are married and that we have two daughters, who are scarecrows. Simon chases them through fields and fields of corn, flicking lit matches at them, trying to light their straw pigtails on fire. I run after him. I try to grab him around the ankles and pull him down. The dream smells of manure and sulfur and when I wake up, I am sweating, but very cold. I get up, take off my uniform, and put on sweat pants and two sweat shirts.

I call the emergency room. The nurse tells me the girl died minutes after we brought her in. I sit on the bed and watch Simon sleeping. Then I dig my toes into his shoulders. "Hey," I say. He lifts his head quickly as if he hadn't been asleep at all. "I don't want you here anymore," I say. "I want you to leave."

301

He doesn't say anything. He gets out of bed and starts putting on his clothes. With my eyes closed, I hear his hands moving into sleeves.

I tell him to shut the front door when he leaves, that I'm going to sit and wait in the backyard until he's gone. He looks hurt, but I refuse to see it.

Outside, the night feels like summer nights in Kansas, the kind that has heat lightning. I sit on the grass and Simon comes out the back door. He looks large and intimidating. I want to shout, "I told you to get outta here," and throw rocks and sticks at him as if he were a mangy dog who might have rabies.

He sits down close enough to touch me. I draw my knees up into my sweat shirt. "That girl died," I tell him, saying it like it's his fault.

"I know, I just called the hospital."

"I wanted her to live," I say, "but I keep thinking she would have felt responsible for the boy. Still, I wanted her to live." Then I can't stop talking, even though I don't want to tell him anything else. I tell him about my dream. I tell him I don't trust him anymore, not after what he told everyone we work with.

He plucks up blades of grass, until I look at him like even that proves he's violent and dangerous. He puts his hands at his side and talks with his head tilted down: "I want to not have said those things. I want to feel like I'll never act like that again. When we were driving that girl to the hospital, I knew just by looking at your neck that you were praying. I thought I might cry. Then I hated you."

He moves towards me. I still want him to leave, but I also want him to love me. There are other things too, that I want. I want us to move to Kentucky where there aren't cities or overdoses or betrayal, where we'd fly over our farm in a biplane that droned and vibrated under our thighs and all we could see would be hills of bluegrass for miles and miles, like the sea.

Simon says in the quietest voice I've ever heard him use, "I saw her there too. I saw her in the window and I wanted to make you think it wasn't true. I just wanted to protect you. Even if only for a minute."

I want to say, who cares, it's too late for being kind. But the truth is, kindness is the only thing that matters. And the truth is that we should be curled up someplace safe, like our parents' bed

302

during a lightning storm, like the back of the ambulance with the doors locked, me on the gurney and him on the couch, not even holding hands, just breathing the same close air that smells of astringent and gasoline.

Nominated by ZYZZYVA.

CHRISTA

by SIGRID NUNEZ

from THE IOWA REVIEW

I AM TOLD THAT my first word was Coca-Cola, and there exists a snapshot of me at eighteen months, running in a park, hugging a full bottle. It seems I snatched this Coke from some neighboring picnickers. I used to believe that I could remember this moment—the cold bottle against my stomach, my teetering, stomping trot, feelings of slyness and joy and excitement fizzing in me—but now I think I imagined all this at a later age, after having looked long and often at the picture.

Here is something I do remember. Coming home from grade school for the lunch hour: It may have happened only once or it may have happened every day. Part of the way home took me through empty streets. I was alone and afraid. The noon whistle sounded, and as at a signal I began to run. The drumming of my feet and my own huffing breath became someone or something behind me. And I remember thinking that if I could just get home to my mother and her blue, blue eyes, everything would be all right.

Here are some lines from Virginia Woolf: "there is nothing to take the place of childhood. A leaf of mint brings it back: or a cup with a blue ring."

Sometimes—now—I might find myself in a strange town. I might be walking down a quiet street at midday. A factory whistle blows, and I feel a current in my blood, as if a damp sponge had been stroked down my back.

Woolf was thinking of a happy childhood, but does it matter? Another writer, members of whose family were killed in concentration camps, recalls how years later, looking through a book, he was touched by photographs of Hitler, because they reminded him of his childhood.

My mother's eyes were enhanced by shapely brows that made me think of angels' wings. Their arch gave her face an expression of skeptical wonder. When she was displeased her brows went awry; the arch fell; the world came tumbling down on me.

I remember a pear-shaped bottle of shampoo that sat on the edge of our bathtub. "With lemon juice. For blonds only." As the years passed and her hair grew darker, she started to use bleach. On the smooth white drawing paper of kindergarten I too made her blonder, choosing the bright-yellow crayon, the yellow of spring flowers: daffodils, forsythia.

Other features: A wide mouth. Good, clear skin. A strong nose. Too big, her daughters said. ("What do you mean? A fine nose. Aristocratic. Same nose as Queen Elizabeth. I don't want a little button on my face.")

And her walk, which was graceful and not graceful. A slight hitch in her gait, like a dancer with an injury.

And her hands: long-fingered, with soft palms and squarish nails. Deft, competent hands, good at making things.

This is the way I see her at first, not as a whole but as parts: a pair of hands, a pair of eyes. Two colors: yellow and blue.

The housing project where we lived. The wooden benches that stood in front of each building, where the women gathered when the weather was fair. The women: not yet thirty but already somewhat worn away. The broad spread of their bottoms. The stony hardness of their feet, thrust into flip-flops. (The slatternly sound of those flip-flops as they walked.) The hard lives of housewives without money. Exhaustion pooled under their eyes and in their veiny ankles. One or two appearing regularly in sunglasses to hide a black eye.

Talking, smoking, filing their nails.

Time passes. The shadow of the building lengthens. The first stars come out; the mosquitoes. The children edge closer, keeping mum so as not to be chased away, not to miss a riddle. *He married his mother. I'm late this month. She lost the baby. She found a lump. She had a boy in the bed with her.*

Finally a husband throws open a window. "You girls gonna yak out there the whole damn night?"

Part of my way of seeing my mother is in contrast to these women. It was part of the way she saw herself. "I'm not like these American women." Her boast that she spoke a better English than they was true. "Dese and dose, youse, ain't. How can you treat your own language like that!" Her own grammar was good, her spelling perfect, her handwriting precise, beautiful. But she made mistakes, too. She said *spedacular* and *expecially* and *holier-than-thoo*. She spoke of a *bone of contentment* between two people. Accused someone of being a *ne'er-too-well*. And: "They stood in a motel for a week." No matter how many times you corrected her she could not get that participle right. She flapped her hands. "You know what I mean!" And her accent never changed. There were times when she had to repeat herself to a puzzled waitress or salesman.

But she would never say youse. She would never say ain't.

Parent-Teachers' Day. My mother comes home with a face set in disgust. "Your teacher said, 'She does *good* in history.' "

My mother liked English. "A good language—same family as German." She was capable of savoring a fine Anglo-Saxon word: murky, smite. She read *Beowulf* and *The Canterbury Tales*. She knew words like thane and rood and sith.

Southern drawls, heartland twangs, black English, all sounded horrid to her.

One or two Briticisms had found their way (how?) into her speech. "It was a proper mess, I tell you." And somewhere she had learned to swear. She had her own rules. Only the lowest sort of person would say fuck. But bastard was permissible. And shit—she said shit a lot. But she always sounded ridiculous, swearing. I was never so aware that English was not her native tongue as when she was swearing at me.

She did not have many opportunities to speak German. We had a few relations in upstate New York and in Pennsylvania, and there was a woman named Aga, from Munich, who had been my mother's first friend here in the States and who now lived in Yonkers. But visits with these people were rare, and perhaps that is why I first thought of German as a festive language, a language for special occasions. The harshness that grates on so many non-German ears—I never heard that. When several people were speaking together, it sounded to me like a kind of music—music that was not melodious, but full of jangles and toots and rasps, like a wind-up toy band.

From time to time we took the bus across town to a delicatessen owned by a man originally from Bremen. My mother ordered in German, and while the man was weighing and wrapping the Leberkäse and Blutwurst and ham, he and she would talk. But I was usually outside playing with the dachshund.

Sometimes, reading German poetry, she would start to say the lines under her breath. Then it no longer sounded like music but like a dream-language: seething, urgent, a little scary.

She did not want to teach her children German. "It's not your language, you don't need it, learn your own language first."

Now and then, on television, in a war movie, say, an American actor would deliver some German lines, and my mother would hoot. If subtitles were used, she said the translations were wrong. When my elder sister took German in high school, my mother skimmed her textbook and threw it down. "Ach, so many things wrong!"

A very hard thing it seemed, getting German right.

In one of my own schoolbooks was a discussion of different peoples and the contributions each had made to American society. The Germans, who gave us Wernher von Braun, were described as being, among other things, obedient to authority, with a tendency to follow orders without questioning them. That gave me pause: I could not imagine my mother taking orders from anyone.

I remember being teased in school for the way I said certain words. *Stoomach.* And: "I stood outside all day." ("Musta got awful tired!") I called the sideways colon the Germans put on top of certain vowels an *omelette.* Later, after I'd left home, I had only to hear a snatch of German, or to see some Gothic script, to have my childhood come surging back to me.

My mother said, "English is a fine language, it gets you to most places that you want to go. But German is—deeper, I think. A better language for poetry. A more romantic language, better for describing—yearning."

Her favorite poet was Heine.

307

She said, "There are a lot of German words for which you have no English. And it's funny—so often it's an important word, one that means such a lot. *Weltschmerz*. How can you translate that? And even if you study German, you can't ever really learn a word like that, you never grasp what it means."

But I did learn it, and I think I know what *Weltschmerz* means.

My first book was a translation from the German: fairy tales of the Brothers Grimm. My mother read these stories aloud to me, before I had learned to read myself. What appealed to me was not so much the adventures, not the morals, but the details: a golden key, an emerald box, boots of buffalo leather. The strangeness and beauty of names like Gretel and Rapunzel, especially the way my mother said them. The notion of enchantment was a tangled one. You couldn't always believe what you saw. The twelve pigeons pecking on the lawn might be twelve princes under a spell. Perhaps all that was lacking in one's own household was the right magic. At the right word, one of those birds might fly to the window bearing in his beak a golden key, and that key might open a door leading to who knew what treasure. My mother shared this with all her neighbors: the conviction that we did not belong in the housing project. Out on the benches, much of the talk was about getting out. It was all a mistake. We were all under a spell—the spell of poverty. What is a home? We project children drew pictures of houses with peaked roofs and chimneys, and yards with trees. My mother said, "Every decent family is getting out," as one by one our neighbors moved away. "We'll never get out, we'll be the last ones left." Meaning: the last white family.

Metamorphosis. First the fairy tales, then the Greek myths—for years my imagination fed on that most magical possibility: a person could be changed into a creature; a tree. In time this led to trouble.

I can still see her, Mrs. Scott, a twig of a woman with a long chin and hollow eyes: my teacher. The way my mother mimicked her. Mrs. Scott became a witch from one of the stories. " 'Your daughter says, In my first life I was a rabbit. In my second life I was a tree. I think she's too old to be telling stories like that.' "

And then my mother, mimicking herself, all wide-blue-eyed innocence: "How do you know she wasn't a rabbit?"

Oh, how I loved her.

Because my mother gave it to me I read a book of German
sagas, but I didn't like them. Heroism on the fierce Nordic scale
was not for me. To Siegfried I preferred the heroes of the *Haus-
märchen:* simple Hanses, farmers and tailors and their faithful
horses and dogs. (In just a few more years I'd prefer to read only
about horses and dogs.) I did not share her taste for the legends
of chivalry or the romances of the Middle Ages. The epic was her
form. She liked stories—legendary or historic—about heroic
striving, conquest and empire, royal houses and courts. Lives of
Alexander and Napoleon were some of her favorite reading. (This
was a mother who for Halloween dressed up her youngest not as
a gypsy or a drum majorette but as Great Caesar's Ghost—
pillowcase toga, philodendron wreath—stumping all of the kids
and not a few of the teachers.) She read piles of paper-back romances, too—what she called her "everyday" reading.

One day I came home to find her with a copy of *Lolita.* The
woman downstairs had heard it was a good dirty book and had
gone out and bought it. Disappointed, she passed it on to my
mother. ("So, is it dirty?" "No, just a very silly book by a very
clever man.")

The "good" books, the ones to be kept, were placed in no particular order in a small pine bookcase whose top shelf was re-
served for plants. To get at certain ones you had to part vines.
Dear to my mother's heart was the legend of Faust. Goethe's version was years beyond me, but what I gathered of the story was
not promising. I liked stories about the Devil all right, but
Faust's ambition struck no chord in me. I was a child of limited
curiosity. I wanted to hear the cat speak, but I didn't care how it
was done. Knowledge equals power was an empty formula to me.
I was never good at science.

Shakespeare in one volume. Plutarch's *Lives,* abridged. In the
introduction to the plays, I read that Shakespeare had used
Plutarch as a source. At first I thought I had misunderstood.
Then I felt a pang: the world was smaller than I had thought it
was. For some reason this gave me pain.

I remember a book given to me by my fourth-grade teacher. A
thick, dark-green, grainy cover, pleasant to touch. A story about

immigrants. One man speaking to another of a young woman just arrived from the Old Country. The phrase stayed with me, along with the memory of the feelings it inspired. I was both moved and repelled. "She has still her mother's milk upon her lips."

My mother never called it the Old Country. She said my country, or Germany, or home. Usually home. When she spoke of home, I gave her my full attention. I could hear over and over (I did hear over and over) stories about her life *before*—before she was a wife, before she was Mother, when she was just Christa.

She was a good storyteller. To begin with, she spoke English with the same energy and precision with which German is spoken. And she used everything—eyes, hands, all the muscles of her face. She was a good mimic; it was spooky how she became the person mimicked, and if that person was you, you got a taste of hell. She talked all the time. She was always ready to reminisce—though that is a mild word for the purposive thing she did. The evocation of the past seemed more like a calling with her. The present was the project, illiterate neighbors, a family more *incurred* than chosen, for there had been no choice. The past was where she lived and had her being. It was youth, and home. It was also full of horror. I cannot remember a time when she thought I was too young to hear those stories of war and death. But we both had been brought up on fairy tales—and what were her stories but more of the same, full of beauty and horror.

She had been a girl, like me—but how different her girlhood from mine. And I never doubted that what she was, what she had been and where she came from, were superior to me and my world. ("What you Americans call an education!" "What you Americans call an ice coffee!")

In memory I see myself always trying to get her to talk. Silence was a bad sign with her. When she was really angry she would not speak to you, not even to answer if you spoke to her.

Towards the close of a long dull day. I have lost the thread of the book I am reading. As so often on a Saturday at this hour, I don't know what to do with myself. Outside, it is getting dark. Nothing but sports on TV. My mother sits across the room, knitting. She sits on the sofa with one foot tucked under her. She is wearing

310

her navy-blue sweater with the silver buttons, which she made herself, and which I will one day take with me, to have something of hers when I go away. (I have it still.) The soft, rhythmic click of the needles. At her feet the ball of yarn dances, wanders this way and that, looking for a kitten to play with. I let the book close in my lap and say, "Tell me again about the time they came to take Grandpa to Dachau."

Motorheads is a word you would use today for the men of my mother's family. In half the photographs I have seen of them there is some sort of motor vehicle. My grandfather and my uncles and many of their friends were racers. In the photos they are wearing leather jackets and helmets. Sometimes someone is holding a trophy. In one astounding photo my grandfather and five other men round a curve, a tilting pyramid, all on one motorcycle. The stories took my breath away. Motorcycle races across frozen lakes. Spectacular, multivictim accidents. Spines snapped in two, teeth knocked out to the last one, instant death. What sort of men were these? Speed-loving. Death-defying. Germans. They slalomed, too.

The year I was born my grandfather opened an auto-repair shop in the Swabian town where he had lived all his life, a business later passed on to the elder of his two sons. I do not remember him from the only time I met him, when I was taken as a child to Germany. The memory of my grandmother on the other hand is among the most vivid I possess. "You took one look at her and called her a witch." So I already knew about witches, at two. Pictures show that she really did have the sickle profile of a witch. And I was right to fear her. She locked me in a dark closet, where I screamed so loud the neighbors came.

My grandparents had grown up together. An illegitimate child, my grandmother was adopted by the childless couple who lived next door to my grandfather's family. In summer, the narrow yard between the two houses was filled with butterflies. My grandparents were said never to have had any interest in anyone but each other, and to have shared a strong physical resemblance all their lives. My grandmother was known for her temper. During the war, when shoes were all but impossible to get and her son Karl lost one of his only pair, she pummeled his head with the other; he still has the scar. Whenever my mother, the eldest child and

311

only daughter, spoke of her mother, she tended to purse her lips. ("We were always at odds." "She didn't like girls.") When I met her for the second and last time, I was in my twenties and she had not long to live. Dying, she was still mean. A habit of reaching out and pinching you as you passed: teasing, hurtful. The pinching malice peculiar to some little old ladies. Revealing things my mother had kept from us: for example, that both of my sisters were illegitimate, and that my mother was too. ("You didn't know?") She suffered all her life from bad circulation and died of a stroke.

My grandparents were Catholics, and at that time in that town, most of the power was in the hands of the Catholic Church. Like other Catholic towns, somewhat slower to embrace National Socialism. I am not sure how much danger my grandfather thought he was courting when, just before the national plebiscite in November 1933, he stood outside the town hall distributing anti-Hitler leaflets. Before this, he had shown little interest in politics. His opposition to the Nazis grew largely under the influence of a friend named Ulli, who planned to leave for America if Hitler got more than seventy-five percent of the vote. My grandfather's two siblings were already in America, having emigrated in the twenties, but neither of my grandparents wished to leave Germany. My grandmother also may have influenced her husband against the Nazis. Her father had been an official of the Social Democratic Party. She had had many leftists among the friends of her youth and had been an admirer of Rosa Luxemburg. She was arrested with her husband immediately after Hitler's victory.

"They woke us up in the middle of the night." "The Gestapo?" "No, no—just the regular town police." My mother was six. "One of the policemen was someone I knew, an old man. I used to see him in the street all the time, he was very nice. But after that night I was so scared of him. Any time I saw him after that I ran the other way."

They searched the house. Earlier that night, while my mother slept, Ulli had come to the door. "Hide these for me." A gun, a typewriter.

A policeman—"not the old one"—opened the hall closet, and the typewriter slid off the top shelf. He covered his head just in time. "I remember, his face turned bright red."

312

"Gerhard and I stood together on the stairs, crying. Karl slept through it all—he was just a baby."

My grandparents were led out to the waiting police van. "It was already filled with people."

"Out of nowhere" a woman appeared. "A complete stranger. She was very stern. She told us to go back to our room and not dare to come out."

The next morning my grandmother returned, alone. Later, after dark, she took the gun hidden in the wall behind the toilet and buried it in the back yard.

Eight months before, Heinrich Himmler had set up the concentration camp at Dachau. It now held about two thousand inmates. My mother said my grandfather never talked much about his time there. ("He was ashamed of having done something so stupid.") In one beating he suffered a broken rib which healed grotesquely—"like a doorknob on his chest." "You are going home," he was told, and put on a truck with a group of fellow prisoners who were then driven to the train station. The train came and went. The prisoners watched it come and go. Then they were driven back to the camp. This happened many times. Meanwhile, there was work to be done. The camp was expanding. My grandfather was put to work installing electrical wiring. And then one day, thirteen months after his arrest, he really was let go. He was sent home in his prison uniform. My mother was playing in the street when another little girl ran up, scandalized. "Christa! Your papa is coming across the field—and he's in his pajamas!"

"He was lucky." Ulli did not get out of Dachau until '45. (And then he left for America.)

My grandparents' house had been confiscated, their bank accounts closed. My grandmother had moved with the children into the house of her in-laws. She had taken a job in a drapery shop.

My grandfather was afraid that no one would hire him. He appealed to an old friend from polytechnic days, now at Daimler-Benz. A relatively quiet time began. Every day my grandfather took the half-hour train ride into Stuttgart. He was not troubled again by the Nazis. And when, after Hitler's speeches on the radio, my grandmother carried on—Hitler-like herself, according to my mother—my grandfather said, "Let Germany follow her own course."

313

Time passed. The town synagogue was closed. The town idiot, a homeless man who begged on the church steps, disappeared. The main department store went out of business. The gardens of the houses where the Jews lived became overgrown. Consternation among the Mendels: They want to go to America, but Oma is stubborn. The very mention of crossing the ocean makes her weep. Finally, a compromise is reached: the Mendels will go with their son to America, Oma will go to Switzerland. Before leaving, she entrusts two trunks to my grandparents' care. "I'll want them back some day."

Nineteen-thirty-nine. My grandfather was called on the first day of the war. He was with the troops that invaded Poland, and would remain in the Army until Germany's defeat.

Meanwhile, my mother was growing up. Away, mostly, at a Catholic boarding school in the Bavarian Alps. The nuns are hard. My mother comes home with a horror tale: a cat smuggled into the dorm, discovered by Sister and thrown into the furnace! Still, her parents send her back.

For many of the girls, returning year after year, from age six to eighteen, the school *is* home. Away, my mother is homesick all the time; but at home, especially over the long summer, she pines for school.

At the end of one summer, the girls arrive to find the nuns replaced by men and women in uniform. The nuns, they are told, have returned to their convent, where they belong. From now on, my mother's education is in the hands of the Nazis.

Over the next few years, many of the new teachers will be soldiers wounded in the war: amputees; a math professor whose face was so scarred, "we thought at first he was wearing a mask."

As she recalls, no one ever made any reference to her father's disgrace; she was not treated any differently from the other girls.

She keeps up her grades but she does not excel. Unlike her brothers, she is not superior in math. She does not seem to have been ambitious, to have dreamed of becoming something.

(Up to this point, I have had some trouble seeing my mother. Even with the help of photographs, it is hard for me to imagine her as a little girl. Unlike a lot of people, she did not much resemble her adult self. The child of six crying with her brother on the stairs, running away from the old policeman—I see that girl,

314

but she could be anyone. But now, she is beginning to be familiar. I can imagine her, her feelings and her moods. I can see her more and more clearly: Christa.)

School trips to the opera. ("He who would understand National Socialism must understand Wagner"—Hitler.) Hot and stuffy in the balcony. The agony of itching woolen socks. She would always hate opera. Today: "All I have to do is hear a bit of it and my feet start to itch like I haven't washed them for weeks!"

Another thing she hated: her turn to tend the rabbits, raised by the school for food. The filth of the cages. The fierceness of one particular buck, known to the girls as Ivan the Terrible.

The Hitler Youth. Uniforms, camping, sports. "Just like your Girl Scouts."

The rallies and the victory parades. "Tell me what kid doesn't love a parade." A little flag on a stick. Flowers for the soldiers. Always something to celebrate. April 20: the Führer's birthday. My mother has just passed her tenth. He marches through the Munich streets, veering right and left with outstretched hand. His palm is warm. Photo opportunity. Later, back at school, a copy of the photo is presented to her. She bears it home, proud, *somebody*. Her mother tears it up. My mother threatens to tell.

School pictures. My mother in her winter uniform, looking, like most of the other girls, comically stout. ("We probably had three sweaters on underneath.")

Trude, Edda, Johanna, Klara—my mother's little band.

Girls becoming women. One's own tiny destiny absorbed into that of the Volk. To be a Frau und Mutter in the heroic mold, champions of the ordered cupboard and snowy diaper. The body: nothing to blush about but always to be treated with respect. My mother earns high marks in gymnastics. She is good at embroidery and crocheting.

Dance lessons. Ballroom steps, the taller girls leading.

The heartswelling beauty of the landscape, especially at sundown. Alpenglow. Someone called it: Beethoven for the eyes.

Lights out at nine. Talking verboten. Whispers in the dark. Confessions, yearnings. Boys back home. Teachers: "I don't care that he has only one arm." Gary Cooper. The Luftwaffe aces. And: "Leni Riefenstahl was so beautiful."

In the summers, you had to work, at least part time. You might be a mother's helper, or work on a farm. You had to bring

315

written proof that you had not idled your whole vacation away. As the war deepened and you got older, you were assigned labor service: delivering mail, collecting tickets on the street cars, working in factories or in offices.

The last year of the war, eight girls assigned to track enemy planes in the same operations room in Stuttgart are killed by a bomb. Among them my mother's best friend, Klara.

The last battles. Only the German victories are announced. But who cannot read the increasingly somber miens of the teachers. Letters from home tell of brothers, still in school themselves, called to fight. "Erich sends his love and asks you to pray for him."

Still, when it comes, the announcement is shocking. "You must make your way home as best you can. Don't try to carry too much with you. And be careful. There are enemy soldiers everywhere—and some of them are black."

My mother had already had a letter from her father at the front. "When the war ends, don't be foolish and try to outrun the enemy. Try if you can to hide until they have passed. Do not let them keep driving you ahead of them. It won't do you any good, they'll just catch up with you anyway. And whatever you do, do not go east."

My mother boarded a train, but long before her hometown station a roadblock appeared and the passengers were put off. Against advice she had packed all her belongings. Now she left two suitcases on the train, keeping only her knapsack; she would soon abandon that, too.

(It is at this point that my mother finally comes in clearly, on this four-day walk home.)

For the first stretch she has company—other people from the train headed in the same direction. But for most of the journey she is alone. She is not afraid. Just days ago she turned eighteen. The sense of having an adventure buoys her up, at least for a time. Also, in the very extremity of the situation, a certain protection: "This can't be happening." Blessings: weather ("That was a beautiful April"), and she is in good shape from Alpine hiking.

Dashing for cover at the sound of a motor. *The enemy is everywhere*.

Hunger. She cannot remember her last good meal. At school, day after day, cabbage and potatoes. The tender early spring shoots begin to resemble succulent morsels. At dusk she knocks at a farmhouse and is given an eggnog and a place to sleep in the barn. The steamy flanks of the cows. Infinity of peace in that pungent smell, in the scrape of hoof against board. Morning. Rain. "Dear God, just let me lie here a little bit longer."

Sometimes she sings out, as people do, from loneliness and for courage. "Don't ask me, for I'll never tell, the man I'm going to marry."

What passes through her mind cannot properly be called thought, though her mind is constantly busy, and she loses herself in herself for hours at a time. Daydreams bring amusement and solace. Her senses are lulled and she is carefree. Funny thoughts do occur to her now and then, and she laughs out loud. Sometimes she watches her feet, and the fact that they can move like that, right, left, right, covering the ground and bearing her along, strikes her as nothing less than miraculous.

Often she is lightheaded. She imagines her head floating like a balloon above her. Attached by a string to her finger. She jerks the string, and her head tilts this way and that, like the head of an Indian dancer.

People met along the way move furtively, every one in a hurry. "No one would look you in the eye."

Straw in her hair, itching between collar and neck. Seams loosening with wear. The smell of the cows mingled with her own. A burning sensation in the folds of her flesh. Will she ever get to change her underwear?

She mistakes a turn, walks for miles down the wrong road before turning back. In the fields, the first wildflowers. A tumult of sparrows. She is seized by the unbearably poignant sensation of déjà vu.

A plane. Nowhere to hide. She squats where she is, arms over her head. The plane swoops down, low, so low she can make out the grinning face of the (British) pilot, who salutes before taking to the sky again. Laughing, she embraces her knees and bursts into tears. In that moment of terror her heart had flown straight to her mother. From now on she will often be struck with fear, foreseeing her house in ruins, and her mother dead.

(A young woman fixed upon reaching home and mother, making her way through a conquered land overrun with enemy soldiers: I read that part of *Gone with the Wind* with a swell of recognition.)

317

At last: the church tower, the wooden bridge. A woman in the *Marktplatz*, weeping, weeping.

My mother beat the Americans by one day.

The Occupation. A time to count your blessings—"at least for us it really was over"—as the refugees streamed in from East Prussia. The Americans: "You know, typical American boys—loud, friendly, vulgar. Every other word was f-u-c-k."

One day an American lieutenant came to the door. "He stood there grinning from ear to ear. 'You don't remember me? I've come for the trunks my grandmother left.' We couldn't believe it. Walter Mendel, all grown up. He brought us our first Hershey bars."

Incredulity, the sense of this-isn't-really-happening, endures. A topsy-turvy time. Dating the enemy. Fräuleins in the arms of American soldiers. Eating themselves sick in the mess hall hung with Stop-VD posters: *Don't Take a Chance, Keep It in Your Pants*.

For my mother, the start of a new life.

(And here I begin to lose her again; I mean, I no longer see her clearly. About this period—so important to me because directly connected to my own coming into being—about this period she hardly spoke at all.)

She has a job, teaching kindergarten, which does not suit her. She doesn't particularly like children, and since these are the children of farmers, she has to keep farmer's hours, going to and coming back from work in the dark.

Whatever energy is left over goes into dating. First in her heart is a boy named Rudolf. He is her own age, a boy from the neighborhood, grown in the years she was away into stripling-handsomeness. Had her life been happy she probably would have remembered her experience of him as a lark; instead he became the love of her life, her one and only.

She said often, "I should have married him"; but just as often, "I couldn't have married him, we would never have got along, we were too much alike." In other ways, too, she hinted at an intense and dramatic entanglement. But I don't think it really was like that. I think she convinced herself that it was, because this helped her: there is consolation in seeing oneself as a victim of

318

love. (Ideally, of course, he should have died—killed, say, as so many other German boys his age were killed, in the last months of the war.)

"After him, I really didn't care what happened to me."

Rudolf. One precious photograph included in the family album. Curly hair and a curl to his upper lip, from a scar, giving him a somewhat cruel expression; and indeed it was by cruelty that he got that scar: he taunted a rooster, who flew in his face. He was fickle, he liked to make my mother jealous. Well, two could play at that game.

Two can play, but for men and women the stakes are not equal.

My mother becomes pregnant.

Lacan says: Only women's lives can be tragic; about men there is always something comic.

Newsreels from this era show that the attempt to turn women who had consorted with Nazis into laughingstocks, by shaving their heads, failed.

*

The next part of her life is the one I have most trouble imagining. I think it also must have been the hardest. "I thought I had died and gone to hell." But it was only Brooklyn. The housing project looked like a prison. "Your father had said something about a house with a little garden. What a fool I was." (She often called herself a fool. Another thing she said a lot: You made your own bed now you have to lie in it. She had little sympathy for people who'd botched their lives, and towards real sinners she was unforgiving. She often complained that criminals in this country got off scot-free. Also: she was suspicious of repentance. You could not escape punishment by confession or apology. She herself rarely apologized. I'm not sure to what degree she applied her own harsh rules to herself. I know only that she suffered a lot.)

She was not the only German war bride in the project. Now and then a group of them would go into Manhattan, to 86th Street, to shop in the German stores. When there was a bit of extra money, a German movie; coffee and cake at the Café Wagner, or at the Café Hindenburg, said to be where the New York branch of the Nazi Party had held their meetings.

319

I am daunted when I try to imagine her pregnant. In those days she was a slender woman, almost frail. In photographs her mouth is dark, the corners lifted, not in a true smile but more of a my-thoughts-are-very-far-away expression. I try to picture her in one of the humiliating maternity dresses of the day ("a large bright bow at the neck or a frilly bib will draw attention away from the stomach"). She wears her long hair pinned back. Not one of her three children was planned.

When I try to imagine her, she becomes stilled: a figure in a painting. She sits in an armchair which she has turned toward the window. From this angle you cannot tell that she is pregnant. Her one-year-old and her three-year-old lie in the next room; she has just got them down. She is exhausted, so heavy in her chair she thinks she will never rise again. Blue smudge like a thumb-print under each eye. What is she looking at? Through the window: water tower against leaden sky. What is she thinking of? Schooldays. A million years ago! Trude, Edda, Johanna, Klara. Klara dead. And the rest? Surely none so unhappy as she? Rudolf! At last she bestirs herself: with a furious gesture she wipes a tear from her eye.

She used to say, "If we had had money everything would have been different." I didn't understand why we didn't get help, like many of our neighbors. "Welfare! Are you mad? Those people should be ashamed." But she was already ashamed. I saw it in her face when she had to tell people my father was a waiter. I thought taking money from the government would be better than always complaining. "You want us to be like the Feet?" (The family next door was named Foot.) "Ten kids to support and the father sits around drinking." But wasn't Mr. Foot better off than my father, who worked seven days a week and never took a vacation? Didn't happiness count for anything in our house?

There were periods when she cried every day. If you asked her why she was crying she would say, "I want to go home." Other times, when she'd "had it" with us, when she made it clear that we were more than any person could bear, with our noise and our mess and our laziness, she would threaten to leave us and go home. (I was one of those exasperating kids who can't bear to be separated from their mothers. More than one teacher lost patience with me. I think I sensed something in those threats to go home that I'm now sure was there: the threat of suicide.)

About the Germans Nietzsche has said: They are either of the day before yesterday or of the day after tomorrow; they have no today. Coming of age, my mother shared in the dream of a grandiose destiny. Now she became one throbbing nerve of longing.

We believed her when she said that every night she dreamed she was back in Germany. She made us promise that when she died we would bury her in Germany. *In German soil*, is what she said. She understood those Russian soldiers who had gone to war with a pouch of soil around their necks so that if they fell, a bit of Russia would be buried with them. She had the Teutonic obsession with blood and soil. She made us promise also that if she was ever in an accident we would not authorize a transfusion. She would rather die than have someone else's blood in her.

Now and then we would receive packages from Germany which might include sweets. Once, a box of small, bottle-shaped chocolates wrapped in colored foil and filled with liqueur. My mother's eyes lit up. "I haven't had these for years!" But before tasting one she wavered, "I shouldn't, it will just remind me of home." A good thing she warned us; from the way she slumped in her chair we might have thought she'd been poisoned. I will never forget the sound she made. Many years later, to thank me for taking care of his plants while he spent Christmas in Denmark, a neighbor of mine brought me back a box of those same chocolate bottles, and at the mere sight of them I felt as if a poison had entered my veins.

Heimweh. "Another word you have no English for." Homesickness? "Yes, but more than that." Nostalgia? "Stronger than that."

In third grade I had a friend named Lore Kaplan. Her mother, too, was from Germany. Mrs. Kaplan's accent was only slightly different from my mother's. "Doesn't she want to go back?" "Oh, no, she would never go back, she hates Germany." Strange!

I was ten when Eichmann went on trial in Jerusalem. My first view of the famous photographs. It was said that all Germans were on trial with Eichmann. Neighbors fascinated by the testimony prodded my mother for details of life in the Reich. She never brought up her father. ("It would be as if I were making excuses.")

"I am still proud to be German." "I do not apologize for being German." But during this time she was depressed. By then we had moved away from Brooklyn, to another housing project, where there were no Germans. My mother might hang out with the women on the benches, but she was not really friends with any of them. She would never feel at home among Americans. She had the European contempt for Americans as "big kids." She found herself constantly having to bite her tongue; for example, when one of the women complained about the war: "I don't know what it was like for youse over there, but here you couldn't even get your own brand of cigarettes."

I don't think a day went by that she did not remember that she was German. Watching the Olympics, she rooted for the Germans and pointed out that, if you counted East and West together, Germany came out ahead of both the Americans and the Russians.

It was not to be hoped that any American—let alone an American child—could grasp what this unique quality of being German was all about. I don't recall how old I was, but at some point I had to wonder: If you took that quality away from her, what would have replaced it? What sort of person might she have been? But her Germanness and her longing for Germany—her *Heimweh*—were so much a part of her she cannot be thought of without them. To try to imagine her born of other blood, on other soil, is to lose her completely: there is no Christa there.

She saw herself as someone who had been cheated in life—but cheated of what, exactly? Not a career. She never missed having a job. She was not one of those women who can say, If I hadn't had a family I'd have gone to med school. (Back then, people would say of certain women: She never married, she was a career girl.) My mother always saw herself as a housewife. During one especially lean spell, when it looked as if she might have to earn some money, the only job she could think of was cleaning houses. But just because she saw her place as in the home doesn't mean she was happy there. The everlasting struggle against the soiled collar and the scuffmarked floor brought on true despair. In that struggle, as every housewife knows, children are the worst enemy. Her big cleaning days were the darkest days of my childhood. She booted us out of one room after the other, her mood growing steadily meaner. We cowered in the hallway, listening to her curses and the banging of her broom, awaiting the inevitable threats to go home.

We offered to help her clean, but she refused. "All you do is smear the dirt around." Besides, she was not going to be one of those parents who use their kids as servants. (Mrs. Foot, for example, who had her six-year-old girl doing the vacuuming.)

Everyone had his proper sphere. "You kids just worry about your schoolwork."

"If we had had money, everything would have been different." In the ads for lotto, people tell their dreams, which often turn out to be of travel, preferably to exotic places. But seeing the world was no more one of my mother's dreams than being a doctor. What would she want? A big house. A big yard. "And a big fence!" No more living on top of other people!

She would live in one housing project or another for most of her adult life.

She never played lotto. She didn't believe in good luck.

I don't know that her life would have been very different if she'd had more money. In later years, when my sister wanted to hire someone to clean for my mother, she refused. Maids: "They just smear the dirt around." (Dirt. Contamination. The horror they inspired in her went deep. When she spoke of dirt encountered somewhere—someone else's house, say— she would shake herself like a drenched dog. We were not allowed to use public toilets, which made going anywhere with her an agony.)

Money. Visiting me in my first apartment, she happened to hear me tell my landlord that the rent would be a little late that month. She didn't understand why I wasn't ashamed of that. She had been uncomfortable, too, about my applying for a college scholarship; she would rather have paid. She would never understand how I could accept loans and gifts of money from other people. *Down to my last penny:* why didn't I blush when I said that? "I don't know how I could have raised a daughter like that."

A simple life. Up in the morning, the first one. Fix the coffee, wake the others, bundle them out the door. Dishes, beds, dust. The youngest child home for lunch. Dishes, laundry. Sometime in the afternoon, between lunch and the children's return, a pause. Lose yourself in a book. Page 50. Page 100. An errant duke. A petty dowager. A handsome and truehearted stepbrother. The heroine swathed in shawls against castle drafts.

Romance. A thing ludicrous to imagine with her husband, with whom she had never been in love. At best she treated him like one of the children. "Wipe your feet off before you step in this house!"

Her early heartbreak (Rudolf) had made her defiant. She didn't owe anyone anything. She didn't have to be nice. "I can't stand the sight of you!" She wasn't going to play the hypocrite. "I wish that we had never met!" A riddle: If it was true what she said, that she expected nothing from her husband, why was she forever seething with disappointment? The threat to divorce him became part of her litany of threats. But she was never interested in anyone else, not even after he died, though she was then just forty-six.

Wife and mother: dissatisfying as that role may have been, it is hard to imagine her in any other. Outside the house she lost her bearings. Any negotiation beyond that required for simple domestic errands flustered her. She hated going out. She hated having to deal with strangers. Even worse: running into people she knew. But she was always cordial. She would stop and chat— often at length—putting on a chumminess that I feared others would see through, and I guess some did.

She was intimidated by authority. My decision to change my major my junior year in college bothered her. "Are you sure you don't get into trouble for that?" "You sure they let us park here?" she would ask, peering anxiously about. Some part of her always remained that child on the stairs watching the arrest of her parents. The ringing of the telephone could stop her heart. An unexpected knock at the door, and she would widen her eyes in warning at us, a finger to her lips. We all held our breath. When the person had gone, she would peek out from behind the window shade to see who it was. Whenever she had to go somewhere she hadn't been before, she was terrified of getting lost. Her fear revealed itself in flushed cheeks and repeated swallowings; I held onto her icy hand. Oh, the trouble you could meet going into the city! Much better stay home. At home *she* was the authority, the only one permitted to do as she pleased, to be herself.

It was as a teenager, I suppose, that I decided that what she needed was the right man. In our neighborhood there were many examples of the rugged type: men with square faces and corded

324

arms, who earned their living by brawn. I thought my mother might have been better off with one of these. (But this was my fantasy; she never expressed any attraction to such men.) Her upbringing had resulted in a paradox: though she feared authority, she approved of it, she would have liked to see more of it. (The trouble with most Americans? They are too free. The trouble with most kids? They are not disciplined enough.) I think her ideal man would have been a cop. At any rate, she needed someone strong, the sort of man with whom a woman feels safe. A scoff-at-your-fears sort of man. She implied that her father had been something like this, before Dachau. My father—fumbling, shy, so fearful of authority himself—would not do. She was the one who had to drive, who carried the kids' bicycles up and down the stairs. She wore the pants. Like so much else, this whetted her scorn. "My lord and master—hah!" No sympathy for him when he was down with a cold—"He sneezes twice and it's the end of the world"—or when for a time he had nightmares and often woke her with his cries. Nor did she expect sympathy from him. Only once did I ever see her turn to him: when her father died.

Outbursts triggered by his forgetfulness, his butterfingers, his superstition against making out a will. Once started, she could not stop herself. Her rage tore like a cyclone through the house. Afterwards we would all sit in a kind of stupor in which the cat and even inanimate objects seemed to share.

My mother sobbed. "I'm not asking for that much." But she was: she was asking him to be someone else.

At times it seemed as if she had but one emotion: loathing. I think she often experienced what Rilke described: "The existence of the horrible in every atom of air."

She had that love for animals that is unmistakably against humans. "Now I know men, I prefer dogs." This remark of Frederick the Great's—quoted by Hitler—expresses a famous German sentiment. My mother: "I feel worse if I see a dog suffering than if it was a man." Said without apology; with a tinge of pride, even. As if it were superior, to prefer dogs. In one of the houses of the Frankfurt Zoo you come to a plaque announcing the animal to be seen in the next cage: the most savage creature

325

of all, the only one to kill its own kind, to kill for pleasure, and so on. A mirror behind bars. When I was there someone had written in English on the wall under the plaque: *You krauts oughtta know!* And under that was written in French: *Of all our maladies, the most virulent is to despise our own being—Montaigne.*

But she was not without pity for humans. Once, she went into the city to do Christmas shopping and gave all her money to an old woman begging outside A & S.

She never forgot the hunger of the war years. "Aren't you going to finish your ice cream? You'll regret it. When the war comes there won't be any ice cream." (I worried a lot about the coming war and had my doubts whether hiding my head in the crook of my arm as we did in school shelter drills was going to save me. At any rate, when the bombs fell I wanted to be home. I knew in case of attack we were supposed to go down to the cellar, but my mother said she would never do that. She remembered raids in which people had drowned in cellars where the pipes had burst. "I'd rather die any way but that—drowning with the rats!" I agreed, and for a time my bad dreams composed themselves out of these elements: sirens, rats, and the water reaching to my chest, to my chin. . . .) At the time of the Cuban missile crisis she went back and forth to the supermarket until the cupboards were jammed. For Easter our school held a contest that involved pairs of children playing catch with raw eggs. "Only in this country do they teach children to throw food around." They say a European housewife could feed her family on what an American housewife throws away. Suppers from my childhood: boiled eggs and spinach, knockwurst, scrambled pancakes with applesauce. My mother's love of sweets would eventually cost her every tooth in her head. Sometimes we made a whole meal out of a pie or a cake. We ate Hershey bars between slices of white bread for lunch. At our house you did not get up from the table until you had cleaned your plate. A common punishment: to be sent to bed without any supper.

I don't think I ever saw her truly relaxed. Some part of her was always going—head, hand, foot. Even when she was sitting still, her breath came a little fast. I suspected that she had high blood pressure. No way to know for sure, since she never had it checked. She wanted nothing to do with doctors. Though she suffered from headaches aspirin couldn't touch, she would not go to a doctor for a stronger prescription. When small growths like blisters appeared on the whites of her eyes, she removed them herself with a sewing needle. "But you'll get an infection!" "Ach, don't be silly, I sterilized the needle." Who needs doctors?

She had good hands and she was always making things. At Christmas she baked and decorated dozens of cookies, storing them in tins with slices of apple to keep them fresh. She copied scenes from children's books onto our t-shirts using magic marker, and covered her bedroom walls with abstract flowers made with crumpled paper dipped in paint. She learned to sew first of all for economy, but then an obsession took hold of her. Day after day we would come home from school to find the beds unmade, dishes in the sink, and my mother hunched at her Singer. After a long day of sewing she would spend her evenings knitting. She made everything from bathing suits to winter coats. She was like a maiden in a fairy tale, spinning, spinning. Soon the closets bulged. All that work ruined those beautiful hands. The scissors raised a great welt on the knuckle of the third finger of her right hand, and crushed her thumbnail. Instead of being proud of her work, she would rather have had others believe the clothes were store bought. I *was* proud, and bragged to my friends that she had made my new red velveteen coat. Liar, they sneered, when they saw the label she had sewn in the lining.

She had a green thumb. Neighbors brought her plants that seemed in danger of dying. And she saved from dying, too, a score of sick or injured animals—squirrels, birds, a cat that had been trapped in a burning house. I remember as blessed those times when she was engrossed in nursing some creature back to health. It was good to see all her gentleness brought out. For those hands that could make plants bloom and heal a broken wing could also destroy and cause pain. They tore things and smashed things. They pinched, slapped, and shoved.

I sit on her bed watching her get ready to go out. The process of putting on her face takes a long time and is always the same, but I never tire of it. Those tempting little pots and tubes with names like desserts: Frosted Cherry; Plum Delight. The magic mascara wand. Abracadabra: blond lashes are black. She says it helps if you keep your mouth open when putting on eye makeup. She is in her slip and stockings, the bumps of her garters standing out on her thighs. When she crosses her legs, there is the hiss of nylon against nylon. She says that European women are better at using cosmetics than American women. "American women look so cheap." She always puts her lipstick on last, but first she rubs a dry toothbrush lightly across her lips to smooth them. I pick up the tissue she uses to blot her mouth and fit my mouth to the imprint. The next part of her toilette I don't like. Before pulling on her dress, to protect it from stains, she ties a scarf over her face. Standing there in her nylons and slip with the scarf over her face she is a disconcerting sight.

People said, "Your mother is so pretty." But she didn't see herself like that. I could tell by the way she spoke of other women that she did not count herself among the pretty ones. She was not flirtatious. She was never charming in a strictly feminine way. She had no use for feminine wiles, and she hated being ogled by men. She would not wear sexy clothing. Her daughters were another story: "When you are young you can get away with anything." Not all agreed. The Dean of Boys stopped me in the hall. "Does your mother know you're walking around like that?" "She made this for me." "Well, tell her this is a high school, not a skating rink." I was chagrined, but my mother laughed. "It's his own guilty conscience that's bothering him."

She didn't like to go to parties where she might be asked to dance. "I don't want a strange man putting his arms around me."

She never complained about getting older. She looked much younger than she was anyway. Once, on her way to the store, she crossed in front of a police car and the patrolman called out through his bullhorn, "Young lady, shouldn't you be in school?" "I gave him a dirty look and kept walking." I knew that look. I'd seen her shoot it at a lot of men. In time her coldness towards men would seem to me a miscalculation: Hadn't she ever considered the possibility that being nice to men could get a woman things she might not otherwise have?

Though she would always color her hair she gave up trying to stay slim. As she put on weight, her jaunty walk became more of a waddle. You would not have thought she had once been good at gymnastics. But she could still bend from the waist with straight knees and touch her palms to the floor.

She might not enjoy going to parties, but she threw herself wholeheartedly into helping me get ready for one. She made my dress. She did my hair. She got into a competitive spirit: "You'll be the prettiest one there." By the time I was in high school her moods in general tended to be brighter. I think it had to do with her children growing up. I was the only one still at home. Young enough to be still under her thumb but old enough not to be a burden. I did well in school, I made her proud. (But if someone complimented me in my presence she would shake her head. "Please. She thinks highly enough of herself as it is.") She was curious about all aspects of my life and took pleasure in those adolescent triumphs: making cheerleaders, being asked to the prom. The carefree, promising youth she herself had not known.

(I spent the summer of my twentieth year in California. One day my friends and I took LSD and went to the beach. At sundown, driving home in our jeep, we were still high. On acid, every passing thought can strike like an epiphany, and this one seemed to fill my head with light: My mother had never known this. To be driving with your friends in an open car, laughing; to be twenty and happy and free with the wind in your hair and your life ahead of you—she had missed all that.)

There may have been another reason why her moods improved with the years. When I first started having periods, I sat down one day and did some math. Once a month times 12 months times 23 years. So she had been through this already 276 times.

I found her everywhere in my reading. Children are said to see images of their own mothers in the stepmothers and witches of fairy tales, but I always saw mine in the innocent blond girl, often the prisoner of the witch, forced to labor at her sweeping or spinning. Later, I would identify her with any damsel in distress, with romantic heroines like Anna Karenina, Emma Bovary, and Scarlett O'Hara. I placed her under the sign of beauty, suffering, and loss.

Sitting on her lap as she pages through a magazine. One ad after another showing beautiful women in beautiful dresses. "You should wear this, Mommy." "You would look nice in that." Her response is gruff. "And where would I wear such a thing—to the laundry room?"

The hours and hours she spent beading the gown I would wear to the country club dance.

She swiftly disabused us of certain notions acquired at school. America is the land of equal opportunity. All men are brothers. The best things in life are free.

Home for lunch, I eat my sandwich while she sits at the kitchen table pasting S & H green stamps into a book.

The hum of her sewing machine. The funny munching sound of her pinking shears. Singing while she works.

Sometimes, I would catch her looking at me with a gently stricken expression. In a sad voice she would say, "You are a good kid, you really are."

She taught me the original German words to "Silent Night," which I sang in a Christmas pageant.

Her favorite English poet was Tennyson.

Back in Germany for the first time in almost twenty years, she realized that she was forgetting her German. "I go into a store, I want to ask for something, and for a second I have to struggle for the German word." With the years she lost more and more German, and at some point—she doesn't remember when—she began thinking in English. After living in America twice as long as she lived in Germany, she finds that German has become her second tongue. She stops reading German. Dining in a German restaurant, she orders in English. But her accent remains as thick as it ever was, and she still makes the same mistakes. "They stood in a motel for a week."

I never saw her at a loss for words. She was always able to say what she wanted to say. She could always say what she was feeling. Her memory was excellent, as were her powers of observation. Nothing escaped her, you could not put anything over on her. I think she had a good mind.

She had no best friend, no one (besides her daughters, as we grew older) to whom she could really talk, no confidante. She didn't trust people. If anyone tried to get close to her she backed off. "People are too much trouble."

Although she insisted that you obey all the rules without question, she was disdainful when you asked to do something because everyone else was doing it. "What are you, a sheep?"

She had strong opinions about everything. Opinions *should* be strong, otherwise they are not worth having (Goethe).

Her people, the Swabians: known for their bluntness and for their love of order.

She was different. She did not *belong*.

She said, "Give women power and they'll turn out to be worse than men." (She always expected the worst of people. She thought humankind was irredeemable. Her punishments were always given more in anger than in sorrow.)

For a while, when I was in grade school, she used to write poems based on themes from mythology. She made the costumes for some of our school plays. Always a supply of pink and blue yarn on hand (in our neighborhood someone was always having a baby). No one I ever knew had such smart hands.

There are times when I seem to remember her as though she were a landscape rather than a person: Those blue eyes filled the entire sky of my childhood.

Once, when we were driving on the highway, another car came hurtling towards us, missing us by a hair. At the moment when it looked as if we would die, she said "Mama."

331

At her lowest she would say, "I feel like a bug crushed under someone's heel."

I believe that, in spite of all her bitter railing against her lot, she never really expected anything different.

You made your own bed now you have to lie in it.

I don't believe my mother made her own bed.

Nominated by Kristina McGrath, H. L. Van Brunt, Iowa Review

BUT BIRD

by PAUL ZIMMER

from THE GEORGIA REVIEW

Some things you should forget,
But Bird was something to believe in.
Autumn 1954, twenty, drafted,
Stationed near New York en route
To the atomic tests in Nevada,
I taught myself to take
A train to Pennsylvania Station,
Walk up Seventh to 52d Street,
Looking for music and legends.
One night I found the one
I wanted. Bird.

Five months later no one was brave
When the numbers ran out.
All equal—privates, sergeants,
Lieutenants, majors, colonels—
All down on our knees in the slits
As the voice counted backward
In the darkness turning to light.

But "Charlie Parker" it said
On the Birdland marquee,
And I dug for the cover charge,
Sat down in the cheap seats.
He slumped in from the kitchen,
Powder-blue serge and suedes.
No jive Bird, he blew crisp and clean,
Bringing each face in the crowd

333

Gleaming to the bell of his horn.
No fluffing, no wavering,
But soaring like on my old
Verve waxes back in Ohio,
He smiled, nodding to applause.

Months later, down in the sand,
The bones in our fingers were
Suddenly X-rayed by the flash.
We moaned together in light
That entered everything,
Tried to become the earth itself
As the shock rolled toward us.

But Bird. I sat through three sets,
Missed the last train out,
Had to bunk in a roach pad,
Sleep in my uniform, almost AWOL.
But Bird was giving it all away,
One of his last great gifts,
And I was there with my
Rosy cheeks and swan neck,
Looking for something to believe in.

When the trench caved in it felt
Like death, but we clawed out,
Walked beneath the roiling, brutal cloud
To see the flattened houses,
Sheep and pigs blasted,
Ravens and rabbits blind,
Scrabbling in the grit and yucca.

But Bird. Remember Bird,
Though of course he was gone
Five months later, dead,
While I was down on my knees,
Wretched with fear in
The cinders of the desert.

Nominated by Lisel Mueller, Dan Masterson, Walter Pavlich

TO THE MUSE

by CAROL MUSKE

from AMERICAN POETRY REVIEW

NEW YEAR'S EVE, 1990

She danced topless, the light-eyed drunken girl
who got up on the bow of our pleasure boat
last summer in the pretty French Mediterranean.

Above us rose the great grey starboard flank
of an aircraft carrier. Sailors clustered
on the deck above, cheering, and the caps rained down,

a storm of insignia: S.S. *Eisenhower.*
I keep seeing the girl when I tell you
the Eisenhower's now in the Gulf, as if

the two are linked: the bare-breasted dancer
and a war about to be fought. Caps fell
on the bow and she plucked one up, set it rakishly

on her red hair. In the introspective manner
of the very drunk, she tipped her face dreamily up,
wet her lips, an odalisque, her arms crossed akimbo

on the cap. Someone, a family member, threw a shirt
over her and she shrugged it off, laughing, palms
fluttering about her nipples. I tell you I barely knew

335

those people, but you, you liked the girl, you
liked the ship. You like to fuck, you told me.
The sex of politics is its intimate divisive plural,

we, us, ours. *Who's over there?* you ask—*not us.*
Your pal is there, a flier stationed on a carrier.
He drops the jet shrieking on the deck. Pitch dark:

he lowers the nose toward a floating strip of
lit ditto marks and descends. Like writing haiku—
the narrator is a landscape. A way of staying subjective

but humbling the perceiver: a pilot's view.
When you write to your friend I guess that
there are no margins, you want him to see

everything you see and so transparent is
your kind bravado: he sees that too. Maybe
he second-guesses your own desire to soar over

the sand ruins, sit yourself in the masked pit
and rise fifteen hundred screaming feet a minute
into an inaccessible shape: falcon, hawk—Issa's

blown petals? Reinvent war, then the woman's
faithless, enslaved dance. Reinvent sailors bawling

at the rail and one intoxicated trick turning in
the dazzling light. Then the psyche re-inventing itself,
breaking the spell, reversing it: Caps on the waves, as if

they'd begun tossing away their uniforms, medals, stars.
See—I can make the girl wake up, dress, face west,
a lengthening, powerful figurehead: swept gold with fire.

I can make everything I thought indefensible change in the waves
of merciless light: the you, the me, the wars. Here is the worst
of it, stripped, humiliated—or dancing on the high deck,

bully-faced, insatiable. Here is the lie that loves us
as history personified, here's the personification: muse,
odalisque
soldier, night fell swear to us this time I can make it right.

Nominated by Jane Hirshfield, David St. John, Sherod Santos

WAR

fiction by MOLLY GILES

from SHENANDOAH

THE FIRST THINGS I noticed when I got back were all the dead plants in the yard. It was as if he'd played God with the garden hose, because the bush beans and peas were all right, but the tomatoes and peppers and corn had dried out. I always like to follow his reasoning when I can, and this, I figured, was his passive-aggressive way of killing what he considered Latin vegetables as a way of punishing me for going to Nicaragua. If I'd gone to Belfast he'd have killed the potatoes, if I'd gone to Lebanon he'd have killed the eggplant. You have to know him to understand how his mind works, and then you have to explain it to him because he pretends not to know himself. I don't bother to do this anymore; since the divorce he's on his own. I just observe.

His truck was gone—only an oil stain to show where he'd parked on the grass—and he'd put a new latch on the gate that was so complicated I had to set my duffle bag down to figure it out. I'd just about decided I'd have to climb over when Cass came running out the front door and down the path toward me. We gripped hands through the gate like two lovers in prison, hopping up and down and trying to kiss through the grids. "Are you all right?" I kept shouting. "I'm fine," she shouted back. She laughed. "Why wouldn't I be?" She slid the gate open and held her arms up, just like she used to do when she was a baby, but her arms came up to my chin now, and she was almost too heavy to lift. "I've missed you so much," she said.

338

I'd missed her too. It had only been ten days but I felt as if I'd returned from another century. Cass felt large in my arms, and solid, and astonishingly American, with her pink cheeks and bubblegum smell and rough blonde hair and new sneakers. At least he bought her decent shoes, I thought, as I swung her around and set her down. The last time he stayed with her he bought her a leather jacket like the Nazis used to wear. We'd had such a fight about it Cass had finally taken the jacket off and thrown it at both of us. Cass—we agree on this at least—deserves better parents.

She helped me with my bag and we went into the house, talking all the way. "You were in the paper," she said. "They had a big article on the peace conference and they had your name and everything, and Mrs. Bettinger read it to my class and said you were a heroine."

"Some heroine," I said. I was pleased, but I'd seen too many real heroes and heroines in the last few days. "All I did was make lists," I told her. "I helped people off one bus and onto another. It was hard work in a way, but it wasn't very exciting." I set my bag down. "How was it for you here? Did you have fun?"

"Not really," Cass said.

I nodded, sympathetic, and glanced across the front room toward the couch. You could tell it had had quite a workout while I'd been gone. There were three big dents in the cushions. The coffee table had been pulled in close, with the remote control at arm's reach, and there was a new circle stain on the wood where his beer had been set down, night after night.

"It looks like he slept on that couch," I said.

"He did."

"Every night?" I stepped closer. I could practically see him there, one hand over his mouth as he snored, the other hand over his crotch. "Just like he used to do when we were married," I marveled. "Did he take his clothes off at least?"

"He said there wasn't any point," Cass said. "He'd just have to wear them the next day."

"What about his shoes?"

"I think he took his shoes off."

"And you?"

"Me?" Cass laughed. "You want to know what I slept in?"

339

"No. I want to know—were you lonely? With him falling asleep in front of TV every night?"

"No," Cass said. "I didn't mind it."

I looked into her face. There were no dark circles under her eyes, no pinch to her lips, no sign of neglect.

"He never talks," I reminded her.

"We had popcorn every night. Kentucky Fried twice. Pizza three times. One night we just had soda and chips."

I shuddered. All those home-cooked casseroles I had left in the freezer with instructions taped on them—ignored. The bran bread and marmalade I'd made, untouched. The sprouts shriveled up in their little glass jar; the tofu amelt in its own sour juice. I pulled off my sweater and looked around. The house felt different but in a way I couldn't define, dirtier somehow, although there were no signs of dirt or disorder. The ferns were all dry in their pots, but alive. The books I'd been studying before I left were still on the table, collecting dust and overdue fines, and the Spanish language tapes Mark had smuggled off an Army base were still threaded through the cassette deck.

"It's good to be home," I said, not too sure. "But it smells funny. Do you smell anything?"

"Like what?"

"Like socks. Old socks. And . . . machine parts? And—I don't know . . . musk?"

"No. It smells like home to me."

"I think I'm going through culture shock," I admitted. "Everything down there smelled like lime trees and sewage. And the people had so little. We have so much more. This room looks . . . jammed."

I had a great urge to start carting things out to the sidewalk— lamps we didn't need, extra chairs, the wicker chest, the TV set, the couch—things other people could use. Then I wanted to scrub and air, and wash all the windows. But I was tired; the flight back had been a long one, and the conference had drained me. I felt if I closed my eyes for a second I'd see Blanca or one of the little soldiers and they'd be more real to me than this room. "It's a strange phenomenon," I said to Cass in my best speaker's voice, "but the more you know the less you know. You know?"

"I know," said Cass.

340

"Brought you some presents." I crouched by my pack and started to pull out the books—as always, I'd bought too many books—"Who," he used to say, "are you going to pay to read them all for you?"—and I had a lot of newspapers too—it's endlessly amazing to me, the news we don't get in the States—and my address book was jammed with new names and there were letters I'd promised to forward and articles I'd promised to try and get published. Finally I found the bright embroidered shirt I'd bought Cass and the friendship bracelets the Mendoza children had woven for her. I also brought out the big seashell I'd found on the beach. "I did have some M-16 bullets to bring you," I confessed, "but I didn't think I could get them through airport security. So I buried them beneath a jacaranda tree just before I left. Maybe someone will find them in a hundred years and make a necklace from them."

Cass smiled, the seashell balanced perfectly in her palm. I straightened and went into the kitchen to see if he'd remembered to feed the cats or water the basil in the window sill. The basil was long gone and it looked like he'd dumped coffee grounds or something on the pots. The cats looked healthy enough but they were so glad to see me, butting their old heads against my throat when I picked them up, that I knew he'd never petted them once. I hugged them close as I went through the mail. There was a long letter from Mercedes, thanking me for my speech, and a card from the head of the Direct Aid Committee. There was nothing from Mark. Unless he took it, I thought. But why would he take a letter from Mark? He doesn't know who Mark is, and even if he did, he wouldn't care. One of your little hippie friends. That's what he called the men I started to see after we split up. One of your little peace-nik pals. If he ever met Mark, who is six years younger than I, he'd call him something like Sonny and he'd shake his hand with this grim pained look on his face as if he were saying, "You poor sucker. Wait till you find out what she's really like."

I put down the mail and glanced at the message pad on the kitchen wall. There in that stingy scrawl I knew so well were two messages—two, in the whole time I'd been gone! One said, "Call your sister Barbara," and I immediately thought, "But I don't have a sister Barbara," just as, in the old days, he would trick me into saying, "But I don't have a meeting tomorrow," and he'd say,

"Oh, did I say tomorrow? I must have meant yesterday, looks like you missed it." The number beneath the name was one digit short, as if he were just too weary to write the whole thing out. The other message, marked, "Important! Don't forget!" was an appointment change from my dentist.

"That jerk," I muttered.

"Don't put my father down," Cass said calmly, slipping into a chair at the kitchen table beside me. "He doesn't put you down."

"Of course he does." I showed Cass the newspaper articles he'd cut out and saved for me. One was about a woman just my age who had single-handedly stopped the destruction of 10,000 acres of rain forest. Another gave new evidence that Joan of Arc was a man. Two were about AIDS, and one was about cigarettes causing facial wrinkles. "He just does it in a way no one but I can understand," I explained. I was remembering the birthday card he'd sent last month. It showed a woman in a black cloak walking toward the edge of a cliff. Inside he'd written, in pencil, "Hope some of your dreams come true," and I'd ripped it from corner to corner, thinking, *All* my dreams are going to come true, and they're not dreams, you fool, they are real choices in a real world and they are going to happen because I'm going to make them happen, and they are going to happen *soon*.

I lit the first cigarette I'd wanted since I'd been home and exhaled, staring out the kitchen window. It was strange to see my own backyard, and again I had the feeling that I wasn't home yet, that Blanca or her mother or one of the men on the bus would be walking in any second, talking to me in a language I did not understand, asking for help I could not give. I glanced at Cass. "He didn't see that article that called me a 'heroine' did he?" Cass half-shrugged and ducked her head. "Good," I said. "Because he would have used it to line the rat's cage with."

"Mom." Cass was shocked, I knew, because the only time she calls me Mom is when I'm not acting like one. I stubbed my cigarette out; I felt ashamed. After all, peace begins at home; that's what I tell everyone I talk to, and it's true, too, in some homes at least. I turned my hand toward Cass, palm up. "I'm sorry," I said. I could see her pet rat's cage in the corner and it was lined, appropriately, with the front page of the *New York Times*. "I'm not being fair," I said. "And anyway," I remembered, "it wasn't the paper that called me a heroine, it was your teacher."

"She did?" Again I felt a rush of pleasure and shame. If I were truly living by my values, I thought, I'd be back in Nicaragua, doing something real about the real horrors I saw there.

Cass looked at me. "What was it like?" she asked.

"Just like here," I said. "Only with people trying to kill you."

Cass waited, patient, and after a second I started to talk. I talked about the young boys in uniform, so playful and shy you think they're joking, and then you notice their carbines. About the flat-bed truck full of men with their hands tied behind their backs, and about the spotted dog that chased that truck, howling, through six blocks of traffic. I talked about the soldiers I'd seen at the beach, patrolling the empty waves, and about the white pig in the Mendoza's front yard, and the bombed-out school house and the bombed-out hospital and the shops full of car parts and Barbie dolls I'd seen in the city. I talked about Blanca, a girl her age who had tuberculosis, and about Blanca's mother, who claimed to see "ghosts" when she prayed, the ghosts of all the men in her village who had disappeared or been killed.

Cass listened, intent. She is a wonderful listener, so different from her father, and she asks all the right questions—questions, that is, I can't answer. "Why can't people," she asked, "just be nicer to each other? Why can't we all get along?"

"I don't know," I told her. "You'd think it would be so simple, but it's not."

Cass nodded and yawned. It was getting dark and we were both tired. She gave me a last hug and went into her room to listen to tapes before she fell asleep, and I peeled off my filthy jeans and T-shirt and went to the bathroom to take a long shower.

The bathroom looked as unfamiliar as the rest of the house, too big by far, and faintly unclean, and cluttered with things we don't need. The shower floor had that sticky tar-like substance on it that he used to bring home on his skin from the shop, so I knew that even if he hadn't slept on a real bed, he'd at least had the sense to wash once or twice. I thought of him standing here, naked, in the same space where I stood, with his eyes open and the water beating down and his bare feet where my feet were, and it gave me the creeps. I saw one of his brown hairs, thin as a spider leg, stuck to the wall, and I aimed the shower at it to hose it down. I wanted every last trace of him out of my house. I turned the water off, glad to step out. As I toweled my hair I noticed a

343

bottle of perfume on the counter, an old bottle of musk stuff I used to wear when we were first married. I sniffed it, curious. Was that what I'd smelled when I first came in the house? Did he wear my perfume when I was gone?

I frowned at the bottle, troubled. It brought back a time I don't think of often, when we were living like gypsies, he and I, traveling up and down the coast in a beat-up old van, picking apples and strawberries, sleeping on beaches, fighting even then, of course, but talking. We did a lot of talking in those years, before he decided to start his own business, before I decided to go back to school, before we had Cass. We did a lot of laughing, and I miss that sometimes, the way we used to roar at each other. Now when he laughs it's this silent wheeze, as if someone just punched him, and he only laughs at the bad news—my car being towed delighted him for days, and the power failure the time I was being interviewed on the radio.

I put the perfume down, pulled on a robe, and went back to the kitchen to see if he'd left any wine. As I passed the guest room I glanced in to see if Cass had been right, and she had been—the guest bed was untouched, the curtains were drawn, the note I'd left to thank him for staying with his own child was still tucked, unread, under the vase where the roses and poppies had dried on their stalks. He never once took what I had to offer, I thought. He never liked the food I cooked or the books I read or the friends I brought home. He wasn't interested in the classes I went to or the papers I wrote or the ideas that made me want to shout all night. "It's such an act," he'd say, when I'd come home late, flushed and hoarse from one of the meetings. "You're such a fake." And his eyes, when he looked at me then from his place on the couch, were almost wide-open, almost alive. Then they'd hood again, and he'd turn from me.

I picked up the vase, crumpled the note, and went into the kitchen. The garbage bag was full of beer bottles and pizza boxes and losing lottery tickets and TV listings. I made some instant coffee. I'd lived on nothing but coffee for weeks, it seemed, and I was used to it; it didn't even keep me awake any more. As I stirred in the honey the phone rang. It was Mark. He was three-hundred miles away, at another conference, and I could hear a woman laughing and two men arguing behind him. "Hey," he said, sounding far-off and rushed, "how was your time down

344

there? I want to hear all about it. But maybe when I get back, okay? Right now I just wanted you to know there's something on TV tonight about the Sandinistas."

"Okay," I said. "I'll watch it. And Mark? What would you think of a man who got into a woman's perfume?"

"I'd think he wanted to be close to her in some way," Mark said. "Got to run. I'll call." He blew me a kiss and hung up.

Close to me? I carried my coffee in to the couch and sat down. The pillows reeked of that old musk stuff and I pushed them away, sickened. The way to be close to me is to talk to me, and let me talk back, and to touch me, and let me reach out. He couldn't do that; it was too hard. The only thing he could do was lie on this couch, night after night, and brush me aside when I wanted to talk. "You're in my way," he'd said once, when I was trying to tell him about an article I was trying to write. "You're blocking the light."

"That's not *light*," I pointed out. "That's the TV. Don't you know the difference?"

"No," he drawled, dumb, "I don't know the difference. I'm just the bozo who brings home the bacon. You know the difference. Right? So why don't you tell me—like you tell everyone, over and over, on and on, all the time. Why don't you educate me?" he said. "Why don't you change my life?"

His life. I remembered something the woman who saw ghosts had asked me. "Do you think," she had asked, "we make our own lives?" And I'd answered, "No, how could we?"—for I was thinking of her, and the horrible things that had happened to her, none of them her fault or her choice. But what about him? Look how he lives. He still sleeps in the shop. He started to sleep there before he moved out, and he hasn't moved since. Why don't you find an apartment, I say, or a little house, some place where Cass could visit you? We could afford it. I make money now, not a lot, not what he calls a "real" salary or a "real" job but the Peace Institute has promised to give me a raise in a month and my articles are starting to sell to the bulletins. He could easily find some place with neighbors and a garden and some sunshine, some place where Cass could have her own room on weekends. But no, he stays put.

He has a television there, of course, a huge color set, and a mattress on the floor in back. He has a refrigerator with nothing in it, and a hot plate he doesn't bother to use. He has some of Cass's art work on the walls, and a photo of the three of us at Disneyland when she was six, and a calendar that still shows snow. There's his desk with tools on it and gritty rags and old invoices everywhere.

He's alone most of the day and most of the night. He meets women in bars, and there was one girl, an aerobics instructor, who lasted almost three months. "She had problems," he said— which means, of course, she had life, she had hope, she moved on. He has no men friends outside the shop. He sees Cass once a week, on Sunday afternoons, and they go to the movies; Cass says he sleeps. He's lost twenty pounds and still wears that old blue jacket with the grease stain on the cuff. He won't see a therapist or get involved in a support group; when I suggest these things he just stares at me, his eyes bright with thoughts he finds very funny.

I set my coffee cup down with a bang on the table and reached for the remote control, wiping it first on my robe. I clicked on the set. There was the end of some comedy show: *stupid*. Then one of those wrestling matches he used to watch all the time: *stupid stupid*. Then the news: *stupid stupid stupid*. Then the show Mark wanted me to see. Some liar from Associated Press was asking some liar from the Pentagon all the wrong questions and getting all the wrong answers and despite myself I started to drift off. My head just kept getting heavier and heavier and I could feel myself fade.

I had this image—not a dream exactly, just an image that kept getting bigger and bigger. It was something I'd seen down there, from the bus, when we were driving through cane fields. It was a turkey vulture, tall and black and ugly the way vultures are, with their bare red necks and bald heads and it was sitting on a fence post hunched over watching something in the dirt below. "Look," the man beside me had said, "he's waiting for his dinner to die," and we'd shivered and talked about other things and I hadn't thought about that bird again, but now it appeared to me, huge as a man, familiar and close, and I realized it was perched on the edge of the couch. It was peering down, patient, waiting for me to get tired and give up. I wanted to, too.

The conference—I could never tell Mark this—but the conference hadn't accomplished a thing. Blanca was still dying, her mother was seeing new ghosts every day, the baby boys were still aiming their guns. What's the point? I thought. What makes me think I can make any difference? I'm as weak and shallow and false as he said I was.

The vulture bent close and I hated him so I jerked up with a start. My head was buzzing and my throat was dry and my legs were numb, but I got to my feet, and even though I knew I was being what he used to call "ridiculous," I watched the rest of that damn show with my arms crossed, standing up, and when that jerk from the Pentagon said, "This is not a war, see, what we have down here is not a war, it's what we call a 'low intensity conflict,' not a war at all," I hooted so hard that I woke Cass up and she came trailing out, still wearing the embroidered shirt I'd brought her, stumbling a little with sleep as she put her arms around me saying, "Come to bed now, Mom. You're home."

Nominated by David Jauss, Shenandoah

347

CRITTERWORLD

fiction by STEVE WATKINS

from MISSISSIPPI REVIEW

FIRST THE rumors.

No, Henry's Meats didn't come around with their knives to carve steaks from the body. Mutt & Jeff's Grill didn't serve elephant-burgers.

Nobody sawed off the feet for umbrella stands. Nobody caught any weird African diseases, no elephantiasis. The little girl from Michigan, the one who got trapped in the car, she might have seen a psychiatrist for awhile, but if she did it was back up North so I don't see how anybody could have known for sure about that story, true or not.

And the elephant's name wasn't Stash, like "trash." It was Stash, like in "lost."

But people will say anything, I know that now, especially in a little town like ours, and I guess the best thing is not to even listen, though I don't see how that's possible unless you go deaf. You could still do everything you wanted if you were deaf. You could even make great music, like Beethoven; you just wouldn't be able to hear it is all.

I told my mother that after what happened to Stash. My mother was the only one I talked to for a long time, maybe about a month. But she just hugged me and said, "Oh Charlie, do you know what? That Beethoven story is so sad it always makes me cry."

We were there when it happened, of course—me and Jun Morse and George Mabry—out by 301 a mile south of town,

348

sitting in the ditch across the road, pretty well hidden behind the tall weeds and under the billboard that said "Critterworld, Florida's First Zoo" which I always thought was kind of a lie because it made you think *first ever* when it was really just the first you got to when you crossed the state line. Jun and George were doing their Advanced Geometry homework. We were all three in the accelerated class. In fact, we *were* the accelerated class. They drove us over to high school from eighth grade so we could sit in a room full of eleventh graders who tried to cheat off our tests. I liked it more than Jun and George, though, because I shared my book with this one girl named Sharla, who was a cheerleader but still pretty nice, and she would scoot her desk right next to mine and sometimes when we were both hunched over the book my elbow touched her boob but she didn't move and either didn't know or didn't mind, and I kept it there as long as I could until I lost all the feeling in my arm.

Anyway, the other guys were doing geometry and I was watching Stash when it happened. One minute he was standing there, this hundred-year-old elephant, not moving except for the ends of his flappy ears, and it might have been a breeze doing that. The next minute he seemed to sort of wobble. He lifted his chained leg, looked at it as if he'd just realized what they'd done to him, even though he'd been chained to that iron ring in front of Critterworld for as long as anybody could remember. He raised his trunk. He swung his head from side to side, made a noise that sounded like all the air rushing from his body, then fell sideways on top of the Volkswagen.

I stood straight up and stepped on George's homework. All I could think about at first was why did they park their car so close to Stash? The explanation later, the one the father of the little girl gave to the Jacksonville paper, was they didn't think Stash was alive. Stash was so still, and so dusty from standing there all those years by the highway, that they thought he was a statue of an elephant, like over in Weekee Wachi they have that brontosaurus that's really a gas station, or like out West my mother told me about a World's Biggest Prairie Dog.

Since there's nothing once you get south of town except scrub brush, slash pine, and Critterworld, and since the little girl's parents were inside the Critterworld snack shop, I was the first to hear her screaming inside the car. And initially I didn't believe it was somebody screaming, because Stash flattened the car so badly and I couldn't see how there could be anybody inside. George was yelling at me to get off his geometry homework, too, so that made it hard to hear anything else. George is just anal about his homework anyway—writes everything out on graph paper in this tiny block print that looks like a computer wrote it, which you might say is sort of the case, because when they did the eighth grade aptitude test it was old George Mabry that not only scored in the 99th percentile, but actually answered all the questions and didn't miss one. They announced it at an assembly. Jun and I and two girls were in the 90th percentile, but Jun— whose real name used to be John until he decided he needed to change it—told me all the tests really measured was your ability to take tests. Somehow to him that meant that being in the 90th or even the 99th percentile was, to use his favorite phrase, a meaningless abstraction, but I didn't see how it was meaningless since my whole life seemed to be about taking tests, so it was comforting to know I was good at it. When you make all As, you just figure they're grading on the curve and most of the kids in class aren't too smart, so your A is a relative thing, to use another one of Jun's favorite phrases. But when they rank you with the whole state of Florida, you have to figure there are some pretty smart people out there that you're up against.

Not that I ever felt as smart as Jun or George. Even though everybody lumped us together as the eggheads of junior high and all because of our grades and because we hung out together and because we played chess in home room, I always thought I was pulling something over on the teachers, working really, really hard to seem like I was as smart as them, when the truth was that I'm not actually all that intelligent. I said that to my mother after the time I got accused of cheating on a science test. A kid had told the teacher I looked on George's answer sheet, when all I was really doing was seeing how far along George was on the test, which of course was a lot further along than me. Nothing happened, though, because Mrs. Crow said she knew I would never cheat, and besides, what was that kid doing looking around during a test anyway? Still, I was pretty upset, and I told my mother I thought I was getting an ulcer from trying to pretend I was as smart as George and Jun.

What she said was, "Of course you're smart, Charlie. Just maybe not in the same way as your friends. You have an intuitive intelligence."

The funny thing was that nobody really cared if I was smart, or if Jun was, or if George was. I mean, teachers cared, and our parents cared, and George and Jun certainly cared about themselves. George already had a correspondence going with the registrar at M.I.T., and I'm not making that up. But other kids didn't care, and I only cared in a weird way because being smart, or pretending to be smart, was about the only thing I was good at. It was all I had. I couldn't play basketball, even though I worked at it all the time. I wasn't big enough or fast enough or strong enough. I didn't know how to talk to girls, except for smart girls about school subjects, and except for that cheerleader, Sharla, who talked to me sometimes about things, like the difference between dancing and dance. Dancing was what she loved to do; dance was what she wanted to study when she got to college. But she had a football-player boyfriend, and whenever she was with him I pretty much ceased to exist.

But there I was, anyway—to get back to the story—standing on George Mabry's graph paper, staring across the road, shaking my head to figure out if that really was somebody screaming. It was Jun who made the first move. He stood beside me and said, "Stash! Wow!" and then he said, "Squashed bug!" He grabbed my arm and we both ran across the highway to the car. George was too busy collecting his papers and books to come right away.

We could just see the little girl's face through what was left of the passenger door window; Stash had pretty much flattened the driver's side. The girl was flat on the floor of the car, screaming in a way that sounded more like squealing—like "Hreeeee-hreeeee-hreeeee"—and I think it was as much to get her to stop as anything else that I started pushing like crazy against Stash to get him off the car. That's how stupid I was.

Jun ran inside Critterworld to get help. He told me later that when he came back out with the parents I was hitting Stash's head with my fists and yelling at him to get up, but that's not how I remember it. I just remember pushing and pushing, and dust rising off Stash in little puffs right in my face, and not really figuring out he was dead until the girl's father shoved me out of

351

the way and I stepped back and looked into one of those big elephant eyes that was wide open but already dusted over, too.

A dozen cars stopped, some of them right there in the highway, before the sheriffs finally showed up. The little girl had quit squealing by then—partly because she'd figured out she wasn't going to die, and partly because Jun got her a bottle of Coke from Critterworld and stuck about ten straws together into one long one to reach her mouth. The father yelled at Jun when he first brought it out, but the mother said, "Let the boy help, Clyde," and the father got a little nicer after that and they threaded the straw through a crack in what was left of the window and down to the girl trapped on the floor.

After that, Jun moved off a short ways from the crowd. He couldn't stand crowds. He told me once that he was an ascetic, and that there were two kinds: the ones that choose it, as a means to something, and the ones that are born to it, the ones like him. That was supposed to explain his aversion to crowds. At the time I didn't even know what he meant by *ascetic*, and when I looked it up I had the wrong spelling so I went around for a long time with the wrong definition in my head. I did the same thing with *cavalry* and *Calvary*, too, but that was in second grade.

I didn't want to leave Stash when Jun moved away. Everybody was so mad at him for dying and crushing the VW and trapping the little Michigan girl, I guess I felt like Stash needed somebody on his side, an advocate or something, even though he was dead.

Not that I said anything to anybody. I laid my hand on the bottom of his foot, which was crusty because it was so old, but still not hard like you might expect, and I tried to remember everything I had read about elephants. The only line that came to me, though, was this one: "The powerful feet can trample an attacker into the ground, but are so softly cushioned that a whole herd of elephants can troop through a forest without making a sound."

George Mabry, meanwhile, wasn't having any problems remembering. He was over in front of the monkey cage where they kept the psycho-monkey that everybody flicked cigarette butts at, and he was lecturing some kids about elephant penises. For such a math-and-science nut, it's amazing how much George Mabry went in for the dirty stuff. He told those kids that an elephant

352

penis weighs sixty pounds, and it gets four feet long when the elephant gets aroused, and sometimes, if the elephant is chasing a cow, he might even step on it. And he told them about how the penis is shaped sort of like an S, and the muscles at the end work on their own to poke around under the cow's belly to find the hole, which is way up underneath, not right there between the hind legs.

For some reason it really bothered me that George was telling them all that. I knew it, too, of course—Jun had given both of us the same book to read—but George was just showing off how much he knew, and what a dirty mind he had. Those kids, though, they didn't deserve to know that stuff. They hadn't earned the right like we had. It didn't seem appropriate, or fair, or something, that they should get it so cheaply, and for a minute I hated George Mabry, standing there in his high-water pants and nerd glasses with that hair he never washed, trying to be cool with those elementary school kids, trying to be cool like I knew none of us would ever be cool, not him or me or even Jun who always knew what to say and never had to show it off like George the M.I.T. nerd.

I saw all of us in that second as these three very brainy but mostly very pathetic guys who didn't have any friends but one another, and even those friendships as a sort of last resort because nobody else would have us. I looked at Stash's old yellow tusks, or what was left of them since they'd been sawed off short before I ever knew him, and I looked down between his legs and saw just this shrivelled worm of a penis, and I felt like crying and I felt like everything that had happened was my fault, as dumb as that may sound, but it was how I felt and in some ways how I still feel, no matter what my mother said later to cheer me up and no matter what sometimes I can think of to tell myself.

The girl was still trapped in the car, and the sheriffs, as it turned out, didn't have a clue for getting her free, and that's the way things stood for awhile, except for one thing I haven't mentioned yet, which is why Jun and George and I happened to be there in the first place, hiding out in the ditch across the highway from Critterworld. It was because we were studying old Stash and looking for a way to kill him ourselves.

Critterworld is the saddest place in Florida, maybe even in America. I only went inside once, and that was on a field trip in elementary school. Stash out front was so familiar to us that we hardly noticed him—all except Jun, who made a point of saying how much Stash disgusted him—and the psycho-monkey in the cage was already mean way back then from picking up lit cigarettes. When people came near he attacked the bars and tried to throw things, but for some reason he couldn't stop himself from picking up cigarette butts and burning his hands. All us kids crowded around the cage and teased him with monkey noises that day of the field trip, which frustrated him and made him crash wildly around, hurling himself at the bars as if he wanted to kill us, or kill himself trying.

Pay a dollar and you could go inside where they had the two-headed turtle collection, and the Siamese piglets disintegrating in a giant jar of formaldehyde. The whole place smelled of formaldehyde, as a matter of fact—that and the vomitty smell of very old, very wet straw. There were the snakes, of course, and all the girls cried when they saw the white rat shivering in a corner of the aquarium where they kept the boa constrictor. And there was the bald eagle with the broken wing that hadn't healed right so it couldn't fly. And the albino squirrels, and the furry chinchillas, and the Shetland pony. In the petting area they kept a lamb and a goat and a calf and a live piglet and a goose, but Jun told me Critterworld sold them all for slaughter except the goose once they grew past the cute-baby stage. Nobody liked the goose because he bit kids.

Our first plan—or rather Jun's first plan—was to get rid of all of Critterworld, maybe burn it down, but we quickly dropped that because it was too ambitious. "And besides," Jun told us, "The point is not to draw attention to ourselves or to the deed."

"Then what is the point?" I asked him—this was in home room a couple of weeks before everything happened, and Jun and George were playing chess while we debated our course of action.

George put Jun in check just then and Jun glared at me as if it was my fault, but also as if to say, "We can't keep going over and over this for you, Charlie." He was mad at me for bringing it up again, but I was still having a hard time figuring out why it meant so much to Jun to kill something. I mean, I understood the reasons he *said*, but Jun seemed so obsessive. That was the word my mother used for it later, anyway, and she said she thought it had something to do with Jun's father, who used to be head of maintenance at the hospital but lost a lot of jobs because of drinking and now ran a service station north of town out by the interstate. That made a lot of sense in a Sigmund Freud kind of way, I guess, but somehow when you're in the middle of things it all seems a lot more complicated, and with Jun, who could talk me into just about anything if he talked long enough, I'm still not sure.

The point, as he had explained a hundred times, was to kill a thing that had compromised itself so much that it no longer had a self. Something that wasn't true to its nature. Jun started talking about "essence" like it was something you could put in your book bag or hide in your locker, and he said Stash represented all those things that had lost their essence, and that's why we had to do away with him. George, who liked the idea from the start—but from a purely scientific perspective, as he kept reminding us—suggested killing the psycho-monkey instead, but Jun got really mad about that and said didn't we understand anything, and said the monkey was the only animal at Critterworld worth living.

Jun had gotten the idea from a story we read in another advanced class on World Literature. It was that Japanese book, *The Sailor Who Fell From Grace With the Sea*, which I personally hated but which Jun read about ten times and carried with him everywhere like a bible. It was about a bunch of kids who dissected their cat because he didn't catch mice anymore, and later they dissected a sailor, I think because he was dating their mom. That was when Jun decided he was an ascetic, which he said made plenty of sense because his family was Catholic and the Catholics had an ascetic tradition of sitting in the desert and fasting and wearing hairshirts, and Jun said he saw a connection between that and the Japanese ascetics, which was what he said those kids were in the book, and he went on his own fast for purification which lasted a couple of days until he went to bed one night and slept through all of the next day and the next night, too, and his parents took him to the emergency room thinking it had something to do with his hemophilia.

Jun said he had a visionary dream about knocking off Stash during his two-day sleep, and he convinced George and me to learn everything we could about elephants. He said we had to understand what Stash was supposed to be to experience the tragedy of what he was instead.

At first I went along because Jun was so persuasive, and because he said all we had to do was kill Stash, not dissect him. Plus it was usually easier to do what Jun wanted than to talk him out of it, and besides, he often lost interest in projects before we saw them through to the end. So we read the elephant book. We discussed elephant lore. We figured out that Stash was an African elephant rather than an Asian elephant—bigger ears—which I was happy about once I learned how they trained elephants to work in India which was to make a hole in the back of their skulls and poke inside the hole with an iron bar.

Studying Stash himself was my idea. We were having a hard time coming up with a way to kill him—George, in an uncharacteristically stupid moment, recommended dynamite; Jun said poison—and I suggested gathering first-hand data on the subject while we tried to figure it out. Jun agreed because, as he put it, we needed to become more elephant than the elephant. And of course the idea appealed to the scientist in George, who must have been the most empirical guy in the state.

So that's what we were doing when Stash died—or what I was doing. Jun just shrugged about it later and said it was coincidence; he said Stash saved us a lot of trouble by dying when he did, but something in his voice sounded false, and I wondered if maybe he wasn't more upset than he was letting on. His mother let him paint a St. George and the Dragon mural on his bedroom wall, which seemed to take his mind off ritual slaughter for awhile, and then we took up the Russians in that World Literature class and Jun decided to become a humanitarian.

My mother believes in God, which means she has a stock answer for things that can't be explained, and I go to church with her every week thinking one day it will rub off on me, too. She said God was watching out for us by taking Stash, but I still have my doubts.

After two hours trapped in the VW under Stash the little girl started squealing again—"Hreeee, hreeee, hreeee"—and nothing her mother or her father said could get her to stop. The sheriffs were useless, talking on their radios, calling more and more sheriffs to come out. They tried pulling Stash off with a wrecker truck, but that didn't work, and they were afraid he might shift and crush the car worse if they jerked at him hard.

Finally, though, Mr. Funderburke, the guy who owned Critterworld, got Steve's Sod Farm to send over three tractors and together they were able to drag Stash off the car. The welder burned the girl's arm with his blow torch cutting through the metal, but just a little, just a spark, and the sheriffs took the whole family to a motel in town, compliments of Critterworld.

Now the problem was what to do with the body. It became like a big joke there in the Critterworld parking lot: people saying, "How do you get rid of a dead elephant?" then cracking up, as if it was the funniest thing in the world. Stash must have weighed a couple of tons.

Woody Riser, the tree-service man, finally showed up with the biggest chain saw I've ever seen. He consulted with the sheriffs and with Funderburke, then he lugged his chain saw over next to Stash. The sheriffs herded everybody back a ways—there must have been a hundred people by then, and more coming all the time—and they formed a line around the body. Woody Riser mixed gas and oil for his tank, slipped on his safety goggles, then pulled the cord. On the third pull it coughed around and caught, and the noise was so loud that the little kids covered their ears. He went for a leg first, aiming carefully just above the knee where the skin was taut, but I guess he should have checked how tough the flesh was because the chain saw kicked back on him and took a bite out of Woody Riser's own leg.

Things got a little crazy after that.

A couple of sheriffs put Woody Riser in their car and left for the hospital, and the rest of the sheriffs gave up on crowd control while they huddled with Funderburke to figure out what to try next. Right away people started pushing close to Stash. They all wanted to touch him, but some pulled out knives and poked at him with their blades. I saw a guy sawing at Stash's tail, and a couple of kids tugging on a tusk. Somebody else went for a piece of the ear.

George and Jun stood next to the psycho-monkey cage—the monkey had gotten hold of a cigar and they were watching him try to smoke it—but I didn't want to have anything to do with

357

them for awhile. I wanted to leave, but I also wanted to stay, and it was about then that I saw Sharla, that cheerleader from my Advanced Geometry class, standing by herself at the edge of the crowd.

I went over to her and stood there for a couple of minutes before she noticed me. "Oh, hi, Charlie," she said. Her eyes were red from wanting to cry, but she hadn't cried yet. I tried to think of something to say back to her—something sensitive or clever—but nothing came except, "How's your geometry?"

She didn't have a chance to answer, though, or to laugh in my face and tell me how stupid I was, because a couple of pick-up trucks pulled into the crowd and a bunch of football players from the high school got out with axes. "Elephant Patrol!" they shouted. Everybody laughed except for me and Sharla, and the crowd pulled back to give the guys room to operate. Even the sheriffs seemed to think it was pretty funny, and they ignored Funderburke, who started yelling at them to stay away from Stash. "He can be stuffed," Funderburke kept saying. "He can be stuffed." Nobody listened.

"Isn't that your boyfriend?" I asked Sharla. I thought I recognized one of the football players.

"Oh, David wouldn't do that," Sharla said, obviously worried that David would. "He's just with them. He wouldn't—"

One of the football players climbed onto the hood of his truck and shouted: "County High one time!" The crowd roared, and an axe ripped into Stash's side.

"County High two times!" Another axe sliced the trunk. "County High three times!" Two football players—one of them Sharla's boyfriend—hacked at Stash's legs.

"County High all the damn time!"

They attacked.

It must have gone on for a long time, guys passing off the axes when they got tired, always somebody new to step in for a few whacks at Stash. A couple of people left, offended, but more came, and the Critterworld parking lot turned black with blood. I didn't see too much, though, because I followed Sharla across the highway where she sat and cried in the ditch where George and Jun and I had been.

I'd never seen a girl that upset before, and I didn't exactly know what to do, so I just patted her on the back like my mother

358

used to do to me when I was little. I wanted to tell her that her sorry boyfriend didn't deserve her anyway, but that didn't seem quite appropriate even though it was true. She cried harder and harder, but nothing could block out the thwack of axes or the pep rally cheers as they worked over Stash in front of Critterworld. I heard the psycho-monkey screaming, too, and figured he'd gotten to the ash-end of his cigar, and then, after a long time, just about when I started thinking I should leave Sharla alone because I was probably just bugging her, sitting there patting on her like I was, she turned her face to my shoulder and she cried onto my t-shirt and I put both of my arms around her as far as they would reach, and we stayed like that for a while longer until it was all over and nearly dark and a couple of her girlfriends came looking for Sharla to give her a ride home.

She wiped her eyes and climbed into the car, and she said something to me through the back window, but they were already pulling away so I didn't catch it. Maybe it was just "Goodbye" or "See you in class," or maybe she just said my name.

Pretty soon I was the only one left, sitting there in the ditch, except for Mr. Funderburke, who just stood in the parking lot like the broken man he was. The crowd was gone, the sheriffs, the football players with their axes, even George and Jun. I got up slowly and walked back across the road to get a last look at what was what. But now here's the really funny part: For all their chopping and their pep rally and everything, Stash was still there. Sure, he was cut to hell and bleeding everywhere, and his trunk and his tail were gone, and the ears were tattered and all like that, but he was still there. They could have swung their axes for another whole day and Stash would still have been there. Even dead he was too much elephant for them, and I wished Jun was there for me to show him, and to tell him that, and to make him understand.

They got those sod farm tractors back the next day and dragged Stash into a field behind Critterworld. They got a bulldozer and dug a big hole and dropped him in on a bed of wood soaked in gasoline. The fire lasted all night, and I got my mother to drive me out to see it. There were cars all up and down the road.

Some people say that Stash haunts that field now, that somebody stole his trunk and he looks for it on full moons, that passing motorists have seen him standing at 3 a.m. on his old spot in front of Critterworld. All that standard ghost story stuff. They even say that nothing will grow on the spot where Stash was cremated, but I guess you can write that off as rumor, too, because I've been out there a couple of times since and the grass is as green there as anywhere.

Nominated by Mississippi Review

QUICK EATS

by CHARLES SIMIC

from BOULEVARD

Trees like evangelists
On their rostrums,
Arms raised in blessing over the evening fields.

I saw that and more
Sitting by the open window
In the back room
Of Herman's Funeral Home.

Every leaf now, every bush
Helps the night
Darken and quiet the world.

Birds of a feather,
Friends of the blues,
Listen, pay attention.

What runs but never walks,
O Mother?
What goes out without putting its coat on?

Winding road, the place of vanishings . . .

I am the original nomad exquisite,
I am setting out astride my phantom Rozinante.

Imponderabilia, old fashioned gal,
Strolling among the lengthening shadows,
I hear your ass was tattooed in Singapore.

It's this sly little wine I sip
Chill with twilight.
Chateau Abracadabra.

No two rain drops,
No two blades of grass
Whisper your name alike.

QUICK EATS in blood-red neon,
Miles away
In the dark-clouded,
Storm-threatening West.

Nominated by David Lehman, Kenneth Rosen, Sherod Santos, Karen Fish, Boulevard

WORLDLY BEAUTY

by T.R. HUMMER

from PLOUGHSHARES

Skin deep, you son of a bitch, I thought, *no more*—but the impure
Tip of his needle tracked its dance. The snake between the ribs,
Anchor, tiger, the daggered heart, *memento mori* of the skull:
In the heat of the body's refusal,
                                  I had to choose among images.
Beyond the window, awl-points of sun incised
San Francisco Bay with patterns of blindingness. I watched
The sea over his shoulder as he touched me with his tools,
The chisel made of the bone
                        of an albatross, narrow,
Very sharp, driven by means of a little mallet—or
An oblong piece of human bone, *os ilium*, an inch and a half broad
And two inches long, one end cut like a small-toothed comb,
The other, fastened to a piece of cane,
                           like a serrated adze.
He leaned above me, rubbing the pigments in,
His own skin clean and golden, untouched by signs or tokens,
Fire on the lake, scarlet penis in a secret place,
No swastika, no *rosa mystica*,
                      no lightning or transparent eye.
He wore no shirt. He was fat as a Buddha. His fleshy nipples
Hung like incipient breasts. How long could I authorize this pain?
I stared at snapshots on the walls: images of the carriers of images,
Those who had come here before me,
                         done this thing and lived.
One was a man, on his chest the cod, split from head to tail,

Laid open: on each thigh the octopus, and below each knee the
    frog.
One was a woman, on her breast the head with forepaws of the
    beaver;
On each shoulder the head
                            of the eagle or thunderbird;
On each arm, extending to and covering the back of the hand,
The halibut; on the right leg the bullhead; on the left leg the
    turtle.
I sat on my small stool, my blouse drawn open. I suffered
The alcohol and the burning, in love
                            with the clean
Lines of boats on distant water, the absolute
Whiteness of sailcloth, anesthetic sting of brine.
I knew I could take the blueprint of the broken tower on my skin,
The profile of the angel of blood.
                            I knew I could carry another
                    flesh
On my flesh, go otherworldly as any bodily shape, male or
    female,
Become a terrible breathing heap of descriptions of God.
In that dirty parlor on the western edge of the empire of the
    chosen,
I finally refused it all—the romance
                            of the past, the heaven of
                    family.
I denied the apocalypse of genes, the passionate resurrection
Of memory, the pierced and reborn body we call *the story*
Of our lives. In his hand, the needle's spasm repeated itself.
He sweated. He held the mirror.
                            What does it matter now
Who I say I am? This may not be done in the presence
Of the dead, or if anyone in the house should dream of floods,
Lest there be excessive bleeding—this may not be done if a man
Should dream of the face of a woman, or a woman
                            of the face of a
                    man,
Lest the shape of another self should shiver between
The soul that is and the soul that is to come. I am the image

364

Of diesels on the Embarcadero, I am the image of water—
So much beauty, and the world is still
                                    only the world.

Nominated by Josip Novakovich, Edward Hirsch, Arthur Smith, Mark Jarman

BODIES

fiction by SUSAN MOON

from FIVE FINGERS REVIEW

WITHOUT A BODY to live in, love is homeless.

I fell in love and then I went shopping for groceries. We were
out of everything. Milk and cold cereal. Bread. Boring. But my
heart was eating images of him—paint on his legs, his tongue in
my ear, the vibrations of his voice moving through the rim of the
hot tub from his chest cavity into mine.

The first time I ever saw him, he came late to the AA meeting.
I saw him suddenly, a luminous apparition in the doorway. Light
was coming out of his eyes and off his purple shirt with white
paint stains on it. He was smiling at the roomful of strangers.

I was irresistibly drawn to the strawberries, red peppers, and
radishes. They were pounding away on their grassy shelves, under the pretty light, waiting to be adopted. The thumping in my
chest got louder and louder as I approached these red cockles,
but luckily the clatter of the shopping cart obscured the sound. I
heaped them into my cart.

The first time he called, the day after the meeting, he said,
"I'd like to see you tonight, or this afternoon, or better yet, this
very minute—but then, I guess I'm just that kind of a guy."

On the way to Safeway, I drove by a young man shuffling bare-
foot along the dark street, his pants hanging in tatters, a dirty
blanket around his shoulders. He hunched his shoulders just the
way my son, moving his body down a dark street, thinking,
hunches his shoulders. I imagined this was the body of my son,
homeless and hungry. And where was the body this body came

366

out of? In the moment that I drove by, he suddenly spun, flapped his blanket, and jumped sideways into the street. I missed him by inches. In the rear view mirror I saw a hand dart out from under the blanket to give me the finger.

I only wanted to buy sexy food. I bought an avocado just ripe enough that the curve of the skin would reverse itself when I peeled it back from the soft meat.

He would ask me what words I liked for certain parts of the body, and I would tell him. We would agree that certain words were boring, and didn't really make much of a contribution to love. "I think penises and vaginas should just go off somewhere and do something together," he would remark.

I bought an eggplant. When I was in college, I went on a date with a dark-skinned heavy man from New Orleans who, when he came to my dorm to pick me up, brought me an eggplant for a present. Ever since, I've thought of eggplants as vegetables of courtship. I like how mushy they get if you cook them long enough.

Let's say eggplants are bodies. Strawberries, too. Then you have your bodies of water, and your heavenly bodies, burning themselves up. Are people bodies, or do people have bodies? Everybody has one, every body is one. Whose body do I have? I have a body of water, 98%. Water's body, earth's body, air's body. He has a body of fire, a heavenly body.

Time to get some brie cheese. Say cheese. Say wheel of brie. Wheel of brie. Say breel of whee. Breel of whee. I'll leave it on top of the refrigerator, so it will be warm and gooey by suppertime.

His body has a life of its own. It does things. It says things. All the while, the heart beats against the bars of its cage. Sometimes it pounds so hard it shakes me, too. The skin keeps glowing, the legs step lively, the eyes shine, the breath moves past the larynx, and is shaped by the mouth and tongue into words: "I love you, darling."

I was sleepy. My knees were weak with desire. I clung to the handle of my shopping cart. Turning a sharp corner to the cheese case, I misjudged the cart's width, and knocked down a tower of paper towels. Forcing myself to work slowly and carefully, I piled them back up on top of each other. My body is happy. They say the body doesn't lie. But my body lies in bed beside him. His

367

back is to me. I tuck my knees behind his knees, put my hand over his hip. Later in the night, he turns on his other side, so he's facing me, and gently turns my body, too, on the spit of my spine, so that my back is to him. Now he fits his body to mine in a mirror image of how we lay before. I awaken just enough to feel him tuck his knees behind my knees and put his arm around my waist, gathering me to him. Our long bodies lie together. Long together. "I adore you," he whispers into my neck. He lies by me. He lies. As I ride by. So he may see her, as she rides by.

Brie went into my shopping cart on top of the red globes. I looked at my list. On the way to the raisin bran I had to pass the seafood. I saw all those slippery bodies. Shiny fishies were not on my list. I saw a rainbow trout between his legs. Neither were little pink shrimp, or scallops gleaming in their viscous juices.

Late at night he calls. His body's at a pay phone, in the rain. His voice is in my ear, in my kitchen. It says, "I love you, darling." He pauses, but I say nothing. I'm putting away groceries. I hear by the challenge in his voice that he's drunk. I put the box of Familia, my son's favorite cereal, in the cupboard. He says, "Say, 'I love you, darling.'" I can't hear the rain falling, but I can hear the sibilance of tires on the wet street behind him.

"I love you, darling," I repeat.

"Not like that. Say it with feeling."

I feel suddenly cold. I say it again, the same only louder and faster: "I love you, darling!" I tumble the bright oranges into the fruit basket.

Perhaps he's satisfied. He says, "I wish I could smell your sweet neck right now." It doesn't matter what he says on the telephone. His body isn't there.

At Safeway I wanted something special. Something special for my body. Food is for bodies, and shampoo, and toothpaste, but they aren't special. Most things at Safeway are for bodies, but not everything—not batteries, for example, or *People* magazine. Flowers are for bodies and flowers are special and I wanted sweet-smelling flowers. But the flowers with fragrance at Safeway that night were ugly—the carnations were an impossible turquoise color, the blooms of the stock looked brown at the outer edges. The other flowers didn't smell—not the daisies, not the iris, not the Peruvian lilies. I had a vulgar thought: "I love him with my twat." But it's the mind that's vulgar, not the body. The words "vulgar" and "twat" mean nothing to the body.

You can have a body for long periods of time without noticing it. And what is it doing all that time? Is it noticing you? Hoping you will buy it flowers? So you can bury your nose in their sweet neck. I get to know my body over and over again, as I get older. I get to know a different body. Every seven years the cells replace themselves. The cheese ripens. The hands wrinkle.

At Safeway, I imagine crawling down the aisles on all fours. I want to steal food off the shelf. I want to eat almonds without paying for them. I want to bring the man something that will make his body happy, to thank him for pouring so much heat into me. A dry salami. He likes spicy things. I'll say, "For a man with a hot sausage between his legs." And I'll bring him mustard, hot mustard. And something to put it on. My thighs. My legs are long. I don't crawl, I walk. My long legs take me around, from place to place, from aisle to aisle, like a pair of scissors cutting through the thick air.

Where is his body now?

Alone in my bed, something will make me stir in the middle of the night. I will get up to turn down the thermostat in the front hall. A water baby, I will be wearing pajamas damp with sweat. I will have been dreaming that I suck his cock, and that it grows longer and longer, unreeling off his body like a garden hose.

At the seafood counter, I took a number, longing for scallops.

I will step into the hall, groggy. I will see him suddenly, a wild man, standing stock still, just inside the open doorway, a statue of himself, and behind this body, a cold wind stirring up the darkness.

"Oh my God!" I will exclaim, and my hand will fly to my heart.

"Don't be scared, darling. I came to get my jacket. It's a cold night."

"Are you all right?" I will ask. I will know he's drunk. But light will still be coming out of his eyes, from the fire still burning inside him.

He will nod. He will not kiss me, because he will not want me to smell his breath. He will take his jacket from the hook by the door. He will say, "Goodnight, baby." He will turn unsteadily and go. I will lock the door behind him. I will turn down the thermostat and go back to bed.

Satisfied desire, that comes from the past, in the form of memory. What we did already. How good it felt. Unsatisfied desire, drawn out of the future, that takes the form of anticipation and imagination. What we haven't done yet—how good it will feel to do it. My body is pinned to the present moment by desire, like a butterfly to a board. Desire the very condition of my breath.

Just myself and my son to feed this night—I'll go home and prepare us a meal of salad made of red things, scallops in a little wine, and brie cheese, soft and ripe. The wind ripens the cheese of the long river.

Maybe the man will come over later on. He'll reach his big hand through the bars of my rib cage to cradle my heart.

The breath joins the body to the universe. With breath we sing, we sigh, we lie. He comes. He tells me stories. He sings me songs. He reads aloud to me, a sad story I have chosen, by Chekov, a story of deceit and disease and ill-fated love.

I turn on my longing, pivot and spin on it. He says, "my darling," over and over and over and over again. I impale myself on my desire. I ride a cock horse to Banbury Cross. So he may see me as I ride by. I see him suddenly. His aglow face looks out of a window of the Birmingham Jail. The Birmingham Jail, dear, the Birmingham Jail. I wheel like a bird, I soar above him, I dive like a kite. I rise again, and the string pulls tight between us.

We dress ourselves in our bodies. We eat, we sleep, we touch each other, we walk, we talk. We spend a pleasant weekend in the country. We do these things together. He washes the dishes, I dry them and put them away. He breaks a plate. I don't care. He doesn't have any shoes, so I give him my son's old basketball sneakers. They fit like a glove, he says happily. I imagine gloves on his feet, and Converse hightops on his big hands. Head over heels. I tore my body away from his body. Fingers from fingers, toes from toes. I went to Safeway, and he went to an AA meeting.

He goes down. On me. His cheeks are always warm. He coughs. He's sick. He pours heat into me.

In the early morning I go for a walk with a friend. In Live Oak Park we pass a body, asleep or dead, in an old sleeping bag, in a nest of leaves. The wind blows so hard it tears the leaves off the live oak trees. The body turns. Suddenly I see him. There's a pair of Converse hightops by his head. He reaches through the bars of the cage with his big hand.

I am always at Safeway. To get to the bathroom, I walk past all those fruits and vegetables, ripening, waiting, through the swinging double doors at the back of the store, past big boxes of cauliflower on dollies, into the ladies' room. On a couch in the ladies' room, a disheveled woman lies, pressing her raw knuckles into her cheeks, moaning very softly.

"Are you all right?" I ask.

"I was out all night in the cold," she answers. "I'm trying to get warm. Don't make me leave."

"I'm just a shopper," I explain. "I came in here to use the bathroom. I don't want you to leave."

It's not very warm in the ladies' room. But I don't offer her my red flowered scarf from Moscow, because my red heart clings to it with clinging desire. When I come out of the toilet stall, I see in the long mirror a long body with flashing hair, a body that flickers with longing, a body getting older and colder, but flaring up in the wind. My eyes see my pretty hair. The woman on the couch doesn't have pretty hair. She doesn't have shampoo, she doesn't have a shower. I am living in the body of a shopper, a person with shelves and cupboards.

But we both have bodies wracked with desire. Perhaps she has a son. Perhaps her son is the young man in the flapping blanket and tattered jeans. Perhaps her son is my lover. She will take my groceries home and put them away on the shelves, and I will stay here in the Safeway ladies' room, waiting till they make me leave. On my way out I will take a handful of almonds from the open bin. The store security officer who is ushering me out will force my hand open. The almonds will fall to the floor. Under his breath, like under sheets and blankets, he will call me a cunt.

My son is gone. I find the man with the big hands in the bushes. I find him by following the sound of his singing. I see him suddenly—his face is on fire. We curl up together in the sweet-smelling leaves. He tucks his knees behind my knees. He gathers my body to his body. I breathe the wind. I sink into his warmth.

The spirit crouches inside the food, the blood, the juice, the secretions of desire, the pounding heart. Biding its time. Love lives in bodies. There's no place else to live. Without a body to live in, love is homeless.

Nominated by Josip Novakovich, Five Fingers Review

A CLARION FOR THE QUINCENTENARY

by ELIOT WEINBERGER

from THE LITERARY REVIEW

IN NOVEMBER 1620, the *Mayflower* is anchored in the shallows off the coast of Cape Cod. The men, terrified of what one of them calls the "hideous & desolate wilderness, full of wild beasts & wild men," must wade nearly three-fourths of a mile through freezing water to reach shore. There, they report back, all is surprisingly calm: no people. The next day is the Sabbath and they pray. The following day the women come ashore to do the washing, and all of them gorge themselves on quahogs, cherrystones and mussels, which make them sick.

Two days later, a small party led by their chief of security, Myles Standish, sets out to explore. They come across a group of six men, who dart into the woods. Pursuing them, the expedition, with their heavy arms, becomes entangled in the thick brush. At last they come out in a clearing: a field of corn. There are freshly-made mounds which they uncover. Some are graves; others are granaries, with baskets full of yellow, red and blue maize stored for the winter. Thanking God for His bounty, they steal the corn.

Having repaired a shallop to carry them along the coast in search of a river they think they've seen, and a possible site for settlement, a larger party pushes off in a snowstorm ten days later. They first return to the place they've named Corn Hill. To loot the mounds again they must break the frozen ground with their cutlasses. They find more corn, a bag of beans, a gourd containing oil.

They discover two round houses, evidently abandoned at their approach. Inside are various mats; wooden bowls, trays and dishes; clay pots; large baskets ingeniously made of crab shells; woven baskets, some of them "curiously wrought with black and white in pretty works"; deer heads, freshly killed; antlers and deer feet and eagle claws; baskets of dried acorns; a piece of broiled herring; tobacco seed; and "sundry bundles" of dried flowers and sedge and bulrushes. They take the "best things" away with them, but decide to leave "the houses standing," as their diarist reports.

Wandering in the snow, in the empty stretches of an uncolonized America, they come across a mound, covered with boards, that is longer and larger than the others they've seen. They dig, and find a mat, and under it a bow. Then another mat, and under that, a board two feet long and "finely carved and painted, with three tines or broaches on the top, like a crown." Then bowls and trays, dishes and trinkets. Another mat, and under that, two sacks, one large, one small. The larger is filled with a fine red powder, and the partially consumed flesh, bones and skull of a man. The man has long blonde hair. Alongside him is a knife, a pack needle and "two or three old iron things," wrapped in a sailor's canvas cassock and a pair of cloth breeches. They open the smaller sack and find the same red powder, and the head and bones of a small child. On his or her legs and arms are bracelets of fine white beads. Beside the child is a tiny bow. Standish and the men take some of the "prettiest things," cover up the grave, and move on. A month later they have found their place in Plymouth.

Who is this sailor? The Pilgrims were the first white settlers, but there had been English and Breton fishermen along the coast for some years. Champlain had explored the area in 1605. Captain John Smith of the Virginia colonies had come in 1614, stolen canoes from the Indians and traded them back for beaver skins, and drawn a detailed map. In 1616 or 1617 a French ship had been wrecked in a local storm. By the time the Pilgrims arrived, it is estimated that 95,000 of the 100,000 Indians in the area had already died of the newly-imported diseases.

And this child? Indian, white or both? The sailor's child, a co-incidental death, a victim? Did they die together, or was the child killed to join the sailor in the other world? Only one thing is certain: both were buried by the Indians, and with honor.

Standish and the sailor: one alive in history, in a linear time that is all future; the other dead in myth, in a cycle of time that has ended abruptly and forever, for him and for a world. At the founding of the New England, this impossibly chance encounter: a point of origin where the road splits into what America did and did not become.

Myles Standish, not a Separatist like the Pilgrims but a Roman Catholic of aristocratic background, a Standish of Standish, who was defrauded of his inheritance and became a mercenary in the Low Countries. The Pilgrims hired him as a military adviser, a bodyguard for the landing. He was one of the few to survive the first winter at Plymouth; he built the fort and oversaw what was for decades the most secure English colony in America. He was sent to England to negotiate the complicated property rights for the colonists, who were supposed to be in Virginia. And he was sent to Merry Mount to destroy the orgiastic colony led by Thomas Morton, where drunken Indian men traded pelts for guns, while drunken white men and Indian "lasses in beaver coats" danced around the Maypole.

Standish who kills for money, who builds the fortress to keep us in and them without, who steals their food and trinkets and—through Samoset and Squanto—their savvy, the businessman who gets laws changed to his advantage and the cop who enforces them, who treats the dead with disdain, who brings order to wilderness and wildness, the true Separatist, the founding father.

Standish standing over the found father, this sailor who crossed over. White skin and red skin, red powder and white beads, iron knife and wooden bow, man and, in death, woman, a dead Madonna with dead child, fair-haired god and goddess of the fair-haired corn nearby.

And the child, symbol of a blending, a future generation that will generally not occur in North America. In his place, the day before his grave is opened, another child is born, the first in the New England colonies. He is named Peregrine (pilgrim and bird of prey) White.

375

And the *Mayflower,* on its next voyage, sailing to Africa to pick up slaves.

And Plymouth Rock, today in the newspapers—"defaced" they say, but "signed" is more accurate—with a huge red swastika. A swastika whose author, in his ignorance, has drawn backwards. Intended clarion for racial purity, for a Pilgrim and Puritan land, it is instead a revenging light: the ancient American Indian symbol for the sun.

Nominated by Lydia Davis

WHEN I WAS SAVED

by ANDREW HUDGINS

from SHENANDOAH

"Do you still have a demon in your heart?"
the preacher asked. I did. My heart
and some place lower too. The demon kicked
inside my body—heart and groin—the way
I'd felt my brothers kick, all three, inside
my Mother's bulge. "Put your hand here," she said.
"Do you feel him?" I did. "That's your new brother."
The demon too was blood-kin and he lived
a fierce life of his own. In my aisle seat,
I sweated and I had no doubt—still don't—
that Satan owned my heart. I burst in tears,
fled—staggered—down the aisle and, blubbering,
was saved. A prayer. A hymn. More tears. And then
the preacher led me like a trophy back
up that long aisle. My father, radiant,
stepped out and bearhugged me so hard I gasped.
Later that day I couldn't breathe at all
when I, damp handkerchief clamped on my mouth,
was lowered into death. I went down easy,
stayed, panicked, struggled and was yanked back up,
red-faced and dripping. After that, each Sunday,
I went to preaching early, so I could sit
behind a boy whose torn right ear did not
attach entirely to his head. Through that
pink gap of gristle, I'd watch the preacher shout,
croon, soothe, between that boy's head and his ear.

More sinners lumbered up the aisle. I longed
to run up and again be purged of Adam,
who was reborn each night, like Lazarus,
by my own hand, beneath the sweat-drenched sheets.

Nominated by Joan Murray, Mark Jarman, John Drury, Linda Bierds, Shenandoah

GOOD HEAVENS

by PATTIANN ROGERS
from THE GETTYSBURG REVIEW

I

The common garden snail can't watch
the heavens and enumerate—600 young
stars in Perseus, one more hour
until full moon. It can't make lists—
pinwheel of Andromeda, comet fireball
of Tempel-Tuttle. It has never called
its slither the soft finger of night
nor its wound shell a frozen
galactic spin. Yet its boneless,
thumb-sized head is filled and totally
deaf with exactly the same tone
and timbre as the sky.

II
Winter Midnight

It seemed I was looking into the face
of a vendor, skin so dark
I couldn't focus at first,
the stark structure of his skull
tighter, blacker even than his eyes.
It was a vendor with his wares—glass
bulbs and seeds, silver goats, loops

and strings of copper, brass-cathedral
charms, polished couples on sticks
copulating, twisted bracelets
and rings—spread like a market
of stars on the blanket at his knees.
I thought I saw borders, ways
and measures in his onyx face
as I looked. A shifty hawker,
a familiar swindler, it was an old,
skinny vendor on folded knees,
kneeling purple bones, a skeleton
of vestments, a posture of spirals
and stocks hovering above and below
his spread of sockets and hoops,
reaching, rocking, merchandising
at my bedside: *Kum, laydee, bye,*
kum bye mine.

III

To imagine stars and flaming
dust wheeling inside the gut
of a blind, transparent fish
swimming out-of-sight in the black
waters of a cave a thousand years ago
is to suggest that the perfect
mystery of time, motion and light
remains perfect.

IV

Good—because the heavy burnings
and fumings of evolving
star clusters and extragalactic
cacophonies—because the flaming
Cygnus Loop, still whipping
and spewing sixty thousand years
after its explosion—because

the churning, disgorging womb
of the Great Nebula and the rushing
oblivions left from the collapse
of protostars—because suffocating
caverns of pulling, sucking gases
and pursuing, encircling ropes
of nuclear bombardments—
because erupting caldrons
of double stars and multiple
stars flinging outward great
spires and towers of searing
poisons—because all of these
for this long have stayed
far, *far* away from our place.

Nominated by Alberto Alvaro Rios, The Gettysburg Review

381

LIKE HANDS ON A CAVE WALL

fiction by KAREN MINTON

from THE GEORGIA REVIEW

In a diner north of Little Rock, people were sitting in booths behind plate-glass windows. A garage and a convenience store sat on either side of the diner, and stretches of fields and briar thickets lay beyond. The diner had been built by the same group of developers who, thinking growth was headed that way, had also built the subdivision of wood-frame houses across the highway. Growth hadn't come, and property values stayed low on what the real-estate agents called "great starter homes." Swing sets, clotheslines, and basketball goals stood in patchy yards, and power lines ran overhead.

Some of the homes' lighted windows were steamed up from cooking, but customers in the diner could see into windows where curtains hadn't been drawn. A waitress poured coffee and looked outside, complaining about the cold snap and the early dark of January. A Michigan woman cooled her coffee and said to her husband, "It's a shame they don't have snow to cover it." She looked beyond the brown field—gray, actually, in the light of dusk. Her gaze settled on a green house where, in a lighted living-room window, a woman stood with her arms raised straight above her head, whether in a rage or a stretch, she couldn't tell.

The earthquake started out some six or more miles beneath west Tennessee and twisted the crust of the earth like a lid on a Mason jar. The force that toppled buildings and twisted steel bridges nearer the Mississippi would dissipate like surf at the shore when it reached the rising escarpment of the Ouachita Mountains to the west. It was already losing strength at this distance. When the Michigan woman set her coffee down, it clinked against the saucer and kept clinking. Mailboxes shook. Power poles swayed. Cracks webbed down the sidewalk, split already by time and sporting dead grass and dandelion weeds.

Beside the green house, a walnut tree shook a few dry leaves to the ground. At the other end of the house—the bright south end, where the grass was thin and the paint faded from the summer sun—the mortar in the concrete block foundation began to crack. The outlines of the blocks, smoothed over by layer upon layer of paint, became more defined as cracks traveled up the wall and outward in both directions while the tremor pulsed under the house. The house, sitting on the foundation but not attached to it nor connected in any way to the ground, was knocked sideways just a couple of inches off-center to the south side of the wall, struck all those years by the sun and maybe built in the first place by a lazy mason using too much water in the mortar mix to keep it from drying out so fast.

Whatever action continued—barking dogs, pots boiling on stoves, the faraway roar of an airplane overhead—was absorbed by the earthquake. When the rumbling ceased, the contrasting silence seemed louder and longer than the quake, silence broken only by the still-barking dogs and the drumming of hooves in the field behind the house as a white horse galloped toward the unmoving headlights on the highway.

A jagged line of concrete blocks jutted from the foundation, and under the redistributed weight of the house, gave way at the weak south end. And that started more crumbling of concrete on around the front and back of the house until the whole building tilted—not falling, but dropping at one end even as it was held at the other end by the north wall. It simply eased down at an angle on a wadding of broken concrete.

Ginny Robinson pushed her boy and girl through the front door, which had been wedged nearly shut by the porch boards. Then she slipped through the opening, carrying a cardboard box that held the cat she'd had to pry off a window screen. The clouds were still pink where the sun had set before the earthquake began. She negotiated the splintered wood and chunks of

383

concrete to the car in the driveway and put her kids into it. Then, still holding the box, she leaned against the fender and looked at her house.

Concrete dust, caught in the gray light of dusk, swirled around the bottom of the house like a fog bank. Some part of Ginny's mind recognized that other houses were standing, that in fact only fallen bicycles and leaning poles and the slight shifting of sheds and lawn furniture gave witness to the earthquake. Some part of her mind remembered she should have shut off the power and water as the civil-defense commercials warned, but mainly she wondered at her house, upright and solid one minute and canted now as if the ground had raised like an ocean wave beneath one end of it. She paid no attention yet to the cold or to the yowling cat, its claw tearing at her bare arm through the flaps in the box. And some part of her mind marveled that an earthquake sounded so much like a human scream—that within the sounds of the quake and rattling glasses, she had heard screams coming right out of the ground.

Down the street, dark now with a power failure, doors opened and closed, and neighbors called to each other. A collie loped around her house and barked a couple of times at the ground where the north wall of the foundation stood intact. The neighbors drifted to Ginny's house, some carrying flashlights even though the sky was still light. They circled the house, speculating on the integrity of the foundation left standing, checking the power lines and water pipes that ran into the house. One man volunteered to drive to the fire department since the phones were down. Someone said the state patrol was closer, but that depended on what bridges might be out. The yowls of the cat never ceased. It scratched the sides of the box and occasionally darted its paw out to snag Ginny's skin. The collie barked into the opening that gave access to the crawl space. Mattie from next door tried to shoo it off. A boy threw rocks at it. It tucked its tail and crept a few steps away but returned barking at the ground.

Someone said, "Listen"—and underneath the noise of the cat and the dog and children, they heard the man under the house yell for help.

He barely breathed when he gained consciousness this time. He had screamed before, when he first realized the significance of the noise that was coming from beneath him instead of from out there, from airplanes or traffic or from the woman in the house above him. He had heard the rumble and then saw, though it was dark as pitch under there, the house start to lean above him. He heard the scraping concrete and the creaking timbers reverberate in the crawl space. He had darted for the piece of plywood, outlined in gray light, that covered the opening in the concrete wall. He scuttled toward it—careful even then to stay low on all fours to keep from bumping against the floor and giving his presence away.

When the house fell on his back, he screamed, then passed out. Each time he had come to, he breathed in the dust, and each time he had coughed, passing out again as pain shot through his chest and back. But this time he barely breathed, not deliberately but instinctively fearing the pain. He was practiced at it—breathing slowly to control the creeps of a closed place so similar to a tunnel or a mine shaft, and he knew the closeness of both. His face was pressed into the damp dirt. He couldn't move. He couldn't raise up or roll over or even gather his knees beneath him, and each try almost knocked him unconscious. Outside the dog barked, and his mind began divorcing itself from panic to count the rhythm of barks. Four barks. Pause. Four barks. Pause. Three barks. Finally he caught the drone of voices outside, and he yelled for help.

Ginny hadn't gone crazy during the earthquake. She sat now in the car with the radio on, the way her Dad used to sit in his Mercury listening to ballgames and smoking cigarettes. Darkness had fallen, but she faced the western horizon where light still fanned across the sky. She had sent her kids to a neighbor's and let the cat loose in the bushes behind the house. Mattie was wrapping her arm with gauze and trying to persuade her to come and sit in her kitchen till the shock wore off. Ginny didn't remember even seeing the cat leave the box, it had darted away so quickly. She just remembered the empty box shredded on the inside by claws. A wet circle of her blood had soaked into the box lid.

She hadn't gone crazy. She had shuffled her mind through insurance policies, through the leave time she'd amassed at the radio station (which was even now broadcasting in her car), and she'd thought of calling her mother in Fort Smith as soon as the phones were working. She thought of the clothes and her purse hanging on the bedroom doorknob, which she needed whenever she could get back in the house. She had forgotten to grab her purse and a coat, so Mattie loaned her John's old coat. Still, she had kept her head. Then they told her there was a man under her house.

She kept potatoes and onions under the floor in a hole dug into the hard-packed dirt. It was cool under there in the summer and safe from frost in the winter—like now, when the temperatures had been in the teens and twenties for too many days running. Her daughter had crawled under the floor last fall after leaving a note that she was running away from home, and exterminators had once spent an expensive day under there when they found termites. She'd also seen a king snake slither through the concrete and thought of it whenever she reached down in the hole for potatoes.

She watched them gather at the end of her house, milling around in the beams of flashlights. She pulled John's coat on and pushed her way over to the house. The sheet of plywood she used as a door to the crawl space was wedged sideways in the opening. John gripped the splintered top of the plywood as he leaned his head and shoulders into the hole. She heard him talking, but the man under the house was quiet now.

When John backed out of the opening, Ginny asked, "Who is it?"

John said he didn't know and motioned her over to the walnut tree. The neighbors followed. He turned around when he reached the trunk and tried to put his hands in his pockets, even the hand that held the flashlight.

"Ginny, how long's it been since you've been under there?"

"Awhile," she said, "I keep potatoes and onions under there, but it's been awhile since I got any. Why?"

John was a big man, but Ginny stood eye-level with him. His coat fell right on her, just a little too long in the sleeves. She looked into his eyes, but while he looked at her face, it seemed in the dim light he was staring at the top of her head.

"A beam's got him pinned to the ground," he said. "It hit him across the shoulders, and all I could see was his head. It looks like his head is sticking right up out of the ground."

Ginny put her hands in the coat pockets and twirled something, a nail or a hinge pin, in her fingers. It was too dark to read the expression on John's face.

She asked, "How bad hurt is he?"

"He might be bad," John said. "The phones are out, but the state patrol ought to be here soon. We might ought to get somebody else to go. Walt didn't know anybody was under the house when he went to report it."

Ginny said, "What's he doing under my house?"

John took a long time to answer. He looked above Ginny's head where the horizon was lined with light. Stars were out.

He said, "Maybe living there. It looked like he had a damned nest built up under there."

Moonlight shafting through cracks in the crumbled concrete showed like color but didn't light the darkness under the house. The collapsed end of the house sat not on solid ground but on jagged chunks of concrete block. The other end didn't sit on the standing foundation but was tilted against the block wall's inside edge, caught midway in its downward slide. Now, the house pushed slowly, imperceptibly outward against the foundation that was left, seeming frozen there until some cosmic second hand started moving again and the house would finish its fall to the ground.

Pinned between the hard earth and the wooden beam, the man seemed to have served as the wedge that halted the house in its slide. He was conscious now, listening to the voices outside—not to the words, but to the drone of human beings. Dirt was in his left eye, and every once in a while, instinctively, he tried to wipe it, but his arms were somewhere behind the beam looming just in back of his head. His face was cold, both from being pressed into the cold dirt and from the wind that blew in the opening, where he could occasionally see light dart from flashlights or the white paws and snout of the barking dog. He was used to the musty, pervading smell of dirt—even liked it now, as one likes the smell of yeast—but he was barely breathing, taking shallow breaths into a chest that couldn't rise. They would see his bed and the onion skins. The woman would crawl under her house and see her potatoes gone. His nose was running, but his arms didn't pull up to wipe it with his sleeve.

Ginny's transmitter had withstood the quake and her backup power system worked. The announcer was broadcasting from the transmitter and had just been joined by a member of civil defense who said in 1811 and '12 it took three earthquakes to

387

release the pressure in the New Madrid fault, so that, at best, they needed to brace themselves for aftershocks. In Mattie's kitchen, Ginny gazed at the transistor radio in the light of a Coleman lantern while Mattie made coffee on a propane stove. No one outside had mentioned the possibility of aftershocks, had maybe not even thought of that yet.

Ginny wrapped both hands around the coffee cup. The oldest of seven kids, she had plowed fields behind a mule and learned the mechanics of a John Deere tractor. She had put herself through tech school waitressing and laying sod, earned her degree in electronics, then helped her brothers and sisters through school. She had worked two jobs after her husband cut out and still got her kids bathed and in bed on time. She had once held a ball bat over her brother-in-law while he packed his clothes and while her little sister nursed a swollen eye. Yet she had fallen apart when John described the pillow the man had made from the straw in her potato hole. She had screamed and shook all over, but in Mattie's kitchen, while she listened to the strong signal on the radio, the shaking stopped. She sucked on a cough drop she'd found in John's coat pocket and tried to remember what she'd heard about aftershocks. They shouldn't wait much longer for help to come.

The state patrol car had pulled off into the grass in her front yard. The siren was off, but the blue lights were flashing around the neighborhood like strobe lights. A couple of neighbors stood by the open car door where a patrolman talked into the radio; she could hear its squawk. The others were grouped around the end of the house. She marched to the house and found John talking to the other patrolman.

"Is he still alive?" she asked.

He was. John didn't see how—mashed in the ground like that. But according to the state patrol, there was a pile-up north on Route 67 and a fire at the cotton mill, so the fire trucks and ambulances were tied up. Ginny's ex worked swing shift at the mill. She knew people there.

The patrolman was young. He had a pocket notebook out but wasn't writing anything. Ginny told him to get hold of the city and get a civil engineer out here. He left for the car.

"They're talking about aftershocks on the radio, John," she said.

She remembered driving to work last summer and watching builders put a new foundation under an old farmhouse. The house had sat on jacks for a week, suspended three feet above the new brick the masons were laying.

"The drawback is the house is just leaning against the block wall on this end," John said, "and it could cave in anytime, tremor or not." He was afraid of trying to hoist the house up—any movement or pressure at all would likely cause the house to fall before they could get a stable hold on it. "We might could shore it up somehow, get the house sitting on something besides the foundation. Then if the block gave or if we knocked the house off, there would be something else holding it up. Then we could chance the jacks."

"Would lumber hold it?" Ginny asked.

"It might."

It would take a lot of jacks. Ginny had a generator and a gallon of gas in the shed. She had cranked it over when the cold weather started to make sure it ran all right. She could borrow a circle saw.

"We'll round up what lumber we can," John said. He started across the yard. Ginny called him back.

"Do you have any idea who he is?" she asked. "I mean, does he have anybody we ought to call?"

"I don't think so, Ginny," John said. He stood there a second, put his hands on his hips. "He's been eating your onions."

Ginny sawed two-by-fours, four-by-fours, whatever scattered pieces of lumber they'd found to build the brace. John had said it had to fit right up against the floor of the house; if the house dropped even half an inch, it would be enough to crush him. A man down the road had a gas compressor in his work van, and John ran his nail gun off it. Even the pneumatic force could knock the house off balance, but the rhythmic beat of a hammer would likely have rocked it on down to the ground.

"We'd do better with sawhorses," Walt told Ginny.

Walt had said he'd do the sawing, but Ginny set him measuring boards and bracing them while she ran the saw.

"These cinder blocks are fine, I think," she said. "We don't have time to go find sawhorses."

Walt pressed his hand into the small of his back and laid a two-by-four across the blocks. Ginny set the saw blade against it. A

389

droplight hung from a tree limb, and she had to crane her shadow left then right to see the pencil mark. Sawdust flew out the back of the saw, bright like mica in the cone of light and dissolving in air when it touched the darkness.

Walt took both hands full of boards to John and his crew, who were building the brace just inside the hole. Ginny wanted more boards, wanted to stand sawing endlessly, to concentrate on keeping her fingers clear of the blade and following the dim pencil line. He must have heard her sing. When she was alone in the house she sang with the radio. She sang on Saturday mornings off-key, loud, all the hymns she remembered from church, old songs about the River Jordan and the tree planted by water. Once she had started crying and kept singing while she washed dishes, singing at the top of her voice and crying. He would have heard that.

Walt came back with measurements for cross-bracing. Ginny held the end of the tape measure.

"John's got to crawl under there now to nail these on," Walt said.

He took the pencil from behind his ear and drew a line using an end piece of lumber for a straight edge. The boards didn't have to be cut precisely, they just had to be the right length. No one would ever inspect their woodwork inside the crawl space or check for flush edges and tight joints.

"I ought to do it," Ginny said. "It's my house and my responsibility."

"You'd have to fight him for it," Walt said. He pulled two more long boards from a pile. "They can't tell when any more shocks will come. They don't know how many minutes between them."

"No," Ginny said.

She yelled at her kids sometimes. And the cat. And she had danced that weekend before having her crying fit. She had put an old record on and danced in the kitchen. He would have heard that. She hadn't danced since high school, so she knew old steps—the pony, stomping dances. She propped a board on the cinder blocks and squatted beside it. The plastic casing of the saw was cold. Her fingers moved slowly. There was enough heat under the floor to keep her onions and potatoes from freezing. He would have heard the television at night, heard the quiet when

390

they went to bed. She couldn't remember hearing him ever. Not even nights she couldn't sleep and lay listening to the creaks or the wind or rain on the roof.

"John said he's mashed flat," Walt said.

"He can't be," Ginny said. "Not and still be alive. The best I can remember, the ground under there's not level. Maybe he's in a hollow."

"That's it," Walt said.

Ginny walked with him to the house. John leaned inside the hole shining his light and talking to the man. John's words were too muffled to be heard outside, but he had a soft voice—Mattie complained about it, said he had to repeat everything he ever said to her. Ginny's voice was loud. Her whole family was loud. Maybe most of the time her voice would have sounded like this to him, a muted hum when she talked on the phone or when she talked to her kids at supper. He would have heard her kids, would know when they fought or made bad grades on homework, would have heard them when they came in crying from falling off their bikes or not getting their way.

The state patrolmen stood with the other neighbors who were still around, waiting to jack the house up. The ambulance still hadn't come. They hadn't gotten hold of a civil engineer either. One of the state patrolmen crossed his arms and leaned his shoulder against the house, then jerked erect. He's so young, Ginny thought. The other one was older—the one who first told them not to do anything until the fire department got there. He had roped orange tape around the front of her yard.

Ginny said, "John."

"It won't take but a minute, Gin. I'll be in and out. Once we get this cross-braced it may hold. A little anyway."

He was too big. He pushed against the plywood and the side of the hole. Someone handed him a board and the air gun. Ginny jumped at the blast of the compressor. He reached out again for another board, just a white shiny hand coming from under the floor.

A wind came up. The droplight swung from the tree, casting shadows of bare limbs in its swinging arc, while the Coleman lanterns fluttered near the house. The moon was higher in the sky now, not quarter or full, just an in-between moon. Down the street houses were lit by candles and flashlights, soft glows in the windows usually bright with fluorescent light. And in the field behind the house, the white horse had returned. This wasn't its pasture—just a place it came to rest after its flight—but in the moonlight the grazing horse was more film than substance. Except for the far-off traffic and the occasional thump of the air hammer, the night was quiet. In summer, the noises of tree frogs and owls would have gone on all night until they gave way to birds at dawn.

A cloud bank slowly spread over the north horizon, covering the stars. The Ozarks lay that way, west a little. It might snow now if the clouds kept moving in. And further west were the old Ouachita Mountains, so old the trees and even the soil were wearing off them. The caves there were also old, old enough to have sheltered the gatherers who once drew stories on their walls, who made paints of mud and left the marks of their hands behind them. This time the moving earth had stopped short of the caves, short of the bones and diamonds and calcified shards within them. Perhaps the handprints had staved off the violent forces as the early people had believed they would.

He heard her outside. He couldn't make out the words, but he knew the pitch and cadence of her voice. He had heard her sing. There was a lamp now pointing to the braces they had built, the flimsy timbers they hoped would hold up the house. Cribbing would have worked better, maybe. For the first time, he could see the grain running sidelong in the beam on top of him— hickory, he thought. From the angle his neck was cocked, he saw the underside of the floor above him, the dark patch of mold which spread from the concrete wall and the cracked and peeling surface of the plywood. The light struck the straw left in the hole near the door and caused a yellow halo to shine around it.

Ginny crawled through the hole. She was shaking now, chilled from the wind and the night, and worn out from the hangover of reaction. Her hand trembled against the plywood as she slid around it, careful not to knock the new scaffolding, careful not to catch her foot on the cords to the lamp and air gun. The light at her back threw her shadow over the entire space in front of her, casting the man in darkness. She was glad for it. She stayed on her hands and knees, moving more slowly than she had to. Trash was pushed against the wall—wadded paper bags, newspapers, and onion skins shining gold when the light struck them. But there was a neatness to it. She would never have seen signs, likely, if she had ducked her head under the floor to fill a bowl with potatoes. She would have thought it was her mistake if she had noticed at all the potato hole was less full, or would have thought it was rats eating them. She wouldn't have searched the dark corners for a human.

She saw the white of his eye and leaned aside against the beam to let the light hit him. Dirt clung to the side of his face next to the ground where his mouth and nose had run, but he wasn't breathing out blood. The nurse down the street had told her to look for that. His eye next to the ground was swollen to a slit and circled in red. John had washed it out well as he could. The man squinted his good eye shut and frowned with deep furrows between his eyebrows. Ginny moved her shadow over him again. John had left a squirt bottle of water near his head. She squirted water into his mouth, squeezing gently. His mouth didn't close around it but his tongue snaked around the water, holding it in.

"They're putting jacks in place," Ginny said.

His tongue slipped against his lower lip, and she gave him more water.

"We're going to jack up this end of the house to lift it off of you."

The way his head was turned sideways, he had to look up at her from the corner of his eye. In the darkness, the way the filtered light struck it, his eye seemed all white without an iris or pupil. He closed it again.

"The state patrol said an ambulance is on the way," Ginny said.

She heard the scrapes and clinks through the wall where they set up jacks. She heard Walt holler for something to wedge his jack handle with. She heard Mattie and realized she couldn't make out her words, but recognized some ineffable quality in her voice—its tone or its rhythm. She knew the cough she heard was John's.

Ginny had thought the man would say something. In fact, she had expected him to reveal secrets, to explain what could have driven him to live under her floor.

"I better go now. It sounds like they're set up." She waited. She felt the closeness of space and air and inhaled deeply, but the air smelled musty, confined, not like the full, cold air of outside.

393

He remained silent. She crawled backwards, not turning away from him. At the door she said, "It won't be long."

She turned her back to him and lifted her knee over the light cord.

"Wait," he said.

Ginny froze, straddling the wire. He'd spoken so low she would never have heard him outside the crawl space, or at least would never have realized the soft words were spoken to her. She looked over her shoulder, but her shadow blocked the light. She crawled back and stayed on all fours looking down at him.

He said, "The cat?"

His voice was gravelly, dry. So he had heard the cat, heard through her floor as if it was glass he could see through. Aloud, Ginny said, "Oh," as she realized it would have crawled up under here. Some nights it didn't come in till daybreak. Some mornings it left mice on the porch.

Ginny said, "I carried it out in a cardboard box." She laughed softly. "Stupid of me—it nearly clawed my arm off. It took off into the bushes, but it'll be back."

She leaned her back gently against the beam that held him down. She had to duck forward, and still her head pushed into the floor above her. Here, she could look at his face, and he could look at her with his good eye without rolling his eyeball too far. She rested her arms on her raised knees. John's coat sleeves covered all but her fingers. The sleeves were filthy now, and the right one had a long tear in it.

"We call it Pansy," Ginny said. "You know that, don't you. My little girl named it. It's a pretty cat, ain't it? Mean, though. It jumps my legs anytime I put hose on."

She pulled at the strings in the torn sleeve. He watched her but didn't say anything.

"I have two kids," she said. "Well, you know that, too. They're down at the Rosens. My boy, he wanted to stay, but I couldn't be worrying about them. You wouldn't believe how hard it is to find a good jack. Cars nowadays come with scissors jacks. You bust your knuckles using them."

She rotated her fist in circles, showing the motion it took to raise a scissors jack, then brought her fist to her forehead. She laughed shortly.

"I'm talking like you've been frozen in an ice cap."

The man didn't say anything.

"So we went everywhere looking for jacks. We lucked up. There's a shop down the road, and they brought over some big old hydraulic jacks. This end here—" she pointed to the standing concrete wall—"it's too high for most of the bumper jacks. I'll never find out who all these jacks belong to."

She stopped. She'd said it off the top of her head. She hadn't thought actually of returning the jacks when this was all over, or even of its being over. And John's coat. She would offer to buy him a new one, and he'd tell her not to worry, an old coat like that. It was quieter out there now.

"The jacks are in place, it sounds like," she said. John had tried to talk her out of crawling under here, and she'd told him she wouldn't be long. While she sawed wood for the bracing, she'd thought the man deserved it. He'd brought it on himself. But nobody had thought to ask him his name. Ginny had told them she would do it; it was her house and her responsibility.

"We don't even know your name," she said.

She didn't look at him, but picked at her sleeve, unraveling the threads and letting them fall to the ground. Then she glanced at him. His eye was open, looking away from her. She put her hands in her pockets.

"I knew somebody had an Escort," he said.

He paused between words to soak his mouth with his tongue. It took Ginny a second to realize he was talking about cars. Ginny had an Escort.

"A tube comes out of the air filter," he said.

Ginny gave him a squirt of water.

"Carries moisture out . . . drips down on the fuel pump."

John hollered, "Gin." His head stuck through the door. "You better come out now. We're ready."

"I'll check it," she told the man.

Her fingers were busy in John's coat pocket, finding screws and coins while they talked. She found another cough drop, gluey and coated with fuzz from the cloth of the pocket. Her finger touched the inside of his lip as she put it in his mouth. His lips were soft but too dry and cold. It would help a little anyway to keep his mouth from drying out.

"Keep it tucked in your cheek or you'll strangle."

She got on her hands and knees to leave.

395

"Millard," the man said.

"Millard what?"

"Royle."

At the door, Ginny paused. The cold air stung her nose. She had stopped noticing the closed musty smell under the house, and now the air from outside hurt.

"It won't be long, Mr. Royle," she said and slid out the opening. She almost waved goodbye to him.

They pulled the light out, leaving the crawl space dark and familiar. In the dark the smells, the feel of damp air, and the gray outlines returned—the place he knew. She was larger than he had thought, big-boned, but when he closed his eyes while she spoke, he saw her as he had always imagined her, with long curly hair and high cheekbones. In another few days the cold front would have passed, and he would have moved on. If she had ever found the newspapers under her house, she would have thought kids had left them.

He felt the aftershock before anyone outside did. At first he thought, just for an instant, that the house was falling from the jolt of jacks, but he felt too much the movement underneath, the pulse shooting through miles of earth below his face where he still had feeling. He knew what a wall of underground coal looked like, and he knew the force it would take to move it—through bedrock and ores and roots and subterranean rivers, through the solid ground against which he was pinned—as if the ground were air or water only. All the overpasses and high-rises, museums and hydroelectric dams, were no more than hands on a cave wall in the path of a shifting earth.

The bones in his face tingled with the vibration. The rumble grew louder, closer, like a train roaring toward him on a track. He couldn't have hopped a train nor read the secret hobo marks on gate posts—those romantic days were gone before he could have lived them. The waves moved through him, as if he were a conduit connecting the earth on either side of him, as if he weren't separate himself from the earth under the floor. He sucked the candy from behind his teeth and held it with his tongue.

The horse flew again across the field. Dogs barked a few seconds before the droplight hanging in the walnut tree shook with vibrations which grew into a rhythmic sway. The circle of light moved back and forth on the dry grass, catching the steel blade of the saw and moving past it, steadily swinging wider. The half circle of people stepped back from the house, then scattered away from it. Under the house, nails pulled out of the newly built bracing, and boards splintered and split in two. The second hand swept again, and the house, released from time, finished falling.

Ginny tried to run to her car, thinking in the first instant of the aftershock there was some safety there, thinking she had to get to her kids. When she reached her car, she held onto the fender, and those few seconds were enough that the tremor subsided, though she still felt the way she had when she'd stepped off a boat down in the Gulf a long time ago and walked as if the land were the ocean. She turned just in time to see the rest of the foundation give way. The north end of the house pushed the blocks to the outside as it fell slowly, lowered by the crumbling of concrete beneath it. She started to dart toward the house as if she could stop it, but her legs wouldn't hold her up. She slid down against the front tire and watched as white dust flew up from the ground and clung like a cloud touching down.

Maybe they could never have saved him. But when the jacks were all set, and she and John stood at the corners to keep the jack handlers working in sync—right then it had seemed as if it might work. She'd been holding her hand up, ready to drop it as soon as John dropped his to signal the start. There she had been—her hand above her head in the artificial light—when the aftershock hit.

He'd known someone with a car, and Escorts hadn't been out that long.

Her fuel pump *had* been freezing up. She'd put two new ones on since the first cold snap, and the last time she'd cut her hands on the cold metal and cussed and banged her ratchet against the ground. She'd called the parts store and bawled out the boy who answered the phone. Then she had carried a cup of coffee outside wrapped in both her hands, breathing the steam. He would have smelled the coffee.

She knew his name.

The dust took a long time to settle. She could go back in now and get her purse and see how bad the damage was inside.

The clouds were nearly overhead. She wished she had thought to tell him it was going to snow. Snow was rare in this part of Arkansas. The past winter the kids had to haul snow from the neighbors' yards to have enough for a snow fort. They would be glad tomorrow.

Nominated by The Georgia Review

LOOK ON THE BRIGHT SIDE

fiction by DAGOBERTO GILB

from THE THREEPENNY REVIEW

THE WAY I see it, a man can have all the money in the world but if he can't keep his self-respect, he don't have shit. A man has to stand up for things even when it may not be very practical. A man can't have pride and give up his rights.

This is exactly what I told my wife when Mrs. Kevovian raised our rent illegally. I say illegally because, well aside from it being obviously unfriendly and greedy whenever a landlord or lady wants money above the exceptional amount she wanted when you moved in not so long ago, here in this enlightened city of Los Angeles it's against the law to raise it above a certain percentage and then only once every twelve months, which is often enough. Now the wife argued that since Mrs. Kevovian was a little ignorant, nasty, and hard to communicate with, we should have gone ahead and paid the increase—added up it was only sixty some-odd bones, a figure the landlady'd come up with getting the percentage right, but this time she tried to get it two months too early. My wife told me to pay it and not have the hassle. She knew me better than this. We'd already put up with the cucarachas and rodents, I fixed the plumbing myself, and our backporch was screaming to become dust and probably would just when one of our little why nots—we have three of them—snuck onto it. People don't turn into dust on the way down, they splat first. One time I tried to explain this to Mrs. Kevovian, without success. You think I was going to pay more rent when I shouldn't have to?

My wife offered the check for the right amount to the landlady when she came to our door for her money and wouldn't take it. My wife tried to explain how there was a mistake but when I got home from work the check was still on the mantle where it sat waiting. Should I have called her and talked it over? Not me. This was her problem and she could call. In the meantime, I could leave the money in the bank and feel that much richer for that much longer, and if she was so stupid I could leave it in the savings and let it earn interest. And the truth was that she was stupid enough, and stubborn, and mean. I'd talked to the other tenants, and I'd talked to tenants that'd left before us, so I wasn't at all surprised about the Pay or Quit notice we finally got. To me, it all seemed kind of fun. This lady wasn't nice, as God Himself would witness, and maybe, since I learned it would take about three months before we'd go to court, maybe we'd get three free months. We hadn't stopped talking about moving out since we unpacked.

You'd probably say that this is how things always go, and you'd probably be right. Yeah, about this same time I got laid off. I'd been laid off lots of times so it was no big deal, but the circumstances—well, the company I was working for went bankrupt and a couple of my paychecks bounced and it wasn't the best season of the year in what were not the best years for working people. Which could have really set me off, made me pretty unhappy, but that's not the kind of man I am. I believe in making whatever you have the right situation for you at the right moment for you. And look, besides the extra money from not paying rent, I was going to get a big tax return, and we also get unemployment compensation in this great country. It was a good time for a vacation, so I bunched the kids in the car with the old lady and drove to Baja. I deserved it, we all did.

Like my wife said, I should have figured how things were when we crossed back to come home. I think we were in the slowest line on the border. Cars next to us would pull up and within minutes be at that redlight greenlight signal. You know how it is when you pick the worst line to wait in. I was going nuts. A poor dude in front of us idled so long that his radiator overheated and he had to push the old heap forward by himself. My wife told me to settle down and wait because if we changed lanes then *it* would stop moving. I turned the ignition off then on again when we moved a spot. When we did get there I felt a lot better, cheerful even. There's no prettier place for a vacation than Baja and we really had a good time. I smiled forgivingly at the customs guy who looked as kind as Captain Stubbing on the TV show "Love Boat."

"I'm American," I said, prepared like the sign told us to be. My wife said the same thing. I said, "The kids are American too. Though I haven't checked out the backseat for a while."

Captain Stubbing didn't think that was very funny. "What do you have to declare?"

"Let's see. A six-pack of Bohemia beer. A blanket. Some shells we found. A couple holy pictures. Puppets for the kids. Well, two blankets."

"No other liquor? No fruits? Vegetables? No animal life?"

I shook my head to each of them.

"So what were you doing in Mexico?"

"Sleeping on the beach, swimming in the ocean. Eating the rich folks' lobster." It seemed like he didn't understand what I meant. "Vacation. We took a vacation."

"How long were you in Mexico?" He made himself comfortable on the stool outside his booth after he'd run a license plate check through the computer.

"Just a few days," I said, starting to lose my good humor.

"How many days?"

"You mean exactly?"

"Exactly."

"Five days. Six. Five nights and six days."

"Did you spend a lot of money in Mexico?"

I couldn't believe this, and someone else in a car behind us couldn't either because he blasted the horn. Captain Stubbing made a mental note of him. "We spent some good money there. Not that much though. Why?" My wife grabbed my knee.

"Where exactly did you stay?"

"On the beach. Near Estero Beach."

"Don't you work?"

I looked at my wife. She was telling me to go along with it without saying so. "Of course I work."

"Why aren't you at work now?"

"Cuz I got laid off, man!"

"Did you do something wrong?"

"I said I got *laid off*, not *fired!*"

"What do you do?"

"Laborer!"

"What kind of laborer?"

"Construction!"

"And there's no other work? Where do you live?"

"No! Los Angeles!"

"Shouldn't you be looking for a job? Isn't that more important than taking a vacation?"

I was so hot I think my hair was turning red. I just glared at this guy.

"Are you receiving unemployment benefits?"

"Yeah I am."

"You're receiving unemployment and you took a vacation?"

"That's it! I ain't listening to this shit no more!"

"You watch your language, sir." He filled out a slip of paper and slid it under my windshield wiper. "Pull over there."

My wife was a little worried about the two smokes I never did and still had stashed in my wallet. She was wanting to tell me to take it easy as they went through the car, but that was hard for her because our oldest baby was crying. All I wanted to do was put in a complaint about that jerk to somebody higher up. As a matter of fact I wanted him fired, but anything to make him some trouble. I felt like they would've listened better if they hadn't found those four bottles of rum I was trying to sneak over. At this point I lost some confidence, though not my sense of being right. When this other customs man suggested that I might be detained further if I pressed the situation, I paid the penalty charges for the confiscated liquor and shut up. It wasn't worth a strip search, or finding out what kind of crime it was crossing the border with some B-grade marijuana.

Time passed back home and there was still nothing coming out of the union hall. There were a lot of men worried but at least I felt like I had the unpaid rent money to wait it out. I was fortunate to have a landlady like Mrs. Kevovian helping us through these bad times. She'd gotten a real smart lawyer for me too. He'd attached papers on his Unlawful Detainer to prove *my* case, which seemed so ridiculous that I called the city housing department just to make sure I couldn't be wrong about it all. I wasn't. I rested a lot easier without a rent payment, even took some guys for some cold ones when I got the document with the official court date stamped on it, still more than a month away.

I really hadn't started out with any plan. But now that I was unemployed there were all these complications. I didn't have all the money it took to get into another place, and our rent, as much as it had been, was in comparison to lots still cheap, and rodents and roaches weren't that bad a problem to me. Still, I took a few ugly pictures like I was told to and had the city inspect the hazardous back porch and went to court on the assigned day hoping for something to ease out our bills.

Her lawyer was Yassir Arafat without the bedsheet. He wore this suit with a vest that was supposed to make him look cool, but I've seen enough Ziedler & Ziedler commercials to recognize discount fashion. Mrs. Kevovian sat on that hard varnished bench with that wrinkled forehead of hers. Her daughter translated whatever she didn't understand when the lawyer discussed the process. I could hear every word even though there were all these other people because the lawyer's voice carried in the long white hall and polished floor of justice. He talked as confidently as a dude with a sharp blade.

"You're the defendant?" he asked five minutes before court was to be in session.

"That's me, and that's my wife," I pointed. "We're both defendants."

"I'm Mr. Villalobos, attorney representing the plaintiff."

"All right! Law school, huh? You did the people proud, eh? So how come you're working for the wrong side? That ain't a nice lady you're helping to evict us, man."

"You're the one who refuses to pay the rent."

"I'm disappointed in you, compa. You should know I been trying to pay the rent. You think I should beg her to take it? She wants more money than she's supposed to get, and because I wanna pay her what's right, she's trying to throw us onto the streets."

Yassir Villalobos scowled over my defense papers while I gloated. I swore it was the first time he saw them or the ones he

403

turned in. "Well, I'll do this. Reimburse Mrs. Kevovian for the back rent and I'll drop the charges."

"You'll drop the charges? Are you making a joke, man? You talk like I'm the one who done something wrong. I'm *here* now. Unless you wanna say drop what I owe her, something like that, then I won't let the judge see how you people tried to harass me unlawfully."

Villalobos didn't like what I was saying, and he didn't like my attitude one bit.

"I'm the one who's right," I emphasized. "I know it, and you know it too." He was squirming mad. I figured he was worried about looking like a fool in the court. "Unless you offer me something better, I'd just as soon see what that judge has to say."

"There's no free rent," he said finally. "I'll drop these charges and reserve you." He said that as an ultimatum, real pissed.

I smiled. "You think I can't wait another three months?"

That did it. He charged the court and court secretary and my old lady and me picked the kids up from the babysitter's a lot earlier than we'd planned. The truth was I was relieved. I did have the money, but now that I'd been out of work so long it was getting close. If I didn't get some work soon we wouldn't have enough to pay it all. I'd been counting on that big income tax check, and when the government decided to take all of it except nine dollars and some change, what remained of a debt from some other year and the penalties it included, I was almost worried. I wasn't happy with the US Govt and I tried to explain to it on the phone how hard I worked and how it was only that I didn't understand those letters they sent me and couldn't they show some kindness to the unemployed, to a family that obviously hadn't planned to run with that tax advantage down to Costa Rica and hire bodyguards to watch over an estate. The thing is, it's no use being right when the US Govt thinks it's not wrong.

Fortunately, we still had Mrs. Kevovian as our landlady. I don't know how we'd have lived without her. Unemployment money covers things when you don't have to pay rent. And I didn't want to for as long as possible. The business agent at the union hall said there was supposed to be a lot of work breaking soon, but in the meantime I told everyone in our home who talked and didn't crawl to lay low and not answer any doors to strangers with

404

summonses. My wife didn't like peeking around corners when she walked the oldest to school, though the oldest liked it a mess. We waited and waited but nobody came. Instead it got nailed to the front door very impolitely.

So another few months had passed and what fool would complain about that? Not this one. Still, I wanted justice. I wanted The Law to hand down fair punishment to these evil people who were conspiring to take away my family's home. Man, I wanted that judge to be so pissed that he'd pound that gavel and it'd ring in my ears like a Vegas jackpot. I didn't want to pay any money back. And not because I didn't have the money, or I didn't have a job, or that pretty soon they'd be cutting off my unemployment. I'm not denying their influence on my thinking, but mostly it was the principle of the thing. It seemed to me if I had so much to lose for being wrong, I should have something equal to win for being right.

"There's no free rent," Villalobos told me again five minutes before we were supposed to swing through those doors and please rise. "You don't have the money, do you?"

"Of course I have the money. But I don't see why I should settle this with you now and get nothing out of it. Seems like I had to go outa my way to come down here. It ain't easy finding a babysitter for our kids, who you wanna throw on the streets, and we didn't, and we had to pay that expensive parking across the street. This has been a mess of trouble for me to go, sure, I'll pay what I owe without the mistaken rent increase, no problem."

"The judge isn't going to offer you free rent."

"I'd rather hear what he has to say."

Villalobos was some brother, but I guess that's what happens with some education and a couple of cheap suits and ties. I swore right then that if I ever worked again I wasn't paying for my kids' college education.

The judge turned out to be a sister whose people hadn't gotten much justice either and that gave me hope. And I was real pleased we were the first case because the kids were fidgeting like crazy and my wife was miserable trying to keep them settled down. I wanted the judge to see what a big happy family we were so I brought them right up to our assigned "defendant" table.

"I think it would be much easier if your wife took your children out to the corridor," the judge told me.

"She's one of the named defendants, your honor."

"I'm sure you can represent your case adequately without the baby crying in your wife's arms."

"Yes ma'am, your honor."

The first witness for the plaintiff was this black guy who looked like they pulled a bottle away from him the night before, who claimed to have come by my place to serve me all these times but I wouldn't answer the door. The sleaze was all lie up until when he said he attached it to my door, which was a generous exaggeration. Then Mrs. Kevovian took the witness stand. Villalobos asked her a couple of unimportant questions, and then I got to ask questions. I've watched enough lawyer shows and I was ready.

I heard the gavel but it didn't tinkle like a line of cherries.

"You can state your case in the witness stand at the proper moment," the judge said.

"But your honor, I just wanna show how this landlady. . . . "

"You don't have to try your case through this witness."

"Yes ma'am, your honor."

So when that moment came all I could do was show her those polaroids of how bad things got and tell her about roaches and rats and fire hazards and answer oh yes, your honor, I've been putting that money away, something which concerned the judge more than anything else did.

I suppose that's the way of swift justice. Back at home, my wife, pessimistic as always, started packing the valuable stuff into the best boxes. She couldn't believe that anything good was going to come from the verdict in the mail. The business agent at the hall was still telling us about all the work about to break any day now, but I went ahead and started reading the help wanted ads in the newspaper.

A couple of weeks later the judgment came in an envelope. We won. The judge figured up all the debt and then cut it by twenty percent. Victory is sweet, probably, when there's a lot of coins clinking around the pants pockets, but I couldn't let up. Now that I was proven right I figured we could do some serious negotiating over payment. A little now and a little later and a little bit now and again. That's what I'd offer when she came for the money, which Mrs. Kevovian was supposed to do the next night by 5 p.m., according to the legal document. "The money to be collected by the usual procedure," were the words, which meant Mrs. Kevovian was supposed to knock on the door and, knowing her, at 5 exactly.

Maybe I was a tiny bit worried. What if she wouldn't take anything less than all of it? Then I'd threaten to give her nothing and to disappear into the mounds of other uncollected debts. Mrs. Kevovian needed this money, I knew that. Better all of it over a long period than none of it over a longer one, right? That's what I'd tell her, and I'd be standing there with my self-confidence more muscled up than ever.

Except she never came. There was no knock on the door. A touch nervous, I started calling lawyers. I had a stack of junkmail letters from all these legal experts advising me that for a small fee they'd help me with my eviction procedure. None of them seemed to understand my problem over the phone, though maybe if I came by their office. One of them did seem to catch enough though. He said if the money wasn't collected by that time then the plaintiff had the right to reclaim the premises. Actually the lawyer didn't say that, the judgment paper did, and I'd read it to him into the mouthpiece of the phone. All the lawyer said was, "The marshall will physically evict you in ten days." He didn't charge a fee for the information.

We had a garage sale. You know, miscellaneous things, things easy to replace, that you could buy anywhere when the time was right again, like beds and lamps and furniture. We stashed the valuables in the trunk of the car—a perfect fit—and Greyhound was having a special sale which made it an ideal moment for a visit to the abuelitos back home, who hadn't been able to see their grandkids and daughter in such a long time. You have to look on the bright side. I wouldn't have to pay any of that money back, and there was the chance to start a new career, just like they say, and I'd been finding lots of opportunities from reading the newspaper. Probably any day I'd be going back to work at one of those jobs about to break. Meanwhile, we left a mattress in the apartment for me to sleep on so I could have the place until a marshall beat on the door. Or soon I'd send back for the family from a house with a front and backyard I promised I'd find and rent. However it worked out. Or there was always the car with that big backseat.

407

One of those jobs I read about in the want-ads was as a painter for the city. I applied, listed all this made-up experience I had, but I still had to pass some test. So I went down to the library to look over one of those books on the subject. I guess I didn't think much about the hours libraries keep, and I guess I was a few hours early, and so I took a seat next to this pile of newspapers on this cement bench not that far away from the front doors. The bench smelled like piss, but since I was feeling pretty open-minded about things I didn't let it bother me. I wanted to enjoy all the scenery, which was nice for the big city, with all the trees and dewy grass, though the other early risers weren't so involved with the love of nature. One guy not so far away was rolling from one side of his body to the other, back and forth like that, from under a tree. He just went on and on. This other man, or maybe woman—wearing a sweater on top that was too baggy to make chest impressions on and another sweater below that, wrapped around like a skirt, and there were pants under that, cords, and unisex homemade sandals made out of old tennis shoes and leather, and finally, on the head, long braided hair which wasn't braided too good—this person was foraging off the cemented path, digging through the trash for something. I thought aluminum too but there were about five empty beer cans nearby and the person kicked those away. It was something that this person knew by smell, because that's how he or she tested whether it was the right thing or not. I figured that was someone to keep my eye on.

Then without warning came a monster howl, and those pigeons bundled up on the lawn scattered to the trees. I swore somebody took a shot at me. "Traitor! You can't get away with it!" Those were the words I got out of the tail-end of the loud speech from this dude who came out of nowhere, who looked pretty normal, hip even if it weren't for the clothes. One of those great, long graying beards and hair, like some wise man, some Einstein. I was sure a photographer would be along to take his picture if they hadn't already. You know how Indians and winos make the most interesting photographs. His clothes were bad though, took away from his cool. Like he'd done caca and spilled his spaghetti and rolled around in the slime for a lot of years since mama'd washed a bagful of the dirties. The guy really had some voice, and just when it seemed like he'd settled back into a stroll like anyone else, just when those pigeons trickled back down onto the lawn into a coo-cooing lump, he cut loose again. It was pretty hard to understand, even with his volume so high, but I figured it out to be about patriotism, justice, and fidelity.

"That guy's gone," John said when he came up to me with a bag of groceries he dropped next to me. He'd told me his name right off. "John. John. The name's John, they call me John." He pulled out a loaf of white bread and started tearing up the slices into big and little chunks and throwing them onto the grass. The pigeons picked up on this quick. "Look at 'em, they act like they ain't eaten in weeks, they're eatin like vultures, like they're starvin, like vultures, good thing I bought three loafs of bread, they're so hungry, but they'll calm down, they'll calm down after they eat some." John was blond and could almost claim to have a perm if you'd asked me. He'd shaven some days ago so the stubbles on his face weren't so bad. He'd never have much of a beard anyway. "They can't get enough, look at 'em, look at 'em, good thing I bought three loafs, I usually buy two." He moved like he talked—nervously, in jerks, and without pausing—and, when someone passed by, his conversation didn't break up. "Hey good morning, got any spare change for some food? No? So how ya gonna get to Heaven?" A man in a business suit turned his head with a smile, but didn't change direction. "I'll bury you deeper in Hell then, I'll dig ya deeper!" John went back to feeding the birds, who couldn't get enough. "That's how ya gotta talk to 'em." he told me. "Ya gotta talk to 'em like that and like ya can back it up, like ya can back it up."

I sort of got to liking John. He reminded me of a hippie, and it was sort of nice to see hippies again. He had his problems, of course, and he told me about them too, about how a dude at the hotel he stayed at kept his SSI check, how he called the police but they wouldn't pay attention, that his hotel was just a hangout for winos and hypes and pimps and he was gonna move out, turn that guy in and go to court and testify or maybe he'd get a gun and blow the fucker away, surprise him. He had those kind of troubles but seemed pretty intelligent otherwise to me. Even if he was a little wired, he wasn't like the guy that was still rolling under the tree or the one screaming at the top of his lungs.

While we both sat at the bench watching those pigeons clean up what became only visible to them in the grass, one of the things John said before he took off was this: "Animals are good people. They're not like people, people are no good, they don't care about nobody. People won't do nothing for ya. That's the age we live in, that's how it is. Hitler had that plan. I think it was Hitler, maybe it was somebody else, it coulda been somebody else." We were both staring at this pigeon with only one foot, the other foot being a balled up red stump, hopping around, pecking at the lawn. "I didn't think much of him gettin rid of the cripples and the mentals and the old people. That was no good, that was no good. It musta been Hitler, or Preacher Jobe. It was him, or it musta been somebody else I heard. Who was I thinkin of? Hey you got any change? How ya gonna get to Heaven? I wish I could remember who it was I was thinkin of."

I sure didn't know, but I promised John that if I thought of it, or if something else came up, I'd look him up at the address he gave me and I filed it in my pocket. I had to show him a couple of times it was still there. I was getting a little tired from such a long morning already, and I wished that library would hurry up and open so I could study for the test. I didn't have the slightest idea what they could ask me on a test for painting either. But then jobs at the hall were bound to break and probably I wouldn't have to worry too much anyway.

I was really sleepy by now, and I was getting used to the bench, even when I did catch that wiff of piss. I leaned back and closed the tired eyes and it wasn't so bad. I thought I'd give it a try—you know, why not?—and I scooted over and nuzzled my head into that stack of newspaper and tucked my legs into my chest. I shut them good this time and yawned. I didn't see why I should fight it, and it was just until the library opened.

Nominated by Sigrid Nunez, Jonathan Penner, Threepenny Review

SNOW FIGURE

by DAVID BAKER

from OHIO REVIEW

1.

A humble night. Hush after hush. Are you listening?
That's what the snow says, crossing the ice.

And the blue creek out back—where my love and I came
early one morning to remember nothing but blue

and the muffled joy of a far night's nothingness—
the blue creek, teasing, wild beneath its ice,

says hush. Snow whiffs around on its glassine surface.
Why did we wish so hard to walk where it deepens?

Why did we want to hold hands here?
My love and I came to learn how to love

the little that skates on the surface,
the nothing that flies, fast and fatal, beneath.

2.

I have put in a poem what has fallen from my life
and what I would change. Are you here?

We left a slender pathway of tracks. It led nowhere,
if not to our bodies, and filled in our emptiness.

What I want most to say is what I never told her.
Don't trust me. Trust me. How could I lie?

3.

A figure of speech is where desire forces a crisis, a crossing—
one world and its weather suddenly brilliant with meaning.

My love and I came out early one morning to forget
the humble one night when the snow fell over us

and we filled each other's body with our own.
So the old snow burns crystal in the sun. So the ice

slipping the creek's edges keeps teasing to be tried—
trust me, it brags, black, thrilling, or empty.

Why do we wish so hard to listen to what isn't here?
Here, the snow says, as if in response. My love was here.

*Nominated by David Jauss, Jim Simmerman, Kathy Mangan, James Solheim, Sherod
Santos, T. R. Hummer, Marilyn Hacker, Reginald Gibbons, Edward Hirsch*

LOST FUGUE FOR CHET

by LYNDA HULL

from THE KENYON REVIEW

Chet Baker, Amsterdam, 1988

A single spot slides the trumpet's flare then stops
    at that face, the extraordinary ruins thumb-marked
with the hollows of heroin, the rest chiaroscuroed.
    Amsterdam, the final gig, canals & countless

stone bridges arc, glimmered in lamps. Later this week
    his Badlands face, handsome in a print from thirty
years ago, will follow me from the obituary page
    insistent as windblown papers by the black cathedral

of Saint Nicholas standing closed today: pigeon shit
    & feathers, posters swathing tarnished doors, a litter
of syringes. Junkies cloud the gutted railway station blocks
    & dealers from doorways call *coca, heroina,* some throaty

foaming harmony. A measured inhalation, again
    the sweet embouchure, metallic, wet stem. Ghostly,
the horn's improvisations purl & murmur
    the narrow *strasses* of *Rosse Buurt,* the district rife

with purse-snatchers, women alluring, desolate, poised
    in blue windows, Michelangelo boys, hair spilling
fluent running chords, mares' tails in the sky green
    & violet. So easy to get lost, these cavernous

413

brown cafes. Amsterdam, & its spectral fogs, its
  softly shifting tugboats. He builds once more
the dense harmonic structure, the gabled houses.
  Let's get lost. Why court the brink & then step back?

After surviving, what arrives? So what's the point
  when there are so many women, creamy callas with single
furled petals turning in & in upon themselves
  like variations, nights when the horn's coming

genius riffs, metal & spit, that rich consuming rush
  of good dope, a brief languor burnishing
the groin, better than any sex. Fuck Death.
  In the audience, there's always this gaunt man, cigarette

in hand, black Maserati at the curb, waiting,
  the fast ride through mountain passes, descending with
no rails between asphalt & precipice. Inside, magnetic
  whispering *take me there, take me.* April, the lindens

& horse chestnuts flowering, cold white blossoms
  on the canal. He's lost as he hears those inner voicings,
a slurred veneer of chords, molten, fingering
  articulate. His glance below Dutch headlines, the fall

"accidental" from a hotel sill. Too loaded. What do you do
  at the brink? Stepping back in time, I can only
imagine the last hit, lilies insinuating themselves
  up your arms, leaves around your face, one hand vanishing

sabled to shadow. The newsprint photo & I'm trying
  to recall names, songs, the sinuous figures, but facts
don't matter, what counts is out of pained dissonance,
  the sick vivid green of backstage bathrooms, out of

broken rhythms—and I've never forgotten, never—
  this is the tied-off vein, this is 3 a. m. terror
thrumming, this is the carnation of blood clouding
  the syringe, you shaped summer rains across the quays

of Paris, flame suffusing jade against a girl's
   dark ear. From the trumpet, pawned, redeemed, pawned again
you formed one wrenching blue arrangement, a phrase endlessly
   complicated as that twilit dive through smoke, applause,

the pale haunted rooms. Cold chestnuts flowering April
   & you're falling from heaven in a shower of eighth notes
to the cobbled street below & foaming dappled horses
   plunge beneath the still green waters of the Grand Canal.

Nominated by David Jauss, Wally Lamb, Maura Stanton, Lou Mathews, David Wojahn, Richard Jackson

I WOULD CALL IT DERANGEMENT

by GERALD STERN

from THE SOUTH FLORIDA POETRY REVIEW

I cut a stick for my love. It is too early
to clear the yard. I pick some lilac. I hate them
dying on the vine. I plan my assault
on the dead maple. I will tie some rope
to the rotting side and I will pull it down so I can
cut it limb from limb without destroying
the phone connections from one state to another
or smashing the new tomato plants and ruining
the asters. She is walking from place to place
and wrapping herself in sheets. If the wind
were free up there it would lift the curtains
just as it bends the poppies and the yearning
iris. I am setting a table. I
am smiling at the Greeks next door. I put
an old gardenia in the center, something
that has some odor. We are in the flowery
state now. I spill half the petals over
her watermelon; only here are flowers
good for eating, here and India
where they are sprinkled over colored ice
and onto the half-cooked fish. I have a system
for counting bricks but this one day I study

the clouds that move from left to right and the swallows
hunting for food. They seem to fly in threes
and alternately flap their wings, then skim
the roofs; they even make a sound, some brief
chipping; I hear it when they come in range,
maybe when they fight for space. One cloud
is black, it goes from a simple skeleton
to a bloated continent. Given my inclination,
I will turn it into a blowfish before
breakfast is over—or an uprooted tree.
Upstairs she sings—she chips—I know she's dancing
with something or other. When she comes down she'll have
the static of the radio on her tongue,
she understands the *words*, she actually sings
those songs—her voice is a high soprano—I
love it going up and down. My voice is ruined
but I can do a kind of quaver. I have
unearthed the wisdom from my second decade,
and though it did the world little good and even
served as a backdrop to our horrors I don't
blame the music, I can't blame the music
if the horrors grow stronger every year.
She listens to me with one hand, eating sugary
pineapple with the other. I listen too,
under the washrag and the dead maple,
hearing the words for the first time, making her scream
with laughter at my words, almost lucid
compared to hers, as hers are labyrinthian
compared to mine. There is this much music
in eastern Pennsylvania and this much love
and this much decadence. I would call it
derangement—the swallows twice a day
have it, and the white delphiniums
turning to blue again and the orange snapdragons.
If we could lie down for a minute we would let
the bastardy of our two decades take over
just as we let the songs do; there is nothing
that doesn't belong with love; we can't help it
if anguish enters; even leaving the world
as we do there is no disgrace, that is

another kind of anguish—just as it was
following a band of swallows, just as it was
bending down to taste the flowers or turning
the clouds into overturned trees or smiling in Greek.

Nominated by Linda Bierds

THE WRESTLER'S HEART

by GARY SOTO

from COLORADO REVIEW

I had no choice but to shave my hair
And wrestle—thirty guys humping one another
On a mat. I didn't like high school.
There were no classes in archaeology,
And the girls were too much like flowers
To bother with them. My brother, I think,
Was a hippie, and my sister, I know,
Was the runner-up queen of the Latin American Club.
When I saw her in the cafeteria, waved
And said things like, Debbie, is it your turn
To do the dishes tonight? she would smile and
Make real scary eyes. When I saw my brother
In his long hair and sissy bell-bottom pants,
He would look through me at a little snotty
Piece of gum on the ground. Neither of them
Liked me. So I sided with the wrestling coach,
The same person who taught you how to drive.
But first there was wrestling, young dudes
In a steamy room, and coach with his silver whistle,
His clipboard, his pencil behind his clubbed ear.
I was no good. Everyone was better
Than me. Everyone was larger
In the showers, their cocks like heavy wrenches,
Their hair like the scribbling of a mad child.
I would lather as best I could to hide
What I didn't have, then walk home

In the dark. When we wrestled
Madera High, I was pinned in 12 seconds.
My Mom threw me a half stick of gum
From the bleachers. She shouted, It's Juicy Fruit!
And I just looked at her. I looked at
The three spectators, all crunching corn nuts,
Their faces like punched-in paper bags.
We lost that night. The next day in Biology
I chewed my half stick of Juicy Fruit
And thought about what can go wrong
In 12 seconds. The guy who pinned
Me was named Bloodworth, a meaningful name.
That night I asked Mom what our name meant in Spanish.
She stirred crackling *papas* and said it meant Mexican.
I asked her what was the worst thing that happened
To her in the shortest period
Of time. She looked at my stepfather's chair
And told me to take out the garbage.
That year I gained weight, lost weight,
And lost more matches, nearly all by pins.
I wore my arm in a sling when
I got bloodpoisoning from a dirty fingernail.
I liked that. I like being hurt. I even went as far
As limping, which I thought would attract girls.

One day at lunch the counselor called me to his office.
I killed my sandwich in three bites. In his
Office of unwashed coffee mugs,
He asked what I wanted to do with my life.
I told him I wanted to be an archaeologist,
And if not that, then an oceanographer.
I told him I had these feelings
I was Chinese, that I had lived before
And was going to live again. He told me
To get a drink of water and by fifth period
I should reconsider what I was saying.
I studied some, dated once, ate the same sandwich
Until it was spring in most of the trees
That circled the campus, and wrestling was over.
Then school was over. That summer I mowed lawns,

Picked grapes, and rode my bike
Up and down my block because it was good
For heart and leg. The next year I took Driver's Ed.
Coach was the teacher. He said, "Don't be scared
But you're going to see some punks
Getting killed. If you're going to cry,
Do it later." He turned on the projector,
A funnel of silver light which showed motes of dust,
Then six seconds of car wreck from different angles.
The narrator with a wrestler's hair cut came on.
His face was thick like a canned ham
Sliding onto a platter. He held up a black tennis shoe.
He said, "The boy who wore this sneaker is dead."
Two girls cried. Three boys laughed.
Coach smiled and slapped the clipboard
Against his leg, kind of hard.
With one year of wrestling behind me,
I barely peeked but thought,
Six seconds for the kid with the sneakers,
Twelve seconds for Bloodworth to throw me on my back.
Tough luck in half the time.

Nominated by Alberto Alvaro Rios, Colorado Review

THE OTHER LEAGUE
OF NATIONS

fiction by ALBERTO ALVARO RIOS

from HAYDEN'S FERRY REVIEW

THE CRAZY PEOPLE had a convention, people later said, and tried to laugh it off. But it was true.

Without prior advertisement, there took place one day in this town a chance gathering of the left-minded. It was a coincidental meeting of those who were famous in this town, prominent in their human loudness as the oblong fruit of retardation and cruelty, and of laughter. Everybody knew them. But nobody said so.

In this way they were ghosts, some of them. Or perhaps all of them. They were ghosts at very least in that nobody saw them. They had the meat of invisibility. And nobody noticed when they were gone, as they were never there to begin with. It is the trick of small towns.

Today, however, they were all here, recognizable as the single-walkers, those who owned the last four hours of the night. They were the bothersome ones who sometimes knocked on the door, loudly, as if to come home or to ask where lunch was, and who were then shushed away in no particular direction.

It was inevitable then, after years of wandering, after this and that here and there, after having taken an interest in stray dogs and trash cans and store windows and glass, the crazy people of this town, as they were called, would all one day bump into each other at the same time and the same place.

And that is what happened on this day.

422

And because of their training of years, at this convention they were all speakers, all group leaders, all fully and duly authorized representatives charged with championing their one cause or another. No one here was a member of the audience. Certainly not Mr. Luder, as anyone could guess.

This was a convention of ideals and a dead squirrel in someone's pocket; a convention of ambitions and desires, and the certainly urgent hand motions that go with them. It was Doña Jesusita's convention on her unending topic of morality, but without a quorum on any of her points one way or the other. It was Mr. Louie's conference on the nature of accident, of circumstance.

Except for Tavo who did not know one way or the other, no one wanted to be at a meeting, but by chance as will happen on summer days the meeting began anyway. First it was two of them bumping one into the other. Then it was the addition and convergence of the rest, coming not to help, but to take sides. It might have been a fight had anyone thought to use fists.

Some took sides against each other. Some took sides against whoever or whatever seemed appropriate to the moment as they saw it: God, the noises, the county commissioner's second wife, who was said to make the real decisions around his house. And a second wife, anyway—who had heard of such a scandal. Several of these crazy people were in complete agreement with the rest of the town, certainly, on that outrage.

Added to all of this were the passing innocent bystanders, who simply wanted to get by along the sidewalk.

Someone might have described this meeting as not anything official, not a meeting at all. If it were not a fight, then it was a simple confusion of people on the street.

But again that was wrong: each person here had something to say, an immediate point to be made, and, more importantly, an answer. Or, in Mrs. Cano's case, there were necessary tricks to be played and people gathered now to play them on.

Each of them had been hurriedly coming to this place all their lives. As the conference began, after the first person bumped into the second, each began talking, in earnest, making apologies for being late, and saying that they knew there was to be a convention, but had never quite precisely known where it would be

423

or when. So they were sorry for their tardiness, and that it was time at last to get on with business, so here was the agenda.

Mrs. Cano simply made an extended obscene sound.

Each person had an extensive list, if not on paper then in mind. And oddly enough, each would leave this meeting satisfied. Conventions are always summed up the same way, that there is never enough time, that just when the good things started to happen it is time to leave.

But not so here. In that each of them spoke simultaneously, in that each of the ideas was of a world-order, in that no one wasted time with the habit of listening: this was the brilliant meeting, and cause for the happy leaving.

Everything had been said, everything had been dealt with, including and among which even the dead squirrel, after a fashion, had been brought back to life on a table, speaking its name loudly as a certain Mrs. Cano from San Luís Potosí. Though as anyone could see she was a squirrel now, she had originally come to this town as a woman looking to visit her cousin.

This might of course have seemed to be a joke, but since nobody was paying attention, there did not seem to be any reason for a joke—and so it was not. And nobody laughed.

This singular meeting was so efficient it did not consume more than twenty minutes, the time it took for the delegates to pass through each other on the way to where they were each originally going on that day. So many crooked walks and faulty postures, so many objects protruding from pockets and held, and protected at all costs and against all odds—with the resulting falls to the ground—that to pass by each other took a little time.

But a twenty minute meeting, this was something. Something for those who met, and something for those who saw them meeting. Something for everybody.

So, as the newspapers finally said, this assembly therefore could not be described as a simple stroll wherein several people meet each other by coincidence, not exactly. It might have been just such a thing for other people, but not this time, not here. This was official business.

That was a phrase someone in fact used: "We are here on official business." There followed applause, but it was for a small trick Mrs. Cano—the deceased squirrel—was playing on the widow Sandoval, concerning a pointedly nasty showing of the teeth through which was being forced some bluish spume, some kind of liquid no one had ever seen before. They had suspected the existence of this liquid in life, of course, but to see it—well, that was the applause.

But official business, or *very* official business, someone said, which was it?

Mrs. Cano again made an extended obscene noise.

Someone else said, No business was already too much business. The assembled adjudged this reasonable, in the same manner that too much business is no business, and so they felt exhausted, all this talk about business. It was time now to relax.

"After not doing so much," they said, "after not doing *very* much," Mr. Luder, who was German and knew these things, corrected, as was his custom. Whichever was correct, the conversation thereby and with its loudness put an emphasis on both "so much" and "very much," which convinced even the hold-outs that something exhausting had in fact taken place, both so much and very much together adding up to a great deal.

But wait, someone said. If, as was being emphasized now, their work here could be characterized boldly as either "so much," in Mrs. Martínez's words, or as "very much," according to Mr. Luder's corrective, should they not then be paid? Something for their time? Had they not in fact heard this all their lives—that if they did either so much or very much work, that there would be some reward, had they not all heard that? Some money, preferably?

But of course no one listened, and so they did not get rich that day. And while the notion of exhaustion was a strong case, no one heard that either, and so exhaustion was what they kept with them. But no one listened to someone saying that no one heard, so everybody left happy, glad to have had the opportunity at last to be given a voice in the world.

This was particularly true of Mrs. Cano, who thereafter would not leave her owner Mr. Louie in peace. A happy squirrel, he would say to anyone who would listen, is too much. She was a dead squirrel, but a happy squirrel, now that she had made her contribution to the assembled.

So Mr. Louie later murdered Mrs. Cano again, and the neighborhood children put him on trial, showing a lack of mercy only children have. He was said to have murdered her in cold blood, though as there was no blood in the dead squirrel to speak of, the issue of this fine point took up the whole of the trial.

After the deliberations of the jury, who also ate some very fine cookies without offering him even one, he was sentenced to carry the body of Mrs. Cano around with him forevermore, a verdict which he accepted though it brought tears to his large face.

The tears were from laughter, but he could not show it. The trick was, after all, on them, he thought. These poor children. How could they have known. That is the way it used to be, in the good old days before Mrs. Cano ever spoke a word. That was when *he* had been happy instead of *her*.

He had fooled these children by letting them think they were the masters of everything after all. How could they have known they were sentencing him to a happy life once more. Children, he would say thereafter on the sly to passers-by, ha, they're not so smart.

And the passers-by, they would agree, and more often than not, give him a wink, so that he began to think he was perhaps onto something bigger than the moment: an underground, a cabal of people who knew what he knew, that in fact children were not so smart as they looked. It made his head hum. They would come to him sooner or later, they would see he was trustworthy and that he had seen the truth finally. He would be given the secret password for which he had been waiting so long.

He wore the body of Mrs. Cano as a necklace, or, better said, as a scapular, since he touched it so much in concert with his prayers. He would be patient.

Mr. Louie would be patient because he understood patience, unlike Tavo, the boy who understood nothing, or everything— but nothing in between. He had found his way to this conference the way he had found his way everywhere else. By walking.

Tavo was not so much of anything or anybody, patient or impatient, just a little bit less all the time, and asking only for simple things, with simple gestures. Tavo, Tavito, they would call him, Gustavo, and Gustavito, and the kids and some of the grown-ups would gesture back at him, not always kindly. He was born to a good family, of a high social class, but out of wedlock, and so his

426

name was therefore unspeakable and he was invisible because no one could see him. He was taken, or rather simply left, at the orphanage, and there he grew up.

In 1940 he was forty years old, and this gave him some cause for small celebration. That he thereafter was as old as the year was always a source of renewed amazement, a charm for his life which he wore with an obvious pride, always smiling even when he was not.

The oddness of his circumstance and of that smiling was, however, that he never grew to be more than the moment of his being left at the orphanage: he stayed a baby, with a baby face and a baby body, bigger and more proportionate as he grew, but a baby's body nonetheless. And his smile was like a baby's, and his words. And as he saw people in the street, first to the ladies, he would say, *"ma,"* or *"amá,"* because he knew them to be his mother. *"Amá,"* he would say, "I'm hungry." And to the men, if he felt comfortable, he would say, *"Pa,"* and then *"Apá."*

He would put out his hand and show them, I'm hungry here, taking his hand from the air and putting it first to his mouth and then to his stomach. And someone always was his mother, and his father. By circumstance and by turns, by coincidence and perhaps even by virtue of the occasional prayers on his behalf, someone always saved something for him, some bit of food, a nicer shirt perhaps.

Sometimes he would move in for a day, and the family would bathe him and change him, and he would find his way of apologizing for having stayed out in the world so long without coming home. One day and for thereafter, the family of Mr. Jesús Cano took him at his word, or his kind of word, and they shushed him and kept him, and told him not to go.

Tavo followed Mr. Cano at first because he wanted to tell Mr. Cano about Mrs. Cano the dead squirrel, did he know her? But Tavo could not get the words and the story straight, and so he simply followed Mr. Cano anyway, hoping that one day he would be able to explain. It gave him great reason to stay.

Mr. Cano made Tavo a small house of wood in back, by the far corner of the yard, and each week made the house a little better. Tavo stayed there, until for other reasons Mr. Cano became mayor of the town. It was said that Mr. Cano became mayor

427

sideways because Tavo so often got lost. And every time he did, Mr. Cano would go out and find him.

In that way Mr. Cano met everybody, as they never failed to help him find Tavo because they did not want the burden of Tavo on his own again. Perhaps, someone said, and at just the right time, a man should be made mayor for just such a thing.

One time Tavo lost himself too well. Neither Mr. Cano nor the town could find him. He reported Tavo missing to the authorities, and even offered a reward for word of his whereabouts, so much had he come to care for Tavo, so much like a family member had he become. And a reward was not too much for a son, and even less so for a baby.

After some sad months he got word that Tavo had been apprehended and taken to Hermosillo or Nogales by one of the social squads which in those days were in charge of rounding up the crazy people. These people were full of the contagion, it was said, but of what they were contagious no one could be certain. Still, no one was sorry. All they knew was to wash their hands well afterward, for a week or two.

It was the one word—crazy—in their lifetimes they later saw fall to the ground like a china teacup and break into a thousand pieces, each with its own name, diabetes, cancer, innocence, and the rest. But in these days they only had the one word, and anyone who was suspect had to be taken away quickly.

Sometimes in a neighborhood where someone like this had wandered, one could smell the gasoline and later hear the hundreds of buckets full of water being spilled into basins all at the same time before dinner, and then so much scrubbing a fast washboard music filled the air, a music that said go away, and do not come here. It was a music that found its way into all the work of the musicians in those days, a music that would not itself go away, just get fancier.

The choices of the squad collecting these people was to take them either to the special green hospital or to jail. But Tavo was not in the hospital, as Mr. Cano had looked for him several times there. Instead, he had been taken to the jail, where people get lost, and at first he could not find him there either.

But he was after all a prisoner there. When Mr. Cano found him after hearing the full story, which was all mixed up, Tavo could only say "*Apá,*" and could only cry. Mr. Cano also could only cry, and they put their arms around each other, in a way that in earlier days would have meant food.

Tavo later died officially in the small house made, now, of wood and of gold.

Afterward, Mr. Cano did not come out very much, and did not keep up with anyone in particular outside of his family. A man like that, people said, should truly be mayor, not thinking one way or another about anything, a fair man, without preconceived ideas, without emotions on the issues of the day. An impartial man.

But of course they knew what they were saying. How now, as the town itself was growing older, sadness increasingly ruled their lives. A sad mayor was something they understood, something they knew how to vote for. Sadness like his was a pleasure, only in that it was an old and more intimate friend.

It is sadness people vote for, not happiness, which always wears a new hat, always ready to move on. No one was opposed to a new hat, certainly, and generally people even liked new hats; like the circus, however, they just never lasted, and there was always the worry, what if some mud should splash onto its brim from a car, or some unmannered bird go by. With happiness there always comes a worry.

That's what Mr. Louie kept trying to say. This damn squirrel Mrs. Cano, she's too damn happy. Doesn't anybody see that there's something wrong with this?

The *loca* Chuy did not think so. She petted Mrs. Cano, and said, call me Jesusita. But mind you, call me Doña Jesusita, or else people will get mad. And then she smiled.

No one called her Doña Jesusita except the priest, who was out of a job anyway with all the churches being closed down in these days by the government. So who listened. Everybody else called her the crazy woman, the *loca* Chuy.

From the Thirties on she made her place. No one took her away because they could not catch her. She had a new cardboard or tin or dog-blanket house every night, and the new morning for a house every day, and since she asked nothing of anyone they stopped trying to catch her, even though they could have, now and again, as she grew older.

She was alone, but talked enough to keep herself company, so that she did not notice that she was alone. Nobody knew how she

429

made it through the night. Sometimes there was a terrible snow in those days, a freezing and a rain, a wind stronger than a man, with a shout loud enough to fill the space in between the hills of this town. Sometimes she would be in the mercado, sometimes in the streets, but never in the same place at the same time, as if she understood her responsibility as equal to the lawyer who was always in his office by eight o'clock in the morning, never once late in his nineteen years of practice.

One day, news would come that the *loca* Chuy had become pregnant, but from whom no one could say. The *loca* Chuy said over and over she was made pregnant by all the women of this town, and that's all she could say about it. Perhaps it was because she had a little girl that she said that, perhaps it was something else.

As her stomach grew, she began to laugh, and could not help but show it to everyone as was her manner. In earlier days, the boys would say to her that they had heard she was not wearing any panties. Liars, she would say, and lift her dress to show them, yes I do, she would say, yes.

But it was work, as under her dress she would wear slips and other skirts and sometimes loose rolls of thick, colorful material, no matter how hot the day, and lifting them all was an effort. And when she was done with the lifting, they would laugh and she would look down, because in fact she was not ever wearing any, and she would laugh too, and lift her shoulders in an oh well. When she was much younger, she had forgotten one day to put any on, and that was enough for the rest of her life. She remembered and forgot things in that way, always for the rest of her life.

She would do it anywhere, lifting her skirts, as she would not tolerate being called a liar. Somewhere in her life she had learned it was not nice to be called a liar, and also that it was good to be nice, and so she never failed her lessons.

Part of the joke for the people who asked her, however, was that many times in combination with the heat of the day the weight of her skirts was so much that they would pull themselves down, sometimes all the way to her upper thighs before she would notice, and with a casual and distracted motion pull them back up. The work of going under them instead of lowering them was the thing, now, as what was to be seen there was already familiar to everyone.

430

But showing her stomach was laughter to her as well, and she liked doing it. But that stomach finally made her too heavy, and she could not run away very well. She would be caught, finally, and taken to the Madre Conchita, which was the name of the house for innocents. Her daughter would have a long life, beautiful but with a serious disposition from the orphanage, and a secret beard like a man, which she had to shave very early every morning, and again in the afternoon as everyone slept.

She would grow up without her mother, about whom no one would hear anything more.

The last man standing presently in the group had not heard about the *loca* Chuy one way or the other, so seeing her did not matter to him.

In making his way through them all, he found Mrs. Cano suddenly in his face, and when he began to say something, Mr. Louie smiled and said he hoped that what the man was about to say to Mrs. Cano would be bad.

But Mr. Luder shushed the new man before he could say anything to Mrs. Cano. You would not be so quickly irritated, Mr. Luder said, if she were your wife, would you. Mr. Louie made a noise of disgust with his mouth and his fingers. Some wife, he said.

This last man, Mr. Calderón, had not thought himself part of this league, and had simply been crossing the street on his way to the butcher's, not knowing that the butcher himself had already ceased functioning as a butcher, his profession pushing him the step too tender; that the butcher was in fact, as they would later say, crazy; and that his state of being was contagious, as evidenced by what happened next.

It was as if the whole town had caught it, the whole town and the whole half of the century, as someone would later say. And then someone else would imitate the late Mrs. Cano, and make an extended obscene sound.

Mr. Calderón was to enter the store, perfectly at ease with his charge of two pork chops for the evening meal. But after his request, and a subsequent discussion with the butcher, a discussion in yellow and in purple, as it was later said, and after seeing a magnificent collection of clocks on the walls instead of cow sectioning charts and white paper rolls, Mr. Calderón would leave

431

the store through the window, so that his own face, his own body, would mirror with bruises and with blood the yellow and the purple of their talk, some truth resident in being, by actions, the sum of one's spoken words.

It had been a discussion first of the eating of meats, then more generally on life itself, then of the clocks, the texture of the fine old woods, the delicate sounds of the movements, and the voices, almost caught in a moment of surprise and yet still able to be calm on the half hour, and then the full and growing conversation of the hours.

In the morning, the butcher said, there was little talk by his clocks after waking, but then more and more into the morning, with full directions for lunch and a discussion of one anecdote or another at noon, with a full twelve moments of voice. Then the sleep after lunch, until in the late evening and after supper there was talk again, into the hours, until midnight, the sometimes heated sometimes loving twelve strokes of conversation again, and then sleep.

That was why, the butcher would say to him, many times now he could not leave his store until so late, for fear and for love he would miss something.

Mr. Calderón would nod in understanding, and it would not be a simple social gesture, not this time. He would understand. And after saying good-bye, he would leave—because the world for him had changed even more than the butcher would know.

It was perhaps nothing the butcher had done. Perhaps it was. Perhaps he had caught this something as a germ, a germ which would turn out to be simply an odd turn of phrase, a curious mispronunciation, or an accidental juxtaposition of words not heard before. That. The kind of thing that changes a life. The school of the Moment.

Mr. Calderón would walk through the glass of the shop's window of his own volition, and it would break as a glass jar thrown against a wall, breaking into so many excited pieces, so that the whole group assembled in front of the store would be covered with a hundred stars each.

After doing so Mr. Calderón would be led to the front of this convention, the front more or less, as much the front of this group as a front was possible.

Though they would all turn left and right, up and down, not looking at him, he would on that day become by acclamation, if only his own, and by virtue of his singular act of the last five minutes, the visible red emperor of everything and everyone.

At that moment, the butcher stopped being the butcher, the town stopped being the town: perhaps forever, perhaps only for the moment. It did not now matter which. They were all suddenly caught in the place with Tavo, everything and nothing, but not in-between.

Like all these other assembled kings and presidents, fieldmasters and divine beasts of the fire, Mr. Calderón in his exultation would then in that moment wear his own squirrel, which was his pants, over his face and head, and his crown, which was the last piece of window—still shined, still clear—would hang pinned by its points like a burr to his skin.

Nominated by David Madden, Hayden's Ferry Review

TWELVE O'CLOCK

by CAROLYN KIZER

from THE PARIS REVIEW

At seventeen I've come to read a poem
At Princeton. Now my young hosts inquire
If I would like to meet Professor Einstein.
But I'm too conscious I have nothing to say
To interest him, the genius fled from Germany just in time.
"Just tell me where I can look at him," I reply.

Mother had scientific training. I did not;
She loved that line of Meredith's about
The army of unalterable law.
God was made manifest to her in what she saw
As the supreme order of the skies.
We lay in the meadow side by side, long summer nights

As she named the stars with awe.
But I saw nothing that was rank on rank,
Heard nothing of the music of the spheres,
But in the bliss of meadow silences
Lying on insects we had mashed without intent,
Found overhead a beautiful and terrifying mess,

Especially in August, when the meteors whizzed and zoomed.
Echoed, in little, by the fireflies in the grass.
Although, small hypocrite, I was seeming to assent,
I was dead certain that uncertainty

Governed the universe, and everything else,
Including Mother's temperament.

A few years earlier, when I was four,
Mother and Father hushed before the Atwater-Kent
As a small voice making ugly noises through the static
Spoke from the grille, church-window-shaped, to them:
"Listen, darling, and remember always;
It's Doctor Einstein broadcasting from Switzerland."

I said, "So what?" This was repeated as a witticism
By my doting parents. I was dumb and mortified.
So when I'm asked if I would like to speak to Einstein
I say I only want to look at him.
"Each day in the library, right at twelve,
Einstein comes out for lunch." So I am posted.

At the precise stroke of noon the sun sends one clear ray
Into the center aisle: He just appears,
Baggy-kneed, sockless, slippered, with
The famous ravelling grey sweater,
Clutching a jumble of papers in one hand
And in the other his brown sack of sandwiches.

The ray haloes his head! Blake's vision of God,
Unmuscular, serene, except for the electric hair.
In that flicker of a second our smiles meet:
Vast genius and vast ignorance conjoined;
He fixed, I fluid, in a complicit yet
Impersonal interest. He dematerialized and I left, content.

It was December sixth, exactly when,
Just hours before the Japanese attack
The Office of Scientific R & D
Began "its hugely expanded program of research
Into nuclear weaponry"—racing the Germans who, they feared,
Were far ahead. In fact, they weren't.

Next night, the coach to school; the train, *Express*,
Instead pulls into every hamlet: grim young men

435

Swarm the platforms, going to enlist.
I see their faces in the sallow light
As the train jolts, then starts up again,
Reaching Penn Station hours after midnight.

At dinner in New York in '44, I hear the name
Of Heisenberg: Someone remarked, "I wonder where he is,
The most dangerous man alive. I hope we get to him in time."
Heisenberg. I kept the name. Were the Germans, still,
Or the Russians, yet a threat? Uncertainty. . . .
But I felt a thrill of apprehension: Genius struck again.

It is the stroke of twelve—and I suppose
The ray that haloes Einstein haloes me:
White-blond hair to my waist, almost six feet tall,
In my best and only suit. Why cavil?—I am beautiful!
We smile—but it has taken all these years to realize
That when I looked at Einstein he saw me.

At last that May when Germany collapsed
The British kidnapped Heisenberg from France
Where he and colleagues sat in a special transit camp
Named "Dustbin," to save them from a threat they never knew:
A mad American general thought to solve
The post-war nuclear problem by having them all shot.

Some boys in pristine uniforms crowd the car
(West Pointers fleeing from a weekend dance?),
Youth's ambiguities resolved in a single action.
I still see their faces in the yellow light
As the train jolts, then starts up again,
So many destined never to be men.

In Cambridge the Germans visited old friends
Kept apart by war: Austrians, English, Danes,
"In a happy reunion at Farm Hall."
But then the giant fist struck—in the still
Center of chaos, noise unimaginable, we thought we heard
The awful cry of God.

Hiroshima. Heisenberg at first refused
To believe it, till the evening news confirmed
That their work had lead to Hiroshima's 100,000 dead.
"Worst hit of us all," said Heisenberg, "was Otto Hahn,"
  Who discovered uranium fission. "Hahn withdrew to his room,
And we feared that he might do himself some harm."

It is exactly noon, and Doctor Einstein
Is an ancient drawing of the sun.
Simple as a saint emerging from his cell
Dazed by his own light. I think of Giotto, Chaucer,
All good and moral medieval men
In—yet removed from—their historic time.

The week before we heard of Heisenberg
My parents and I are chatting on the train
From Washington. A grey-haired handsome man
Listens with open interest, then inquires
If he might join us. We were such a fascinating family!
"Oh yes," we chorus, "sit with us!"

Penn Station near at hand, we asked his name.
E. O. Lawrence, he replied, and produced his card.
I'd never heard of him, but on an impulse asked,
"What is all this about the harnessing
Of the sun's rays? Should we be frightened?"
He smiled. "My dear, there's nothing in it."

So, reassured, we said goodbyes,
And spoke of him in coming years, that lovely man.
Of course we found out who he was and what he did,
At least as much as we could comprehend.
Now I am living in the Berkeley hills,
In walking distance of the Lawrence lab.

Here where Doctor Lawrence built the cyclotron,
It's noon: the anniversary of Hiroshima:
Everywhere, all over Japan
And Germany, people are lighting candles.

437

It's dark in Germany and Japan, on different days,
But here in Berkeley it is twelve o'clock.

I stand in the center of the library
And he appears. Are we witnesses or actors?
The old man and the girl, smiling at one another,
He fixed by fame, she fluid, still without identity.
An instant which changes nothing,
And everything, forever, everything is changed.

Nominated by Barbara Thompson

438

TRAIN WHISTLES IN THE WIND AND RAIN

by HENRY CARLILE

from SHENANDOAH

In some Havana of the heart I still
imagine my father, his broken English
explaining why that morning he left
he never looked back but went on
into his life. And was it a good life?
The last time I saw him was before
the war, on Christmas Day. I was two,
watching the toy train he'd brought
slow down until, minutes after he left,
my mother wound it too tight and broke it.

I gave his name up for a stepfather's, but
whenever I thought of it, and I tried not to,
I hated him for leaving, for not writing.
I hadn't a photo, even, to tell what he had
looked like, only his shadow, and images
of trains. Later, in Klamath Falls,
my mother told me tales to scare me
from the tracks: horrible stories of hoboes
who tortured children, and of a kid with
both legs cut off at a crossing.
But nothing kept me away. On my tricycle
I watched the trains roar past, huge

439

Mallets, four-eight-eight-fours, with pusher
engines to scale the Siskiyous, until
my mother, missing me, switched me home,
pedaling and howling for my life.

In Seattle, Uncle Andrew took me to the yards
to watch the engines shuttling boxcars.
And standing by the tracks, clutching his hand
as the switchers passed, bathing us in steam,
I didn't know I wouldn't see him again, that
somewhere in the Ardennes a German mortar
round would fall behind the lines where
he stood drinking coffee beside his tank.
Mother, not his mother, though she had nurtured
him after my grandmother's religion tore the
family apart, hung a gold star in our window.
That Seattle morning's all I remember of him.
I can almost see his face, almost hear him,
mother's youngest brother, explaining
the complicated mechanisms of pistons
and drivers, of boilers and steam valves,
as the engines rumbled and huffed, bellowing
steam and smoke, their bells clanging.

And years later, a young man, just broken up
with my fianceé, I took my grief to a river,
as I always had, and stood knee-deep
in the chill winter current, casting
toward a far bank where the steelhead lay,
their icy blue backs freckled with black,
their noses aimed upstream, fins sculling
them in place. But nothing hit that day.
One by one they broke ranks to let my lure
drift past, then reclaimed their places.

I was almost ready to leave when I heard
the far whistle of a freight, one of the
last steam engines, surviving dinosaur,
its carboniferous breath blooming beyond
a far curve of pinkish, bare alders,

where the tracks followed the river,
then curved to cross a bridge upstream
from where I stood. Like soot, a flock
of crows started from the deep boom of
its drivers, the screech of trucks on rails,
the headlight, though it was almost noon,
swiveling its lizard's eye. And suddenly,
something, not nostalgia for trains,
or the woman who had left me, or my
father, or my uncle, caused my eyes to brim
and scald as they had once in St. Paul
when I leaned off an overpass to stare down
a passing engine's funnel and got an eyeful.

So tell me why, this late at night, I love
to hear that far hoot through the rain.
Why does it comfort me, when it's not steam
but air sounds the whistle, not coal
but diesel quakes the house and rattles windows?
Tell me why so late in life, engine, father,
uncle, lover, your loss gathers to a sweetness
in one voice to sing a past more
perfect than it was.

Nominated by Vern Rutsala, David Jauss

KERFLOOEY

fiction by SHARON SHEEHE STARK

from THE ANTIOCH REVIEW

FOR MANY YEARS my father operated the cable tool for Genoca Drilling. The tool was a big percussing brute that went *kerwham, kerwham,* hammering down through the substrata after good water. One night he came home slit-eyed, groping for aspirin. We suspected a "granite" headache. If only it was, he told us. What his crew had come up against was worse than granite. They'd hit air. *Air?* He had to be kidding. Wearily he explained what was known in the trade as a "void." It was resistance that kept the tool tracking. "When it meets with the void, it wanders off, goes kerflooey." My sister Mo, known for giant leaps, shrugged and said, "Sounds like Sundee to me."

Leap then to Sunday. The stringy length of us reflected in the dusty shop fronts of Duchesne Street, on our way home from Mass. If we are anchorless, unreal, the feeling is fed by the long communion fast and the premature warmth of the June morning. But isn't the real malaise the day itself? We enter every Sunday like the Dead Zone. Even the word *leisure* is a slow leak. We breathe it in, it soaks the brain, and the world lists like the vision of a tippler.

We're a lackluster bunch, nondescript except for the here-come-the-Ryan-girls hats. On the subject of hats, my mother is adamant, backing her convictions with a private deal: a week of ironing thrice a year in exchange for three Lillyanns from Madame Millinery. Though we suspect Madame of cheating, stockpiling a month's dirty linen, my mother always keeps her end to the letter, taking, indeed, open pleasure in Mr. Madame's shirts, of imported pima, soft as silk.

We are seven, my father in the lead, Lizzu, tiny for thirteen months, dusky-lipped, hypnogogic, slung over his shoulder. She has a bad heart. Her trinity of defects makes every step treacherous.

At home the hats are sailed onto sofas and chairs. Already the day's gone sloppy. We could eat the withers off a running horse. Breakfast is instant, and cold: cornflakes and day-old crullers. "Bless us O Lord" runs too long, so Tim recites what's come to be known as "Jello Instant Grace": "Rub a dub dub. Thanks for the grub. Yea Jesus!" Mo lives on crackers and black tea, but the rest of us make a single, many-tentacled beast reaching into the bakery box.

My father, chomping, gobbles up the book propped against the toaster. At the moment he's deep in the Harvard Classics, a red freight train of a set bought on time from the Colliers man. And this is just one of the ways my father skips out on us.

Mugs stuffed, my brothers leap up, light out for town, hell bent for trouble. Predictably, they're back in jigtime, riding in on the lazy hum of the Hystone trolley and the carillon medley from the Nazarene-Church. "Rock of Ages." "Jesus Loves Me." But it's a Protestant Jesus, pickled-faced, author of Blue Laws designed to tranquilize the Pisscutter Mick. Or so I've been told. The peace of the Lord is final. The door slams shut and Tim, victimless thus far, has to settle for petty domestic violence. "MA!" I cry, whacking my own behind. "The little creep has your cake tester."

Though Mo and I have already wiped up, my mother scrubs avidly along behind us. In a smooth, swiveling move, she disarms my brother. "Why don't you soak your head?" she says, rehanging the tester. She checks for petrifactions under the highchair tray, wipes ten bluish baby fingers the way she pares carrots. She keeps order as if Heaven's judgment hung on something like the furtive hanky test we watched Mrs. Cahill apply to a dead woman's mantelpiece at her wake.

She carries Lizzu up to her crib and with arms that will not suffer emptiness, hurries back down and plucks the chicken from the fridge. Cradling it, she swings and sways it to the cutting board. "Oh, I said to myself, sit down. Sit down," she sings out.

443

"You're rocking the boat." Slipping into a hum, she rubs the chicken with salt, gives it a sisterly pat. We insist on this chicken, and the chicken, like the hats, speaks for us: *Life is sweet. We are rich.* "Oh, I said to myself—" She stuffs and sutures, returns the bird to the cold.

With the same vague discontent that took my brothers outdoors, my father circumnavigates the house. Upstairs, downstairs, now his cheap shoes squeak the floorboards overhead. Tilting back to listen, my mother frowns. "The heat." she says and starts through her rooms, setting all the fans to thrumming. Essence of musty mohair eddies with the dangerous scent of a restless man. Ten minutes later he ambles out to the kitchen where four of us are busy keeping the teeth in our mouths. Mo, the Maker, deep in her needlework stage, vexedly scans for a lost crochet stitch.

Hands in pockets, he jiggles his change, fakes a sympathetic interest in Mo's dilemma. Then, as if the thought just struck, he says. "Hey, I'm just in the way here. Why don't I wander down to Pahula's, see the Buckos through another humiliation."

"The Buckos, God love them," my mother says.

It will be another two years before we own a TV, another five before Mazeroski cracks the big one.

"God bless Pahula's," from Mo. Indeed!

In Pahula's front window is a squiggle of pink neon that turns out to be a badly articulated palm tree rooted to the T of the word SPIRITS. And spirits are what haunt this family. Both my grandfathers died the same year, one from "liver," the other shot dead by a drunk provoked by lethal wit to run home for a gun.

Still, it's an easy jaw my mother lifts to him, and it's sweetly she says, "Jack, take your time, we'll not be sitting down for a bit."

Her evenness unnerves him. "You sure now, Kate?"

"My best to the Communion of Saints," she says in reference to the fact that one of the Sunday guzzlers has convinced his wife that the Nocturnal Adoration Society holds its weekly meetings at Pahula's. "Go, go, go," she says, shooing him with a flock of long white fingers.

Our stove, bow-legged and mangy, comports itself with the entitled, spiteful cunning of an elderly pet past caring to please. Only my mother can outthink it. At three, with a hexing growl,

444

she spins the oven control, bangs the door thrice, to confuse the technology. Then, quick, before it catches on, she inserts the roaster, eases the door shut, makes praying hands.

Then smoothing her apron front, she summons me over. "Queenie," she says, "think His Nibs might care to know I've set dinner for five or thereabouts?"

"I'm on my way."

"Why don't you just call?" I asked several weeks ago, the first time she put me up to this.

"Mercy," she said. "In thirteen years, you haven't figured it out? Why, there's no finer prod to an Irishman's folly than a bossy woman." She tapped a finger to her lips as if sealing the secret between us. "Shackle him," she whispered, "with permission."

And now, in the same woman-to-woman tone: "Give him to understand, dinner in this house is by invitation, *never* command."

It's a haul on a hot day. Down into the dip at the Bijou and then a five-block hike up a nearly perpendicular hill. Pahula's sits in a cluster of ornate, porchless rowhomes and shares with the Ray Beziks and Pingatore's Shoe Repair a warm wall each. Take shoes for soles and you'll find Pingatore's door standing wide, especially on a day like this one, Flag Day banners awilt all the way down to the Monongahela. The heavy damp, rot of windowboxes and garbage, the wash of axle grease, glue, and cowhide. Oh, and add the sulfurous stench rising off the river and you have a Duchesne Street summer bouquet. But the penny loafers, poor things. Their need is acute and Pingatore's tiny shop vibrates without him. Nonetheless, you know to go next door, rap twice on the window of Pahula's Spirits, bellow *customer, customer,* until you've flushed the cobbler out. Each rectified shoe looms as proof of God. But we who occasion hope with the wearing of hats will negotiate our own miracles, thank you. Still it's a lovely image, angels stitching while Pingatore sleeps it off.

But Sundays even angels lock up. From the curb opposite, the shop looks still as death, the Cat's Paw clock off an hour, emphatic with standard time. Pahula's, with its straight face, its haphazardly drawn shades, projects a demeanor of winking innocence that sets my own devils to leaping. I cut across Duchesne, dawdle to fake out the neighborhood neb-noses, then duck with breathless glee into Pingatore's alley. It's deserted except for an old-timey buff-and-tan roadster reminiscent of the wingtips worn by the snooty manager at the five-and-dime.

Pingatore's yard is a weedy mess since his Mrs. died, the wheelbarrow left where she fell. Dandelion seedheads rubberneck through rusted spokes. I follow a path trampled through to the break in the privet, and with a furtive turreting glance, step through the hedge, onto the Pahulas' property.

The Sunday entrance is through two ground-level cellar doors. Mossy stone steps descend into low clearance, into the sudden updraft of humusy rooty rot from the earthen floor. A single bare bulb cuts a jagged passage past boxes of bar trash, beer kegs, a sack of yellow onions sprouting foot-long snakes. Shouldering close to the wall, I feel my way up narrow stair treads to the door at the top. It's been left ajar, but I knock politely before squeezing through into Bubby's room. The room used to be Mrs. Pahula's larder and Bubby used to be Mr. Pahula's mother, from up the line, in Slabtown.

"Afternoon," I say, sidling past the ugly iron bed. In her envelope of yellowed muslin Bubby raises hardly a bump, she's that insubstantial. Her face isn't wrinkled so much as worn to a translucent, tallowy sheen. Cracking an eye, she rattles her beads, mumbling devoutly in, I forget, Polish or Slovenian, one of those things.

"Holy-Mary-all-over-the-place," her daughter-in-law calls her. Which she is between episodes, when she's old-lady-from-hell.

"Amen," I say, all but hurtling into the kitchen, where due to the truncated proportions of her divided house, Mrs. Pahula, the younger, holes up. On her nicked enamel tabletop sits a tray of shriveled pork links left from breakfast for the men who came directly from Mass.

She's standing back to a sinkful of brown-speckled froth and protruding pothandles. Grease rings bracelet her forearms. "How do," she says, sucking from a damp Camel. Through a forceful scroll of smoke she adds, "Your Highness." The words are insinuating, snide. Does she know they named me Regina as a prod to a haughty bearing? Does she know something I don't? She's a big frazzle-headed harridan, the kind of Irish that keep the rest of us stepping, the kind we feel driven to live down. But she's a wonder, with those glittery little pig eyes, that jutting stemless head,

446

cheekbones flaring above a cudgel-like jaw. Earrings the size of demitasse cups. "I like your earrings," I say, tossing flattery like a moldy cheese rind to a guard dog. Then I back through the swinging doors into the business section.

The taproom takes up what would otherwise be living and sitting rooms. Four skinny posts bisect the area: The L-shaped bar takes up one side, and off to the right three tables (two Formica, one Ping-Pong) and a battered upright piano bespeak Pahula's vague aspirations to entertainment and fine dining. In the far corner a cased stairwell leads to the rental rooms on the second floor.

"Well, worry the bushes and see what ventures out," says Packy Carroll, lifting his glass to me. He's someone's cousin, just off the boat from Connemara, which they say is like being from the moon. At the long leg of the bar, between Regis T. Quilty and Mr. Pingatore, Packy looks dug in, perfectly at home. "Jack," he says, "it's your Queenie."

The stools are stationary types and my father has to crank around to take me in. The motion unleashes a shock of hair, snow-white now for several years. It curtains his left eye but the other blazes a flame-blue welcome such as I never get at home. "Be damned," he says, patting the adjacent seat. "Quick, girl, sit with me." When I've slid in beside him, he sizes me up. His smile is a tight rictus of dingy teeth. "Aren't you the shiny bit," he says. "In this company of bums."

"The usual?" Pahula plants himself before me, a generous mezzanine of midsection resting on the speckled linoleum bar top. Rumor has it he found his soul the day he gave up his bread route to run a bar. Not that it's loosened his tongue any. In a neighborhood thick with the gloom of taciturn men, he's famous for silence. But his product unhinges other men's jaws and here, in the vortex of stories, his moon face glows and he radiates a perfect, incorruptible bliss. He moseys over to the fridge for my Nehi orange. With the methodical precision of a gem setter he positions it before me. He puts the same finesse to filling my glass as he does to tapping a draft. Then, winking at my dad, into the pristine fizz, he shakes a single drop from the Seagram's bottle.

Yikes. A highball. My life will be a string of Christmases set end to end. But I don't let on, not me. Instead, I take a small

447

indifferent sip. "Mum's set supper for quarter past five," I tell my father. "Just so you know."

I have always been amazed by the gullibility of men. Sometimes I think they use up their IQs on the Big Questions, so they don't have to think about personal matters at all.

He regards me with penetrating interest for a second. Then the palaver I've shattered starts up again and he's swept away. It's a zestful exchange of hideous demise. Industrial mishaps, mostly, abundant back then. My father contributes a complicated tale about some fellow well-digger who took "a portly rap on the bean. Lucky devil recovered everything but one essential acuity. Lost his sense of smell, you know. Granted it's not the same as taking a nosedive into boiling steel, but it *has* changed the man. He's gone cross-eyed. And lugubrious. Goes about the livelong day like a beagle in search of his nose."

The telling, I note, is much enriched by all the reading he does at table. After three slugs of fortified orange, I feel like one of the boys. "Maybe he left his nose in a book," I say. The remark looms huge to me, scurrilous, brazen, clever. But it's only a reed in the storm of horror stories and it blows right by them all.

I steal a glance across the way. Regis T., a courtly fellow buttoned tight in his Sunday best. Mr. Pingatore's half-deaf from the racket of his big machines. His twitching mustache seems a sort of revving to speak, if only he could catch the drift. And Packy. He might be twenty-five, maybe younger. A thin, sweetly crimped mouth, dimpled chin. His green eyes I dare not meet with my own lest he read into them. Last week he brushed the round bone of my left shoulder as he tottered past on his way out. All week I've kept busy resummoning that touch. I close my eyes and fill, as from the lip of a pitcher of fire.

In Packy's mouth, everything—religion, Christmas, nylon socks—splits into two automatic halves, if you can imagine the blessing side of a sock, or the curse of it. "A blessing and a curse," he's saying now, about his new convertible top. As it turns out, the car in the alley is his, a thirty-nine Essex purchased Monday through an ad. When Packy speaks, they lean to him, the light under his skin, the blue of the black of his hair, the music he puts to his wishy-wash nonsense, those dense, sensuous gerunds. *Oh, there at the road's turning.* My father clamps my waist, the tickling between our ribs. Sunday at Pahula's is Sunday with a skin. It lifts like the Goodyear blimp and I am launched on a single drop of blended rye.

Pahula's operation is strictly make-do. No finialed, filigreed backbar to showcase the potables. A modest array of barstock lines the shelves of an apple-green hoosier set against the wall next to a square icebox crowned with a round motor. The Pirates are, indeed, playing ball, on a small-screen blond floor model TV set on a high corner shelf. But the contest is obliterated by a staticky blizzard that struck several Sundays back after my brothers "adjusted the vertical." In any case, the set is no more attended to than is Pardo, Pahula's mongrel, over by the front door muzzling after body vermin.

The doors whisper open and Mo slips through like a stiff breeze. Mary's my twin, both of us thickset like our dad, yet she manages to project an aura of weightlessness, an almost saintly detachment that can turn, in a flash, to a crookedness of the eye, a lascivious interest in, well, catastrophe, grief. She can detect the buckling of a fender on the south side of town. Ha, I'm thinking. You missed the good stuff, men getting decorticated, bonked, parboiled, baked into bridge supports.

Skimming past, she dips to me, bumps me with her hobby bag. "Ma says watch the time." She wafts across to Pardo, already galvanized by the sight of her. He stands now rigid and quivering, eyes drilled with light. He drops to his back, Mo to her knees, and she proceeds to slather him with goony talk, dog gibberish. "Sweetboy Pardobelly. Kiss, kiss," Yechh, right on the lips. If that girl's got love in her heart, she's bled of it now, and my father and I watch her rise, snap up her bag as if to say, So much for that jazz.

She settles in at the table by the piano, with its stubborn preponderance of depressed keys, bench stuffed with wartime sheet music and two decks of cards, the polka-dotted pinochle and the standard deck backed with fifty-two raunchy Esquire cartoons. As usual, she's planted herself at a safe remove from the rest of us, yet close enough to keep tabs. My father puts a finger to his lips. "Mo, girl," he ventures. "Is there green stuffing?" He's partial to parsley.

"There's always that," she says, upending her bag. "Now ask me something you don't know."

449

"Okey doke," he says. "What in harry are you going to do with all those—?"

"Doilies," I fill in. "Doilies, Dad." Her inventory must number in the hundreds by now. "Cripes, Mo. Nobody wants those things any more, except maybe immigrants, or something."

But that little hook's pecking happily along now, on my sister's face the grim, God-dazed determination of a land-locked Noah pegging the boards of a big boat.

The wall phone caws, startling me. Hiking his pants, Pahula chugs to get it. "Eh?" he says. Then, "Hmfff. Hey, there, I said hello. You. Who are you?" An audible click. Holding the receiver at arm's length, he screws up his face. Then, shrugging, he hangs up.

"Was that the phone?" Mrs. Pahula's disheveled horse head pokes from between the doors.

"Yup."

"Well?"

"Well what?"

"Hell's bells, man, who did they want?"

"Nobody," says he.

"Nobody, is it? Well, I devoutly hope you told them they had the right man." She recoils with a snort, the doors chattering in her wake.

Shuddering deeply, Packy downs the dregs of his ale, jiggles his glass. "And this time put a whiskey to it." He leans confidingly down the line. "And you wonder now why I'm not after tyin' the knot." And I'm thinking of the woman my father married, that quiet, ladylike guile, the intricate wisdom with which she pilots our destiny from ten blocks away.

Two abreast, my brothers crash through. Flushed from racing the uphill leg, with a triumphant "Yeah!" they make straight for the Ping-Pong table. They think they've beat someone to it. But these men are philosophers. They have to sit to think and drink to pontificate and Ping-Pong is just Pahula's penurious answer to Noonan's at the corner installing pocket billiards.

Tim cups his mouth. "Yo, Queenie. Grab us a coupla pops."

"Who was your nig—*negro* last year."

Tim, whose eyes flash challenge from every family photo, skips sideways to the bar, slots in between me and our dad as Pahula uncaps two Yoo Hoo chocolates. Tim closes a fist over their frosty

450

lips. At fourteen he's a stunner but only half as pretty as he'll get. My father's proud regard unsettles him. Stepping back, he cuts his discomfort with a swinish guzzle of pop. He's shorn so flat on top he looks bald under the lights.

Tim forces a disgusting belch. "You two scags are supposed to get home and set the table."

In the meantime, Johnny Pat's dancing around, warming up his backhand. For all his efforts he will never achieve the supreme miserableness of his older brother. "Ma wouldn't say scags," he says quietly.

"Who the dickens?" someone whispers when the new man comes in. An elfin fellow in a snappy black suit. The regulars stiffen, pretend not to see him. When he understands, the stranger cracks the silence with a laugh. "Whoaa there, boys. There might be revenuers about, but you're not looking at one. Name's Joe. I'm brother-in-law to Tripper Lynch and I drove all night to get here. Tripper cashed in, you know. Last night, twenty past ten. A busted aorta. Caught us a bit shy, he did. Whatever you can spare will help relieve the—tensions."

Pahula bows his head for a respectful second. Then he bags a couple of fifths, on loan, a cold quart of Iron City, free of charge. When the stranger is gone, Regis T. clears his throat. "Mr. Rattigan," he says, "wasn't the late Mr. Lynch a chum of your own? You might have said something."

Rattigan, who combines nastily with alcohol, gives back with a black look. "See here," he says. "Ask anyone, I'd cut off a toe if my friend could use an extra. Let him kick on me, though, I'm quit with the bum. Hell, I won't stand for it."

Regis T. nods uneasily. "Yes, indeed." Poggety pock. The Ping-Ponging is like a bouncing ball over singalong lyrics.

I check my father's watch. Four twenty-three. The subject has come around to a popular one. Nothing these men relish more that enculturating Packy Carroll. Pingatore drinks muscatel from a blind cup. His eyes dart from face to face. He's trying to figure should he laugh or cry. Stymied, he holds to a sort of rapt absorption even though Rattigan has just counseled Packy against "any and all dealings with the eyetalian sector. One dirty look and they go blubbering to the mob."

Poggedy pock. "That ball was out!"

'You swung at it, dummy."

451

"Hey, wait a minute!" I am indignant. "The Pope's Italian. Does the Pope blubber to the mob? I don't think so."

And Rattigan glances down, that oblique, bitten smile hinting the extent to which he's privy to Vatican affairs. Then the doors squeak open. "Guess who?" he says sourly without troubling to look up.

My mother is jonquil-bright in yellow piqué with a wide white patent cinch. Her skirt, pouffed at the waist, tapers sleeky to mid-calf. From the humidity her head is a helmet of girlish corkscrews. She looks ingenuous, just tumbled from sleep. Bracing Lizzu against her slung left hip, she fixes on each of her children. "Did you forget the way home?" she says.

"What? Well, for God's sake, it's herself." My father's forehead rises, hiking thick brows, stunningly black in contrast to the dead white of his hair. "Christ Jesus!" You'd think he hadn't seen her in years. He squeezes my shoulder. "Scoot over like a good girl." He lunges forth for Lizzu.

The shift bumps Rattigan off the end stool. Grumbling, he removes to the other side. "What is this?" he says in a stage whisper. "Family day at the rink?" Pingatore nods yes, shakes his head no, then baring rattlesome dentures, slaps the bar in hearty agreement.

"Katherine Meagher Egan," my father says. "The one woman on earth I'd bounce a check for."

Flapping her hand, my mother slips in beside him. The dress is so vibrant, its line so acute, she looks cut out and pasted, like the Jane Russell someone stuck to The Last Supper in the school cafeteria. When Pahula approaches, she makes a show of shrinking from him. But he's already got the crème de menthe in hand. Eyes on my mother, he tips the neck to within an inch of the glass.

She sighs. "Have it your way, then. A finger and not a drizzle more. I've got my chicken in." There's a hurried, impermanent air about her, but she's taken pains with her make-up, and a flush of pleasure laps the circles of liquid rouge.

To her left sits a man they call Upstairs Mike in honor of his lengthy tenure as the Pahula's star boarder. "Say," he asks her, with slurry earnestness. "What's it doing out there?"

Oddly enough, the question makes sense to me. Outside, the lowering light leans against the window blinds, nuggets of red-gold burn through the worn spots. In this beery, bottled air she shows the patinaed mystique of someone passing through from a distant place.

"Why, it's still Sunday," she says. "And Clara Bezik out thinning her greens without a thought for shame." Said tongue-in-cheek. Yet the men shy from her. They stare into their drinks. *Ah, yes, a disgrace, this thinning.*

Pahula gears up for the frontal thrust of a full sentence. "Clara's getting even with God," he says. "For tossing her boy back not a month before ordination."

"Ho," my father says. "Tommy Bezik was by the Saturday last. He's door-to-door for Kirby's, you know. Katherine needs another sweeper like she needs—'Well,' I said to the boy, 'now, Tommy,' I said, 'didn't the Jesuits tell you, Nature abhors a vacuum, especially one that runs two hundred bucks.' "

"Cheapcheap," Rattigan chirps. "When you consider the prevailing tariff on redemption." Rattigan's rumored to be an atheist. And when an Irishman defects, it's with a reaction equal and opposite. With the whole of his heart and soul and mind. And he will love his bitterness as himself.

Wrapping his hand around my mother's glass, Pahula waits. She laughs, clacks her tongue. "Very well, but just a finger, mind you."

The Ping-Ponging has stopped. Four dungareed boy-legs gangle out from the corner hidden by the lap of the piano. They're too quiet, but whatever they're up to, I don't want to know about it. The banter has me, this light shadow-dance of wit and opinion that today will keep within the limits of decency. No one feels duty bound to impugn a motive or needle a man at his roots, no articulate, malicious triggering someone to high-horse it home for a pistol. Communion of saints. Company of bums. I'm plush with love for them all.

The bartalk builds, filling with miscellany the way the rush from a busted dam gathers all and sundry in its path. There's speculation as to the length of the new Cadillacs due in September. They razz Packy about his new old Essex. The "Beau Brummel Junker" my father calls it. But Packy's unpredictable. He abides it all with a lipless, simpleton grin. Inevitably, someone gets theological, deep. If God is the author of all virtue, is He also humble? *Huh? Huh? Gotcha there, didn't I?*

453

And "Yes, indeed," says the decorous Regis T. Or "No, indeed."

"Dee dah," echoes Lizzu, all pretzeled up in my father's lap. Folded in three, knees to chin, she doesn't get dandled like other kids. In one, two. Out three, four. My father squeezes his babe like a concertina. It's a maneuver the heart man taught us, a simple trick to force the thwarted blood through faulty valves. "Who knows, who knows?" he says dreamily to nothing and everything. But since taking Lizzu he hasn't once touched his beer.

Dee dah, like a weak echo from far away. Lizzu's eyes, elderly in their purpled depths, struggle open. She seems always trying to lift the lid on her weary young life. My father glances up. "Packy," he says, "might you have something in your repertoire, for the tyke here? Something in the grand old tongue."

Packy's guppy-eyed by now. But he never has to be asked twice. "A lay from the Time of Trouble," he tells us and his boozy throat is a boon to its mood. Who knows what the words mean, but they clog the room like soft weather and even the cobbler picks up on the melancholy. Pingatore sets down his wineglass to wipe an eye.

Packy's an able player, fixing woeful eyes on the most receptive face in the room, my mother's. And yes, she nods when Pahula tags her glass. She gives the air a signifying pinch. And yes, again, distractedly, not two minutes later. Packy deepens his tone to get under the *Oh*. The "Oh" rolls away like a stone from the grave. Dead men rumble among us.

"Shit to you. Sunzybeeches!"

"Oh," Packy says, crossing himself.

"Timber," I whisper, "Bubby's loose."

I can feel the heat of Mo's piqued expectation as the curses mount. English broken into a rubble of saints and sins of the flesh. A largesse of obscenity requiring of a pious type, a lifetime of saving up. *Thwack!* Bubby comes hacking through from the kitchen. Wielding a wooden cane, she's one weird three-legged flamingo in a pink nightgown and matching sleep socks. Astonishingly fleet, she leaps the sullen dog, hammers the door bolt through, and with a wicked cackle she's off the stoop and on the street before we can mobilize to stop her.

"Damn you lazybunchalushes." It's Mrs. Pahula in grim pursuit. She's not running exactly but the cant of neck and jaw, that

454

erect rocking mass makes her both figurehead and ship, steady as she goes. She stops short, swerves off to the right. "Urchins," she says, looming over my brothers. She gives each a cuff. "Will you drop that dirty deck and get cracking. You know I can't catch her.

It's a challenge they meet with brio. Kipping into position, they spring off in their scrubbed hightops, Mrs. Pahula plowing crossly behind. Pahula turns red to the rims of his ears. "Mother," he says softly. "Oh Ma!" With the mystified regret of a dying man.

Sunday comes full through the flung door, the Protestant calm holding for an instant before shattering like dawn when the cat catches the rabbit. The shriek of brakes. That inhuman wail. Moments later they troop back in, the old woman passive as a prom date on Johnny Pat's arm, all wildness gone but for the ruff of brindle hair pushed up by her pillow. At the kitchen door, Mrs. Pahula shakes off her goons and, seizing Bubby by the armpit, turns back to the bar. "Next time," she says, "you'll be the one to pursue or so help me, Paul Pahula, I'll let her hotfoot it back to Slabtown. Hear?"

Packy sits staring through one glinty eye slit. Then he's pinching one cheek, slapping the other. *Rise and shine.* With the perky dignity of the practiced drunk he gathers his body parts, one by one. He settles his crush cap to his crown, pushes up from the bar. My mother straightens. "Aw, stay now," she says, darting a pleading look from face to face. For these drinkers are mysteriously linked. A single break and they scatter like a string of cheap pearls. Pingatore, triggered, disembarks as cautiously as if he were descending a forty-foot ladder. He takes careful aim before casting himself into the path behind Packy. "Sit down, you two," from my mother.

Yes, yes, I'm thinking. Sit down, you're rocking the boat. My shoulder aches to steady Packy's exit.

When they're gone, my mother turns distant and with a thoughtful shrug, nudging her glass, indicates another tap from the green bottle. Overhead the Pirates must be into the second of the double header but the action crackles like the mouth of a garbled God.

Pahula, panicked, tries to hold the hanger-on with one on the house. My father blocks with a hand over his glass. He turns Lizzu bellydown on his lap. Pahula rocks back on his heels, casts

455

a quizzical glance over my head, towards the door. "Don't tell me," he says, "you forgot something."

I turn to see Packy braced between the door jambs, body cocked as if to counterbalance his sliding cap. "They did it again," he says. The boy is weeping real tears.

"Dear me, what did they do?" my mother asks in that tone she uses to deflate a child's idea of dire.

"The devils, they lifted me shifting gear and me steering wheel."

Pahula's smile is indulgent, avuncular as he bends to my father's ear. When my father understands, he nods. "Ah Packy," he says, "don't you know a blessing and a curse when you're pinched between them. You're in no shape to be cruising the streets. By the grace of God, you'll walk home. Leave us to collar the thief. On my honor, you'll get your belongings back."

Packy blows his nose, tries to look sober. "A man could do worse in his choice of friends. But, Mother of Christ—this is a daunting neighborhood."

When he's out of earshot the place cracks up. Tim, who recently stole a case of roofing shingles from a construction site, lets out a whoop.

"Never you mind," my mother calls back. "And it better be *pinochle* you're playing, you two." Vivified, my sister rises, ecru thread trailing. She approaches the bar, that look in her eye, a moth to another's loss.

"Well, shame on you all!" I say. "That's mean to laugh. A poor immigrant—how can he afford to keep himself in steering wheels."

"Look at me, Madam Fair and Right." My father motions my mother forward so he can meet my eyes across her back. "According to Mr. Pahula here, who should know, the lad's been wrestling with his problem nearly every day since he got that dapper machine of his. Unless he's in full possession, you see, he tends to forget that unlike the old sod, by U.S. law, we drive on the right, keep our steering apparatus on the left. So Mr. Carroll climbs in, and reaches out—" my father's laughing so hard he can hardly finish—"all heck breaks loose. *Help, haha, help, I've been robbed.* Sleep well tonight, sweet girl, for there's no steering-wheel thief on Duchesne Street."

"Oh, Daddy."

456

The afternoon has passed in a raking rhythm of peaks and dips. This will be the last full rise. Then silence. The men breathe deep, drink of this silence. It is what they carried here, what they must take back, the very stuff of their souls. My father pockets his smile along with a stack of small change. Before him his glass stands three-quarters full, but lifeless and flat after all that magic. Well, hasn't it cracked the man, lavished him upon us?

"Upsy," he says, easing Lizzu vertical against his chest. My Nehi buzz shrinks to a single drilling word: Home.

He stands. "Katherine?"

"Ummm," she says. "The chicken's on low." And she takes her blessed time with those final drops and, draining her glass, she flashes a smile full of Day-Glo-green teeth. "Okay, okay," she tells my father, letting on as though leaving is his idea. Nor has it escaped me that, a finger at a time, my enterprising mother has siphoned from her duties a full glass. "Let's march," she says resolutely.

We queue up and move single file through the kitchen, past Bubby, fast asleep after her exertions; down through the dim, constricted cellar. Tim holds the door as, one by one, we rise out of the hole. Before me, my mother's yellow melts into buttery sunlight, the sky from below so blindingly bright and unreal my elbows tingle. A round moment, its radiance mixed with the magnified power of my first real drink and the good emptiness of hunger running to an oven on low. Lord!

But my pleasure is ridiculous, the moment dangerously overblown. Look, already it's ripping away, ramifying into its numberless, unknowable strains, high in the Sunday blue as we trudge in blissful weariness up the long hot hill, my mother puffing with effort. She will be quick with dinner, the Sunday grace abridged to the bones of gratitude. *Thanks for the grub. Yea Jesus.*

There it is, Sunday, studded even to the least observant with seeds of assorted ruin. Ignore the portents: we grew up. And, as my mother so devoutly willed, we "turned out." Tim, the little criminal, learned to like the law enough to marry it. He made a crackerjack, exceedingly handsome trial lawyer. The Jesuits got our Johnny Pat. Mo made a slow, multi-staged transition from stitchery to literature. She's a poet, of some repute, I hear. Her lines, according to one reviewer, "pump freon straight to the heart." Lizzu, bless her, overcame preposterous odds to survive

457

highly experimental heart surgery. Between the two of us we have five healthy children upon whom my father spends his *sober* self with ridiculous, buffoonish, enviable abandon. His career took him well into the era of the high-speed rotary drill, which augers nicely through granite but, like the old cable tool, continues to lose itself in air. Kerflooey.

And kerflooey tells as well as anything what happened to my mother, though some might allow how pride can blind and cleverness kill. And irony keeps a long stick for tripping the ones who try too hard. Who knows? Who knows? Not us, no how, but we carry a full grudge against Sunday nonetheless. It's good to blame. Blame cordons off horror. And don't the ones who go on, those who think and work and love and hope, don't we have to believe that on some days on earth, some streets are humanly navigable?

So go back to that Sunday in June. Now jump ahead six months. A ceramic Christmas tree blazes from atop Pahula's TV, still on the blink. The same bunch, less one, sitting as if they never left. The mood is, by turns, dirgeful, jocular, elegiac, and nasty, depending on who's doing the eulogizing. It's been a full week since Packy Carroll, having finally made his cultural adjustments, took steering wheel in hand and drove through Madame's plate-glass window, scattering hats like birds.

Regis T.'s cheeks are shiny, impetigo pink. His mouth is pinched awry. His little eyes jitter and swim and he's silly faced from mixing bar whiskey and grief. "Poor Pack," he says. "Poor, poor boy." Then he puts great effort into aligning himself. He clears his throat. "The broken ones," he says sternly. "They'll find the pieces, boys. Sweep them into heaven with a silver broom." He narrows his eyes, glances around. Then oh so tenuously, "Won't they?"

But Rattigan's no friend to the dead. "Dumb shit," he says. "Good riddance."

Lizzu is cranky, Johnny Pat bored without Tim, who's off to the Bijou with his first girlfriend. Finally, my father, so shrewdly tooled to make the first move, does. "Katherine?" These days he handles her name like a hot potato.

"Why don't you go soak your head!" she snaps, flagging around with her empty glass. "Yoo hoo, there, yoo hoo, Mister Pahoooola."

And it will be long after dark before we drag her home to a bird as sere as old Bubby.

"Say grace."

"Yea Jesus."

The breast meat shreds like rotten softwood. We rake it into piles. So much for the saving gravy. Goodbye highstepping hats. Our faces are dumb with the dawn of the bad years. Atop her two propped elbows my mother holds a drumstick. Head cocked, tipsily, she contemplates the nibbled bone, and she's humming, a broken, toneless *Sit down* under her breath. Then suddenly she looks up and blurts something. Food bits fly.

"What?"

"Sliver broom," she says.

I remember Regis T. "She means sill. Sil-ver. As in gold?"

"Sill," she says. "Sill ver buh-room." With proud, almost bellicose precision. "Sill-silly man," she adds. And she starts to giggle, the drum-stick, in splinters, swings from her left fist.

"Huh?" Johnny Pat screws up his face. "What's so funny about a broom?"

In her highchair Lizzu rocks back and forth. "Boom boom," she chants happily.

My mother's laugh is rubbery and wet. Her chin keeps bouncing on her chest and the bone lies under the table.

"Silver broom," my father says, hesitantly. Then "Bloody goddammed broom," tight-lipped, trying to ignore Johnny Pat and me, in fits now, all but falling off our chairs. With a high, hiccoughing yelp, he too cracks up, and Mo follows, dissolving in a soundless slide to the floor. Tim, giddy in love these days, is the silliest one of all. And this is the silliest thing we ever heard. Every time the laughter slacks off, someone belts out another one. Silver broom! Silver broom! and we cannot let go of it.

Nominated by The Antioch Review

THE LOOM

fiction by R. A. SASAKI

from THE LOOM AND OTHER STORIES (Graywolf Press)

It was when Cathy died that the other Terasaki sisters began to think that something was wrong with their mother. Sharon and Jo were home for the weekend, and when the phone call came they had gone up to her room with the shocking news, barely able to speak through their tears. Sharon had to raise her voice so her mother could hear the awful words, choked out like bits of shattered glass, while Jo watched what seemed like anger pull her mother's face into a solemn frown.

"You see?" their mother said. Her voice, harsh and trembling with a shocking vehemence, startled the two sisters even in their grief. "Daddy told her not to go mountain climbing. He said it was too dangerous. She didn't listen."

Recalling her words later, Jo felt chilled.

They had always known about their mother's "ways"—the way she would snip off their straight black hair when they were children as soon as it grew past their ears, saying that hair too long would give people the wrong idea. Then later, when they were grown and defiant and wore their hair down to their waists, she would continue to campaign by lifting the long strands and snipping at them with her fingers. There was also the way she would tear through the house in a frenzy of cleaning just before they left on a family vacation, "in case there's a fire or someone breaks in and *yoso no hito* have to come in." They never understood if it was the firemen, the police, or the burglar before whose eyes she would be mortally shamed if her house were not spotless. There

460

was even the way she cooked. She was governed not by inspiration or taste, but by what "they" did. The clothes she chose for them were what "they" were wearing these days. Who is this "they"? her daughters always wanted to ask her. Her idiosyncrasies were a source of mild frustration to which the girls were more or less resigned. "Oh, Mom," they would groan, or, to each other: "That's just Mom."

But this.

"It was as though she didn't feel anything at all," Jo recounted to her eldest sister, Linda, who had come home from Germany for the funeral. "It was as though all she could think about was that Cathy had broken the rules."

It wasn't until their father had come home that their mother cried, swept along in the wake of his massive grief. He had been away on a weekend fishing trip, and they had tried to get in touch with him, but failed. Jo had telephoned the highway patrol and park rangers at all his favorite fishing spots, saying, "No, don't tell him that his daughter has died. Would you just tell him to come home as soon as possible?" And it was Jo who was standing at the window watching when his truck turned the corner for home. The three women went down to the basement together. He and his fishing buddy had just emerged from the dusty, fish-odorous truck, and he was rolling up the garage door when they reached him. He was caught between the bright spring sunlight and the dark coolness of the basement. His hand still on the garage door, he heard the news of his daughter's death. Their mother told him, with a hint of fear in her voice. He cried, as children cry who have awakened in the night to a nameless terror, a nameless grief; for a suspended moment, as he stood alone sobbing his dead daughter's name, the three women deferred to the sanctity of his suffering. Then Sharon moved to encircle him in her arms, clinging flimsily to him against the tremendous isolation of grief.

It was only then that their mother had cried, but it seemed almost vicarious, as if she had needed their father to process the raw stuff of life into personal emotion. Not once since the death had she talked about her own feelings. Not ever, her daughters now realized.

"It would probably do Mom good to get away for a while," Linda said. "I was thinking of taking her to Germany with me when I go back, just for a few weeks. She's never been anywhere. A change of scene might be just what she needs. Don't you think?"

"I suppose it's worth a try," Jo said.

So it was decided that when Linda flew back to join her husband, who was stationed in Heidelberg, their mother would go with her and stay a month. Except for a visit to Japan with her own mother when she was sixteen, it was their mother's first trip abroad. At first she was hesitant, but their father encouraged her; he would go too if he didn't have to stay and run the business.

It was hard to imagine their mother outside the context of their house. She had always been there when the children came back from school; in fact, the sisters had never had babysitters. Now, as they watched her at the airport, so small and sweet with her large purse clutched tightly in both hands and her new suitcase neatly packed and properly tagged beside her, they wondered just who was this little person, this person who was their mother?

She had grown up in San Francisco, wearing the two faces of a second-generation child born of immigrant parents. The two faces never met; there was no common thread running through both worlds. The duality was unplanned, untaught. Perhaps it had begun the first day of school when she couldn't understand the teacher and Eleanor Leland had called her a "Jap" and she cried. Before then there had never been a need to sort out her identity; she had met life headlong and with the confidence of a child.

Her world had been the old Victorian flat in which her mother took in boarders—the long, narrow corridor, the spiral stairway, the quilts covered with bright Japanese cloth, and the smell of fish cooking in the kitchen. She had accepted without question the people who padded in and out of her world on stockinged feet; they all seemed to be friends of the family. She never wondered why most of them were men, and it never occurred to her child's mind to ask why they didn't have their own families. The men often couldn't pay, but they were always grateful. They lounged in doorways and had teasing affectionate words for her and her sister. Then they would disappear, for a month, for six months, a year. Time, to a child, was boundless and

462

unmeasurable. Later, crates of fruit would arrive and be stacked in the corridor. "From Sato-san," her mother would say, or, "*Kudoh-san kara.*"

The young men sometimes came back to visit with new hats set jauntily on their heads, if luck was good. But often luck was not good, and they came back to stay, again and again, each stay longer than the last; and each time they would tease less and drink more with her father in the back room. The slap of cards rose over the low mumble of their longing and despair. All this she accepted as her world.

The Victorian house which contained her world was on Pine Street, and so it was known as "Pine" to the young adventurers from her parents' native Wakayama prefecture in Japan who made their way from the docks of Osaka to the lettuce fields and fruit orchards of California. "Stay at Pine," the word passed along the grapevine, "Moriwaki-san will take care of you."

It was a short walk down the Buchanan Street hill from Pine to the flats where the Japanese community had taken root and was thriving like a tree whose seed had blown in from the Pacific and had held fast in this nook, this fold in the city's many gradations. When she was a little older her world expanded beyond the Victorian called Pine. It expanded toward the heart of this community, toward the little shops from which her mother returned each day, string bag bulging with newspaper-wrapped parcels and a long white radish or two. She played hide-and-seek among the barrels of pickles and sacks of rice piled high in the garage that claimed to be the American Fish Market while her mother exchanged news of the comings and goings of the community over the fish counter. "Ship coming in Friday? Do you think Yamashita-san's picture bride will come? She's in for a surprise!"

At the age of five she roller-skated to the corner of her block, then on sudden impulse turned the corner and started down the Buchanan Street hill. Her elder sister, Keiko, who had expected her to turn around and come right back, threw down her jump rope and ran after her, screaming for her to stop. But she didn't stop. She made it all the way to the bottom, cheeks flushed red and black hair flying, before shooting off the curb and crumpling in the street. Her hands and knees were scraped raw, but she was laughing.

463

Before that first day of school there had been no need to look above Pine Street, where the city reached upwards to the Pacific Heights area and the splendid mansions of the rich white people. The only Japanese who went to Pacific Heights were the ones employed to do housecleaning as day laborers. She had always known what was on the other side of Pine Street, and accepted easily that it was not part of her world.

When it came time for her to go to school, she was not sent to the same school as the other Japanese-American children because Pine was on the edge of Japantown and in a different school district. She was the only Japanese in her class. And from the instant Eleanor Leland pulled up the corners of her eyes at her, sneering "Jap!", a kind of radar system went to work in her. Afterward she always acted with caution in new surroundings, blending in like a chameleon for survival. There were two things she would never do again: one was to forget the girl's name who had called her a Jap, and the other was to cry.

She did her best to blend in. Though separated from the others by her features and her native tongue, she tried to be as inconspicuous as possible. If she didn't understand what the teacher said, she watched the other children and copied them. She listened carefully to the teacher and didn't do anything that might provoke criticism. If she couldn't be outstanding she at least wanted to be invisible.

She succeeded. She muted her colors and blended in. She was a quiet student and the other children got used to her; some were even nice to her. But she was still not really a part of their world because she was not really herself.

At the end of each school day she went home to the dark, narrow corridors of the old Victorian and the soothing, unconscious jumble of two tongues that was the two generations' compromise for the sake of communication. Theirs was a comfortable language, like a comfortable old sweater that had been well washed and rendered shapeless by wear. She would never wear it outside of the house. It was a personal thing, like a hole in one's sock, which was perfectly all right at home but would be a horrible embarrassment if seen by *yoso no hito*.

In the outside world—the *hakujin* world—there was a watchdog at work who rigorously edited out Japanese words and mannerisms when she spoke. Her words became formal, carefully chosen and somewhat artificial. She never thought they conveyed what she really felt, what she really was, because what she really was was unacceptable. In the realm of behavior, the watchdog was a tyrant. Respectability, as defined by popular novels and Hollywood heroines, must be upheld at all costs. How could she explain about the young men lounging in the doorways of her home and drinking in the back room with her father? How could she admit to the stories of the immigrant women who came to her mother desperate for protection from the beatings by their frenzied husbands? It was all so far from the drawing rooms of Jane Austen and the virtue and gallantry of Hollywood. The Japanese who passed through her house could drink, gamble, and philander, but she would never acknowledge it. She could admit to no weakness, no peculiarity. She would be irreproachable. She would be American.

Poverty was irreproachably American in the Depression years. Her father's oriental art goods business on Union Square had survived the 1906 earthquake only to be done in by the dishonesty of a *hakujin* partner who absconded with the gross receipts and the company car. The family survived on piecework and potatoes. Her mother organized a group of immigrant ladies to crochet window-shade rings. They got a penny apiece from the stores on Grant Avenue. Her father strung plastic birds onto multi-colored rings. As they sat working in the back room day after day, they must have dreamed of better times. They had all gambled the known for the unknown when they left Japan to come to America. Apparently it took more than hard work. They could work themselves to death for pennies. Entrepreneurial ventures were risky. They wanted to spare their sons and daughters this insecurity and hardship. Education was the key that would open the magical doors to a better future. Not that they hadn't been educated in Japan, indeed some of them were better educated than the people whose houses they cleaned on California Street. But they felt the key was an American education, a college education. Immigrant sons and immigrant daughters would fulfill their dreams.

She and her peers acquiesced in this dream. After all, wasn't it the same as their own? To succeed, to be irreproachable, to be American? She would be a smart career girl in a tailored suit, beautiful and bold—an American girl.

After the Depression her father opened a novelty store on Grant Avenue, and she was able to go to college. She set forth into the unknown with a generation of immigrant sons and daughters, all fortified by their mutual vision of the American dream.

They did everything right. They lived at home to save expenses. Each morning they woke up at dawn to catch the bus to the ferry building. They studied on the ferry as it made the bay crossing, and studied on the train from the Berkeley marina to Shattuck Avenue, a few blocks from the majestic buildings of the University of California. They studied for hours in the isolation of the library on campus. They brought bag lunches from the dark kitchens of old Japantown flats and ate on the manicured grass or at the Japanese Students' Club off campus. They went to football games and rooted for the home team. They wore bobby socks and Cal sweaters. The women had pompadours and the men parted their hair in the middle. They did everything correctly. But there was one thing they did not do: they did not break out of the solace of their own society to establish contact with the outside world.

In a picture dated 1939 of the graduating members of the Nisei Students' Club, there are about sixty of them in caps and gowns standing before California Hall. She is there, among the others, glowing triumphantly. No whisper of Pearl Harbor to cast a shadow on those bright faces. Yet all these young graduates would soon be clerking in Chinatown shops or pruning American gardens. Their degrees would get them nowhere, not because they hadn't done right, but because it was 1939 and they had Japanese faces. There was nowhere for them to go.

When the war came, her application for a teaching job had already been on file for two years. Since graduation she had been helping at her father's Grant Avenue store. Now she had to hand-letter signs for the store saying "Bargain Sale: Everything Must Go." Her father's back slumped in defeat as he watched the business he had struggled to build melt away overnight. America was creating a masterpiece and did not want their color.

They packed away everything they could not carry. Tom the Greek, from whom they rented Pine, promised to keep their possessions in the basement, just in case they would be able to come back someday. The quilts of bright Japanese cloth, Imari dishes hand-carried by her mother from Japan, letters, photos, window-shade rings made in hard times, a copy of her junior college newspaper in which she had written a column, her Cal yearbook, faded pictures of bright Hollywood starlets—she put all her dreams in boxes for indefinite keeping. As they were told, they took along only what was practical, only what would serve in the uncertain times to come—blankets, sweaters, pots, and pans. Then, tagged like baggage, they were escorted by the U.S. Army to their various pick-up points in the city. And when the buses took them away, it was as though they had never been.

They were taken to Tanforan Racetrack, south of the city, which was to be their new home. The stables were used as barracks, and horse stalls became "apartments" for families. As she viewed the dirt and manure left by the former occupants, she realized, "So this is what they think of me." Realization was followed by shame. She recalled how truly she had believed she was accepted, her foolish confidence, and her unfounded dreams. She and her *nisei* friends had been spinning a fantasy world that was unacknowledged by the larger fabric of society. She had been so carried away by the aura of Berkeley that she had forgotten the legacy left her by Eleanor Leland. Now, the damp, dusty floor and stark cots reminded her sharply of her place. She was twenty-four. They lived in Tanforan for one year.

After a year they were moved to the Topaz Relocation Center in the wastelands of Utah. Topaz, Jewel of the Desert, they called it sardonically. Outside the barbed wire fence, the sagebrush traced aimless patterns on the shifting gray sands. Her sister Keiko could not endure it; she applied for an office job in Chicago and left the camp. Her brother enrolled at a midwestern university. She stayed and looked after her parents.

After a time she began to have trouble with her hearing. At first, it was only certain frequencies she could not hear, like some desert insects. Then it was even human voices, particularly when there was background noise. She couldn't be sure, but sometimes she wondered if it was a matter of choice, that if she only concentrated, she would be able to hear what someone was saying. But the blowing dust seemed to muffle everything anyway.

She left camp only once, and briefly, to marry the young man who had courted her wordlessly in the prewar days. He was a *kibei*, born in America and taken back to Japan at the age of

467

eight. He had then returned to San Francisco to seek his fortune at the age of eighteen. He got off the boat with seven dollars in his pocket. He was one of those restless, lonely young men who would hang out at the Japantown pool hall, work at odd jobs by day, and go to school at night. He lived with a single-minded simplicity that seemed almost brash to someone like her who had grown up with so many unspoken rules. He wanted this sophisticated, college-educated American girl to be his wife, and she was completely won over. So she got leave from camp, and he from his unit, which was stationed at Fort Bragg, and they met in Chicago to cast a humble line into the uncertain future, a line they hoped would pull them out of this war into another, better life. Then they each returned to their respective barracks.

As defeat loomed inevitable for Japan, more and more people were allowed to leave the camps. Some of them made straight for the Midwest or East Coast, where feelings did not run so high against their presence, but her family could think only of going back home. The longing for San Francisco had become so strong that there was no question as to where they would go when they were released. They went straight back to Pine, and their hearts fell when they saw the filth and damage caused by three years of shifting tenancy. But they set about restoring it nevertheless because it was the only thing left of their lives.

The three years that had passed seemed like wasted years. The experience had no connection to the rest of her life; it was like a pocket in time, or a loose string. It was as though she had fallen asleep and dreamed the experience. But there was certainly no time to think about that now; they were busy rebuilding their lives.

She was pregnant with her first child. Her husband pleated skirts at a factory that hired Japanese. Later he ventured into the wholesale flower business where the future might be brighter. His hours were irregular; he rose in the middle of the night to deliver fresh flowers to market. Her sister, who had come back from Chicago to rejoin the family, took an office job with the government. Her parents were too old to start over. Her father hired out to do day work, but it shamed him so much that he did not want anyone else to know.

Then she was busy with the babies, who came quickly one after another, all girls. She was absorbed in their nursing and

468

bodily functions, in the sucking, smacking world of babies. How could she take time to pick up the pieces of her past selves, weave them together into a pattern, when there were diapers to be changed and washed, bowel movements to be recorded, and bottles sterilized? Her world was made up of Linda's solicitude for her younger sister Cathy, Cathy's curiosity, and the placidity of the third baby Sharon. Then there was Jo, who demanded so much attention because of her frail health. The house was filled with babies. Her husband was restless, fiercely independent—he wanted to raise his family in a place of his own.

So they moved out to the Avenues, leaving the dark corridors and background music of mixed tongues for a sturdy little house in a predominantly *hakujin* neighborhood, where everyone had a yard enclosed by a fence.

When first their father, then their mother, died, Keiko also moved out of Pine and closed it up for good. The old Victorian was too big for one person to live in alone. But before all the old things stored away and forgotten in the basement were thrown out or given away, was there anything she wanted to keep? Just her college yearbook from Cal. That was all she could think of. She couldn't even remember what had been so important, to have been packed away in those boxes so carefully when the war had disrupted their lives. She couldn't take the time with four babies to sift through it all now. It would take days. No, just her yearbook. That was all.

Sealed off in her little house in the fog-shrouded Avenues, the past seemed like a dream. Her parents, the old Victorian, the shuffling of slippered guests, and the low mumble of Japanese, all gone from her life. Her college friends were scattered all over the country, or married and sealed off in their own private worlds. But she felt no sense of loss. Their lives, after all, were getting better. There was no time to look back on those days before the war. The girls were growing. They needed new clothes for school. She must learn to sew. Somer & Kaufman was having a sale on school shoes. Could she make this hamburger stretch for two nights?

Linda was a bright and obedient child. She was very much the big sister. Jo, the youngest, was volatile, alternating between loving and affectionate, and strong and stubborn. Sharon was a quiet child, buffered from the world on both sides by sisters. She

469

followed her sister, Cathy, demanding no special attention. Cathy was friendly and fearless, an unredeemable tomboy. When she slid down banisters and bicycled down the big hill next to their house in the Avenues, her mother's eyes would narrow as if in recognition, watching her.

As a mother, she was without fault. Her girls were always neatly dressed and on time. They had decent table manners, remembered to excuse themselves and say thank you. They learned to read quickly and loved books because she always read to them. She chose the books carefully and refused to read them any slang or bad grammar. Her children would be irreproachable.

She conscientiously attended PTA meetings, although this was a trial for her. She wasn't able to tell people about her hearing problem; somehow she was unable to admit to such a deficiency. So she did her best, sometimes pretending to hear when she didn't, nodding her head and smiling. She wanted things to go smoothly; she wanted to appear normal.

Linda, Cathy, and Jo excelled in school and were very popular. Linda held class offices and was invariably the teacher's pet. "A nice girl," her teachers said. Cathy was outgoing and athletic, and showed great talent in art and design—"a beautiful girl," in her teachers' estimation. Jo was rebellious, read voraciously, and wrote caustic essays and satires. Teachers sometimes disliked her, but they all thought she was "intelligent." Sharon was termed "shy." Although she liked the arts, Cathy was the artist of the family. And though Sharon read quite a bit, Jo was thought of as the reader. Sharon was not popular like Linda, and of all the Terasaki girls, she had to struggle the hardest, often unsuccessfully, to make the honor roll. But all in all, the girls vindicated their mother, and it was a happy time, the happiest time of her life.

Then they were grown up and gone. They left one by one. The house emptied room by room until it seemed there was nothing but silence. She had to answer the phone herself now, if she heard it ring. She dreaded doing so because she could never be sure if she was hearing correctly. Sometimes she let the telephone ring, pretending not to be home. The one exception was when her sister called every night. Then she would exchange news on the phone for an hour.

470

When her daughters came home to visit she came alive. Linda was doing the right things. She had a nice Japanese-American boyfriend; she was graduating from college; and she was going to get married.

Cathy was a bit of a free spirit, and harder to understand. She wore her hair long and straight, and seldom came home from Berkeley. When she did she seemed to find fault. Why didn't her mother get a hearing aid? Did she enjoy being left out of the hearing world? But Cathy had friends, interesting friends, *hakujin* friends, whom she sometimes brought home with her. She moved easily in all worlds, and her mother's heart swelled with pride to see it.

Sharon sometimes came home, sometimes stayed away. When she did come home she did not have much to say. She was not happy in school. She liked throwing pots and weaving.

Then there was Jo, who would always bring a book or notebook home, and whose "evil pen" would pause absently in midstroke when her mother hovered near, telling her little bits of information that were new since the last visit. Jo, whose thoughts roamed far away, would gradually focus on the little figure of her mother. She had led such a sheltered life.

And then Cathy had died, and her mother didn't even cry.

Linda sent pictures from Germany of their mother in front of Heidelberg Castle, cruising down the Rhine. "She's just like a young girl," her letters proclaimed triumphantly. "She's excited about everything." But when their mother came home she talked about her trip for about a week. Then the old patterns prevailed, as if the house were a mold. In a month, Germany seemed like another loose thread in the fabric of her life. When Jo visited two months later, her mother was once again effaced, a part of the house almost, in her faded blouse and shapeless skirt, joylessly adding too much seasoned salt to the dinner salad.

"If only," Jo wrote Linda facetiously, "we could ship her out to some exotic place every other month."

In the fall Jo went to New York to study. "I have to get away," she wrote Linda. "The last time I went home I found myself discussing the machine washability of acrylics with Mom. There has got to be more to life than that." In the spring she had her mother come for a visit. No trip to the top of the Empire State

Building, no Staten Island ferry, with Jo. She whisked her mother straight from Kennedy Airport to her cramped flat in the Village, and no sooner had they finished dinner than Jo's boyfriend, Michael, arrived.

Her mother was gracious. "Where do you live, Michael?" she asked politely.

He and Jo exchanged looks. "Here," he said.

Despite her mother's anxiety about the safety of New York streets, the two of them walked furiously in the dusk and circled Washington Square several times, mother shocked and disappointed, daughter reassuring. At the end of an hour they returned to the flat for tea, and by the end of the evening the three of them had achieved an uneasy truce.

"I knew you wouldn't be happy about it," Jo said to her, "but I wanted you to know the truth. I hate pretending."

"Things were different when we were your age," her mother said. "What's Daddy going to say?"

She stayed for two weeks. Every morning Michael cooked breakfast, and the three of them ate together. Her attitude toward the situation softened from one of guarded assessment to tentative acceptance. Michael was very articulate, Jo as level-headed as ever. Their apartment was clean and homey. She began to relax over morning coffee at the little round table by the window.

She remembered the trip she made to Chicago during the war to get married. She had traveled from Topaz to Chicago by train. It was her first trip alone. Her parents and camp friends had seen her off at Topaz, and her sister and future husband had met her at the station in Chicago. But as the train followed its track northeastward across the country, she had been alone in the world. She remembered vividly the quality of light coming through the train window, and how it had bathed the passing countryside in a golden wash. Other passengers had slept, but she sat riveted at the window. Perhaps the scenery seemed so beautiful because of the bleakness and sensory deprivation of Topaz. She didn't know why she remembered it now.

Jo took her to the Metropolitan and to the Statue of Liberty. In a theater on Broadway they sat in the front row to see Deborah Kerr, her all-time favorite, and afterwards she declared she had heard every word.

472

When she left she shook Michael's hand and hugged Jo, say-ing, "I'll talk to Daddy."

But by the time Jo came home to visit a year later, the house, or whatever it was, had done its work. Her mother was again lost to her, a sweet little creature unable to hear very well, relaying little bits of information.

"I give up," said Jo. "We seem to lose ground every time. We dig her out, then she crawls back in, only deeper."

Linda loyally and staunchly defended the fortress in which her mother seemed to have taken refuge.

Jo wanted to break through. "Like shock treatment," she said. "It's the only way to bring her out."

Sharon, the middle daughter, gave her mother a loom.

And so, late in life, she took up weaving. She attended a class and took detailed notes, then followed them step by step, bend-ing to the loom with painstaking attention, threading the warp tirelessly, endlessly winding, threading, tying. She made sampler after sampler, using the subdued, muted colors she liked: five inches of one weave, two inches of another, just as the teacher instructed.

For a year she wove samplers, geometric and repetitious, all in browns and neutral shades, the colors she preferred. She was fas-cinated by some of the more advanced techniques she began to learn. One could pick up threads from the warp selectively, so there could be a color on the warp that never appeared in the fabric if it were not picked up and woven into the fabric. With this technique she could show a flash of color, repeat flashes of the color, or never show it at all. The color would still be there, startling the eye when the piece was turned over. The back side would reveal long lengths of a color that simply hadn't been picked up from the warp and didn't appear at all in the right side of the fabric.

She took to her loom with new excitement, threading the warp with all the shades of her life: gray, for the cold, foggy mornings when she had warmed Jo's clothes by the heater vent as Jo, four, stood shivering in her pajamas; brown, the color of the five lunch bags she had packed each morning with a sandwich, cut in half and wrapped in waxed paper, napkin, fruit, and potato chips;

dark brown, like the brownies they had baked "to make Daddy come home" from business trips. Sharon and Jo had believed he really could smell them, because he always came home.

Now when the daughters came home they always found something new she had woven. Linda, back from Germany, dropped by often to leave her daughter, Terry, at "*Bachan's* house" before dashing off to work. When Linda's husband picked her up, Terry never wanted to leave "Bachi" and would cling to her, crying at the door.

She continued to weave: white, the color of five sets of sheets, which she had washed, hung out, and ironed each week—also the color of the bathroom sink and the lather of shampoo against four small black heads; blue, Cathy's favorite color.

Sharon came by from time to time, usually to do a favor or bring a treat. She would cook Mexican food or borrow a tool or help trim trees in the garden. She was frustrated with the public school system where she had been substitute teaching and was now working part time in a gallery.

Sometimes Sharon brought yarn for her mother to weave: golden brown, the color of the Central Valley in summer. The family had driven through the valley on their way to the mountains almost every summer. They would arrive hot and sweating and hurry into the cool, emerald green waters of the Merced River. The children's floats flashed yellow on the dark green water. Yellow, too, were the beaten eggs fried flat, rolled, and eaten cold, with dark brown pickled vegetables and white rice balls. She always sat in the shade.

Jo was working abroad and usually came home to visit once a year. She and Michael had broken up. During the visits the house would fill with Jo and her friends. They would sit in the back room to talk. Jo visited her mother's weaving class and met her weaving friends.

"So this is the daughter," one of them said. "Your mother's been looking forward to your visit. The only time she misses class is when her daughters are home."

Soon it was time for Jo to leave again. "Mom's colors," she remarked to Sharon as she fingered the brown muffler her mother had woven for her.

"Put it on," said Sharon.

Jo did, and as she moved toward the light, hidden colors leaped from the brown fabric. It came alive in the sunlight.

"You know, there's actually red in here," she marveled, "and even bits of green. You'd never know it unless you looked real close."

"Most people don't," Sharon said.

The two sisters fell silent, sharing a rare moment together before their lives diverged again. Their mother's muffler was warm about Jo's neck.

At the airport, Jo's mother stood next to Jo's father, leaning slightly toward him as an object of lighter mass naturally tends toward a more substantial one. She was crying.

When Jo was gone she returned to the house, and her loom. And amidst the comings and goings of the lives around her, she sat, a woman bent over a loom, weaving the diverse threads of life into one miraculous, mystical fabric with timeless care.

Nominated by Graywolf Press

THE PULL

by SHARON OLDS

from POETRY

As the flu goes on, I get thinner and thinner,
all winter, till my weight dips
to my college weight, and then drops below it,
drifts down through high school, and then
down into junior high,
down through the first blood,
heading for my childhood weight,
birth weight, conception. When I see myself naked
in the mirror, I see I'm flirting with my father,
his cadaver the only body this thin
I have seen—I am walking around like his corpse
risen up and moving again, we
laugh about it a lot, my dead
dad and I. I do love being like him,
feeling my big joints slide
under the loose skin. My friends don't
think it's funny, this cakewalk
of the skeletons, and I can't explain it—
I wanted to lie down with him,
on the couch where he lay unconscious at night
and there on his deathbed, let myself down
beside him, and then, with my will, lift us both
up. Or maybe just lie with him
and never get up. Now that his dense
bones are in the ground, I am bringing
my body down. I'm not sure

how he felt about my life. Only twice
did he urge me to live—when the loop of his seed
roped me and drew me over into matter;
and once when I had the flu and he brought me
ten tiny Pyrex bowls with
ten leftovers down in the bottoms.
But when, in the last weeks of his life,
he let me feed him—slip the spoon of
heavy cream into his mouth
and pull it out through his closed lips, I
felt the suction of his tongue, his palate, his
head, his body, his death pulling at my hand.

Nominated by Brenda Hillman, Len Roberts, Diane Williams

BLACK AND BLUE

by CHARLES WRIGHT

from POETRY

Rain is a dangerous thing.
>>> It shrinks and squats the years
We've come to count on.
With its good eye and its bad eye,
>>> it settles them back to size.

Like deer in a leafy light,
>>> window and looking glass,
Yesterdays flash and reflect,
Ready to bolt, ready to empty out.
>>> Horizon them black and blue.

White water like white flags,
>>> streamers, little prayer beacons,
Back in the North Fork of Basin Creek,
Beckons our memory.
>>> But never the same flag twice.

Hawk planes over marsh grass,
>>> low over marsh grass and meadow weed.
Hawk pivots, folds and unfolds, drops and rises like string.
Unseen, under the dun mat and wattle runs,
>>> something is always there.

The road to Damascus runs through
>>> the veins in the lilac's leaf.

Ararat pokes through the daisy's eye.
Crows at the salt block
                pick their way through the back streets of Carthage.

Sunglasses. Hands on his hips
                        like Montgomery Clift. Levis.
Cistercian courtyard. St. Something or other. Weeds.
A chainsaw clears its throat.
                Like blue balloons, we disappear in the sky.

The dead have lives of their own.
                They glide, like round, radiant pearls of light,
Under our feet, stopping, from time to time, to handcup an ear.
Listen, they think, on the room roof,
                        faint footfalls of the unborn.

Beautiful stars of the Bear,
                Dipper
Unchanged of all the waters that blessed my youth, sprinkle
Me now,
        cross and burn.

The wind shifts, the landscape turns in its sleep.
                        Seasons slough and rinse.
Like trees, we fall in the dark forest and make no sound.
The deer never raise their heads.
    The voles never miss a step through the mystical sloughgrass.

Two boys in sateen bathing suits.
                Lunch box. Stringer of sunfish.
Father-shadow. Half father-shadow
Draining out of the photograph.
                Summer. It's always summer.

Our lives are an emptiness
                at rest in the present.
Dark cloud, bright cloud, sunlight, rain.
Great wind keeps carrying us
                where we don't want, where we don't know.

Nominated by Arthur Smith

479

HELEN

by C. K. WILLIAMS

from HELEN (Orchises Press)

1

More voice was in her cough tonight: its first harsh, stripping
    sound would weaken abruptly,
and he'd hear the voice again, not hers, unrecognizable, its
    notes from somewhere else,
someone saying something they didn't seem to want to say, in a
    tongue they hadn't mastered,
or a singer, diffident and hesitating, searching for a place to start
    an unfamiliar melody.

Its pitch was gentle, almost an interrogation, intimate, a plea, a
    moan, almost sexual,
but he could hear assertion, too, a straining from beneath, a
    forcing at the withheld consonant,
and he realized that she was holding back, trying with great
    effort not to cough again,
to change the spasm to a tone instead and so avert the pain that
    lurked out at the stress.

Then he heard her lose her almost-word, almost-song: it became
    a groan, the groan a gasp,
the gasp a sigh of desperation, then the cough rasped everything
    away, everything was cough now,
he could hear her shuddering, the voice that for a moment
    seemed the gentlest part of her,

480

choked down, effaced, abraded, taken back, as all of her was
    being taken from him now.

2

In the morning she was standing at the window; he lay where he
    was and quietly watched her.
A sound echoed in from somewhere, she turned to listen, and
    he was shocked at how she moved:
not *enough* moved, just her head, pivoting methodically, the
    mechanisms slowed nearly to a halt,
as though she was afraid to jar herself with the contracting
    tendons and skeletal leverings.

A flat, cool, dawn light washed in on her: how pale her skin was,
    how dull her tangled hair.
So much of her had burned away, and what was left seemed
    draped listlessly upon her frame.
It was her eye that shocked him most, though; he could only see
    her profile, and the eye in it,
without fire or luster, was strangely isolated from the rest of her
    face, and even from her character.

For the time he looked at her, the eye existed not as her eye, his
    wife's, his beloved's eye,
but as *an* eye, an object, so emphatic, so pronounced it was
    separate both from what it saw
and from who saw with it: it could have been a creature's eye, a
    member of that larger class
which simply indicated sight and not that essence which her
    glance had always brought him.

It came to him that though she hadn't given any sign, she knew
    that he was watching her.
He was saddened that she'd tolerate his seeing her as she was
    now, weak, disheveled, haggard.
He felt that they were both involved, him watching, her letting
    him, in a depressing indiscretion:

481

she'd always, after all their time together, only offered him the
images she thought he wanted.

She'd known how much he needed beauty, how much presumed
it as the elemental of desire.
The loveliness that illuminated her had been an engrossing
narrative his spirit fed on;
he entered it and flowed out again renewed for having touched
within and been a part of it.
In his meditations on her, he'd become more complicated, fuller,
more essential to himself.

It was to her beauty he'd made love at first, she was there
within its captivating light,
but was almost secondary, as though she was just the instance of
some overwhelming generality.
She herself was shy before it; she, too, as unassumingly as
possible was testing this abstraction
which had taken both of them into its sphere, rendering both
subservient to its serene enormity.

As their experience grew franker, and as she learned to move
more confidently towards her core,
became more overtly active in elaborating needs and urges, her
beauty still came first.
In his memory, it seemed to him that they'd unsheathed her
from the hazes of their awe,
as though her unfamiliar, fiery, famished nakedness had been
disclosed as much to her as to him.

She'd been grateful to him, and that gratitude became in turn
another fact of his desire.
Her beauty had acknowledged him, allowed him in its secret
precincts, let him be its celebrant,
an implement of its luxurious materiality, and though he
remained astonished by it always,
he fulfilled the tasks it demanded of him, his devotions
reinvigorated and renewed.

3

In the deepest sense, though, he'd never understood what her
    beauty was or really meant.
If you only casually beheld her, there were no fanfares, you were
    taken by no immolating ecstasies.
It amused him sometimes seeing other men at first not really
    understanding what they saw;
no one dared to say it, but he could feel them holding back their
    disappointment or disbelief.

Was this Helen, mythic Helen, this female, fleshed like any
    other, imperfect and approachable?
He could understand: he himself, when he'd first seen her,
    hadn't really; he'd even thought,
before he'd registered her spirit and intelligence, before her
    laughter's melodies had startled him—
if only one could alter such and such, improve on this or that: he
    hardly could believe it now.

But so often he'd watched others hear her speak, or laugh, look at
    her again, and fall in love,
as puzzled as he'd been at the time they'd wasted while their
    raptures of enchantment took.
Those who hadn't ever known her sometimes spoke of her as
    though she were his thing, his toy,
but that implied something static in her beauty, and she was
    surely just the opposite of that.

If there was little he'd been able to explain of what so
    wonderfully absorbed him in her,
he knew it was a movement and a process, that he was taken
    towards and through her beauty,
touched by it but even more participating in its multiplicities,
    the revelations of its grace.
He felt himself becoming real in her, tangible, as though before
    he'd only half existed.

Sometimes he would even feel it wasn't really him being
    brought to such unlikely fruition.

Absurd that anyone as coarse and ordinary as he should be in
    touch with such essential mystery:
something else, beyond him, something he would never
    understand, used him for its affirmations.
What his reflections came to was something like humility, then a
    gratitude of his own.

4

The next night her cough was worse, with a harsher texture, the
    spasms came more rapidly,
and they'd end with a deep, complicated emptying, like the
    whining flattening of a bagpipe.
The whole event seemed to need more labor: each cough
    sounded more futile than the last,
as though the effort she'd made and the time lost making it had
    added to the burden of illness.

Should he go to her? He felt she'd moved away from him,
    turning more intently towards herself.
Her sickness absorbed her like a childbirth; she seemed almost
    like someone he didn't know.
There'd been so many Helens, the first timid girl, then the
    sensual Helen of their years together,
then the last, whose grace had been more intricate and difficult
    to know and to exult in.

How childishly frightened he'd always been by beauty's absence,
    by its destruction or perversity.
For so long he let himself be tormented by what he knew would
    have to happen to her.
He'd seen the old women as their thighs and buttocks bloated,
    then withered and went slack,
as their dugs dried, skin dried, legs were sausaged with the
    veins that rose like kelp.

He'd tried to overcome himself, to feel compassion toward them,
    but, perhaps because of her,

he'd felt only a shameful irritation, as though they were
  colluding in their loss.
Whether they accepted what befell them, even, he would think,
  gladly acquiescing to it,
or fought it, with all their sad and valiant unguents, dyes and
  ointments, was equally degrading.

His own body had long ago become a ruin, but beauty had
  never been a part of what he was.
What would happen to his lust, and to his love, when time came
  to savage and despoil her?
He already felt his will deserting him; for a long time, though,
  nothing touched or dulled her;
perhaps she really was immortal, maybe his devotion kept her
  from the steely rakings of duration.

Then, one day, something at her jowls; one day her hips; one
  day the flesh at the elbows . . .
One day, one day, one day he looked at her and knew that what
  he'd feared so was here.
He couldn't understand how all his worst imaginings had come
  to pass without his noticing.
Had he been looking at her all this while, or had he not wanted
  to acknowledge what he'd seen?

He'd been gazing at her then; in her wise way she'd looked back
  at him, smiled, and touched him.
She knew, she'd long known, what was going on in him, and
  another admiration for her took him,
then another fire, and that, simply, he felt himself closer to her:
  there'd been no trial,
nothing had been lost, of lust, of love, and something he'd never
  dreamed would be was gained.

5

With her in the darkness now, not even touching her, he sensed
  her fever's suffocating dryness.

485

He couldn't, however much he wanted to, not let himself
    believe she was to be no more.
And there was nothing he could do for her even if she'd let him;
    he tried to calm himself.
Her cough was hollow, soft, almost forgiving, ebbing slowly
    through the volumes of her thorax.

He could almost hear that world as though from in her flesh: the
    current of her breath,
then her breastbone, ribs, and spine, taking on the cough's
    vibrations, giving back their own.
Then he knew precisely how she was within herself as well, he
    was with her as he'd never been:
he'd unmoored in her, cast himself into the night of her, and
    perceived her life with her.

All she'd lived through, all she'd been and done, he could feel
    accumulated in this instant.
The impressions and sensations, feelings, dreams, and memories
    were tearing loose in her,
had disconnected from each other and randomly begun to float,
    collide, collapse, entangle;
they were boiling in a matrix of sheer chance, suspended in a
    purely mental universe of possibility.

He knew that what she was now to herself, what she
    remembered, might not in truth have ever been.
Who, then, was she now, who was the person she had been, if
    all she was, all he still so adored,
was muddled, addled, mangled: what of her could be repository
    now, the place where she existed?
When everything was shorn from her, what within this flux of
    fragments still stayed her?

He knew then what he had to do: he was so much of her now
    and she of him that she was his,
her consciousness and memory both his, he would will her into
    him, keep her from her dissolution.
All the wreckage of her fading life, its shattered hours taken in
    this fearful flood,

486

its moments unrecoverable leaves twirling in a gust across a
  waste of loss, he drew into himself,

and held her, kept her, all the person she had been was there in
  his sorrow and his longing:
it didn't matter what delirium had captured her, what of her was
  being lacerated, rent,
his pain had taken on a power, his need for her became a force
  that he could focus on her;
there was something in him like triumph as he shielded her
  within the absolute of his affection.

Then he couldn't hold it, couldn't keep it, it was all illusion, a
  confection of his sorrow:
there wasn't room within the lenses of his mortal being to
  contain what she had been,
to do justice to a single actual instant of her life and soul, a
  single moment of her mind,
and he released her then, let go of this diminished apparition
  he'd created from his fear.

But still, he gave himself to her, without moving moved to her:
  she was still his place of peace.
He listened for her breath: was she still here with him, did he
  have her that way, too?
He heard only the flow of the silent darkness, but he knew now
  that in it they'd become it,
their shells of flesh and form, the old delusion of their
  separateness and incompletion, gone.

When one last time he tried to bring her image back, she was as
  vivid as he'd ever seen her.
What they were together, everything they'd lived, all that
  seemed so fragile, bound in time,
had come together in him, in both of them; she had entered
  death, he was with her in it.
Death was theirs now, she was herself again; her final, searing
  loveliness had been revealed.

Nominated by Orchises Press

GLIMPSES:
RAYMOND CARVER

interviews by SAM HALPERT
edited by JAMES LINVILLE

from THE PARIS REVIEW

*T*HE FOLLOWING EXCERPTS *of conversations with close friends and family of Raymond Carver have been edited and rearranged from the interviews conducted by Sam Halpert for the collection . . . When We Talk about Raymond Carver, published by Peregrine Smith Books.*

Some additional material was supplied by the subjects for this feature.

—J.L.

Maryann Carver, *Raymond Carver's first wife:*

I was almost fifteen. I was working at my first real job at a place called the Spudnut Shop, a doughnut store, in Union Gap, Washington, June of 1955. This very good-looking young man walked in with his younger brother and sat down on a stool. The moment I saw him I had this incredible intuition that he was going to be the father of my children. Of course, in those days I didn't know about past lives, and that sort of thing. We just looked at each other and smiled.

Ray always wanted to be a writer, from the third grade on. He had been taking a home-study course from the Palmer Institute of Writing, paid for by his father who worked at a lumber mill.

Ray would do those assignments religiously, and feel very guilty if he skipped any. I had a reading list of twenty books for summer break from school—Tolstoy, Flaubert and Chekhov. Ray would come to the library with me and, well, he had never heard of these writers before. I told him what they were about, explained to him their styles and so forth. He began to realize there was more to read than Thomas Costain and Edgar Rice Burroughs.

Ray didn't want to go to college. He wanted money to buy a car, a phonograph and clothes. He had seen the movie *King Solomon's Mines* about fourteen times and so he and two friends decided that they were going to South America to pick diamonds out of the mouth of the Amazon River. They expected to be gone for two years on this great adventure. We shared a very melancholic Christmas in 1956 before he left. One of the boys had a beat-up old car that took them to Mexico as far as Guaymas, but they had a falling out. Three weeks after he left, Ray arrived back, absolutely broke and without having had a thing to eat for three days.

While I finished at the St. Paul's School for Girls in Walla Walla, Ray was staying with an aunt in Yakima. He took me to the formal dances at the school. We had a lovely spring and were married four days after I graduated.

When I got a scholarship from the University of Washington to study law, I told Ray that I wouldn't be happy with anyone who didn't want to go to college. Nobody in his family had ever gone. Ray didn't particularly like school. He hoped he could just read a lot, which he always did, and that that would prepare him adequately to be a writer (he had an absolutely extraordinary vocabulary). But in the fall of 1957 he entered Yakima Community College for a year, then transferred to Chico State in California for two years. Ultimately, he graduated from Humboldt State College in Arcata, California, in 1963.

He had written some science-fiction stories, but when he got into John Gardner's writing class at Chico, he no longer was interested in writing about little green monsters. He began to write literary stories, his He/She stories. He wrote "Furious Seasons" at Chico. Gardner thought it was outrageously good, taught the hell out of it in class and included it in the college literary magazine.

489

Almost always, we rented a house with an extra bedroom for Ray to use as a study. In addition to that, whenever he could afford it, Ray would rent a room where he could be alone to do his writing. All those stories about his having to write in his car are part of a "poor me" syndrome to add to the drama of his success. Even when we had our first big house in Arcata, he rented a room somewhere else for his writing: in Sacramento, Palo Alto, Cupertino. We sacrificed necessities and certainly luxuries so he could rent space to write; but for the first thirteen years of our marriage, one or the other of us was in college, without any money. Thirteen years . . .

Ray's first story accepted by a real magazine was "Pastoral," in *Western Humanities Review*. He received two copies for payment. On the very same day, a magazine in Arizona named *Target* accepted Ray's poem "Brass Ring," another first. That evening it seemed that if we did the right things, the right things would happen. We went to our friends David and Charlene Palmer's house and burst in on their dinner. They dropped everything and called some friends who called other friends. We celebrated for three days.

I edited every one of Ray's stories before anybody else. Ray would encourage me to do what John Gardner did—take a pencil and strike out any words I thought didn't belong. He would invariably take fifty percent of my suggestions and ignore the other fifty percent.

In 1963 Dick Day helped Ray get a grant for a thousand dollars at the University of Iowa Writers Workshop. We piled all of our belongings onto the roof rack of our '53 Chevy, "Old Faithful," and, with our son and daughter, we were on our way.

We stayed at a trailer park until our application for student housing was approved. After all the moves we'd made, when I saw the Quonset hut, a World War II relic that served as university married-student housing, I just sat down on a bed and cried. There were cement floors, open cupboards in the kitchen, and the hot-water tank was in the middle of the living-room floor. The children's room was like a cell with two little bunks and a tiny window.

Whenever we'd land in some godforsaken little room like this, I'd ask Ray jokingly how would we ever survive in such a place, and he'd smile and pull a little can of roast beef hash or whatever out of his pocket and prepare a lunch for us.

That spring, after we had had such a desperate time financially, I checked around and found out that Ray had more publications than anybody else in the workshop. He had written "Sixty Acres," "The Student's Wife," "Will You Please Be Quiet, Please?" But he was very quiet in class. People did not know about him. One weekend, they were reading manuscripts to give out fellowships and Ray hadn't been invited to participate. So I got my hair done, put on my best dress, and gathered all his published stories and the rest of his manuscript-in-progress, which was *Will You Please Be Quiet, Please?* and I went down to director Paul Engle's office at 8:00 A.M. and asked to see him. He wasn't there, but I said, "That's fine, I'll wait." I waited all day. Finally, around four in the afternoon, Paul Engle showed up. He picked up his mail and invited me into his office. He asked me what was on my mind, but as I started to tell him, he kept his nose in his mail. So I stopped talking and after a couple of minutes he noticed. I said, "It's okay, why don't you just finish reading your mail." He pushed it aside. I asked him if he remembered what happened when Tennessee Williams came to Iowa. Everybody there knew how Williams had written *The Glass Menagerie* and his teachers at Iowa had rejected it, refused to give him his degree, and had virtually ridden him out of town on a rail. Engle straightened up in his chair, half insulted and half interested. I told him that he had another situation almost exactly like that with my husband, that Ray had more published stories and poems than any other student in the workshop and that he was a far better writer than many on the faculty. Engle agreed to give Ray's manuscript to a faculty reader over the weekend. The upshot was that John Clellon Holmes came back on Monday raving about Ray's work. They offered Ray a stipend for the following year, but Ray had already decided to move on. He had itchy feet and a short attention span. He could never stand to be bored. We left for California.

Ray tried all kinds of little jobs . . . as a desk clerk in a hotel, and as a stockboy at Weinstock's Department Store, until his crew was fired when one of them stole some cookies.

After the cookie thing, there was no money. Our lights were turned off and when we couldn't pay the rent, I took the children

491

to my mother's in Paradise, California. We were in debt. With tears running down my cheeks, I withdrew from all my classes at Sacramento State, and found a job as a barmaid. Ray suggested bankruptcy. I was adamantly opposed. My family upbringing was different. Still, we went into bankruptcy twice.

Ray got a job as janitor at Mercy Hospital mopping, house-keeping, and changing sheets. The night shift was the gravy train, and he had his days free to write. Things began to turn; I became office manager at *Parents Magazine's* Cultural Institute where I worked with Werner Erhard, who later founded EST. Werner and I were good friends. We'd fly around to major cities to deliver addresses at various hotels. There was an opportunity to make money, dress well, use my intelligence, and I went for it. I made lots of money, and before long I was wearing hundred-dollar dresses from I. Magnin's. I had a maroon Pontiac convertible that was faster than the wind . . . living the high life, you know. These two handsome, brilliant men were in my life: Werner Erhard and Raymond Carver. While that was going on, Ray had this janitor job, which was okay for him, for a while, as it gave him time to get some writing done, but certainly had no prestige. He got jealous of my job, the power, the attention. So he got a job as an editor in Palo Alto, the first white-collar job he ever had. Then he gave me an ultimatum: either give up your marriage or your job. Werner and I didn't have a romance; it was just a work association, no hanky-panky whatsoever. But Ray had decided to become head of the family with a vengeance, and *his* career came first.

I was used to running an office, making good money, and now all of a sudden, nothing. To create some excitement in my life, I entered San Jose State, and in the spring, I applied for a scholarship to study abroad. I was such a good student that we had our choice to go anywhere: Uppsala, Sweden, or Florence, Italy, or Tel Aviv, Israel. We went to Israel because that fellowship offered an extra five hundred dollars. Israel was the absolutely perfect place for me given my later interest in spiritual realities. But Ray and my daughter both became very disgruntled. He'd say, "I don't know what I'm doing in *Asia!*" He resented that we didn't have the villa on the Mediterranean we had been promised. We had an apartment that seemed small by our standards, only two bedrooms, but actually it was the apartment of the conductor of the Israel Philharmonic, filled with paintings and wonderful art objects. Ray would sit out on the balcony reading *Life on the Mississippi*.

The children went to school in the old Arab city of Jaffa, an hour and a half bus ride with three transfers. One day a bomb went off in a wastebasket at the bus depot, killing six people, just fifteen minutes after our children had been there. Ray said, "This may be the high time of your life, studying at the university, learning Hebrew, listening to Golda Meir speak, dancing Jewish folk dances, but I'm taking my children and going home."

Chuck Kinder, *author, professor at the University of Pittsburgh:*
After he returned from abroad, we were on Stegner fellowships at Stanford together. He was a big shambling fellow, always wore shades. He looked like someone whose lunch money I'd have taken away when I was a kid. I'd seen him sitting around mumbling a lot, smoking, and biting on his thumbnail. Corduroy pants. Shirts that he had buttoned up to the collar, like he didn't care what he looked like. One day I needed a ride to El Camino Real and I asked if anyone was going in that direction. Ray raised his hand and said he was, and I said to myself, "Dear God, not this goofy guy."

Douglas Unger, *author of* Leaving The Land *and other novels:*
Some of his stories in the first collection had been around in some form from the time he was eighteen. Sometimes he'd simply change a few elements of a story, or he'd add a frame to the story, maybe change character names. He'd send out the version he thought best. Years later he might send out the other version.

Chuck Kinder:
He was always pulling stunts. He was teaching at Berkeley while he had his Stegner at Stanford, which he wasn't supposed to do, or he'd send his stories out to a half-dozen magazines at once. That story "So Much Water So Close To Home" was published in two separate journals before he sold it to *Playgirl*. The same story.

493

Douglas Unger:

When I was the managing editor at *The Chicago Review*, his story "They're Not Your Husband" came into the office. Most of the manuscripts we were reading in those days were so-called experimental fiction—highly textured prose, with highly innovative and surreal subjects. Ray's story was nothing like that. It was straightforward, realistic, with an unadorned style and humorous implications. There was also a strange, dark quality to the writing that I felt myself immediately drawn to. The editor-in-chief, Richard Hack, and I, and the other editors accepted the story that same day. We had never acted that quickly before.

Maryann Carver:

We had worked so hard and, by 1972, we had both become teachers; we had enough money and we owned a lovely home. Then when everything was in place and the great challenge gone, all we had worked for was knocked down.

We had always drunk socially but it was always a safe thing because we'd look out for each other, and when we did get drunk we thought it was funny. Ray's father was an alcoholic, but we didn't know that alcoholism was a disease. When Ray would write a story about drinkers, as far back as 1967, it wasn't about us. He'd known enough drinkers growing up. But Ray was very shy; to be up in front of a class or an audience was terrifying for him, at first. It was when he started to teach, his first year at Santa Cruz, that his drinking habits changed.

Douglas Unger:

The first fall after I had met Maryann's sister, Amy, we were invited to their home in Cupertino for Christmas. Ray met me at the airport in a broken-down Mercury Comet station wagon full of dents and rattles, barely running. He looked like a man at the edge of death from drinking. The whole San Francisco and Stanford writers' scene was there at one time or another over the holidays—Bill Kittredge, Chuck Kinder, Jim Crumley, Lenny Michaels, Thomas Sanchez, Gurney Norman, Ed McClanahan. Their parties would go on for weeks sometimes, moving from one place to another. Because of all the drinking, it was a very rough holiday. Ray stood up for me in a drunken fight with one of Amy's former boyfriends. But there were a lot of good times, too. As soon as Ray got up in the morning, everyone in the house had to get up to keep him company. He'd knock on the door and shout, "Hot doughnuts! Steaming hot cups of coffee! How about a little heart starter?" And he'd have Bloody Marys, coffee and doughnuts and platters of food out on the table.

Maryann Carver:

In 1970, when I began to teach, Ray had a whole year off to write. He wrote prodigiously and finished the bulk of *Will You Please Be Quiet, Please?* during that year. In the fall of 1971, Ray began teaching at the University of California, Santa Cruz. But that spring, Ray went through another bout of depression. We'd studied existentialism. Angst and melancholy went with the trade in those days and Ray was good at them.

Leonard Michaels, *author, professor at the University of California:*

What can I say? When I was low, I read Hegel. When he was low, he got drunk.

Douglas Unger:

Maryann taught English for eight years. She had always worked, but ends just didn't meet in that house. Ray began to hang paper all over town, writing hot checks just to get enough liquor to get through the day.

Chuck Kinder:

I remember one night we had to carry them home and literally put them in bed. Maryann was so impressed by that. She said their other friends would just dump them on the porch for their kids to find them in the morning.

Maryann Carver:

During the summer of 1972 Ray took a trip to Montana to visit Bill Kittredge, and he met a group of writers who did a lot of drinking. These men got up, showered, shaved and dressed in fresh starched shirts at eight in the morning as if they were going off to work; what they were doing was going off to drink. They were into their second and third wives, too. "Another wife, another life." Remember, this was the seventies. Ray and I seemed like the last holdouts and were ridiculed for being "sweet and quaint," by all sorts of people. High school sweethearts. These people would take scenes from our life and satirize them in their novels.

Douglas Unger:

It was amazing to me as a young writer to sit at a table with Bill Kittredge, Ray, Chuck Kinder and the others, and hear them telling stories and topping each other. Ray, or one of the others, would ask, "Are you going to use that one? Because if you're not, it's mine."

William Kittredge, *author, screenwriter:*

Ray and I were sitting at a bar in Missoula when a woman bartender told us about being arrested the night before because she and her boyfriend had gotten stoned and moved all their furniture out on the lawn, set up lights and all. After a while the neighbors got annoyed and called the cops. I looked at Ray and told him that one had to be his. So he wrote it, changed it a little. It became the one about the guy moving all his stuff out in the driveway for a yard sale, "Why Don't You Dance?"

Douglas Unger:

In those days, Ray often used to say, "I never had a problem that money couldn't solve." But I think a bigger problem was that no publisher anywhere in the country would accept his book, *Will You Please Be Quiet, Please?* The collection represented fourteen years of work. Editors found the stories too depressing, or not in tune with what the culture wanted to read. Short-story collections were very hard to get published back then. Ray had sent it to the Iowa Short Fiction Award contest. Even though the preliminary judges selected his book to win, their decision was reversed. Jack Leggett, who succeeded Engle as director of the workshop, was so outraged that he told everyone that not only did he think Ray's manuscript should have won first prize, hands down, but that he was going to offer Ray a teaching job.

Maryann Carver:

Ray was flattered to get the job, but he would drink the moment he got out of class. He drank around his job.

William Kittredge:

Ray flew back and forth between teaching jobs in Iowa City and Santa Cruz. Some of his friends and I would go down and get him off the plane on Thursday afternoon. He'd always come home loaded. On Friday he'd be supposed to teach at Santa Cruz. A couple of times he made it, but most of the time we'd pin a note to the door saying, "Mr. Carver is too sick to teach." Then he began to not show up at all. Chuck Kinder and I taught the class together and it was a disaster. I think Ray must have met that class twice. The provost of Santa Cruz got wind of what was going on and that Ray was also teaching at Iowa City. Fired him. Deservedly so.

Maryann Carver:

He flew back and forth. His friends called him Running Dog.

Leonard Michaels:

He even managed to con United into flying him for free, telling them he'd put United into his stories. Of course, he never wrote a word about them. He also had a lover in Denver where he changed planes. So there he was, holding on to two teaching jobs, a couple of thousand miles apart, and drinking and carrying on a love affair, and conning United into flying him back and forth.

Chuck Kinder:

On their fifteenth wedding anniversary Ray and Maryann came sweeping over to my house. They'd had a few. Maryann invited us to go out and celebrate with them at a Greek restaurant. She had obviously been to this place before, but she wouldn't come clean as to who she'd been there with or why, and Ray was getting very suspicious. This restaurant had a floor show, a strongman who picked up tables with his teeth. He would do a backbend and invite people from the audience to come up and step on his stomach. The strongman's assistant took Ray by the hand and dragged him up there. Ray was so drunk he couldn't stand on the guy's stomach. Stumbled and tumbled all over him.

Despite the fact that it was their anniversary, Ray began to sulk. He didn't want to pay and said we should walk the check. He went out and laid in the back seat of the car. My wife was the designated driver and we were the designated drunks. When the waiter came out after us, before Maryann had made it to the door, Ray called out to my wife from the back seat, "Step on it! Step on it!" He was perfectly willing to leave his wife behind, anniversary or not.

At this point, Ray and Maryann were having trouble. Ray was deeply in love with another woman he'd been involved with for a couple of years. Maryann had found a pack of letters from her, so Ray gave me some stuff to take back to her for safekeeping in Montana. I delivered the stuff from Ray and I fell madly in love with her. That was Diane, my present wife. Ray was real pissed at me. He said that they always called him Running Dog but that I was the real running dog.

Ray phoned one day. He called me names like backstabber and asshole and all that, but we were laughing. When Diane and I moved back down to Palo Alto, Ray had moved back in with Maryann and we were all closer than we had been when I was with my first wife.

Douglas Unger:
Gordon Lish had gone from *Esquire* to McGraw-Hill, and I believe one of the conditions of his accepting the job was that he could publish Ray's book. So Ray had the book, finally, on its way to being published, but I think he felt this was happening way too late.

Maryann Carver:
Will You Please Be Quiet, Please? wasn't published until 1976, and for years, leading up to that, Ray didn't draw a sober breath.

Leonard Michaels:
When we first met he owned a VW bug. It was always strewn with unpaid traffic tickets and emergency room receipts.

Chuck Kinder:
Maryann had started to go to AA and, when she found out about Diane and Ray, she had a fling with someone down there. She told Ray about it and there had been black eyes. The drinking got heavier and heavier. At our place one night, Maryann was wearing a beautiful white dress and trying to keep everything

498

afloat, break the tension by being witty and lively. But I could sense Ray was in a lot of pain. The rage and pain was so deep within him, it would truly frighten him. Maryann started flirting with a guy called Shorty Ramos—a couple of kisses at the table. Later, Maryann said something, and Ray hit her on the side of her head with a bottle. The bottle shattered, glass flying across the room. Maryann ran outside. Diane found her standing in the alley, bleeding heavily, her white dress drenched in red. She said, "Look what Ray did." Diane called for an ambulance and went with her to the hospital. Ray was devastated by what he had done. He couldn't talk. This time she would have bled to death. Funny thing, even years later, after he stopped drinking, he couldn't remember hitting her with the bottle.

Douglas Unger:
He made so many attempts over that year and a half to stop drinking. Once I went with Chuck Kinder and Ray to a summer home up in Tiburon, loaned to us for that purpose. Chuck and Ray were going to try to stop drinking together, but they weren't there four hours before they discovered a fully stocked liquor cabinet and the whole thing turned into a kind of drinking contest between them.

Chuck Kinder:
Once we talked about getting tattooed and we drew little pictures of the tattoo we wanted. Mine was a heart with Diane's name across it. Ray drew a picture of a real heart, an anatomical heart, not a valentine, with Maryann's name in it.

They'd have their sweet times together, but it was the last of the sweet times. They used to go down to Market Street and spend afternoons watching porn movies. There were a lot of breakups. There'd be a shattering of glass, yells and screams, and then howls in the night, and the next minute they'd be ordering pizza. She'd say, "Did you see what he just did?" He and Maryann would tell these horrific stories about what they'd gone through, laughing about them, and the stories took on the tall-tale quality of legends.

When Ray was drinking, he'd blank out a lot. So very often Ray would question her, like in an interview, "Then what did I do after that?" I could see the story taking root in Ray's mind as

Maryann would plumb her memory. With them there was a sense of play, but, toward the end, with all that booze, it got dark and evil, really destructive.

Douglas Unger:

Ray had suffered from seizures at least twice, with convulsions, just like the character Tiny in "Where I'm Calling From." That's where he got that detail. Ray was terrified to quit drinking then, because of these dangerous seizures when he tried to quit. So that was one of the reasons he kept on drinking.

Chuck Kinder:

Ray was in and out of hospitals. He had collapsed in a doctor's office. They gave him several stitches and said he had a wet brain.

Maryann Carver:

When alcohol became a problem, he couldn't write. No stories were written when he was desperately drunk. He wrote those stories about people drinking when he was sober.

Douglas Unger:

They were going to separate. Then they were going to stay together. They were going to split up again. A lot of it is shown in the stories in *What We Talk about When We Talk about Love*—the infidelity committed by the man that destroys trust, followed by all the guilt and heavy drinking. I can think of only two or three stories he wrote that were not in some way drawn from incidents in his own life or in his own family.

Maryann Carver:

After *Will You Please Be Quiet, Please?* was nominated for the National Book Award, and all those reviews came out in *Newsweek, Time*, and elsewhere, it was a shock to me. It was exactly all that we had always prayed for, what we had worked so hard for, sacrificed for, but the fact of the matter was that it was tough to read those reviews and see our lives held up and analyzed. Characters were called "inarticulate members of the working class, involved in violence and doomed to go nowhere," for

500

example; and it was kind of hard for me to relate to this kind of classification. Ray was surprised by it, too.

After all the reviews came out, I read the book again, with new eyes. I felt as if I were in a fishbowl, but that my identity was somehow invisible. However, I could accept the notoriety as long as Ray and I were together. It went with my territory, so to speak. Ray and our marriage were my protection and security.

I read many of Ray's later stories and poems with a very thin skin after we'd separated, and I'd see how his family was "done in" for his capital gain. When "Fires" came out, for example, one of our son Vance's professors was so concerned for him that he took him to lunch and tried to comfort him and explain what poetic license was all about.

I know Ray did what he needed to do to write captivating stories and poems. Profit, personal catharsis and hurt to family members were secondary considerations at best. He wrote whatever came to him, and if he could use anything, he did. Later, after Ray became famous, I became supersensitive as to how I was depicted on the page. But now as I look back, I see Ray did not hesitate to portray himself either, in any position, humiliating or not. But he was a man and could get away with it better. He also had a voice. What did it matter if Ray Carver humiliated himself? He *was* Ray Carver.

Life was different than it had been before anybody knew of us, and our lives had not been held up for scrutiny. I always knew Ray was going to be a great writer, and I insisted on that. All the time he was drinking, I'd tell him that it would be the worst catastrophe that could possibly happen if he ended up as a second-rate writer.

Leonard Michaels:
The people he lived with were all participants in his writing. Maryann lived through a hell of a lot of that material with him. She and Ray paid for those stories with their lives.

William Kittredge:
Ray and the late poet Richard Hugo were in so many ways alike. They both were guys writing from a kind of disenfranchisement, some sense of not being part of the major-league world. Writing was a way of justifying your life, but at some point in

their careers they began to have some success, and both of them had trouble with that success because it forced a change in self-image. They had seen themselves as failures, as people who lived on the margins. For a time, they both reacted as if to say, "If you think I'm terrific, well, watch this." They'd be invited to read at Yale or somewhere and they'd immediately get drunk for two weeks, as if to deny they were this terrific guy who got invited to Yale. It was, I think, a fear of becoming someone else, someone who could negotiate with the world well and easily.

Douglas Unger:

Things fell apart, also, because the children were in such terrible difficulty. His daughter, Chris, and her boyfriend ran into trouble and all of Ray and Maryann's money had to go into bailing her out of her trouble. And with the family problems, there was the guilt he felt that, once again, they had no money. He was so desperate for money that he took a job as clerk in the Tides bookstore in Sausalito, but he didn't stay there for more than a couple of weeks. His hunger for books either ate up too much of his salary, or he was liberally "borrowing" books from the store. He never stopped reading, no matter how much he drank, and he'd bring home armloads of books.

To keep himself sober, he had to get out and get away. He had rented a small apartment on Castro Street in San Francisco. In "Careful" he describes that apartment exactly. He had somehow convinced himself that if he only drank champagne, he'd be able to taper off and quit. He'd go out in the morning and buy bottles of the cheapest Andre, but this wasn't working, and he knew it. We all thought he would keep on drinking until it killed him. And he thought so, too.

He tried to stop drinking from the summer of '76 through the fall and into '77. He would stay with Amy and me or with Chuck and Diane Kinder, who had a big apartment across the street. Amy and I rented our flat from the St. James Episcopal Church where meetings of Alcoholics Anonymous were held. Maryann was in recovery first, and was willing to do anything to save Ray. She had heard of a place called Duffy's, an alcoholic rehabilitation center in Myrtledale, California. She was selling the house in Cupertino and had scraped together the money for a rehab center for Ray, and Ray had nowhere else to go.

502

She and Amy and I drove Ray up to Duffy's. He was scared, terrified that he was going to die if he stopped drinking, or end up brain-damaged from the seizures, the convulsions. But if he kept drinking, the doctors had given him six months and he'd be dead, maybe sooner. I remember when we checked him in at Duffy's, Ray was dead drunk. He'd been drinking all the way up as we drove through the Napa valley. As I recall, he was in rehab for about three weeks the first time.

Ray checked himself out, concerned about the money it cost, and also believing that he had learned enough about the disease of alcoholism that he could quit now. He didn't last long without a drink that first time. For a certain number of alcoholics, especially the heaviest drinkers, their nervous system has become so adjusted to having alcohol that when they stop drinking, they go into seizures as though with epilepsy. These seizures are very dangerous, since brain damage can occur during the convulsions.

Ray moved in with us when he tried to quit drinking again. He'd learned at Duffy's how to taper himself off more safely by having what he called "hummers," time-controlled shots of liquor. Ray had bottles of a kind of booze he hated to drink, the cheapest possible bourbon. There was a time schedule. He'd start with a drink every half hour. Then a day later, he'd taper off to a shot every hour, after that, one every two hours, then later, every three hours, and so on. He gave the bottles to Amy and me, so he couldn't get at them, and he explained the schedule. Those days and nights were the lowest for Ray, sitting alone in our living room feeling his marriage was gone, fearing he'd never write again. Whatever he owned—about one carload of books, manuscripts, a few personal items, some old clothing, a few artworks— had been packed in about six boxes and stored in the garage of the church next door.

He'd been at our house a week, tapering off on his hummers, and going to AA meetings at St. James church, when he looked out the window one morning and saw the church was having a bazaar. His few belongings had been spread out on tables in the churchyard, ready to be sold. His manuscripts, his books, his few items of clothing, his artwork. So he and Amy had to go up to the ladies running the bazaar and convince them not to sell them, and get his few belongings back. That evening I found him in our

503

living room, in the dark, crying. That was his bottom; I don't think he ever felt that low again.

When he was off all the hummers and completely dried out, he only hung around San Francisco for a few weeks before he fled north to a house in McKinleyville, the inspiration for the one in "Chef's House," that Richard Day had helped get him. A few months later, he went to Dallas and the Southern Methodist University Writers' Conference, where he met Tess Gallagher for the first time.

Richard Ford, *author:*

I met Ray in Dallas. Nineteen seventy-seven, in the autumn, Southern Methodist had a writers' conference of some sort, and a mutual friend of Ray's and mine, Michael Ryan, invited us. We'd published one book apiece, and didn't know each other, though I'd read some stories of Ray's and liked them, and Ray, God love him, *said* he'd read *A Piece of My Heart,* and maybe he had. Anyway, there were the usual writers' conference high jinx. I remember seeing Ray leave a party one night by climbing out a window. Two women were involved in that particular exit, one he wanted to see, who was, I believe, going out that window just ahead of him; and one he didn't want to see, who was just coming in the front door looking for him. He was sober then, and for good. But he was still Ray. Certain things don't dry up in a person, I guess.

That was a memorable time for me, because Ray and I went on to be great friends for the rest of his life. But it was probably more memorable for Ray because in addition to being out in the world for the first time since he'd been sober, and finding out he could do that, he met Tess Gallagher then. Tess was at the conference, and that's where they first laid eyes on each other. I don't exactly know what Ray's marital situation was then. He was by himself in Dallas, and I'm sure he was still married. And, for truth, he and Tess only met there and palled around like we all did. Their romance didn't spark up until later, when Ray had gone down to El Paso to teach, and Tess was teaching in Tucson.

Ray and I used to say that we were such natural friends, in part, because our families had pretty much been the same kind of people, in fact, were from the very same place. Rural Arkansas. They'd all left there to find work in the thirties. And Tess's family was of that background, too. They were from the Ozarks and eastern Oklahoma, and like Ray's folks, had come out to the Northwest to go to work. I'm not really much of a believer in this kind of destiny. But they were a lot alike, Tess and Ray, in instinctual ways. They knew a lot of the same things, just from growing up the way they did. Writing and literature could be said to have saved them both from perhaps glummer lives. They'd each had their licks. That's not a formula for affection, but still it's not surprising they loved each other so much.

Douglas Unger:

That conference seemed to be a turning point for Ray. He managed to get through his reading, and all the socializing, even having the antique, cherrywood bed he was sleeping on collapse into broken sticks under him one night and then trying to hide the damage from his hosts, all without having a drink. He was proud of himself for that. He was openly amazed and surprised by the good reception for his work there. He talked a great deal about Richard Ford, Donald Justice and other writers he had spent time with. Also, there was something already in the air concerning Tess Gallagher. I remember Ray gave Amy and me and many friends T-shirts from the conference. Maryann kept asking him about who Tess Gallagher was, reading her name off the T-shirt, suspicious that Tess seemed to be the only writer he had met that Ray was reticent about. Maryann sensed something had happened between them. Years later, Ray always said that nothing more than a friendly meeting with Tess took place. But it was clear that, in his mind, the seeds were already sewn for their future relationship.

After the conference, Ray returned to the house in McKinleyville. He had a room all set up for writing. He wasn't writing very much, but he had pulled off a kind of scam. He had written an outline for a novel which was something like the German side of the story told in *The African Queen,* and he had received an advance for the book from McGraw-Hill. I'm not sure he had every intention of writing the novel when he wrote the proposal, but anybody could look at this outline, and look at Ray's stories, and wonder how in the world he was going to write that kind of book. He often joked, years later, that he was still getting notes

505

every so often from McGraw-Hill asking how the novel was coming along. He'd tell them it was going just fine.

Maryann went up and lived with him that summer and fall.
They went fishing almost every day, visited old friends, played
bingo, went to meetings, and he never had a drink again.

William Kittredge:

I remember asking him after he had been sober for about six
months if he had been writing at all. He said, "I can't. I can't
convince myself enough that it is worth doing."

Maryann Carver:

I lived with Ray in McKinleyville, California. At Christmastime
1977 Ray saw John Cheever on the Dick Cavett show. He had
been close friends with Cheever back in Iowa, had drunk with
him, and here was his old friend on TV, sober and successful. It
had a great impact. He had already begun to write again, had
written "Why Don't You Dance?" and "Viewfinder" there in
McKinleyville in "Chef's House" where we were living. Seeing
John Cheever on a TV show made Ray want to leave California
and go to New York to be a writer there.

Chuck Kinder:

Ray had a teaching job lined up in El Paso. Maryann had some
money coming from her teachers'-retirement fund, so she said,
"You go off and have a good life in El Paso. I'm going to California." She set him adrift. He got into this old car that his son
Vance had left there and drove off and that pretty much was the
end of it.

Maryann Carver:

After five treatment centers, Ray was sober from June 3, 1977
to the end of his life. After a sick and shaky start, by the summer
of 1978 he was writing again as well as ever, and I checked out in
late July 1978 to let him have his life, to experience all he could,
because he was forty then, and who knew how long he had. He
would always say "I'm going to die young, but you're going to live
to be a mean old lady."

You know, not only was I the first lady he ever had, but I can
modestly say from the time we were first together that I was his

lifelong muse. I wondered what was going to happen after we had divorced—to see where his writing would take off then.

Douglas Unger:

That summer in Iowa City was tough on everyone. Amy and I landed there, broke and without prospects, knowing we could at least get minimal jobs and subsist somehow in that town where we had both gone to graduate school. We joined Ray and Maryann, who were just barely skimping along on some grant money and on his checks from the Goddard College M.F.A. program where he had been teaching. We managed to line up three house-sitting arrangements, complete with lawns to mow and dogs to bail out of the pound. Ray was trying very hard to get his writing going again. Then it seemed the whole family came crashing in, his son, his mother-in-law, everyone with needs and problems. There was chaos and turmoil, with a major move every month. How he managed to stay sober through all of this was a miracle. Ray had a word for the kind of life we were living. He called it *milling*. "We're just milling around and getting nowhere," he'd say.

He was terribly frustrated. And he and Maryann were fighting. Ray took off in a rush for El Paso, where he had a job waiting. Maryann left him then, for the last time, to go back to California. Ray's old car broke down on the way to El Paso. As the story goes, Tess Gallagher rescued him. It was there that they struck up that working partnership that lasted for the rest of his life.

That was a strange crossroads for him, and really a kind of paradigm of how he lived. Ray told me that when that old car broke down, he traded it for a bicycle, traded it right on the spot. That's the way it was with him—disaster happened, but then he had a great story about how he had once actually traded his car for a bicycle.

Geoffrey Wolff, *critic and novelist:*

Ray was a great liar, a wonderful liar. Ray, Richard Ford, my brother Toby and I once sailed my boat to Block Island. We went ashore the next morning to do some drinking, but of course Ray couldn't be interested in that. He stayed on board but he wanted to know where the coffee was. I told him the stove was pretty complicated, that it could easily blow up and so I'd bring him back some coffee since I didn't want him to use the stove. He said, "Oh, Jesus, I wouldn't dream of touching that stove. I don't need the coffee that bad anyway." So we left and went into town and drifted into a bar. My brother wanted to talk about literature, and Richard and I wanted to talk about the waitresses at the bar, The Oar. When we went back to the boat, we brought along one of them to take our picture. As the dinghy approached, I noticed Ray back in the stern of the boat, as far back as he could go, looking awful, covered with soot. I asked him what the hell had happened. He said, "Don't worry about a thing. I've just been shooting smack into my eyeballs." The waitress was terrified, didn't know he was joking. I went below to get my camera. Below decks it used to be all white, but now it was covered with black soot everywhere, completely black. I was very cross. I said, "Jesus, Ray, why did you have to light that stove?" And he said, "What are you talking about? I didn't do a damn thing." I said, "Come on, Ray, you lit that stove." "I don't know what you're talking about," he said. "I was asleep. Maybe someone came aboard." I told him to look down below. He said, "That's just the way it looked when you guys left." It took me and my sons ten years to scrape all that damn soot off, to scour that boat down clean. Sometimes I wonder if I shouldn't have left it the way it was that day in the harbor at Block Island—Carvered.

Douglas Unger:

When Geoffrey Wolff reviewed *Will You Please Be Quiet, Please?* in the *New York Times*, Ray called me up and said, "Did you see that? Would you believe it? Who would have thought it five years ago?" With every good review or piece of good news, he was like a child at Christmas. After so many years of rejection, the financial struggles, the drinking, even giving up writing, now when he least expected it, the world embraced him. He never ceased to be amazed at that.

Leonard Michaels:

His early work is more musical. More terrifying. Terrifying in the Kierkegaardian sense, like life itself. Actually, forget that.

When his work came out there were heavy blows at first. There's a Russian saying: "When you enter the city, the geese begin to cackle." A number of established sensibilities didn't want him in the city. But then some big names weighed in on his side. Soon thereafter right opinion seized the mental masses, high and low.

Geoffrey Wolff:

I wasn't more than three sentences into the first story in the collection, before I knew I was hearing a voice I'd never heard before. Not merely what people mean when they say they know what a minimalist is—a taker-outer rather than a putter-inner. Ray liked to lean things down, but not always. He was certainly capable of being a putter-inner too. Stanley Elkin said a wonderful thing: "Less is less. More is more. And enough is enough." Ray wrote enough.

Douglas Unger:

After they moved to Syracuse, Tess was instrumental in getting his life organized. From all the chaos of the past, Tess was able to step in and establish order, manage things so Ray wouldn't have to worry about bill collectors or other distractions—how to make ends meet, or how to find writing time. Tess would unplug the phone and later put up a sign that said, "No Visitors." Ray wrote much of the main body of his work during this new life.

I had a chance to get a close look at his work patterns, when I first visited him in Syracuse in the Spring of 1982. We were writing a screen treatment together, a possible project for the director Richard Pearce. Ray was then hard at work on finishing stories for his collection *Cathedral* and had another screenplay going about the life of Dostoyevski. He was always up very early in the morning. He stayed at his desk long periods of time then with little breaks for meals and coffee. He said that he preferred, if he could, when working on a first draft to get it all down in one sitting. Then he could tinker away at that draft with great patience, month after month, never seeming to tire of making changes.

Later, he told me how he worked on poems, sometimes so hard at it that he could get a draft of one poem in the morning, and another in the afternoon. Two poems in a day! He was astounded and satisfied with how productive he was. He'd be whipped out afterward, exhausted, of course. Then he would

509

keep several poems going in the rewriting stages. As far as I know, Tess read them and made comments on them, and he did much the same for her, an atmosphere between them as though they were sharing their secrets.

Sometimes, when he talked about his work, which wasn't often, Tess would jump into the conversation and claim something as her own. "He got that story from me," she often said about "Cathedral." Or the detail of the woman, Olla, and the grotesque plaster casting of her teeth before her husband had them fixed in "Feathers." "That's mine," Tess would say. The macabre casting of her own teeth was right there, brought down off a bookshelf and shown off to prove her case.

They worked together very intimately. It was a quiet, peaceful life. Ray had an unnatural paranoia about the telephone ringing, and sometimes he would bury the phone rather than simply unplug it. He would take the receiver off the hook, shove the phone in a drawer, muffle it with dish towels, then shut the drawer on it before he was satisfied. "The telephone rings and your life changes," he'd say. It was clearly implied that he had had enough changes in his life by then. He wanted to stay pretty much fixed in one place, in his study. She would rove around the house from one writing place to another, wandering as she wrote, and there were at least five good spaces set up for writing in their Syracuse home.

He got a lot of work done, seriously, living and breathing, it seemed, only to write during those years he divided between his house in Syracuse and his homes in Port Angeles. When he got the Strauss Living Award from the American Academy, he was able to redouble his writing efforts. He was so relieved not to have to teach, which he never really felt comfortable doing. He was proud of himself that he could now spend almost all of his time writing. And, in my opinion, writing poetry, more than fiction, was his first love. Even after Ray was turned down for financial aid as a young poet that year at Iowa, he never gave up his youthful dream of being accepted by the world as a poet. Later, writing poetry was the open expression of his new freedom, from alcoholism, from financial insecurity, from family troubles. There was also something of his outlaw mentality involved. The world seemed to be pressuring him to write more fiction, even after he had spent months concentrating only on his stories, painstakingly laboring away at them, through as many as fifteen or more drafts. But Ray was going to write what he felt like writing. He wasn't going to compromise his instincts now. The more he felt pressured by critics and editors and even his friends to write fiction, the more he used his new freedom to turn back to writing poems with joy and with a vengeance.

Tobias Wolff, *author:*

For the two or three years before he moved to Syracuse Ray was all over the map, living here, living there. But when he got to Syracuse he dug right in. He was determined to make a home for himself, a place where he could live in peace and have his friends over for some gossip and get his work done. And so he did. When I think of Ray in those years, I think of comfort—I think of a sleek, pampered cat preening by the fire, slit-eyed with contentment.

He loved fires. He'd have a fire going from September till June, and on cool nights in the summer. Once I was over visiting and the fire was burning low and he went down to the basement for more wood. He was down there a long time, and all the while I kept hearing these terrible crashing sounds. Finally I decided I'd better investigate, and what he was doing, he was lifting these big logs over his head and smashing them down on the cement floor until they split. I said, "Jesus, Ray, why don't you use an ax?" "I will," he said, a little impatient. "I will. I've been meaning to get one."

That's how he'd been splitting his firewood for at least a year, maybe two.

Fires and candy. If he had a fire and some good chocolate, Ray was in heaven. He was a boy, a very large boy. And like a boy, he didn't always want to share. He could be pretty cagey with his candy—cagey and secretive. On Halloween he turned all the lights out and pretended he wasn't home so he wouldn't have to shell out to the kids. Catherine and I brought our sons over one year and gave them permission to bang on the door and throw gravel at the windows until he showed himself, which he finally did, in a bathrobe, pretending he'd been asleep. He tried to buy them off with some peppermint drops but Catherine and I kept badgering him to break out his stash. Finally he gave in and let

511

the boys have some of his better confections. He was laughing like crazy. He loved it when someone really got his number.

He was content, happy with Tess and his work and the respect his work began to inspire in all kinds of people. He grew fat on the land, but not arrogant. His manner was open and gentle and somewhat cunning. He never killed off the rascal in him, but he didn't let the rascal run his life. He knew exactly how fragile the peace was. In the best of times—sitting around the fire with friends, telling stories—he unfailingly wonderingly, said, "Things could be worse." He knew whereof he spoke. He knew the value of this gift of quiet time, and he didn't waste a minute of it. Look at what he did in those last ten years. When I drove by his house in those days I could feel him at work in there.

Jay McInerney, *author, former student of Carver's:*
I first met him here in New York. Oddly enough, it was the day that John Lennon died. I opened the door of my apartment in Greenwich Village, and standing there was Raymond Carver, who at that time was my favorite writer. It wasn't quite as coincidental and weird as that. My friend Gary Fisketjon was working at that time as an editor at Random House and he had had lunch with Carver. After lunch Ray didn't really have much to do so Gary called me up and asked if I would take Raymond Carver around and show him the city. I thought he was kidding and hung up on him. Within moments there was a knock on my door and there was this giant bear of a man in my door frame. We just sat down and started talking about one thing or another, mainly about books and writing, and never stopped.

He'd been through so much by the time I met him, and he'd come out the other side. He insisted that what he'd been through had only distracted him from writing. I think his writing improved as he sobered up, so he was also a steadying influence on my life, in giving me a model of the writer who wasn't a self-destructing meteor. Living in New York I had felt I was in the center of the media and publishing world. Sometimes it's easy to confuse that with the literary world. The literary world exists wherever there is a man or a woman alone in a room writing. I was a little foolish in confusing the one thing with the other.

Ray said if I really wanted to make it as a serious writer, commit myself to the act of writing fiction, I would have to arrange my life accordingly. He felt that living in New York and having to support myself in the most expensive city in the country was draining away a lot of my energy. I changed my whole life to follow him to Syracuse, hardly at the top of my list of favorite places to live if Ray hadn't been there.

I think it's quite possible that if I hadn't met Ray I would have gone down another road. I'd be an editor of a magazine today or something like that. One thing Ray did for me was to pound away at the idea that the only way to be a good writer was to write every day, sit down and put black on white. Sometimes he'd even call me up and ask, "Did you write today?" Many years later as a joke, I called him to ask if he'd written that day and he said, "No—you have to write every day until you *are* a writer, then you can take a day off every now and then."

Ray was a somewhat unwilling teacher. He almost didn't trust himself to give advice. He thought it strange that so many American writers supported themselves by teaching. On the other hand, he thought it was better than sweeping floors or pumping gas, which he had done in the past.

William Kittredge:

William Abrams, in his introduction to the O. Henry collection in which "A Small Good Thing" was the lead story, said something about the courage of Ray to take a brief story from his previous book and enlarge it this way. Well, in fact it was just the opposite. He had written the story, but his editor Gordon Lish had cut it down to the short version. The short version of that story is enormously diminished in its emotional power. It's no coincidence that, when he was able to, Ray changed contractual agreements, changed editors and all that. As he told me afterward, "They can't change a comma from now on."

Richard Ford:

He would listen to his editors—Chip McGrath at *The New Yorker* for one, a man he admired very much. He certainly listened to Tess. Finally, though, it doesn't make much difference how the stories came into being, because they were Ray's and only Ray's.

513

Jay McInerney:

It was with some trepidation that I first visited Syracuse along with Gary, to try to find a place for me to live. We were to stay with Ray and Tess for the weekend, but I was driving this old MG that kept overheating, and we arrived late. Ray had already eaten one supper but he was happy to join us for another. He liked five or six meals a day and often said his idea of heaven was breakfast anytime. I remember his grace"—"Here's hoping the phone don't ring and the food don't get cold—Amen." A big old carton of milk sat on the table. While we were eating Ray told us about his visitor the weekend before—a friend of Tess's, a blind man. He couldn't get over it—it seemed to him the most extraordinary condition, the man's blindness, he just couldn't take it for granted. He told us how the guy smoked, which made Ray wonder if it was as much fun when you couldn't *see* the smoke. That was one of Ray's great gifts—he hardly took anything for granted. Some of us might try to be cool about having a blind man visit, but not Ray. He told us how the first thing he'd done, before he realized his mistake, was ask the blind man if he sat on the right or left side of the train coming up from New York—the left being the scenic, river side. Ray was basically telling stories on himself, making fun of his own reactions to having a blind man around. It was very funny stuff, but you could see he was agitated by the experience too. He was trying out the material.

Tobias Wolff:

When I read "Cathedral" for the first time I was lying on a couch, and when I came to the end I had the feeling that I was levitating. Of course, literally, I wasn't; but I felt as if I were lifting off the couch. I was so charged by the story and drawn up by it that I ran to the phone and spent about half an hour trying to track Ray down. I finally found him at Yaddo, and I had to tell him what he'd done to me.

Douglas Unger:

So many people all over the world are still just discovering his work. In Buenos Aires there's a bookshop that also serves coffee and sandwiches. They serve a salad called "The Carver" and a sandwich called "Cathedral." The Cathedral Sandwich is cheese and lettuce on white bread—the simplest things. Ray's on a restaurant menu in Argentina. . . .

Leonard Michaels:

When I last saw him in Port Townsend, it was quite clear that he was enjoying himself enormously. He looked very very good, in an Eddie Bauer country-gentleman outfit. He had this big Mercedes and he told me about his two boats. He was triumphant and his French editor was right there walking around, admiring Ray every minute.

Mona Simpson, author of *Anywhere but Here:*

I never paid for a meal. Neither did anyone else when Ray was around. I met him in his second life. He was what William James called "the twice born" and he had a childlike gratitude, a sort of caved-in look to his mouth. Restaurants, taxis, coats, good cars—they were all a joke and a toy to him.

I met Ray at a reading he gave in New York. I was a first-year graduate student at Columbia but one of his students invited me along to the dinner afterward. When Ray guest-edited an issue of *Ploughshares,* he accepted a short story of mine, the first I ever published. He knew how to save people from small humiliations. He edited a few lines and called me up about the changes; then he sent his suggestions so I could see them on the page, sent them overnight mail. He never lost his joy at publishing one story in a journal only a few faithful readers would ever see and he protected that feeling in others. He knew how a writer can feel smallest in his moment of victory. That was what was best about Ray: he knew how to celebrate. "That's one for our side!" he'd say. He never stopped feeling like one of the unfortunates, one of the guilty undeserving. He was too far in. None of his people were getting lucky. And so he had this mischievous, incredulous laugh. "Here's one for our side."

He never forgot the others. He could bitch and gossip but never blame.

I visited Ray and Tess once in Port Angeles but he never took me fishing. Once in a while, though, in the dead of winter, I'd get a padded envelope with Ray's little up-slanted writing on it. Inside, in a plastic vacuum pack, would be a side of a smoked salmon. He'd catch a bunch of fish and send some to each of his friends.

515

Jay McInerney:

I came to Syracuse just as he was starting to be showered with laurels, and so we were always celebrating some new triumph of Ray's or Tess's in their big old Victorian house. It was a lovely thing to behold, the genuine happiness of Ray's later life. Shortly after I moved down the street the world started knocking at Ray's door, and eventually he and Tess had to retreat a little to get their work done. Tess would sometimes check into a motel down on Eerie Boulevard when she was really cooking on a project, but Ray liked his creature comforts and he'd stay at home, not always answering the door or the phone. It was kind of ironic, here was a man who, like so many of the characters in his stories, used to be afraid to answer the door for fear of bill collectors, now reverting to his old furtive behavior because some reporter from the Frankfurter *Zeitung* had flown all the way to Syracuse to get an interview with the master. The really funny thing is that I would always see him looking out from behind the curtains to see if it was safe.

Ray and Tess had a famous sign they put out when they were working—a big painted piece of sheetrock which said NO VISITORS PLEASE. It was born one morning after I paid, or tried to pay, a late night visit. I had a girl visiting me from New York one weekend shortly after I moved to Syracuse. We went out to dinner and had a few drinks. Suddenly it seemed absolutely essential to me to introduce this girl to Ray and Tess, or vice versa. Or maybe it was her idea, I can't remember. Anyway, we rolled up the hill to their house. It was probably ten-thirty or eleven o'clock at night, which in New York is, or was, a perfectly respectable hour to visit your friends. There were a couple of lights on, so we thought nothing of hammering on the door. After the second set of knocks I realized they weren't coming, although my escort was not easily dissuaded. She wanted to meet Ray. She gave the door a few more good whacks. Finally I convinced her to retreat, realizing that the Carver-Gallagher household was perhaps on a different schedule than we were. I was now worried that they would know it was me who had shattered their sleep. I snuck away, hoping no one was looking out the window and trying to subdue my boisterous companion.

I woke up the next morning mortified. I didn't want to go near Ray's house but my girlfriend insisted, unable to understand my reluctance. Finally we walked up to the house to be greeted with the freshly painted NO VISITORS PLEASE sign. A week later Mona Simpson came up to visit and to interview Ray for the *Paris Review;* she put the sign in her introduction. I never told anyone how it came into being, though Ray liked to tell his version. When I finally worked up the courage a few days later to visit, he told me how a bunch of students had pounded on his door at midnight. "Can you believe that?" Ray asked. "Twelve-thirty in the morning for God's sake, pounding on the door." I shook my head nervously. "Terrible," I said. "So we decided to make that sign," Tess explained. Later I would hear Ray improve on the story. A gang of thesis-hunting graduate students from out of town kicking the door at one in the morning. A team of drunken Manhattan journalists seeking an interview at two in the morning. And so on. I felt sort of ashamed about it, and then I forgot and never got to tell him the real story.

Douglas Unger:

He was fascinated by this turnaround and by the smallest kinds of pleasures it enabled him to enjoy. He'd check into a nice hotel room in New York. He'd laugh and quote his version of the Pinter line, "A person feels like he has a chance in a room like this." Just going out to dinner was a big occasion. And he'd always want to share this feeling with his friends.

Leonard Michaels:

He may have intended to sound that way only to hold off the demonic forces, the ones that are sure to punish you if you take any pleasure in anything in your life.

Douglas Unger:

There is a tremendous sadness in Maryann now, and there has been for some time, about how the world considers her relationship with Ray. She read all the reviews describing these down-and-out people in Ray's work, treating them like ragged lowlifes, most of them, saying how heartbreaking they were. Maryann is a proud, capable woman, an educated person, has a master's degree, and can quote from Jung and Blake and the major poets off the top of her head. She was his first sounding board, and helped to edit all those early poems and stories. She worked for nineteen years to keep Ray and the family together. Then to see their lives and his work so refracted and distorted to the world by critics, reviewers, and now even biographers, to see the most intimate portions of their lives shown in Ray's work treated that way, all of that really hurt her pride. That's what Ray's story "Intimacy" is about, the writer asking forgiveness for having allowed their lives to be so used and abused in his stories and by the world. Then, of course, there is the ironic twist of making use of that very apology as fresh meat for another story.

William Kittredge:

He knew he owed Maryann a great debt. She had kept his life together for years and years. She'd helped him imaginatively, yet she was clearly portrayed in many of those stories in all kinds of unflattering ways. He used her so ruthlessly in those stories. It's just so sad that after a long series of emotional betrayals of various kinds, great anger developed. It got so that they couldn't be in the same room together, essentially. Ray felt great sadness, but it made his life impossible to live, impossible for him to work, impossible for him to do the things he felt he had to do. He knew he had to do his work, but back there all the time was somebody he had left behind. They'd been entwined in an emotional compact about getting the work done yet he was the one who had walked away with all the skills. One gets to leave with all the success, and the other gets to stand out in the rain.

Douglas Unger:

I was at Yaddo when "Errand" came out, and it so happened there was a copy of Henri Troyat's biography of Chekhov around. James Salter noticed that the death scene in the biography and a large part of the death scene in "Errand" were almost exactly alike, almost word for word. That caused quite a stir and discussion among the writers there. Ray had read the biography, was fascinated by it, and had decided to use it when he got the idea for his story. To his mind, it was no different than using parts of a story one of his friends had told him around the table. The interesting thing is that he turned it so completely into a Ray Carver story. He laughed at how someone had actually caught him at it, then said he might just do that same kind of story with the biographies of other writers he admired, like de Maupassant, Dostoyevski and Kafka.

518

After he finished the manuscript of *Where I'm Calling From,*
he wanted more than anything to complete another book of poems. A lot of people kept urging him to write less poetry and
more fiction but he wasn't sure if he had another story in him.
He told me that he had to fill his well again; for Ray that always
meant going back to writing poetry.

Jay McInerney:
One of the things I learned from reading Ray's critics is how
often even our best literature is caricatured. And how even a
writer as widely admired as Ray is so often misunderstood, even
when he is being praised. Some of us felt frustrated by what we
considered to be the awkwardness and stupidities of some of the
more casual criticism, though overall I'd say it was a joy to see so
good a writer so well appreciated.

Richard Ford:
In the summer of '87, Kristina and I and Tess and Ray had
been to England and France together. We had a very good time,
but I noticed Ray looked thin and kind of gaunt. I had a sense
that something was amiss with him. Ray was never a healthy-
seeming man. He ate horrible things, smoked a million cigarettes, he'd been through the ravages of liquor. He'd given his
body a lot of big whacks. Sometimes I'd go over to his house and
he'd go to the store and come back with a sack of doughnuts and
Twinkies and God knows what else. I'd say, "Jeez, Ray, I hate to
see you buy that stuff," and he'd say, "You'll feel different about
it at twelve o'clock tonight."

Chuck Kinder:
One night he called me up and told me. He told me that he
had something dark down there.

Geoffrey Wolff:
He was going to be operated on for lung cancer; they had to
crack his chest and I'd had my chest cracked during my heart
surgery and I wanted to tell him as much as he wanted to know
about that particular operation. He asked me some questions
about it, but he also told me exactly what he did not want to

know about it. I'd want to know all I could; after all, knowledge is power. But not Ray. He wanted, as he said, to wake up three months later and find out it was all fixed, that it was all over.

Douglas Unger:

Amy and I had lunch with Ray, the day before his surgery. He seemed in good spirits, and optimistic, hoping for the best. Then when the food came, it was like the reality of his condition hit him. His face turned gray. A dark and somber mood came over us all and we fell silent. Ray was staring down at his food, fixed on it sadly, stirring his spoon around and around. We asked him if he was all right. "I'm looking at this soup and thinking I'm in the soup," he said.

The next morning, very early, Amy and I and Tess were at St. Joseph's hospital. Ray was waiting in his room, all prepped, with like a blue shower cap on his head. He had been given his first injections, which were making him drowsy. He held hands with each of us in turn. He was joking with us, too, philosophically, looking back at his life. He had spoken often of the years of his youth, and later of his alcoholism, as "the old life." There were the years in Syracuse and Port Angeles; sober years of literary success, which he called "the new life." He spoke of each of these lives he had lived, and how lucky he thought he had been, how amazing it seemed to him, clear in this how much he had loved his life, and it seemed as though he were ready now for anything. When the orderly came to wheel him off to his surgery, we all hugged and kissed him, wished him luck. He smiled at us sleepily. "I'm on to my next new life," he said.

Leonard Michaels:

His surgeon told Ray he had read his stories. He had loved them.

Douglas Unger:

When they gave him his honorary doctorate at the University of Hartford, he turned to everyone and said, "Well, it's Dr. Carver now. You'll all have to start calling me doctor." It was just over two months before he died. From Hartford, he went on to give a reading at the Endicott bookstore and sign copies of *Where I'm Calling From*. People were spilling out into the street. He was exhausted from the illness and could barely read, but he signed books for hours. The next day, he was inducted into the American Academy and Institute of Arts and Letters. That was a miracle to him. Then there was another book signing at the Scribner's bookstore. About twenty writers were there signing books, but there were as many people lined up at Ray's table, waiting for a handshake and signature, as you might see in line for a first-run movie. He kept turning to me and saying, "Can you believe this? Isn't this just amazing? Who would have thought this?" Finally, they had to shut the bookstore down. We were out in the street later, and there were still people waiting.

Ray had managed to convince both the press and his editors that he had beaten his cancer. Up until mid-June, maybe he had even convinced himself, as well as the world, that he had beaten it. He'd say, "I feel fine. I'm getting stronger every day."

Maryann Carver:
He did not want to die, of course. But I think he had written out all his themes and didn't have a whole lot more to say, or he would have stuck around to do it. I think his higher self knew when it was time to go—at the very pinnacle of his life as far as his career was concerned.

The last time I saw him alive was April 22, 1988 when he was receiving radiation treatment in Seattle. Chris, our daughter, and her little girls, Windy and Chloe, and I went down to see him. I had received a letter from him earlier, right after he'd had his surgery, in which he had tried to counsel me and advise me how to behave, consolidate property, and so on, now that we were sort of over the hill. When I read that, I thought, well, speak for yourself. I was very saddened to read that negative letter, for, after all, I did not think that was the right attitude for fighting cancer.

So I was determined when I went to The Four Seasons in Seattle to meet for lunch that I'd show him. I got this absolutely stunning outfit from this store in town called A Touch of Class, and wore incredible gold earrings from Turkey that four people in the restaurant complimented me on. A friend said I looked like I'd just stepped out of a Ferrari.

We arrived before he did, so I waited for him up on the balcony, and when he walked in, oh, it was the most tragic sight I had ever, ever, ever seen. His face was so swollen from the steroids he had been taking. He had a big coat on, with a scarf around his neck, and a cap to cover his loss of hair from the radiation treatments. He looked at me and tears flooded his eyes. He said, "If you're not a sight for sore eyes."

But then he managed to put on a real party for the little girls. Ray insisted we all have a different dessert; then we took a bite of everyone else's as we laughed and enjoyed the treats. We were thrilled to be together, holding hands as we ate. They all looked at me at the beginning of the meal, so I said grace. I finished by saying, " . . . in Jesus's name." At one time, Ray would have been embarrassed perhaps, but he was right in there this time. I told him it was important to pray in Jesus's name because it was the consciousness involved and invoked, as well as the literal instruction of Jesus in the Bible. I said a prayer for his life and health, and we all very solemnly and sensitively said "Amen."

Later that afternoon I gave him a Reiki treatment. He would have scoffed at that too in the past. Reiki in the first degree is the laying-on-of-hands technique that Jesus used to heal. It was rediscovered by a Japanese Christian professor, Dr. Mikao Usui, after many years of research. Ray laid his head on the palms of my hands and, ironically, I was holding the exact part of his head where he was daily being zapped with radiation treatments. My hands got hot. And he absolutely loved lying with his head in my lap, his head in my hands. He kept saying, "This feels so good, oh, this feels so good."

Chuck Kinder:
Ray had a premonition long ago that he'd die young. I'm not into this touchy-feely business, but I think that was pretty genuine.

Douglas Unger:
During the last month of his life, we talked with Ray only a few times on the telephone. When asked about his illness, he kept saying he was doing well, his hair was growing back after the radiation treatments, and he was working hard on his new book of poems. That continued to be his news for everyone. But there were so many hints that this wasn't true. Amy and I were

stricken by a house fire in Idaho in which our two German shepherds died and we just barely got out alive. Ray was concerned for us, offered us money and help, if we needed it, and we thanked him. At one point in the conversation, he said mysteriously, "I'm thinking a lot about those dogs."

We wanted to come to Port Angeles to visit, and had tentatively planned a visit for early August in any case, but he told us no, he was on his way to Alaska for a salmon fishing expedition to celebrate completing the manuscript of his book of poems of *A New Path to the Waterfall*. He sounded happy, and satisfied, and said, "Wish me luck." He told us to take care and promised to catch a big one for us.

Nominated by The Paris Review

SPECIAL MENTION

(The editors also wish to mention the following important works published by small presses last year. Listing is in no particular order.)

POETRY

Mastectomy—Lawrence Gonzalez (New Letters)
In The Park—Tom Sleigh (Ploughshares)
Mercies—Charlie Smith (Mississippi Review)
History Lessons—Yusef Komunyaaka (Kenyon Review)
Chrysanthemums—Jane Kenyon (Iowa Review)
The Burning Man—William Logan (Sewanee Review)
Them—Kim Addonizio (Prairie Schooner)
The Loop—Bruce Weigl (New England Review)
Wijiji—Greg Pape (Cutbank)
To Pasolini—David St. John (Pequod)
Consummation—Corrine Hales (New England Review)
Christmas Carol for the Severed Head of Mangas Coloradas— Adrian C. Louis (Guadelupe Review)
Big Romance—Maggie Anderson (Women's Review of Books)
Naming The Stone—Cecile Goding (Georgia Review)
Wartime Photos of My Father—David Wojahn (Gettysburg Review)
Just Say No To Insect Sex—Sheryl St. Germaine (Guadelupe Review)
Big Black Car—Lynn Emanuel (Georgia Review)
The Summer of Celia—Elizabeth Spires (New Criterion)
Spilled—Roland Flint (North Dakota Review)
Daylilies On The Hill—Donald Hall (Michigan Quarterly Review)
Indios Con Levita—Ricardo Pau-Llosa (Missouri Review)

525

The Generosity of Souls—Renee A. Ashley (New England Review)

Negative Confession—William Olsen (Iowa Review)

The Greek Statuette—Andrew Feld (Ploughshares)

Saturday Night—Thom Gunn (Tikkun)

Ten Years After Your Deliberate Drowning—Robin Behn (Indiana Review)

At The Writers' Conference—Marvin Bell (New England Review)

Hymn To The Sun—Randy Blassing (Paris Review)

Jim Barnett's Pigs—Boyd White (Iowa Review)

From A Paper Boat—Reginald Gibbons (Poetry East)

ESSAYS

Husbands—Andre Dubus (Epoch)

Mountain Spirits—James Kilgo (Sewanee Review)

Leaving the Ranch—William Kittredge (Cutbank)

Families And Prisons—Robert Hass (Michigan Quarterly Review)

Edmund Wilson—Mary McCarthy (Paris Review)

An Album—Ron Carlson (Tampa Review)

Nihilism In Black America—Cornel West (Dissent)

When I Was A Child—Marilynne Robinson (The Brick Reader)

Hard Being Good: Reaganomics, Free Expression, and Federal Funding of the Arts—David Bosworth (Georgia Review)

Nabokov and Memory—Robert Alter (Partisan Review)

A Sister's Story—Virginia DeLuca (Iowa Review)

My Main Man—Frank Standiford (New Letters)

Letters to Mutti—Edith Milton (Tikkun)

Infamous Liberties and Uncommon Restraints—C. D. Wright (AWP Chronicle)

Living Root—Michael Heller (Parnassus: Poetry in Review)

The Redemption Center, Inc.—Victoria Nelson (Agni)

Looking Around Our Corridor of Freedom—Carol Ascher (Boulevard)

Something That Will Last—Nancy Willard (Prairie Schooner)

Correctionville, Iowa—Michael Martone (North American Review)

The Ground Sense Necessary . . . Marvin Bell (American Poetry Review)

The Ark of What Has Been—Rachel Hadas (AWP Chronicle)

FICTION

You Drive—Christine Schutt (The Quarterly)
Easter Dresses—Kent Meyers (Georgia Review)
Kerensky on Broadway—Matthew Goodman (New England Review)
The Wrecking Yard—Pinckney Benedict (Ontario Review)
The House Behind—Lydia Davis (Antaeus)
Beauty—Julie Brown (Michigan Quarterly Review)
The Meat Eaters—Michael Collins (Chicago Review)
From The Diary of Gene Mays—Richard Burgin (TriQuarterly)
Past Useless—Nanci Kincaid (Missouri Review)
Lázaro In Paris—Alberto Alvaro Ríos (Blue Mesa Review)
The Witch of Owl Mountain Springs: An Account of Her Remarkable Powers—Peter Taylor (Kenyon Review)
The Way Out—Steven Millhauser (Story)
Tanks—Phil Condon (Georgia Review)
Have You Seen Me?—Elizabeth Graver (Antaeus)
Lena—Joan Wickersham (Story)
The Act of Solitude—Joyce Carol Oates (Agni)
Clearwater and Latissimus—Alison Baker (Ontario Review)
A Sense of Aesthetics—Eileen Pollack (New England Review)
Debts and Payments—Suzanne Berne (Threepenny Review)
The Horror Age—Richard Burgin (Another Chicago Magazine)
Outings—Jeanne Schinto (Boulevard)
The Virtue of Cool—Joseph Olshan (Boulevard)
Woman Found Dead In Elevator—Ruth Tarson (Paris Review)
From Hunger—Gerald Shapiro (Quarterly West)
Swimming—Louis Berney (Quarterly West)
The Communist—Bonita Friedman (Another Chicago Magazine)
Books—Paula Sharp (Threepenny Review)
The Statue—Nicholas Shakespeare (Paris Review)
Poet On The Mountain—Rolaine Hochstein (Ohio Journal)
The Famous Thing About Death—Lisa Sandlin (Shenandoah)
The First Indian Pilot—Diane Glancy (Farmer's Market)
Sisters—Abigail Thomas (Columbia)
Just Married 1960—Abigail Thomas (Glimmer Train)

527

No Permanent Bad Thing—Kim Edwards (Missouri Review)
Tigers—Catherine Browder (*The Clay That Breathes*, Milkweed)
One Sunday—Barbara Hudson (Quarterly West)
Questionnaire To Determine Eligibility for Heaven—Rosellen Brown (*Street Games*, Milkweed)
The Salem Letters—Diane Keating (Exile Editions)
From Man Who Died—C. E. Poverman (Ontario Review)
A Love Song—Andre Dubus (Crazyhorse)
Le Rocket Nègre—Peter LaSalle (Boulevard)
Still There Is Grace—J. Carol Goodman (Nebraska Review)
The Cleanest House—Karen Brennan (Sonora Review)
Max and Lulu—Terry Engel (Product)
Flambé—Brent Beebe (Sonora Review)
The Density of Sunlight—Rosa Shand (Nimrod)
Dreams of Heaven—Steve Heller (Laurel Review)
Blackbeard—Joyce Winer (Crazyhorse)
The Photojournalist—Richard Neumann (Laurel Review)
Waterdog Writers—Denis Trudell (Quarry West)
El Ojito del Muerto, Eye of the Dead One—Melissa Pritchard (The Southern Review)
Fair Hunt—Antonya Nelson (The Southern Review)
My Marilyn—Emily Hammond (Fiction)
In The Land of Men—Antonya Nelson (TriQuarterly)
Murdock's Wife—Tom McNeal (Black Warrior Review)
Painted Pony—Dwight Yates (Quarterly West)
In The Valley of Kings—Terrence Holt (TriQuarterly)
The Dreaming Dog—Melinda Rooney (Santa Monica Review)
Hunter's Park—Stephen Dunning (Witness)
Ah Liberated Man—Marvin E. Williams (Caribbean Writer)
Sailors Take Warning—Pamela Dell (Alaska Quarterly Review)
Five Pears or Peaches—Reginald Gibbons (*Five Pears or Peaches*, Broken Moon)
Area Man Found Crucified—Joyce Carol Oates (Southern California Anthology)
The Tryout—Jack Driscoll (Witness)
The Dream Sweep—Scott Lasser (Alaska Quarterly Review)
Batteiger's Muse—Gordon Weaver (Mānoa)
Enfleurage—Aryeh Lev Stollman (Puerto Del Sol)
Sally At the Bullfight—Thomas E. Kennedy (Paris Transcontinental)

Feral Cats—David Michael Kaplan (Story)
A Roadside Resurrection—Larry Brown (Paris Review)
Peanut's Fortune—Amy Tan (Grand Street)
Love—Robert Olen Butler (Writers' Forum)
Moratorium—Wayne Karlin (Vietnam Generation)
The Perfect Tenant—Mary McGarry Morris (Glimmer Train)
Gwen—Stephen Dixon (Story Quarterly)
The Heat Death—Thomas E. Kennedy (New Letters)
Flames—Dean Albarelli (Hudson Review)
Holy Week—Deborah Eisenberg (Western Humanities Review)
The Chimney In The Sand—Lewis Turco (Beloit Fiction Journal)
Black Is The Color—Irving Wexler (*Will The Morning Be Any
   Kinder Than The Night?*, Sheep Meadow Press)
A House of Mirrors—Gary Pak (Hawaii Review)
Instead of Men—Vicki Lindner (The Little Magazine)
Memorial—Marianne Villanueva (*Ginseng & Other Tales*, Calyx)
Songs People Sing When They're Alone—Carolyn Osborn (Amer-
   ican Literary Review)
Small Talk—Sharon Solwitz (Stand Magazine)
Someone to Watch Over Me—Melissa Lentricchia (New England
   Review)
For Colored Only—Nanci Kincaid (Emry's Journal)
Tall Tales—Johnny Payne (TriQuarterly)
Rainy Day—Guy Malet de Carteret (Exile Editions)
Catalogue of the Exhibition: The Art of Edmund Morrash (1810–
   1846)—Steven Millhauser (Salmagundi)
The Clutch—Dick Scanlan (Other Voices)
Quiet and Listening—Ann Darvy (Malahat Review)
The Clown—Enid Harlow (TriQuarterly)
The Death of Hieronymous Bosch—Lance Olsen (Another Chi-
   cago Magazine)
Toughing It—Jerry Bumpus (Kansas Quarterly)
The Train—Akhil Sharma (Fiction)
Marina—Greg Johnson (Virginia Quarterly Review)
Magic and Hidden Things—Kevin McDermott (Missouri Review)
Death By Vending Machine—Alyce Miller (Kenyon Review)
The Death of Them Yet—Ferenc Sánta (TriQuarterly)
People—Daniel Meltzer (Gettysburg Review)

PRESSES FEATURED IN THE PUSHCART PRIZE EDITIONS (1976–1992)

Acts
Agni Review
Ahsahta Press
Ailanthus Press
Alaska Quarterly Review
Alcheringa/Ethnopoetics
Alice James Books
Ambergris
Amelia
American Literature
American PEN
American Poetry Review
American Scholar
The American Voice
Amicus Journal
Amnesty International
Anaesthesia Review
Another Chicago Magazine
Antaeus
Antietam Review
Antioch Review
Apalachee Quarterly
Aphra
Aralia Press
The Ark
Ascensius Press
Ascent

Aspen Leaves
Aspen Poetry Anthology
Assembling
Bamboo Ridge
Barlenmir House
Barnwood Press
The Bellingham Review
Bellowing Ark
Beloit Poetry Journal
Bennington Review
Bilingual Review
Black American Literature Forum
Black Rooster
Black Scholar
Black Sparrow
Black Warrior Review
Blackwells Press
Bloomsbury Review
Blue Cloud Quarterly
Blue Unicorn
Blue Wind Press
Bluefish
BOA Editions
Bookslinger Editions
Boulevard
Boxspring
Bridges

Brown Journal of the Arts
Burning Deck Press
Caliban
California Quarterly
Callaloo
Calliope
Calliopea Press
Canto
Capra Press
Carolina Quarterly
Cedar Rock
Center
Chariton Review
Charnel House
Chelsea
Chicago Review
Chouteau Review
Chowder Review
Cimarron Review
Cincinnati Poetry Review
City Lights Books
Clown War
CoEvolution Quarterly
Cold Mountain Press
Colorado Review
Columbia: A Magazine of Poetry
    and Prose
Confluence Press
Confrontation
Conjunctions
Copper Canyon Press
Cosmic Information Agency
Crawl Out Your Window
Crazyhorse
Crescent Review
Cross Cultural Communications
Cross Currents
Cumberland Poetry Review
Curbstone Press
Cutbank
Dacotah Territory
Daedalus
Dalkey Archive Press

Decatur House
December
Denver Quarterly
Domestic Crude
Dragon Gate Inc.
Dreamworks
Dryad Press
Duck Down Press
Durak
East River Anthology
Ellis Press
Empty Bowl
Epoch
Exquisite Corpse
Fiction
Fiction Collective
Fiction International
Field
Firebrand Books
Firelands Art Review
Five Fingers Review
Five Trees Press
The Formalist
Frontiers: A Journal of Women
    Studies
Gallimaufry
Genre
The Georgia Review
Gettysburg Review
Ghost Dance
Goddard Journal
David Godine, Publisher
Graham House Press
Grand Street
Granta
Graywolf Press
Green Mountains Review
Greenfield Review
Greensboro Review
Guardian Press
Hard Pressed
Hayden's Ferry Review
Hermitage Press

Hills
Holmgangers Press
Holy Cow!
Home Planet News
Hudson Review
Icarus
Iguana Press
Indiana Review
Indiana Writes
Intermedia
Intro
Invisible City
Inwood Press
Iowa Review
Ironwood
Jam To-day
The Kanchenjuga Press
Kansas Quarterly
Kayak
Kelsey Street Press
Kenyon Review
Latitudes Press
Laughing Waters Press
Laurel Review
L'Epervier Press
Liberation
Linquis
The Literary Review
The Little Magazine
Living Hand Press
Living Poets Press
Logbridge-Rhodes
Lowlands Review
Lucille
Lynx House Press
Magic Circle Press
Malahat Review
Mānoa
Manroot
Massachusetts Review
Mho & Mho Works
Micah Publications
Michigan Quarterly

Milkweed Editions
Milkweed Quarterly
The Minnesota Review
Mississippi Review
Mississippi Valley Review
Missouri Review
Montana Gothic
Montana Review
Montemora
Moon Pony Press
Mr. Cogito Press
MSS
Mulch Press
Nada Press
New America
New American Review
The New Criterion
New Delta Review
New Directions
New England Review and Bread
    Loaf Quarterly
New Letters
New Virginia Review
New York Quarterly
Nimrod
North American Review
North Atlantic Books
North Dakota Quarterly
North Point Press
Northern Lights
Northwest Review
O. ARS
Obsidian
Oconee Review
October
Ohio Review
Ontario Review
Open Places
Orca Press
Orchises Press
Oxford Press
Oyez Press
Painted Bride Quarterly

Painted Hills Review
Paris Review
Parnassus: Poetry in Review
Partisan Review
Penca Books
Pentagram
Penumbra Press
Pequod
Persea: An International Review
Pipedream Press
Pitcairn Press
Ploughshares
Poet and Critic
Poetry
Poetry East
Poetry Northwest
Poetry Now
Prairie Schooner
Prescott Street Press
Promise of Learnings
Puerto Del Sol
Quarry West
The Quarterly
Quarterly West
Raccoon
Rainbow Press
Raritan: A Quarterly Review
Red Cedar Review
Red Clay Books
Red Dust Press
Red Earth Press
Release Press
Review of Contemporary Fiction
Revista Chicano-Riquena
River Styx
Rowan Tree Press
Russian *Samizdat*
Salmagundi
San Marcos Press
Sea Pen Press and Paper Mill
Seal Press
Seamark Press
Seattle Review

Second Coming Press
The Seventies Press
Sewanee Review
Shankpainter
Shantih
Sheep Meadow Press
Shenandoah
A Shout In The Street
Sibyl-Child Press
Small Moon
The Smith
Some
The Sonora Review
South Florida Poetry Review
Southern Poetry Review
Southern Review
Southwest Review
Spectrum
The Spirit That Moves Us
St. Andrews Press
Story
Story Quarterly
Streetfare Journal
Stuart Wright, Publisher
Sulfur
The Sun
Sun & Moon Press
Sun Press
Sunstone
Tar River Poetry
Teal Press
Telephone Books
Telescope
Temblor
Tendril
Texas Slough
13th Moon
THIS
Thorp Springs Press
Three Rivers Press
Threepenny Review
Thunder City Press
Thunder's Mouth Press

Tikkun
Tombouctou Books
Toothpaste Press
Transatlantic Review
TriQuarterly
Truck Press
Undine
Unicorn Press
University of Pittsburgh Press
Unmuzzled Ox
Unspeakable Visions of the
    Individual
Vagabond
Virginia Quarterly
Wampeter Press
Washington Writers Workshop

Water Table
Western Humanities Review
Westigan Review
Wickwire Press
Wilmore City
Witness
Word Beat Press
Word-Smith
Wormwood Review
Writers Forum
Xanadu
Yale Review
Yardbird Reader
Yarrow
Y'Bird
ZYZZYVA

534

CONTRIBUTORS' NOTES

AYLA NUTKU BACHMAN grew up in Istanbul, Turkey. She lives in New York City, is a recent Yaddo Fellow and has just completed her first novel.

DAVID BAKER teaches at Denison University in Ohio. He is the author of three poetry collections and is currently Consulting Poetry Editor of the *Kenyon Review*.

YOLANDA BARNES lives in Los Angeles. Her stories and a novella have appeared in *TriQuarterly* and *Ploughshares*.

STEVEN BARTHELME teaches at Southern Mississippi University. His stories were collected in *And He Tells the Little Horse the Whole Story* (Johns Hopkins University Press, 1987).

KEN BERNARD's most recent work is published by Asylum Arts. He lives in New York City.

EAVAN BOLAND lives in Dublin with her husband and two daughters. Norton published her *Outside History: Poems 1980–1990* recently.

HENRY CARLILE is the author of the forthcoming *Rain* (Carnegie Mellon). He teaches at Portland State University in Oregon.

HAYDEN CARRUTH'S poem is part of his collection just out from Copper Canyon. He lives in Munnsville, New York.

LYDIA DAVIS is the author of *Break It Down*. She teaches at Bard College.

LARS EIGHNER was homeless for several years. He is at work on a book titled *Travels With Lizbeth*.

535

PETER EVERWINE is the author of *Collecting The Animals* and *Keeping the Night*. He lives in Fresno, California.

CAROL FROST's two books of poetry are *Day of the Body* (Ion Books) and *Chimera* (Peregrine Smith).

WILLIAM GASS is the author of several works of fiction and criticism, most recently *Habitations of the Word*. He lives in St. Louis.

TIMOTHY GEIGER has published two chapbooks of poetry, *Proving The Light* and *Catechism Days*, both from Aureole Press. He won a 1991 Breadloaf Writers Conference Fellowship.

DAGOBERTO GILB is a journeyman union carpenter, a native of Los Angeles, who lives in El Paso. He is a frequent contributor to *The Threepenny Review* and other western journals.

MOLLY GILES won the Flannery O'Connor Award for her story collection *Rough Translations* (1985). She has recently published stories in ZYZZYVA, *The Greensboro Review,* and *Mănoa*.

LOUISE GLÜCK lives in Plainfield, Vermont. Her most recent poetry collection, *The Wild Iris,* is just out from Ecco Press.

SAM HALPERT has published stories in *The Kansas Quarterly* and *The Aspen Flyer*. His recent collection of interviews is *When We Talk About Raymond Carver.*

ANDREW HUDGINS was Alfred Hodder Fellow at Princeton University in 1989–90. He is the author of three books of poetry, all from Houghton Mifflin.

LYNDA HULL's poetry collection, *Star Ledger,* is just out from the University of Iowa Press. She lives in Chicago.

T.R. HUMMER is editor of *New England Review* and lives in Middlebury, Vermont.

RICHARD JACKSON is the author of *Dismantling Time* (1988). He teaches at the University of Tennessee.

MARK JARMAN's most recent collection is *The Black Riviera* (Wesleyan). He teaches at Vanderbilt University.

HA JIN is from mainland China. This is his first story published in English and it won the 1991 Agni Fiction Prize.

MARY KARR's next book, *The Devil's Tour*, will soon appear from New Directions. She teaches at Syracuse University and was a Bunting Fellow at Radcliffe.

CAROLYN KIZER won the 1985 Pulitzer Prize for her poetry collection, *Yin*. She was last year's co-editor of poetry for the Pushcart Prize. She is the recipient of the Frost Medal from the Poetry Society of America.

NORMAN LAVERS holds 1991 fellowships from the Arkansas Arts Council and the National Endowment for the Arts. He lives in Jonesboro, Arkansas.

GRETCHEN LEGLER is at work on *A Sportswoman's Notebook*, a collection of essays about human relationships and the natural world. She lives in St. Paul.

PHILIP LEVINE is a former poetry co-editor of this series. He is the author of several poetry collections. This essay was the keynote address at a recent John Berryman Conference.

LARRY LEVIS's most recent poetry collection is *The Widening Spell of Leaves*. He lives in Salt Lake City.

JAMES LINVILLE is the managing editor of *The Paris Review* and a former editor of *The Harriton Forum*.

WILLIAM MATTHEWS teaches at the City University of New York. His most recent book is *Curiosities*, a collection of essays from the University of Michigan Press.

CAMPBELL MCGRATH worked as a pig farmer, a snake handler, a gandy dancer, a cocktail waiter and an astronaut, he informs us. His poetry has appeared in *Antaeus, Big Wednesday*, and *Caliban*

KAREN MINTON is a native of Georgia. She recently returned there after eleven years in Alaska.

SUSAN MOON is the author of *The Life And Letters of Tofu Roshe* (1988). She lives in Berkeley, California, teaches at St Mary's College, and is the editor of *Turning Wheel*.

CAROL MUSKE is the author of *Dear Digby* and *Applause* (1989). She teaches at the University of Southern California.

SIGRID NUNEZ was the recipient of a 1990 GE Foundation Award for younger writers. She lives in New York City.

ED OCHESTER is the author of two books from Carnegie-Mellon Press. He lives near Pittsburgh.

SHARON OLDS teaches at New York University and Goldwater Hospital for the physically disabled. Her next collection is *The Father*, soon out from Knopf.

JANET PEERY won a 1992 NEA fellowship. Her work has appeared in *New Virginia Review, Black Warrior Review, Quarterly West* and elsewhere.

FRED PFEIL lives in Seattle. He has published work in *Georgia Review, Fiction International* and *Sewanee Review*.

STANLEY PLUMLY's poetry collection, *Boy On The Step*, is now available from Ecco Press. His *Out-of-the-Body-Travel* was nominated for an NBCC Award.

FRANCINE PROSE is the author most recently of the novel *Primitive People*. She is currently a Guggenheim Fellow and lives in upstate New York.

ALBERTO ALVARO RIOS is Professor of English at Arizona State University. His most recent book is *Teodoro Luna's Two Kisses*.

PATTIANN ROGERS has published recently in *TriQuarterly, Georgia Review, New England Review, Missouri Review* and *Prairie Schooner*. Her fourth book is *Splitting and Binding*.

R. A. SASAKI lives in Berkeley, California. "The Loom" is part of her collection *The Loom And Other Stories* (Graywolf Press.)

PERDITA SCHAFFNER's essays have appeared in *Grand Street, Paideuma*, and *Iowa Review*. She has written several introductory essays for the re-published works of her mother, the poet H. D.

LAURIE SHECK's *Io At Night* was published by Knopf in 1990. She was a 1991–92 Guggenheim Fellow.

CHARLES SIMIC lives in Strafford, New Hampshire. He is the author of *Selected Poems* (Braziller, 1989).

GARY SOTO's sixth book of poems, *Home Course in Religion,* is out from Chronicle Books. An essay collection is available from Dell.

SHARON SHEEHE STARK is the author of a collection of stories and a novel (Morrow). She has been featured in O'Henry and Best American Short Story collections.

GERALD STERN teaches at The Writers' Workshop, University of Iowa and is the author of several poetry collections. He is a former poetry co-editor of this series.

ALEXANDER THEROUX is the author of three novels. His most recent book is *The Lollipop Trollops and Other Poems.*

MARY MICHAEL WAGNER's story is her first in print. She lives in San Francisco.

STEVE WATKINS has recently completed work on his first novel, *Something With Wings.* His work has appeared in *Quarterly West, Crescent Review,* and elsewhere.

ELIOT WEINBERGER's essays are collected in *Works On Paper* and *Outside Stories* (both from New Directions). He has translated work by Octavio Paz, Vicente Huidobro and Xavier Villaurrutia.

LIZA WIELAND's first novel, *The Names of The Lost,* is due out soon from Southern Methodist University Press. Her work has appeared in *Ploughshares, Missouri Review* and elsewhere.

C. K. WILLIAMS is the author of five poetry collections including *Flesh and Blood* (1987) winner of the National Book Critics Circle Award for poetry.

CHARLES WRIGHT's *The World of The Ten Thousand Things: Poems 1980–1990* was recently published by Farrar, Straus and Giroux. He teaches at The University of Virginia.

ROBERT WRIGLEY lives in Idaho. His most recent book is *What My Father Believed* (University of Illinois, 1991).

GARY YOUNG is editor of Greenhouse Review Press. Copper Beech Press published his poetry collection, *The Dream of A Moral Life,* in 1990.

PAUL ZIMMER directs the University of Iowa Press. His most recent poetry collection is *The Great Bird of Love* (University of Illinois Press).

CONTRIBUTING SMALL PRESSES

(These presses made or received nominations for this edition of *The Pushcart Prize*. See the *International Directory of Little Magazines and Small Presses*, Dustbooks, Box 1056, Paradise, CA 95969, for subscription rates, manuscript requirements and a complete international listing of small presses).

A

ABS Press, 12 N. Union St., Lambertville, NJ 08530 (Alpha Beat Soup)
Adventure Bus. Systems, POB 26, Angels Camp, CA 95222
Agni. Boston Univ., 236 Bay State Rd. Boston, MA 02215
Ahsahta Press, Boise St. Univ. 1910 Univ. Dr., Boise, ID 83725
Alabama Literary Review, 253 Smith Hall, Troy St. Univ., Troy, AL 36082
Alaska Quarterly Review, Univ. of Alaska, Anchorage, AK 99508
Alice James Books, 23 Richdale Ave, Cambridge, MA 02140
Amador Publishers, POB 12335, Albuquerque, NM 87195
Ambergris, POB 29919 Cincinnati, OH 45209
American Poetry Review, 1721 Walnut St., Philadelphia, PA 19103
American Scholar, 1811 Q Street NW, Washington, DC 20009
The American Voice, 332 W. Broadway, Ste. 1215, Louisville, KY 40202
Ander Publications, 202 View Pointe Ln, La Grange, GA 30240
Another Chicago Magazine, 3709 N, Kenmore, Chicago, IL 60613
Antaeus, 100 W. Broad St., Hopewell, ND 08525
Antietam Review, 82 W. Washington St., Hagerstown, MD 21740
The Antioch Review, POB 148, Yellow Springs, OH 45387
Apalachee Quarterly, POB 20106, Tallahassee, FL 32316
Aralia Press, 928 Marie Rochele Dr, West Chester, PA 19382
Artful Dodge, Eng. Dept. College of Wooster, Wooster, OH 44691
Ascension Publishing, POB 3001, Burbank, CA 91508
Ascent, POB 967, Urbana, IL 61801
Asylum, POB 6203, Santa Maria, CA 93456
The Atlantic Advocate, POB 3370, Fredericton, NB E3B 5A2 *CANADA*
Avec, POB 1059, Penngrove, CA 94951

B

Bamboo Ridge Press, POB 61781, Honolulu. HI 69839
Beloit Poetry Journal, RFD 2, Box 154, Ellsworth, ME 04605
Bennett & Kitchel, POB 4422, E. Lansing, MI 48826
Berwick Publ. Co., 501 Spinnaker Ln, Ft. Collins, CO 80525
The Bilingual Review, Hispanic Research Ctr, Tempe, AZ 85287
Black American Literature Forum, Indiana St. Univ, Terre Haute, IN 47809
Blue Heron Publishing Inc, 24450 NW Hansen Rd, Hillsboro, OR 97124
Blue Light, Red Light, 496 Hudson St., Ste. F42, NY-NY 10014
Bluestem Press, Eng. Dept. Emporia St. Univ, Emporia, KS 66801
Bluestone Press, POB 1186, Hampshire College, Amherst, MA 01002
BOA Editions, Ltd, 92 Park Ave, Brockport, NY 14420
Bomb, 594 Broadway, Ste. 1002A, NY-NY 10012
Borderline, 425 W. Meyer, Kansas City, MO 64113
Bottom Dog Press, Firelands College, Huron, OH 44839
Boulevard, 2400 Chestnut St., Apt. 2208, Phila., PA 19103
Breakthrough Magazine, 204 Millbank Dr. SW, Calgary, Alberta, CAN T24 2H9
Brick Books, Box 38, Sta. B, London, Ont. N6A 4V3 CAN
The Bridge, 14050 Vernon St, Oak Park, MI 48237
Broken Moon Press, POB 24585, Seattle, WA 98124
Burning Deck, 71 Elmgrove Ave, Providence, RI 02906

C

Café Solo, Box 2814, Atascadero, CA 93422
Calliope, Creative Writing Prog, Roger Williams College, Bristol, RI 02809
Calyx, POB B, Corvallis, OR 97339
Canio's Editions, POB 1962, Sag Harbor, NY 11963
Caravan Press, 15445 Ventura Blvd, Ste. 279, Sherman Oaks, CA 91403
The Caribbean Writer, Univ. of the Virgin Islds, RR02, Box 10,000, Kingshill,
    St. Croix, Virgin Islands, 00850
Center Press, 309 Johnson St, Santa Fe, NM 87501
Chaminade Literary Review, Univ. of Hawaii, 3140 Waialae Ave, Honolulu, HI
    96816
The Chattahooche Review, DeKalb College, 2101 Wonack Blvd, Dunwoody, GA
    30338
Chelsea, Box 5880, Gr. Cent. Sta, NY-NY 10163
Chelsea Green Publ. Co, POB 130, Post Mills, VT 05058
Cheops Books, 977 Seminole Trail, Ste. 179, Charlottesville, VA 22901
Chicago Review, 5801 S. Kenwood, Chicago, IL 60637
Cimarron Review, Okla. St. Univ. Stillwater, OK 74078
Cincinnati Poetry Review, Eng. Dept. 069, Univ. of Cin., Cincinnati, OH 45221
The Clamshell Press, 160 Calif. Ave, Santa Rosa, CA 95405
Cleveland St. Univ. Poetry Center, Eng. Dept., Rhodes Tower, Cleveland, OH
    44115
Cliffhanger Press, POB 29527, Oakland, CA 94604
Coach House Press, 401 Huron St, Toronto, Ont M5S 2G5 CAN
Coffeehouse Quarterly, POB 15123, San Luis Obispo, CA 93406
Colorado Review, Eng. Dept. Colo. St. Univ, Ft. Collins, CO 80523
Comforter Publishing, 515 Crocker Ave, Daly City, CA 94014
Concho River Review, Eng. Dept, Angelo St. Univ, San Angelo, TX 76909
Confrontations, Eng. Dept, Long Island Univ, Brookville, NY 11548
Conjunctions, 33 West 9th St., New York, NY 10011
Copper Canyon Press, Box 271, Port Townsend, WA 98368
Cornerstone Magazine, 939 W. Wilson, Chicago, IL 60640

Cottonwood, Box J, Kansas Union, Univ. of Kansas, Lawrence, KS 66045
Crab Creek Review, 4462 Whitman N, Seattle, WA 98103
Crazy Horse, Eng. Dept., Univ. of Ar., Little Rock, AR 72204
Cream City Review, VW-Milwaukee, POB 413, Milwaukee, WI 53201
Creeping Bent, 433 W. Market St, Bethlehem, PA 18018
The Critic, The Thos. More Assoc, 205 W. Monroe, 6th Pl., Chicago, IL 60606

D

Dalkey Archive Press, Illinois State University, Normal, IL 61761
Damascus Works, 1101 N. Calvert St, #1605, Baltimore, MD 21202
Dawn Rose Press, 12470 Fiori Ln, Sebastopol, CA 95472
W. S. Dawson & Co., POB 62823, Virginia Beach, VA 23462
Delos, POB 2880, College Park, MD 20741
Denver Quarterly, Eng. Dept. Univ. of Denver, Denver, CO 80208
Diarist's Journal, 102 W. Water St, Lansford, PA 18232
Doublestar Press, 1718 Sherman #205, Evanston, IL 60201
Dragon's Teeth Press, El Dorado Nat'l Forest, Georgetown, CA 95634
Drew Blood Press Ltd, 3410 First St., Riverside, CA 92401
Druid Books, POB 231, Ephraim, WI 54211
Drumm, Chris (Books), POB 445, Polk City, IA 50226

E

Ecco Press; see Antaeus
18th Moon, Eng. Dept. SUNY, Albany, NY 12222
the eleventh muse, POB 2413, Colorado Springs, CO 80901
Embers, Box 404, Guilford, CT 06437
Emerald City Review, POB 4724, Louisville, KY 40202
The EOTU Group, 1810 N. State, #115, Boise, ID 83702
Epoch, 251 Goldwinsmith Hall, Cornell Univ., Ithaca, NY 14853
The Equator, 509 Cultural Center, 509 Ellis St, San Francisco, CA 94109
Event, POB 2503, New Westminster, BC CAN V3L 5B2
Exit 13 Magazine, 22 Oakwood St., Fanwood, NJ 07023

F

The Family Therapy Networker, 7705 13th St. NW, Washington, DC 20012
Fiction, Eng. Dept, City College of NY, Convent Ave at 138th St, NY-NY 10031
Fiction International, English Dept., San Diego State Univ., San Diego, CA 92182
Fine Madness, POB 31138, Seattle, WA 98103
Firebrand Books, 141 The Commons, Ithaca, NY 14850
Five Fingers Review, 853 Greenwich St., San Francisco, CA 94133
The Florida Review, Eng. Dept. Univ. of Central Fla., Box 25000, Orlando, FL 32816
Flume Press, 4 Casita, Chico, CA 95926
For Poets Only. POB 4855, Schenectady, NY 12384
The Formalist, 525 S. Rotherwood, Evansville, IN 47714
Free Focus, 224 82nd St. Apt. #2, Brooklyn, NY 11209
Free Lunch, POB 7647 Laguna Niguel, CA 92607
Frogpond, 87 Bayard Ave, North Haven, CT 06473
Fromm Int'l Publ. Corp., 560 Lexington Ave, NY-NY 10022

G

Galileo Press, 15201 Wheeler Ln, Sparks, MD 21152
Gamut, 1218 Fenn Tower, 1983 E. 24th St, Cleveland, OH 44115
The Georgia Review, Univ. of GA, Athens, GA 30602
Gettysburg Review, 249 N. Washington St, Gettysburg, PA 17325
Golden Isis Press, 23233-105 Saticoy St, Ste 137, West Hills, CA 91304
Graham House Review, Box 5000, Hamilton, NY 13346
Grand Street, POB 2140, Knoxville, IA 50198
Grasslands Review, POB 13706, Denton, TX 76203
Graywolf Press, 2402 Univ. Ave., Ste. 203, St. Paul, MN 55114
Great Stream Review, Box 66, Lycoming College, Williamsport, PA 17701
Green Mountains Review, Johnson State College, Johnson, VT 05656
Greenhouse Review, 3965 Bonny Doon Rd, Santa Cruz, CA 95060
Green's Magazine, Box 3236, Regina, Sask., S4P 3H1, CAN
The Greensboro Review, Eng. Dept., 134 McIver, UNCG, Greensboro, NC
  27412

H

Haight-Ashberry Literary Jour., 558 Joost Ave, San Francisco, CA 94127
Harp-Strings, 310 S. Adams St, Beverly Hills, FL 32665
Hayden's Ferry Review, Matthews Ctr, Ariz. St. Univ, Tempe, AZ 85287
Haypenny Press, 211 New St., W. Paterson, NJ 07424
Heatherstone Press, POB 215, Whately, MA 01093
Heaven Bone, POB 486 Chester, NY 10918
Helicon Nine, POB 22412, Kansas City, MO 64113
Helikon Press, 120 W. 71st St, NY-NY 10023
Hermitage, POB 410, Tenafly, NJ 07670
Heyday Books, POB 9145, Berkeley, CA 94709
High Plains Literary Review, 180 Adams St. Ste 250, Denver, CO 80206
Hob-Nob, 994 Nissley Rd, Lancaster, PA 17601
Hubbub, 5344 S.E. 38th Ave, Portland, OR 97202
The Hudson Review, 684 Park Ave, NY NY 10021
Hurricane Alice, 207 Lind Hall, 207 Church St. SE, Minneapolis, MN 55455

I

Icarus, 29 E. 21st St., NY-NY 10010
Igneus Press, 310 W. Amherst Rd, Bedford, NH 03110
Illinois Writers Review, Eng. Dept, Illinois St. Univ, Normal, IL 61761
Infinity ∞ Limited, POB 2713, Castro Valley, CA 94546
Invisible City / Red Hill Press, POB 2853, San Francisco, CA 94126
The Iowa Review, Univ. of Iowa, Iowa City, IA 52242
Iowa Woman, POB 2938, Waterloo, IA 50704

J

The Jacaranda Review, Eng. Dept. Univ. of Calif., Los Angeles, CA 90024
The Journal, Eng. Dept., Ohio St. Univ, 164 W. 17th Ave, Columbus, OH
  43210
Journal of New Jersey Poets, County College of Morris, Rte. 10 7 Center Grove
  Rd, Randolph, NJ 07869

K

Kaimana, Hawaii Literary Arts Council, POB 11213, Moiliili Sta., Honolulu, HI 96828
Kalliope, Fla. Community College, 3939 Roosevelt Blvd, Jacksonville, FL 32205
Kansas Quarterly, Eng. Dept, Kansas St. Univ, Manhattan, KS 66506
Karamu, Eng. Dept, East Illinois Univ, Charleston, IL 61920
Kelsey Review, Mercer Comm. College, POB B, Trenton, NJ 08690
Kelsey Street Press, POB 9235, Berkeley, CA 94708
The Kenyon Review, Kenyon College, Gambier, OH 48022

L

Laurel Review, Northwest MO St. Univ. Maryville, MO 64468
The Ledge, 64–65 Cooper Ave, Glendale, NY 11385
LIPS, POB 1345, Montclair, NJ 07042
The Literary Review, Fairleigh Dickinson Univ, Madison, NJ 07940
The Little Magazine, Eng. Dept, SUNY, Albany, NY 12222
Long Shot, POB 6231, Hoboken, NJ 07030
The Long Story, 11 Kingston St, No. Andover, MA 01845
Lucidity, Rte 2, Bx 94, Eureka Springs, AR 92632
Luna Bisconte Prods, 137 Leland Ave. Columbus, OH 43214
Lynx, POB 169, Toutle, WA 98649
Lynx House Press, c/o C. Howell, 1326 West St, Emporia, KS 66801

M

The MacGuffin, Schoolcraft College, 18600 Haggerty Rd., Livonia, MI 48152
Mad River, Dept. of Philosophy, Wright St. Univ., Dayton, OH 45435
The Magazine of Speculative Poetry, POB 971, Stevens Point, WI 54481
The Malahat Review, Univ. of Victoria, POB 3045, Victoria, B.C. CAN V8W 3P4
Manhattan Review, 440 Riverside Dr, NY-NY 10027
Mānoa, Univ. of Hawaii, 1733 Donaghho Rd, Honolulu, HI 96822
Massachusetts Review, Univ. of Mass., Amherst, MA 01003
McFarland & Co., Publrs, Box 611, Jefferson, NC 28640
Mercury Publ'g Co, 3319 Emerson Ave S., Mnpls, MN 55408
Mho & Mho, Box 33135, San Diego, CA 92103
Micah Publications, 255 Humphrey St, Marblehead, MA 01947
Michigan Quarterly Review, Univ. of Mich., 3032 Rackham Bldg, Ann Arbor, MI 48109
Mid-American Review, Eng. Dept. Bowling Green State Univ, Bowling Green, OH 43403
Midwest Farmer's Market, POB 172, Galesburg, IL 61402
Milkweed Editions, POB 3226, Mnpls, MN 55403
Mind Matters Review, 2040 Polk St, Box 234, San Francisco, CA 94109
Mississippi Review, Box 5144, Southern Sta., Hattiesburg, MS 39406
The Missouri Review, 1507 Hillcrest, Univ. of Missouri, Columbia, MO 65211
Momentum Books Ltd, 210 Collingwood, Ste. 106, Ann Arbor, MI 48103

N

Naiad Press, Inc, POB 10543, Tallahassee, FL 32302
Nebo, Eng. Dept. Arkansas Tech. Univ, Russellville, AR 72801

Nebraska Review, Creative Writing Prog, Univ. of Neb., Omaha, NE 68182
New American Writing, 2920 W. Pratt, Chicago, IL 60645
New England Review, Middlebury College, Middlebury, VT 05753
New Letters, UMKC, 5100 Rockhill Rd, Kansas City, MO 64110
New Poets Series, Inc., 541 Piccadilly Rd, Towson, MD 21204
the new renaissance, 9 Heath Rd, Arlington, MA 02174
New Rivers Press, 420 N. 5th St, Ste. 910, Mnpls, MN 55401
Night Roses, POB 393, Prospect Heights, IL 60070
Nightshade Press, POB 76, Ward Hill, Troy, ME 04987
The Nihilistic Review, POB 1074, S. Sioux City, NE 68776
Nimrod Arts & Humanities Council of Tulsa, 2210 S. Main, Tulsa, OK 74114
The Nocturnal Lyric, Box 2602, Pasadena, CA 91102
North American Review, Univ. of Northern Iowa, Cedar Falls, IA 50614
North Dakota Quarterly, POB 8237, Univ. of No. Dak., Grand Forks, ND
   58202
The North Stone Review, D Sta., Box 14098, Mnpls, MN 55414
Northern Lights, Inc., 493 College Ave, Orono, ME 04473
Northwest Review, 369 PLC, Univ. of Ore., Eugene, OR 97403
Now and Then, Box 70556, East Tenn. St. Univ., Johnson City, TN 37614

O

O.A.R.S. 21 Rockland Rd, Weare, NH 03281
Ocean County Poets Collective, POB 1342, Pt. Pleasant Beach, NJ 08742
The Ohio Review, Ellis Hall, Ohio Univ, Athens, OH 45701
Old Red Kimono, Box 1864, Floyd College, Rome, GA 30162
Omega Cat Press, 904 Old Town Ct., Cupertino, CA 95014
The Ontario Review, 9 Honey Brook Dr., Princeton, NJ 08540
Orchises Press, POB 20602, Alexandria, VA 22320
Osiris, Box 297, Deerfield, MA 01842
Other Voices, Eng. Dept., Univ. of Ill, Box 4348, Chicago, IL 60680
Ox Head Press, Rte. 3, Box 136, Browerville, MN 56438
Oxalis, POB 3993, Kingston, NY 12401
Oxford Magazine, Bachelor Hall, Miami Univ., Oxford, OH 45056

P

The Pacific Review, Eng. Dept., Calif. St. Univ., San Bernardino, CA 92407
Painted Hills Review, POB 494, Davis, CA 95617
Panic Button Press, POB 14318, San Francisco, CA 94114
Panther Press Ltd, POB A44, Wantagh, NY 11793
Papier-Mache, 795 Via Manzana, Watsonville, CA 95076
The Paris Review, 541 E. 72nd St., NY-NY 10021
Parnassus, POB 1384, Forest Park, GA 30051
Partisan Review, 236 Bay State Rd, Boston, MA 02215
The Pegasus Review, POB 134, Flanders, NJ 07836
Perceptions, 1530 Phillips, Missoula, MT 59802
Persephone Press, 22-B Pine Lake Dr., Whispering Pines, NC 28327
Phoebe, Eng. Dept, George Mason Univ, Fairfax, VA 22030
The Pikestaff Forum, POB 127, Normal, IL 61761
Pine Grove Press, POB 40, Jamesville, NY 13078
Pittsburgh Quarterly, 36 Haberman Ave, Pittsburgh, PA 15211
Ploughshares, 100 Beacon St., Boston, MA 02116
The Plum Review, POB 3557, Wash, D.C. 20007
Poet Lore, see The Writer's Center

Poetic Page, POB 71192, Madison Heights, MI 48071
Poetpourri, Box 3737, Taft Rd', Syracuse, NY 13220
Poetry, 60 West Walton St., Chicago, IL 60610
Poetry Harbor, 530 E. Skyline Pkwy, Duluth, MN 55805
Poetry Northwest, University of Washington, Seattle, WA 98105
Poets On, 29 Loring Ave, Mill Valley, CA 94941
Portmanteau Editions, POB 159, Littleton, NH 03561
Potpourri Publications Co., POB 8278 Prairie Village, KS 66208
Prairie Fire Press Inc, 423-100 Arthur St, Winnipeg, MB R3B 1H3 CAN
Prairie Schooner, 201 Andrews, Univ. of Neb., Lincoln, NE 68588
Primavera, 700 E. 61st St, Box 37-7547, Chicago, IL 60637
Product, SS Box 5144, Hattiesburg, MS 39406
The Prospect Review, 557 10th St, Brooklyn, NY 11215
Provincetown Arts, POB 35, Provincetown, MA 02657
Puckerbrush Press, 76 Main St., Orono, ME 04473
Peurto del Sol, Creative Writing Ctr, Box 3E, N.M. St. Univ, Las Cruces, NM
  88083

Q

Q.E.D. Press, 155 Cypress St., Ft. Bragg, CA 95437
The Quarterly, 201 3. 50th St, NY-NY 10022
Quarterly West, 317 Olpin Union, Univ. of Utah, Salt Lake City, UT 84112

R

Raccoon, POB 11327, Memphis, TN 38111
Raritan, Rutgers Univ, 31 Mine St, New Brunswick, NJ 08903
Red Dirt, 1630 30th St., Ste. A 307, Boulder, CA 80301
Red Dust, POB 630, NY-NY 10028
Redneck Review, 2919 N. Downer Ave, Milwaukee, WI 53211
Review of Contemporary Fiction, see Dalkey Archive Press
Ritz Publishing, 202 W. 5th Ave, Ritzville, WA 99169
Riverside Quarterly, 807 Walters, #107, Lake Charles, LA 70605
Rowboat, MFA Writing Prog., Univ. of Mass., Amherst, MA 01003

S

Samisdat, 456 Monroe Trnpke, Monroe, CT 06468
San Diego Poets Press, POB 8638, LaJolla, CA 92038
Sandhills Press, 219 S. 19th St., Ord, NE 68862
Santa Monica Review, Santa Monica College, Santa Monica, CA 90405
Saturday Press, POB 884, Upper Montclair, NJ 07043
Schmaga, POB 8062, Vallejo, CA 94590
Scripsit, Wallace 217, East Ky. Univ, Richmond, KY 40475
The Seal Press, 3131 Western Ave, #410, Seattle, WA 98121
Sedna Press, 5522 Cope St, Anchorage, AK 99518
Seems, Lakeland College, POB 359, Sheboygan, WI 53082
Seneca Review, Hobart & Wm. Smith College, Geneva, NY 14456
Sheep Meadow Press, POB 1345, Riverdale, NY 10471
Shenandoah, Box 722, Lexington, VA 24450
Silver Wings, Box 1000, Pearblossom, CA 93553
Silverleaf Press, Inc., POB 70189, Seattle, WA 98107
Simple Cooking, POB 88, Steuben, ME 04680

Sing Heavenly Muse!, POB 13320, Mnpls. MN 55414
Singing Horse Press, POB 40034, Phila, PA 19106
Singular Speech Press, 10 Hilltop Dr, Canton, CT 06019
Sisyphus, 8 Asticou Rd, Boston, MA 02130
Sites, 446 W. 20 St., NY-NY 10011
Skylark, Purdue Univ. Calumet, 2200 169th St, Hammond, IN 46323
Snake Nation Press, 110 #2 W. Force St, Valdosta, GA 31601
Somersault Press, POB 1428, El Cerrito, CA 94530
Sonora Review, Eng. Dept. Univ. of Ariz, Tucson, AZ 85721
South Coast Poetry Journal, Eng, Dept, Calif. St. Univ, Fullerton, CA 92634
South Florida Poetry Review, Oak Hollow Rd., Bullard, TX 75757
Southern Calif. Anthology. Prof. Writ. Prog., WPH 404, USC, Los Angeles, CA 90089
The Southern Review, 43 Allen Hall, Louisiana State Univ., Baton Rouge, LA 70803
Sou'wester Magazine, Eng. Dept., So. Illinois Univ, Edwardsville, IL 62026
Sow's Ear Press, 245 McDowell St, Bristol, TN 37620
Sparrow Press, 103 Waldron St, W. Lafayette, IN 47906
Spear Shaker Review, POB 308, Napanoch, NY 12458
Spoon River Quarterly, Eng. Dept, Ill St. Univ, Norman, IL 61761
St. Martin's Press, 175 Fifth Ave, NY-NY 10010
Wallace Stevens Journal, Clarkson Univ, Potsdam, NY 13699
Still Waters Press, 112 W. Duerer St, Galloway, NJ 08201
Story, 1507 Dana Ave, Cincinnati, OH 45207
Suburban Wilderness Press, 1619 Jefferson St, Duluth, MN 55812
Sucarnochee Review, Sta. 22, Livingston Univ, Livingston, AL 35470
Sun Dog, FL. St. Univ, 406 Williams Bldg, Tallahassee, FL 32306

T

Tabula rasa, 4 Marshall Dr., Camp Hill, PA 17011
Talisman, Box 1117, Hoboken, NJ 07030
Tampa Review, Univ. of Tampa, POB 19F, Tampa, FL 33606
Tar River Poetry, Eng. Dept. E. Carolina Univ, Greenville, NC 27858
Tender Buttons, Box 1290, Cooper Sta, NY-NY 10276
III Publishing, POB 170363, San Francisco, CA 94117
Threepenny Review, POB 9131, Berkeley, CA 94709
Tikkun, 5100 Lerna St., Oakland, CA 94619
Times Change Press, POB 1380, Ojai, CA 93023
Toad Highway, Eng. Dept. Bowling Green State Univ, Bowling Green, OH 43403
Translation, 412 Dodge Columbia Univ, NY-NY 10027
TriQuarterly, Northwestern Univ, 2020 Ridge Ave, Evanston, IL 60208
True Directions, 2215 R Market St, Box 115, San Francisco, CA 94114
Tucumcari Literary Review, 3108 W. Bellevue Ave, Los Angeles, CA 90026
Turning Wheel, c/o Buddhrst Peace Fellowship, P.O. Box 4650, Berkeley, CA 94904
Turtle Point Press, Tuxedo Park, NY 10987

U

Union Steel Review, POB 19078, Alexandria, VA 22320
University of No. Texas Press, POB 13856, Denton, TX 76203
University of Phoenix Press, POB 52069, Phoenix, AZ 85072
University of Wisconsin Press, 114 N. Murray St, Madison, WI 53715

V

Vandeloecht's Fiction Magazine, POB 515, Montross, VA 22520
Verve, POB 3205, Simi Valley, CA 93093
The Vincent Brothers Review, 4566 No. Circle, Mad River Twnshp, Dayton,
   OH 45424
Voices in Italian Americana, For. Lang. & Lits., Purdue Univ, West Lafayette,
   IN 47907

W

Warthog Press, 29 S. Valley Rd, West Orange, NJ 07052
Washington Review, Box 50132, Wash. D.C. 20091
Washington Writers' Pub. House, POB 15271, Wash. D.C. 20003
Wayland Press, 675 S. Sherman, Denver, CO 80209
We Press, POB 1503, Santa Cruz, CA 95061
West Branch, Eng. Dept., Bucknell Univ, Lewisburg, PA 17837
Western Humanities Review, Univ. of Utah, Salt Lake City, UT 84112
Whetstone, Barrington Area Arts Counc., POB 1266, Barrington, IL 60011
Whispering Wind, 8009 Wales St, New Orleans, LA 70126
White Cross Press, Rte. 1 Box 592, Granger, TX 76530
Willamette River Books, POB 605, Troutdale, OR 97060
The William & Mary Review, POB 8795, Campus Ctr, Williamsburg, VA 23187
Willow Springs Magazine, MS-1, E.W.U., Cheney, WA 99004
The Windless Orchard, Eng. Dept, Purdue Univ, Ft. Wayne, IN 46805
Wisconsin Academy Review, 1922 Univ. Ave, Madison, WI 53705
The Wise Woman, 2441 Cordova St, Oakland, CA 94602
Witness, Oakland Comm. College, 27055 Orchard Lake Rd, Farmington Hills,
   MI 48334
Woodbine House, 5615 Fishers Ln, Rockville, MD 20852
The Worcester Review, 6 Chatham St, Worcester, MA 01609
The Word Works, POB 42164, Wash. DC 20015
Words of Wisdom, 612 Front St, Glendora, NJ 08029
The Wormwood Review, POB 4698, Stockton, CA 95204
Writ Magazine, Two Sussex Ave, Toronto, Ont M5S 1J5 CAN
The Writer's Center, 7815 Old Georgetown Rd, Bethesda, MD 20814
Writers Forum. Univ. of Colo., POB 7150, Colorado Springs, CO 80933

Y

Yellow Silk, POB 6374, Albany, CA 94706

Z

Zeitgeist Press, 4368 Piedmont Ave, Oakland, CA 94611
Zirlinson Publishing, 1447 Treat Blvd, Walnut Creek, CA 94596
ZYZZYVA, 41 Sutter, Ste. 1400, San Francisco, CA 94104

INDEX

The following is a listing in alphabetical order by author's last name of works reprinted in the first seventeen *Pushcart Prize* editions.

Abbott, Lee K.—X (fiction)   XI, 317
    —THE ERA OF GREAT NUMBERS (fiction)   XIII, 308
Abish, Walter—PARTING SHOT (fiction)   III, 261
Acker, Kathy—NEW YORK CITY IN 1979 (fiction)   VI, 396
Ackerman, Diane—ZÖE (poetry)   VIII, 379
Adams, Alice—MOLLY'S DOG (fiction)   XI, 357
Adisa, Opal Palmer—DUPPY GET HER (fiction)   XII, 277
Ai—ICE (poetry)   IV, 81
Alcosser, Sandra—APPROACHING AUGUST (poetry)   XIII, 134
Aleixandre, Vicente—THE WALTZ (poetry)   III, 106
Aleshire, Joan—TO CHARLOTTE BRONTË (poetry)   XIII, 379
Alfau, Felipe—THE STUFF MEN ARE MADE OF (fiction)   XVI, 218
Allman, John—MARCUS GARVEY ARRESTED AT THE
        125TH STREET STATION (poetry)   VIII, 210
Anania, Michael—OF LIVING BELFRY AND RAMPART:
        ON AMERICAN LITERARY MAGAZINES SINCE 1950
        (nonfiction)   V, 138
Anderson, Jack—CITY JOYS (poetry)   I, 374
Anderson, Jon—LIVES OF THE SAINTS, PART I (poetry)   II, 73
Andrews, Bruce—KEY LARGO (poetry)   III, 510
Antin(ova), Eleanor(a)—A ROMANTIC INTERLUDE (fiction)   VI, 289
Appleman, Philip—THE TRICKLE DOWN THEORY OF
        HAPPINESS (poetry)   IX, 203
Ascher/Straus Collective—EVEN AFTER A MACHINE IS
        DISMANTLED IT CONTINUES TO OPERATE,
        WITH OR WITHOUT PURPOSE (fiction)   III, 402
Ashberry, John—ALL KINDS OF CARESSES (poetry)   II, 257
Atkinson, Jennifer—THE DOGWOOD TREE (poetry)   XIII, 304
        —IMAGINING THE OCEAN (nonfiction)   XIV, 425
Atlas, James—from THE GREAT PRETENDER (nonfiction)   X, 260
Atwood, Margaret—THE MAN FROM MARS (fiction)   III, 490
Auster, Paul—IN THE COUNTRY OF LAST THINGS (fiction)   XI, 278
Baber, Asa—TRANQUILITY BASE (fiction)   V, 227
Baca, Jimmy Santiago—43 (poetry)   XIV, 153
Bachman, Ayla Nutku—BLOOD BROTHER (fiction)   XVII, 74
Bailey, Jane—LATE TRACK (poetry)   I, 274
Baker, David—SNOW FIGURE (poetry)   XVII, 411
Baker, Donald—DYING IN MASSACHUSETTS (poetry)   XV, 389

Baker, Will—FIELD OF FIRE (fiction)   XV, 161
Balaban, John—DOING GOOD (nonfiction)   III, 445
     —FOR THE MISSING IN ACTION (poetry)   XV, 486
Ball, Bo—WISH BOOK (fiction)   V, 124
     —HEART LEAVES (fiction)   X, 278
Banks, Russell—SARAH COLE: A TYPE OF LOVE STORY (fiction)   X, 362
Baranczak, Stanislaw—IF PORCELAIN, THEN ONLY THE
     KIND (poetry)   VII, 393
Barnes, Jim—THE CHICAGO ODYSSEY (poetry)   V, 374
Barnes, Julian—PLAYING CHESS WITH ARTHUR KOESTLER
     (nonfiction)   XIV, 140
Barnes, Yolanda—RED LIPSTICK (fiction)   XVII, 63
Barthelme, Donald—NOT KNOWING (nonfiction)   XI, 23
Barthelme, Steven—HUSH, HUSH (fiction)   XVII, 223
Bass, Rick—WHERE THE SEA USED TO BE (fiction)   XIII, 3
     —WEJUMPKA (fiction)   XV, 451
Batey, Kristine—LOT'S WIFE (poetry)   IV, 129
Baxter, Charles—HARMONY OF THE WORLD (fiction)   VII, 181
     —WESTLAND (fiction)   XIV, 212
     —THE DONALD BARTHELME BLUES
     (nonfiction)   XVI, 363
Beauvais, John H.—AUTUMN EVENING (poetry)   I, 352
Becker, Jillian—THE STENCH (fiction)   VIII, 309
Bedway, Barbara—DEATH AND LEBANON (fiction)   VII, 118
Bell, Marvin—FIVE AND TEN (nonfiction)   V, 432
     —THREE PROPOSITIONS, HOOEY, DEWEY, AND
     LOONY (nonfiction)   XVI, 83
Bellow, Saul—SOME QUESTIONS AND ANSWERS (nonfiction)   I, 295
Benítez-Rojo, Antonio—HEAVEN AND EARTH (fiction)   X, 231
Bennett, John—BEAUTIFUL PEOPLE (poetry)   I, 403
Bentley, Nelson—THIRD DUNGENESS SPIT
     APOCALYPSE (poetry)   XVI, 286
Berg, Stephen—VARIATIONS ON THE MOUND OF CORPSES
     IN THE SNOW (poetry)   I, 144
     —AND THE SCREAM (poetry)   VII, 244
Berger, John—HER SECRETS (nonfiction)   XII, 443
Berger, Suzanne—THE MEAL (poetry)   X, 358
Bergland, Martha—AN EMBARRASSMENT OF ORDINARY
     RICHES (fiction)   XII, 211
Bergman, Susan—ANONYMITY (nonfiction)   XVI, 48
Bernard, Ken—PROLEGOMENA (fiction)   XVII, 136
Berriault, Gina—THE INFINITE PASSION OF EXPECTATION
     (fiction)   V, 360
     —THE ISLAND OF VEN (fiction)   XI, 193
Berrigan, Daniel—CONSOLATION (poetry)   IX, 69
Berry, D. C.—PIER (poetry)   X, 357
Berry, Wendell—STANDING BY WORDS (nonfiction)   VII, 46
     —PROPERTY, PATRIOTISM AND NATIONAL
     DEFENSE (nonfiction)   XI, 81
Bierds, Linda—MID-PLAINS TORNADO (poetry)   XI, 95
Birtha, Becky—JOHNNIERUTH (fiction)   XIII, 138
Blaise, Clark—MEMORIES OF UNHOUSEMENT (nonfiction)   VIII, 121
Blandiana, Ana—DON'T YOU EVER SEE THE BUTTERFLIES
     (poetry)   II, 256
Blei, Norbert—THE GHOST OF SANDBURG'S PHIZZOG (fiction)   XII, 229
Blessing, Richard—TUMOR (poetry)   IX, 272

Bloch, Chana—THREE STUDIES FOR A HEAD OF JOHN
  THE BAPTIST (poetry)   VI, 470
Blumenthal, Michael—STONES (poetry)   V, 358
  —FISH FUCKING (poetry)   IX, 121
Bly, Carol—MY LORD BAG OF RICE (fiction)   VX, 464
Bly, Robert—THE EIGHT STAGES OF TRANSLATION
  (nonfiction)   VIII, 451
Boland, Eavan—THE WOMAN POET: HER DILEMMA (essay) XIII, 336
  —INSCRIPTIONS (poetry)   XVII, 138
Booth, Philip—PROCESSION (poetry)   VIII, 339
  —SHORT DAY (poetry)   XII, 380
Booth, Wayne C.—THE COMPANY WE KEEP: SELF-MAKING
  IN IMAGINATIVE ART, OLD AND NEW (nonfiction) VIII, 57
Boruch, Marianne—MY SON AND I GO SEE HORSES (poetry) XIII, 210
Boston, Bruce—BROKEN PORTRAITURE (fiction) I, 346
Bosworth, David—THE LITERATURE OF AWE (nonfiction) V, 244
Bowden, Michael—MILLER CANYON TRAIL NO. 106 (poetry) XV, 337
Bowles, Jane—THE IRON TABLE (fiction)   III, 521
Bowles, Paul—TANGIER, 1975 (fiction)   XIV, 335
Boyle, T. Coraghessan—CAVIAR (fiction)   IX, 102
  —THE HECTOR QUESADILLA STORY
  (fiction)   X, 203
Brandt, Pamela—L. A. CHILD (fiction)   IX, 351
Bringhurst, Robert—THE STONECUTTER'S HORSES (poetry) IV, 495
Brodkey, Harold—INTRO (fiction)   I, 419
Brodsky, Joseph—LAGOON (poetry)   VI, 69
Bromige, David—ONE SPRING   V, 156
Brondoli, Michael—SHOWDOWN (fiction)   V, 458
Brooks, Gwendolyn—JANE ADDAMS (poetry) XVI, 216
Brown, Clark—A WINTER'S TALE (fiction)   IX, 289
Brown, Rosellen—ONE OF TWO (fiction)   XII, 316
Brown, Wesley—GETTING FREEDOM HIGH (fiction) III, 87
Browne, Michael Dennis—BAD POEMS (poetry) I, 324
  —"TALK TO ME BABY"(poetry)   III, 222
Buckley, Christopher—WHY I'M IN FAVOR OF A NUCLEAR
  FREEZE (poetry)   X, 360
  —APOLOGUES OF WINTER LIGHT (poetry) XV, 449
  —SUN SPOTS (poetry)   XVI, 489
Bukowski, Charles—DOG FIGHT (poetry)   X, 258
Bulatovic-Vib, Vlada—THE SHARK AND THE BUREAUCRAT
  (fiction)   V, 356
Bumpus, Jerry—LOVERS (fiction)   II, 358
Burgin, Richard—NOTES ON MRS. SLAUGHTER (fiction) VII, 464
  —THE VICTIMS (fiction)   XI, 300
Burkard, Michael—DIM MAN, DIM CHILD (poetry) XIII, 306
Burlingame, Robert—SOME RECOGNITION OF THE JOSHUA
  LIZARD (poetry)   III, 356
Burroughs, Franklin—A SNAPPING TURTLE IN JUNE (nonfiction) XIV, 61
Callaghan, Barry—A MOTIVELESS MALIGNANCY (nonfiction) XV, 202
Callaway, Kathy—HEART OF THE GARFISH (poetry) V, 219
Calvino, Italo—THE NAME, THE NOSE (fiction) II, 321
Campbell, Anneke—CRANES (poetry)   X, 224
Cannon, Steve (with Ishmael Reed and Quincy Troupe)—THE
  ESSENTIAL ELLISON (interview)   III, 465
Carew, Jim—THE CARIBBEAN WRITER AND EXILE (nonfiction) V, 287

552

Carlile, Henry—OFF PORT TOWNSEND ONE MONTH BEFORE
    THE ARRIVAL OF THE U.S.S OHIO (poetry)   XI, 38
    —TRAIN WHISTLES IN THE WIND AND RAIN
    (poetry)   XVII, 439
Carruth, Hayden—MENDING THE ABODE (poetry)   II, 505
    —SONG: SO OFTEN, SO LONG I HAVE
    THOUGHT (poetry)   V, 397
    —FOREVER IN THAT YEAR (poetry)   VII, 427
    —PAUL GOODMAN AND THE GRAND
    COMMUNITY (nonfiction)   IX, 410
    —PLAIN SONG (poetry)   XI, 224
    —RAY (poetry)   XVII, 140
Carter, Jared—FOR STARR ATKINSON, WHO DESIGNED
    BOOKS (poetry)   X, 389
Carver, Raymond—SO MUCH WATER SO CLOSE TO HOME
    (fiction)   I, 50
    —WHAT WE TALK ABOUT WHEN WE TALK
    ABOUT LOVE (fiction)   VI, 88
    —A SMALL, GOOD THING (fiction)   VIII, 33
    —CAREFUL (fiction)   IX, 306
Cassady, Carolyn—POOR GOD (nonfiction)   III, 386
Cassens, Denise—GIRL TALK (fiction)   VI, 325
Castle, Sandi—WHAT THE SHADOW KNOWS (fiction)   XIII, 388
Cedering, Siv—UKIYO-E (poetry)   IX, 408
Cervantes, Lorna Dee—MEETING MESCALITO AT OAK HILL
    CEMETERY (poetry)   IV, 183
Chandonnet, F. L.—STORIES (fiction)   XVI, 292
Chapman, Diane—VETERAN'S HEAD (poetry)   I, 305
Cherry, Kelly—WHERE THE WINGED HORSES TAKE OFF
    INTO THE WILD BLUE YONDER FROM (fiction)   II, 164
Chock, Eric—CHINESE FIREWORKS BANNED IN HAWAII
    (poetry)   XVI, 212
Chowder, Ken—WITH PAT BOONE IN THE PENTLANDS
    (fiction)   XV, 395
Cisneros, Antonio—SUNDAY AT ST. CHRISTINE'S IN BUDAPEST
    AND A FRUITSTAND NEARBY (poetry)   XI, 93
Clampitt, Amy—THE REEDBEDS OF THE HACKENSACK
    (poetry)   VIII, 398
    —GRASMERE (poetry)   X, 291
Clark, Naomi—THE BREAKER (poetry)   III, 167
Clausen, Christopher—POETRY IN A DISCOURAGING TIME
    (nonfiction)   VII, 129
Codrescu, Andrei—ANESTHETIC (nonfiction)   V, 432
    —SAMBA DE LOS AGENTES (fiction)   VIII, 214
Cofer, Judith Ortiz—MORE ROOM (nonfiction)   XV, 366
Coffey, Marilyn—PRICKSONG (poetry)   I, 49
Cohen, Marvin—THE HUMAN TABLE (fiction)   I, 210
Cohen, Robert—SHAMSKY AND OTHER CASUALTIES (fiction)   XII, 3
Cohen, Ted—THERE ARE NO TIES AT FIRST BASE (nonfiction)   XVI, 440
Cole, Henri—ASCENSION ON FIRE ISLAND (poetry)   XV, 460
Collier, Michael—THE CAVE (poetry)   XV, 121
Collins, Kathleen—STEPPING BACK (fiction)   III, 418
Collins, Martha—DICKINSON (poetry)   X, 288
Cooley, Peter—THE ELECT (poetry)   X, 133
Cooper, Jane—THE CONVERSATION BY THE BODY'S LIGHT
    (poetry)   III, 352
    —LONG, DISCONSOLATE LINES (poetry)   XVI, 146

Cope, David—CRASH (poetry)   II, 500
Corkery, Christopher Jane—THE ANNUNCIATION (poetry)   IX, 407
Cotez, Jayne—THREE DAY NEW YORK BLUES (poetry)   II, 471
Costanzo, Gerald—DINOSAURS OF THE HOLLYWOOD DELTA
    (poetry)   X, 136
       —THE RISE OF THE SUNDAY SCHOOL
    MOVEMENT (poetry)   XIII, 131
Coulette, Henri—THE DESIRE AND PURSUIT OF THE PART
    (poetry)   VIII, 401
Cowley, Malcolm—JOHN CHEEVER: THE NOVELIST'S LIFE
    AS A DRAMA (nonfiction)   IX, 531
       —HEMINGWAY'S WOUND—AND ITS
    CONSEQUENCES FOR AMERICAN LITERATURE
    (nonfiction)   X, 32
Crase, Douglas—CUYLERVILLE (poetry)   II, 51
Creeley, Robert—THIS DAY (poetry)   VI, 492
       —SONG (poetry)   XIV, 279
Crumley, James—WHORES (fiction)   III, 427
Cuelho, Art—LIKE A GOOD UNKNOWN POET (poetry)   I, 334
Currey, Richard—BELIEVER'S FLOOD (fiction)   XV, 339
Dacey, Philip—THE SLEEP (poetry)   II, 369
       —THE LAST STRAW (poetry)   VII, 490
Daniel, John—THE LONGING (poetry)   VIII, 345
Daniels, Kate—MY FATHER'S DESK (poetry)   VII, 423
Dauenhauer, Richard—KOYUKON RIDDLE-POEMS (poetry)   III, 308
Davenport, Guy—CHRIST PREACHING AT THE HENLEY
    REGATTA (fiction)   VII, 94
Davidson, Jean—ROBO-WASH (fiction)   VIII, 300
Davis, Lydia—MOTHERS (fiction)   III, 443
       —FIVE STORIES (fiction)   XIV, 233
       —THE CENTER OF THE STORY (fiction)   XV, 195
       —FOUR STORIES (fiction)   XVII, 286
Davis, Melinda—TEXT (fiction)   XVI, 310
Davis, Thadious M.—FOR PAPA (AND MARCUS GARVEY)
    (poetry)   IV, 289
Day, R. C.—ANOTHER MARGOT CHAPTER (fiction)   IV, 332
Deal, Susan Strayer—SOME CARRY AROUND THIS (poetry)   IV, 493
DeAndrade, Carlos Drummond—THE ELEPHANT (poetry)   I, 342
DeLoria, Vine—CIVILIZATION AND ISOLATION (nonfiction)   IV, 389
Dennis, Carl—HENRY JAMES ON HESTER STREET (poetry)   XIII, 302
Derricotte, Toi—CAPTIVITY: THE MINKS (poetry)   XV, 447
Desaulniers, Janet—AGE (fiction)   VIII, 404
Des Pres, Terrence—POETRY IN DARK TIMES (nonfiction)   VII, 351
       —SELF/LANDSCAPE/GRID (nonfiction)   IX, 43
De Veaux, Alexis—THE WOMAN WHO LIVES IN THE
    BOTANICAL GARDENS (poetry)   VIII, 476
Dickey, William—THOSE DESTROYED BY SUCCESS (poetry)   VIII, 116
Dickstein, Morris—FICTION HOT AND KOOL: DILEMMAS OF
    THE EXPERIMENTAL WRITER (nonfiction)   I, 309
Digges, Deborah—VESPER SPARROWS (poetry)   X, 443
Dixon, Jeanne—RIVER GIRLS (fiction)   XVI, 281
Dixon, Stephen—MILK IS VERY GOOD FOR YOU (fiction)   II, 179
Dobler, Patricia—CAROLYN AT TWENTY (poetry)   VIII, 271
Dobyns, Stephen—WHERE WE ARE (poetry)   X, 323
       —THE NOISE THE HAIRLESS MAKE (poetry)   XI, 398
       —QUERENCIA (poetry)   XII, 302
"Domecq, H. Bustos"—MONSTERFEST (fiction)   III, 152

Doty, M. R.—THE MAN WHOSE BLOOD TILTED THE EARTH
    (poetry)   IV, 313
Doty, Mark—TURTLE, SWAN (poetry)   XI, 348
    —BILL'S STORY (poetry)   XIV, 416
Doubiago, Sharon—GROUND ZERO (poetry)   IX, 54
    —THAT ART OF SEEING WITH ONE'S OWN
    EYES (fiction)   X, 90
Dove, Rita—DUSTING (poetry)   VII, 268
Drury, John—THE BIBLICAL GARDEN (poetry)   XI, 245
Dubie, Norman—THERE IS A DREAM DREAMING US (poetry)   III, 164
Dubus, Andre—THE FAT GIRL (fiction)   III, 357
    —ROSE (fiction)   XI, 116
Duesing, Laurie—SEND PICTURES YOU SAID (poetry)   XIII, 213
Dugan, Alan—THE DECIMATION BEFORE PHRAATA (poetry)   VIII, 98
    —AGAINST THE TEXT 'ART IS IMMORTAL' (poetry)   XVI, 125
Dunn, Stephen—TENDERNESS (poetry)   XIII, 176
    —WHAT THEY WANTED (poetry)   XVI, 335
Dybek, Stuart—HOT ICE (fiction)   X, 53
Eastlake, William—THE DEATH OF THE SUN (fiction)   I, 175
Eberhart, Richard (with William Carlos Williams—)—MAKING
    POETRY A CONTINUUM: SELECTED
    CORRESPONDENCE (letters)   IX, 170
Edson, Russell—THE NEIGHBORHOOD DOG (fiction)   II, 308
Eighner, Lars—ON DUMPSTER DIVING (nonfiction)   XVII, 88
Eigner, Larry—A PUDDLE (poetry)   III, 398
Einzig, Barbara—LIFE MOVES OUTSIDE (fiction)   XIII, 393
Ekstrom, Margareta—DEATH'S MIDWIVES (fiction)   X, 428
"El Huitlacoche"—THE MAN WHO INVENTED THE
    AUTOMATIC JUMPING BEAN (nonfiction)   II, 371
Emshwiller, Carol—YUKON (fiction)   XII, 407
Engberg, Susan—IN THE LAND OF PLENTY (fiction)   VI, 219
Engels, John—THE COLD IN MIDDLE LATITUDES (poetry)   V, 550
    —WINTER FLIGHT (poetry)   IX, 78
Edrich, Louise—INDIAN BOARDING SCHOOL: THE
    RUNAWAYS (poetry)   VIII, 450
Essary, Loris—UNTITLED   III, 487
Everwine, Peter—FROM THE MEADOW (poetry)   XVII, 62
Federman, Raymond—THE BUICKSPECIAL (fiction)   II, 402
Feld, Ross—LOWGHOST TO LOWGHOST (nonfiction)   II, 430
Feldman, Irving—THE TORTOISE (poetry)   V, 376
Ferry, David—THE GUEST ELLEN AT THE SUPPER FOR
    STREET PEOPLE (poetry)   XIII, 172
Fiedler, Leslie—LITERATURE AND LUCRE (nonfiction)   VI, 429
Field, Edward—THE SAGE OF APPLE VALLEY ON LOVE
    (poetry)   II, 241
Finley, Michael—GISE PEDERSEN SETS ME STRAIGHT ON A
    MATTER OF NATURAL HISTORY (poetry)   IX, 405
Fish, Karen—WHAT IS BEYOND US (poetry)   XV, 425
Flanders, Jane—THE STUDENTS OF SNOW (poetry)   V, 546
    —CLOUD PAINTER (poetry)   X, 227
    —THE HOUSE THAT FEAR BUILT, WARSAW,
    1943 (poetry)   VIII, 272
Forché, Carolyn—MIENTRAS DURE VIDA, SOBRA EL TIEMPO
    (poetry)   VIII, 209
    —EL SALVADOR: AN AIDE MEMOIR (nonfiction)   VII, 159
Ford, Richard—COMMUNIST (fiction)   XI, 65
Fowler, Gene—THE FLOWERING CACTI (poetry)   I, 97

Fox, Siv Cedering—THE JUGGLER (poetry)   II, 459
Francis, H. E.—A CHRONICLE OF LOVE (fiction)   I, 31
    —TWO LIVES (fiction)   V, 524
Frost, Carol—APPLE RIND (poetry)   XVII, 101
Gallagher, Tess—BLACK MONEY (poetry)   I, 276
    —THE RITUAL OF MEMORIES (poetry)   IV, 178
    —EACH BIRD WALKING (poetry)   VIII, 96
    —THE LOVER OF HORSES (fiction)   XII, 480
    —GIRLS (fiction)   XIII, 50
Galvin, James—EVERYONE KNOWS WHOM THE SAVED ENVY
    (poetry)   III, 249
Gangemi, Kenneth—GREENBAUM, O'REILLY & STEPHENS
    (fiction)   X, 295
Garber, Eugene—THE LOVER (fiction)   II, 288
Gardner, Isabella—THE WIDOW'S YARD (poetry)   VI, 217
Gardner, John—MORAL FICTION (nonfiction)   III, 52
Gass, William—I WISH YOU WOULDN'T (fiction)   I, 98
    —UNCLE BALT AND THE NATURE OF BEING
    (fiction)   VIII, 384
    —SOME SNAPSHOTS FROM THE SOVIET UNION
    (nonfiction)   XII, 146
    —SIMPLICITIES (nonfiction)   XVII, 142
Geha, Joseph—THROUGH AND THROUGH (fiction)   XV, 147
Geiger, Timothy—INSOMNIA (poetry)   XVII, 172
Gibbons, Reginald—A NOTE IN MEMORIAM: TERRENCE DES
    PRES (nonfiction)   XIII, ix
Gilb, Dagoberto—LOOK ON THE BRIGHT SIDE (fiction)   XVII, 396
Gilbert, Celia—LOT'S WIFE (poetry)   IX, 63
Gilbert, Jack—HUNGER (poetry)   VI, 392
Gilchrist, Ellen—RICH (fiction)   IV, 502
    —SUMMER, AN ELEGY (fiction)   VIII, 180
Gildner, Gary—SOMEWHERE GEESE ARE FLYING (fiction)   XI, 254
Giles, Molly—WAR (fiction)   XVII, 335
Gilson, William—GETTING THROUGH IT TOGETHER (fiction)   VII, 342
Glasscock, Sarah—BROKEN HEARTS (fiction)   XV, 427
Glowney, John—AT DAWN IN WINTER (poetry)   I, 216
Glück, Louise—THE DREAM OF MOURNING (poetry)   III, 169
    —WORLD BREAKING APART (poetry)   VI, 216
    —CELESTIAL MUSIC (poetry)   XIV, 333
    —VESPERS: PAROUSIA (poetry)   XVII, 268
Godshalk, C. S.—WONDERLAND (fiction)   XIII, 215
Godwin, Gail—OVER THE MOUNTAIN (fiction)   IX, 252
Goedicke, Patricia—THOUGH IT LOOKS LIKE A THROAT IT IS
    NOT (poetry)   II, 91
Goldbarth, Albert—THE FORM AND FUNCTION OF THE
    NOVEL (poetry)   IX, 349
    —THE ALIAS: A SURVEY (poetry)   XII, 254
    —AFTER YITZL (essay/poem/fiction)   XIII, 187
    —A LETTER (poetry)   XV, 56
Goldensohn, Barry—THE LIBRARIAN OF ALEXANDRIA (poetry)   X, 200
Goldensohn, Lorrie—LETTER FOR A DAUGHTER (poetry)   III, 220
Goodison, Lorna—BY LOVE POSSESSED (fiction)   XIV, 419
Goodman, Paul—THE TENNIS-GAME (fiction)   II, 387
Gordett, Marea—THE AIR BETWEEN TWO DESERTS (poetry)   V, 545
Gordon, Mary—NOW I AM MARRIED (fiction)   I, 227
Goyen, William—ARTHUR BOND (fiction)   VI, 242
    —RECOVERING (nonfiction)   IX, 124

Graff, Gerald—THE POLITICS OF ANTI-REALISM (nonfiction)   IV, 203
Graham, Jorie—I WAS TAUGHT THREE (poetry)   V, 316
    —MY GARDEN, MY DAYLIGHT (poetry)   VII, 264
    —REMEMBERING TITIAN'S MARTYDOM OF
ST. LAWRENCE (poetry)   VIII, 296
Graham, Matthew—TRANSLATION (poetry)   VII, 177
Gray, Patrick Worth—I COME HOME LATE AT NIGHT (poetry)   I, 214
Gregg, Linda—BEING WITH MEN (poetry)   VII, 477
    —THE RIVER AGAIN AND AGAIN (poetry)   VI, 441
    —RONDO (poetry)   X, 448
    —STRONG POMEGRANATE FLOWERS AND
SEEDS OF THE MIND (poetry)   XVI, 179
Groff, Ben—A CALL FROM KOTZEBUE (fiction)   XVI, 451
Grossman, Allen—BY THE POOL (poetry)   V, 221
    —POLAND OF DEATH (poetry)   XII, 38
    —DUST (poetry)   XV, 488
Grossman, Barbara—MY VEGETABLE LOVE (fiction)   V, 347
Guber, Susan—BLESSINGS IN DISGUISE: CROSS DRESSING AS
REDRESSING FOR FEMALE MODERNISTS (nonfiction)   VII, 492
Gunn, Thom—ON A DRYING HILL (nonfiction)   VII, 249
    —A SKETCH OF THE GREAT DEJECTION (poetry)   XII, 425
Gusewelle, C. W.—HORST WESSEL (fiction)   III, 228
Gussow, Adam—BOHEMIA REVISITED: MALCOLM COWLEY,
JACK KEROUAC, AND ON THE ROAD (nonfiction)   X, 390
Hacker, Marilyn—AGAINST SILENCE (poetry)   XIV, 81
Haines, John—RAIN COUNTRY (poetry)   X, 318
Hall, Donald—POETRY AND AMBITION (nonfiction)   IX, 317
    —SHRUBS BURNED AWAY (poetry)   XII, 100
Hall, James B.—MY WORK IN CALIFORNIA (fiction)   IV, 267
Hall, James Baker—SITTING BETWEEN TWO MIRRORS (poetry)   VIII, 175
Hallerman, Victoria—TALKING TO GOD (poetry)   XIII, 174
Halliday, Mark—ONE THOUSAND WORDS ON WHY YOU
SHOULD NOT TALK DURING A FIRE DRILL (fiction)   XVI, 141
Halpern, Daniel—DEAD FISH (poetry)   VI, 334
    —AMARYLLIS (poetry)   XI, 248
    —WALKING IN THE 15TH CENTURY (poetry)   XII, 423
Halpert, Sam—GLIMPSES: RAYMOND CARVER (nonfiction)   XVII, 485
Hamill, Sam—ONLY ONE SKY (nonfiction)   XIV, 247
Handsome Lake—FARMING (poetry)   V, 499
Hardison, O. B.—A TREE, A STREAM-LINED FISH, AND A
SELF-SQUARED DRAGON: SCIENCE AS A FORM OF
CULTURE (nonfiction)   XII, 342
Harjo, Joy—EAGLE POEM (poetry)   XIII, 178
    —FOR ANNA MAE AQUASH WHOSE SPIRIT IS
PRESENT HERE AND IN THE DAPPLED STARS
(poetry)   XV, 362
Harmon, William—EIRON EYES (nonfiction)   V, 503
Harper, Michael—MADE CONNECTIONS (poetry)   IV, 352
    —CHIEF (poetry)   VII, 241
Hartman, Yuki—CHINATOWN SONATA (poetry)   III, 354
Hashim, James—THE PARTY (fiction)   II, 258
Hass, Robert—LOWELL'S GRAVEYARD (nonfiction)   III, 332
Hathaway, James—COOKING (poetry)   XI, 354
Havazelet, Ehud—WHAT IS IT THEN BETWEEN US? (fiction)   XIII, 179
Hayes, Daniel—WHAT I WANTED MOST OF ALL (fiction)   XV, 235
Head, Gwen—NIGHT SWEATS (poetry)   XVI, 101

Heaney, Seamus—SWEENEY ASTRAY (poetry)   III, 251
          —THE OTTER (poetry)   V, 84
          —THE IMPACT OF TRANSLATION (nonfiction)   XII, 289
          —ATLAS OF CIVILIZATION (essay)   XIII, 363
Hejinian, Lyn—SELECTIONS FROM MY LIFE (fiction)   VI, 151
          —FROM THE PERSON (poetry)   XII, 492
Hellerstein, David—DEATH IN THE GLITTER PALACE
          (nonfiction)   VI, 53
Hemley, Robin—INSTALLATIONS (fiction)   XV, 258
Hempel, Amy—TODAY WILL BE A QUIET DAY (fiction)   XI, 212
Hendrie, Jr., Don—MORAL CAKE (fiction)   III, 76
Henley, Patricia—THE BIRTHING (fiction)   XII, 124
Henry, DeWitt—WITNESS (fiction)   XIV, 355
Herbert, Anne—SNAKE (fiction)   III, 281
Hernández, Felisberto—THE DAISY DOLLS (fiction)   IV, 88
Herzinger, Kim—THE DAY I MET BUDDY HOLLY (fiction) XV, 27
Hewat, Alan V.—THE BIG STORE (fiction)   II, 95
Hillman, Brenda—ANONYMOUS COURTESAN IN A JADE
          SHROUD (poetry)   IV, 354
          —AT A MOTEL (poetry)   XIV, 210
          —MIGHTY FORMS (poetry)   XVI, 144
Hirsch, Edward—IN A POLISH HOME FOR THE AGED (poetry) XI, 178
          —BIRDS OF PARADISE (essay)   XIII, 247
Hirschfield, Jane—JUSTICE WITHOUT PASSION (poetry)   XIII, 264
Hitchcock, George—MARATHON OF MARMALADE (poetry)   V, 154
Hoagland, Edward—LEARNING TO EAT SOUP (nonfiction) XIV, 401
Hoagland, Tony—SWEET RUIN (poetry)   XVI, 122
Hogan, Linda—FRIENDS AND FORTUNES (fiction)   XI, 150
Hogan, Michael—SILENCE (poetry)   I, 273
          —SPRING (poetry)   I, 30
Hollander, John—BLUE WINE (poetry)   V, 222
          —THE POETRY OF RESTITUTION (nonfiction) VII, 295
Hongo, Garrett Kaoru—MORRO ROCK (poetry)   XI, 180
Hood, Mary—SOMETHING GOOD FOR GINNIE (fiction)   XI, 370
Hoover, Judith—PROTEUS (fiction)   IV, 368
Howard, Richard—LINING UP (poetry)   VIII, 340
Howe, Marie—MENSES (poetry)   XIII, 351
Howe, Susan—HELIOPATHY (poetry)   XII, 459
Howell, Christopher—THE WU GENERAL WRITES FROM FAR
          AWAY (poetry)   III, 85
Hudgins, Andrew—from A SEQUENCE ON SIDNEY LANIER
          (poetry)   VIII, 177
          —WHEN I WAS SAVED (poetry)   XVII, 377
Hugo, Richard—MEDICINE BOW (poetry)   II, 145
          —CONFEDERATE GRAVES AT LITTLE ROCK
          (poetry)   VIII, 153
Hull, Lynda—TIDE OF VOICES (poetry)   XI, 101
          —HOSPICE (poetry)   XV, 199
          —LOST FUGUE FOR CHET (poetry)   XVII, 413
Hummer, T. R.—AUSTERITY IN VERMONT (poetry)   XV, 157
          —WORLDLY BEAUTY (poetry)   XVII, 363
Huss, Sandy—COUPON FOR BLOOD (fiction)   XIV, 387
Hyde, Lewis—ALCOHOL AND POETRY: JOHN BERRYMAN
          AND THE BOOZE TALKING (nonfiction)   I, 71
          —SOME FOOD WE COULD NOT EAT: GIFT
          EXCHANGE AND THE IMAGINATION (nonfiction)   V, 165
Ignatow, David—A REQUIEM (poetry)   VII, 266

Illyes, Gyula—WHILE THE RECORD PLAYS (poetry) III, 304
Inez, Collette—WHAT ARE THE DAYS (poetry) XI, 400
Inness-Brown, Elizabeth—RELEASE, SURRENDER (fiction) VII, 150
Irving, John—THE PENSION GRILLPARZER (fiction) II, 25
Jackson, Angela—THE LOVE OF TRAVELLERS (poetry) XIV, 231
Jackson, Richard—THE PROMISE OF LIGHT XII, 204
—CIRCUMSTANCES (poetry) XVII, 205
Jacobsen, Josephine—A MOTEL IN TORY, N.Y. (poetry) VI, 336
—THE LIMBO DANCER (poetry) XVI, 337
Jaffe, Harold—PERSIAN LAMB (fiction) XII, 472
Jarman, Mark—BETWEEN FLIGHTS (poetry) XIII, 265
—GRID (poetry) XVII, 273
Jauss, David—FREEZE (fiction) XIV, 433
—GLOSSOLALIA (fiction) XVI, 27
Jensen, Laura—THE CROW IS MISCHIEF (poetry) III, 459
—CHEER (poetry) XIII, 70
Jin, Ha—MY BEST SOLDIER (fiction) XVII, 125
Johnson, Denis—THE THRONE OF THE THIRD HEAVEN
OF THE NATIONS MILLENNIUM GENERAL
ASSEMBLY (poetry) XI, 40
Johnson, Diane—THE IMPORTANCE OF PLOT (nonfiction) XIV, 102
Johnson, Willis—PRAYER FOR THE DYING (fiction) VIII, 100
Jolley, Elizabeth—MY FATHER'S MOON (fiction) XII, 389
Jones, Rodney—A HISTORY OF SPEECH (poetry) IX, 347
Jones, Rodney Hale—FRANCIS: BROTHER OF THE UNIVERSE
(fiction) XV, 371
Justice, Donald—PSALMS AND LAMENT (poetry) XII, 500
Kalpakian, Laura—THE BATTLE OF MANILA (fiction) XV, 490
Karr, Mary—POST-LARKIN TRISTE (poetry) XV, 423
—AGAINST DECORATION (nonfiction) XVII, 245
Kauffman, Janet—MENNONITE FARM WIFE (poetry) V, 155
—THE EASTER WE LIVED IN DETROIT (fiction) X, 245
Kaufman, Shirley—LAWRENCE AT TAOS (poetry) IV, 316
Kearney, Lawrence—AFTER THE INTERROGATION (poetry) VI, 443
Keeley, Edmund—CAMBODIAN DIARY (fiction) IX, 355
Keithley, George—WHEN THEY LEAVE (poetry) XVI, 181
Kelly, Dave—MOTHER TERESA (poetry) XIII, 267
Kennedy, J. Gerald—ROLAND BARTHES, AUTOBIOGRAPHY,
AND THE END OF WRITING (nonfiction) VII, 429
Kennedy, Thomas E.—MURPHY'S ANGEL (fiction) XV, 348
Kennedy, William—WRITERS AND THEIR SONGS (nonfiction) XVI, 165
Kent, Margaret—LIVING WITH ANIMALS (poetry) IV, 547
Kenyon, Jane—THE POND AT DUSK (poetry) VIII, 174
—AT THE IGA: FRANKLIN, N.H.(poetry) XV, 393
Kermode, Frank—INSTITUTIONAL CONTROL OF
INTERPRETATION (nonfiction) V, 107
Kiely, Benedict—FIONN IN THE VALLEY (fiction) VI, 276
Kilodney, Crad—THE CIRCUMCISION RITES OF THE
TORONTO STOCK EXCHANGE (nonfiction) X, 165
Kinnell, Galway—THE SADNESS OF BROTHERS (poetry) VI, 329
—THE FUNDAMENTAL PROJECT OF
TECHNOLOGY (poetry) X, 51
Kinsella, W. P.—PRETEND DINNERS (fiction) V, 424
Kirstein, Lincoln—CRANE AND CARLSEN, A MEMOIR
(nonfiction) VIII, 238
Kitchen, Judith—HIDE-AND-GO-SEEK (nonfiction) XV, 290

Kittredge, William—AGRICULTURE (fiction)   X, 215
       —REDNECK SECRETS (essay)   XIII, 201
Kizer, Carolyn—RUNNING AWAY FROM HOME (poetry)   IV, 435
       —EXODUS (poetry)   X, 85
       —TWELVE O'CLOCK (poetry)   XVII, 434
Kleinzahler, August—SHOOTING (poetry)   X, 134
Kloefkorn, William—OUT-AND-DOWN PATTERN (poetry)   V, 501
Knight, Etheridge—WE FREE SINGERS BE (poetry)   II, 93
Knott, Bill—MY MOTHER'S LIST OF NAMES (poetry)   III, 460
Koch, Kenneth—FROM "THE DUPLICATIONS" (poetry)   II, 382
Komunyakaa, Yusef—TU DO STREET (poetry)   XIII, 349
Konwicki, Tadeusz—FROM A MINOR APOCALYPSE (fiction)   IX, 83
Kooser, Ted—AS THE PRESIDENT SPOKE (poetry)   IX, 62
Kopp, Karl—CLOE MORGAN (poetry)   I, 325
Kornblum, Cinda—IN IOWA (poetry)   II, 503
Kostelanetz, Richard—OLYMPIAN PROGRESS   II, 456
Kranes, David—CORDIALS (fiction)   I, 3
Krysl, Marilyn—LEDA (poetry)   VI, 119
Kumin, Maxine—ANOTHER FORM OF MARRIAGE (fiction)   II, 347
       —THE MAN OF MANY L'S (poetry)   VIII, 382
Kunitz, Stanley—QUINNAPOXET (poetry)   IV, 378
       —THE SNAKES OF SEPTEMBER (poetry)   VII, 179
Kusz, Natalie—VITAL SIGNS (nonfiction)   XV, 82
Lamb, Wally—ASTRONAUTS (fiction)   XV, 128
Lane, Mary—HOW IT WILL BE (poetry)   II, 368
Lasch, Christopher—THE FAMILY AS A HAVEN IN A
   HEARTLESS WORLD (nonfiction)   II, 194
Laughlin, James—IN ANOTHER COUNTRY (poetry)   IV, 83
Laux, Dorianne—QUARTER TO SIX (poetry)   XI, 219
Lavers, Norman—THE TELEGRAPH RELAY STATION (fiction)   XVII, 181
Lazard, Naomi—THE PILOT (poetry)   I, 307
LeClair, Thomas—AVANT-GARDE MASTERY (nonfiction)   VIII, 368
LeGuin, Ursula K.—BILL WEISLER (fiction)   XVI, 70
Lee, Li-Young—PERSIMMONS (poetry)   VIII, 150
       —THE GIFT (poetry)   IX, 274
       —EATING TOGETHER (poetry)   XI, 97
       —FURIOUS VERSIONS (poetry)   XIV, 184
       —THE CLEAVING (poetry)   XVI, 60
Legler, Gretchen—BORDER WAR (nonfiction)   XVII, 274
Lehman, David—HEAVEN (poetry)   XV, 161
Lentricchia, Melissa—THE GOLDEN ROBE (fiction)   XIII, 353
Lessing, Doris—UNDER ANOTHER NAME (nonfiction)   X, 313
Levertov, Denise—INTERWEAVINGS (nonfiction)   VI, 258
Levin, Bob—THE BEST RIDE TO NEW YORK (fiction)   II, 115
Levine, Miriam—THE STATION (poetry)   II, 427
Levine, Philip—A WOMAN WAKING (poetry)   II, 457
       —I SING THE BODY ELECTRIC (poetry)   VII, 488
       —A POEM WITH NO ENDING (poetry)   X, 414
       —MINE OWN JOHN BERRYMAN (nonfiction)   XVII, 37
Levis, Larry—THE OWNERSHIP OF THE NIGHT (poetry)   IV, 284
       —WHITMAN (poetry)   VII, 478
       —THE POET AT SEVENTEEN (poetry)   XI, 355
       —TO A WREN ON CALVARY (poetry)   XVII, 241
Lewisohn, James—THEODORE ROETHKE (poetry)   II, 501
Licht, Fred—SHELTER THE PILGRIM (fiction)   VII, 324
Linney, Romulus—HOW ST. PETER GOT BALD (fiction)   V, 368

Lish, Gordon—HOW TO WRITE A POEM (fiction)   VIII, 145
    —THE MERRY CHASE (fiction)   XI, 273
    —MR. GOLDBAUM (fiction)   XII, 138
Liu, Stephen Shu Ning—MY FATHER'S MARTIAL ARTS (poetry)   VII, 146
Locklin, Gerald—THE LAST ROMANTIC (fiction)   II, 461
Logan, John—THE PAPERBOYS (poetry)   XI, 251
Long, David—ECLIPSE (fiction)   VI, 413
Lopate, Philip—ODE TO SENILITY (poetry)   II, 131
    —AGAINST JOIE DE VIVRE (nonfiction)   XII, 81
Love, John—A VISION EXPRESSED BY A SERIES OF FALSE
    STATEMENTS (nonfiction)   IV, 291
Lovell, Barbara—A WOMAN IN LOVE WITH A BOTTLE
    (nonfiction)   IV, 356
Lux, Thomas—BARRETT & BROWNING (poetry)   II, 463
    —AT THE FAR END OF A LONG WHARF (poetry)   VI, 275
    —FOR ROBERT WINNER (1930–1986) (poetry)   XIII, 347
MacDonald, D. R.—THE FLOWERS OF BERMUDA (fiction)   XI, 103
MacDonald, Susan—HIM & ME (poetry)   II, 212
MacLeod, Alistair—ISLAND (fiction)   XIV, 31
Macmillan, Ian—MESSINGHAUSEN, 1945 (fiction)   II, 464
Madden, David—ON THE BIG WIND (fiction)   V, 377
Mairowitz, David—HECTOR COMPOSES A CIRCULAR
    LETTER . . . (fiction)   XIII, 230
Major, Clarence—FUNERAL (poetry)   I, 275
    —MY MOTHER AND MITCH (fiction)   XV, 110
Major, Devorah—A CROWDED TABLE (poetry)   XII, 306
Malaparte, Curzio—THE SOROCA GIRLS (fiction)   IX, 276
Mandel, Oscar—BEING AND JUDAISM (nonfiction)   VIII, 415
Mandell, Arnold J.—IS DON JUAN ALIVE AND WELL?
    (nonfiction)   I, 199
Manfredi, Renèe—BOCCI (fiction)   XVI, 104
Mangan, Kathy—ABOVE THE TREE LINE (poetry)   XV, 256
Manley, Frank—THE RAIN OF TERROR (fiction)   XIV, 453
Marcus, Adrianne—A LETTER HOME (poetry)   II, 498
Marshall, Jack—SESAME (poetry)   XVI, 252
Martel, Yann—THE FACTS BEHIND THE HELSINKI
    ROCCAMATIOS (fiction)   XVI, 396
Martin, Robert K.—WHITMAN'S SONG OF MYSELF:
    HOMOSEXUAL DREAM AND VISION (nonfiction)   I, 379
Martone, Michael—THE SAFETY PATROL (fiction)   XIV, 86
Mason, Bobbie Ann—GRAVEYARD DAY (fiction)   VIII, 156
Masterson, Dan—THE SURVIVORS (poetry)   III, 69
    —HERON (poetry)   XIII, 74
Mathis, Cleopatra—GRANDMOTHER (1895–1928)   IV, 500
Mathews, Lou—CRAZY LIFE (fiction)   XV, 324
Matthews, William—THE THEME OF THREE CASKETS (poetry)   XI, 402
    —THE DREAM (poetry)   XVI, 148
    —MY FATHER'S BODY (poetry)   XVII, 292
Mattingly, George—NUMBER SEVENTEEN (poetry)   I, 209
Mayer, Bernadette—CARLTON FISK IS MY IDEAL (poetry)   III, 485
McBrearty, Robert—THE DISHWASHER (fiction)   VIII, 168
McBride, Mekeel—WHAT LIGHT THERE IS (poetry)   III, 399
McCann, David—DAVID (poetry)   III, 260
McClure, Michael—WHITE BOOT (poetry)   XVI, 485
McElroy, Colleen J.—THE GRIOTS WHO KNEW BRER FOX
    (poetry)   I, 19
McFall, Lynne—STAR, TREE, HAND (fiction)   XIII, 269

McFee, Michael—SILO LETTER IN THE DEAD OF A WARM
WINTER (poetry)   VI, 489
McGarry, Jean—WORLD WITH A HARD K (poetry)   XII, 449
McGrath, Campbell—WHEATFIELD UNDER CLOUDED SKY
(poetry)   XVII, 179
McGrath, Kristina—HOUSEWORK (fiction)   XIV, 267
McGrath, Thomas—TRINC: PRAISES II (poetry)   V, 268
   —THE END OF THE WORLD (poetry)   VIII, 56
   —TOTEMS (poetry)   IX, 81
   —THE UNDERGROUND (poetry)   XII, 208
McHugh, Heather—BREATH (poetry)   V, 342
   —I KNEW I'D SING (poetry)   VIII, 294
   —20-200 ON 707 (poetry)   XIII, 68
McLaughlin, Joe-Anne—GREAT-AUNT FRANCESCA (poetry)   VIII, 449
McMahon, Lynne—HOPKINS AND WHITMAN (poetry)   XV, 250
McMahon, Michael—RETARDED CHILDREN IN THE SNOW
(poetry)   I, 400
McNair, Wesley—MUTE (poetry)   X, 385
McPherson, Sandra—FOR JOHANNES BOBROWSKI (poetry)   V, 456
   —FOR ELIZABETH BISHOP (poetry)   VI, 442
   —LEDGE (poetry)   X, 253
   —EVE (poetry)   XII, 452
Meagher, Thomas—STRAND: EVIDENCE OF BOOKS AND
BOOKSTORES (nonfiction)   XIV, 306
Meek, Jay—THE WEEK THE DIRIGIBLE CAME (poetry)   II, 470
Merrill, Christopher—BECAUSE (poetry)   XV, 419
Merrill, James—THE PYROXENES (poetry)   XVI, 483
Messerli, Douglas—EXPERIMENT AND TRADITIONAL
FORMS . . . (nonfiction)   VI, 304
Metcalf, Paul—THE HAT IN THE SWAMP (fiction)   IV, 472
Michaels, Leonard—LITERARY TALK (essay)   XIII, 359
   —I'M HAVING TROUBLE WITH MY
RELATIONSHIP (nonfiction)   XV, 123
Milam, Lorenzo—from THE CRIPPLE LIBERATION FRONT
MARCHING BAND BLUES (nonfiction)   X, 325
Miller, Henry—JIMMY PASTA (nonfiction)   II, 243
Miller, Leslie A.—EPITHALAMIUM (poetry)   XIII, 136
Miller, Mark Crispin—BIG BROTHER IS YOU, WATCHING
(nonfiction)   X, 171
Milosz, Czeslaw—THE GARDEN OF EARTHLY DELIGHTS
(poetry)   XII, 505
Milton, Barbara—THE CIGARETTE BOAT (fiction)   IX, 155
Minkoff, Robert—BETTER TOMORROW (fiction)   XIV, 324
Minot, Stephen—HEY, IS ANYONE LISTENING? (nonfiction)   III, 239
Minot, Susan—HIDING (fiction)   IX, 31
Minton, Karen—LIKE HANDS ON A CAVE WALL (fiction)   XVII, 382
Mitchum, Judson—EXPLANATIONS (poetry)   XIV, 385
Mitchell, Susan—THE EXPLOSION (poetry)   IX, 270
   —LEAVES THAT GROW INWARD (poetry)   XIII, 384
Moffett, Judith—SCATSQUALL IN SPRING (poetry)   VI, 273
Molesworth, Charles—CONTEMPORARY POETRY AND THE
METAPHORS FOR THE POEM (nonfiction)   IV, 319
Montag, Tom—LECTURING MY DAUGHTER IN HER FIRST
FALL RAIN (poetry)   I, 69
Montale, Eugenio—XENIA (poetry)   I, 439 (cloth ed. only)
Moon, Susan—BODIES (fiction)   XVII, 366
Moore, Jim—FOR YOU (poetry)   XIV, 116

Morley, Hilda—THAT BRIGHT GREY EYE (poetry)   VIII, 446
Morris, Herbert—DELFINA FLORES AND HER NIECE
    MODESTA (poetry)   XI, 184
Morris, Mary—COPIES (fiction)   IX, 506
Moss, Howard—SHORT STORIES (poetry)   II, 354
    —IT (poetry)   XI, 353
Moss, Thylias—INTERPRETATION OF A POEM BY FROST
    (poetry)   XIV, 379
Mowry, Jess—ONE WAY (fiction)   XVI, 491
Mueller, Lisel—THE END OF SCIENCE FICTION (poetry)   II, 49
Mura, David—LISTENING (poetry)   XV, 391
Muravin, Victor—THE RED CROSS NIGHT (fiction)   II, 78
Murray, Joan—COMING OF AGE ON THE HARLEM (poetry)   IX, 522
Muske, Carol—BOX (poetry)   XIII, 381
    —TO THE MUSE (poetry)   XVII, 335
Myerhoff, Barbara—THE RENEWAL OF THE WORD (nonfiction)   IV, 48
Nathan, Leonard—SEASON'S GREETINGS (poetry)   X, 439
Nations, Opal—THE U.S. CHINESE IMMIGRANT'S BOOK OF
    THE ART OF SEX (fiction)   II, 310
Nelson, Kent—THE MIDDLE OF NOWHERE (fiction)   XV, 306
Nelson, Lynn—SEQUENCE (poetry)   XIV, 448
Nemerov, Howard—MEDIA (poetry)   XVI, 378
Neville Susan Schaefer—JOHNNY APPLESEED (fiction)   IV, 486
Ng, Fae Myenne—A RED SWEATER (fiction)   XII, 332
Nickerson, Sheila—SONG OF THE SOAPSTONE CARVER (poetry)   I, 399
    —KODIAK WIDOW (poetry)   X, 257
Nin, Anaïs—WASTE OF TIMELESSNESS (fiction)   III, 312
Norris, Helen—RAISIN FACES (fiction)   XVI, 265
Nourbese, S—WHEN I WAS A CHILD (poetry)   VI, 395
Novakovich, Josip—RUST (fiction)   XV, 69
Nunez, Sigrid—THE SUMMER OF THE HATS (fiction)   XIV, 196
    —CHRISTA (nonfiction)   XVII, 304
Nye, Naomi Shihab—MAKING A FIST (poetry)   VII, 461
    —TRYING TO NAME WHAT DOESN'T
    CHANGE (poetry)   IX, 520
    —MAINTENANCE (nonfiction)   XVI, 240
Oates, Joyce Carol—THE HALLUCINATION (fiction)   I, 404
    —DETENTE (fiction)   VII, 270
    —NOTES ON FAILURE (nonfiction)   VIII, 194
    —AGAINST NATURE (nonfiction)   XII, 242
    —PARTY (fiction)   XIV, 381
    —THE HAIR (fiction)   XVI, 150
O'Brien, Tim—GOING AFTER CACCIATO (fiction)   II, 53
    —QUANTUM JUMPS (fiction)   X, 3
Ochester, Ed—OH, BY THE WAY (poetry)   XVII, 280
Ohle, David—THE BOY SCOUT (fiction)   II, 464
    —THE FLOCCULUS (fiction)   VI, 79
Olds, Sharon—THE GENTLEMEN IN THE U-BOATS (poetry)   VI, 472
    —THE QUEST (poetry)   VII, 175
    —MAY, 1968 (poetry)   XIII, 48
    —THE DEAD BODY ITSELF (poetry)   XVI, 333
    —THE PULL (poetry)   XVII, 476
Oles, Carole—MARIA MITCHELL IN THE GREAT BEYOND
    WITH MARILYN MONROE (poetry)   XI, 405
Oliver, Mary—WINTER SLEEP (poetry)   IV, 232
    —THE GARDENS (poetry)   VII, 246
    —MOLES (poetry)   VIII, 119

—LITTLE OWL WHO LIVES IN THE ORCHARD
(poetry) XVI, 99
Oliver, Raymond—DREAM VISION (poetry) VIII, 400
Olson, Charles—ENCOUNTERS WITH EZRA POUND (nonfiction) I, 353
Orr, Gregory—PREPARING TO SLEEP (poetry) II, 504
Ortiz, Simon—SELECTIONS FROM SAND CREEK (poetry) VII, 480
Ostriker, Alicia—THE NERVES OF A MIDWIFE:
CONTEMPORARY AMERICAN WOMEN'S
POETRY (nonfiction) IV, 451
Otto, Lon—PLOWING WITH ELEPHANTS (poetry) IV, 181
Oz, Amos—THE AUTHOR ENCOUNTERS HIS READING
PUBLIC (fiction) VII, 414
Ozick, Cynthia—A LIBERAL'S AUSCHWITZ (nonfiction) I, 149
—LEVITATION (fiction) V, 29
—HELPING T. S. ELIOT WRITE BETTER (fiction) VII, 103
—WHAT LITERATURE MEANS (nonfiction) VIII, 289
Packard, Steve—STEELMILL BLUES (nonfiction) I, 278
Paino, Frankie—WHAT THE BLUE JAY SAID (poetry) XV, 364
Palmer, Michael—FOUR FROM THE BAUDELAIRE SERIES
(poetry) XII, 251
Pape, Greg—MAKING A GREAT SPACE SMALL (poetry) XIII, 402
Pastan, Linda—I AM LEARNING TO ABANDON THE WORLD
(poetry) VII, 321
Pavlich, Walter—ON THE LIFE AND DEATH OF STAN
LAUREL'S SON (poetry) XV, 288
Payerle, George—WOLFBANE FANE (fiction) III, 318
Paz, Octavio—HURRY (poetry) I, 95
—LAUGHTER AND PENITENCE (nonfiction) II, 146
Peery, Janet—NOSOTROS (fiction) XVI, 185
—WHITEWING (fiction) XVII, 104
Penner, Jonathan—EMOTION RECOLLECTED IN
TRANQUILITY (fiction) IX, 335
Perillo, Lucia—JURY SELECTION (fiction) XI, 98
Perkins, David—WRAPPED MINDS (nonfiction) V, 212
Perseroff, Joyce—MAKING A NAME FOR MYSELF (poetry) III, 400
Pershin, Laura—UNTITLED (poetry) I, 271
Peterson, Mary—TO DANCE (fiction) III, 143
Pfeil, Fred—FREEWAY BYPASS (Detail from map) (fiction) XVII, 209
Phelan, Francis—FOUR WAYS OF COMPUTING MIDNIGHT
(fiction) VI, 338
Phillips, Jayne Anne—SWEETHEARTS (fiction) II, 317
—HOME (fiction) IV, 29
—LECHERY (fiction) IV, 381
—HOW MICKEY MADE IT (fiction) VII, 376
Phillips, Robert—THE STONE CRAB: A LOVE POEM (poetry) IV, 131
Piercy, Marge—MY MOTHER'S NOVEL (poetry) III, 488
Pilcrow, John—TURTLE (fiction) III, 458
Pinsky, Robert—DYING (poetry) VI, 487
—LAMENT FOR THE MAKERS (poetry) XII, 427
Plante, David—JEAN RHYS: A REMEMBRANCE (nonfiction) V, 43
Planz, Allen—LIVING ON THE LOWER EAST SIDE . . . (poetry) II, 336
Plumly, Stanley—WILDFLOWER (poetry) IV, 223
—SONNET (poetry) VIII, 209
—THE FOUNDRY GARDEN (poetry) XI, 351
—READING WITH THE POETS (poetry) XVII, 105
Poirier, Richard—WRITING OFF THE SELF (nonfiction) VII, 213
Pollack, Eileen—PAST, FUTURE, ELSEWHERE (fiction) XVI, 339

Pollitt, Katha—TURNING THIRTY (poetry)   VII, 389
          —VISITORS (poetry)   XVI, 120
Pope, Robert—FLIP CARDS (essay)   XIII, 407
          —POPOCATEPETL (poetry)   I, 174
Porter, Joe Ashby—SWEETNESS, A THINKING MACHINE
          (fiction)   IV, 306
          —DUCKWALKING (fiction)   IX, 70
Porter, T. E.—KING'S DAY (fiction)   II, 214
Poverman, C. E.—BEAUTIFUL (fiction)   XII, 259
Powell, Padgett—TYPICAL (fiction)   XV, 58
Prose, Francine—OTHER LIVES (fiction)   XI, 45
          —LEARNING FROM CHEKHOV (essay)   XIII, 157
          —RUBBER LIFE (fiction)   XVII, 164
Puig, Manual—FROM KISS OF THE SPIDER WOMAN (fiction)   IV, 400
Pulaski, Jack—FATHER OF THE BRIDE (fiction)   I, 218
Quagliano, Tony—EXPERIMENTAL LANGUAGE (poetry)   I, 333
Quillen, Ruthellen—WEST VIRGINIA SLEEP SONG (poetry)   III, 108
Ramke, Bin—THE CONSOLATION OF TOUCH (poetry)   X, 202
Ramsey, Jarod—RABBIT TRANCE (poetry)   II, 191
Ratushinskaia, Irina—ON THE MEANING OF LIFE (fiction)   XII, 46
Ray, David—TAKE ME BACK TO TULSA (poetry)   I, 197
Redmond, Eugene B.—FIVE BLACK POETS: HISTORY,
          CONSCIOUSNESS, LOVE AND HARSHNESS (nonfiction)   I, 154
Reed, Ishmael (with Steven Cannon and Quincy Troupe)—THE
          ESSENTIAL ELLISON (interview)   III, 465
          —AMERICAN POETRY: LOOKING FOR A CENTER
          (nonfiction)   IV, 254
Reid, David—THE SECRET SHARER (nonfiction)   XII, 415
Reilly, Gary—THE BIOGRAPHY MAN (fiction)   IV, 441
Retallack, Joan—HIGH ADVENTURES OF INDETERMINANCY
          (nonfiction)   IX, 470
Revell, Donald—A SETTING (poetry)   X, 289
Reyzen, Avrom—THE DOG (fiction)   I, 115
Rich, Adrienne—POWER (poetry)   I, 438
          —VESUVIUS AT HOME: THE POWER OF
          EMILY DICKINSON (nonfiction)   III, 170
Richard, Mark—HAPPINESS OF THE GARDEN VARIETY
          (fiction)   XIII, 144
Ríos, Alberto Alvaro—THE SECRET LION (fiction)   X, 159
          —WHAT SHE HAD BELIEVED ALL HER
          LIFE (poetry)   XIII, 405
          —INCIDENT AT IMURIS (poetry)   XIV, 341
          —THE OTHER LEAGUE OF NATIONS
          (fiction)   XVII, 422
Roberts, Len—GIFT SHOP IN PECS (poetry)   XVI, 250
Robinson, Mary—HAPPY BOY, ALLEN (fiction)   VII, 449
Rogers, Pattiann—THE OBJECTS OF IMMORTALITY (poetry)   X, 387
          —THE POWER OF TOADS (poetry)   IX, 118
          —THE FAMILY IS ALL THERE IS (poetry)   XIV, 475
          —GOOD HEAVENS (poetry)   XVII, 379
Roh-Spaulding, Carol—WAITING FOR MR. KIM (fiction)   XVI, 382
Romero, Leo—WHAT THE GOSSIPS SAW (poetry)   VII, 322
Romtvedt, David—1989, GILLETTE, OUR NAVY (poetry)   XVI, 214
Rooke, Leon—THE BLUE BABY (fiction)   XIII, 292
Root, William Pitt—MEETING COOT (poetry)   III, 227
          —DEAR JEFFERS (poetry)   VII, 115

—THE UNBROKEN DIAMOND: NIGHTLETTER
TO THE MUJAHADEEN (poetry)   IX, 207
Rosen, Kenneth—CASTRATO (poetry)   XV, 403
Rosenfeld, Alvin—"ARMED FOR WAR": NOTES ON THE
ANTITHETICAL CRITICISM ON HAROLD BLOOM
(nonfiction)   III, 372
Roszak, Theodore—ON THE CONTEMPORARY HUNGER FOR
WONDERS (nonfiction)   VI, 101
Ruark, Gibbons—A VACANT LOT (poetry)   XV, 462
Ruch, Teri—CLAIRE'S LOVER'S CHURCH (fiction)   IX, 462
Rudnik, Raphael—AMSTERDAM STREET SCENE, 1972 (poetry)   V, 318
Rueckert, William—LITERATURE AND ECOLOGY: AN
EXPERIMENT IN ECOCRITICISM (nonfiction)   IV, 142
Russell. Sharman Apt—ALIENS (nonfiction)   XV, 408
Russell, Thomas—LAVONDER (poetry)   IX, 346
Rutsala, Vern—WILDERNESS (poetry)   X, 446
Ryan, Margaret—PIG 311 (poetry)   IV, 522
Ryan, Michael—THE PURE LONELINESS (poetry)   II, 144
Sadeh, Pinchas—FROM A JOURNEY THROUGH THE LAND OF
ISRAEL (nonfiction)   III, 110
samizdat—THE DEATH OF YURY GALANSKOV (nonfiction)   I, 22
samizdat—THE DEPORTATION OF SOLZHENITSYN (nonfiction)   II, 339
samizdat—THE TRIAL OF ROZHDESTVOV (nonfiction)   IV, 549
samizdat—ON THE METROPOL ALMANAC (nonfiction)   VI, 386
Sanders, Ed—CODEX WHITE BLIZZARD (nonfiction)   V, 338
—THE MOTHER-IN-LAW (fiction)   I, 248
Sandor, Marjorie—ICARUS DESCENDING (fiction)   XIII, 77
Saner, Reg—THEY SAID (poetry)   II, 395
Sanford, John—THE FIRE AT THE CATHOLIC CHURCH (fiction)   II, 473
Santos, Sherod—MELANCHOLY DIVORCÉE (poetry)   V, 86
Sasaki, R. A.—THE LOOM (fiction)   XVII, 460
Savory, Teo—THE MONK'S CHIMERA (fiction)   II, 396
Scalapino, Leslie—THAT THEY WERE AT THE BEACH:
AEOLOTROPIC SERIES (poetry)   XII, 110
Schaffner, Perdita—A DAY AT THE ST. REGIS WITH DAME
EDITH (nonfiction)   XVII, 196
Scheick, William J.—BOOKS OFT HAVE SUCH A CHARM:
A MEMORY (nonfiction)   XVI, 206
Schmitz, Dennis—BIRD-WATCHING (poetry)   XIII, 211
Schott, Max—EARLY WINTER (fiction)   IV, 239
Schultz, Philip—ODE (poetry)   VI, 469
Schutt, Christine—THE WOMEN (fiction)   IV, 473
Schutzman, Steve—THE BANK ROBBERY (fiction)   IV, 464
Schuyler, James—SONG (poetry)   II, 429
Schwartz, Lloyd—SIMPLE QUESTIONS (poetry)   XII, 310
Schwartz, Lynne Sharon—ROUGH STRIFE (fiction)   III, 29
Schwartz, Rhoda—NOTHING VERY MUCH HAS HAPPENED
HERE (poetry)   I, 417
Schwartz, Sheila—MUTATIS MUTANDIS (fiction)   XIV, 280
Scruggs, Charles—"ALL DRESSED UP BUT NO PLACE TO GO";
THE BLACK WRITER AND HIS AUDIENCE DURING
THE HARLEM RENAISSANCE (nonfiction)   III, 283
Scully, James—THE DAY OF THE NIGHT (poetry)   I, 377
Siedman, Hugh—EMBARKMENT (poetry)   III, 425
Selzer, Richard—MERCY and THE WITNESS (fiction)   VII, 205
Shacochis, Bob—HOT DAY ON THE GOLD COAST (fiction)   X, 333
Shainberg, Lawrence—EXORCISING BECKETT (essay)   XIII, 98

Shange, Ntozake—TOUSSAINT (poetry)   II, 332
Shannon, Beth Tashery—BONS (fiction)   III, 73
—ASILOMARIAN LECTURE (THE
DIRMAL LIFE OF THE INHABITANTS) (fiction)   IX, 518
Shapiro, Harvey—MUSICAL SHUTTLE (poetry)   I, 417
Sharp, Constance—I SHOW THE DAFFODILS TO THE
RETARDED KIDS (poetry)   IV, 545
Sheck, Laurie—RUSH HOUR (poetry)   XV, 253
—MANNEQUINS (poetry)   XVII, 240
Shelnutt, Eve—ANDANTINO (fiction)   XIII, 325
Shixu, Chen—THE GENERAL AND THE SMALL TOWN
(fiction)   VI, 473
Shyne, Gerard—COLUMN BEDA (fiction)   V, 89
Silko, Leslie—DEER DANCE/FOR YOUR RETURN (poetry)   III, 49
—COYOTE HOLDS A FULL HOUSE IN HIS HAND
(fiction)   VI, 142
Silliman, Ron—SITTING UP, STANDING, TAKING STEPS   IV, 346
Silverman, Maxine—A COMFORT SPELL (poetry)   III, 423
Simic, Charles—A SUITCASE STRAPPED WITH A ROPE (poetry)   V, 198
—BIRTHDAY STAR ATLAS (poetry)   X, 229
—THE TOMB OF STÉPHEN MALLARMÉ (poetry)   VI, 121
—QUICK EATS (poetry)   XVII, 361
Simmerman, Jim—CHILD'S GRAVE, HALE COUNTY, ALABAMA
(poetry)   X, 198
Simpson, Louis—PHYSICAL UNIVERSE (poetry)   IX, 528
—HIS FUNNY VALENTINE (poetry)   XII, 455
Simpson, Mona—LAWNS (fiction)   XI, 3
Sleigh, Tom—DON'T GO TO THE BARN (poetry)   XI, 191
Smiley, Jane—JEFFREY, BELIEVE ME (fiction)   IV, 299
Smith, Arthur—ELEGY ON INDEPENDENCE DAY (poetry)   XI, 243
—A LITTLE DEATH (poetry)   XIII, 403
Smith, Dave—SNOW OWL (poetry)   IV, 127
Smyth, Gjertrud Schnackenberg—FROM LAUGHING WITH ONE
EYE (poetry)   IV, 43
Snodgrass, W. D.—A VALEDICTION (poetry)   VIII, 293
Solheim, James—CAMBRIAN NIGHT (poetry)   XV, 421
Solotaroff, Ted—WRITING IN THE COLD (nonfiction)   XI, 228
Sorrentino, Gilbert—THE GALA COCKTAIL PARTY (fiction)   IX, 246
Soto, Gary—MEXICANS BEGIN JOGGING (poetry)   VII, 117
—ORANGES (poetry)   IX, 344
—THE WRESTLER'S HEART (poetry)   XVII, 419
Southwick, Marcia—THE BODY (poetry)   VII, 462
Spain, Chris—ENTREPRENEURS (fiction)   XIII, 90
Spencer, Elizabeth—JACK OF DIAMONDS (fiction)   XII, 50
—THE GIRL WHO LOVED HORSES (fiction)   V, 320
Spicer, Jack—A POSTSCRIPT TO THE BERKELEY
RENAISSANCE (poetry)   I, 436
Spires, Elizabeth—BLAME (poetry)   VI, 393
Sprunt, William—A SACRIFICE OF DOGS (poetry)   III, 84
Stafford, Jean—WODEN'S DAY (fiction)   VI, 447
Stafford, William—THINGS THAT HAPPEN WHERE THERE
AREN'T ANY PEOPLE (poetry)   IV, 380
—WAITING IN LINE (poetry)   VI, 73
—GROUND ZERO (poetry)   IX, 53
—THE GIFT (poetry)   XVI, 103
Stahl, Jerry—RETURN OF THE GENERAL (fiction)   II, 485
Stanford, Ann—THE WEAVER (poetry)   VIII, 212

Stanton, Maura—BATHROOM WALLS (poetry)   III, 421
        —SORROW AND RAPTURE (poetry)   X, 88
Starbuck, George—OYSTER BAR ON THE ROAD TO
        MURURUA (poetry)   XII, 41
Stark, Sharon Sheehe—KERFLOOEY (fiction)   XVII, 441
Steele, Timothy—SAPPHICS AGAINST ANGER (poetry)   VIII, 479
Stefanile, Felix—THE NEW CONSCIOUSNESS, THE NEA AND
        POETRY TODAY (nonfiction)   II, 491
Steinbach, Meredith—VESTIGES (fiction)   II, 133
Steiner, George—THE ARCHIVES OF EDEN (nonfiction)   VI, 177
Stern, Gerald—PEACE IN THE NEAR EAST (poetry)   I, 146
        —I REMEMBER GALILEO (poetry)   V, 88
        —HIDDEN JUSTICE (poetry)   VIII, 274
        —BELA (poetry)   XII, 43
        —I WOULD CALL IT DERANGEMENT (poetry)   XVII, 417
Sternberg, Ricardo—THE ANGEL AND THE MERMAID (poetry)   III, 307
Stewart, Pamela—THE PEARS (poetry)   V, 435
St. John, David—ELEGY (poetry)   IV, 176
Strand, Mark—VIEWING THE COAST (poetry)   XII, 502
Straight, Susan—THE BOX (fiction)   XVI, 127
Sukenick, Ronald—THE MONSTER (fiction)   I, 255
Suleri, Sara—EXCELLENT THINGS IN WOMEN (essay)   XIII, 31
Swift, Joan—ON THE GÖTA CANAL, 1986 (poetry)   XIV, 322
Szerlip, Barbara—THE GARMENT OF SADNESS (poetry)   II, 400
Taggart, John—GIANT STEPS (poetry)   V, 343
Taggart, Shirley Ann—GHOSTS LIKE THEM (fiction)   IV, 161
Tall Mountain, Mary—THERE IS NO WORD FOR GOODBYE
        (poetry)   VII, 425
Tallent, Elizabeth Ann—WHY I LOVE COUNTRY MUSIC (fiction)   VI, 247
Tanner, Ron—GARBAGE (fiction)   XIV, 343
Targan, Barry—DOMINION (fiction)   VI, 154
Taylor, Eleanor Ross—TO FUTURE ELEANORS (poetry)   X, 451
Terrill, Kathryn—TO MY DAUGHTER (poetry)   II, 162
Thacker, Julia—IN GLORY LAND (fiction)   VI, 126
Theroux, Alexander—LYNDA VAN CATS (fiction)   I, 139
        —A NOTE ON THE TYPE (fiction)   XVII, 268
Thomas, Elizabeth—WITHOUT END (poetry)   VII, 148
Thompson, Barbara—TATTOO (fiction)   VII, 31
        —CROSSING (fiction)   IX, 216
Tichy, Susan—AT A P.C. SERGEANT'S HOUSE (poetry)   XII, 384
Tinsley, Molly Best—ZOE (fiction)   XV, 219
Tremblay, Bill—UNWRITTEN LAWS (poetry)   XII, 256
Troupe, Quincy (with Steven Cannon and Ishmael Reed)—THE
        ESSENTIAL ELLISON (interview)   III, 465
Tyler, Anne—THE ARTIFICIAL FAMILY (fiction)   I, 11
Tysver, Peter—AFTER THE STATIONS OF THE CROSS (fiction)   XIV, 156
Updike, John—TO ED SISSMAN (poetry)   IV, 311
Upton, Lee—THE IMAGINATION OF FLOWERS (poetry)   XII, 387
Valentine, Jean—SEEING YOU (poetry)   XVI, 263
Vallejo, Cesar—THE SPANISH IMAGE OF DEATH (poetry)   IV, 287
Van Brunt, H. L.—THE SPRING (poetry)   I, 195
Van Duyn, Mona—LETTERS FROM A FATHER (poetry)   IV, 235
Van Walleghen, Michael—ARIZONA MOVIES (poetry)   II, 279
Vannatta, Dennis—THE DAVID OF MICHELANGELO (fiction)   XV, 443
Vaughn, Stephanie—SWEET TALK (fiction)   V, 201
Vega, Ana Lydia—LYRICS FOR PUERTO RICAN SALSA AND
        THREE SONEOS BY REQUEST (fiction)   XI, 59

568

Venn, George—FORGIVE US . . . (poetry) IV, 470
Vine, Richard—FROM THE DEATH OF LOVE: A SATANIC
    ESSAY IN MOBIUS FORM (nonfiction) V, 405
Vishniac, Roman—THE LIFE THAT DISAPPEARED
    (photographs) III, 512 (cloth only)
Vogan, Sara—SCENES FROM THE HOMEFRONT (fiction) V, 437
Voigt, Ellen Bryant—QUARREL (poetry) VIII, 155
    —WOMAN WHO WEEPS (poetry) XVI, 183
Wagner, Mary Michael—ACTS OF KINDNESS (fiction) XVII, 294
Wagoner, David—MISSING THE TRAIL (poetry) I, 10
    —WHISPERING SONG (poetry) V, 5230
    —PEACOCK DISPLAY (poetry) IX, 120
Walcott, Derek—CANTINA MUSIC (poetry) VI, 50
    —EUROPA (poetry) VII, 113
Walser, Robert—TWO STRANGE STORIES (fiction) III, 441
Walsh, Marnie—VICKIE LOANS-ARROW, FORT YATES,
    NO. DAK. 1970 (poetry) II, 284
Waniek, Marilyn—I SEND MOMA HOME (poetry) XI, 222
Wantling, William—STYLE THREE AND STYLE FOUR (nonfiction) I, 328
Warren, Robert Penn—THE ONLY POEM (poetry) V, 548
Waters, Michael—THE MYSTERY OF THE CAVES (poetry) IX, 76
    —MILES WEEPING (poetry) XV, 406
Watkins, Barbara—JOSEFA KANKOVSKA (poetry) V, 403
Watkins, Steve—CRITTERWORLD (fiction) XVII, 348
Watson, Richard—ON THE ZEEDIJK (nonfiction) XV, 41
Weaver, Gordon—WHISKEY, WHISKEY, GIN, GIN, GIN (fiction) X, 138
Weaver, Marvin—LOST COLONY (poetry) I, 376
Weigl, Bruce—TEMPLE NEAR QUANG TRI, NOT ON THE MAP
    (poetry) V, 199
Weinberger, Eliot—AT THE DEATH OF KENNETH REXROTH
    (nonfiction) XI, 339
    —PAPER TIGERS (nonfiction) XII, 23
    —JAMES JESUS ANGELTON (1917–1987)
    (nonfiction) XIV, 350
    —A CLARION FOR THE QUINCENTENARY
    (nonfiction) XVII, 370
Weinstein, Jeff—A JEAN-MARIE COOKBOOK (fiction) IV, 185
Weissmann, David—FALLING TOWARD THANKSGIVING (poetry) I, 401
Weizenbaum, Joseph—SCIENCE AND THE COMPULSIVE
    PROGRAMMER (nonfiction) I, 122
Welch, Susan—THE TIME, THE PLACE, THE LOVED ONE
    (fiction) VIII, 347
West, Paul—THE PLACE IN FLOWERS WHERE POLLEN
    RESTS (fiction) XII, 430
    —PORTABLE PEOPLE (nonfiction) XVI, 316
Wheeler, Kate—JUDGMENT (fiction) VIII, 275
White, Edmund—A MAN OF THE WORLD (fiction) VII, 394
Whittier, Gayle—LOST TIME ACCIDENT (fiction) VI, 29
    —TURNING OUT (fiction) X, 111
Wiebe, Dallas—NIGHT FLIGHT TO STOCKHOLM (fiction) IV, 133
Wieland, Liza—THE COLUMBUS SCHOOL FOR GIRLS (fiction) XVII, 23
Wilbur, Ellen—FAITH (fiction) V, 275
    —SUNDAYS (fiction) X, 81
Wilbur, Richard—HAMLEN BROOK (poetry) VIII, 381
Wilkins, Anita—TUTKA BAY, ALASKA (poetry) VIII, 481
Willard, Nancy—HOW THE HEN SOLD HER EGGS TO THE
    STINGY PRIEST (poetry) III, 306

Williams, C. K.—FLOOR (poetry)   VI, 213
   —FROM MY WINDOW (poetry)   VII, 143
   —LE PETIT SALVIÉ (poetry)   XII, 194
   —HELEN (poetry)   XVII, 480
Williams, Diane—TWO STORIES (fiction)   XVI, 360
Williams, William Carlos (with Richard Eberhart)—MAKING
   POETRY A CONTINUUM: SELECTED
   CORRESPONDENCE (letters)   IX, 170
Wilson, John—DREAM (poetry)   IX, 546
Wilson, Barbara—MISS VENEZUELA (fiction)   XIV, 124
Wilson, Jr., Robley—THE UNITED STATES (fiction)   III, 197
Witt, Harold—STATIONERY, CARDS, NOTIONS, BOOKS (poetry)   I, 418
Wojahn, David—WELDON KEES IN MEXICO (poetry)   VI, 124
   —ARMAGEDDON: PRIVATE GABRIEL CALVIN
   WOJAHN 1900–18 (poetry)   XV, 108
Wolff, Tobias—LEVIATHAN (fiction)   XI, 201
"Workers University"—THE OTHER FACE OF BREAD (nonfiction)   III, 208
Wrigley, Robert—RAVENS AT DEER CREEK (poetry)   XVI, 487
   —PARENTS (poetry)   XVII, 137
Wright, Charles—PORTRAIT OF THE ARTIST WITH LI PO
   (poetry)   V, 315
   —THE SOUTHERN CROSS (poetry)   VII, 81
   —DECEMBER JOURNAL (poetry)   XIII, 65
   —BLACK AND BLUE (poetry)   XVII, 475
Wright, James—YOUNG WOMEN AT CHARTRES (poetry)   V, 136
   —THE JOURNEY (poetry)   VII, 459
Wuori, G. K.—AFRIKAAN BOTTLES (fiction)   I, 336
Yates, Richard—OH, JOSEPH, I'M SO TIRED (fiction)   IX, 132
Young, Al—MICHAEL AT SIXTEEN MONTHS (poetry)   V, 346
Young, Gary—FOUR DAYS: EARTHQUAKE (poetry)   XVII, 207
Youngblood, Shay—SNUFF DIPPERS (fiction)   XV, 280
Yurkievich, Saul—TENEBRAE (poetry)   IX, 205
Yvonne—THE TEARING OF THE SKIN (poetry)   III, 462
Zacharia, Don—MY LEGACY (nonfiction)   XI, 161
Zagajewski, Adam—LAVA (poetry)   XVI, 380
Zawadiwsky, Christine—WITH THE REST OF MY BODY (poetry)   II, 192
Zelver, Patricia—STORY (fiction)   V, 399
Zimmer, Max—UTAH DIED FOR YOUR SINS (fiction)   III, 135
Zimmer, Paul—ZIMMER DRUNK AND ALONE, DREAMING
   OF OLD FOOTBALL GAMES (poetry)   II, 72
   —THE EISENHOWER YEARS (poetry)   VII, 391
   —BUT BIRD (poetry)   XVII, 333
Zimmon, Howard—GRANDPARENTS (poetry)   I, 245